A Diplomatic
History of Europe

A Diplomatic History
of Europe Since
the Congress of Vienna

REVISED EDITION

RENÉ ALBRECHT-CARRIÉ
Professor Emeritus,
Barnard College,
and the School of International Affairs,
Columbia University

Harper & Row, Publishers
New York   Evanston   San Francisco   London

To the Memory of My Mother

CONTENTS

Part Two. THE ERA OF STABILITY, 1871–1914

PREFACE TO THE REVISED EDITION

The fifteen years that have passed since the first publication of this book have been a period of continued peace, at least in the sense that no open conflict has occurred among the major Powers, though wars have been and still are being waged. These have, however, been contained at the level of local, or at least limited, disturbances. The purpose of this new edition is to bring up-to-date the record of the intervening years.

Granting the inevitable lack of perspective in dealing with so proximate events, some major trends are nonetheless discernible. Most important of all is the change from the bipolar situation that was produced by the Second World War to one in which the solidity of both blocs has proved to be but a passing condition; the satellites, or clients, of the two superpowers have in their various ways been straining at the leash of control and have succeeded in varying degrees in asserting some measure of independence. While the power of these states remains in a lower category, the United States and the Soviet Union have both been compelled to acknowledge the limitations of their own. The consequence of this state of affairs has been a greater fluidity of relations and the search for a new equilibrium. The process, as might be expected, has been a fumbling one and contains varied possibilities of alignments; which may materialize we cannot know, but the fact of their existence can be confidently asserted. The new closing pages, therefore, have attempted to sketch the process of transformation; to do more would be rash.

In writing this updated survey the author gratefully acknowledges the benefit of the perceptive observations that have been given him by Dr. Aleksander Rudzinski. The responsibility for interpretations remains, however, his own.

RENÉ ALBRECHT-CARRIÉ

New York
January, 1973

PREFACE TO THE FIRST EDITION

However much the United States may have developed a culture *sui generis*, that its roots and institutions are essentially of European derivation is a generally accepted commonplace. Quite properly, therefore, considerable attention is devoted in America to the study of European history. That history, like any history, has many facets, and the tendency has been to enlarge the narrower aspect of politics to include those of economic, social, cultural, and other approaches. Fashion, too, plays a part in these matters; the history of ideas is greatly favored at the moment, to a degree that some would call distortion.

But, among the various specialized aspects of history, that which is called diplomatic has, until recently, been relatively neglected. There has, in fact, been not a little popular distrust and suspicion of diplomacy in America, where the profession has often been associated with such pejorative aspects of political activity as the epithet "Machiavellian" describes. The picture of an America "bamboozled" into the First World War, and that of Wilson, the innocent abroad, falling victim to the crafts and wiles of European diplomats, preferably wicked, are myths that achieved considerable popularity and die hard.

Such an outlook should be no cause for surprise, for it is merely expression and consequence of the fact that America has been able to develop and grow while maintaining a minimum of political contact with the outside world. Contacts there were, inevitably, but their significance loomed small by comparison with the place that domestic issues commanded. America was, in a real sense, different from Europe, and it is also quite true that it entered into the first great conflict of our century with clean hands, uninvolved in, if not wholly unaware of, the prior arrangements contrived by the belligerents. The Wilsonian crusade "to make the world safe for democracy" and to insure that the decision of peoples' fate in future would only be the subject of "open covenants, openly arrived at" ended in failure in 1919. Apart from recriminations, this outcome was well-calculated to confirm the dislike and suspicion of old-world diplomats and diplomacy.

If understandable, this view was in the main naïve. But it took time—and another world conflict—for the realization to come that the American experience of the nineteenth century had been a unique and accidental, if fortunate, phenomenon, the result of a peculiar combination of circumstances, and a condition the passing of which is as inevitable as it may be regrettable. That American power has come of age is another platitude, equally recognized in and outside America. But what is more important is the final acceptance in America of the fact that power entails inescapable responsibility. The American people may be congenital anti-imperialists—in their own eyes at least—but they find themselves involved in commitments that encompass the planet.

The issues and commitments in which America finds itself enmeshed are less of America's making than they are the inheritance of a long historic development. And since, for a long time, Europe was the dominant and driving force of change in the world, these issues derive in large measure from the activities and mutual relations of the Great European Powers. To be sure, it has been said that for Americans all history is ancient. There is some basis for this view, and, in the light of the modern rapidity of change, perhaps even some virtue in it. I, for one, harbor considerable suspicion of the value of the so-called lessons of the historic past; human experience in general is too complex and the component parts of it are too varied and changeable for one to feel confidence in the identity of repetition. But, however, that may be, knowledge and understanding remain not only useful, but often indispensable.

Also, we have been forced to realize that, for all the nobility of the Wilsonian League of Nations—which incidentally ended in failure—and the renewed attempt that the United Nations embodies, or alternatively despite the hope of world revolution, the world remains very much a world of nations, or states. So long as they exist states must deal with each other. This they occasionally do by force, at other times by peaceful negotiation; in any case power remains the prime determinant of the outcome of either violent or peaceful dealings. From this standpoint, war and diplomacy are but two aspects of one central activity, not even so distinct and unrelated as they are often conceived to be.

The impact of the Second World War on America, especially in the form of the acceptance of the responsibilities of power, has had the effect of inducing an increased interest in what had been the relatively esoteric domain of international affairs, on the current state of which a large and steady stream of literature is constantly pouring from the presses. The fact that America has fallen heir to many problems the roots of which lie in the European past may be regarded as the fundamental reason for this book. The history of American foreign relations and policy has been analyzed in lengthy and competent detail, and the study of it is flourishing. The realization of the importance of the European roots of many current issues has given a corresponding, though naturally somewhat smaller, fillip to the study of European diplomatic history.

Interestingly enough, despite a wealth of monographs, there is in English a dearth of general treatments of the subject for the entire period of the nineteenth and twentieth centuries, the period covered in the present work, the outcome of a course of lectures I have been giving for some years. The present treatment does not pretend to be more than an introduction; in view of the dimensions of the subject no more could be attempted in the compass of a single volume. It is designed to give an organized picture of development and, while not avoiding personal interpretations and views, it has endeavored to take into account the up-to-date, and sometimes shifting, results of latest scholarship.

A further caution should be issued. Power, it has been said, lies at the center of the relations among states. But power is not an empty abstraction that operates in a vacuum. Rather it is the result of numerous components, geographic, economic, and moral, to mention only some. The state of industrial development, the cohesion of a society, the strength of an ideology or myth, are all equally relevant considerations when it comes to assessing the power of a state; it is the sum total of these that stands behind its armies and its negotiators. These forces must therefore always be borne in mind. But to attempt to deal with them in detail would lead into general history. The purpose of this book is by intention definitely limited to the study of the operation of the resultant of the complex of forces the totality of which constitutes the power of the state. The significant words in the title are *diplomatic* and *history*; the accent is on analysis and explanation. However, occasional reference will inevitably be made to matters economic, for instance. Also, in order to help keep the broader background in proper focus, each of the three main sections of the book is introduced by an initial chapter which is devoted to a general survey of the period, a consideration of the dominant tendencies that prevail in it, and of the major alterations that changing circumstances and conditions produce in the conduct of the relations among states.

For it must be remembered that diplomacy, like other aspects of human activity, operates in a changing context. The development of communications has brought a revolution in diplomatic methods and procedures, and there is no need at this writing to emphasize the role of applied science in altering the bases of power. But, in historic times, human nature may be regarded as a constant. With aircraft surpassing the speed of sound instead of with horse-drawn artillery, with missiles bearing nuclear charges instead of with swords, men still pursue basically unaltered purposes. The added means that science has placed in their hands have given in our day unwonted significance, responsibility, and interest to the activity of statesmen and of diplomats; unless they succeed we all fail.

The manuscript of this book has been read by Professor Lynn M. Case. His observations and comments have often proved of value and I wish to express my appreciation of them. The labor that goes into the stage between the initial putting of thoughts on paper and the appearance of the printed page, if not the most exciting, is none the less indispensable. It is one that requires much patience and time; for assistance in performing it a debt of gratitude goes to my wife.

RENÉ ALBRECHT-CARRIÉ

New York,
March 3, 1958

Part One

THE SEARCH FOR

EQUILIBRIUM,

1815–1870

I

Introduction:
Europe in 1815

I. Diplomacy and the Relations Among States

Whether as individuals or in organized groups men have always had dealings with each other; when their contacts have not taken the form of the open contest of brute force it has been necessary for them to establish some accommodation in their mutual relations. In this broad sense, diplomacy, the art of finding such accommodation, is timeless. But in the recent period with which the present treatment will concern itself, the nineteenth century and our own, a narrower definition may be given of diplomacy as the management of the relations among sovereign entities through negotiations conducted by the appropriate agents.

The terms used in this definition warrant some examination. During our period sovereign entities are states, and the concept of sovereignty, as well as the development and nature of the modern state system, must be borne in mind. This last may be said to have gradually taken shape during the so-called modern period of history, more particularly during the seventeenth and eighteenth centuries. It meant the disappearance in effect of the concept of universality inherited from Rome. Despite the irretrievable collapse of the unity of civilized mankind (Western at least) that Rome had meant, the stamp of Rome was so profound that the concept of a single allegiance as constituting the proper ordering of society long survived in the minds of men as an ideal, the restoration of which was to be sought. Both Emperor and Pope long stood for it, long vying for supremacy between them. But with the coming of Islam and the occurrence of the Eastern schism, the Papal claim at its widest encompassed little more than the European West; the imperial domain was even more restricted.

In the western chaos that the barbarians introduced in Europe the accent was on force and arms, where Rome had meant law, order, and peace. The exchanges between Charlemagne and Harun al-Rashid were not part of an established and continuing pattern. But once the nadir of disintegration had been reached reconstruction and the rebuilding of civilization, albeit painfully and slowly, began anew. One aspect of this revival was the renewal of trade. The trader will normally prefer negotiation to strife, and since the most important center of this trade was located in Italy, it was appropriate that the Italian towns and city states should cultivate more than others the peaceful art of diplomatic dealing. The home of modern diplomatic practice is Venice which early initiated a system of representation abroad and organized what may be called a permanent foreign service; the Papacy likewise, by its nature involved in dealings with numerous and diverse entities, was a forerunner in the development of the modern diplomatic art.

That art was sufficiently flourishing in the high Renaissance to command the attention of a Machiavelli, and this early period has properly been characterized as Italian.[1] But if diplomacy stresses negotiations, these have no meaning divorced from the background of power. The time when the Italians were raising to a fine art the conduct of their mutual relations[2] was also one that witnessed the consolidation and emergence of the great Western monarchies of Europe whose power was far greater than that of city states, whether Italian or Imperial. If Spain dominates the sixteenth century, the turn from that century to the next saw her displacement by France. France fought the Habsburgs, whether Spanish or Austrian, and her success was registered in the settlement of Westphalia that put a close to the Thirty Years' War.

That settlement is often regarded as marking the birth, or at least the formal institution, of the modern state system of Europe. More important from our point of view than the successful accomplishment of Richelieu's purpose[3] is the form that this accomplishment took. The success, partial but extensive, of the Protestant Revolt had further restricted the area over which any claim

---

[1] A useful discussion and survey of the changing aspects of diplomatic practice will be found in Harold Nicolson, *The Evolution of Diplomatic Method*, New York, Macmillan, 1954.

[2] For an analysis of this period reference may be made to Garrett Mattingly, *Renaissance Diplomacy*, Boston, Houghton Mifflin, 1955.

[3] Richelieu died in 1642, but the Thirty Years' War was essentially concluded by that time, and the negotiations finally registered in the treaties of 1648 were in fact initiated as early as 1643. It is therefore appropriate to regard the settlement of Westphalia as in large measure Richelieu's accomplishment.

of Papal supremacy could be asserted; even where allegiance to
the Pope was maintained his influence had been curbed; thus, the
Concordat of 1516 gave the French crown extensive rights in
the affairs of the Catholic Church in the French kingdom. With the
settlement of Westphalia the power of the Emperor was so much
further weakened as to make his position little more than nominal:
by receiving at Westphalia the unfettered control of their foreign
policy the member princes of the Empire became sovereign. The
Emperor henceforth had sovereignty, but only over the domain
that he held in his own personal right as heir of the Austrian
branch of the house of Habsburg; the Prussian Elector, for instance, soon to assume the royal dignity, was wholly free to make
alliances and treaties, with or against, the Emperor, which he soon
did. The Pope likewise was sovereign, but only over the limited
territory that constituted the States of the Church. The asset of his
spiritual position he could exploit, but save for this he was and for
some time had been but one among many Italian princes; the Renaissance Popes had acted in that capacity, joining with or against
other Italian rulers. With the final devaluation of the imperial
title the Treaty of Westphalia left Europe a collection of sovereign
entities.

Sovereignty, by its very nature, means the denial of any higher
authority; the sovereigns of Europe owed allegiance to no one.
To no one, save possibly their maker, could they be held accountable for their acts and decisions,[4] else they would not have been
sovereign. This fact is of overwhelming importance and represents
a condition that largely prevails to our day. Subsequent alterations in the domestic ordering of states, important as they have
been otherwise, have not altered this state of affairs: be it an absolute divine right monarchy or a constitutional one, a democratic
republic or our present-day people's democracy, the state still
claims the attribute of sovereignty.[5] A community of sovereign
entities must of necessity exist in a state of anarchy, the denial of
the subjection to law. Yet Europe was not chaos and one may

[4] Among important Powers England constitutes an exception, for during
the seventeenth century she introduced in her constitutional practice the beginnings of effective limitation on the power of the Crown.
[5] This is the rock on which have foundered the attempts at international
organization of our time. Strictly speaking, the very phrase, "an international
organization of sovereign states," involves a contradiction if it is meant to imply
an organization with laws.

even speak of the laws that governed her existence, but the word law must be taken in the context of natural science, an observable and to a point predictable manner of behavior, rather than in the legal sense.

Power is the great regulator of the relations among states. But in a situation where a number of Powers existed, roughly of a comparable order of magnitude, it came to be an accepted convention that all, great and small alike, had an equal right to this existence; the balance of power may be regarded as a theory, or law, that none could break with impunity. The suspectedly too far-reaching ambitions of a Louis XIV produced a coalition of others against him that succeeded in containing those ambitions; Napoleon met with the same fate eventually and so did pre-1914 Germany. The very real, if elusive, sense of community that was the legacy of the past to modern Europe helped to maintain the theory in practice. States will strive to enhance their position and to secure advantages at each other's expense, but under the circumstances just mentioned we find that the eighteenth-century wars were contests of limited scope: total victory, the destruction of the adversary, would defeat their own purpose for they would radically alter the balance of power and endanger the very right, acknowledged by all, of all to exist. To this there are exceptions, but they are relatively few: the obliteration of the Polish state by its neighbors during the latter part of the eighteenth century is the most outstanding and was widely condemned as a blunder as much as a crime.

If the logical consequence of sovereignty is anarchy, not a little order existed in practice that made it possible to speak of law among nations. As early as 1625, in the midst of the chaos of the Thirty Years' War, Grotius had written his famous *De Jure Belli et Pacis*, for which he has been credited with fathering international law. There has been continued accretion to this development, but it must ever be borne in mind that international law, so-called and such as it is, does not rest on the same basis as ordinary law for the simple reason that no enforcing agency can, in the last analysis, exist among sovereigns. The respect for international law, for *jus gentium*, has been greatest under conditions of stability and of broad agreement about methods and legitimate aims such as prevailed in large measure during the eighteenth or the nineteenth century; that law fares ill when that agreement ceases, or when large new forces take over and break the bounds of accepted practice.[6]

To the extent that law exists among states it is registered in international treaties. But, as often pointed out, treaties are in large measure the expression of conditions and relationships of power in existence at the time of their making; they cannot hope to freeze forever the *status quo* of any particular moment of time. Treaties, to be sure, are supposed to retain their validity under the tacit qualification *rebus sic stantibus*, conditions persisting that prevailed at the time of their making. When these conditions alter, as in time they will, there is no agency with power to adjudicate the measure of the change or the consequences that should ensue from it. Against the breach of a treaty there is only one recourse, force, and to speak of the sanctity of treaties is to make a purely moral judgment that carries no foreseeable or previously known sanction with it.[7] Thus, as a consequence, conquest in history has been the source of legitimate right. Treaties nevertheless remain of the highest importance and the drafting of them one of the principal tasks of diplomatic activity.

Conditions of at least relative stability are conducive to the establishment of settled practice. The conduct of the relations among states thus became highly formalized during a period that was also that of the preponderance of French power in Europe, so that it is appropriate to speak with Nicolson of the French system following or superseding the Italian.[8] The foreign office as a domestic agency for directing relations with the outside world took shape, as well as the office of the ambassador, or envoy, ordi-

---

[6] The time of the wars of religion, that of the French Revolution, and our own are all illustrations of the intrusion of powerful ideas that have the effect of questioning the former bases of legitimacy and whose impact is not spent until sufficient agreement has been produced on a new basis of legitimacy.

[7] This has opened in our time the large question of the significance of world opinion, an important but clearly not regulated or codified element. When, in 1914, Germany decided to violate the neutrality of Belgium, she claimed no other justification than the higher law of necessity. Her action, coming at the end of a long period of relative stability, earned her widespread opprobrium. Since the first World War the respect for treaties has been a much devalued commodity. The attempts after that war, and even more after the last, to introduce the concept of "war criminality" and the holding of trials of war criminals constitute interesting innovations that have been highly questioned. Whether this will turn out to have been a first step in the direction of introducing morality and law in the relations among states, or a modern form of *Vae victis*, remains to be seen.

[8] Nicolson, *op. cit.*

nary or extraordinary, representative of one sovereign to another. Spanish etiquette and Louis XIV served to make the manner of conduct of these men very rigid and formal. Much has been written, especially in French, on the proper behavior and the desirable characteristics of the good ambassador, who should be honest, cautious and forthright, quick-witted yet master of his tongue, alive to the defense of the interests entrusted to his care, yet eschewing trickery and deceit and the temptation to take undue advantage. Until quite recently, the slowness of communications made the ambassador a very important personage, provided with detailed and carefully elaborate instructions, but also granted considerable latitude in the exercise of his powers. The fussiness and punctilio of precedence may appear humorous in some of their manifestations; there was in them a delicate gauge of power standing, hence their real importance.

Also, the gradual supersession of Latin by the various vernaculars, in combination with the eighteenth-century prestige of French culture, caused the French language to become the one that was universally adopted for the transaction of affairs among states. The advantages of a common medium of expression, whatever it might be, Latin, French, or some other, have often been pointed out, to which some would add certain qualities, such as precision, of the French tongue in particular. It is one of the less attractive aspects of our contemporary hypersensitive nationalisms that this aspect of universality has ceased to exist in our day.

The quarter of a century interlude that precedes the opening of the present subject of discussion, the period of the French Revolution and the Napoleonic episode, was a major convulsion in the annals of Europe. Revolutionary and Napoleonic diplomacy were at times highhanded and crude; Napoleon did not abide by the established rules, least of all by that which acknowledged the equal right of all to existence. Napoleon did not succeed in uniting Europe, and when the dust had settled on the conflict, great as in many respects its impact was to be, from the limited standpoint of the conduct of relations among states, the effects of it seemed relatively small. The system which had taken shape prior to the outburst of 1789 in France continued to prevail during the nineteenth century: a community of sovereign states, all equally legitimate, pursuing goals of a limited nature, still making treaties and conducting their transactions in French. Of the underlying new forces that were to shape the nineteenth century, more will be said presently, but diplomatic method was little disturbed. It will be useful at this point to examine briefly the shape of the settlement which registered the close of the Napoleonic epic.

II. The Settlement of Vienna

In one respect at least, the Napoleonic episode, as pointed out before, falls into the classical pattern. From the British point of view in particular, what Napoleon meant was not so much the threat of a novel ideology as the danger of a united continent. But if other Continental Powers would, either from necessity or free will, come to terms with Napoleon and adjust themselves to a radically altered distribution of power in Europe, their wishes did not differ fundamentally from the British. Restoration of the *status quo ante bellum* was therefore the ostensible order of the day in Vienna.

Broadly speaking, the purpose was carried out successfully, though not without certain difficulties in the process of its accomplishment. The fundamental aim of the victorious coalition, the containment of France, was essentially achieved with the campaign of 1814, to which the first Treaty of Paris, of May 30, put an end. With minor alterations to her advantage, France was restored to her prerevolutionary frontiers,[9] while the allies brought her back the legitimate king, Louis XVIII, brother of the unfortunate Louis XVI. It will be noted that France was not partitioned, let alone destroyed; no one questioned her right to independent existence since, ostensibly, the allies sought no more than the restoration of the proper, or "legitimate," order of things.

But, as usual, the successful accomplishment of the purpose of the coalition also destroyed its chief *raison d'être*. Two things therefore were done. Lest France should again threaten the order of Europe, the Treaty of Chaumont, in March, 1814, had reasserted the ties of the coalition; in addition, Article 32 of the Treaty of Paris provided for the holding of a European congress in Vienna. It was all very well to assert the general purpose of restoring the *status quo ante bellum*; twenty-five years of turmoil, during which much of the map of Europe had been redrawn as if it

[9] Actually, the frontiers of 1792 rather than those of 1789 were used. This meant some gain in the East and no attempt to undo the incorporation of Papal Avignon. Napoleon himself was sent to the island of Elba, the rule of which, not without some humor perhaps, was made his.

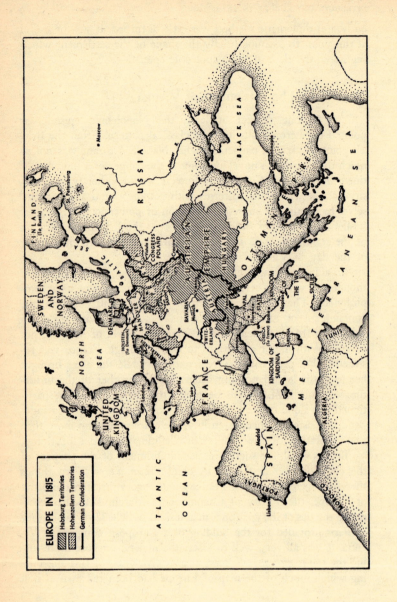

EUROPE IN 1815

▨ Habsburg Territories

∴ Hohenzollern Territories

— German Confederation

ATLANTIC OCEAN

UNITED KINGDOM

London

NORTH SEA

SWEDEN AND NORWAY

BALTIC SEA

FINLAND (To Russia)

St. Petersburg

● Moscow

RUSSIA

DENMARK

HOLSTEIN (To Denmark)

HANOVER

Amsterdam

NETHERLANDS

Berlin

PRUSSIA

CRACOW & CONGRESS POLAND

AUSTRIAN EMPIRE

HUNGARY

BLACK SEA

OTTOMAN EMPIRE

FRANCE

Paris

Lyon

Loire R.

BAVARIA

Munich

SWITZERLAND

PAPAL

TUSCANY

Florence

Rome

KINGDOM OF THE TWO SICILIES

Naples

SICILY

KINGDOM OF SARDINIA

SPAIN

Madrid

PORTUGAL

Lisbon

MEDITERRANEAN SEA

MOROCCO

ALGERIA

TUNIS

were mere paper, called for a major task of readjustment. There were also some awkward mortgages in the way of simple restoration: the partition of Poland had not been completed until 1795; the Russo-Prussian Treaty of Kalisch of February, 1813, was a purely bilateral arrangement, and Metternich had also made commitments to the Napoleonic King Murat of Naples for the sake of his assistance in the war. Austria and Bavaria had entered into a separate understanding, the Treaty of Ried, in October, 1813.

The Congress duly met at Vienna, in September, 1814, and its work was largely accomplished during the next six months although the signature of the final Act did not take place until June, a few days before Waterloo, last flare-up of the Napoleonic episode. That footnote had relatively little effect. It conveniently removed the embarrassment of Murat who once again, mistakenly this time, shifted his allegiance, and the first Treaty of Paris was superseded by a second, in November, 1815: France had to go back to the frontiers of 1790 instead of those of 1792 and she was saddled with the penalties of an indemnity and occupation while Napoleon was more securely put away in distant St. Helena, his active career irretrievably closed. The Hundred Days did not affect the arrangements contrived at Vienna.

Metternich was host to the Congress. Authentic representative of the *ancien régime*, he saw to it that proper form, due pomp, and suitable entertainment surrounded its more important purpose: the Congress danced. Behind the avowed aim of restoration, the reality of power intruded and the problem of its adjustment was the main concern of the diplomacy of Vienna. Outwardly, there was no French problem since peace had been restored with France, but France was represented at the Congress in the person of one of the ablest diplomats of all time, the Prince of Talleyrand, ex-bishop of the *ancien régime*, Napoleon's ex-foreign minister, and now filling the post of representative of the restored legitimate king of France. That France should be present was no more than reasonable: restored to her former place and dimensions, she remained a very major European Power and no arrangement of Europe could well be made without her.[10] She was nevertheless, and of necessity, on probation, and Talleyrand was shrewd enough

[10] The above-mentioned Article 32 of the first Treaty of Paris provided for French representation at Vienna, but a secret clause also provided for the exclusion of France in the reaching of decisions, an arrangement that circumstances, and Talleyrand's use of them, soon nullified.

to be content at first with a role of effacement: France, at the moment powerless, had no desires or claims beyond her general support of the enactment of justice for all; the professed dedication of the victors to restoration based on legitimacy had already put into his hands a powerful weapon when it had come to the terms meted out to France: Louis XVIII could hardly be restored to his "legitimate" inheritance if he were at the same time deprived of any part of it.

The legitimate right of all to exist is a very different concept from the democratic notion of equality, whether applied to individuals in the state or to states among themselves. The democratic idea was anathema in Vienna, where instead the concept that power implies rights no less than responsibilities was frankly acknowledged. Britain, Austria, Russia, and Prussia, the four greater Powers, intended to make the decisions; France soon joined them, and the five Great Powers dominated the Congress whose business was mainly done by them, in private meetings rather than in plenary sessions. It is difficult to achieve results otherwise, as a later Congress, just a century after that of Vienna, was to discover for all its proclaimed stress on open covenants openly arrived at. In the signature of the final Act the Five were joined by three others, Spain, Portugal, and Sweden; these three states had once enjoyed Great Power rank, but their decline and the measure of their current standing were thus accurately reflected.

If Restoration founded on Legitimacy was the avowed intention of the Congress, the fact did not exclude two things. Some of the alterations that Napoleon had made represented a long-postponed recognition of reality as much as his arbitrariness: the Holy Roman Imperial title was not revived, nor was the multitude of German principalities which made up the Empire reëstablished; a substantial consolidation took place instead which reduced their number from over three hundred to less than two score. This process of simplification gave rise to little difficulty for the dispossessed were too small. Also, restoration and the balance of power did not preclude the individual seeking of at least limited advantage. The three Eastern Powers had no intention of restoring Poland, but fear of Russian power was felt no less by Austria than by Britain. If Prussia did not share in this it was because of the above-mentioned arrangement of Kalisch; she was willing to leave all Poland to the tsar who was in turn amenable to the Prus-

sian absorption of Saxony whose king had unwisely adhered to
the Napoleonic cause too long. In the pursuit of his Polish ambitions the tsar enjoyed the substantial advantage of a large Russian
army in Poland. The Polish-Saxon issue was the most difficult of
resolution and split the Four into Anglo-Austrian and Russo-
Prussian camps.

Thus Talleyrand was presented with his opportunity, for both
camps were anxious to secure French support. For this the Prussian delegate, Hardenberg, was willing to pay the price of compensating the Saxon king with the territories on the left bank of
the Rhine. But this arrangement was equally unpalatable to Metternich, inimical to Prussian expansion, and to the British Castlereagh, who was concerned lest the device provide a cover for
the extension of French influence on the Rhine. Talleyrand would
not incur Austrian and British displeasure and therefore threw his
lot with the Anglo-Austrian camp.[11] In high secrecy—Castlereagh
penned the instrument in his own hand—a treaty of alliance was
concluded between the three Powers on January 3, 1815,
whereby each obligated itself to supply 150,000 troops in the
event of hostilities.[12] But these did not occur—too much warfare
had been the lot of all—and the momentary relationship of power
resulted in a compromise: the tsar received the bulk of Poland,
save a small western segment (West Prussia and Posen) to Prussia, and Austrian Galicia; Prussia absorbed two-fifths of Saxony,
the rest remaining to her legitimate ruler, while the relative loss to
Prussia was made good to her in the Rhineland[13] where much of
the ecclesiastical territory secularized by Napoleon, together with
imperial cities and small principalities, was merged into a solid
block.

This arrangement provides a good illustration of that other
principle, compensation, which, with legitimacy and restoration,
dominated the proceedings of Vienna. For the rest, if the Holy
Roman Empire was not revived, the Germanic Confederation, of

[11] For this he has been charged by some with missing a supreme opportunity
for France who could have secured a friendly buffer between herself and future
Germany.

[12] The secret remained until found and revealed by Napoleon during the
Hundred Days. Considering the long struggle against France just concluded, few
neater illustrations can be given of the operation of power.

[13] This suited the British book especially, for Prussia, now coterminous with
France, would be in a better position to act as guardian against any French designs on the Rhine.

which the Austrian emperor was *ex officio* president, was virtually identical with it. There were other examples of compensation, to a degree of simplification if one will. The Hanoverian crown reverted to the British ruler, but Britain had no claims in Europe apart from the eccentric bases of Malta and the Ionian Islands. Britain retained, however, imperial acquisitions resulting from the Napoleonic Wars, South Africa and Ceylon, formerly Dutch.[14] The former Austrian Netherlands, roughly modern Belgium, furnished suitable compensation for Holland whose House of Orange would henceforth rule over the united Kingdom of Holland and Belgium.[15]

This meant in turn an Austrian loss, for all that the responsibility was awkward for the defense of so eccentric a position as Belgium. Suitable compensation was found for Austria in her acquisition of Venice: like the destruction of many German states, the death of Venice, also Napoleon's work in 1797, may be viewed as an instance of bringing up to date, of bringing the law nearer reality. Otherwise, restoration prevailed in Italy, be it in Naples, whence Murat had conveniently eliminated himself, in Rome, whither the Pope returned in full sovereignty, or in the Duchies, where the former dynasties were brought back. However, like superseded Venice, the Genoese Republic also ceased to exist, being incorporated into the Kingdom of Sardinia.

To complete this survey of the European map as it emerged from the deliberations of Vienna, the Scandinavian states must be mentioned. The Danish like the Saxon king had remained faithful to Napoleon too long. For this he had to pay a price in the form of the dissolution of the union of his country with Norway. This last was joined to Sweden where Bernadotte, unlike Murat in Naples, continued to reign,[16] Sweden meanwhile relinquishing Finland to the tsar. Finally, the Congress set up a Swiss committee. Here again, retaining the Napoleonic change, the Constitution of 1803, to the former cantons were added those of Geneva, Valais, and Neuchatel, although this last remained a possession of the Prussian king. In addition, the Eight guaranteed the perpetual neutral-

[14] In connection with the Napoleonic wars Britain also acquired some Caribbean islands, Mauritius and Guiana.

[15] The further purpose was thereby served of creating another, and stronger, barrier against France.

[16] Denmark received some compensation from Sweden in the form of a financial payment and the cession of former Swedish Pomerania, which latter she subsequently exchanged with Prussia for the Duchy of Lauenburg. Britain retained formerly Danish Heligoland.

ity of the reorganized Switzerland, an arrangement destined to prove highly durable.

The map of Europe had been redrawn and, with relatively minor qualifications, its new shape may indeed be said to have represented a return to the *status quo ante bellum.* It will be noted that the work of the Congress was confined to Europe.[17] There were other matters that exceeded the confines of Europe, the revolt of Spain's American possessions for one. The legitimacy of Spanish rule in the New World could hardly be questioned, even if Britain was not blind to the advantages that could accrue to her from American emancipation. The matter was simply not dealt with at Vienna. Similarly, and largely in deference to Tsar Alexander's wishes, Ottoman affairs were left outside the purview of the Congress.

Its work accomplished, the Congress disbanded after the signature on June 9 of the hurriedly drafted Final Act. A sense of urgency prevailed, for Napoleon had gathered a large army that was moving to meet the enemy in the North. But Napoleon only marched to his Waterloo with the consequence, as mentioned before, that the Hundred Days was a mere passing interlude of no effect on the decisions of Vienna. The episode nonetheless had significance as a gauge of the state of opinion and feeling in France, a condition that would have consequences in the long-term future.

Much has been written about the charter that the Congress of Vienna wrote for the future of Europe, and appraisals of it have varied, reflecting the circumstances of the time when they were made. During the latter part of the nineteenth century, after the great nationalistic triumphs that the unifications of Italy and Germany represented, the shortcomings of Vienna were largely emphasized. In our time of greater trouble and uncertainty, when the nineteenth century as a whole appears by contrast with the present as a period of relative stability and minor disturbances, the point is often made that, altered as they had become by 1914, the settlements of 1815 served Europe for a century; the contrast certainly is arresting between the mere twenty-year truce that followed the 1919 settlements and the story enclosed by the years 1815 to

[17] Britain and France had agreed to seek the abolition of the slave trade but all that could be obtained was a general declaration of intent that such was a desirable end, leaving the individual states to decide on the appropriate time for implementation.

1914. Metternich's stock has risen as a consequence and some have rediscovered the merits of the conservative outlook that was his.[18] History is forever rewritten.

III. The Forces of the Future

Metternich was indeed a conservative, an avowed and intelligent one; to put the work of Vienna under his sign is wholly fair description. What had happened in France after 1789 was to him clearly and undebatably dangerous aberration, and the word "liberal" contained the quintescence of all that was nefarious and perverse in the domain of politics, international or domestic. Against the international of peoples the international of rulers had won; that its solidarity should persist was obviously desirable. But the comment of Galileo is also apt, *Eppur si muove;* there were limits, in 1815 as always, to the degree to which the course of change could be arrested.

The internal condition of France remained, therefore, a factor of paramount concern to Europe as a whole. Louis XVIII sat again on the French throne after the Hundred Days, returned to his legitimate inheritance. But Louis XVIII had had enough of travel and understood that much that had happened in France could not be undone with impunity. The ex-nobles might be compensated for the effects of confiscation, but the Code Napoleon was not abrogated. The French people in fact were to be allowed a measure of control in the management of their affairs: if the king remained in theory absolute and irresponsible, and if the Charter that he granted, because granted could presumably be withdrawn, in actual practice representative institutions were established in France. This was far from a democratic ordering, and the franchise was highly restricted, even more than in Britain, but the wedge of representation was firmly driven into the absolutistic theory. France being France—meaning by this her power and her role in the twenty-five years just elapsed—she was during the ensuing century to remain the standard-bearer of the revolutionary ideal, and Paris the lodestar whither all European liberals turned their glance, in that respect displacing and superseding Britain, hitherto sole example of constitutional practice in government. The great upheaval left lasting memories in France where

[18] As a good illustration of this tendency may be cited the book of Peter Viereck, *Conservatism Revisited*, New York, Scribner's, 1949.

the passage of time would tend to make the Napoleonic epic a legend that would become an active force in politics; revolution likewise was to take on *per se* the power of respectable tradition. Unlike England, France was henceforth to be, and still remains for that matter, irreconcilably cleft between the broad antagonistic tendencies of conservation and change; she was during the nineteenth century the prime European battleground of these forces. The phrase was apt, "When Paris catches cold, Europe sneezes."

The government of France after 1815 was in effect not very different from that of Britain. Britain was less sensitive than Metternich to ideological considerations, and if the Revolution was generally considered to have degenerated into regrettable excesses, its initial purpose and actions appeared in Britain less cause for alarm than the pleasing compliment of imitation. "Boney" had been another matter; an enlightened despot rather than a starry-eyed radical, he had raised the specter of power that would control the continent. To that aspect of things Britain was very sensitive indeed, and she had fought Napoleon with far greater tenacity than had Metternich. This state of things introduced a measure of cleavage into the operation of the Concert of Europe. From the long-term point of view and in regard to Europe as a whole, Britain and France had much in common; they represented, broadly speaking, what may be described as the liberal tendency in opposition to the conservative and reactionary emphasis that held sway in the Eastern Great Powers of Austria, Russia, and Prussia.

But the major part of the century was to elapse before the ideologically kindred Western states were to find themselves in close and lasting association *vis-à-vis* the outside. If our time is accustomed to the view that France and Britain have for some time been fundamentally in a similar position, in 1815 the emphasis was on antagonism, in the secular record of which the struggle just ended was but another episode: traditional enmity was much more evident and real on the shores of the Channel than on the banks of the Rhine. Also, of capital importance is the fact that after 1815 the star of British power was to continue in the ascendant while French power embarked on the path of at least relative decline.

Britain, therefore, was a genuine supporter of the Quadruple Alliance, but she thought of that association primarily in limited terms of power and was most interested in the provisions of it that committed its members to the supplying of definite contingents should there be need again to contain France. If Britain, like Austria, was opposed to an undue accretion of Russian power, it would be highly premature to speak in 1815 of any widespread consciousness of a Russian danger that might engulf all Europe.

Metternich felt more keenly than the British the desirability of insuring the existence of proper—read "conservative"—governments within the various states,[19] but it was left to the volatile tsar to stress the common interest of all in the sound governance of all states. Tsar Alexander I was not immune to the influence of the Enlightenment of the preceding century; he was still toying with a vague liberalism, a tendency in him of which Metternich was suspicious. These yearnings, combined with his religious propensities, caused him to sponsor that association to which the name "Holy Alliance" is given. That loose statement of common intent, dating from November, 1815, had little reality by comparison with the concrete content of the Quadruple instrument, and Britain would have no truck with its vagueness. Castlereagh thought it nonsense, but more politely the British government pleaded the limitations of its constitutional nature as an excuse for declining to join it. The ideological cleavage, to use a modern phrase, of Europe between East and West, if of little immediate consequence and by its nature elusive of concrete measurement, was nonetheless an underlying element whose importance was to increase with time.

It has been one of the standard criticisms of the arrangements made in 1815 that they showed total disregard of the factor of nationality. That was indeed the case, but this result was deliberate and the logical consequence of the Metternichian outlook. To Metternich, nationalism, the claim to self-determination, was heresy on a par with other aspects of the French Revolution. Rulers were the legitimate claimants to certain lands, hence to the government of peoples therein residing; the sovereignty of peoples, of which self-determination is an easy corollary, was another dangerous doctrine. In addition, the Austrian state was more than any other vulnerable to the assertion of such claims, being the one state in Europe devoid of any national foundation. The mer-

---

[19] England was not wholly immune to the ideological influence, and for some time the excesses of the French Revolution induced in her a fear of revolution as such comparable to Metternich's. But while Metternich continued to adhere to this view Britain soon returned to her more liberal tradition.

its or shortcomings of self-determination need not be examined here. It was not God-ordained from creation that the state should be identified with the ethnographical fact of diverse nationalities; the fact remains that, for good or ill, nationalism was destined to be one of the dominant forces of the nineteenth century, the effects of which were to be felt with special virulence in the Central European world. Through her presidency of the Germanic Confederation, her direct holdings in Italy, and her connection with ruling houses in the Peninsula, Austria, or the house of Habsburg, was dominant in Central Europe. The story of that entire area during the first half of the century may fairly be centered on the national theme; but the convulsions and drastic rearrangements that involved so large a part of Europe could hardly fail to embroil the rest. Here again the cleavage between East and West appears. Russia, save in the Balkans, was generally unsympathetic to the claims of nationality; conservative in her outlook, though unlike Austria not made up of a congeries of disparate peoples, she too controlled substantial numbers of non-Russian subjects, of whom the Poles were the largest contingent.

But in the West the identification of state and nation had long since taken place. The degree to which the French Revolution and Napoleon had given encouragement to the nationalistic force cannot be overstressed; our modern nationalism, with all its aberrations, really dates from them. Nineteenth-century France was in substantial degree sympathetic to the struggle for independence of subject nationalities. And so was England in considerable measure.

Yet in this matter also power considerations often cut athwart the lines of sentiment and sympathy. It has been mentioned that Russia was generally favorable to the struggle for emancipation of the Balkan peoples subject to the Ottoman Turk. The tendency in Russia that made for sympathy for brother Slavs is a reality that must not be ignored; but it was also highly useful to the expansive aims of the Russian state, which at times and depending upon circumstances could play fast and loose with these brother Slavs. In British eyes, and in French sometimes, the Austrian state was a vital and necessary component of the European community, a fact determinant of policy decisions even when it ran counter to sympathy for independence struggles. This element is also very marked in the British policy of support for Ottoman integrity. Moreover, popular opinion carried more weight in Britain and in France, ahead of others on the democratic path. The weight of this opinion must at times be considered by the foreign office; it could make itself felt in elections, intrude into and complicate the operation of domestic politics, though it must be acknowledged that popular opinion interfered relatively little with the conduct of foreign affairs. Even in the Western countries, the foreign office and the foreign service, manned by a competent few, drawn overwhelmingly from a very restricted section of society, remained in very large measure a closed and esoteric preserve.

Prussia was clearly in a special position in the matter of nationality. Conservative also, hence sharing the Austrian outlook in her domestic organization, she had long been engaged in a struggle with the Habsburg dynasty. Unlike the Austrian, the Prussian state was essentially Germanic, and as the largest German state, a Great Power in its own right, would be a logical candidate for the promotion of the national ideal from which, in addition, it stood to reap individual benefit. The intrusion of nationalism was to give a new twist to the old Hohenzollern-Habsburg contest.

The judgment that democracy, or liberalism,[20] and nationalism are the two basic and dominant forces of the nineteenth century is fundamentally warranted. But to these a third must be added, that the term "industry" best describes. The Congress of Vienna and the settlements there contrived were essentially innocent of economic considerations. Compare them with a modern major treaty, that of Versailles, for instance, and an important part of the story of the nineteenth century stands revealed. Economic clauses constitute a large part of Versailles, but it was not necessary to proceed likewise in Vienna, for the simple reason that European society at the beginning of the nineteenth century was still predominantly agrarian. To be sure, international commerce had undergone a marked expansion during the course of the eighteenth century, but the so-called Industrial Revolution, revealingly a term of relatively recent coinage, had only just been initiated in England in the latter part of that century. The movement was to grow to gigantic proportions, in Britain herself first, whence it spread on an eastward course. During the first half of the nineteenth century Britain was by far the dominant industrial state of Europe and the world; in northern France and Belgium next, across the Rhine, the movement got under way. The significance

[20] The two concepts are by no means identical, but during the nineteenth century they tended to become equated or at least intimately related.

of industry is too familiar a phenomenon for it to need explanation or emphasis; that its development should bring in its train a host of problems, domestic no less than external, and a modification of old, it is enough to mention. It may be indicated, however, that the imperial activity of Europe, to which industrial development would eventually give an added fillip, was at a relatively low ebb at first, before 1870, at least by comparison with its manifestations during the second half of the century. Europe could absorb much of the domestic production before the search became imperative for remoter outlets.

But of greatest importance from the standpoint of our approach is the fact that industry means power, not only in the most elementary form of producing the increasingly elaborate engines of warfare, but because industry means wealth, and wealth as ever is power. Under a simpler and more primitive economic dispensation greater stress could be placed on mere numbers: the fact that France had long been and still was the most populous country of Europe, Russia excluded, is not unrelated to the French role in Europe; and the power of Prussia was magnified out of proportion to its real dimensions from the fact that, though far smaller, she had maintained as large an army as that of greater states. Nor must those other components of power be forgotten, the role of which has ever been important: geography for instance, the nature and quality of frontiers, of which the enormous asset for Britain of her island position is the clearest example; France has seldom been invaded save from the northeast, and nature has given no boundaries to Poland. The value of the technical competence of management when the test of arms must be met had received recent and telling illustration from the Napoleonic performance. Nor is the more elusive factor of morale, to a degree at times related to that of ideology, undeserving of mention.

For the rest, as already indicated, the states of Europe during the nineteenth century continued to conduct their relations as they had in the past. The community that was Europe was dominated by the constellation of its major units, the so-called Great Powers, of which there were just five, Great Britain or the United Kingdom, France, Austria, Russia, and Prussia. There is no abstract definition of the term "Great Power," yet the criterion of greatness is of the simplest: a Power has such rank when acknowledged by others to have it. The fact of a Power belonging in that category makes it what has been called a Power with general interests, meaning by this one which has automatically a voice in all affairs, by contrast with a Power of lower rank, or Power with limited interests.

The nineteenth century opened with a clearly defined charter, that of the settlement of Vienna. In outlining the terms of that charter and the manner in which they were contrived stress has been laid on the territorial aspect. This is legitimate, for, in the relations among states, frontiers are the item most recalcitrant to alteration, to the extent that one is hard put to find examples of peaceful change in the boundaries of states. Diplomacy is apt to be thought of in contrast to war; yet the distinction is only valid in part, for states pursue their aims by what means seem to them the most suitable. If war is power in action in its crudest form, diplomacy is only once removed from that condition; it too is an exercise in the use of power, and even war, a break in diplomatic relations, by no means excludes the continuation of diplomatic activity, even among belligerents, especially when these pursue aims of a limited nature. Total war, total victory, and unconditional surrender are practices of the twentieth century, but not of the nineteenth. In studying the exercise of power as we are about to do in that century, it must ever be borne in mind that power is the resultant of a multitude of components, of which the military, the *ultima ratio regum,* is but one.

II   *The Restoration Period*

I. The Concert of Europe

Waterloo definitely eliminated Napoleon, and Europe could again envisage the prospect of a lasting peace. Louis XVIII, returned once more to France, shared the coalition's desire to avoid renewed upheavals in that country with whom the second Treaty of Paris, of November 20, 1815, once more restored formal peace. The short-lived Napoleonic flare-up of the spring served to confirm the wisdom of the ties forged among the allies a year earlier at Chaumont; these were accordingly reaffirmed. The Quadruple Alliance, the arrangements of the Congress of Vienna, and the second Treaty of Paris among them constituted the instruments that would govern the subsequent relations of the European states.

As a formal tool of international relations, the vague declaration of the Holy Alliance, expression of the tsar's mood of the moment, strongly influenced by the mysticism of Madame de Krüdener of whom the tsar saw much while in Paris, had little influence on the future course of events. Metternich himself set little store by that instrument of which it must be said, however, that the spirit of it was adequate expression of the dominant conservative orientation of the Eastern empires and of their common wish to keep others on the proper path. Alexander was given to dreams; for that reason his influence on the concrete was evanescent. More realistic Metternich, like the tsar anxious to maintain the proper order in all states, was better qualified to act as guide of a restored conservative Europe; the description of the period that follows 1815 as the Era of Metternich is on the whole quite suitable. He, or Austria, and Britain, more specifically Castlereagh at the moment, were the dominant influences of the immediate aftermath of Napoleon, while Prussia for many years would only play a relatively secondary role, one of effacement greater than her power warranted, in part because of the timidity of her ruler who was content to leave initiative in other hands and generally followed Metternich's lead.

Should France again threaten the European peace and equilibrium, whether because of internal disturbance or of meddling in the affairs of other states, the allies agreed that they would take joint action; specifically, they each undertook to supply a force of 60,000 men for the purpose, but apart from the clear *casus foederis* that a breach of the Treaty of Paris would constitute, the proper cause for joint action was none too clearly specified, hence might give rise to divergent interpretations. The specific guarantee against France appealed especially to Britain, otherwise loath as ever to undertake too far-reaching commitments; there was no general guarantee of the provisions of the settlement of Vienna. It was also agreed among the allies that they would meet on subsequent occasions: the so-called Concert of Europe was thereby given formal recognition. It functioned successfully for a while, though not for long, roughly it may be said so long as the fear of France and revolution persisted. The record of a quarter-century of strife naturally gave that fear reality at first, and even in England, long accustomed to representative institutions, reaction was for a while in control.[1]

But France behaved and gave no cause for alarm though she was torn by factions. Louis XVIII was a moderate man and some of his difficulties arose at first from supporters more royalist than the king; the *Chambre introuvable* of 1816, too reactionary, he dissolved, in doing which he had the approval of both Metternich and the tsar; the former was merely sensible while the tsar had not yet rid himself of his liberal sympathies. From the French point of view, if the terms of the Treaty of Paris caused no great satisfaction, the main task was to regain acceptance in the European community; a policy of fulfillment of her obligations, under the guidance of the Duc de Richelieu, was adopted as the device best calculated to allay suspicions and to remove the taint of unrespectability associated with revolution. More narrowly and immediately, France wished to rid herself of the burdens of indemnity and foreign occupation.

THE CONCERT IN OPERATION

The second Treaty of Paris had imposed upon France the payment of 700,000,000 francs over a period of five years, a large sum

---

[1] In 1819 Parliament enacted the Six Acts, curbs on the traditional British liberties, which were the expression of the fear of popular agitation and influence.

but one well within her capacity to discharge, especially in view of her recovery after 1815. Moreover, while the armies of occupation acted as guarantee of both good behavior and payment, their permanence in the home of revolution exposed them to possibly subversive influences. Thus, by 1818, it was proposed that the time was suitable for a meeting of the five Great Powers. Though various issues might have been considered, a review of the French situation was the only accomplishment of the Congress that met at Aix-la-Chapelle in September, 1818. Agreement was promptly reached on the remainder of the payment of the French indemnity and the armies of occupation were withdrawn in November.

The Treaty of Aix-la-Chapelle of October 9, 1818, between the four allies and France may be said to have finally liquidated the episode of the Napoleonic wars. Moreover, the allies collectively invited the French king to join in their deliberations, which the Duc de Richelieu promptly did. France was thus formally admitted to the Concert of Europe as an equal member in full and good standing. To be sure, lingering suspicion of France led to the secret renewal, on November 1, of the Quadruple Alliance. But there was no occasion for the use of that instrument which therefore fell into desuetude. Instead, France could henceforth participate in the discussion of the paramount issues of Europe.

As much as the rivalries of individual states, those issues were the legacy of the French Revolution: liberalism did not stop at frontiers to the stability of which the force of nationalism offered a different kind of threat. Correctly and consistently from his point of view Metternich detested both of these forces and would gladly have led all Europe in the suppression of them wherever their manifestation occurred. The liberal spirit flourished in the Germanic Confederation where it achieved certain local successes.[2] Understandably, it appealed to the young, and the *Burschenschaft*, an association of university students, reflected German nationalism as well. The assassination of Kotzebue, an agent of the tsar, in March, 1819, gave Metternich occasion for the institution of the Carlsbad decrees.[3]

In doing this, Metternich was acting within his own domain. But the Italian situation raised problems of a different nature, just

[2] Constitutions were granted in Baden and in Bavaria.
[3] Like the British Six Acts of the same year, these decrees instituted curbs on political freedoms. The subsequent Act of Vienna, in 1820, gave the federal Diet the right of intervention, in certain circumstances, in the domestic affairs of the member states.

as did the course of events in Spain. There was no Italy as yet, but liberals in general, secret societies, the *Carbonari*, were beginning to think of union of some sort; however, at this stage, the agitation did not yet visibly threaten the international order of Italy, rather confining itself to the demand for reform within the framework of the existing units. "Constitution" was in those days the slogan of liberalism, a word seemingly laden with magical content. In July, 1820, in Naples, a virtually unopposed rising had extracted from King Ferdinand the granting of a charter.

This touched on a sensitive and concrete Austrian interest, that of the paramountcy in the Peninsula. Metternich was anxious to intervene and to use Austrian force to restore the Neapolitan king to full power. But the tsar, though not necessarily opposed to constitutions, was more favorable to concerted European action, a prospect none too pleasing to Metternich.[4] The Concert of Europe gathered at Troppau in October-November, 1820, to examine the situation and continued its deliberations at Laibach at the turn of the year.[5] The outcome of these meetings was a mandate to Austria for the restoration of order in Italy. This Austrian troops had little difficulty in accomplishing in February, 1821. They rendered a similar service to the king of Sardinia in April, for Turin had also been the scene of revolution in March.[6] The consequence of this was to reaffirm the dominance of the Austrian influence in all Italy, but another important issue had been raised at Troppau and Laibach, that of the merits and legitimacy of the intervention of one state in the internal affairs of another.

THE BREAKDOWN OF THE CONCERT

Metternich had been docilely supported by Prussia at these congresses and he began to make some headway in winning Tsar

[4] Austro-Russian rivalry cut across the wider interest in the maintenance of proper order everywhere. Metternich suspected the tsar of being desirous of extending Russian influence in general. There was the basis of a bargain between a free hand for Austria in Italy in exchange for a Russian free hand in the Balkans. Already at Aix-la-Chapelle the tsar's wishes of general European coöperation had been sidetracked.
[5] King Ferdinand of Naples, appearing before the Congress, repudiated the concessions extracted from him and asked for Austrian assistance to reëstablish order in his state.
[6] King Victor Emmanuel I had abdicated in favor of his brother Charles Felix, naming at the same time Charles Albert, the next in the line of succession, as regent. The latter, liberally inclined, proclaimed a constitution, but the Austrian intervention established Charles Felix and reaction in control. In their own Italian domain, Lombardo-Venetia, the Austrians indulged in severe persecution of liberals.

Alexander away from his dangerous liberal proclivities. But Castlereagh had strongly opposed the principle of intervention while the French government, catering to its own liberal opinion, refusing to take a stand inimical to liberalism in Italy, had maintained a noncommittal attitude. What emerged, therefore, might be regarded as an alliance of sorts between the three conservative courts of Vienna, St. Petersburg, and Berlin. Then and since the issue of intervention has troubled the relations of states.

More consistently than any other state, island and commercial Britain has adhered to the policy of nonintervention, tending to recognize whatever system or regime happens to be in *de facto* control; generally speaking, the principle of nonintervention has been honored in periods of stability. But when novel ideas or ideologies seize control of a state it becomes difficult for them to be contained within its boundaries for they will command the allegiance of individuals in other states as well. Quite naturally, therefore, a major upheaval like the French Revolution or the Russian of our own time, leads to the reciprocal intervention of the revolutionary state in the affairs of others and of that of the others in the home of the revolution. War generally ensues, but even after peace is restored it may take long before the impact of the new ideology becomes absorbed into the normal political life of states. At such times the merits of intervention versus nonintervention are vigorously debated; the actual practice varies with individual circumstances while the debate remains forever unresolved.

If Aix-la-Chapelle had dealt with France alone and if Italian affairs had been the only object of decision at Troppau and Laibach, unrest and revolution, whether potential or actual, were active elsewhere as well. Spain had like others felt the impact of French ideas; she was, in addition, embroiled in a struggle to retain the control of her rebellious transatlantic possessions. Even before rebellion occurred in Naples, it had flared up in Spain in January, 1820.[7] Restored King Ferdinand VII had been forced to grant a constitution, the operation of which was badly strained by the contentions of extremes of the Right and Left, *apostolicos* and *exaltados*, as they styled themselves. An attempted coup of the Right in July, 1822, though failing in Madrid, established control in the North.

---

[7] The Spanish rising started in 1819 with the mutiny of troops assembled for transportation to America at Cadiz, whence it spread through much of the country.

Spanish affairs were naturally of special interest to neighboring France. In that country the relatively liberal Duc de Richelieu had been succeeded in October, 1821, by the more reactionary Villèle.[8] Assistance in restoring King Ferdinand in full control, attractive to the conservatives in France, might in addition redound to the prestige of French power. For that very reason the prospect of it was unwelcome in Britain. Another European congress met in Verona in October, 1822, to consider the Spanish situation. The tsar, as usual, would gladly intervene in Spain; but no one in Europe, not even Metternich, relished the prospect of a Russian army marching across the Continent; if Europe was to intervene in Spain her mandate would logically devolve on France. Castlereagh had elected to commit suicide on the eve of the Congress, but his successor, Canning, was even more strongly opposed to intervention in Spain. He was alone, however, and the determined stand of France was supported by the three eastern Powers. Though Wellington proclaimed the British opposition to intervention, Britain would hardly go the length of using force to prevent it; but Britain had clearly dissociated herself from the Concert of Europe.

A French army marched into Spain[9] in 1823 and accomplished its task with ease, after which it withdrew,[10] giving the lie to certain British fears. Even among the four Continental Powers, agreement was largely a fiction that diplomatic formulas endeavored to maintain; France had received a European mandate, but she herself minimized that aspect of things, and the rift in the Concert of Europe was made even sharper in connection with the other aspect of the Spanish question, that of the American colonies.[11]

That Spain's title to her colonies was legitimate was not open to question, but the fact was also irrelevant. By its very nature any revolution is illegal since its purpose is to alter the foundations of legitimacy. Rebellion against the rule of Spain in the New World had begun as early as 1810 and continued with alternating

[8] The relatively liberal tendency of the French government was brought to a halt following the assassination of the king's nephew, the Duc de Berri, in 1820. The ensuing reaction proceeded to institute measures inspired by the same spirit as the British Six Acts and the Carlsbad decrees.

[9] Some qualms were felt in France on the score of the loyalty of the army in such an operation, but no difficulties occurred.

[10] Repression in Spain was extremely brutal and harsh, to the extent that the French commander, the Duc d'Angoulême, endeavored, though without success, to counsel moderation.

[11] The Congress of Verona did little more than mention the Italian and the Greek situations. Of the latter more will be said presently, see below, pp. 43 ff.

prospects during the following decade. The end of the Napoleonic Wars, freeing Spain in Europe, enabled her to reassert herself overseas, but after 1817 the South American leaders, San Martin and Bolivar, achieved increasing success, to which the mutiny at Cadiz and revolution in Spain was a fillip. Not until 1823 was Spain in a position to renew her effort, but it was too late by that time; under any dispensation at home, the Spanish policy of intransigeance had rendered any accommodation with her rebellious colonies unlikely to succeed.

American affairs involved no concrete interests of the Eastern Powers of Europe. Among them, the tsar alone showed a desire to provide material assistance to Spain, partly because of principle, partly with an eye on rival Britain. For Britain, having in mind the advantages that would accrue to her own trade, was entirely favorable to the destruction of the commercial monopoly of Spain. France, also an Atlantic and a commercial Power, was not insensitive to such considerations, but her policy was more tortuous and laden with political overtones: the establishment of republics in America she did not view with sympathy, but monarchies might be created for which French princes could be made available. The French intervention of 1823 in Spain destroyed the possibility of a common Anglo-French policy.

THE MONROE DOCTRINE. But here another element intrudes. The young American republic, but recently emancipated from Britain, because of its own origin was sympathetic to the struggle for independence going on to the South. Ideological sympathy, commercial considerations, the general dislike of European intrusion on the American continent as a whole, all pointed to an orientation of American policy similar to the British. The United States had but recently been at war with Britain and could even humor Spain for a while,[12] but we have here an early instance of what was destined to grow into one of the major factors at a later time, the large coincidence of British and American interest for all that rivalry exists within the larger common interest. In the third decade of the nineteenth century America was still small and weak, not in a category with either Britain or the major European Powers, but as early as April, 1822, the American government announced its intention of recognizing the South American states,

[12] While negotiations were proceeding for the acquisition of Florida from Spain, which was effected in 1819.

which the following year it urged to adhere to republican forms of government like its own, a statement that betokened suspicion of French designs.

Nothing had come in 1817 and 1818 of Russian and Franco-Russian proposals of mediation, but the French action in Spain in 1823 had the effect of bringing closer together the United States and Britain. Canning would have liked a common declaration of policy which minor differences prevented.[13] He therefore went on to notify the French government that Britain would not brook any French intervention overseas; Polignac and Villèle meekly submitted, even putting their acquiescence in writing. But persisting American suspicion of Britain, plus Secretary Adams' pride in independence, overcoming the objections of some of his colleagues, resulted in the message that President Monroe sent to the Congress on December 2, 1823, the Monroe Doctrine: any European intervention in the Americas would be regarded as an unfriendly act.

This was a daring gesture in view of the extent of American power, but the gesture was safe owing to the French commitment to Canning, of which the American government was informed. It is therefore correct to assert that the American position was taken under cover of the protection of British naval power, though Canning's grandiloquent claim that he had called the New World into existence to redress the balance of the Old was an exaggerated boast. But for the longer future, as American power grew and America became capable of enforcing the Doctrine by her own means, the Monroe Doctrine must be viewed as a statement of the highest importance. Some considerable time was to elapse, however, before the reality would match the proclaimed intentions; during that interval, the solid fact of British naval power was what actually counted.

Like Spain, Portugal was possessed of vast South American holdings. But the story of the emergence of Brazil to independence was different from that of the Spanish-speaking part of the continent. In 1808 the Portuguese government had sought refuge in Rio de Janeiro, where it remained after the restoration of 1814. When Prince John returned to Lisbon in 1820, he left his son Dom Pedro in control in Brazil. When the Brazilians, following the example of the surrounding Spanish lands, claimed independence, Dom Pedro, taking the leadership of the movement, proclaimed himself

[13] Britain felt some reluctance in granting recognition to republican governments.

emperor. To this step the government in Lisbon granted peaceful recognition in 1825, with the consequence that Brazilian independence did not become a concern of the Powers. Having obtained confirmation of the commercial advantages secured in Brazil during the Napoleonic Wars, the British government had urged the Portuguese to recognize Brazilian independence.

II. The Revolutions of 1830

The international scene was quiescent during the second half of the decade of the twenties. Tsar Alexander died in December, 1825; the military rising that followed, the Decembrist movement, lacked sufficient foundation in Russia to produce significant results; it was promptly put down by Alexander's successor, Nicholas I, a confirmed autocrat. The war that Russia waged against Turkey in 1828–1829 will be dealt with more conveniently in connection with the survey of the Near Eastern Question.[14] In the Central European domain of the Habsburgs, the hunting down of the exponents of liberal ideas proceeded with success; the Metternichian system seemed in firm control. But mention must be made of a Prussian initiative, the consequences of which were both lasting and considerable: having already established a uniform tariff in all her territories, in response to the needs of growing trade, Prussia initiated the movement of customs union, the *Zollverein*, that would shortly include nearly all Germany.[15] The first beginnings of the *Zollverein* may be dated to 1818; by 1834 the movement was successfully launched.

Britain had been least affected among European states by the ideas that, from France, had spread over the Continent. Nevertheless, revolutionary excesses helped strengthen conservatism across the Channel. The Six Acts of 1819 betokened fear of the mob, but it was not long before more liberal tendencies began to reassert themselves. The Catholic Emancipation of 1829 is one of their manifestations, but of greater concern to Englishmen were issues rising out of economic change. England was fortunate in the head

[14] In 1826–1828 Russia waged against Persia a successful war to which the Treaty of Turkmanchai put an end. By it Russia obtained a portion of Armenia and the exclusive right to a naval establishment on the Caspian, as well as commercial concessions.

[15] In Germany proper, exclusive of Austria, there was opposition and rivalry between reactionary Prussia and the more liberal Southern states which set up a rival union. The year 1829 marks the turning point when Prussia began to secure the adherence of other states to her union.

start she had in the development of industry; she could successfully meet the competition of others and the increasing place of industry in her economy went with the growing demand for free trade. The old mercantilistic system was under mounting attack while the pressure was also rising, not for a change in the fundamentals of the system, but for a distribution of representation that would give a better reflection of the existing reality of economic power.

France, by contrast, seemed bent on increasing reaction that the advent to the throne of Charles X in 1824 appeared to establish in secure control. France remained torn between irreconcilable extremes and the British record of unlimited, but gradual and peaceful, change within the framework of an existing constitution was not to be hers. Reaction in successful control merely meant that explosive pressure was generated; when change occurred in France, the form of it was to be violent. The explosion took place in July, 1830.[16] Charles X took the road of exile, to be replaced by a member of the Orléans branch, Louis Philippe. The change constituted a clear success of bourgeois liberalism, expression as in England of the rising power of a new class of industry and trade; the fact is significant that the new ruler was not king of France but king of the French: the supremacy of popular sovereignty was thus once more asserted.[17]

But what is of especial interest from the point of view of this treatment is the fact that the Parisian events had widespread repercussions abroad; it was an encouraging signal to liberals throughout the Continent, some of whom thought the time propitious for imitation of the French example. In matters governmental Britain does not follow France, although the liberal success in the latter country was not without some effect in encouraging similar forces in the former; the great Reform Bill of 1832, though constitutionally enacted, registered the success of tendencies quite similar to those that had won the day in France. But on the Continent risings were both widespread and numerous. The one that was to furnish the occasion for major international activity occurred next door to France herself and led to the emergence of a new political unit on the map of Europe.

[16] The occasion for it was the king's refusal to heed the verdict of an election, following which Charles X attempted to assert the power of the executive. Decrees dissolving the Chamber, restricting the franchise, and curbing the press were answered by a Parisian rising.

[17] The franchise was also enlarged, raising the French electorate to some 200,000, and the hereditary peerage was abolished.

THE INDEPENDENCE OF BELGIUM

The settlement of 1815 had united under one sovereign the Dutch Netherlands and the former Austrian Netherlands, modern Holland and Belgium. Whether a separate Belgian nationality exists might be debated; it has in fact been denied, for in what came to be Belgium there were, and are, two distinct ethnic groups, Walloon and Flemish, separated by language. They were both Catholic, however, unlike the predominantly Calvinist Dutch; moreover, the government of the Dutch king, William I, had been unwise in its management, causing Walloons and Flemings alike to resent their rule by what they looked upon as alien Dutch administrators. Despite the divergence between the more conservative and strongly Catholic inclination of the Flemish section and the more liberal, sometimes anticlerical, tendency of the Walloon, the two eventually joined in the common focus of opposition to the Dutch, hence the desire for union.[18]

At any rate, a rising occurred in Brussels on August 25, 1830, which expelled the Dutch garrison. The uncompromising attitude of King William soon turned relatively moderate demands for the redressing of grievances and a measure of autonomy into a struggle for complete national independence which a provisional government proclaimed in October. The following month a constituent assembly pronounced itself in favor of a constitutional monarchy for the country.

This situation confronted the Powers with a major issue. According to the existing law of Europe, King William was undoubtedly the legitimate ruler of Belgium. The Dutch ruler, in fact, appealed to his legitimate brother rulers—all, that is, but the French —for assistance in putting down the rebellion. Tsar Nicholas was most responsive: like his predecessor he was prepared to send troops; the Prussian king was not unfavorable, but both he and the tsar eventually insisted that action must be collective; Metternich was even less enthusiastic, confining himself to expressions of moral support. The three Eastern rulers had for that matter cause for concern nearer home, as there will presently be occasion to mention.

The British and the French attitudes were thus of greatest consequence. The possibility could not but present itself to all of a

[18] Economic factors also played a role, the divergence between the interests of primarily commercial Holland and those of increasingly industrial Belgium.

repetition of 1792 when the French had overrun Belgium as liberators, and there were indeed those on both sides of the Franco-
Belgian frontier to whom such a course was attractive. But French
intervention in support of a rebellion might easily spill over into a
French incorporation of Belgium. Be it on the score of legitimacy
or on that of excessive French power, French intervention would
likely result in that of others. If liberal Britain could contemplate
with equanimity, or even sympathy, a Belgian struggle for independence, French power in Belgium would certainly evoke strong
British opposition. But, conversely, active intervention by one or
more of the Eastern Powers would likely cause the French to
intervene. The situation for a while was quite delicately balanced.

But Louis Philippe, the bourgeois king, was peacefully inclined.
French interventionist opinion he resisted, announcing at the end
of August that he favored nonintervention by all, but also making
it clear that France would not tolerate the intervention of others.
The effect of this was to put Britain in an arbitral position. Britain
in general felt no desire to assist the Dutch king, let alone to engage
in general war; once the one paramount condition—no French
control of Belgium—was assured, British and French policies were
engaged on similar paths and it became in fact Britain's concern to
prevent the intervention of others, lest that in turn produce French
interference. It fell to Talleyrand, the same old Talleyrand, nomi-
nated to the London embassy, to urge on Wellington these considerations of common policy. But as a French initiative might be
impolitic, it was left to the British government to propose the
holding of an international conference to deal with the question.

The conference met in London and, as early as November,
agreed upon a protocol that recognized the Belgian state.[19] There
remained details to be settled, Anglo-French differences in the
main, for Britain wanted reinsurance against possible French designs in the future, but their adjustment proved not too difficult
since both she and Louis Philippe, in spite of pressure in France in
the case of the latter, were bent on conciliation. The conference
essentially concluded its labors with the Protocol of January 21,
1831, birth certificate of present-day Belgium. From the standpoint of the Powers the chief provisions of this agreement were
two: they jointly guaranteed the perpetual neutrality of Belgium,

[19] Tsar Nicholas' interventionist enthusiasm was curbed by two facts, the lack
of eagerness, especially on the part of Austria and of Prussia, and the rising that
took place in Poland, of which more will be said presently, see below, pp. 36–37.

and they agreed that the new Belgian ruler should not be a member of the ruling family of any of the major states. This last provision gave rise to some difficulty though it proved easier to fulfill it than it was to establish the frontiers of the new state.

The Powers reached a decision on this latter score on January 27; Belgium would not include either Limburg or Luxembourg. The Belgians did not accept this decision, and with an eye to the enlistment of French help for the satisfaction of their claims, on February 3 their assembly offered the crown to the Duc de Nemours, a son of Louis Philippe, thereby contravening another of the Powers' decisions. Britain could be counted upon to veto French acceptance, and Palmerston[20] made it clear that he would envisage war to prevent it. But Louis Philippe had no desire for conflict, the possibility of which was removed when, speaking for his son, he declined the Belgian offer. The issue was finally resolved with the offer of the Belgian crown to a candidate acceptable to England, Leopold of Saxe-Coburg.

It was now the turn of the Dutch king to object; in August he once more resorted to the use of force. But Anglo-French understanding was such by this time that Britain had no objection to the appearance in Belgium of a French army that went there to enforce the joint verdict of Europe. The treaty of November 15, 1831, embodying the protocol of twenty-four articles of the preceding month, once more registered the agreement of the Powers and settled the frontiers of Belgium on the basis of a compromise that divided both Limburg and Luxembourg. The eastern section of this last, including the city of Luxembourg, continued as a Grand Duchy in personal union with Holland under the rule of the Dutch king.[21] This settlement proved final, and though a joint Anglo-French armed intervention was needed to evict the Dutch from Antwerp, they eventually recognized the treaty of 1831, but not until another eight years had elapsed.

In peaceful fashion, where the Powers at least were concerned, an alteration had been made in the political map of Europe that had been drawn in 1815. The episode may therefore be regarded as an instance of the successful operation of the Concert of Europe. Nevertheless it also emphasized the cleavage between the more

[20] In mid-November Wellington's Cabinet had fallen and Palmerston took charge of the foreign office in the succeeding Grey ministry.
[21] Holland also retained the left bank of the estuary of the Scheldt but not the city of Antwerp.

liberal Western Powers and those still under the successful sway of reaction. In fact, one reason for the passivity of the eastern states was the fact that their rule was challenged in their own domain.

1830 IN EASTERN AND CENTRAL EUROPE

THE POLISH INSURRECTION.   It has been said, with some exaggeration, that Belgian independence was secured by the Poles; a connection exists nonetheless between events in Brussels and Warsaw. It had been one of the manifestations of Tsar Alexander's romantic liberalism that, instead of simply incorporating Poland into his own domain, he had set himself up as constitutional king of that country, though he too, like Louis XVIII, had "granted" the constitution of Poland. The Poles enjoyed freedom of the press and religion, there was a distinct Polish army, Polish-officered save that its head was a Russian general, administration of the country was in Polish hands as well, and there was a Polish Diet, elected under the customarily restricted suffrage of the day where the suffrage existed at all. Though ultimate power remained in the hands of the tsar's representative in Warsaw, the Poles were hardly an oppressed people.

Nevertheless, there were some elements in Poland, army officers, smaller nobility, intellectuals, that were attracted to the liberalism of Western Europe and resented the alien Russian control, relatively light though it was; Polish nationalism has long been a sturdy growth. The Polish opposition was neither well organized nor even in agreement within itself upon a clear program of action, reflecting the aspect of romantic individualism often associated with Poland. The tsar's mobilization of the Polish army in connection with the possibility of intervention in Belgium gave the malcontents their opportunity. In November, 1830, a rising caused the Russian viceroy to withdraw. The provisional government, under the dominance at first of the more moderate elements, sought initially a negotiated compromise.[22] But the tsar's refusal produced a declaration of independence by the Polish Diet on January 25, 1831.

The only hope of success for the Poles lay in outside assistance. Clearly, this would not be forthcoming from either Prussia or Austria which in fact closed their Russian frontiers lest their own

---

[22] On the basis of the full restoration of the constitution of 1815, on which some encroachments had occurred, and also of the restoration of territories lost in 1772.

Polish subjects assist those in the anti-Russian rebellion. There was substantial sympathy for Polish independence in the West, in Britain, and even more in France. But Palmerston wanted no complications, the advantage of which might redound to France, while in the latter country Louis Philippe was mainly anxious to convince others of his peaceful intentions. French intervention did not go beyond the offer of moderating advice to the tsar—advice, needless to say, rejected—and the vote of a resolution of sympathy for the Poles by the Chamber in August, 1831. As early as December, 1830, the French government had stated through its foreign minister, Sébastiani, its advocacy of nonintervention.

The Poles were therefore left to their own insufficient resources.[23] What assistance they had was no more than the indirect one that resulted from the tsar's concern with the general European situation—events in Italy and Belgium—that caused him to refrain for a time from committing large forces in Poland lest they be needed for a larger war. Once the full weight of Russian power was brought into action the fate of the Polish insurrection was sealed; in September, 1831, the Russians entered Warsaw. Russian repression was harsh and the Polish grievance had greater justification after than before the abortive uprising; the Polish desire for freedom was rather exacerbated than stilled.[24] The episode registered a deep impression on the tsar in whose mind the memory of it persisted; more immediately, the Polish insurrection had served to curb the Russian freedom of action on the larger European scene.

DEVELOPMENTS IN CENTRAL EUROPE. The general unrest that manifested itself at the opening of the fourth decade of the century was not without effects in the central section of Europe as well, the region of more direct Metternichian control, but the disturbances in this case were of smaller proportions than in the cases just related of either Belgium or Poland.

The events in Paris of July, 1830, gave encouragement to liberals throughout the Italian Peninsula. There was insurrection in the Papal domain, in Romagna, which soon spread to neighboring Modena and Parma; the focus of this agitation was mainly the demand for domestic reform rather than a manifestation of unitary

[23] The Provisional Government even sought the assistance of Turkey with whom Russia had recently been at war, see below, pp. 46 ff.
[24] Thousands of Poles sought the shelter of emigration to other European states. Disagreeing among themselves as usual, the Polish émigrés nevertheless kept up active and intense propaganda.

Italian nationalism. As ten years earlier in Naples, Metternich wanted to suppress these movements and Austrian troops made their appearance in the Papal States. But, just as Britain was suspicious of any possible extension of French influence in Belgium, so likewise France disliked any further enhancement of the Austrian position in Italy. The threat of her own intervention produced an Austrian withdrawal after order had been restored.

But a renewed outbreak brought the Austrians to Bologna. The French answer this time was a landing of troops in Ancona, the length of whose stay it was announced would be determined by the duration of the Austrian intervention. The rulers of the Italian states felt no great love for the Austrian power, but neither did they like revolution, a commodity likely to be found, in their estimation, in the baggage of any French army, especially of one that would represent the July Monarchy whose origin was, after all, revolutionary. And the appearance of the French on the scene did in effect encourage the hopes in Italy of those who were at once anti-Austrian and liberal. The wish to protect their own positions easily overcame among the rulers whatever desire they may have felt for emancipation from Austrian tutelage, and even Charles-Albert of the Kingdom of Sardinia concluded a secret treaty with Austria by way of reinsurance against the possible French peril. But Metternich was content with the restoration of order in Italy where France had no intention of engaging in any adventures. The Italian situation therefore did not give rise to any further complications.

What repercussions were felt in Germany of the events of 1830 were even feebler than in Italy. Liberals there were in Germany as well, but they were neither organized nor very numerous; talk, meetings, banquets, resolutions were sufficient outlet for their activity. What interest attaches to these repercussions is as an occasion for the testing of Austro-Prussian relations. The timid Prussian king was not minded to assert independence of policy; like his Italian counterparts he agreed with the governmental philosophy of Metternich whose initiative he was content to follow. Metternich therefore used the occasion of whatever agitation there was to reassert and strengthen the Carlsbad decisions of 1819. To a degree, nevertheless, he may be said to have paid a price for his success.

Mention has been made of the spreading of customs unions in the Germanic world. There were three such unions in 1830: the

Prussian, one of the intermediate central states, and the southern one of Württemberg and Bavaria. By the beginning of 1834 the three had been merged, but Austria was not part of the union.[25] Metternich was not unaware of the significance of this economic development: a tacit *quid pro quo* was effected out of Austrian acquiescence to this development in return for Prussian support of the Metternichian order in politics; but the appearance of Austrian leadership was to prove less solid than the substance of the development taking place under the sponsorship of Prussian initiative. Put it another way perhaps: as the nineteenth century was unfolding, economic factors assumed increasing importance over the more purely political.

From the point of view of Europe as a whole, the disturbances that occurred in the opening years of the fourth decade of the century had relatively small effect. The avoidance of any major conflict was due in considerable part to the moderate and peaceful policy of the new French regime of Louis Philippe. Once its intentions were established, Britain had no cause for objection, and in fact, despite continuing suspicion, Britain and France found themselves drawn together in opposition and contrast to the Eastern regimes. The Belgian episode brought out this disharmony in the Concert of Europe; yet it may also be cited as an instance of the Concert in successful operation. The Powers eventually agreed in London, and once they had agreed their will was enforced upon the recalcitrant, but undeniably legitimate, Dutch king.

On balance Metternich could still feel satisfied that his system was in successful operation, especially in the Central European domain of his more immediate control. Liberals were too few in that portion of Europe, whether Italian or Germanic, they lacked a widespread basis of support, as well as organization and practice. But, despite the setback that it suffered, liberalism was not dead; rather it continued to grow and gather strength and was, under the surface, one of the vital forces of the future. The better part of two decades was to elapse, however, before liberalism would give the European structure a major jolt with consequences equally important for the internal ordering of states as for their mutual relations. Meantime the chancelleries of Europe had cause to busy themselves with events on the fringes of the Continent, mainly in the Mediterranean region, and especially in the eastern portion of

[25] Among the dissident states were Baden, Hanover, Mecklenburg, Nassau, and Frankfort.

it. These events had already been unfolding for some years before 1830 and to them we must turn our attention.

III. Mediterranean Problems

THE EASTERN QUESTION

The Congress of Verona in October, 1822, had dealt mainly with the Spanish problem, choosing to ignore the contemporaneous disturbance of which Greece was the center. In Metternich's words, the Ottoman Empire was beyond the pale of civilization and moreover the sultan was the legitimate ruler of Greece, hence the trouble might be allowed to burn itself out. But the Greek rising was only a limited aspect of the larger Eastern Question which, more than any other single issue, was the continuing concern of the diplomacy of Europe in this period.

In simple form, the Eastern, or Near Eastern, Question is the problem of the fate of the Ottoman Empire. The Turks had once threatened to overcome all Europe, but the danger was checked during the sixteenth century, mainly by Habsburg resistance. Things became stabilized for a time, roughly along the Danube boundary, and the Turks remained established in the European Balkans. Despite the size of their European holdings their main base was outside Europe, a fact to which emphasis was added by the contrast between their own Islamic religion and the Christianity of Europe. After a time, while the power of Europe went on increasing, that of the Ottoman state entered upon a process of decay and the initiative of aggression passed from their hands into those of the Habsburgs first, then of Russia, these two Powers generally coöperating in pushing back the area of Ottoman control. The Treaty of Carlowitz in 1699 may be regarded as the turning point; the whole eighteenth century registered fairly consistent Austrian and Russian encroachment, and the Treaty of Kutchuk Kainardji of 1774 marks an important step along the Russian road toward the Straits as well as the intrusion of Russian power into internal Ottoman affairs.[26] In addition to the interest of Austria and of Russia, an interest deriving from the simple fact of territorial contiguity, France was the other European Power with

---

[26] The Treaty of Kutchuk Kainardji gave Russia control of lands north of the Black Sea and acknowledged her right to the protection of some churches in Constantinople; a Turkish promise or reform in the Principalities implied an undefined Russian right of interference.

substantial interests in the Near East, interests of long standing, the continuity of which may be traced back to the Crusades through the sixteenth-century alliance of Francis I with Soleiman. The British, too, had at one time created a Levant Company, but their interest until the nineteenth century, whether commercial or political, was still secondary to the Russian, the Austrian, and the French.

The Ottoman Empire remained essentially extraneous to the great European upheaval that closed in 1815. The effect of French revolutionary ideas was nonexistent in Constantinople though faint repercussions were felt among some of the subject Balkan peoples. Napoleon, to be sure, went to Egypt, but that was an abortive experience[27] and the tsar was at war with the sultan from 1806 to 1812, when the Treaty of Bucharest registered the Russian acquisition of Bessarabia. It has been indicated that the Ottoman question was not discussed at the Congress of Vienna; this was in deference to Russian wishes but did not mean that there was no awareness of the Turkish problem, for continuing decadence had reached such a stage in the domain of the sultan that the question arose of the eventual disposition and fate of the inheritance of the "Sick Man of Europe," the prospect of whose demise had become a not too distant possibility.

For Ottoman possessions were still vast. Besides the European Balkans, the rule of the sultan extended over the entire Near East, in terms of current political divisions, Turkey and all the Arab states from Iraq and Arabia to Libya; even beyond this, modern Tunisia and Algeria had still some nominal connection at least with Constantinople. The Napoleonic episode had the effect of increasing the British awareness of the importance of the Eastern Mediterranean; after 1815 Britain retained the bases of Malta and the Ionian Islands. As it opened, the nineteenth century therefore found four Powers with definite interests in the Ottoman Empire and its fate: Russia, Austria, France, and Britain. There was no direct or immediate Prussian interest other than the fact that, as one of the Great Powers, Prussia had a voice in all European problems.[28]

But in the evolution of the Eastern Question throughout the nineteenth century another element intrudes. The Turkish con-

[27] It had significance nevertheless as a manifestation of French interest in the Near East for the later extension of which it also laid further bases.
[28] Even after the unification of Germany, German interest was slow in developing and did not become substantial until the decade from 1890 to 1900.

quest of the European Balkans went back to the fourteenth century, but in spite of their long subjection the Balkan peoples had for the most part retained their religion, Christianity, of the Eastern, or Greek Orthodox, persuasion. In view of the nature of the Ottoman state, one in which the sultan was caliph and the Koran the basis of the law, the Christian subjects of that state could not be subject to Islamic law; the millet was the answer, a system whereby the state acknowledged the existence within itself of communities to whom a different type of law must apply, a concept alien to European thought and practice, since the basis of law in Europe is territorial. As head of the Christian community, the Greek Patriarch of Constantinople was in effect an important official of the Ottoman state.[29]

But these Balkan Christian subjects of the sultan belonged to a variety of distinct ethnic groups. The memory of distant events and past glories, Bulgarian Tsar Simeon, Serbian Dushan and Kossovo field, to say nothing of the glory that was Greece, persisted, often carried about in popular ballads. These peoples had in common the fact of their Christianity and their objection to Turkish control, often maladministration rather than outright oppression, yet they differed among themselves. In the course of their nineteenth-century struggle for emancipation from Ottoman control, in proportion to the degree of the success of that struggle the accent came to be increasingly on their mutual differences.

The Balkans were to become a microcosmic replica of the larger European scene of power competition, with the consequence of introducing unwonted complications in the affairs of Europe. For international relations operated on the Balkan scene at two levels: the local, where a group of small Powers were engaged in mutual competition; the European, where the Great Powers were concerned, first with the defense and promotion of their respective interests, secondly with an adjustment of their rivalries that would prevent open conflict among them. They did not always succeed. In this involved situation the Balkan peoples and states assumed the status of pawns or clients of the greater Powers, but they in turn had it in their power to use and exploit the rivalries among the larger states for their own ends. It will appear quite understandable in this context that the Balkans should have earned the description of "powder keg of Europe."

[29] His stewardship extended to Greek Orthodox Christians only. Other Christian communities, the Armenians, for instance, were organized separately.

Vis-à-vis the Balkans Russia enjoyed a unique position. One reason for this was the community of religion, the other the fact that a goodly proportion of the Balkan peoples were Slavs. Moscow, the third Rome, ancient capital of the tsars (caesars), would not be loath to claim—and exploit—the right to act as protector of brother Christians and Slavs. This could be used, when expedient, in furtherance of the more sharply defined Russian aim of gaining control of the Straits, or at least unimpeded passage through them. For a long time Russia and Austria had generally coöperated against the Turks, but with the disappearance of any threat from the latter, this coöperation turned into competition. To an extension of Russian control over the Straits the staunchest opposition was to come from Britain. French interest in this respect coincided with British, but elsewhere in the Near East France and Britain engaged in bitter rivalry. Thus a set of firmly established differences, Austro-Russian, Anglo-Russian, and Anglo-French came to surround the evolution of the Eastern Question; against this, Anglo-Austrian similarity of views may be regarded as a constant, while on specific issues and occasions Britain, Russia, and France might join in pairs against the other Power. In the Balkans themselves Britain had no direct interest and France but little.

This is the general background and the broad framework within which the story of the Eastern Question was to unfold during most of the nineteenth century. Christian grievances against the ruling Turks and simple nationalism struggling for independence were the chief elements that, within the Ottoman Empire itself, furnished occasion for specific developments, crises, and wars, and at all times much diplomatic activity of the Powers. Already by 1815 a measure of autonomy had been secured by the small nucleus of Serbia.[30] The first major development after that date had its focus in Greece.

THE INDEPENDENCE OF GREECE. Among the Christian Balkan subjects of the Turks the Greeks held a special position. Like others, they had fallen to a low estate in Greece proper, but the old maritime tradition they had never lost nor the classical skill and nimbleness of traders. An important Greek colony, the Phanariote, in the Phanar, a section of Constantinople, commanded

[30] The Serbs were largely abandoned by Russia in 1812, but after the rising of 1815 Milosh Obrenović was recognized by the sultan as hereditary prince of Serbia in 1817.

substantial wealth and position,[31] and in the eighteenth century one may already trace the beginnings of Greek national revival in the customary literary form that such phenomena commonly take, especially in the case of small and long-submerged ethnic groups; the glory of ancient Greece and the prestige that it commanded among all Western civilized mankind were valuable assets for the Greeks. Following in this respect also a common pattern of the time, the *Hetairia Philiké*, a secret revolutionary society, was organized in Odessa in 1814 with the connivance of the tsar, one of whose close advisors, Capo d'Istria, was a Corfiote by origin.

The movement was led by Alexander Ypsilanti, of a Greek Phanariote family established in Moldavia, at the time an officer in the Russian army. He and a brother of his simultaneously sought to raise the standard of revolt in 1821 in Moldavia and in the Morea. The failure of hoped-for Russian assistance caused the Moldavian movement to be promptly crushed by the Turks,[32] but the Morean rising had better success. An ultimatum sent by the tsar to the Turks in July, though rejected by the latter, did not lead to war; the tsar allowed himself to be restrained and convinced by Metternich's consideration of the legitimacy of Turkish rule and the general undesirability of supporting revolution, arguments that Castlereagh underwrote.

This is not the place to dwell on the details of the local aspects of the struggle. It was one of unwonted brutality on both sides, justifying in some degree the Metternichian description of it as taking place beyond the pale of civilization. But despite reciprocal massacres the Greek revolt maintained its hold on the Morea, and an assembly proclaimed independence on January 13, 1822. The Greeks benefited in considerable measure from the sympathy of opinion in Europe, especially the liberal opinion of the West, whence individual enthusiasts went to join the war of independence. Lord Byron, who died in Missolonghi, is perhaps the most famous of them, but there were others. As time passed and the struggle went on with varying but inconclusive fortunes, it became further complicated by the injection of that normal component of Greek politics, internecine quarrels.

So far, Europe had watched the conflict from the sidelines

[31] The Greek Patriarch of Constantinople usually came from the Phanariote community, from which were also drawn the hospodars of the Principalities.
[32] The Phanariote hospodars of Moldavia were regarded locally as Turkish administrators, hence commanded little popular allegiance.

despite the pressure of pro-Greek opinion. From combined motives of sympathy and national interest Russia was favorably inclined to the Greeks in their struggle for emancipation. If Austria and Britain were opposed to an extension, in whatever form, of Russian influence in the Balkans, France was less concerned and the tsar was not blind to the possibility of Franco-Russian coöperation; but France was on her side reluctant to commit herself in opposition to British and Austrian wishes. The opposition of these Powers to another scheme of the tsar, his proposal, in January, 1824, to set up three distinct Greek principalities under Turkish suzerainty, a scheme acceptable neither to Greeks nor Turks for that matter, caused it to be set aside. Unable to subdue the Greeks, the sultan appealed for assistance to his vassal, Mohamed Ali of Egypt, whose son, Ibrahim, landing in the Morea in 1825, proceeded to reconquer that region.

Tsar Nicholas I, who came to the throne in December, 1825, was disposed, unlike his predecessor, to put greater stress on the purely Russian interest than on the undesirability of supporting rebellion. In March, 1826, he sent an ultimatum to the Porte, stressing, however, the situation in the Principalities of Moldavia and Wallachia rather than Greek affairs. In face of the difficulty of Anglo-Austrian coöperation,[33] Britain elected to seek accommodation with Russia as a preferable alternative to conflict. Wellington's mission resulted in the protocol of April, 1826, which envisaged Anglo-Russian mediation for Greek autonomy under Turkish suzerainty.[34] The move was partly dictated by British fear lest Russia act alone, an element that will reappear in the future as inducing joint action by these rival Powers.

The Turks, meantime, sought to come to terms directly with Russia; the Convention of Akkerman of October 7, 1826, gave Russia satisfaction in the Principalities. But this attempt to divide the Powers did not succeed. On July 6, 1827, the Treaty of London, in which France joined Britain and Russia, provided for the enforcement of mediation by the resort to a blockade. The Turkish refusal of the three Powers' proposal[35] brought an Anglo-French fleet to the Morea where, by accident rather than design,

[33] If opposition to Russia was a common Anglo-Austrian interest, Britain was unwilling to support Metternich's policy in Central Europe.

[34] It was at this time, in June, that the sultan succeeded in ridding himself of the excessive power of the Janissaries, a result that was accomplished through the time-honored eastern method of massacre.

[35] With the assistance of Egyptian forces the Morea was being successfully reconquered at this time.

an action took place in Navarino Bay, on October 20, 1827, as the result of which the Turco-Egyptian fleet was destroyed. This unpremeditated act of intervention saved the Greeks, but the news of the victory caused dismay in London where the government characterized it as a deplorable event; for the effect of it was that in a matter of primarily Russian concern the initiative of armed action had passed into English and French hands.

The tsar could hardly be pleased at this turn of affairs; he reasserted the primacy of Russian interest by declaring war upon Turkey on April 26, 1828. The possibility of awkward complications appeared: Britain did not want war with Russia, but neither would she meekly acquiesce in the possible fruits of Russian victory; she reinforced her fleet in the Mediterranean, but France was rather bent on a compromise on the basis of giving Russia a free hand on the Danube while retaining the control of Greece for the West. Following an agreement with Mohamed Ali in August, the Egyptians withdrew from the Morea where their place was taken by a French expeditionary corps.

The Russians had meantime crossed the Danube but found their progress impeded by the condition of their forces;[36] they could not advance beyond Varna before the winter set in. Domestic considerations were making for restraint in London as well as in St. Petersburg. On March 22, 1829, the London Protocol ratified the agreement reached by the ambassadors of the three Powers: an autonomous Greek state, bounded in the north by a line from the Gulf of Volo to that of Arta, and tributary of the sultan, was to be ruled by a hereditary prince who would not be a member of the ruling family of any of the three states.

However, Britain balked at the sending of a tripartite ultimatum to the Porte, and Russo-Turkish hostilities were resumed in the spring. The Russian capture of Adrianople on August 20, in addition to Russian successes in the Caucasus, where Kars and Erzerum were also taken, resulted in the conclusion of a bilateral agreement, the Russo-Turkish Treaty of Adrianople of September 14, 1829. Russia acquired no territory in Europe beyond access to the southern mouth of the Danube; she would, however, pending the payment of an indemnity of 15,000,000 ducats, remain in occupation of the Principalities, whose fortifications

---

[36] The Persian war had the effect of a diversion on Russian military action in the Balkans. To this diversionary effect British influence was not extraneous.

were to be dismantled and whose hospodars would be appointed for life under a Russian supervisory right of guarantee; Greece was to be dealt with in accordance with the earlier Protocol of London.[37] The relative mildness of these terms was dictated by the exhausted state of the Russian forces and by the fear of inducing European complications.

This was the time that witnessed the elaboration of an ambitious French scheme, of which Polignac, the French Prime Minister, was the author. The Russian successes and the prospect of a complete collapse of the Ottoman Empire, combined with the possibility of a Russian orientation of French policy were the occasion for Polignac's design. It proposed that the Ottoman Empire should be partitioned, creating a very large Greece that would extend to Constantinople, while Russia would absorb the Principalities and Asiatic territory; Austria would receive Serbia and Bosnia. But this far-reaching readjustment was only part of a much wider European reshuffling: the king of the new Greece would be King William of the Low Countries, whose existing possessions would be partitioned, the colonies to Britain, Holland to Prussia, and Belgium to France; in addition, Prussia would complete the incorporation of Saxony, compensating her king with her own holdings on the left bank of the Rhine which would thus constitute a Franco-Prussian buffer. What Polignac was seeking was an advantage for France in the form of territorial gain in combination with an undoing of the 1815 arrangements. The scheme was clearly fantasy; neither Britain nor Prussia were likely to entertain such proposals and the tsar would not listen to them. It deserves no more than passing mention as a picturesque footnote to the unfolding of the Eastern Question.

The Powers, soon to meet in London in connection with the Belgian situation, set about disposing of the Greek problem as well. Their agreement, registered in the London Protocol of February 3, 1830, established a somewhat reduced[38] but completely independent Greece. The crown of it was offered to Leopold of Saxe-Coburg, shortly to mount the Belgian throne, who declined

[37] Russia also obtained Poti on the Black Sea, the right to trade in the Ottoman Empire, and the freedom of passage for her merchantmen through the Straits.

[38] The northern boundary was pushed southward to a line from the Gulf of Lamia to Aspropotamos, but Greek objections resulted in a restoration of the Arta-Volo frontier in 1832.

the offer. In March, 1832, Otto, the second son of the king of Bavaria, became the choice of the Powers; having accepted the offer he became king of Greece.[39]

Two new states, Belgium and Greece, had thus almost simultaneously made their appearance on the map of Europe. The emergence of both represented definite successes of nationalism, which provided the initial motivation of revolt against their legitimate sovereigns; yet both ultimately owed their existence to the joint will of Europe. The clash of interests that the process of their emergence produced had, in the end, been resolved without open conflict among the Great Powers. Partly impeded in the pursuit of foreign policy by their respective domestic preoccupations, they also showed a preference for the avoidance of a major clash among themselves. It will be noted, in the case of the Greek episode, that Austria played a surprisingly inactive role despite her major interest in Ottoman affairs. This tendency on Austria's part to remain in the background where Eastern affairs were concerned and to let others take the initiative, leaving them to court her assistance in the uncertainty of what she might elect to do, is characteristic of her eastern policy; it will appear on more than one occasion, generally to the annoyance of all. The reason for it lay in part at least in the fact that the East held second priority of interest for Austria who looked upon Central Europe as the prime concern of her policy. Not until her eviction from Italy and from Germany was she to put first emphasis on the Near East.

THE FRENCH ESTABLISHMENT IN ALGERIA.   If the Ottoman Empire had suffered the loss of Greece and of some other outlying parcels, it had escaped disintegration. But the tale of its difficulties was not ended even for the moment. It is out of the Greek situation that the Egyptian trouble arose, a major concern of the Turkish state no less than of the European Powers. Before dealing with that next chapter in the Eastern Question, brief mention may appropriately be made at this point of a development in the Western Mediterranean, in Algiers.

Whether or not the Regency of Algiers was still part of the Ottoman domain might be regarded as a fine point of law; it is a measure of the tenuousness of whatever links may have existed that the French conquest of Algeria gave rise at no point to Otto-

[39] For a time Capo d'Istria was virtual ruler of Greece until his assassination in October, 1831, in connection with internal Greek political feuds.

man involvements. Virtually the whole North African coast, save Egypt, had become independent under the rule of local powers, the home of Barbary corsairs whose activity was a source of common annoyance to the maritime nations of the day. Even the far removed United States had found cause for intervention in this piratical activity,[40] and in 1816 a British fleet, under mandate from the Congress of Vienna, had bombarded Algiers. The French had trading interests in Algiers, which were highhandedly treated at times;[41] in 1830 the government decided on a show of force. In July, 1830, Algiers was taken by a French expedition.

No great issue was initially involved, let alone the conquest of Algeria. The government of Charles X, which resolved on the action, was rather motivated by considerations of internal conditions at home, classical illustration of the resort to a foreign diversion for domestic unrest. That aspect of the matter was a failure and Charles X had to abandon the throne less than three weeks after the capture of Algiers. Economic considerations were largely nonexistent in France and those who entertained imperial designs were few, to be found mainly in naval circles. The new government of Louis Philippe was somewhat embarrassed by this particular legacy of its predecessor, yet felt that mere withdrawal would bespeak unwarranted timidity. The French therefore stayed on in Algiers, but several years elapsed before they could make up their minds to expand from that initial base. The capture of Constantine in 1837 may be regarded as the real beginning of a North African policy that was to lead in time to the foundation of a vast empire.

France's Algerian expedition gave rise to no international complications; one other Power alone, Britain, had any possible interest in the matter. The British government was not blind to the possible implications of a French establishment in North Africa; it clearly foresaw the widening circle of involvement into which France might be entering and even made a feeble show of objection, insufficient to deter the French. In face of their determination the issue was not pressed, and Britain acquiesced.[42] One

[40] The depredations of the Barbary corsairs had caused the sending of an American naval expedition to Tripoli in 1801.

[41] In 1827 a complaint of the French consul had been answered by the dey with a slap from a fly whisk, for which insult the French government had been unable to procure satisfaction.

[42] Britain did not seek to interfere with the foreseen extension of the French conquest in Algeria proper, showing no interest, for instance, in the struggle of Abd-el-Kader during the thirties.

condition alone did she insist upon: the French conquest must be confined to Algeria and not extend to either Tunisia or Morocco. Thinking primarily in terms of Mediterranean strategy, Britain wanted to retain for herself unchallenged control of the western entrance to that sea and of the Sicilian Strait in the middle, which her possession of Gibraltar and Malta insured. For the rest, like later Germany, Britain could detect possible advantages in the diversion of French interest and power away from Europe that a colonial undertaking entailed.

THE PROBLEM OF EGYPT.   This favorable climate of Anglo-French relations did not, however, extend to the extremities of the Mediterranean, Egypt and Spain, especially the former.

The Egyptian question, next specific development in the larger Eastern problem, grew out of the Greek settlement of which it was an aftermath. Egypt was undoubtedly part of the Ottoman Empire, but in the decadent condition of that state, making for weak control at the center, the governor of that province may best be described as a powerful vassal of the sultan, therefore possessed in his own right of substantial power that he could use to bargain with his suzerain. This vassal was Mohamed Ali, of Albanian origin, who, through his own capability, had risen by way of the army to his present position.

Mohamed Ali was an able and ambitious man, if a ruthless one. He was also in many respects a modern man who had a proper understanding of the ways and bases of power in the world of his day; if the methods of Western governments at home seemed to him simple foolishness for Egypt—a correct judgment—he had the shrewdness to secure the help of Western advisers for the organization of his armed forces, military and naval, and even for the development of the economic possibilities of Egypt. In other respects he remained a typical oriental despot and tyrant.

Mohamed Ali had been willing to assist the sultan put down the rebellion of Greece; for this service he was to have a price, the Pashalik of the Morea, in addition to Crete, already his.[43] The intervention of the Powers, procuring independence for the Greeks, had frustrated this arrangement. If he could not have the Morea, Mohamed Ali requested Syria instead; from that demand, war was eventually to ensue between the vassal and his suzerain.

[43] Actually, his adopted son Ibrahim led the expedition to the Morea and was to hold the expected Pashalik.

But this was more than a mere internecine Ottoman dispute; for Mohamed Ali, already past sixty and growing impatient, entertained very large ambitions indeed. Precursor of later Egyptian rulers, he thought he might extend his sway over the Arab world;[44] even beyond that, he might supplant the very sultan and put new life into the whole Ottoman structure just as he had in the Egyptian.

In the face of such possibilities the Powers could hardly remain indifferent. The prospect of a revived Ottoman state commanded less than enthusiasm in Britain[45] and in Russia; if the latter country might envisage schemes of Ottoman partition, Britain was opposed to them, especially if they might entail the creation of an Arab state extending to the Persian Gulf. Britain and Russia had in fact managed to reach agreement, in connection with the Greek disturbance, on what might be described as the preservation of the Ottoman state in a condition of endemic decay. France did not wish to destroy the Empire, but the French stake in Egypt was substantial: apart from many Greeks, the bulk of Mohamed Ali's advisers in his task of reorganization had been French. France was not loath to exploit the possibilities of the situation and, on his side, when Mohamed Ali found no response in Britain he sought his main support in French quarters.

It was under these conditions that Mohamed Ali launched into the adventure of open clash with the sultan. His superior military preparations soon bore fruit; at Konieh, in December, 1832, a Turkish army was crushed by the Egyptians, leaving open the road to Constantinople. It was Russian intervention that saved the day for the sultan; the Russian offer of assistance was conveyed by Muraviev in Constantinople, whence he went on to Alexandria to express clear warnings to Mohamed Ali. In February, 1833, a Russian squadron appeared in the Bosporus to the alarm of the British and French. The latter favored mediation on a basis advantageous to their Egyptian protégé, the granting to him of Syria and Adana,[46] but persisting Turco-Egyptian differences brought the landing of Russian troops on the Bosporus, in response to which development British and French squadrons made their ap-

[44] The Egyptians reached Khartum in 1822 and had previously sent an expedition in Hejaz in 1815.
[45] Britain had just concluded an advantageous commercial treaty with the sultan, whereas Mohamed Ali maintained firm state control of foreign trade in Egypt.
[46] Convention of Kutahia of April 8, 1833.

pearance in the Eastern Mediterranean. The tension was relieved by a direct Turco-Egyptian agreement which restored peace in all quarters; it removed the need for Russian assistance, hence that of British and French opposition to Russia.

But as the Russians left the Straits they took back with them an agreement with the Turks, the Treaty of Unkiar-Skelessi of July 8, 1833. Ostensibly, this was a defensive alliance between the two states; but it was not an alliance between equals and like all such arrangements it implied a condition of dependence of the weaker partner upon the stronger. This relationship was in fact clarified in a secret (not well kept or for long) article of the treaty which provided for Russian armed assistance in the event of an attack by a third party against Turkey, which in exchange undertook merely to close the Straits in the event that Russia found herself at war.

Even so qualified a measure of Russian protection was bound to produce British objections, yet the British reaction was surprisingly mild. The reason for this lay in the fact of Anglo-French divergence elsewhere,[47] while Austria on her side had also come to terms with Russia; the Münchengrätz agreement of September, 1833, envisaged the *quid pro quo* of Russian support for Austria's policy in Central Europe in exchange for Austrian support of Russia in Ottoman affairs. Those in England, Palmerston himself, who opted for a policy of patience were to prove justified. The passage of time went to show that Russia did not seek to press her advantage[48] while Britain reasserted a measure at least of influence in Turkey: a commercial treaty in August, 1838, secured for her further advantages, putting a 3 percent limitation on Turkish customs duties, while the reorganization of the Turkish fleet was entrusted to British officers in 1839.[49] Little was left of the substance of Unkiar-Skelessi when the next crisis occurred in the Near East. Being a sequel and aftermath of the one that has just been related, it will conveniently be dealt with at this point.

The new crisis was the result of Turkish initiative. Sultan Mahmoud II had never become reconciled to the setbacks of 1832

---

[47] Largely over the Spanish situation, on which see below, pp. 55–58.

[48] Metternich's support of Russia became lukewarm once he felt reassured over German matters. At the meeting at Teplitz in September, 1835, he declined to associate himself with Russian policy toward the Ottoman Empire.

[49] For the reorganization of the army the Turkish government enlisted Prussian assistance.

and the arrangements that ensued from them. With the assistance of Reshid Pasha he busied himself for some years with projects of reform for his Empire, the reorganization of its armed forces among other things. Having brought these to what he thought a satisfactory pitch, in April, 1839, he took the initiative of hostilities in Syria. His calculations proved mistaken for, in June, the Turkish forces were completely defeated by those under the command of Ibrahim, while a week later he sustained the further disillusion of seeing his fleet join the Egyptians in Alexandria. Mahmoud died heartbroken in the midst of these reverses and his successor, a mere child, found himself confronted with confusion in the state. But the Powers would not allow matters to rest in this fashion.

The crisis of 1832 had been primarily an Anglo-Russian affair, with France hedging between the two but on the whole aligning herself with Britain. On the present occasion France elected to give her Egyptian protégé more determined support. What prompted her to do this was a greater consciousness of Mediterranean interests that the Algerian establishment, now pursued with greater determination and vigor, served to enhance, as well as domestic considerations. In Parliament Louis Philippe was criticized for the timidity of his foreign policy, and the cause of Mohamed Ali took on in France the color of a national issue. Palmerston would grant Algeria to the French, but that possession combined with a preponderant influence on the Nile and in Syria raised the specter of French control over the entire southern Mediterranean shore; this Britain would not tolerate and from that situation there arose a sharp Anglo-French crisis.

The prime mover this time was Britain rather than Russia, which for that matter perceived in the issue the possibility of disrupting the too close Anglo-French understanding of the immediately preceding years. As early as July 27, 1839, the Powers, still in ostensible agreement, had sent a collective note to the Porte reserving their right to review any settlement. But behind this agreement stood Palmerston's determination that Syria must be regained for the sultan and France's corresponding insistence to the opposite effect. The advent of Thiers to the ministry in February, 1840, augured ill for a compromise: Thiers represented at this time the aggressive aspects of French foreign policy, success in which he would use to bolster the regime. Thiers was therefore uncompromising and thought to cut the ground from under Palmerston's feet by using pressure on the Porte to procure an agreement with

Ibrahim—along the lines of French and Egyptian wishes—thereby facing the Powers with a *fait accompli*. In this intrigue Palmerston got the better of him. By the Treaty of London of July 15 all the Powers—save France and unbeknown to her—agreed to use force if necessary in order to secure the acceptance of their terms by Mohamed Ali. These terms included the hereditary rule of Egypt for him and that of southern Syria for life; but he must yield the rest of that province, as well as Crete and Arabian possessions, and he must also return the Turkish fleet.

These terms were put to Mohamed Ali as a virtual ultimatum. Unless he accepted them within ten days the offer of southern Syria would be withdrawn; the lapse of another ten days would entail complete freedom for the sultan to make his own decisions. Relying on French support,[50] Mohamed Ali rejected the proposal.

The French reaction to the news of the London agreement was violent in the extreme. Revived visions of the coalition of 1815 led to pointing out that France under Napoleon had conquered Europe and to recalling that France had in her arsenal the powerful weapon of the revolutionary idea. Thus events on the Nile led to talk of war on the Rhine. But Palmerston was not to be intimidated; in September[51] a British fleet bombarded Beirut where troops were also landed. Ibrahim was forced to withdraw from Syria, while from France he got no more than verbal fulminations in which Thiers still indulged. The more pacific Louis Philippe, using the occasion of a disagreement with Thiers over the speech from the throne, forced the latter's resignation on October 20.

The crisis was resolved and Mohamed Ali had to be content with the hereditary rule of Egypt. Britain had no desire to push her advantage unduly; for, to a large extent, the contest had been bluff on both sides, not devoid of considerable danger—bluff can easily get out of hand, especially with public opinion involved— but in reality neither side wanted war. If the French reaction to the London agreement is understandable, to maintain a belligerent attitude in the face of that arrangement was also less than realistic. Having obtained his victory, one of prestige in large measure, Palmerston did not attempt to destroy Mohamed Ali, and he would

[50] Thiers had declared in April that France would not tolerate the use of force by the Powers to coerce Mohamed Ali.

[51] The relatively slow development of the crisis was due to British hesitation, for Palmerston encountered considerable opposition in the Cabinet to his fire-eating tactics.

even let France, having taught her a lesson, rejoin the Concert of
Europe. The Convention of the Straits of July 13, 1841, was
signed by all the Powers.

That Convention stipulated the closure of the Straits to men-
of-war of all Powers so long as the Ottoman state was at peace;
but if itself at war this provision no longer applied; an allied fleet
could then enter the Straits. This new arrangement registered a
further British advantage, at the expense of Russia this time, for
Unkiar-Skelessi was dead. Altogether, the episode represented a
clear British victory: determined and most resolute guardian of
Ottoman integrity, Britain had preserved the Ottoman Empire,
even enhanced the authority of the sultan, and in the process she
had checked further encroachments of French influence at the
eastern end of the Mediterranean and also written into the Convention of the Straits the cancellation of Russia's privileged position, substituting for it the common guardianship of Europe.[52]
Whatever one may think of the man and his methods, Palmerston's
boldness must be recognized as mainly responsible for this enhancement of British prestige, and the accomplishment naturally
redounded to his personal credit.

BRITAIN, FRANCE, AND THE IBERIAN PENINSULA

After this contest, mainly Anglo-French, that had been waged
at the eastern end of the Mediterranean,[53] relations between the
two countries seemed to improve to the extent that the phrase
"first Entente Cordiale" has been used to describe them. But the
long-term rivalry and suspicion that always underlay the mutual
outlook of France and Britain found cause to manifest itself at
the other end of the inland sea, in Spain. The struggle in that
country was relatively mild, it rather lacked dignity at some points,
and some aspects of it are not devoid of the humor of a comedy
of errors. It is usually known as the affair of the Spanish marriages.
The source of it lay in Spanish domestic affairs.

Following the reëstablishment of order in 1823, King Ferdinand lived out in peace the remaining ten years of his life until
his death in September, 1833. Spain, long declining, eccentric to
the main currents of Europe, did not share in the activity of the

[52] The Russian loss may be said to have been partly theoretical in view of
the weakness of Russia's Black Sea fleet and was compensated by locking out of
the Black Sea any enemy fleet.

[53] In Greece also an Anglo-French contest of influence was taking place
through the association of Greek parties with these outside Powers.

Powers, which is why there has been little occasion to make mention of her. But, when King Ferdinand died, he had no male issue, only an infant daughter, Isabella. In order to insure for her the succession, the king, under the prodding of his more energetic spouse, Queen Christina, had resorted to the device, used on other occasions in other European states, of setting aside the Salic law of succession. Else his own brother, Don Carlos, would have worn the crown.

In 1833, Queen Christina, as regent, held power for her daughter, but in order to consolidate her position, thought it desirable to intrude into the country's politics. Broadly speaking, she sought support among liberal ranks, while the pretender, Don Carlos, became the rallying point of conservative forces whose base was mainly in the north. The Carlist war that ensued[54] was the occasion for an interesting, if minor, outside intervention that was connected with Portuguese affairs as well.

For Portugal's course was also troubled in this period. The death of King John, in 1826, gave the Portuguese crown to Dom Pedro of Brazil. But Dom Pedro chose to remain in that country; he gave Portugal a British-type constitution and turned over the throne to an infant daughter, Maria, under the regency of his brother, Miguel. But Dom Miguel was allied with conservative forces and wanted to rule in his own right; the result, as in Spain, was the Miguelite wars, ending in the restoration of Maria in 1833.[55]

The aspect of these involved and similar Spanish and Portuguese disturbances that warrants mention here is the consistent British support of the liberal, or constitutional, faction, going at times to the length of active intervention.[56] In 1834, the state of relations between Britain and France was such as to make possible the formation of the so-called Quadruple Alliance, consisting of those two Powers and the "legitimate" holders of the Spanish

[54] The Carlist war went on from 1834 to 1839 to the accompaniment of a juggling of constitutions, that of 1812, the new ones of 1834 and 1837, results of the internecine divisions of Spain between liberals and conservatives and among shades of liberals.

[55] This was accompanied by a British intervention in Lisbon in 1828, followed by Dom Miguel's *coup d'état*, then the return of Dom Pedro to Europe, where with British and French assistance he defeated the Miguelite faction, reinstating his daughter Maria.

[56] In 1834 the British suspended the Foreign Enlistment Act in order to allow the formation of a foreign legion that went to Spain.

and Portuguese crowns. What this meant was that Britain and France saw eye to eye in the matter of throwing the weight of their influences on the side of the more liberal forces in the whole Iberian Peninsula. Emphasis was thus placed on the ideological cleavage, mild though it was, of Europe into the Western liberal and the Eastern conservative types of governments. The Quadruple Alliance was concluded in April and the agreement of Münchengrätz had taken place in September; to a degree, one arrangement was the counterpart of and answer to the other, broad assertion of solidarity among certain types of regimes.

Britain and France fell out in 1840 while Palmerston and Thiers matched their wits and their power. But when the dust had settled on the Near Eastern issue the entente of the two Powers resumed. Spain now provided the occasion for dissension. The two countries and their governments had not a little in common: constitutional monarchies in which the commercial element held much power, bent on industrial growth and commercial expansion, both preferred peace in which to pursue their endeavors. After the flare-up of 1840, Guizot in France, anglophile and milder than Thiers, found in Aberdeen,[57] less fiery than Palmerston, a suitable compeer.

After renewed domestic disturbances in Spain, in 1843, Isabella, though a mere thirteen and under the virtual control of General Narvaez, the real ruler, was declared of age. During the course of that same year, Queen Victoria paid a visit to the French king, at Eu, outward manifestation of the amicable state of the two countries' relations. In connection with this meeting,[58] the question came up for discussion of a suitable candidate for the hand of Queen Isabella. Among the possibilities, the Duc de Montpensier, one of Louis Philippe's sons, and a prince of Saxe-Coburg, cousin of the English prince consort, were outstanding. But the same objections arose over either arrangement that had appeared in connection with the choice of rulers for Belgium and for Greece. The same solution was adopted in this case: both candidates would be eliminated in favor of a member of the Bourbon house of Spain and Naples.

[57] Aberdeen was foreign secretary in Peel's second ministry, which lasted from 1841 to 1846.
[58] The visit was returned by Louis Philippe in 1844 and Queen Victoria came again to Eu the following year.

But Guizot's second thoughts led him to propound the idea of a marriage between the Duc de Montpensier and Isabella's sister, the Infanta Luisa. A new compromise was achieved between Guizot and Aberdeen: Luisa could marry Montpensier, but not until her sister had herself first been married and borne issue; the Coburg prince remained eliminated. However, Palmerston returned to the foreign office with the formation of the Russell ministry in June, 1846. Unlike Aberdeen, Palmerston was not averse to the use of forceful methods, while in intrigue he could indulge with the best; he revived the idea of the Coburg candidacy while criticizing the alleged French interference in the domestic politics of Spain, as usual involved with the private affairs of royalty.

The British and the French ambassadors in Madrid were kept very busy watching each other and intriguing at Court,[59] until the common French and Spanish suspicion of Palmerston's designs resulted in the announcement of the engagements, followed by the simultaneous marriages in September of Isabella to the Duke of Cadiz and of Luisa to the Duc de Montpensier. Palmerston had overreached himself; he and his envoy in Madrid had succeeded in conveying to Louis Philippe the impression that he was being double-crossed, with the consequence that he was willing to follow Guizot's advice in the matter. Palmerston was incensed, but the *fait accompli* could hardly be undone, and his references to the Treaty of Utrecht that forbade the union of the French and Spanish crowns were empty threats. In terms of relative importance the incident was minor, but it sufficed to put an end to the Anglo-French entente, such as it was.

IV. Extra-European Developments

It has been mentioned that the period of the July Monarchy of France was one of considerable economic growth for that country no less than for the prime industrial state of the day, Britain. But this growth did not yet result in imperial activity of major proportions; the British Empire was by now long established, but the impact of the loss of the American colonies

[59] The close watch kept on the situation may be judged from a dispatch sent by the French envoy to his government on April 3, 1846: "*La reine est nubile depuis deux heures.*" Cited in R. B. Mowat, *A History of European Diplomacy*, London, Edward Arnold, 1922, p. 83.

had not fully evaporated; the emphasis was more on free trade than on empire building, and the former was the dominant issue of British politics at the time, until the great debate that resulted in the repeal of the Corn Laws in 1848, registering the definite victory of the industrial-commercial interests over the agrarian, irrevocably wedded Great Britain to a doctrine that was to serve her well. France had lost her empire and, in France as in England, many held the belief that empire building was not a worthwhile undertaking; the French decision to create a firm establishment on the opposite shore of the Mediterranean had only been arrived at slowly and amid much questioning. The Mediterranean for that matter is a unit, as much European as African, and falls therefore in a category different from that of distant overseas possessions. At the eastern end of that sea French designs had been checked.

Nevertheless, if the imperial urge of the period was feeble, certainly by comparison with either earlier or later times, it was not wholly dormant. In so far as such activity existed, its manifestations were chiefly British and French; they were, if small and relatively weak, world-wide. Brief mention must be made of them, also because they laid some of the bases of the far more intense activity and struggle of the latter part of the century that will be considered in the second part of this book.[60]

NORTH AMERICA

Across the Atlantic, the young United States had definitely embarked on the task of filling a continent, a process in which the Louisiana Purchase had been a major step. Settlement proceeded with both rapidity and vigor, but if the West was empty there was contact in the South with the empire of Spain; the Sabine River had been the agreed frontier since 1819. The viceroyalty of Mexico soon liberated itself from Spanish control and proceeded to incorporate the region of Texas, a fact given recognition by the United States in 1828. Texas, however, soon became the locale of substantial American colonization, until American settlers outnumbered the Mexicans, with the consequence that Texas proclaimed its independence in 1836 and soon followed this step with a request, not granted at the time, for union with

[60] The Russian expansion in Asia falls in a different category and mention of it will be made later.

the United States.[61] Here were clearly the makings of a conflict between the United States and Mexico, a matter wholly extra-European, and which would not be mentioned here save for a measure of European involvement. The life of the Texan state was precarious, and assistance, especially financial assistance, might be forthcoming from British or French sources.

Britain was reticent at first, reluctant to antagonize Mexico where British interests existed; not hampered by similar considerations and on bad terms with Mexico besides, France concluded with Texas a treaty of commerce and friendship in November, 1839. Palmerston was annoyed—he was trying to check France in Egypt at the moment—and Britain entered into relations with Texas, which failed, however, to secure the desired assistance of loans on any European market. Britain, perceiving the possibility of using Texas as a pawn in her negotiations with the United States over the northwestern frontier,[62] granted recognition to Texas and offered a loan, asking, however, that slavery be abolished.

This British move caused alarm in the United States where visions appeared of the undesirable economic consequences of a free Texas under some British influence, a Texas without slavery to boot. The outcome was the American decision to proceed with the annexation of Texas, which took place in 1845, after the election of the preceding year had put Polk in the Presidency. Aberdeen went the length of proposing joint action with Guizot in defense of Texan independence, but both men realized in time the unwisdom of any such action and resigned themselves to the *fait accompli*. The episode may be seen as a successful test of the Monroe Doctrine and was occasion for an extension of it in the form of denying the right of European interference in the possible voluntary union of territory on the American continent with the United States.

A somewhat comparable state of affairs—suspicion of British designs—prevailed in the matter of California. There was war between the United States and Mexico as a result of which another

[61] The aspect of the matter having to do with slavery, which had been abolished in Mexico but restored in independent Texas, and with the gathering storm in the United States over the issue of slavery, does not fall within the scope of this treatment.

[62] Some difficulties had also arisen over the northeastern frontier with Canada but these were eventually settled by the Webster-Ashburton Treaty in August, 1842.

vast territory in the Southwest became part of the Union. Britain did not seek to interfere, merely using the possibility of action as a means to secure a settlement of the western Canadian frontier, which was effected by the Oregon Treaty in June, 1846.[63]

THE FAR EAST

Though not yet a Great Power by European standards of the day, the United States was an important mercantile nation. Its ships carried on a fruitful trade with the Far East, their share in the maritime trade of Canton being estimated at some 25 percent of the total, though a far larger share was British. The vast and largely unknown bulk of China could not but be attractive to traders, those of the two countries just mentioned, to which must be added the Russians whose trade with China was by land. By 1840, the French also had a small but growing interest in the Far East. The main issue for all was the "opening" of the Chinese Empire to greater trade. In view of the relative dimensions of existing interests it was only natural that the most active outside agency should be British.

Britain's trade with China was conducted in Canton through the intermediary of the British East India Company and of a Chinese merchant association; the Chinese government had no official dealings with foreign barbarians. Moreover, in 1839, that government took the decision to enforce the ban on the importation of opium, one of the chief articles of trade.[64] The method of enforcement gave Palmerston occasion for protest; the result was the Opium War of 1839.

With the internal conditions of the Chinese Empire there is no need to deal; it will suffice to say that it was thoroughly incapable, partly because of its inner difficulties, partly for simple reasons of technical deficiency, to deal with even a small British force. The difficulty of any sort of meaningful communication between such antipodic structures as the Chinese and the British

[63] The war between the United States and Mexico was concluded by the Treaty of Guadelupe Hidalgo in February, 1848. There was some feeling in the United States for annexation of Mexico, and the expansionist tendencies of the United States in the Carribbean gave rise to negotiations with Britain which, however, were not concluded until some years later and, for that reason, are not mentioned here. See below, p. 117.

[64] The ban had long been in existence but the law had been a dead letter. In 1834 the East India Company's monopoly of Chinese trade was ended by the British government with the result that Britain sought to obtain recognition of her official representative by China, a recognition that China refused to grant.

served to prolong for some time a wholly futile and unequal contest, until, when finally convinced that British aims did not envision any conquest of China, the court of Peking came to terms. These were registered in the Treaty of Nanking of August 29, 1842: in addition to Canton, four other Chinese ports, Shanghai among them, would henceforth be open to British merchants who would enjoy in them the benefits of extraterritorial status; Chinese duties would be limited to 5 percent *ad valorem,* and the island of Hong Kong, future naval base and commercial entrepot, was ceded outright to Britain. A small indemnity— £21,000,000—completed the arrangement.

These were not drastic terms, but the significance of the Treaty of Nanking is considerable. Albeit in limited fashion, it broke open to outside influence the ancient, decadent, and fossilized Chinese structure, thereby initiating a chapter in Chinese annals the last pages of which are being written in our day. Others were not slow to take notice of these developments. A French mission, led by Lagrené, obtained in the Treaty of Whampoa, in October, 1844, in addition to commercial advantages, the toleration of Catholics in China.[65] Almost simultaneously, Caleb Cushing's mission obtained similar grants for the United States in the Treaty of Wanghsia in July, 1844. Another decade was to elapse before the opening up of Japan to Western influence would initiate a development of character wholly different from the Chinese.

This Far Eastern activity of the West gave added interest to the vast expanse of the Pacific Ocean, not yet wholly known at the beginning of the century. While the British established themselves in Australia and the Dutch annexed western New Guinea in 1828, the French Dumont d'Urville conducted extensive explorations in the twenties and thirties. Access to the Far East also gave added interest to the possibility of opening a passage through the Central American Isthmus,[66] but the Pacific islands might be so many steppingstones on the lengthy highways of that ocean. In New Zealand, the British, largely to forestall French designs, established their formal control in 1840, while the French began to assert their own in the Society Islands in 1842. This led to a sharp, if also minor, encounter for which the politico-

[65] Faced with competition by others, the British, in October, 1843, obtained an extension of the Treaty of Nanking that insured them most favored nation treatment.

[66] This will be more conveniently dealt with a little later, see below, p. 117.

religious activity of British missionaries provided the occasion. The expulsion of Pritchard by the French from Tahiti was strongly protested in England: Pritchard was indemnified but French control remained.

Farther north, the Sandwich Islands were a meeting point of American, British, and French interests. American missionaries, from 1820, established themselves in the islands where they prospered economically. The United States concluded a treaty of friendship and commerce in 1820, followed by Britain and France, in 1836 and 1839, respectively. The United States was not yet prepared to extend a formal claim to that region, but recognizing in 1842 the independence of the islands, it assumed, in effect, the position of protector against the possible encroachment of any other Power. In this one may see a transitional or evolutionary stage from the Monroe Doctrine to the later American doctrine of the Open Door in the Far East.

India, under the rule of the British East India Company, was an established British holding. The course of her internal development may be regarded as an internal aspect of British imperial affairs and for that reason will not be considered.[67] But around the periphery of India activity went on; the Burmese war of 1824–1826 extended the reach of British control, but the war with Afghanistan in 1839–1842 did not have a similar result. British and Russian influences were yet to meet in the interior reaches of Asia. Farther away from India, the British, highly sensitive to the significance of naval power and to the value of naval outposts, had established themselves in Malaya, in the highly strategic position of Singapore, as early as 1819.[68] At the opposite end of the Indian Ocean, Aden was occupied in 1839, but this was partly with an eye on developments in the Ottoman Empire and on Mohamed Ali's dreams of an Arab empire.

All this activity, scattered in the four corners of the planet, may nevertheless be summed up as relatively minor and of secondary importance to that which was the main concern of the chancelleries of Europe, their mutual relations *in Europe*. It is impor-

[67] There is no space in this treatment to consider the evolution of the British Empire in which the Durham Report of 1839, origin and basis of later change, constitutes an important landmark. Nevertheless, in view of the world spread of that empire, the course of its internal change assumes considerable importance and must be borne in mind.

[68] In 1826, a treaty of commerce with Siam established the independence of the local sultanates of Perak and Selangor. A similar treaty of commerce was concluded by the United States with Siam in 1833.

tant nonetheless, but rather as a prelude to what would happen later in the century, when imperial rivalries would become one of the major sources of international activity. Much of the world was still impreëmpted and there was room for all. Nevertheless, bases were being laid, possession taken of valuable positions from which influence would expand and radiate. Even at this early stage it will be noticed that Britain and France most often met each other in a variety of quarters, a fact expressive as much of continuing past tradition as of future possibilities. If one thinks of the conditions of our own time, the appearance of the young United States on the imperial scene appears full of both interest and significance. But to the more important affairs—in terms of their own time— and relations of the European states at home we must now return.

III   *The Mid-Century Crisis*

I. Europe in Mid-Century

If imperial rivalry was the cause of minor flurries only, in Europe herself the international scene was also fairly quiescent during the forties. Even the great outburst of 1848, once the smoke of battle had settled, did not appear to have given rise to open clash among the major Powers. This relaxation of international tensions is attributable to a variety of causes, some of which are the very sources of later tensions and conflicts.

In the Western states, Britain and France especially, economic activity absorbed much of the energy of the nations. Such activity may itself lead to conflict, and one might fairly mention the interest in Texan cotton as having played a role in British, French, and American foreign policy. But there was room for economic expansion at home, and in terms of relative importance and by comparison with later times, the generalization may be made that domestic issues absorbed a greater part of the attention and energy of the governments than did foreign affairs. The stuff of British politics is to be found in the great debate over the respective merits of the free versus the mercantilist approach to trade, to which may be added the beginnings of the problems of labor; the Chartist movement, though unproductive of results at the time, had flourished in the 1830s. The French bourgeois, entrenched in control of the state, and aptly represented by the bourgeois king, were quite content to follow his advice, *enrichissez-vous*.

In the Europe of the time, Britain and France, restricted as the franchise may have been in both countries, were the liberal states, where power in the last analysis derived its legitimacy from the people. It would be premature to speak of these two countries at this time as having a general common interest *vis-à-vis* the rest of the world. If the relative decline of French power had already

65

set in, the consciousness of it did not yet exist in France, where the memory of Napoleon was still vivid.[1] Britain was clearly still in the ascendant. It is all the more interesting to observe the relatively good state of Anglo-French relations, in spite of Palmerston and Thiers.

This similarity in practice of the two regimes militated in favor of a common outlook of broad sympathy toward forces struggling for recognition elsewhere on the Continent. For Metternich and his system were in control of Central Europe, where the Prussian king was wholly in agreement with the Metternichian outlook, while the tsar adhered to the same principles in Russia. Liberalism, in broad terms adherence to the principles of 1789, was not unknown in the domain of Metternichian dominance, but it lacked there the basis of support from which it drew its main strength in the Western states; the correlation is close between the state of economic development of these sections of Europe, to say nothing of the diverse condition of the peasant masses in them, and the nature of their political institutions. Among intellectuals liberalism had much support, and universities were hotbeds of infection, but these at any time could only represent a minute fraction of the people. European liberals were apt to look to France, especially to Paris, for example, and even more important, for material assistance in achieving their ends. The response to the July Revolution has been indicated. Constitution, as mentioned before, was their fetish.

But between Central Europe and the West there was another point of difference. For Europe as a whole the nineteenth century may indeed be characterized as the age of nationalism. But the establishment of national states in the West had been so long a fact as to be no longer the source of significant issues. The tendency in them was, again broadly speaking, for nationalism as we have come to think of it to become connected with the more conservative tendency in their domestic politics, though the French case needs a qualification from the association between revolution and nationalism that was a legacy of the course of the Great Revolution.[2] But in Central Europe the larger meaning of freedom found expression in the desire for constitutions that would curb

---

[1] The transfer to Paris of the ashes of Napoleon in 1840 was the occasion for a manifestation of national feeling and a measure of the standing of what had by that time become the Napoleonic legend.

[2] This introduced a complicating and confusing factor in the operation of domestic French politics, and to some extent of foreign policy as well.

arbitrary power and guarantee the rights of the citizen, as well as in the wish to be rid of alien control. The association of liberalism with nationalism was natural and logical in Central Europe. Metternich's feeling was the same about both tendencies, and, quite apart from any abstract merits of the concept that insists upon the rightness of identifying state and nation, no Habsburg state could be sympathetic to the force of nationalism, of necessity a disintegrating factor from its point of view.

In this respect again Britain and France, in view of their own nature, could easily accept and even sympathize with the national idea; its application held no threat for them, nor did they have claims against others.

But if it be true that these two forces, liberalism and nationalism, between them dominate the direction of the nineteenth-century evolution of Europe, if they were the leaven at work under the seemingly tranquil surface of Metternichian control, the operation of them was not smooth. In the abstract, Italian or Hungarian nationalism could enlist much sympathy in the West, but was not the preservation of the Austrian state as a bulwark against Russian power a British interest? And was it not better for France, for her power at least, to have weak states for neighbors? Considerations such as these intruded into the unfolding of the great disturbance of 1848 to which we may now turn; if they made for complexity they also had the ultimate effect of minimizing the impact of that disturbance on the international scene.

Events in France may be regarded as having given the revolutions of 1848 their European character, though actually the first specific outbreaks occurred in Italy, in Naples at the end of January, in Turin at the beginning of the following month. Already for some time before this, there had been indications of illness in the European body politic. The year 1846 was one of economic crisis in Europe: crop failures resulting in higher food prices; decreased purchasing power reflected in lower industrial production, hence unemployment; financial crisis as well; all these contributed to create a climate suitable to political and social unrest. As Metternich put it, in 1847, "The world is very ill, and the sickness is spreading every day." While taking repressive measures, especially in Italy, he judged the danger greatest since the time of the Great Revolution in France.

The Swiss situation, in 1847, provided an interesting test of the international condition. The *Sonderbund*, a league of seven

Catholic cantons, had been organized in 1845.[3] A vote in the Diet for the dissolution of the *Sonderbund*, a success of the liberals, resulted in civil war. The war was brief, concluded by the clear victory of the federal forces, and the victorious liberals proceeded to reorganize the state, drafting a new constitution in 1848 to replace the existing statute of 1815. But this liberal victory was made possible by the nonintervention of the Powers, a result for which Palmerston was largely responsible, for he had used his influence to restrain Metternich, ready to intervene in Switzerland. Metternich and Palmerston stood in sharpest contrast at this point; in France, however, Guizot was in favor of the Metternichian view.

II. The Revolutions in France, Italy, and Austria

THE FIRST PHASE

But this position of Guizot, in turn, meant that the government of Louis Philippe was out of step with the country's feeling. Opposition to the government had been gathering for some time and came from many and disparate quarters, while the pedestrian quality of the regime commanded little active support. *La France s'ennuie*, "France is bored," was an appropriate comment. On February 22 demonstrations occurred, then barricades made their appearance, in Paris.[4] The struggle was brief; three days sufficed to make the workers masters of Paris, and on the 24th Louis Philippe abdicated in favor of his grandson. Ignoring this decision, the Chamber, or a rump of it, under popular pressure, the same day created a provisional government which, fusing with more radical elements, proclaimed France for the second time in her history a Republic. In the provisional government the foreign ministry was held by the poet Lamartine, a moderate republican himself.

Such a development in France was naturally cause for alarm elsewhere on the Continent, be it on the score of the example of revolutionary ideology or on that of the danger to the existing international order. On March 5, however, Lamartine issued a proclamation to Europe disclaiming any aggressive French intent, but warning against foreign interference in domestic French affairs.

[3] This was itself an episode in the struggle for revision of the constitution, desired by the liberals; in the Swiss context this struggle took the form of a contest along lines of religious difference.

[4] The immediate occasion was the ban on a banquet in Paris, the form that the campaign of the opposition had taken.

The treaties of 1815 were declared abrogated, but the territorial effects of them would be respected, a neatly balanced statement, calculated as much to allay fears as to entertain their existence.

France did not interfere. The struggle between the forces that had joined in overthrowing the July Monarchy was sufficient to absorb her own energies; as on earlier and later occasions in France the initial role of Paris and the more radical Left was no adequate reflection of the state of the country at large. The election of April for a National Assembly—first instance of the use of universal suffrage—was a decisive victory for the moderates; when the workers rose again in June they were ruthlessly put down, and the outcome was in turn an undue rightward oscillation of the political pendulum, while General Cavaignac temporarily held the powers of dictator.

But the news of the Parisian events of February was the spark that was needed in Central Europe. Metternich judged the end to have come; seventy-five years of age, he did not feel that he could effect reform: unless the army could maintain the *status quo* unchanged, the game was wholly lost. From Budapest and Prague came demands that combined the expression of liberal and national desires; these gave encouragement in turn to liberals in Vienna, where clashes occurred on March 12 between demonstrators— largely students—and troops.[5] Metternich resigned and left to join Louis Philippe in the shelter of foreign exile.

The Emperor yielded to demands from all quarters; to his Austrian subjects he gave a constitution in March, while he granted the wishes of the Hungarian liberals, making that country virtually independent save for the remaining personal union. Having done these things he fled from his capital to the shelter of Innsbruck. The Slavs were neither Austrian nor Magyar: a Croatian National Committee sought separation from Budapest while a Pan-Slavic Congress, stressing distinction from and opposition to the Germanic element, met in Prague. This gathering, in June, was the high-water mark of revolutionary success, the tide of which began to turn sharply at that point.

Trouble elsewhere faced the Habsburgs as well. Nearly all Italy seemed to have succumbed to the revolutionary fever: in Naples, Rome, Florence, and Turin constitutions were granted

[5] Even then the use of the armed forces by the government was half-hearted, a fact that has been credited to opposition to Metternich within the government.

in February and March though the existing rulers were not ousted. In the Austrian domain proper, Milan saw the Five Days in March, as the result of which the Austrians were expelled from the city, Radetzky retreating to the Quadrilateral fortresses[6] while simultaneously Venice proclaimed itself a Republic under Manin. Too occupied nearer the center, the Austrians were unable to prevent or suppress these outbreaks. Worse still, the national component seemed to have penetrated the Italian movement: responding to Milanese appeals, and yielding to the urgings of his own radicals, King Charles Albert of Sardinia declared war against Austria on March 22. From all quarters of Italy, with much enthusiasm if little organized and effective strength, recruits flocked to the Sardinian standard, which might thus become the Italian; even a Papal contingent joined for a brief moment.[7] Initial Italian successes caused even the Austrian government to make a pessimistic estimate of the situation to the extent of instructing Radetzky in June to seek an armistice on the basis of Lombard independence.

One important consideration was that of the attitude of outside Powers, Britain, Russia, and France, especially this last.[8] Lamartine's declaration of March 5 has been mentioned, which was not devoid of ambiguity; the French concentrated an army on the Alps. Charles Albert of Sardinia did not want French help, fearful of its revolutionary aspect, and the prospect of it had been a deterrent rather than encouragement to his own action. This same consideration of the possibility of French intervention was the paramount concern of British policy, directed at this time again by Palmerston. Palmerston had no particular objection to the emancipation of Italy, or even to the demise of the Metternichian system, but the liberation of Italy must not be done by France. Beyond this, he did not wish to see a disintegration of the Austrian state, necessary counterweight to Russia.

The tsar had no sympathy with revolution, in either its liberal

---

[6] These consisted of the group of the four fortresses of Mantua, Legnano, Verona, and Peschiera on the borders of Lombardy and Venetia.

[7] The Pope, however, soon yielded to Austrian protests and, disclaiming any desire to participate in hostilities among members of his Catholic faith, in effect withdrew his contribution to the Italian national cause.

[8] Prussia was mainly concerned with the narrowly Germanic aspect of the situation. For reasons of clarity and simplicity of exposition, this aspect of the matter will be dealt with separately. It did not involve Austrian forces in the way that developments in Italy and in the purely Austrian domain did.

or its nationalistic aspect. He was somewhat contemptuous of what he regarded as the panicky and cowardly behavior of Central European princes who had so easily yielded to the liberal cry for constitutions and would allow the establishment of radical regimes next to his own borders, while he was equally concerned with the possibility of territorial readjustments. But his own troubles at home, mainly financial, and the initial rapid spread of the revolutionary wave paralyzed his action. In the last analysis, Russian policy, like British, became one of watchful waiting of the unfolding of events.

THE TURNING OF THE TIDE

So long, therefore, as France remained inactive abroad, the possibilities of European conflagration were greatly minimized. The "second revolution" in France, in June, did not enhance the prospects of French assistance to revolutionary forces. Moreover, after this same June, the Austrian situation seemed to be righting itself, at least from the point of view of the forces of order. It was in June that Prince Windischgrätz, after bombarding Prague, established firm military control in Bohemia. Meanwhile, Radetzky in Italy proved justified in refusing to follow the advice of Vienna by completely defeating the Piedmontese forces—now largely alone—at Custozza, on July 24, thereby regaining the control of Lombardy.[9]

This, for a moment, revived the possibility of French intervention; there was much feeling in France for assistance to the Piedmontese, which found expression in a vote in the Chamber in favor of it on September 2. But, in actuality, this vote became a useful means for effecting a compromise. Palmerston had been urging such a solution on a reluctant Austrian government; he could now point to the danger of the French mood; since the French government was desirous of avoiding foreign complications, it and the British could easily agree, and the principle of Anglo-French mediation was accepted by Austria. This was sufficient to maintain the peace for the moment, though it did not close the Italian chapter of the episode as we shall see presently.

There was reason for Austria's reluctance to accept compro-

[9] Following this defeat, General Salasco concluded an armistice with Austria on August 9, relinquishing Lombardy, which, however, Charles Albert still hoped to regain as the consequence of Anglo-French mediation.

mise, for the situation was developing quite favorably for the counterrevolutionary forces. Having successfully dealt with Italy, they could now turn to the Hungarian situation. This last was to furnish a prime example of the successful application of the policy of divide and rule, for which the rivalries of colliding nationalisms offered a perfect opportunity. The logic of the Hungarian wish for independence applied no less to the Croats; the Diet of Croatia-Slavonia wanted to be freed from subjection to Hungary. This was in a sense rebellion against the emperor, king of Hungary as well. But Hungarian nationalism, for all its liberal content, failed to see the equal legitimacy of the Croatian cause, to whose demands it responded by merely reasserting the integrity of the lands of the crown of St. Stephen. Consistency is a desirable but often lacking human trait. The opportunity thereby was opened for the emperor to exploit this cleavage; in September, Ban Jellachich was reinstated in Croatia[10] to lead an army against Hungary.

Hungarian resistance was at first successful, and the Hungarians even managed to invade Austria whither they might effect a junction with the Viennese liberals. But at this juncture Windischgrätz was in a position to repeat with his army the June performance of Prague. At the beginning of November reaction was in secure control in the Austrian capital; the advent of Prince Felix Schwarzenberg to the chancellorship was expression of the turn of the situation. Metternich's judgment that the game was lost had been premature. Schwarzenberg was determined and able; he could be ruthless as well, and he believed in the full restoration of the imperial power. The abdication of Emperor Ferdinand in favor of eighteen-year-old Francis Joseph was his work, symbolic of his determination to turn over a new leaf in the management of the state: neither Schwarzenberg nor the emperor, both new men, were to consider themselves bound or committed by any prior engagements, in Italy or elsewhere: no concessions in any quarter was Schwarzenberg's simple policy.

THE EVENTS OF 1849

While the application of this policy was successful, the implementation of it did not go without some complications. In Austria proper the Reichstag was dissolved and a new constitution

---

[10] Initially appointed in March, he had been suspended owing to his advocacy of Croatian demands against Hungary in June.

proclaimed;[11] meanwhile Windischgrätz had entered Budapest in January and Hungary was nearly overrun. But Schwarzenberg's constitution aroused a last flare-up of resistance; in April the Hungarian Diet proclaimed a republic of which Louis Kossuth was head. This was the one occasion for major outside intervention, for Tsar Nicholas' offer of assistance was accepted by the emperor. Accordingly, a Russian army marched into Transylvania in June.[12] In desperation, the Hungarians appealed for assistance but found a deaf ear in the West;[13] caught between the Austrian army of Windischgrätz and the Russians, led by Paskievich, their surrender to the latter at Villagos in Transylvania wrote finis to the Hungarian episode. The Russian intervention was no cause for wider complications; their task accomplished, the Russians withdrew. The tsar's understandable expectation of gratitude was soon to be disappointed by Schwarzenberg who, as he was to put it, would astonish Europe by the extent of Austria's ingratitude.

While these events were taking place in the East, the Italian scene continued unsettled. The principle of Anglo-French mediation, accepted by Austria in September, was rejected by Schwarzenberg. Italian affairs were to lead to a rather unpredictable outcome, in the form of a French intervention in Rome. In that city agitation continued, which flared up into insurrection in November, 1848. The Pope fled to Gaeta, and in February, 1849, a constituent assembly proclaimed a Roman republic. A month later, Charles Albert in Piedmont was induced to denounce the armistice with Austria and to resume hostilities. The decision proved highly unwise, for at Novara, before the month was out, Radetzky decisively crushed the Piedmontese forces. There was nothing for it but to capitulate again, which Piedmont did. Negotiations were somewhat protracted, for Austria was bent on revenge, the effects of which Britain and France endeavored to mitigate. Peace was finally made in August, Piedmont having to

[11] The Austrian Assembly had fled from Vienna and continued its deliberations at Kremsier in Moravia; it even went on to elaborate a constitution which, in the circumstances, remained a dead letter. Schwarzenberg's constitution, applicable to the entire Habsburg domain, emphasized uniformity and centralization, though it allowed for a representative Diet.

[12] In the summer of 1848 the Russians had moved into the Principalities for the purpose of suppressing a revolutionary movement. A success of Hungarian liberalism and nationalism, with its likely repercussions in the Principalities, was an added incentive to Russian intervention.

[13] Kossuth even sought to enlist British help with the offer of economic concessions, but the preservation of Austria was a more important British interest than sympathy for Hungarian nationalism or some economic advantage.

pay an indemnity, but escaping territorial loss. It is worth mentioning, because of its later significance, that the new king, Victor Emmanuel,[14] was steadfast in refusing the Austrian demand that he abolish the *Statuto* of March, 1848.

The Roman situation meanwhile was the object of outside interest, mainly Austrian and French. The former Power, restored to inner confidence, was not loath to assist the Pope, in doing which it would have merely continued the earlier Metternichian policy in Italy. But French events had also taken a new turn. After the definite success of the moderates in June, the Assembly drafted a new constitution, completed in November, and elections took place in December for the presidential office.[15] The outcome of the free consultation of the French people was the election by an overwhelming majority of Prince Louis Napoleon Bonaparte to the Presidency of the Second Republic.

The course of the Great Revolution and the fate of the first Republic of France were sharply and inevitably brought to mind by this development, unforeseen at the beginning of the year. To the rest of Europe the possibility of French aggression, or at least of French interference was of foremost concern, all the more to be feared in view of the strong feeling in France on the score of the "iniquitous" settlements of 1815. Louis Napoleon will often reappear in the following pages; for the moment it will suffice to say that his attention was mainly absorbed in the domestic scene and that his chief concern toward the outside world was to give it reassurance of wholly peaceable intent. At home likewise Napoleon presented himself mainly as the savior of order.[16] The outcome in the foreign field was perhaps not devoid of some humor, for, following the vote of necessary credits by the French Assembly, a French force appeared before Rome, which, after some misunderstanding and rather confused negotiations, was taken.[17] This

---

[14] After the defeat of Novara, Charles Albert had turned over the crown to his son.

[15] The constitution maintained universal suffrage but provided for a strong executive to be elected popularly.

[16] In January the Assembly had dissolved itself under threat of military intervention, and the subsequent election, in which the various conservative tendencies joined hands, was a substantial parliamentary victory for the forces of "order."

[17] In Rome, a relatively moderate regime had been established after the Piedmontese defeat of Novara, a triumvirate of which Mazzini was a member. A peaceable arrangement was negotiated with the Roman Republic by the French representative, Ferdinand de Lesseps, but he was recalled and disavowed, after which Rome was attacked by the French forces of General Oudinot. Despite

was in June, 1849. Order being restored in Rome, the Pope returned the following April; he had been thoroughly frightened by what appeared to him the excesses and the dangers of liberalism unleashed; completely disillusioned, he had learned his lesson and could henceforth be counted a dependable advocate and supporter of Metternichian ideas.

But the outcome was odd. By the time the disturbance originating at the beginning of 1848 had finally subsided, its remaining effects in Italy were two: in Piedmont a liberal constitution survived; in Rome the Pope was dependent on French bayonets. To this extent French influence may be said to have displaced the Austrian in the Peninsula. But it was a conservative influence, not a revolutionary one as might have been feared two years earlier. This unexpected turn is traceable directly to the domestic situation in France: catering to the forces of order, Louis Napoleon had enlisted conservative Catholic support. But herein lay a fundamental ambiguity in the domestic operation of France; the ambiguity was never really resolved and remained to confuse and bedevil in turn the operation of French foreign policy throughout the period of Louis Napoleon, another twenty years.

III. The Revolution in the Germanies

While events were unfolding in the Habsburg domain and in Italy, Germany was the scene of similar disturbances. To these German events, which have so far been left aside for the sake of clarity of presentation, we must now turn. Needless to say, Germany was of no less concern to Austria than Italy. The line of Austrian policy in the German case may be summed up in the general observation that it was one of biding time and watchfulness while attending to more pressing matters elsewhere, after which Austria could reassert herself in Germany as well. From another point of view, the episode is one in the long tale of rivalry between Hohenzollern and Habsburg, between Prussia and Austria, for supremacy in the Central European domain.

The news of the Parisian revolution of February, 1848, had in Germany the same effect of giving encouragement to suppressed but hopeful liberal elements as elsewhere in Central Europe. Widespread liberal successes, peaceably effected in gen-

---

vigorous resistance, Garibaldi, judging the situation hopeless, yielded and made good his withdrawal and eventual escape.

eral, seemed to sweep the land where the rulers had been caught by surprise. Also, in general, the national factor was strongly marked: as in the case of Italy it was a force of integration, by contrast with Austria where it could only have the contrary effect. It was this aspect of the matter that made the events of 1848–1849 in Germany a question of European concern.

THE FRANKFORT PARLIAMENT

In Berlin, the March days found King Frederick Willian apparently quite willing to accede to the wishes of his "beloved Berliners," at least of those who had set up barricades to express their desires, and on the 21st he issued a proclamation significantly addressed to his and to the German nation, the leadership of which he promised to assume. It was ten days later that the *Vorparlament* met in Frankfort whence it proceeded to issue the call for elections on the basis of universal suffrage. The National Assembly, a large body of over eight hundred men,[18] that issued from this consultation, met in Frankfort on May 18, almost simultaneously with the meeting of a Prussian constituent assembly. It proceeded to substitute itself for the Diet of the Germanic Confederation and went through the motions of organizing a government, appointing various ministers and an imperial Regent in the person of Archduke John of Austria.

This seemingly smooth operation was only such because no force was available to impede its enactment. For Frankfort was possessed of no power; though recognized by the German states, it could command no army of its own. The choice of Archduke John was an evasion of the paramount issue: what constituted Germany? In other words, should Austria or should she not be included in Germany? The ethnic facts were simple: a part of Austria, the Austria of our day, was undeniably Germanic, and just as undeniably the rest of the Austrian state was not. The ruler of that state, by the provisions of the Act of Vienna, held in perpetuity the presidency of the Germanic Confederation. Clearly, the Austrian state would have to have an important say in the matter, which in any event could hardly be settled by default.

[18] Despite the refusal of conservatives to participate in a revolutionary body, the Frankfort Assembly was overwhelmingly a body of middle-class men—lawyers, professors, officials, etc. The individual quality of its members has caused it to be described as "the most distinguished constituent body in history," a fact which, however, also contributed to the ineffectiveness of its operation in practice

Much would therefore depend upon the shape in which, and under what control, that state would emerge from the disturbance that confronted it at the moment. As pointed out before, the tide in Austria began to turn in June, but it took time before control was reëstablished. All the while the debate could go on between the respective advocates of the *gross* and *kleindeutsch* solutions.

On a smaller scale, there had already been a testing of the vexed problem of the precise frontiers of would-be Germany; the Duchies of Schleswig and Holstein provided the occasion for it. These small states, of which the latter was wholly Germanic in population and the former partly so, were attached to the Danish crown in a personal union. The death of the Danish king in January, 1848, which brought Frederick VIII to the throne, was the occasion for launching an attempt at closer integration of the Duchies with Denmark. This led to a revolt and the setting up of a provisional government,[19] which event brought in Danish troops. German national feeling was aroused and the Frankfort Assembly entrusted Prussia with the execution of its mandate of resistance to Danish encroachment.

War between Prussia and Denmark pleased neither Russia nor Britain, the former anxious to keep Prussia away from the Baltic, the latter concerned over control of the Danish Straits. But this common anti-Prussian interest did not suffice to overcome mutual Anglo-Russian suspicion, and both states were content with separate pressure on Prussia that never exceeded the bounds of diplomacy. To this pressure Frederick William was not loath to yield, and in August the armistice of Malmö provided for evacuation and joint Danish-German administration pending a final settlement. Frankfort protested this arrangement at first but eventually acquiesced.

In general terms, the tsar viewed with suspicion the whole German movement, mainly because of its liberal content. That aspect of things or, for that matter, the prospect of unification, did not displease Palmerston who soon began to cool, however, toward the wordy debates of Frankfort.[20] France, too, was of two

[19] The situation was further complicated by the fact that the Duchies claimed the application of the Salic law, with the consequence that they supported the claim of the Duke of Augustenburg to the succession.

[20] English opinion on the score of German unity was divided. Some favored it, though not necessarily to the benefit of Prussia (the prince consort); Disraeli considered it dangerous nonsense, agreeing in this respect with Metternich and Nesselrode.

minds. French liberals tended to sympathize with the national aspirations of their trans-Rhenish counterparts, but the classical tradition that preferred a collection of weak neighbors in the East was strong in France. Talk of German Alsace and the Prussian refusal to entertain Polish demands for autonomy helped to raise doubts, even in Lamartine, about the future of German nationalism. In any case, things did not go beyond a guarded attitude of noncommittal suspicion.

THE AUSTRO-PRUSSIAN CONFLICT

German affairs were thus enabled to develop without external interference and the debate went on in Frankfort around the related issues of the constitution and the extent of the future Germany. It was a lengthy debate, and although conducted on a high level, was one that was becoming increasingly abstract and divorced from reality as the old order was becoming reëstablished in Austria. Windischgrätz' military victories and the advent of Schwarzenberg toward the end of the year were soon reflected in the tone of communications from Vienna. Schwarzenberg's insistence on the *grossdeutsch* solution—the inclusion of the totality of Austria—resulted in a compromise in the Frankfort Assembly under the sponsorship of its president, von Gagern: Austria would be included, but only for her German territories. In effect, this represented a victory for the *kleindeutsch* solution, for Austria could be counted upon to decline, leaving Prussia the logical candidate for leadership of the alternative.

This in fact is what happened. Having adopted, on March 27, 1849, a constitution that created a federal German state to be presided over by an emperor of the Germans, the Frankfort Parliament chose the Prussian king for that office. This was to invite a showdown between the rival influences of Austria and of Prussia. But the showdown did not occur at once.

The Prussian king would have liked to assume the German crown but he was loath to embark upon an open clash with Austria. He resorted to some tergiversation, but finally discovered at the end of April that, ruler by divine right, he could not accept a crown the legitimacy of which stemmed from an elected body, the "crown from the gutter." This refusal spelled the end of the Frankfort body, which most of the German states ceased thereupon to acknowledge, as well as the end of the effort to create a united Germany under any kind of liberal auspices. The future price of this failure was to be high, for Germany and for others as well.[21]

But the idea of unity was not dead and now led to a sharp Austro-Prussian clash. A Prussian scheme was now produced, the credit for which goes to von Radowitz, close to the king. Having sent his troops to assist his Saxon and Hanoverian colleagues to restore order in their respective domains, in May, 1849, the Prussian king formed with them in Berlin the so-called League of the Three Kings. Starting from this initial combination, and on the basis of the consent of the princes, the scheme of German unity could be revived. A larger union, taking in all of Austria, would also be created, the affairs of which would be in the hands of a Directorate made up of representatives of three entities: Austria, Prussia, and the "middle" states. This was a compromise of sorts and raised the prospect of a vast Middle Europe.

The response to the Prussian scheme of German union was not unfavorable, Bavaria alone remaining aloof. But Austria, having finally dealt with the Hungarian problem, was now freer to assert herself, and her increased assurance and power were reflected in various German defections, those of Hanover and Saxony being the most important. Undeterred, the Prussian king and Radowitz persisted, now seeking to create a more limited union of Prussia with the smaller states. A call was issued for an assembly to meet at Erfurt. When the Erfurt Assembly gathered, in March, 1850, to adopt the constitution proposed by Prussia, it was confronted by a rival gathering in Frankfort, held under Austrian auspices. Bavaria, Saxony, Württemberg, and Hanover, as well as some smaller states, had taken sides with Schwarzenberg. Middle Europe was rent in two, and for the moment Frederick William would not press the issue which would have meant war with Austria.

OLMÜTZ. It is at this juncture that an incident revived the possibility of a clash. An internal issue in Hesse-Cassel, a dispute between the ruler and the Parliament, caused the former to appeal to Frankfort for federal assistance, which Prussia claimed an equal right to give. Both sides mobilized, but the determination of Schwarzenberg, expressed in an ultimatum, caused Prussia to retreat. On November 29, Manteuffel, who had meantime replaced Radowitz, went to Olmütz to sanction the Prussian surrender;

[21] The Frankfort body disbanded and a rump, meeting in Stuttgart, was shortly dispersed by armed force.

the order of mobilization was recalled and Prussia agreed to an
open conference of all the member states of the Germanic Confederation. The meeting, when held, merely resulted in a restoration of the *status quo ante*. In the open and final showdown,
Austria had won a clear-cut victory; the "humiliation of Olmütz"
was long to rankle in Prussia.

It was at about the same time that the Danish issue was settled.
The Danes having denounced the armistice of Malmö, hostilities
had been resumed. A fresh armistice was concluded and with the
intervening assistance of Britain, Russia, and Sweden, peace was
established between Prussia and Denmark on July 2, 1850. This
was little more than a truce, for, while Prussian troops were withdrawn, both sides reserved their rights and the disputed issue of
succession was not settled. Two years later, on May 8, 1852, a
London Protocol signed by the Great Powers, Sweden, and Denmark, purported to settle the succession to the Danish throne and
in the Duchies, all of which were to acknowledge the rule of the
Duke of Glücksburg, the Danish king being without issue.[22]

IV. The Balance Sheet of 1848

Thus, within two years of the outbreak that had seemed
for a while to threaten the stability of much of the European
structure, order had been reëstablished and the outward remaining signs of the disturbance were impressively few. Britain had
been affected not at all, and likewise Russia; in Central Europe,
where the turmoil had been most pronounced, Austria had ridden
out the storm and stood as before at the head of the restored Germanic Confederation. What constitutional changes survived in
the whole Central European world, from the Baltic to Sicily, were
for the most part of very little significance.

Even in France, where the force of liberalism was strongest,
the Second Republic seemed to be in the hands of dependably
conservative, or at least moderate, elements. "The revolution that
failed" may therefore be said to be apt characterization of these
events. The reason for this failure must be seen in the fact that
the forces of change lacked a sufficient basis of support among the
peoples: universal suffrage returned assemblies, be it in Paris or
Frankfort, whose membership was on the whole of a more mod-

---

[22] The Duke of Augustenburg yielded his claims for a money payment. For
the later development of the Schleswig-Holstein question, see below, pp. 127–129.

erate bent than that of those who had called them into existence. In this respect the role of France was crucial, for in France lay the hope of liberals throughout the breadth of Europe; France, by deceiving the hopes of movements outside her borders, had saved the peace but let the revolution die. Nevertheless, if 1848 was a failure, the long-term trend of change could not be easily arrested. Liberal principles, broadly speaking and in their various aspects, would continue to assert themselves and in time steadily to increase the area over which they prevailed. Viewed in that context, 1848 appears as an important and far from a useless step in a continuing process.

But from the point of view of Europe as a whole and the relations of her component parts, the most remarkable thing about the 1848 revolutions is the fact that the peace was not broken among the major states. Some interventions there were, French in Rome, Russian in Hungary, Prussian in Denmark, but in no case did the disturbances spread. In this respect, also, the French role of abstention was crucial. For, naturally, the likelihood seemed greatest that revolutionary France, venting her discontent with the treaties of 1815, would be the disturber of the existing international order. Once France had decided not to intervene, since Austria and Prussia were fully occupied with Central European affairs, that left Britain and Russia free to undertake any action. The tsar was highly unsympathetic to revolution as such and anywhere, while the prospect of it found not a little sympathy in Britain, where even Palmerston would shed no tears over the demise of the Metternichian system. But Russia and Britain agreed in not wishing to see either themselves or others involved in major conflict; accordingly, they threw the weight of their influence in favor of the preservation of peace. No one thought of interfering in purely French affairs, and the Central European disturbance was left to work itself out within its own confines.

One major conflict might have developed in that area, which the Prussian surrender at Olmütz avoided. Russia was not extraneous to that particular event. The tsar assumed an arbitral position, stating that he might throw his force against the disturber of the peace, making clear at the same time that this did not necessarily mean the initiator of hostilities, but he that was in reality responsible for a clash. This was tantamount to taking sides with Austria. Yet Austria did not have her way completely at Dresden where Schwarzenberg restored the Germanic Confederation as it had been before, for he failed in his desire to secure the inclusion of all the Austrian possessions. The period from 1848 to 1850 therefore witnessed considerable diplomatic activity among the major Powers, but no more than diplomatic activity.

THE ENIGMA OF FRANCE

Nevertheless, to a degree, the French enigma remained, to which the person of the President gave added point. Whether in France or abroad, Louis Napoleon could not but be the symbol of what the first Napoleon had stood for. Louis Napoleon, soon to be Napoleon III, was a complex personality; he and the two decades of his rule have been and are the objects of widely divergent estimates. Unlike his uncle, he was himself no military man, had in fact little stomach for the battlefield; intrigue and diplomacy were to him more congenial. He was in some respects a very modern man, one who would have fitted well in the practice of later politics, adept at playing on the feelings of the mass, a demagogue if one will. He, too, was a son of the Revolution. The short, if spectacular, career of the first Napoleon did not create for his nephew a solid claim to rule; he was conscious that what legitimacy he could claim had the will of the nation as its sole foundation; like any parvenu, he was highly aware of his uncertain standing and craved the acceptance of longer established rulers. Also, unlike the first Napoleon, the tendency to trim and compromise, the reluctance to make clear decisions, to see their consequences, and to adhere to them were important parts of his make-up. Predilections of his own, sentimental sympathies one might say, he had, and to a point would yield to them. Nationalism in general appealed to him; had he not been a *carbonaro?* But he was the head of the French state, hence must naturally promote the interests of that entity, now identified with his own, both personal and dynastic. The mixture of these elements led to not a little confusion and inconsistency. Skillful as he may have been, there are limits to the degree to which one may mean all things to all men.

Some of these contradictory elements appeared early in his policy. In rising to the Presidency of France he had known how to exploit to the utmost the asset of the Napoleonic legend. But he had soon allied himself with the forces of moderation and even of reaction; the Roman episode is a case in point. On the plane of national feeling, he might unite all Frenchmen in support of himself and of the desire to undo the settlement of 1815; this view he cherished and it became a lasting component of his motivation. It is revealing that, in 1849, in the midst of the German confusion, he toyed with schemes of a Prussian alliance for the price of some compensation on the Rhine; he reverted to the possibility again in 1850 when the Austro-Prussian clash seemed imminent, and he also felt the ground in Bavaria. His offers were not entertained; Prussia was on her side championing German nationality. But these projects were to be taken up again at a later date. In the end he contented himself with announcing that France would not intervene in an Austro-Prussian conflict so long as the equilibrium was not broken, meaning so long as Russia did not intervene.

No one intervened in the end and Louis Napoleon succeeded in reassuring other Powers on the score of his intentions. Once order had been restored in Europe, domestic affairs commanded his attention for a while, and this is not the place to tell the tale of his quarrels with the legislature, and of his skillful exploitation of them, through the *coup d'état* of December, 1851, to the ultimate conclusion of the reëstablishment of the Empire in France on December 2, 1852, a date symbolically chosen as the anniversary of Austerlitz. As usual, a plebiscite endorsed the outcome.

The act itself was calculated to revive once more abroad the fear of French, or Napoleon's, intentions, but for a time he continued to adhere to the policy of reassuring all and, on the whole with success, to cultivate good will in all quarters. But not for long.

Successes
of Nationalism

The story of the two decades that end in the proclamation of the German Empire in 1871 might be written around a variety of centers. French foreign policy would be such an adequate focus, for the reason that France is involved in most of the conflicts that occurred in that period. Nevertheless, if French policy is either at the center of, or at least importantly connected with, most of the international developments of the period, it is not its guiding influence, partly for the reason that the director of it, Napoleon III, was not of comparable stature with other statesmen of his time. From another standpoint, Britain, preferring peace and quite content to promote her economic and imperial development, is more than ever the upholder and arbiter of European equilibrium.

But there would seem to be little question that the time is most markedly characterized by the great success of the nationalistic force, of which the simplification of the map of Europe that was produced by the consolidation of the Italian and the German states is the clearest expression. These developments dominate the European scene and the manner of their achievement was conditioned in part by the course of events that has been related in the preceding chapter. All the while the interests of all existing states are involved, and, as during the revolutionary period just ended, the clash of rival nationalisms cuts across and complicates the operation of international relations.

I. The Eastern Question

BACKGROUND OF THE CRIMEAN WAR

It took some years before the ground was properly prepared for the collapse of the structure that existed in the Italian Peninsula and a few more before Bismarck could undertake the corresponding task in Germany. Meanwhile, in a different quarter, and in rather unexpected fashion, the Eastern Question once more was to absorb for a time the attention of Europe.

The issue that was to develop into a war that involved three major European Powers has been called disparagingly "a quarrel of monks," and the war itself the most unnecessary war. If it is true that the monks quarreled and that the war had largely the effect of merely preserving the Ottoman state, the preservation of that state was no minor question for Europe. The status of the whole Near East had been regulated in 1840, but the efforts of the Ottoman Empire to revive itself had not, on the whole, been successful; so long as it continued to be the Sick Man of Europe, the problem of its fate was bound to continue a prime concern of the Powers. Nevertheless, matters had remained quiescent through the whole decade of the forties and even the great disturbance of 1848 had had no repercussions in Turkey. The Russian intervention in the Principalities, like that in Hungary, was a passing episode of temporary nature; intended as it was to counter revolutionary activity, it may even be regarded as an act designed to preserve Ottoman stability and integrity.

But with the opening of a new decade matters began to change. In point of time, though certainly not of importance, the quarrel of the monks came first and therefore warrants brief mention. It grew out of the fact that Jerusalem is a Holy City for Christians, but that Christians belong to a variety of persuasions. In Moslem eyes the Western Christians had for long been Franks, but without going back to the Crusades, the French king—emperor as he styled himself in dealing with the sultan—had obtained the right of representation and protection of Christians *vis-à-vis* the Ottoman power.[1] It was only natural, however, that Eastern (Greek) Christians should correspondingly look to the Russian tsar to perform a similar service for them; and that is what happened as Russian power grew and began to assert itself successfully against the Ottoman. The treaty of Kutchuk Kainardji, though none too precise in this respect, registered Russian rights in the matter.

In Jerusalem itself, a situation had developed as the result of which monks of the two Christian branches, Catholic and Greek, shared the care of the Holy Places. The precise spots with the guardianship of which they were entrusted were narrowly defined and the various orders eyed each other in watchful jealousy. From the 1830's one may speak of something in the nature of a Catholic

[1] This was confirmed in the Capitulation of May, 1740.

offensive, in the form of intensified activity of Catholic orders in Jerusalem. This is the quarrel of the monks: who was entitled to what gate and which key, who was encroaching on whose rights? a quarrel often less than dignified in its local manifestations—the monks would sometimes come to blows—and hardly calculated to enhance the regard for Christianity of the Turks whose main concern was to preserve the peace. But the monks had protectors.

This situation was ready-made pretext for outside intervention; it fitted to a nicety the temporarily dormant, but never dead, Russian interest in Ottoman affairs. If the narrowly religious aspect of the matter was calculated to elicit a wide response in Russia, more concrete interests were not lacking: Russian trade was growing at an appreciable rate—the export of grain from the Black Sea ports and the corresponding import of manufactured goods, in large part British. This meant increased importance for the passage through the Straits. In this entire affair one may fairly speak of Russian initiative, which in the end induced the adverse reaction of others.

But the French President, about to become emperor, was first to take up the defense of his Catholic protégés. There is no evidence that Napoleon had any large or well-thought-out scheme in mind, let alone war or the demise of the Sick Man of Europe; but a minor advantage in that quarter would please Catholic opinion at home and generally redound to national prestige. The sultan had resort to a peculiar expedient: a public firman favoring the Catholic monks; and another one, not public, but communicated to the tsar, doing likewise for the Orthodox. This was hardly designed to clarify matters, but the cultivation of differences among the Powers had long become a standard ingredient of the foreign policy of the Porte.

Russian initiative now broadened the issue, for the tsar began to entertain large schemes that dealt with the Ottoman Empire as a whole. Any drastic rearrangement of it would be most likely to encounter British opposition above all. For Britain consistently adhered to the policy of Ottoman integrity, a policy which, for that matter, would serve her growing economic interest in that quarter.[2] The tsar, therefore, quite properly since he was not desirous of conflict, broached the matter to the British ambassador at the beginning of 1853. The Russian schemes lacked precision

[2] British exports to the Ottoman Empire had grown from £1,400,000 in 1829 to nearly £12,000,000 in 1848. Britain's Russian trade was also growing.

and conveyed the impression of feeling the ground rather than of firm intent. Britain consenting, Russia might go to the length of war with Turkey, the outcome of which might be the eviction of the Turk from Europe: a Serbian and a Bulgarian state would emerge, Russia would have the Bosporus, and Austria the Dardanelles; on another occasion the tsar proposed that Britain might have Egypt and Crete. While Britain did not accept these proposals, neither did she flatly reject them, and the failure of a clear refusal is the ground for the claim that Russia was misled.[3] It will be noted that in the tsar's proposals there was no room for French interests; the tsar had not taken kindly to the new French emperor and even less to the latter's support of the Western monks in Jerusalem.

It is at this point that Constantinople was startled by the news, given out by the Russian representative at the Porte, of the impending arrival of a special mission from Russia. Within a week, at the end of February, Prince Menshikov arrived with an imposing retinue, obviously meant to impress all in the Turkish capital, not least the sultan himself. In view of the display and of the personality of the Russian delegate,[4] the explanation was less than convincing that minor matters only were entrusted to him, and the British and French *chargés d'affaires* conveyed their alarm to their respective capitals.[5] Lord Clarendon, the British foreign minister, refused to be alarmed, though his French counterpart, Drouyn de Lhuys, was inclined to take a more serious view of the matter, and the Russian chancellor, Nesselrode, endeavored to minimize the significance of the whole affair.

Of British interest in the quarreling monks, there was none; the British tendency in that particular matter may be described as mildly pro-Russian. But de Redcliffe, the British representative, returning to Constantinople, immediately perceived that large stakes were involved and urged a prompt settlement of the smaller quarrel. This was done through a firman of May 4 that apportioned the rights of the local contenders, purported restoration of the *status quo ante*. Menshikov had not been idle meanwhile; using a mix-

[3] Palmerston had left the foreign office in 1851. After the short-lived Derby ministry in 1852, Aberdeen was in office at this time with Lord Clarendon at the foreign office.

[4] Prince Menshikov was one of the most important personages in Russia where he had occupied a number of high positions.

[5] Both the British and the French ambassadors happened to be away when the Menshikov mission arrived in Constantinople. The former, Lord Stratford Canning de Redcliffe, promptly returned and played in the whole crisis a major role, the interpretation of which is still the subject of controversy.

ture of cajolery and threats[6] he went about the pursuit of his aim: Russia demanded not only the rights that were hers under the treaty of Kutchuk Kainardji, but the extension of these rights to a protection of all Orthodox Christians under the sultan's rule. The implications of this request were clear: Russia claimed a standing right of intervention of which she might be counted on to make use when the occasion would seem suitable. The issue of the fate of the Ottoman Empire had indeed been raised.

The sultan did not yield. Bolstered by British support—to what extent de Redcliffe acted on his own initiative is debated—he stood firm on his decree of May 4 and refused to grant a special position to Russia. Having failed in his mission, Menshikov thereupon departed, figuratively slamming the door and muttering dark threats. These were not long in being implemented, for the tsar decided, as a means of pressure on the Porte, to occupy the Principalities, which Russian forces began to enter in June. Simultaneously, British and French fleets were sent to Besika Bay, in readiness to enter the Straits.

The situation which had developed was this: the Russian initiative of aggression was being resisted by Britain, a resistance in which France associated herself, though she no longer was a prime mover in the unfolding of events. But no one was anxious for war[7] and the Turks were advised by their Western supporters not to resist the Russian advance into the Principalities. No mention to this point has been made of the one other major Power, Austria, to whom Eastern affairs were of significant concern. Austria never participated actively in the conflict, and Vienna remained throughout the episode the center of diplomatic activity where the antagonists, even when engaged in hostilities, could continue discussions. She entered the picture at this juncture, the Austrian chancellor, Count Buol, calling the ambassadors of the Powers to discuss the issue with him. The outcome of these consultations, the Conference of Vienna, was the so-called Vienna Note of July 28;[8] it was a document, rather vague in its language, which sought to give Russia satisfaction in a fashion not unacceptable to the Turks. The

---

[6] The sultan was sufficiently impressed and frightened to dismiss his minister of foreign affairs, whom Menshikov had ostensibly slighted.

[7] The British Cabinet was divided, with Aberdeen conciliatory toward Russia and Palmerston in strong opposition. Public opinion was turning strongly against Russia. As to Napoleon, he was moved quite as much by the desire not to let Britain act alone as by other considerations.

[8] By this time the Principalities had been completely occupied.

French authorship of the text is revealing, for France, though following Britain, actually held a middle position.

THE DIPLOMACY OF THE CRIMEAN WAR

The tsar would have been satisfied, but the Turkish reply—under British, specifically de Redcliffe's, suggestion—was a skillful rewording that in effect reversed the intent of the note.[9] This version was in turn unacceptable to the Russians, and, despite continued negotiations,[10] tension was mounting in Constantinople. Confident of sufficient support from the Western Powers the Turks declared war on Russia on October 4.

Even after this step the situation was slow in developing. The British and French fleets entered the Straits but did not pass into the Black Sea until January, 1854, long after the incident of Sinope.[11] It took another month before Russia broke relations with the Western Powers, and not until February 27 did the Powers demand the evacuation of the Principalities in the form of an ultimatum. As no answer was forthcoming to this, Britain and France, having concluded a formal alliance, finally took the step of a declaration of war against Russia at the end of March. Rather reluctantly three of the major states of Europe had allowed themselves to come to the point of hostilities. The issue at stake was a real one that they had been incapable of compromising: basically it was a case of Britain's feeling that she would not allow certain Russian encroachments, with France somewhat half-heartedly joining, mainly because she felt that she must not allow Britain to oppose Russia alone.

War having been declared, the question was to find a battle-ground for it. Since the Western Powers had fleets it was clearly for them to bring the war to Russia, and the fact that territorial contact existed between Russia and Turkey would point to the Principalities, specific final cause of the conflict, as the logical meeting place for the opposing armies.[12] In this connection the

[9] Where the original note spoke of the sultan's willingness to recognize again the Russian interest in his Christian subjects, the Turkish reply spoke of the sultan's care in observing the privileges that he had *spontaneously* granted to the Orthodox Church.

[10] Tsar Nicholas and Emperor Francis Joseph met at Olmütz in September.

[11] The Russians had destroyed a Turkish squadron on its way to the eastern end of the Black Sea on November 30.

[12] Some thought was given to the possibility of action in the Baltic, but this was soon abandoned, especially as Sweden showed no inclination to join the anti-Russian coalition.

attitude of Austria was evidently of capital concern to the belligerents. The question in this case was whether Austria would maintain neutrality or join the allies, a result which they endeavored to contrive at this time and throughout the conflict, though never with success. The first Austrian step took the form of an alliance with Prussia, concluded in April: the two states gave each other mutual guarantees of their territories and undertook jointly to oppose Russian extension in the Balkans. Austria went to the length of mobilizing her forces and the pressure that she exerted on Russia had the effect of causing the latter to evacuate the Principalities, where her place was taken by the Austrians.[13]

This rearrangement had in turn the consequence of separating the belligerents while Vienna continued to be the center of negotiations. There, on August 8, a new agreement was reached between Buol and the British and French representatives, which was to form the basis of negotiations with Russia. The Four Points of Vienna provided for a collective, instead of a Russian, protectorate of the Principalities; free navigation of the mouths of the Danube; a revision of the Convention of the Straits of 1841 with a view to establishing a better equilibrium by redressing the Russian preponderance in the Black Sea; Russia's renunciation of the exclusive claim to protection of the Christian subjects of the sultan, instead of which again collective arrangements should be made.

These proposals proved of no interest to Russia, who had not yet suffered military setbacks, and the allies came to the decision to carry the war to the Crimea, where their forces landed in September. Of the war itself little need be said. It provided occasion for heroic fighting on both sides, for intense suffering and hardship from the inclement forces of nature and from the ravages of pestilence, but also for the display of not a little incompetence and mismanagement at the higher levels of commands. On the whole the allies, though operating under the handicap of extended overseas lines of communications, were able to best the Russians on their home ground.

But the protracted duration of hostilities intensified the task of diplomacy and especially the attempt of the allies to enlist the assistance of Austria, matched by the Russian effort to maintain Austrian neutrality. Russia was successful in this contest, but Austria was not loath to exploit the advantage that accrued from the

[13] With the consent of Turkey, with whom Austria had meantime concluded a treaty in June.

uncertainty of all in her regard. The directors of Austrian policy were divided, some favoring intervention, others advocating some direct arrangement with Russia, all agreeing on the desirability of checking the extension of her influence. To a degree, Austria was hampered by fears, despite the Prussian alliance, that Prussia might take advantage of the situation in her rear should she allow herself to become involved in the war.[14]

These circumstances were propitious to the intrusion of a new participant, none other than little Sardinia. Cavour directed the affairs of that state at this time and already envisaged the possibility of insinuating himself into the current conflict. Sardinia had no quarrel with Russia, and any pretext for intervention must be farfetched; Cavour's interest was not with Russian, or even Eastern affairs, but with matters much nearer home. It might be as difficult to "sell" the idea of intervention at home as to convince the Western Powers that the Sardinian contribution was worth while. Negotiations proceeded quite slowly, but in the end various factors contributed to their success. The British were not altogether happy about the larger French contingent in the Crimea; a Sardinian force would help redress the balance. More important, Sardinia could be used as a pawn to exert pressure on Austria, to the enlistment of whose assistance far more importance was attached.

Out of this situation came two results. On December 2, 1854, Austria committed herself to the extent of entering into an offensive and defensive alliance with Britain and France. But one condition that she obtained was a guarantee of her Italian possessions. The news was less than welcome to Cavour and, to a point, the tables were now turned, pressure being put upon him by the Western Powers. On January 26, 1855, Sardinia entered the war.

This intervention could hardly be decisive and Austria would not go beyond mobilization. While hostilities therefore continued in the Crimea, the desire was growing stronger, especially in Russian and French quarters, to extricate themselves from the conflict. In January, the tsar went the length of accepting the Four Points of Vienna as a basis for negotiations. A conference gathered in Vienna on March 15, where the chief belligerents met with Buol, though not even an armistice had been concluded between them. The death of Tsar Nicholas at the beginning of the month

[14] In February, 1855, the federal Diet, at Prussian instigation, refused to decree mobilization, thus largely nullifying the intent of the Austro-Prussian alliance of the preceding year.

might have been expected to enhance the prospects of agreement, but the allies failed of success in the Crimea at this time, and the Vienna meeting had, by June, proved barren of results. The limitation of Russian forces in the Black Sea was more than Gorchakov, the Russian delegate, would consider; as he put it, only a major reverse would warrant its acceptance.

The final capture of Sebastopol in September might be considered such a reverse, for which the later Russian success in Kars, in November, was hardly compensation; the fact of the greater effectiveness of the Western Powers had to be faced by the Russians. Moreover, the possibility of Swedish intervention[15] was again brought into the picture, while Napoleon threw out hints of espousing the cause of nationality toward Russia in Poland, toward Austria in Italy.[16] As the year 1855 drew to a close, Austria finally confronted Russia with an ultimatum; this last pressure sufficed to bring Russian acceptance of the Four Points of Vienna.

THE CONGRESS OF PARIS

The Powers met in Paris, not in Vienna, hitherto the center of negotiations; the Austrian government, with its tergiversations and its refusal to take a clear position in the conflict, had discontented all, whereas Franco-Russian relations, despite the war, were not wholly unfriendly. The tone of the Congress was, in fact, generally amiable and relaxed; its work was light, and social amenities occupied much of its time;[17] agreement had largely been reached in advance and all save perhaps Britain[18] were anxious to have peace. The Congress met on February 25 and its first act was the conclusion of an armistice. Within a month the work was finished and the final treaty was signed on March 30.

The Four Points of Vienna were the basis of the settlement. No indemnities were imposed and, save for one qualification, the *status quo ante bellum* was to be restored: Russia lost access to the Danube by being deprived of the small strip of territory between

---

[15] The possibility of Swedish intervention, considered in the earlier stages of the conflict but abandoned at the time, was brought up anew at this point.

[16] Despite the guarantee given Austria, she was still neutral. In the Sardinian treaty the Western Powers had not committed themselves beyond the promise of good services in the Italian question. Toward the end of 1855 Napoleon announced the forthcoming visit of the king of Sardinia to Paris.

[17] Sessions were suspended from March 14 to 18 on the occasion of the birth of the Prince Imperial, a pretext for festivities.

[18] Palmerston was almost alone in his belligerent intransigeance. But for his insistence on certain conditions, accommodation might have been found earlier.

the northernmost mouth of that river and the Pruth; this land was added to Moldavia.[19] Nothing was left of the Russian claim to an exclusive right of protection of Christians; instead of this, the Powers collectively disclaimed any interfering intentions between the sultan and his subjects and took note with satisfaction of his "solicitude" and of his "spontaneously" manifested good will.[20] The Sublime Porte was, in addition, formally recognized as a rightful member of the Concert of Europe.

The Principalities and Serbia were guaranteed their privileges while remaining under Turkish suzerainty, but the guarantee again was collective. A commission of the signatory Powers was created to attend to the mouths of the Danube, to the navigation of which the provisions of the Act of Vienna of 1815 in regard to international rivers were extended. Most significant of all, perhaps, was the provision which established the demilitarization of the Black Sea. This registered the full extent of the Russian defeat.

The Congress of Paris was a highly important episode in the development of the Eastern Question. It marked a very considerable Russian setback, in the form of the Black Sea clause and in the total elimination of any Russian position of privilege in the Ottoman Empire which correspondingly was granted a new lease on life: simultaneously, it was admitted to the Concert of Europe and in effect placed under the joint protectorate of Europe.[21]

Having completed its main work, a settlement of the Eastern Question, the Congress went on for a while to deal with matters of more general interest. The Aland Islands in the Baltic were not to be fortified by Russia, and the question of mediation as a means to avoid future conflicts was also considered. The Powers agreed that they should have recourse to it, circumstances permitting.

Of more precise effect than this broad declaration of intent were the provisions dealing with maritime law, which the Powers

[19] This and the return of Kars to Turkey were presented as exchanges for the return of the Crimean conquests of the allies.

[20] On February 18, 1856, the sultan, under inspiration of the British, French, and Austrian ambassadors in Constantinople, had issued a decree, the Hatti-Humayun, which embodied a program of reforms that seemed to be unexceptionable in all respects: freedom of conscience, accessibility of all to civil and military positions, equality in taxation, etc. This far-reaching decree, like other similar ones before and after, was destined never to go far beyond the paper stage, but served the purpose of providing the Powers with a convenient alibi for inaction.

[21] On April 15 an Anglo-Franco-Austrian treaty agreed to consider any infringement of Turkish integrity or independence a *casus belli* and a cause for consultation among them.

signed on April 16. Privateering remained abolished; in war, enemy goods, save contraband, were to be protected by a neutral flag; neutral goods, save contraband of war again, were not to be liable to capture under enemy flag; blockade was recognized, but only if effective. These were valuable contributions to the development of international law.

Since the Congress had within its competence the right to examine any and all affairs of interest to Europe, mention was made of the Italian Question. It was Lord Clarendon, the British representative, who, in somewhat dramatic terms, called the attention of the Congress to the condition of Italy. Walewski, the French delegate, though with less enthusiasm, also mentioned the subject. Nothing was done, no action taken or resolution passed; the Congress merely registered the existence of an Italian problem. This was small coin in payment for the Sardinian contribution to the Crimean War; yet Cavour was wise enough to be content with an endorsement of the British delegate's comments. A small seed had been planted which, under his nurturing guidance, would not be many years in bearing fruit. To the Italian scene we must therefore now turn.[22]

II. The Unification of Italy

THE ITALIAN QUESTION

When Lord Clarendon called the attention of Europe to the Italian Question, the political status of the Peninsula was still as it had been established by Europe in 1815: in the South, a branch of the House of Bourbon ruled in the Kingdom of the Two Sicilies; the Pope's domain extended as far as the Po River, and, with the Grand Duchy of Tuscany, accounted for the middle third; the valley of the Po in the North comprised the Duchies of Parma and Modena,[23] the Kingdom of Sardinia, to which the island of that name was attached, and the Austrian lands of Lombardo-Venetia. As in the German world, the tradition of particularism was strong in Italy, quite apart from the dynastic interests of the rulers. It had deep historical roots, but there was such a thing as an Italian people, and unity also had roots in the far-distant, though never completely

[22] For convenience of exposition, other developments of relatively minor importance, the emergence of Rumania to independence, as well as certain imperial developments taking place during the fifties and the sixties, will be treated together in another section. See below, pp. 108 ff.

[23] In 1847 Lucca had been incorporated into Tuscany.

forgotten, past. The wish of the Italian people to constitute themselves into a single state we may therefore take as simple fact,
characteristic instance of nineteenth-century nationalism, though
the qualification is important that the consciousness of unity, hence
the desire to use it as a basis for action, did not deeply affect the
mass of the Italian people; it was largely confined to the politically
conscious, the literate minority, and especially strong among those
to whom cultural matters, the memory of Rome, were a reality.
The phrase was wholly apt, uttered after unification was accomplished: "We have made Italy, all that remains to do is to make
Italians."

It may also be said that the initial impetus toward unity came
from across the Alps, in the form of the French Revolution and
Napoleon. Whether the French were welcomed as liberators, as
they were initially by some, or whether their rule was resented as
alien, the effect of abetting the growth of common consciousness
was the same. The arbitrariness with which Napoleon had treated
the political boundaries of Italy was also useful in breaking the
mold in which the land had long been held. But, to repeat, Vienna
had essentially restored the *status quo ante* in Italy, both in the form
of reëstablishing boundaries and in that of reinstating the dominance of Austrian influence.

The Italian Question had two aspects: the struggle to secure
liberal constitutions and that for unity; in large measure the two
merged into one and Italy offers one of the best illustrations of
liberalism and nationalism combined. The half-century that it took
to bring into existence a united Italian state in the form of a constitutional monarchy goes in Italian annals under the name of the
Risorgimento, the rebirth, or resurgence, of Italy. Either aspect of
the Italian question made it a European problem. On the constitutional aspect of the matter, the Powers naturally tended to take
positions in accordance with their domestic predilections, and the
broad cleavage between the Western states, Britain and France,
and the Eastern monarchies, more staunchly wedded to conservatism, appears fairly consistently in the Italian problem. Appropriately, it was Metternich who intervened to restore order in Italy
in 1820.

But Metternich had another interest as well, the purely Austrian. Quite rightly from his point of view he regarded liberalism
and nationalism as equally nefarious in Italy and did his best to
stamp them out. Clearly, the making of a united Italy would be a

major readjustment in the balance of Europe which would concern all the Powers. Russia would be affected least of all and Prussia
little more, save that Italian developments, being of major significance to Austria, bore an important relation to her own position
toward that country. But Prussia, until the advent of Bismarck, was
largely acquiescent, not to say subservient, to Austrian leadership.
Britain was in the main sympathetic, for reasons partly sentimental
that affected British opinion, but Britain was not blind to the factor
of commercial advantage that might accrue to her from the liberation of Italy. Britain did not wish to see any substantial diminution
of the Austrian position of power, but her own view may be said
to have been that Austria could afford the loss of Italy, or perhaps
even would be better rid of the fettering burden of a reluctant
Italy.

If the Austrian position toward Italy was clear and simple, the
French was more complex. There was in France widespread sympathy for Italian nationalism, but those in control of the policy of
the French state tended to adhere to the view that a fragmentation
of power, in Italy as well as in Germany, was the more desirable
condition. In 1830 and in 1848 we have seen France frustrating the
hopes of Italian liberals.

In Italy herself a special situation existed the implications of
which were far-reaching. The Pope ruled a segment of Italy, but
the Pope in addition was the Pope, head of the Roman Church.
The theory behind the Papal power, apart from the specious legitimacy of Constantine's donation, was that the possession of some
territory in full sovereignty was essential to the proper fulfillment
of the Pope's spiritual, and more important, function. Most Italians were Catholics, but there were in addition Catholic millions
spread throughout the world, more particularly in neighboring
France and Austria. This aspect of the matter, the Roman situation,
was therefore calculated to introduce a special twist into Italian
affairs. For Austria, support of the Pope fitted well into the general
scheme of Austrian interest and policy. In France, the Roman
question fitted into the stuff of French domestic politics; France
was at once the eldest daughter of the Church and the home of
the Revolution.

Those who in Italy set their hearts on the making of a united
country evolved a variety of schemes for the purpose. Especially
in the earlier phase of the *Risorgimento*, till the upset of 1848, they
tended to concentrate on the domestic side of the question, giving

a minimum of attention to its larger, European, aspect. *Italia farà da sè*[24] fairly sums up this approach. The Roman question might be solved through some scheme of federation, wherein the Pope, in deference to his special dignity, would preside over the whole; this was the Giobertian solution.[25] In opposition to this moderate view stood the extreme, or radical, solution that would make a *tabula rasa* of the Italian situation and erect in its place a republic. Mazzini[26] was the standard-bearer of this improbable and premature expectation. A third possibility stemmed from the fact that Piedmont, or the Kingdom of Sardinia, was the only Italian state that could be called authentically independent; around the Kingdom of Sardinia all Italy should aggregate.

Eighteen forty-eight was a vital turning point in the story which served in the outcome to clarify and simplify the situation. The events themselves, in their Italian and European aspects, have been related earlier and need not be repeated.[27] When order was again restored, by 1850, it appeared that two of the three possibilities had been discredited and therefore eliminated. Pius IX, the liberal Pope of 1846, had learned his lesson and was to be henceforth a staunch supporter of order, not to say reaction; moreover, the quality of government in the Papal States, as well as in the Kingdom of Naples, was such as to have been compared to that of the sultan's domain, a stench in the nostrils of Europe,[28] therefore hardly of a nature suited for leadership or model. The radical approach of Mazzini had fared little better; the idealism of the man and the nobility of his outlook were generally granted, but it was also felt increasingly that they were far removed from any practical

[24] The phrase, meaning "Italy will manage alone," was used to describe the tone of the movement in its earlier and optimistic stages, before the failure of Italy acting alone had been established and Cavour, in more realistic fashion, set about accomplishing the task through the skillful use of diplomacy and foreign power.

[25] Vincenzo Gioberti was a priest of liberal inclination whose *On the Moral and Civil Primacy of the Italians*, published in 1843, was one of the influential books of the *Risorgimento*.

[26] Mazzini was also impressed by the historic role of Italy and early became an advocate of unity. His nationalism was not confined to the Italian variety, and from the exile in which he spent most of his life he organized the Young Europe movement (Young Italy, Young Germany, Young Poland, etc.). He placed his reliance on the people and, where Italy was concerned, much of his activity went into abortive conspiracies and plots. His effectiveness was small in the accomplishment of unification, but his ideas exerted considerable influence.

[27] See Chap. III.

[28] To the extent that the Powers had made joint representations to the Pope with a view to inducing reforms by him, just as they made representations to the sultan.

reality. In contrast, little Piedmont had gone to war with Austria and, though defeated, had stood her ground and kept her constitution. The credit of the House of Savoy emerged greatly enhanced in Italy.

FRANCE AND THE ITALIAN QUESTION

Considering the strength of the nationalistic wave one may well take the view that at some point of time the making of a united Italy could not in any case have been prevented. The imminence of this event did not seem high, however, around the year 1850 and it would have seemed rash to predict that another decade would see the task essentially accomplished. High credit for this goes to one man, Cavour, final architect of Italian unification; master of statecraft that he was, his accomplishment was in the last analysis a skillful exercise in the use of power and a display of the diplomatic art at its best.

Cavour was a man keenly aware of the direction of change in his time; essentially a realist by nature, his view was that the only possibility of directing events lay in working with, instead of, like Metternich, against the active forces of the time. His own views in matters of government may best be described as typical of mid-nineteenth-century British liberalism, and the British outlook and scene he found the most congenial in Europe. But having early come to the conclusion that there were no prospects for him in politics, practical man that he was, he turned to the care of his private affairs and estates, in doing which his awareness of the economic changes of his day, plus his ability, caused him to prosper. Not for him plots, barricades, and wordy speeches, in which respect he stood in sharpest contrast to Mazzini.

His opportunity came out of the events of 1848. In the constitutional monarchy of Sardinia that emerged from that crisis, he became a member of the Cabinet in 1850, as minister of agriculture. Within two years he was Prime Minister, a post that he retained, save for a brief interruption, until his death in 1861. Endowed with considerable energy, he set about the task of modernizing Piedmont[29] in all its aspects—economic, administrative, and military.

---

[29] Strictly speaking, one should speak of the Kingdom of Sardinia, but Piedmont being so much the more important and effective part of the kingdom, in contrast with remote and backward Sardinia, its name is in effect often used to describe the whole.

CAVOUR AND NAPOLEON.   But Cavour did not hold to the slogan, *Italia farà da sè*. That the making of Italy, or even more modestly an extension of Piedmont to include the entire North, would entail Austrian opposition needs no explanation; Italian nationalism could not be other than anti-Austrian. But since Piedmont alone, or even with other Italian assistance, lacked the power to evict the Austrians, help must be sought in other quarters. Had Cavour had his choice, he would have preferred British aid, but he soon came to the conclusion that from Britian he would obtain sympathy, but no more, hardly a weapon suitable for dealing with Austrian bayonets. He must, therefore, turn to France. The uncertain quantity that was the French emperor, generally sympathetic to nationalism, especially the Italian, desirous of prestige and of revising the settlements of 1815, might offer possibilities suitable for exploitation. However, Napoleon now stood for French interest and his first concrete action in Italy had been the restoration of the Pope in Rome. Cavour must bide his time.

The Crimean War was another opportunity that he knew how to seize, though it may be called a long gamble. Cavour was present at the Congress of Paris, but the satisfaction he obtained on that occasion was small and he had hoped for better. The Italian question had in general terms, but inconclusive fashion, been brought to the attention of Europe, for all that Lord Clarendon had spoken in vigorous language. Cavour had the good sense not to press the issue for the moment. It was useful from his point of view that in Paris neutral Austria rather than defeated Russia should be surrounded by coldness. Piedmont did not seek revolution; quite the contrary, she was devoted to order, but the objectionable aspects of Austrian, Papal, or Neapolitan rule were the very things that were most likely to foment revolutionary explosions, hence for the sake of the preservation of order stood in need of reform.

It would be incorrect to credit Cavour with a clear and firm plan to which he adhered with steadfastness for the making of Italy; he understood too well that politics is the art of the possible and would pursue at first what seemed to him more limited and realistic ends. For this he was later accused of having little interest in Italy as a whole, being concerned with the mere enhancement of Piedmont, pursuing an "artichoke" policy whereby Piedmont would incorporate bits of Italy leaf by leaf. But Cavour also knew how to seize opportunity by the forelock.

PLOMBIÈRES.   Napoleon's natural sympathy for Italy has been mentioned, but his friendly predisposition encountered much opposition at home: Catholic opinion was powerful in France and the Empress herself was one of its most determined exponents; his own foreign minister, Walewski, was less than enthusiastic and had only seconded Lord Clarendon in 1856 upon Napoleon's insistence. It took another two years after the Congress of Paris before Cavour's patient and persistent diplomacy began to bear fruit.[30] At Plombières, on July 20, 1858, he and Napoleon had a highly secret meeting in the course of which a plan, or plot, was evolved, of which the term "clever" is not an unfair characterization. Napoleon consented to the formation of a Kingdom of Upper Italy made up of Piedmont and the Austrian possessions; another Kingdom would arise in Central Italy; the Pope would continue to rule over a diminished domain, and the Kingdom of Naples would remain unaltered. These four units would then join in a federation presided over by the Pope but of which the North would be the effective leader. For her services France would receive Nice and Savoy and the hand of the daughter of the Sardinian king, Princess Clotilde, for Napoleon's cousin, Prince Jerome.[31]

The realization of the scheme meant war with Austria and for this purpose peace in the rest of Europe must be assured. Cavour might see to it that the war came about ostensibly as the result of Austrian provocation, but with the other Powers Napoleon himself must deal. His calculation was that Prussia would not be displeased at Austrian difficulties, and might even take advantage of them, while the tsar was still laboring under his resentment at Austria's "ingratitude" during the Crimean War; Britain, he thought, was sufficiently occupied with the difficulties of Empire.[32] These estimates proved correct only in part: from the tsar he could obtain no more than a promise of benevolent neutrality in the event of an Austro-Sardinian war[33] instead of the alliance that

[30] In January, 1858, an attempt was made on the life of Napoleon by Orsini, an Italian, who used this means to publicize the Italian cause and arouse Napoleon's interest in it. From Orsini's point of view his efforts were wholly successful for Napoleon allowed, during the trial, the publication of Orsini's appeal to him.

[31] There was some idea that a place could be found for Prince Jerome in the Central Italian Kingdom envisaged in the rearrangement of the Peninsula.

[32] The Sepoy rebellion in 1857 had resulted in a major rearrangement in the organization of India, the crown taking over the position hitherto occupied by the East India Company.

[33] And this not until March, 1859, though Prince Jerome's mission to the tsar in the preceding September had furnished some reassurance.

he sought; Prussia remained noncommittal, fearing the possible applicability of the revisionist precedent to matters on the Rhine; in Britain, the Conservative Derby ministry that had come into office in February, 1858, was generally unsympathetic to disturbance in Italy. These are the reasons that caused Napoleon to hesitate and taxed Cavour's ingenuity and patience in holding him to the Plombières plan.

However, as the year was drawing to a close, Napoleon seemed to be holding to his earlier purpose; all Europe took notice of his remark to the Austrian Ambassador at the New Year's reception: the emperor regretted that relations between the two countries were no longer as amicable as they had been. This caused alarm and resulted in British exertions to save the peace. But on January 26, 1859, a formal treaty of alliance was signed between France and Sardinia. Yet to the last Napoleon hesitated and entertained alternative solutions of European congresses and rearrangements in Italy that would leave Austria in possession of her own. Cavour was sorely tried by the congenital irresolution of the imperial character.

THE MAKING OF ITALY

THE WAR WITH AUSTRIA AND THE ARMISTICE OF VILLAFRANCA. Austria resolved his difficulties and saved the day for him. The state of relations between Sardinia and Austria was one of friction that could easily provide occasion for more violent dispute. The issue of Italian subjects of Austria who found shelter in Piedmont was allowed to become embittered, and when Austria resorted to an ultimatum on April 23, demanding Sardinian demobilization, she walked into Cavour's trap. The rejection of the ultimatum and the subsequent declaration of war brought into play the French alliance. The Austrian forces failed to act with speed, giving time for the French to arrive; by the end of May they were pushed back into Lombardy, and after the engagements of Magenta and Solferino, unsuccessful for them though not fatally so, they began to retreat to the shelter of the Quadrilateral.

Thereupon a *coup de théâtre* took place. On July 11, the two emperors, Napoleon and Francis Joseph, meeting at Villafranca, came to a direct understanding:[34] Lombardy, save Peschiera and Mantua, would be ceded to France, who might then turn

[34] Preliminary negotiations, of which the Villafranca meeting was the outcome, had been going on for some days.

them over to Sardinia, while Austria would retain possession of Venetia; for the rest, the rulers of Italy would remain undisturbed in their respective positions. This understanding was achieved without consultation with either Cavour or the Sardinian king, to

UNIFICATION OF ITALY
1859-1870

Kingdom of Sardinia
Ceded to France 1860
Incorporated 1859
Incorporated 1860
Incorporated 1860
Incorporated 1866
Incorporated 1870

whom the *fait accompli* naturally came as a shock. Even realistic Cavour was not prepared for this; in a fit of rage—authentic or pretended—he resigned, leaving Victor Emmanuel to accommodate himself to the inevitable, which he had the good sense to do.

Such behavior on Napoleon's part was, to say the least, startling;

nevertheless there were for it good reasons which account for, even if they do not justify, the clumsiness of the procedure.[35] In May, peaceful revolutions, to the occurrence of which the hand of Cavour was not wholly extraneous, had taken place in the Duchies and in Tuscany, whence the rulers had fled, and the following month saw insurrection in the adjacent section of the Papal States; quite understandably, the war had awakened a response of expectancy throughout the whole Peninsula. This hardly suited Napoleon, who did not want a revolution out of control and who was not without justification in thinking that Cavour had perhaps had the better of him.[36]

The military aspect of the war caused him concern as well, for he must now envisage a protracted siege of the Quadrilateral fortresses, a situation that increased the uncertainty of complications on the Rhine. Prussia did not seem loath to exploit for her own purposes the opportunity of the Franco-Austrian War, though how she might do this appeared unclear. Negotiations were taking place between herself and Austria, during the course of which Prussia strengthened her hand by decreeing partial mobilization in June, while a veiled warning, in the form of an inquiry of intentions, was directed to France. Should an Austro-Prussian agreement materialize, the possibility of Prussian intervention had to be envisaged. France could not entertain the prospect of war in Italy and on the Rhine at the same time; the connection between the Rhine and the Po was wholly real. This, more than any other single reason, explains the Villafranca settlement.

The situation was not less awkward for that. If Napoleon had cause to complain of Cavour's less than open proceedings, he had nevertheless put himself in the position of being the defector in the alliance. Because of his mode of procedure there could be little cause for him to expect gratitude in Italy. Napoleon, neither an unkind nor an unreasonable man, was sensitive to his position; embarrassed, he did not press for payment in Savoy and Nice,

[35] Napoleon is said to have been deeply impressed by the sight of the battlefields of Magenta and Solferino, where casualties had been substantial. If it is true that he was impressionable and no warrior, reasons of policy were more important than his own impressions.
[36] These risings were the work of the National Society to which Cavour had given encouragement. Cavour could be a master of evasion when such tactics suited his book. The Tuscan situation was particularly disturbing, for that state was supposed to constitute the kernel of the Central Italian Kingdom which Napoleon had thought of reserving for Prince Jerome. Also, as a means of pressure on Austria, Cavour had established contact with Kossuth, raising the possibility of a revolt in Hungary.

while the Treaty of Zurich on November 10 restored peace on the basis of the Villafranca compromise.

The unfolding of Italian events furnished the means of a revised arrangement with Napoleon. While out of office, Cavour was not idle; in fact, he resumed his position in January, 1860. During the preceding autumn assemblies in the Duchies, Tuscany, and Romagna,[37] where Piedmontese influence had a hand in guiding events, called for union with Piedmont. Piedmont felt some hesitation at incorporating these territories, but they could be used as substitutes for Venetia, which Napoleon had failed to secure. This was the basis of the Treaty of Turin of March 24, 1860, which may be regarded as a revised version of that of December, 1858. Plebiscites held in March in Tuscany, in the Duchies, and in Romagna endorsed the demand for annexation, and Piedmont having received, if not the original price at least a fair equivalent, Napoleon could have Nice and Savoy.[38]

THE UNION WITH THE SOUTH.   Napoleon might consider that he had extricated himself from an awkward situation with comparative success. But Italy and Cavour would not let him rest. In April, agitation directed against Bourbon rule broke out in Sicily. Cavour had contemplated initially no action in the South, but opportunity he would not forego; his handling of this particular operation was truly masterful. The situation was delicate, for the Sicilian rising was in large measure of Mazzinian, hence radical, inspiration. Garibaldi, the colorful patriot, though neither deep thinker nor shrewd politician, was smarting at this time under the outcome that had made him a stranger in his native Nice. But filibustering was a congenial activity to him and he was gathering an expedition in Genoa under the watchful, though officially unseeing, eye of Cavour. On May 5, he and his Thousand set out for Sicily. The Sardinian navy had instructions, both official and unofficial, and the Red Shirts landed safely at Marsala.

There was no very serious war in Sicily, which was overrun with relative ease, while a provisional government was set up in

[37] The situation was especially delicate in Tuscany where feeling was by no means unanimous for union with Piedmont, and skillful though surreptitious Piedmontese guidance was needed to procure the desired outcome.

[38] In deference to the principle of nationality, ostensible basis of all these territorial reshufflings, the incorporation of Nice and Savoy into France was also ratified by plebiscites. Some minute areas that were excluded formed the basis of the French claims for frontier rectifications that were effected after the Second World War.

Palermo. The crossing to the mainland in August and the march on Naples created a delicate situation; King Ferdinand, belatedly and futilely, sought to save himself by restoring the constitution of 1848; his army dissolved, Naples was entered in September, and Garibaldi, undaunted and careless of international complications, made ready to march on Rome and even eventually toward Venice.

Garibaldi in Rome raised the prospect of a clash with the French forces still in that city, as well as the possibility of intervention by an Austria still smarting from the defeat of the preceding year. It raised in addition the specter of an Italy torn between the rival tendencies that Sardinia and the Garibaldian-Mazzinian alliance respectively embodied. Using the pretext of disturbances in the Papal States, Cavour sent Piedmontese troops across the Papal territory. Despite Roman resistance, easily overcome, the Piedmontese expedition had the purpose of minimizing the extent of the whole Italian disturbance. Garibaldi, giving his patriotism priority over his republican predilection, yielded to King Victor Emmanuel.

THE KINGDOM OF ITALY. Despite this peaceful outcome in Italy, a difficult problem remained in which France presented the greatest uncertainty. What had happened far exceeded anything contemplated by Napoleon:[39] French interest as such did not favor a united Italy, and the Roman situation in particular stood to discredit Napoleon with a large section of opinion in France. The French attitude was therefore Cavour's foremost preoccupation, and to secure French acquiescence he used the British card. Britain had viewed with sympathetic complacency the formation of a larger Italian state in the North, while to the Pope's fate she could easily remain indifferent; but she had reservations about a whole united Italy. What Palmerston[40] feared most of all was an Italy under primarily French influence. Napoleon's schemes for the South he opposed, and realizing the weakness of a Neapolitan state in which France might insinuate herself, possibly in the form of a Murat restoration, he came to feel that a united Italy might develop into a counterweight to France in the Mediterranean, hence a prop

[39] He sought to save matters in the middle of 1860 by toying with schemes of rearrangement in the South, such as setting up a separate Sicily and a distinct Kingdom of Naples that Piedmont would recognize.

[40] After the fall of the second Derby ministry in June, 1859, Palmerston was again Prime Minister.

of his own policy, rather than a French satellite. He even offered Piedmont reassurance against the possibility of an Austrian intrusion. Cavour knew how to exploit Napoleon's desire to retain some vestige of influence in Italy; the price for this must be his consent to complete union, including the bulk of the Papal States. Caught in the coils of his own miscalculations, Napoleon had little choice; *faites vite* ("get it over quickly") was his advice.[41]

These circumstances made possible the proclamation of the Kingdom of Italy on March 17, 1861. Victor Emmanuel of Sardinia became king of Italy and the simple device was adopted of merely erasing all the old boundaries and of making the Italian kingdom a unitary state, largely patterned on the French centralized model, while doing away likewise with all internal political arrangements in place of which the Piedmontese *Statuto* of 1848 was extended to the whole land. Cavour barely lived long enough to witness the full fruit of his endeavors. He died on June 6.

The making of Italy may be regarded as the first radical and substantial alteration of the territorial arrangements of 1815.[42] It undoubtedly represented an important setback for Austria, prime guardian of the order established in these agreements, and to that extent might be thought to constitute an equivalent French success. But this was not the case. The Plombières *combinazione* had miscarried, and in the execution things had, from the French point of view, got completely out of control. France had undoubtedly been the chief agent in causing a united Italy to appear at this time, but the manner of the operation, such things as Villafranca, served to attach to French policy, from the Italian point of view, a wholly understandable quality of disingenuousness instead of being a source of gratitude.[43] The acquisition of Nice and Savoy was small compensation for this.

But there were even deeper implications to the reshuffling of the Italian states. Napoleon may certainly be said to have completed in Italy the task begun by his earlier namesake. But the accomplishment, clear success of nationalism that it was, was also a dangerous precedent. The first Napoleon had also rudely shaken the structure that he had found in Germany; it was not to be long before changes in Germany, also along the lines of satisfaction of national desire,

[41] At the end of 1860 the French were aiding in the defense of Gaeta besieged by Garibaldi.

[42] Allowing for the emergence of Belgium which, however, did not produce a major European state.

[43] The same largely applied to the domestic French aspect of the operation which earned Napoleon Catholic disapproval.

but of far greater moment than the Italian accomplishment, were to take place. In that story, with which we shall presently deal, France was to be also deeply involved. Put it another way, the restless and muddling policy of Napoleon III, largely his own policy, was not conducted by one possessed of adequate competence in the field of diplomacy. In that domain, Napoleon was no match for either Cavour or Bismarck.

But even of the Italian question he was not rid in 1861. Before Cavour's death, Napoleon had endeavored to contrive with him another *combinazione*, the focus of which was Rome: a scheme must be evolved which could be presented at once as renunciation of Rome by Italy and the persistence of hopes of Rome for Italy, the two faces of the coin to be used for purposes of domestic consumption in France and Italy respectively. It is perhaps no wonder that it took some time to contrive an agreement.[44] This was finally achieved in September, 1864, when a Franco-Italian convention stipulated the evacuation of the French forces from Rome within two years from the following February, in exchange for which Italy undertook to respect the independence of Rome; by way of ostensible token of Italian intentions, the national capital was moved from Turin to Florence. Outwardly, Italy had renounced Rome, and the agreement was the cause of a loud outcry in the country; actually, this meant that Italy must be patient, bide her time, and watch for opportunities. These were not long in coming, but the final incorporations of Venice and of Rome were no more than footnotes to far greater events that will be dealt with presently.[45]

III. Some Secondary Issues

At this point it will be convenient to turn to a variety of developments, of relatively secondary importance by comparison with such matters as the unification of Italy and Germany, but which nevertheless involved the Powers in their interests and relations.[46]

[44] Matters were not helped by the agitation that went on in Italy and in which Garibaldi, as might be expected, took a prominent part. In 1862 he organized an abortive raid which ended in his defeat and capture at Aspromonte.

[45] These annexations were the results of the Austro-Prussian and Franco-Prussian Wars. See below, pp. 131, 140.

[46] These matters occurred during the fifties and sixties, simultaneously, it must be remembered, with the more important developments of the international scene; some distortion is therefore entailed in this mode of presentation, but that factor is compensated for by the greater simplicity and clarity of exposition that the arrangement will make possible.

EUROPEAN QUESTIONS

THE OTTOMAN EMPIRE AND THE BALKANS.   One of the minor issues that the Congress of Paris had been called upon to consider was that of the Danubian Principalities of Wallachia and Moldavia. Both in the end remained under Ottoman suzerainty, but the former Russian right of supervision was turned into a collective European. It was part of Napoleon's anti-Austrian orientation, of which his Italian policy was another aspect, to espouse the cause of union in the Principalities;[47] this also went naturally with his general predisposition in favor of nationalism anywhere. Both Austria and the Turks were opposed to any such arrangement, nor was Britain sympathetic to it; the tsar, however, was favorably inclined and this fitted into that other facet of Napoleonic policy, a Franco-Russian *rapprochement*. At any rate, it was provided that elections should take place to consult the wishes of the population, and this was duly done after the Austrian evacuation in March, 1857.

That the consultation was unusually fraudulent was not questioned,[48] and France demanded its annulment, in which demand she was supported by Russia, Prussia, and Sardinia, while Britain took the opposite position of endorsing the sultan's refusal. Not a little friction developed between France and Britain, but a compromise was arranged in August, 1858: Britain agreed to new elections and the Principalities might have common institutions but must remain separate. The Powers ratified this arrangement, setting up the ambiguous creation of the United Principalities of Moldavia and Wallachia. Thereupon, the Moldavians having chosen Alexander Cuza for their prince in January, 1859, the Wallachians proceeded to make the same choice the next month. Napoleon promptly recognized the outcome and what was left of separateness became hard to perceive. No one was sufficiently exercised to take action and, by default so to speak, united Rumania was allowed to be born.[49] No doubt French support had been useful and Napoleon could derive whatever satisfaction he would from this success of his diplomacy.

In not far distant Greece, Otto of Bavaria had been king since

[47] He even entertained a scheme that would have placed the ruler of Parma in the Principalities, leaving Parma free to join Piedmont.
[48] It resulted in a victory for the opponents of union.
[49] In 1862 the sultan sanctioned the fusion of the Moldavian and Wallachian legislatures, and the name "Rumania" came into use for the new state.

1832. He meant well, but found it difficult to shed his German ways, and the retinue of foreign advisers that he brought in his train found little popularity among the Greeks. Greek politics pursued their troubled and confused course, while local parties tended to rely on the assistance of outside influences, Russian, British, and French, especially the last two, for which, to a degree, Greece became a battleground of rivalry, as was the rest of the Near East.

It was in 1850 that the Don Pacifico affair[50] provided Palmerston with an opportunity for unusual bluster. A blockade brought the Greeks to surrender, and the speech that Palmerston delivered in Parliament in June in explanation of his action was a perfect expression of arrogant and confident imperial British pride. The Greeks sought to insinuate themselves into the Crimean War, sending bands across the Turkish border, but their efforts were checked, this time by a combined Anglo-French occupation of the Piraeus in 1854. Domestic unrest eventually burst out into a military coup that put an end to the reign of King Otto. The filling of the vacant throne was occasion for rival diplomatic activity of the Powers who, however, finally united on the person of George I, a Danish prince, who became king in 1863. He opened his reign by bringing Greece the present of the Ionian Islands, voluntarily retroceded by Britain, under whose protectorate they had been since the settlement of 1815. It was no longer felt in Britain that this base was essential, hence its gracious surrender.

In general it may be said that the British devotion to the preservation of the integrity of the Ottoman Empire was not matched by a similar French steadfastness of purpose, and if the British wish prevailed it was because, in the test, the Powers were unable to agree on any other solution, thus giving the deceptive appearance of unanimity. There were religious troubles in Syria, between Druses and Christian Maronites,[51] for the protection of whom France felt entitled to a special claim. France in fact intervened,

[50] Don Pacifico, a Portuguese Jew but a British subject, availed himself of this fact in pressing claims against the Greek government. When his house was burned in Athens during an anti-Semitic riot, in December, 1849, Palmerston ordered a squadron to Greece. Unmoved by Greek recalcitrance and French attempts at mediation, Palmerston ordered a blockade that eventually forced a Greek surrender.

[51] The Lebanon was inhabited by Moslem Druses and Christian Maronites who had long lived under their respective chieftains. Turkish attempts at administrative reorganization in Syria after the expulsion of Mohamed Ali were the cause for difficulties between the two communities.

sending forces to Syria in August, 1861, but she only did so under the cover of a European mandate which, even then, only alleviated in part British suspicion. However, order having been restored, the French withdrew and the special constitution elaborated for the Lebanon was under the joint guarantee of the Powers.

The reign of Sultan Abdul Aziz, which opened in that year, was a period that witnessed domestic attempts at reform of the tottering Ottoman structure. These bore little effective fruit, but outside influence made steady progress in penetrating the Empire. It was economic and financial, and cultural as well, and a large share of it was French. The *Banque Impériale Ottomane* dates from 1863 and the Ottoman National Debt administration was organized two years later.

The island of Crete provided another occasion for the action of the Concert of Europe. The islanders were Greek and they revolted in 1866, demanding union with the motherland. Fighting of the kind customary in such a locale went on for some time on the island, until the revolt was put down and the Convention of Halepa,[52] in 1868, promised certain liberties to the Cretans.

THE SUEZ CANAL. But the development of greatest significance in the Near East, an economic enterprise, though one fraught with political implications, was the opening of the Suez Canal. The cutting of a water route across the Isthmus of Suez was an idea that had a long and ancient history; it was only natural that the great increase of commercial exchanges of the nineteenth century should give it added point.[53] Some French projects in the earlier part of the century had had no results, partly because of the opposition of Mohamed Ali, fearful of the intrusion of a multitude of foreign interests in Egypt. But the advent of Khedive Mohamed Said in 1854 brought in control a more receptive personality. It was a French diplomatist, engineer, and general promoter, Ferdinand de Lesseps,[54] who finally obtained from him, in 1854, the concession for building a canal. This was a private undertaking, and the projected Canal Company, registered in Egypt, would have an international administrative board whose president

---

[52] The Convention or Pact of Halepa, proclaimed by the sultan in 1868, allowed Christian officials to assist the Turkish and provided for an elective assembly.

[53] For the opening up of the Far East, see above, pp. 61–62, and below, pp. 114–116.

[54] De Lesseps had been consul in Alexandria at an earlier period. It was Khedive Said who contracted the first foreign loans from British banks.

would be of the nationality that furnished the largest share of capital.

Such an enterprise was obviously of concern to many nations, and most of all to Britain, whose imperial and maritime interests far exceeded those of others; logically, if a canal was to be built at Suez, it might have been expected that the initiative of the undertaking would be in British hands. Palmerston had been antagonistic to the project, and after the grant of the concession his attitude was one of opposition to its realization,[55] though certain British interests saw the project with favor in view of its obvious utility to British trade. Here was a new development in the long tale of Franco-British rivalry in the Near East.

Napoleon at first seemed to take little interest in the matter, mainly because he wished to avoid arousing British suspicion, but when the Suez stock was offered for sale on the various financial markets of Europe, the overwhelming bulk of it was subscribed by French purchasers, thus insuring French control of the company.[56] Palmerston's calculations proved mistaken. He at first discouraged British participation; then, after work was begun in 1859, he sought to raise a variety of obstacles[57] that caused some interference and delay but could not prevent the execution of the scheme. Accepting the inevitable, after 1862, British opposition relented and Britain strove instead to obtain guarantees that the Canal would not serve as a base for the extension of French political interest. From 1866, the sultan having ratified the concession, the additional necessary funds were provided and the work proceeded apace. The Canal was officially opened in November, 1869, to the accompaniment of spectacular international festivities.

The significance of this event was considerable and the Canal was soon to prove a notable success. To a degree at least, the opening of the Suez Canal restored the Mediterranean to the position of importance that it had had as a highway of eastern trade some centuries before. Britain, however, not Italy, was now the great trading nation, and of necessity the Mediterranean must re-

[55] He had done his unsuccessful best at Constantinople to prevent the granting of the concession.

[56] Of 400,000 shares, 54,000 went to the khedive and 32,000 were reserved for Egyptians. Of the remaining 314,000 shares put on the open market 219,000 only were bought, 207,000 of them by French purchasers. The block of unsold shares was taken by the khedive in 1860.

[57] French policy during the Syrian episode of 1860–1861 was not unrelated to the Canal; it was in part used as a means of counterpressure on the sultan whom British influence was trying to sway in the matter of Suez.

ceive increased attention from her, though the expression "life line of Empire" is of a later vintage. Napoleon's vision of the Mediterranean as a French lake, as he put it to Bismarck, could hardly leave Britain indifferent, should it show signs of taking real shape. However, nothing concrete was done by France, save perhaps some intensification of Algerian development, and it is to be noted that, on the whole, Mediterranean developments during the sixties did not give rise to major friction among the Powers.[58]

THE POLISH INSURRECTION OF 1863.   A rather more severe testing of the relations of the Powers took place during this period in connection with Poland.

After the failure of 1830 Poland had been ruled with a stern hand, losing her constitution and what liberties she had. Tsar Alexander II, unlike his predecessor, was ever torn between the alternatives of a repressive policy and one of enlightened concessions. This latter tendency prevailed in the earlier part of his reign and one aspect of it was an effort to make his rule acceptable in Poland. The virtual restoration in 1862 of the 1815 arrangement did win for him some moderate support, but the more radical Polish party that would not be content with less than complete independence remained unreconciled. An attempt to deal with this opposition— students were a large part of it—by drafting it into the army precipitated violence which began with an insurrection in Warsaw in January, 1863.

While the Poles had no army, not a little sympathy existed for them abroad, especially in the Western countries, and the spread of the disturbance was cause of concern to the tsar. He was quite pleased, therefore, to find Prussia willing, not to say anxious, to enter into an agreement in February, the Alvensleben Convention, which would control Polish activity in her own Polish lands. Bismarck was even willing to give active assistance to Russia; this was declined, but the agreement marks an important change in the orientation of Russia and a turn away from what had been Franco-Russian coöperation.

For reasons of his own, largely domestic, courting at once

[58] The opening of the Canal gave added importance to the Red Sea. As early as 1859 the French established themselves in Obock, at the southern entrance of the Red Sea, opposite the British possession of Aden. Italian interests also began to appear in the Red Sea with the acquisition of a station at Assab. The bases were thus being laid for East African rivalries which, however, did not develop until somewhat later. See below, Chap. VI.

liberal and Catholic support, Napoleon saw fit to insert himself into the Polish matter in the form of issuing advice, even a warning, to the tsar and of proposing schemes for rearrangement in Poland. Beyond this, Napoleon thought of cajoling or worrying Britain into joining him in exerting pressure on Russia. He succeeded in obtaining the presentation of similar British and French views to the tsar,[59] but Britain would not agree to joint action. In the end the Poles were deceived in their hopes of Western assistance and their rising was crushed in 1864.

The episode turned into another manifestation of ill-contrived Napoleonic interference: Britain was made suspicious and the tsar definitely annoyed, while Napoleon conveyed the impression that he was an irresponsible meddler.[60] As if bent on confirming this impression, he went on to express in public his dislike of the settlements of 1815[61] and in November circularized the Powers with a note presenting the view that, since the structure of 1815 was in the process of collapsing, in order to avoid divergence among themselves, the Powers should meet in congress to deal with all pending issues. The claim that his intention was to make change possible in peaceful fashion convinced no one; though there was point in his contention, he merely succeeded in arousing universal suspicion of French aims and his initiative turned into a damaging fiasco.

The imperial mind never seemed at a loss for the production of schemes, preferably of a complicated nature. This restless striving for initiative and for some concrete advantage in connection with it was largely motivated, apart from the aspect of personality, by the sense of domestic insecurity. Even outside Europe France found occasion to become involved in a variety of problems.

DEVELOPMENTS OUTSIDE OF EUROPE

In middle southern Asia British India constituted the largest European interest. But from the North Russian influence was beginning to make itself felt. Direct contact and clash between Brit-

---

[59] Austria, too, sent a similar note to Russia.

[60] Ever fertile in schemes and ideas, Napoleon used this occasion to toy with projects of far-reaching territorial rearrangement: a reconstituted Poland under an Austrian archduke; the cession of Venice to Italy, for which the Principalities would compensate Austria; a buffer state on the Rhine and a division of Belgium between France and Holland; compensation for Prussia with Hanover. Austria, when approached, would not entertain such proposals, preferring peace to the prospect of unlimited disturbances.

[61] In a speech at Auxerre on May 6, 1863.

ain and Russia did not yet occur at this time during which the preliminary bases were being laid for sharper conflict. It was in 1858, after the great mutiny, that the East India Company finally ended its days, the British government henceforth assuming the direct control of Indian affairs. But meantime in the West, British protecting influence had been extending itself over neighboring Afghanistan, in the form of support of that country against Persian encroachment. The Persian seizure of Herat in 1855 led to a British declaration of war and the successful assertion of Afghan independence, while Britain obtained recognition of a mediating position in the event of future disputes.[62]

THE FAR EAST. In farther Asia the expanding economy of Europe served as a prod to penetration. Britain was the spearhead of this activity; the limited concessions extracted from China in 1842 have been mentioned.[63] It was hardly to be expected that neighboring Japan would succeed in maintaining the very tight isolation in which she had for long enclosed herself. The initiative of opening Japan to external contact was contested by the two Powers whose own shores abutted on the Pacific and one may almost speak of a race between the United States and Russia to be the first to reach Japan.[64] The story is familiar of Commodore Perry's first visit to Japan in July, 1853, anticipating a Russian squadron on its way from the Baltic. There was no need of violence in this case and when Perry returned the following year the Treaty of Kanawaga, of March 31, 1854, granted some limited concessions for trade. These were extended four years later when further ports were opened, extraterritoriality granted, and diplomatic relations established. Britain, Russia, France, and Holland immediately followed suit.

The decisions had not been taken without qualms on the part of the Japanese, and even after 1858 opposition remained strong to the intrusion of outsiders;[65] it went the length of some violence directed against the Western barbarians and the decision to

[62] Treaty of Paris of March 4 ,1857.

[63] See above, p. 62.

[64] The United States had become a Pacific power after the Mexican War, while Russia was pursuing an active and aggressive policy in eastern Siberia. It was in 1851 that Washington and St. Petersburg decided to open Japan, by force if necessary.

[65] Japan was in the throes of internal readjustment, of which her "opening" is one facet. In addition, she, like China, was wholly incapable of meeting the power of Western arms.

expel them in 1863. The British bombardment of Kagoshima and the appearance of American and French squadrons disposed with both expedition and ease of any will to resistance; by 1864 the Emperor had ratified the earlier concessions. Thereafter no more Japanese opposition was encountered and the most significant aspect of this episode was the deliberate acceptance by Japan, not only of trade with, but of many of the ways of, the West. The tale of Japanese success in this endeavor is unique, and the consequences of this success were to be very great indeed, but the unfolding of them belongs to the next section of this book.[66]

Unlike Japan, China tried to refuse acknowledgment of the inevitable. For the better part of two decades, from about 1850, China was in the throes of the Taiping rebellion of which, in this connection, we need only retain the disorganizing effect. The rebel capture of Shanghai led to the setting up of a foreign inspectorate of customs in 1854, and further incidents were sufficient pretext for armed intervention. This was jointly Anglo-French and of modest dimensions, the United States having declined to associate itself in the use of force. The Treaties of Tien-Tsin in June, 1858, were the outcome which, however, China did not ratify, receiving European negotiators with gunshot instead. The answer could only be greater pressure, which took the form of a seizure of Peking by an Anglo-French corps in October, 1860, on which occasion the behavior of the Western contingent went some distance toward justifying the appellation of "barbarians." But barbarian or not, the greater Western force had to be acknowledged and this was done by the Treaties of Peking with Britain and France in the same month.

Apart from punitive indemnities, the balance sheet of the episode was this: more ports (eleven new ones) were opened to foreign commerce and ships could ascend the Yang-Tse to Hankow; foreigners might travel in the interior of China where, in addition, Christian missionaries could reside, and they would enjoy the privilege of extraterritorial rights; legations were to be established in Peking and a maritime customs service was set up under foreign supervision, while the importation of opium was legalized.

The military intervention had been British and French, but the United States and Russia shared in the Chinese grant of privi-

---

[66] A *coup d'état* in January, 1868, resulted in the abolition of the Shogunate and the deliberate and conscious embarking by Japan on the path of imitation of the West.

leges and China could be thereafter the field of foreign competition.[67] The Russians, in addition, obtained in separate arrangements the territory north of the Amur River where the vigorous Muraviev, governor of Siberia, founded the town of Khabarovsk and the naval base of Petropavlovsk. The Powers had considered at one point whether or not to take sides in the Taiping rebellion and the possibility of using it to set up a wholly new and western-minded regime in China. They opted for noninterference and, having come to terms with Peking, threw the weight of their influence in the latter's favor. Unlike Japan, China was long to remain the impotent object of pressures from the Western world.

The large region that constitutes the southeastern extremity of Asia, meeting place of Chinese, Indian, and even Tibetan influences, in current terms Burma, Siam, and Indochina, also began to fall in this period under outside, mainly British and French, influence. Established in India as they were, the British naturally showed an interest in Burma and Siam; Rangoon was occupied in 1852, following a minor incident, and in 1855 Siam was induced to grant privileges similar to those that had been extracted from China and Japan, privileges that were promptly extended, in this case also, to others as well.

The French turned their attention to the eastern section where Annam was the only political unit of substance. Spreading north and west from Saigon, where a landing was effected in 1859, by 1867 they had established themselves in control of Cochin-China and Cambodia. The scheme of reaching the Chinese interior by following the course of the Mekong River proved to be a fallacy, but the bases had been laid for later expansion at the expense of China, in Tonkin, and for the meeting of rival British and French influences in and around Siam.[68]

THE AMERICAN CONTINENT: TEXAS, MEXICO, AND THE UNITED STATES.   While this imperial activity was taking place in Asia, the American continent, especially during the decade of the sixties, was likewise the scene of European interest, again mainly British and French. The Texas episode and its aftermath have been mentioned.[69] The establishment of the United States on the Pacific Coast, as a consequence of the Mexican War, gave added or re-

---

[67] Despite this coöperation, not a little mutual suspicion attended the operation.
[68] See below, Part II, p. 219.
[69] See above, pp. 59–60.

newed point to the possibility of opening a passage through the Central American Isthmus of Panama. This project was the source of considerable Anglo-American rivalry, the United States fearing British encroachment in an area that it regarded as its own preserve.[70]

Despite a British landing in Nicaragua in 1849, neither side was desirous of conflict and the result of the Anglo-American competition was the compromise registered in the Clayton-Bulwer Treaty of April, 1850: neither country was to seek exclusive control of a future canal which could be built by an Anglo-American company. The ambiguous behavior of the American Secretary of State in connection with the ratification of the treaty gave rise to misunderstanding and a controversy that was not settled for some years. The final outcome of it was that Britain remained established in Honduras, abandoning her other positions, and for the time prevented the building of an exclusively American canal.

This was the era of Manifest Destiny in America, one aspect of which envisaged American control of European possessions on the American continent. Central American possibilities enhanced the importance of Cuba where Spain was already meeting with difficulties. Nothing came of the contemplated possibility of the purchase of the island from Spain, nor of the Ostend Manifesto in 1854,[71] but this was in large measure due to the effects of the great domestic controversy raging at the time in the United States and about to erupt into the violence of civil war.

The American Civil War was a development of capital importance which, paralyzing the United States, opened possibilities of unimpeded European action on the American continent. What issues there had been since the proclamation of the Monroe Doctrine forty years earlier had been of a relatively mild nature and in the end composed through compromise without resort to force. The young American Republic was growing at a rapid rate but its energies were overwhelmingly absorbed by the immense task of establishing itself within what may be called its natural boundaries. On the European side, especially the British, commercial

[70] By 1848 the British had established themselves on the Mosquito Coast and at the entrance of the San Juan River, while the United States obtained in 1848 a railway concession across the Isthmus from New Granada and in 1849 had negotiated an agreement with Nicaragua with a view to establishing a route through that country.

[71] A statement drawn up by the American ministers to Britain, Spain, and France that advocated the forcible seizure of Cuba in the event of Spanish refusal to sell the island.

interests of a substantial nature had grown up, while British capital found a profitable field of employment in the economic growth of the United States. Such interests were on the whole of greater value than the possible extension of direct control over bits of American territory, and this factor served to soften and minimize the frictions that developed.

It was to be many decades before America would register on the popular consciousness of Europe an impression commensurate with her true importance and power. But there were some nevertheless,[72] especially in the seats of government, who understood the possibilities of American growth that would lead to the eventual emergence of a rival power. Viewed in this light, the diminution of American power that secession would entail could be regarded with a not unfavorable eye. But there was also another interest, of a more limited but more immediate nature, connected with the Civil War. The Northern blockade of the South had the effect of producing a cotton famine in the textile mills of Britain and France, with all the consequences of such a condition, high prices and severe unemployment. This might in turn point to the possible desirability of breaking through the blockade and granting the South recognition.

No action was taken, however, by either Britain or France, partly because of uncertainty and divided opinion which pointed to the desirability of waiting upon the military course of events. Both countries proclaimed their neutrality and declined the Southern request for recognition despite the initial military successes of the Confederacy. One consideration of significance was that of identity or divergence of British and French policy.[73] A test of this was provided by the Mason and Slidell affair. The forcible removal of these two Southern representatives from the British steamer *Trent* evoked sharp recriminations from Britain, a demand for apologies, and the surrender of the men. Washington was embarrassed, both by the nature of its case and by the pressure of Northern opinion to which British opinion responded with similar excitability. In the end Secretary Seward decided to yield, a decision in the taking of which the French support of the British position had some effect.

[72] De Tocqueville's *Democracy in America*, which showed a proper appreciation of American possibilities, was first published in 1834.

[73] From the French point of view a strong United States would stand a better chance of becoming eventually an effective counterweight to British naval power.

The seeming continued inability of the North to redress the military course of events encouraged Napoleon to consider the possibility of dealing with the South; he had discussions to this end with Slidell in 1862. British reluctance served to restrain the French design at this point, though Britain seemed to be veering toward the acceptance of a joint offer of mediation. The Southern capture of the Federal capital would have been a suitable occasion for such a move, but the failure to accomplish this caused the opportunity to pass. Once the crisis of 1862 was overcome Britain adhered to her previous attitude of cautious watchfulness; when, ill-advisedly, Napoleon persisted in making a single-handed offer of good services in January, 1863, he received from the American Congress a sharp rebuke for his pains. He had the good sense not to insist, and in the ultimate failure of joint European action the American Civil War was allowed to unfold unimpeded by any extraneous interference.[74]

But this was not the end of the connection between American affairs and those of Europe at this time, for the American preoccupation with the major domestic crisis that was the Civil War furnished an opportunity for the enactment of another far-fetched Napoleonic scheme, the ill-starred French intervention in Mexico.

The course of Mexican affairs had been troubled since the emancipation of the country from the control of Spain, changes of government often being accompanied by violence. The alternation of extremes of conservative and liberal control continued after the unfortunate war with the United States, until another civil war led to the establishment of a liberal government under Benito Juarez, definitely in control after 1860. This domestic turmoil served to accentuate the financial difficulties of the government of Juarez which, along with other confiscatory measures at home, refused to acknowledge the validity of the foreign debts contracted by its predecessor. This, together with claims for compensation of damage incurred during the civil war, offered an easy pretext for intervention.[75]

The interested Powers were three, Britain, Spain, and France,

[74] In 1862 some ships, the *Alabama* among them, were allowed to "escape" from British ports whence they proceeded to act as raiders on Northern commerce. This situation gave rise to the *Alabama Claims* that were eventually settled as a result of the agreement embodied in the Treaty of Washington of May, 1871.

[75] In 1838 a French expedition had already gone to Vera Cruz to enforce the payment of claims.

but the operation as it developed was essentially a French, more narrowly a Napoleonic, enterprise. As frequently was the case with Napoleonic projects, this one was characterized by complexity: a monarchy might be set up in Mexico, though not under a French prince, but such as to make Mexico a zone of French influence; along with the monarchy, clerical interests would be favored, and this would please Catholic opinion in France, in some measure be compensation for the wrong turn taken by Italian affairs. In the process, injured financial interests would receive compensation, but this last, though the ostensible pretext for intervention, was hardly its prime motivation.[76]

In October, 1861, France, Britain, and Spain agreed to joint action which took the form of an occupation of Vera Cruz. But the latter two countries had no such far-reaching designs as Napoleon and disagreement soon became apparent in 1862: the British and the Spanish withdrew, leaving the French alone in pursuit of their project. The French moved on to occupy Mexico City in June, 1863, and Archduke Maximilian of Austria was offered the Mexican crown by a hand-picked assembly. Emperor Maximilian commanded no support in his own right; what control he had of the country was of very limited extent and wholly dependent on the presence of French troops, which Napoleon promised him for as long as might be necessary.

These proceedings, needless to say, appeared in the United States as in the nature of unwarranted interference and unfriendly acts toward the asserter of the Monroe Doctrine. With the conclusion of the Civil War through a complete Northern victory, from 1865 the American government was once more able to assert itself; it refused recognition to Maximilian and demanded the recall of the French expeditionary force in Mexico. It would have been clear folly for Napoleon to engage in conflict with the United States and he had the good sense to yield. Having informed Maximilian that he would have to withdraw the support of French forces, these gradually went home. Left to his own means, the luckless Maximilian was captured at Queretaro in June, 1867, and soon thereafter executed. The whole project, Napoleon's very own, had ignominiously collapsed and turned into a heavy blow

---

[76] Among the French claims for damage were those of the Swiss Jecker, which Morny had had included in exchange for a 30 percent commission. This aspect of the matter, though secondary, gives nevertheless a peculiarly obnoxious odor to the episode.

to the prestige of his regime, no less at home than abroad. Punishment is the normal price of failure in political activity.

At this time Napoleon already had far more serious causes for concern, much nearer home, than the loss of prestige that the somewhat absurd Mexican adventure entailed. Bismarck had for some time been in charge of Prussian affairs which he was guiding on his chosen course with ruthless determination and skill. Napoleon was no match for Bismarck, and to this closing episode of the first half of the century, most important single development between the settlement of Vienna and the outbreak of war in 1914, we must now turn.

IV. Europe and the Making of Germany

THE GERMAN PROBLEM

At Olmütz, in November, 1850, Schwarzenberg had scored a clear Austrian victory, of which the extent of Prussian humilia-

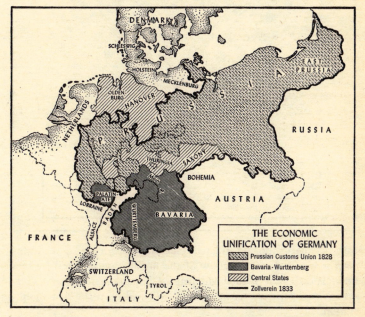

THE ECONOMIC
UNIFICATION OF GERMANY

Prussian Customs Union 1828
Bavaria-Wurttemberg
Central States
Zollverein 1833

tion and rancor was the measure; yet this was but a step, a passing episode in the long tale of the Habsburg-Hohenzollern contest. The dominant forces of the nineteenth century had placed that old dynastic conflict in a new framework. There was such a thing as a German people, just as there was an Italian, and the force was strong, though operating here also particularly at the level of the literate segment of the population, that tended to weld it together as one. Again, in the German as in the Italian case, the impact that came from across the Rhine had played a crucial

THE POLITICAL UNIFICATION OF GERMANY

Prussia, 1815-1866
Annexation of, 1866
North German Confederation, 1867
South German States, 1871
Alsace-Lorraine, 1871
Austrian Section Excluded, 1866
German Confederation, 1815-1866
German Empire, 1871

role. While Napoleon treated German territory like malleable clay, it was under the shadow of the humiliation inflicted by him upon Prussia that Fichte had penned his *Addresses to the German Nation*, and the campaign of 1813 had been the war of liberation.

After the Congress of Vienna and the reconstitution of the Holy Roman Empire under the guise of the Germanic Confederation, the stress of the forces of movement was at first rather more on constitutional reform than on union. There was no Roman Pope in Germany, but in the German world Austria was involved in a manner that she was not in Italy; she was an integral part of it through a part of herself, the original domain of the Habsburgs. The making of any Germany must therefore find a solution for the Austrian problem as well. The discussions of Frankfort in 1848 that centered on that issue have been mentioned as well as the failure of the revolutions of that year.[77] Of necessity, Austria could not do other than oppose the *kleindeutsch* solution; at most she might entertain the alternative possibility that would include the totality of herself in *gross Deutschland*. But *gross Deutschland* would in considerable part be non-Germanic; it was better to temporize, keep matters as they had been, then at Olmütz force a showdown with Prussia. That event had restored in Central Europe the *status quo* of 1815.

Two more considerations must be added which contrast the German with the Italian case. Piedmont and the house of Savoy made Italy, but Piedmont lacked the power to carry out the task by herself; *Italia farà da sè* had been an illusion and the assistance of external force, French in the event, proved indispensable. In many respects the role of Prussia in Germany is comparable with that of Piedmont in Italy; but Prussia was a major Power in her own right, far the largest and strongest of the purely German states; unlike Piedmont, she could in the final test manage alone. Also, and in contrast with the Italian case again, the economic factor played a vital role in Germany. The events of 1848 did not interfere with that aspect of development; it was in 1852 that the German *Zollverein* was completed with the inclusion of the Northern states, Hanover, Brunswick, and Oldenburg. This itself constituted a defeat for Austria which had endeavored, and failed, to induce the South German states not to remain in the customs union. The economic growth of Germany during the fifties, expanding industry and much railway building, served to consolidate this connection that all found satisfactory save Austria, unable to compete and excluded.[78]

Nevertheless, the domestic policy of Prussia during this same decade of the fifties was one little calculated to enlist the support

[77] See above, pp. 76 ff.
[78] The Franco-Prussian treaty of commerce of 1862 provided an interesting testing of the solidity of the *Zollverein*. When Bismarck proposed its reorganization on the basis of those states only that accepted the treaty, all, in the test, adhered.

of the liberal forces of Germany which, unsuccessful as they had been in 1848, had not ceased to exist. The operation of the Prussian constitution of 1850, not an outstandingly liberal document in the first place, was hemmed in by limiting encroachments and restrictions.[79] In 1858 the Prussian king, Frederick William IV, was adjuged incompetent and his brother William assumed the regency, to become king in his own right in 1861. Himself of a highly conservative inclination, he had nevertheless a measure of good sense and balance that was to stand Prussia and Germany in good stead.

The Italian events of 1859 had the effect in Germany of stimulating by the example of success the forces of liberalism and nationalism which, as in Italy, had their main support in the bourgeoisie. But in a more limited, though ultimately more important, sense the uncertainties of the international situation had military consequences of importance. Though Prussia mobilized at one point, thereby influencing Villafranca,[80] she did not participate in hostilities; but it was thought desirable to strengthen the army with an eye on possible future developments. It was for this purpose that von Roon was made minister while his friend, von Moltke, became chief of staff.

THE ADVENT OF BISMARCK. Army reform means money, and out of this situation there developed between the King and the *Landtag* a concrete issue over the vote of army credits, which in turn took the form of a constitutional issue over the power of the purse. The situation in some of its aspects is reminiscent of that which had existed two centuries earlier in England, but in contrast with the English development it is characteristic of the German that the elected bodies of Germany did not know how to make successful use of this power of the purse for political ends. The king was distressed to the extent of contemplating abdication, but he eventually accepted the advice of von Roon, which was to call Bismarck from the Paris Embassy and to put him in charge of affairs.

Among the statesmen of nineteenth-century Europe the figure of Bismarck is towering, owing to the combination of his person-

---

[79] Repeal of the municipal system in 1852, reorganization of the Prussian Upper House in 1854, curbing of freedom of the press and of the right of assembly, are illustrations of the reactionary tendency.

[80] See above, pp. 101–102.

ality and of the power that was his to use. Bismarck has often been compared to Cavour and the comparison is valid in that both men had a sound understanding of the operation of power. But the differences between them are also very substantial: where the Piedmontese is best characterized as a mid-nineteenth-century British liberal, Bismarck may be described as a Prussian Junker; to the conservative outlook he steadfastly adhered and for the chatter of the people's representatives he had little regard. But, again like Cavour, Bismarck understood the active forces of the time and realized that mere blind opposition to them would be futile. Bismarck could endow Germany, once he had made her, with the most advanced social legislation of Europe, well ahead of liberal Britain or France, but this he did in the same spirit of enlightened despotism as the great Frederick in whose tradition he fits well.

In many respects Bismarck was a limited man whose cultural horizon was highly circumscribed—even in history, surprisingly in view of his own role, his interest was relatively small—in which he differed from that other master of statecraft, Richelieu, to whom he may also be compared; power was Bismarck's concern and little else did he seem to appreciate. His training had been useful and served to make him overcome the limitations of the Junker outlook that was initially his own; German unification he viewed at first with suspicion, fearing that it might serve to contaminate and dissolve the character and virtues of the Prussian state. But his contacts soon broadened his outlook, and he gained a proper understanding and perspective of the problems of the Germanic world while he was Prussia's representative at Frankfort. Then he became acquainted with the larger world of Europe, serving first in St. Petersburg, then in Paris; while in those posts he took the proper measure of the Russian state and of the French Emperor.

When, at the age of forty-seven, he received the call to take charge of Prussian affairs in September, 1862, Bismarck already had a clearly formulated design in his mind; with the forthrightness, even brutality, which he knew how to turn into an asset, he informed the Austrian ambassador that the house of Habsburg must transfer the focus of its interest from German affairs to those that would be better viewed from Budapest. The first part of his scheme may therefore be described as the rearrangement of the structure of Central Europe. In order to do this, Central Europe must be isolated from outside interference. This meant dealing with, or neutralizing, Russia and France. At the same time, within Central Europe, Prussia must make herself capable of settling scores with Austria. This last implied in turn two things: the creation of adequate Prussian military power; the use of such diplomacy as would maneuver Austria into a position of disadvantage. As he put it with complete frankness, not by speeches and resolutions, but by blood and iron, was German unity to be achieved.[81] Yet Bismarck was not primarily a military man; he was a statesman who, like any competent craftsman, would use the tool best suited to the task. War was indeed one such tool, but there were others, and it is in keeping with this outlook that after 1871, his task accomplished, Bismarck should have become the staunch and sincere supporter of peace. But until that time war was best suited to his purpose and war he would use.

THE SETTLEMENT OF THE AUSTRO-PRUSSIAN ISSUE

The very first task, that for which he had in effect been called to office, was the securing of credits for the Prussian army. For the *Landtag* he felt a combination of dislike and contempt;[82] if the *Landtag* was not amenable Bismarck would dispense with its concurrence, and it is significant that he was able to do so, suspending in effect for four years the operation of the Prussian constitution. It is also significant and characteristic of the man that, having in the course of his unconstitutional rule created the tool of an adequate army and put it to successful use, he would restore the constitution. By then, how many in Germany would take the doctrinaire type of Mazzinian position of denying the validity of the results accomplished merely because they disapproved of the method?

Of the management of these domestic affairs he kept firm and effective control. But simultaneously the foreign situation must be attended to. Here Bismarck may be said to have been favored by good fortune, but it is also true that the ability to recognize and exploit opportunity is no less a test of statesmanship than the ability to create it. Bismarck had barely been in charge of affairs a few months when the Polish rebellion broke out at the

[81] Bismarck thus described his approach to the problem of Germany in addressing the Prussian parliament upon becoming Minister President in 1862.

[82] In 1849 Bismarck had voted in a minority of two against a vote of thanks to the king for his promise to grant a constitution. Later, he was wholly in favor of the king's refusal of the German crown offered "from the gutter," that is by the Frankfort Parliament.

beginning of 1863. He put this incident to excellent use in the form of the Alvensleben Convention[83] the main significance of which, in connection and in contrast with the Napoleonic handling of the Polish affair, may be described as a step in the displacement of France by Prussia in the Russian scheme of things; at any rate Russian good will was created toward Prussia which had rendered the tsar valuable service when it came to standing up to French, British, and even Austrian pressure.

THE PROBLEM OF THE DANISH DUCHIES AND THE GASTEIN CONVENTION. When the Austrian Emperor proposed a congress of the rulers to consider rearrangement in the Germanic Confederation Bismarck felt that he could be cavalier: the simple Prussian refusal to attend clearly robbed the suggestion of all point. This was in August, 1863, but by that time the Danish king had already presented him with another opportunity, the complicated aspects of which were ideal for the exercise of his skill.

The Duchies of Schleswig, Holstein, and Lauenburg, in personal union with the Danish crown, had been the object of dispute and even armed activity in connection with the widespread disturbances of 1848. A settlement had been eventually contrived, the London Protocol of 1852, which had essentially confirmed the status of 1815.[84] But the Danish king, Frederick VII, persisted in efforts to assimilate the Duchies into the rest of his domain, placing the whole under a common constitution. These efforts quite naturally produced opposition in the Duchies as well as in Germany where the matter, as in 1848, appeared as the simple defense of German nationality. Britain was the Power most interested in this affair, and in September, 1862, Lord Russell offered his country's mediation. Ostensibly the move had universal approval, save in Denmark, where in March, 1863, King Frederick made a new move tantamount to the annexation of Schleswig.[85]

While Denmark was proving recalcitrant, feeling mounted in Germany, and in July the Germanic Diet demanded the withdrawal of the March decree. In the midst of these complications, Frederick died, in November, to be succeeded by the Duke of Glücksburg, as Christian IX; this event was cause of added con-

[83] See above, p. 112.
[84] See above, p. 80.
[85] This was encouraged in part by the Danish belief in the support of British opinion, a belief that Palmerston's statements, his speech in Parliament of July 23, for instance, were calculated to encourage.

fusion, for at this point the Duke of Augustenburg claimed the succession in Schleswig and Holstein,[86] while Napoleon III put forward the idea of a European congress. The involved situation recalls Palmerston's quip.[87]

Mistakenly relying on Palmerston's bombast, Denmark let matters drift; but the Germanic Diet having meantime espoused the cause of Augustenburg, its decree of federal execution took effect in December through the agency of federal troops, Saxon and Hanoverian. It will be noted that Prussia had hitherto not committed herself, but the Danish breach of the Protocol of 1852 was used by Bismarck as justification for his intervention, carefully dissociated, however, from that of the federal Diet.

All possibilities of European mediation were nullified by the failure of Russia, Britain, and France to take joint action, a result largely due to the Polish affair. The tsar was in Prussia's debt; Napoleon had irked Britain with his reference to the outmoded settlement of 1815, in connection with his congress proposal, and he had been in turn annoyed by Britain's reluctance to join him in putting greater pressure on the tsar over the Polish matter. Napoleon was in addition involved in Mexico at this time. The result of it all was that the German-Danish quarrel was allowed to unfold itself without external interference.

In January, 1864, Bismarck took joint action with Austria, a highly skillful move intended to have later consequences. Denmark's refusal to restore the separateness of the Duchies resulted in a joint Austro-Prussian attack and a Danish defeat. A conference in London, where the Powers met from April to June, was barren of results,[88] and hostilities were resumed that ended in total Danish defeat and surrender. Again Bismarck saw to it that no simple solution would put an end to the matter. The Treaty of Vienna, in October, merely provided for the surrender of Schleswig, Holstein, and Lauenburg *collectively* to Austria and Prussia.[89]

[86] For the bases of his claim and the issue of the Danish succession, see above, p. 77.

[87] He is credited with the observation that only three men in Europe had ever understood the question: the prince consort, now dead; a Danish statesman, currently in an asylum; and he himself, who had by now forgotten it.

[88] Partly because of Bismarck's proposal of independence for the Duchies, a proposal generally disapproved of and which misled the Danes into counting on outside (British) support.

[89] A provision for the holding of a plebiscite in Schleswig was never honored. It became the basis for the clause of the Treaty of Versailles of 1919 which resulted in the plebiscite of 1920.

Altogether, the imbroglio of the Duchies, if an unusually complex affair, contained little of concrete substance. Its main significance lies in the role it played in the much larger calculations of Bismarck, now ready to move for the showdown with Austria. Bismarck was determined that Prussia should acquire the whole of the Duchies and was contemplating an open conflict with Austria during the early part of 1865. He was restrained for the moment by opposition at home as well as by uncertainties over the Italian and the French attitudes in the event of actual war; he therefore had to be content with a prolongation of the existing ambiguity. Extended negotiations with Austria resulted in the conclusion, on August 14, of the arrangement known as the Convention of Gastein. The provisional arrangement of the preceding October was ostensibly clarified by the decision that Austria would be in charge in Holstein and Prussia in Schleswig, but without prejudice to the rights jointly acquired over both Duchies.[90]

Austria had badly misplayed her hand. Having first sought and failed to obtain entry into the *Zollverein* and toyed with the idea of compensation for herself in Silesia, her consent to a division of the Duchies with Prussia robbed her of the asset of posing as the defender of Germandom. She could only maintain her newly acquired interest by opposing the union of the Duchies; moreover, a glance at the map will show the awkwardness of an Austrian enclave in Prussian territory, a ready-made occasion for dispute.

THE WAR WITH AUSTRIA AND THE TREATY OF PRAGUE. Before the test of arms, however, Bismarck had to make quite sure that no outside interference would thwart his operation. This meant insuring French neutrality. To this end Bismarck went to see the French emperor at Biarritz in October, 1865. Napoleon could not have been more obliging; allowing himself to be lured by vague hints of possible compensation for France, he gave Bismarck sufficient reassurance to make him feel that an Austro-French alliance was not a possibility.

To be sure, Napoleon had made no formal commitment, but his virtual *placet* to an Austro-Prussian war must nonetheless seem strange. The key to his behavior seems to have been the Italian situation which had left him with a "bad conscience." To make

[90] Lauenburg was to go to Prussia outright in exchange for a money payment. To add to the complications, Prussia was entitled to build a canal (the Kiel Canal) through Holstein.

assurance doubly sure, Bismarck was seeking an Italian alliance that would compel Austria to fight on two fronts. He was having considerable difficulty in achieving this aim for the Italians had little trust in him. It was Napoleon who extricated him by guaranteeing the acquisition of Venetia to Italy, whereupon, on April 8, 1866, Italy entered into an alliance with Prussia that committed her to participate in hostilities against Austria provided Prussia took the initiative within three months.

There was little difficulty in picking a quarrel with Austria. On April 9 Prussia introduced a motion in the Frankfort Diet with a view to reform in the federation. Feeling that war was inevitable, Austria began to mobilize, in which she was followed by Prussia. When, in June, the Holstein Diet was summoned by the Austrian governor to consider the fate of the Duchy, Bismarck denounced the action as a violation of the Gastein agreement and sent his troops into Holstein.

In desperation Austria had turned to France with whom a secret agreement was made: France promised to remain neutral but only for a price, the cession of Venetia to Italy, whatever the outcome of the war. If Austria were successful she might rearrange Germany to her liking, though France retained a right of consultation and might perhaps obtain the formation of a buffer state on the Rhine. Austria gained one more futile satisfaction when, on June 14, the Germanic Diet voted federal execution against Prussia for her aggression in Holstein. Austria declared war on the 17th, Prussia the next day, and Italy on the 20th.

The fate of war is ever uncertain, but Bismarck was in possession of an adequate tool. While a Hanoverian force was disposed of at the end of June, the bulk of the Prussian forces marched into Bohemia, where, on July 3 at Königgrätz (or Sadowa) Moltke defeated the Austrian army of Marshal Benedek. To all intents and purposes the Seven Weeks' War was ended—the German states had had no chance to enter it—the Austrian emperor having offered terms of peace through the mediation of the French. The acceptance of these terms, however, did not go without a bitter inner Prussian struggle. Bismarck wanted neither to destroy nor even to humble Austria beyond the point already reached; but he had the greatest difficulty in persuading the Prussian king, let alone the Prussian generals, flushed with victory and insistent on marching upon Vienna. Alone in his position, he was almost driven to despair at what he considered the failure of his plans. But he had his way in the end,[91] and the position that he took on this occasion is one reason why his place stands as high as it does among statesmen. The Preliminaries of Nikolsburg, signed on July 26, were essentially incorporated into the Treaty of Prague of August 23, 1866, which restored peace and finally settled the century-long contest for Germany between the houses of Hohenzollern and of Habsburg.

The Austrian domain was not in any way diminished[92] nor did Austria have to pay an indemnity, the contribution of 60,000,-000 crowns being quite insignificant. But she agreed to the one purpose for which Bismarck had fought the war, the dissolution of the Germanic Confederation. Bismarck showed further moderation, toward Austria and toward the German states, by undertaking the formation of a new confederation that would remain confined north of the Main River and by renouncing the incorporation of Saxony; the South German states might in turn form another confederation that could enter into agreements with the Northern. Austria renounced all rights in the Duchies, original occasion for the conflict, and agreed to accept any Prussian enlargement within the confines of the Northern organization. These arrangements were implemented in 1867 with the formation of the North German Confederation in which Prussia, having annexed outright Hanover, Nassau, Cassel, and Frankfort, held a dominant position by virtue of her mere relative dimensions in the whole and of the constitutional rights that were hers.[93]

The Italian role in the war had been less than glorious, the Italians having suffered defeat at the hands of the Austrians both on land and at sea. However, in compliance with prior arrangements, Venetia, through the intermediary of Napoleon, passed to Italy. But Bismarck would not support the Italian claim beyond the administrative boundaries of the former Kingdom of Lombardo-Venetia. The result was that Italy was left with a militarily weak frontier in the Alps and with the slogan *Trento e Trieste* for the use of future irredentist agitation.

[91] The acceptance of his views by the crown prince and the latter's intervention saved the day for him.

[92] Save for Venetia, which Italy obtained.

[93] There were also small annexations at the expense of Bavaria and Hesse-Darmstadt, and Prussia secured a corridor connecting her Rhenish section with the rest. In the North German Confederation the king of Prussia was President and commander-in-chief of the federal forces.

FRANCE AND THE GERMAN QUESTION

FRANCE AND THE AUSTRO-PRUSSIAN WAR. The Prussian success had been made possible in large measure because the conflict had remained confined to the Central European arena. Though both Russia and Britain had been largely inimical to Prussian encroachment in the Duchies, the substance of that issue was in itself not very great, and Bismarck had put to good use the Polish insurrection in securing Russian good will for himself. Britain felt great reluctance in the contemplation of an Austro-Prussian conflict, but she was even more concerned with the uncertainties of French meddling. Regarding both Russia and France as the most likely disturbers of the peace, she looked upon a strong Prussia as a useful stabilizing element. Britain, therefore, like Russia, maintained a passive attitude in the affair.

By far the greatest doubts attached to French intentions. If a segment of French opinion, the liberal, felt sympathetically inclined toward a united Italy, the prospect of a stronger Prussia, let alone a united Germany, commanded little enthusiasm in any quarters in France. French policy at this time, and from this time until the Franco-Prussian War, can only be described as incompetent, standing in greatest contrast with the unusual diplomatic skill of Bismarck. The reason for this lies in the fact that the direction of French policy was wholly in the hands of the emperor. Napoleon had many qualities, some of them far from unattractive, but, even allowing that he was already a sick man at this time, steadfastness and clarity of purpose were not among his attributes.

In exoneration of him it may be said that his calculations were based on false, though not necessarily unreasonable, estimates. At Biarritz he had not formally committed himself, and he contemplated the coming Austro-Prussian conflict with a degree of equanimity: it would be a long-drawn-out affair, a match between equals which would supply the opportunity of mediation from which he could extract some advantage.[94] But even within this calculation, his encouragement of the Prusso-Italian alliance was a gratuitous blunder.

---

[94] It may even be pointed out that at Sadowa the Austrians kept the advantage for a good part of the day, until the arrival of Prussian reinforcements. Sadowa foiled the possibility of effective intervention by the South German states; these and Hanover were in the war against Prussia whose prompt action against the latter frustrated the plans of the German states.

Napoleon, as usual, had a plan. It was a reorganization of the Central European world that contemplated Prussian aggrandizement, limited to the Rhine, but still balanced by an Austrian state; between the two larger units the South German states could form a third bloc within which French influence might penetrate in support of its independence against the other two; finally, France herself would receive some compensation on the Rhine. But in the negotiations that he initiated with Bismarck before the outbreak of war he could obtain no firm commitment in exchange for the French promise of neutrality, save the declaration in June that compensation for France at the expense of German territory was not feasible.

Then came the war and Sadowa which destroyed the basic assumption of Austro-Prussian equality of force. There remained the possibility of armed intervention, or at least of the threat of it, matching the Prussian mobilization of 1859. This was indeed considered in France, and the foreign minister, Drouyn de Lhuys, favored mobilization accompanied by the declaration that France would oppose any modification of the *status quo* without being consulted. But, for a variety of reasons,[95] after the crucial meeting of his council on July 5, Napoleon chose to confine himself to a policy of amicable and diplomatic intervention.

The French ambassador to Prussia, Benedetti, was at Nikolsburg and saw Bismarck during his negotiations with the Austrians. His instructions were to obtain some compensation, and a variety of possibilities was suggested: first the left bank of the Rhine; then, when Bismarck objected to this, the frontier of 1814, Luxembourg, and Belgium were all mentioned. Napoleon was even willing to offer a French alliance in return. This mean and ineffective begging has been properly described by the phrase *la politique des pourboires*. But if Bismarck would not bargain German territory, he did not oppose a flat refusal to other possibilities. He could even remain quite urbane and suggest to the French ambassador that he put his proposals in writing, which he promptly did.

By August no conclusion had been reached, but by the time Bismarck and Benedetti parted and went on their respective holidays, Bismarck was in possession of other valuable documents as

[95] Among them the state of French opinion in which Austria enjoyed no special popularity and which failed to appreciate at first the significance of the Prussian victory.

well, secret treaties of alliance with the South German states, which may be regarded as a "liberal" interpretation of the promise he had made to Napoleon to respect their independence. But who indeed was the better defender of that independence when Napoleon had been quite willing to obtain compensation at their expense? That Bismarck had retained the initiative throughout the negotiations and led them along the path that would be most suitable to him is clear. He had already come to the conclusion that an open conflict with France was a necessary accompaniment of his ultimate purpose; for this, therefore, he must prepare in the same shrewd and calculating manner that had led Austria to her undoing.

THE LUXEMBOURG QUESTION.   The coming Franco-Prussian conflict was the great issue of the diplomacy of Europe during this period. Napoleon, though disillusioned on the score of Bismarck, still persisted in his search for compensation. The reorganization of Germany that was effected at the beginning of 1867 gave him an opportunity, for the North German Confederation did not include the Grand Duchy of Luxembourg[96] of which the king of Holland was ruler. A negotiation was consequently undertaken with him which, by March, 1867, had promising prospects: in exchange for a money payment that would take care of his own debts, and after consultation of the people, King William of Holland was willing to relinquish Luxembourg to Napoleon.

But in view of the previously existing status of Luxembourg, the agreement of the king of Prussia ought to be obtained for the transaction.[97] The interpellation of deputy Bennigsen in the Reichstag, an act to which Bismarck was not foreign, was useful in crystallizing German feeling, before the opposition of which, and presumably of Prussia, the Dutch king thought it wise to withdraw his offer. Another *pourboire* had failed to materialize for Napoleon. French face was saved through the Prussian acquiescence in the demand that the Prussian garrison be withdrawn from Luxembourg; Bismarck was not quite prepared for the final test of force and let France score a diplomatic victory of sorts. Thus what seemed for a moment a crisis threatening the peace

[96] It had been part of the German Confederation and garrisoned by Prussian troops which might now, therefore, be withdrawn.

[97] He was planning to visit the Paris exhibition in the summer. Also, the Luxembourg question had aroused objections in Germany on the score of nationality.

was overcome. The Powers meeting in London in May promptly extended to Luxembourg the perpetual neutralization that they had guaranteed to Belgium in 1831.

If a Franco-Prussian showdown must take place, the attitude of the other Powers became of paramount importance. Though, to quote his own words, "I took as assured that war with France would necessarily have to be waged on the road to our further national development at home as well as the extension beyond the Main,"[98] Bismarck was content to bide his time, watch and direct events, and seize what opportunity might offer. One useful accomplishment was the conclusion in March, 1868, of an agreement with Russia whereby, in the event of war with France, Russia undertook to neutralize Austria by gathering her troops on the frontier.

THE FRENCH SEARCH FOR ALLIANCES. On the French side diplomacy was not idle and was directed for more than two years toward the conclusion of an Austrian alliance. On the simple theory that Austria would welcome the possibility of revenge for the defeat of 1866, in April, 1867, Napoleon held out the prospect of an offensive alliance. The Austrian chancellor, Beust, of Saxon origin, was not averse to the idea, but, also as a consequence of its defeat, the Habsburg state was undergoing a constitutional reorganization which, in October, took the form of the *Ausgleich*, or compromise, whereby the state was transformed into the Dual Monarchy, Austria-Hungary, in which the two component parts had positions of equality. The Prussian victory had thus the indirect effect of being advantageous to Hungarian nationalism, and Andrássy, the Hungarian Premier, was less interested in revenge than in Balkan affairs. When Napoleon hinted at the Rhine for himself and Silesia for Austria, Austria countered with Balkan considerations, in which, conversely, France had little interest, especially as this would have implied taking an anti-Russian position. When Napoleon and Francis Joseph met in Salzburg in August the awkward liquidation of the Mexican adventure[99] was at the forefront.

The negotiation dragged on, Napoleon reducing his ambition to a defensive alliance and a guarantee of the *status quo*. But Beust

[98] Bismarck's *Reflections and Reminiscences*, published in English as *Bismarck the Man and the Statesman*, New York, Harper, 1898, Vol. II, p. 57.
[99] See above, p. 120.

felt that Austria must be secure in her rear and therefore introduced the condition of Italian participation in the alliance. Italy was thus brought into the negotiation, but Rome was her price for participation in the alliance, a request that Napoleon could hardly be expected to grant when French forces had made their appearance in that city after the Garibaldian attempt of 1867. Thus nothing came in the end of the projected Austro-French alliance, save an innocuous exchange of friendly letters between the rulers in September, 1869. Some military conversations in 1870 were equally inconclusive, for Austria intended to adjust her behavior to the military course of events should war break out; the discussion was still half-heartedly proceeding when this actually happened.

The British view of continental affairs was that there was no cause for prior commitment. Some suspicion of Bismarck did exist, but the traditional climate of Anglo-Prussian relations was generally favorable, and the tendency was to accept the accomplishment of German unity as fated to occur. There was in Britain far greater suspicion of Napoleon, his revisionist tendencies, and his propensity to indulge in large, complicated, and potentially troublesome schemes, of which not a few illustrations existed by this time. The affair of the Belgian railways[100] at the beginning of 1869 evoked alarm in Britain and the response of a sharp warning to France, while the desirability of a Prussian alliance also received some passing thought. Napoleon did not insist and the Belgian scheme was abandoned.

Thus, by the end of 1869, nothing concrete had been accomplished other than the Russo-Prussian convention of 1868. Bismarck had cause to be satisfied with the international situation, and in the same year, 1868, he had secured the adherence of the South German states to the *Zollverein* and the formation of a *Zollparlament*. His earlier view that war with France was inevitable need not be equated with an active desire for war, but rather may be taken as a judgment of probability. What if France should, like Britain, reconcile herself to the prospect that German unity was unpreventable? On the French side there were those who took precisely that view, and the seeming evolution of the Empire in the direction of parliamentary constitutionalism might make

[100] A French scheme for the purchase of some Belgian railway lines. Though of very limited scope in itself, the project opened up vistas of French economic penetration as a wedge to more far-reaching influence.

France more pacific.[101] But against this must be set the persisting uncertainties of the French situation as well as those of the German, where signs of reviving opposition to Prussia could be discerned. For Germany, war could be the cement of union. The French plebiscite in May, which seemed to give the Empire a new lease on life, and the almost simultaneous appointment of the more aggressive Gramont to the foreign office, were taken as unfavorable signs by Bismarck. If war had to come an issue was at hand for him to use.

THE FRANCO-PRUSSIAN SHOWDOWN

THE HOHENZOLLERN CANDIDACY IN SPAIN. There had been revolution in Spain in 1868, as the result of which Queen Isabella had fled and been deposed. The Constituent Cortes having opted for the retention of the monarchy, the search for a candidate began, which, after a number of refusals, finally produced an offer of the Spanish crown to Prince Leopold of Hohenzollern-Sigmaringen.[102] France could hardly be expected to remain indifferent to the accession of a Hohenzollern to the Spanish throne and her objection to it may indeed be regarded as reasonable. However, the refusal of Prince Leopold would have closed the matter had not Bismarck taken it up again, in May 1870, procuring a new offer followed this time by an acceptance. When the news became official, the French reaction, as expressed by Gramont in the *Corps législatif,* was one of immovable opposition. Prussia was therefore faced with the choice of either fighting or suffering a diplomatic defeat. Much to Bismarck's annoyance and against his opposition the Prussian king elected to back down; on July 12 the withdrawal of Prince Leopold's candidacy was announced. This could have easily closed the matter and Napoleon might have rested content.

Bismarck was indeed disappointed that the occasion had escaped him, but with incredible and inexcusable obtuseness Napoleon once more came to his rescue. In an attempt to push the French advantage, Benedetti was instructed to demand from King William I a guarantee that the matter would not recur in the future. At Ems where William I was vacationing, Benedetti had

[101] It was by way of encouragement of this trend in France, of which the advent of the Ollivier ministry in January, 1870, was an expression, that Bismarck put off the admission of Baden into the North German Confederation.

[102] His brother Charles had taken the Rumanian crown in 1866, after the ousting of Cuza, with the agreement of both Bismarck and Napoleon.

virtually to waylay the king to present his request. Though quite desirous to be done with the troublesome issue and allowing that he had no intention to reopen it, King William nonetheless could only oppose a refusal to so sharp a demand as the French ambassador made.

Bismarck had left Ems on the 12th and only received in Berlin the news of the withdrawn Prussian candidacy to the Spanish throne. He was greatly dejected at seeing the chance of his war disappear, but in the king's account of his last meeting with Benedetti he saw a ray of hope. He had authorization to publish the dispatch, and this he did, but only after having edited the document—not actually falsifying it, but making use of the blue pencil. This is the story of the Ems despatch.

THE FRANCO-GERMAN WAR AND ITS EFFECTS ON EUROPE.   The results were fully as expected by Bismarck. In the edited document opinion in both France and Germany could read reciprocal insults. The decision was for war in France, and she took the initiative of declaring it on July 19. Bismarck's diplomacy now bore fruit and the war remained isolated. To make assurance doubly sure he saw to it that on July 25 the (London) *Times* published the text of the draft treaty that Benedetti had submitted to him wherein a French annexation of Belgium was considered. This news produced the intended alarm and Gladstone hastened to conclude agreements with both Prussia and France, in August, pledging Britain to oppose whichever Power should violate Belgian neutrality.

For all that Bismarck wanted the conflict and had done his utmost to bring it about, the last French insistence seemed generally unwarranted and to that extent weakened the French position in the eyes of others. Nevertheless, the participation of Austria was not wholly excluded. But the Russian willingness to abide by the agreement of 1868 with Prussia served to restrain Austrian action; Austria would therefore wait for a better season and for French successes. Likewise Italy, where the possibility of intervention was also considered, again put as a prior condition the solution of the Roman question; this France would not accept, for she "could not defend her honor on the Rhine and sacrifice it on the Tiber."[103]   Whatever illusions Napoleon may have had on

[103] It is of interest that, despite his earlier experiences, Garibaldi led a corps of Italian volunteers to the assistance of France in the war against Prussia.

the score of the South German states were dispelled from the first; Bismarck had little difficulty in posing as the defender of Germandom in the light of Napoleon's willingness to annex Rhenish territory.

As in 1866, Bismarck's tool, the army, proved wholly adequate for the purpose, whereas in France preparations had indeed been considered but had gone little beyond the paper stage. French reverses began almost immediately, and on September 2, at Sedan, a large French army with the emperor himself surrendered.

The disaster of Sedan essentially sealed the fate of the war, but it also altered its complexion and its significance in Europe. The news of Sedan reached Paris and caused the fall of the Empire and the emergence of a provisional government of national defense. Further French resistance was futile and Paris was besieged; the war might in fact have ended and peace been quickly restored but for the Prussian demand for annexation. This was largely disapproved of by other Powers, Britain among them, who viewed a French defeat as such with equanimity; but if to put troublesome France in her place, teach her a lesson, seemed desirable, too great a diminution of France and corresponding augmentation of Germany would be no less detrimental to the balance of Europe. Bismarck feared the formation of a league of neutrals that would seek to interpose its mediation; for that reason he was anxious to make peace, though still on his own terms, and was annoyed at the French delay in accepting them. France, on her side, sought to foster the possibility of intervention, but both Favre's appeal in September and Thiers' tour of the European capitals the next month were barren of results.

One important reason for this failure lay in the Eastern Question. Russia, though not oversympathetic to substantial Prussian aggrandizement, preferred to collect immediate benefit for herself in the form of abolition of the 1856 provision that had demilitarized the Black Sea. Bismarck was quite willing to pay this price to Russia, but fearful of complications that would involve Britain, sought to delay the Russian move until his war was ended. The Russians, distrustful, would not wait; on October 20, Gortchakoff announced the denunciation of the demilitarization clause of the treaty of 1856.

British policy may perhaps be described as timid at this time. Just as Britain declined to object to the Prussian demand for annexation in France, in the lack of means to oppose it, so in the question of the Straits she was content with verbal protestations. For that matter, she found no support in Austria paralyzed by her internal stresses; Beust in the end acted like Gladstone, with words alone. Bismarck therefore proposed the meeting of a conference to settle the issue of the Black Sea, a proposal that was accepted by the British Cabinet in November.

The conference met in London in January, 1871, but its very meeting contained in Bismarck's eyes the danger that the occasion would be used to bring up the French question and give reality to the league of neutrals. He therefore opposed the presence of a French representative at the meeting and instructed his own delegate to quit the conference if Franco-German issues were raised. He had his way[104] and by March the conference put the sanction of Europe's approval on the unilateral Russian initiative, thereby saving at least the fiction of legality.

Like Russia, Italy endeavored to derive profit from the Franco-German conflict. The French garrison in Rome having been withdrawn in August, once French defeat was insured by Sedan, Italian forces entered Rome, the Pope offering no more than token resistance.[105] The Pope yielded to superior force and did no more than denounce the illegal act; no one in Europe took up his cause and Rome became henceforth the capital of Italy.

THE TREATY OF FRANKFORT AND THE GERMAN EMPIRE. While the London conference was gathering, Jules Favre in Versailles was conducting armistice negotiations with Bismarck. The armistice was signed on January 28 and made possible the holding of elections in France for an Assembly that met in Bordeaux. Favre and Thiers were meantime engaged in negotiations for peace with Bismarck. They had little to bargain with and, save for minor concessions,[106] had no choice but to bow to his dictates.

The debate was sharp in Bordeaux where there was vigorous opposition to the terms of peace. But what else could be done, given the circumstances? The terms were accepted in March, and the Treaty of Frankfort that formally ended the conflict was

[104] The French were invited to participate, but Favre, occupied with the armistice negotiations, neglected to send a representative.

[105] A plebiscite on October 2 ratified the annexation of Rome to Italy.

[106] Thiers obtained a reduction of the war indemnity from 6 to 5 billion francs and the retention of Belfort in exchange for the German right to march through Paris.

signed in the city of that name on May 10.[107] By it France ceded to
Germany the whole of Alsace and a part of Lorraine, putting the
Franco-German frontier on the crest of the Vosges Mountains.
The deputies of Alsace protested in Bordeaux, just as they were
to do later on in the German Reichstag, and on the score of the
territorial cession French feeling was unanimous that it was a
moral wrong. By some it has been characterized as worse than
a crime, a blunder. Whether or not a blunder be worse than a
crime, the acquisition of this territory by Germany may fairly be
described as unwise, for it made it impossible to restore normality
in Franco-German relations; it was a latent source of infection
that was introduced into the body politic of Europe.

It is enlightening to contrast the treatment meted out to France
by Bismarck in 1871 with the manner in which he had dealt with
Austria five years earlier. Austria he would neither punish nor
humiliate, but to France he did both. No better calculated way
to rub salt into wounds could have been found than the ceremony
that took place on January 18, 1871, in the Hall of Mirrors of the
great palace of the French kings at Versailles. For there, upon
motion of the king of Bavaria, the Prussian king was proclaimed
German Emperor. It was to take half a century before that
stain was erased in France, when the second Reich was to sign its
death warrant in the very same spot on June 28, 1919. No better
illustration, or more appalling, could be cited of the continuity of
history.

But the significance of the Franco-German War far exceeded
the limited aspect of that conflict between two European Powers.
It meant that at one stroke Germany appeared as a unit on the
map of Europe and, on the Continent at least, definitely the most
powerful unit. Little wonder that for the rest of the century, until
the First World War, Germany, either positively and by her own
initiative, or negatively through the reactions of others to her
and her intentions, or her supposed intentions, lies at the center of
the record of European affairs.

[107] A Franco-German conference met in Brussels on March 28 to settle outstanding matters. Meantime the episode of the Commune took place in Paris,
from March to May, and was an embarassment to the French negotiators, for
Bismarck proved to be a hard bargainer, demanding a price for any concessions,
such as the modification of the terms of the armistice that would enable
French troops to move against Paris.

Part Two

THE ERA OF

STABILITY,

1871–1914

V *The Period as a Whole*

I. Some General Characteristics of the Period

The overwhelming mass of the peoples of Europe did not, in 1871, have the clear consciousness that they were entering a new period basically different from another that the year 1870 had just brought to a close. The continuity of life does not accommodate itself to the artificial divisions of historic periodization; yet these divisions are convenient and useful, and they are not devoid of a measure of validity.

If we apply the label "nineteenth century" to the hundred-year span enclosed between the dates 1815 and 1914, then the date 1870 may properly be taken as midpoint in the course of that century. The present story is primarily concerned with the record of the relations among states and from that limited viewpoint the Franco-Prussian War is of particular importance as marking the division of the century into two nearly equal but appreciably different and distinct parts. They differ mainly for two reasons: because of the altered relationships of power obtaining in the second when compared with the first; because also of changes in the basic forces that stand behind the operation of international affairs and of their tool, diplomacy.

The first part of the century had to a large extent been characterized by the search for some equilibrium to take the place of that which the twin forces of nationalism and democracy, unleashed by the Great Revolution in France and its Napoleonic aftermath, had fundamentally disturbed. The impact of these forces was by no means spent in 1871—in some ways their effect was to be deeper after that date than before—but with the achievement of Italian and German unity a point of some stability was reached. Between the Franco-Prussian War and the great explosion of 1914 there were no wars among the great Powers of Europe. If it is clear in retrospect that the hope of lasting peace was an illusion, nearly a half century of unbroken peace betokens a state of equilibrium rarely achieved among the Powers. This condition is one of the outstanding characteristics of the second half of the nineteenth century and the study of the manner in which it was maintained will form the object of the middle section of this book, a record of stability achieved.

Yet, within this stability, the period as a whole presents changing characteristics. Stability and peace may be attained through the agency of superior unchallengeable power residing in one place, or may be the result of a balance of forces. The latter state is the more delicate and fragile and more at the mercy of accident, while the former may seem tantalizingly durable. But power feeds upon itself; if unchecked, it tends to overstep the limits of reasonableness and can become the very agent that gives rise to the combination of forces that will contrive its overthrow. These varying conditions will be observed in operation.

Whether diplomacy be the continuation of war, or the reverse be true, in their mutual dealings with each other states cannot but be everlastingly aware that the factor of power, their own and that of others, must receive primacy in their considerations. Power consists of many things—this has been indicated earlier— and it is relevant to bear in mind those changes that took place during the period now under consideration in the relationships of power among the major states of Europe, as well as the changes occurring in the component factors of this power.

The saying that God favors the larger battalions is old. Certainly numbers continued to retain importance, an importance, however, increasingly qualified by other factors. The growth of Europe's population continued at a rapid rate, from some 250,-000,000 to 400,000,000, aside from emigration. The fact alone of this increase, not its causes, need be retained here. The increase was fairly evenly distributed with the marked exception of France. For a long time France had been the most populous state of Europe, a fact not unrelated to that country's role. When she emerged as a united nation in 1871, Germany's population was but slightly larger than France's; but France had by this time achieved virtual stability of numbers. It is significant that in 1914 there were 40,000,000 Frenchmen and 65,000,000 Germans. Among the major Powers France in 1914 was ahead of Italy alone which was fast catching up with her.

But the unit of power that is the man with a rifle was ever more qualified with the passage of time. The growth of industry, heavy industry most of all, must now be reckoned with, whether because of the arms-manufacturing capacity that it entailed, should it come to the ultimate test of force, or more broadly as a major creator of wealth. The growth of industry and its spread during the second half of the nineteenth century were such as to constitute a new phase of the industrial revolution. But this growth was characterized by greater irregularity than that of population.

One basic distinction, the consequences of which were to appear during and after the First World War, is that sometimes expressed by the phrase "inner and outer Europe." Inner Europe, the Europe of steam and machinery, was the region roughly bounded by a line running through Glasgow, Stockholm, Danzig, Trieste, Florence and Barcelona; this boundary was steadily expanding into the domain of primarily agricultural outer Europe. All Russia essentially belonged to outer Europe, but the last two decades of the period witnessed the beginning of industrial development in that country; it makes for interesting, if now idle, speculation to consider what the course of events might have been had this growth been allowed to continue undisturbed by the impact of a conflict that the Russian economy could not stand.

Within inner Europe changes were considerable. If Britain maintained her long-established primacy, she was no longer *the* workshop of the world and her primacy was challenged during this period with increasing seriousness by the remarkable growth of German industry. Here again, the French growth lagged behind both the British and the German, with the effect that the relative decline in man power was compounded, instead of being compensated, by the slower development of industry in France. The shifts in power resulting from the changed relationship of its fundamental components could not but cause stresses and strains in the process of readjustment: declining power will strive to cling to its prerogatives, while rising power tends to be impatient of the achievement of these and of the recognition of its status by others.

This is the proper place to make mention of the emergence of two foci of power, both extra-European, whose influence on world affairs remained, however, largely potential until 1914. The Civil War in the United States, the decision of Japan to westernize herself, and the Franco-Prussian war were almost simultaneous occurrences, and the parallel is arresting between the outburst of economic activity and expansion in Germany, Japan, and the United States during the half century before 1914. For reasons largely historic, however much the Americans and the Japanese, especially the former, built up potential, this did not in a major sense qualify the fact that, up to 1914, Europe remained essentially the powerhouse of the planet. The sharp and overwhelming American impact on the whole world, including Europe, was to be one of the major results of the First World War.

The rapidly growing numbers of Europe and the vastly increased production of her factories also created problems, not wholly new indeed, but the increased intensity of which was tantamount to the creation of different conditions. Economics has ever been important and the middle of the nineteenth century is the time that witnessed the formulation of that view so pregnant with future consequences, mainly associated with the name of Karl Marx. Marxist or otherwise, inner Europe had to call upon the food and raw material resources, not only of outer Europe, but of the other continents, old and new, to an unusual degree. Thus the volume and value of commercial exchanges assumed an importance without precedent with the consequence that the conditions of life, not to say the very possibility of existence, of vast numbers became inextricably entangled with a multitude of commercial relationships that encompassed the earth.

Britain is the best, or most extreme, example of this state of affairs. Having accepted earlier the implications of free trade, the great mass of her people had become dependent on industry and trade to a unique degree. The price and availability of cotton from Egypt and America, of wheat, meat, and wool from Argentina, Canada, and Australia, to cite but random illustrations, became of overwhelming importance, not only to the commercial classes of Liverpool and London, but to the factory hands of Lancashire as well. Empire, trade, banking, commercial and naval fleets were matters of vital concern to the millions dwelling in the British Isles. The safeguarding of these interests—on the growth of their magnitude and complexity lies the stress—of necessity assumed larger proportions by comparison with more purely political cares. The growing importance of the position of commercial attaché is reflection of this situation. Much has been said and written on the role of Anglo-German commercial rivalry as one of the causes of the First World War.

The generally and on the whole steadily expanding economy,

allowing for the normal fluctuations of the business cycle, meant accumulation of wealth. Here again the emphasis is on quantity and size rather than innovation. Finance and banking assumed in their own right unprecedented importance, and accumulating capital, in accordance with the laws of its nature, sought profitable employment in home investment in the expanding industry just mentioned, but overflowing to the far corners of the earth as well. American, Russian, and Argentine railways, no less than rubber plantations in Asia, absorbed billions of European capital, and this development also created new and complex relationships that increasingly absorbed the attention of foreign offices and embassies: the role of French capital in Russia and the intrusion of German finance in the Ottoman Empire loom large in the diplomacy of the period. Money is power and the role of British gold is long familiar; in the case of France, for instance, the considerable wealth of the country served to mitigate in appreciable measure some of the previously mentioned deficiencies of her power.

It is worth mentioning, especially with an eye to later, post–First World War developments, that in matters financial Britain enjoyed a place of undisputed primacy. London had become the financial capital of the world, filling a role at once profitable to Britain and highly useful to all. Also, stability prevailed, of which the gold standard was symbol, expression, and consequence rather than source of equilibrium.

Alongside the effect of these immediately and narrowly material factors, there were other forces at work that the adjectives "social" and "cultural" best describe. If we think of the related, but distinct, forces of nationalism and democracy as those that had mainly provided the motive power of European change since the French Revolution, these forces during the second half of the nineteenth century appear no less active and potent, but their effect is altered. The great and clear triumphs of nationalism up to 1871 were the achievements of Italian and German unity. In both cases nationalism had been an integrating force, leading to a simplification of the map. This result fitted well the economic tendencies of the whole century: increased facility of transportation and communication; technical developments suited to the organization of large units of production. Hence, from the economic point of view, these effects of nationalism may be called desirable, while conversely the tendency of economic development gave added solidity to the new creations.

But, after 1871, there is a pause; thereafter nationalism and economics are at odds and working in opposing directions. In the cases of the Habsburg and Ottoman Empires, the success of nationalism could mean complete disintegration; the process, already successfully at work in the latter during the earlier part of the century, continued to register further gains before 1914. But it was not until the First World War that both empires finally exploded into their component parts. The second half of the nineteenth century meant in both cases a generally losing struggle to hold together a congeries of disparate nationalities. The economic virtues of the Danubian Monarchy have often been pointed out since 1918, but the contrast is significant between the cases of Germany and Italy on one side and that of Austria-Hungary on the other. The fate of the Sick Man of Europe was an old problem and the observation of Sorel was apt—that upon his demise his place in the sickbed would be taken by Austria. The disappearance of either could not but have repercussions of the deepest magnitude and importance for the other states of Europe; the Austrian and the Ottoman situations loom large in the period from 1871 to 1914, as international no less than domestic problems.

But rather novel was the diversion of nationalistic enthusiasm into imperialistic channels. Imperial overseas expansion is an old tale for Europe, but here also the contrast is arresting between the relatively weak manifestations of the imperial urge during the early part of the century and its extraordinary vigor during the last third. Though it is true that actively conscious imperialism was the appanage of a relatively small section of the nation, even that much of the nation was often indifferent if not antagonistic to the activity, the encounter of a rival imperialism at the far ends of the earth could easily arouse national pride and anger. South African setbacks and condemnation by others produced a surge of national unity in Britain; many in France who had little interest in Morocco and even preferred yielding to German demands in that region reacted strongly to German interference and methods. In varying degrees and ways all the major Powers of Europe were, by the end of the century, deeply affected by the imperialistic virus; much space will have to be devoted to the course and effects of Europe's imperial rivalries, which in fact tended to become more serious sources of differences than specific national claims on the continent.

The concept of the sovereign people served to transform rulers' quarrels into rather more dangerous peoples' disputes. It had other effects as well. The seeds of 1789 could not be uprooted, and the first half of the century had been dominated by the contest between reaction and liberalism, with the former fighting on the whole a losing battle. The battle of democracy was by no means won in 1870; in some respects, in fact, the achievement of German unity through Bismarck's blood and iron methods was a serious setback to the liberal cause. Nevertheless, if we think of democracy in the broad sense that will include the economic and social, as well as purely political, connotations of the word, the trend seemed unmistakably established during the second half of the century, a fact most appropriately expressed by the First World War slogan, "to make the world safe for democracy." Everywhere the franchise was introduced and widening, in generally decreasing measure as one went from west to east; even the autocrat of all the Russias had to allow, during the decade before 1914, the hesitant beginnings of popular representation.

No less significant was the growing recognition of the human rights of the people; the concept that the state has a measure of responsibility to its members increasingly tended to supersede the earlier liberal notion that labor was a commodity subject to no other law than that of a free market. A certain amount of confusion was introduced in this connection: relatively autocratic Germany was more advanced in social legislation than constitutionally far more liberal democratic Britain or France; by the turn of the century, it was the Liberal party in Britain that mainly espoused the cause of social legislation. But in one form or another it may fairly be said that everywhere the people were more and more coming into their own; the standard of living was steadily rising, literacy and education were spreading, bringing ever-widening circles within the reach of the popular press. The success of the socialistic idea may be regarded as another manifestation of the same phenomenon; though distinct from, it may be seen as closely related to, the spread in the broad sense of the democratic theory and practice.

The effects of this success of the democratic idea were of the highest importance, though not the simple ones that had been expected with what now would be called optimistic naïveté. Much time would have to pass and much blood to be shed before the perverted concept of national socialism could establish its successful hold on some peoples; but even before 1914, when nationalism and socialism were everywhere accepted as long and well established rivals, opposite ends of the political spectrum, sitting in parliaments on opposite sides of the house, the early notion that if only people could really control their governments peace would automatically reign, a notion derived in turn from the Rousseauian eighteenth-century belief in the fundamental goodness of man, stood in obvious need of qualification. In simplest form, the success hitherto achieved by the democratic idea raised the question, become still more acute in our time, of the conduct of foreign policy under a democratic system. To be sure, the success of democracy was much qualified, and the fact remained that, to a perhaps surprising degree, even in the most advanced democracies, the tradition continued to hold that foreign policy was the esoteric preserve of a small group of men. The foreign offices and the diplomatic services remained largely staffed from a minute section of society. But however much autonomy these organs of the state might have, parliaments existed endowed with certain rights and periodic elections took place. At certain intervals at least, opinion, however formed, could not but be an influence that, beyond a certain point, it would be fatal to ignore.

This raised in turn the question of what the chief concerns of this opinion were and of the manner in which these dominant preoccupations would be shaped. If foreign affairs were felt to be largely beyond its competence, more immediate and more readily apprehended issues of a domestic character were likely to limit its horizon. This gave at once greater freedom and scope to the direction of foreign policy while limiting the possibilities of action. The quip that the British people in their mass were inclined to regard foreign affairs as something, usually unpleasant, that happened to other peoples, held good to a considerable degree for others as well. For the rest, opinion could easily be aroused or dragooned to feel strongly through the oversimplified presentation of issues in terms of blacks and whites, rights and wrongs, justice versus the opposite, threatened aggression from across the border. At this point the press assumed considerable importance. This press enjoyed a large measure of freedom, but much of it was controlled by a variety of vested interests; governments often exercised over it a substantial influence, and some of it was simply venal. The argument of domestic necessity, genuine or manufactured, became a tool in the arsenal of diplomacy.

Those in charge of the conduct of the foreign affairs of the countries of Europe were for the most part honorable men, well trained and competent, though the degree of their individual ability varied. These men were in addition torn between two divergent forces and loyalties. On the one hand, representatives as they were of rival and competing entities, their first task was to promote and defend the interests of the unit with which they were associated; but the concept of a common heritage and unity in the civilization of Europe, if loose and vague, was also a reality, especially among a group of men enjoying much in common by way of training, background, and outlook, to the point that they formed an international of sorts. How to reconcile the defense of rival interests with the larger common interest that was the preservation of peace was their dilemma. To take but one illustration among many possible ones, the Balkan rivalry between Russia and Austria was deep and of long standing; but the thought was not unknown in Vienna of the possibly undesirable consequences of too severe a jolting of the Russian regime.

In view of the very different methods which have come to characterize the conduct of the relations between states in our day, it may be worth mentioning that considerable formality and punctilio were typical of pre–First World War diplomacy. The American phrase, "striped pants diplomacy," and Mussolini's "gardenia school," both of derogatory intent, are apt expressions of our changed, more pedestrian and popular, presumably more democratic practice; whether it is a gain might be questioned. Also, and this is more important, much secrecy prevailed, not only over negotiations—an inevitable condition—but over the results, agreements and treaties, which grew out of the dealings of the Powers among themselves. The need of secrecy, real or supposed, was hard to reconcile with the constitutional procedures of Western parliamentary democracies and was a source of considerable difficulty. Withal, from London and Paris, through Berlin and Vienna, to St. Petersburg, the area of agreement was large on the score of what constituted the proper aims of international business. Not in the literal sense alone of the prevalent use of the French tongue, but in the broader sense of basic understanding, the statesmen of Europe before 1914 may be said to have spoken a common language.

II. The Individual Powers and Their Problems

The purpose of the brief foregoing sketch has been to give an indication of the atmosphere and conditions in which the states of Europe were conducting their relations during the half-century before 1914. It will be of use at this point to give the sketch additional precision by surveying the scene from the standpoint of the individual Powers, indicating the principal concerns of each during this period.

The whole nineteenth century is sometimes labeled the British century. The description has much justification and the British consciousness of superior power was aptly reflected in the phrase "splendid isolation." British power and wealth were the result of a long and proud story of successful empire building. But this is the period during which the supremacy of Britain began to be challenged. If the processes of empire building, industrial growth, and accumulating wealth went on uninterrupted, in relative terms British power diminished. The slowly growing awareness of this diminution and the consequent effort at adaptation to meet the changing circumstances constituted the central problem of British foreign policy at the turn from the nineteenth to the twentieth century. In more limited fashion Britain was much affected by the problem of Ireland.

The diminution of France was sharper and more drastic, though a distinction must be made in this case. For the longer term, the relative decline of French power continued, with the result that the standing of France was considerably lower in 1914 than it had been in 1870. More immediately, the Franco-Prussian War was for France a disaster that definitely demoted her from the position of continental primacy. By itself, military defeat might, however, be but passing incident, not even necessarily irretrievable. In any case, and apart from any hopes of *revanche* that she might entertain, the central problem of France was that of reconstruction and of the recovery of her position, or of as much of that position as might be regained. The constitutional change that came with the defeat absorbed much of the energy of the nation, but the peace of Frankfort left a festering sore which, however mitigated by the passage of time, ever prevented a normalization of Franco-German relations.

By contrast with France, Germany emerged at the same time united and victorious. More important is the fact that she was about to embark on a career of unprecedented development. Domestic growth and integration could for a time absorb the vast energies released by the fact of unification, but the problem of growth was the dominant issue of the Second Reich. For this meant adaptation to and by others; any growing organism will tend to infringe upon its surroundings. What was the proper place of Germany under the sun, in her own and in others' eyes, and how would she set about gaining that place? This in a sense was the basically new as well as the most central problem of the entire period for Europe as a whole because of the rate and extent of development of the power of Germany. Adjustments must be made, and in sufficient time, if conflict were to be avoided.

Unlike the German, the Habsburg Empire was old. Shortly before 1870 it had undergone the drastic reorganization of the *Ausgleich*. During the period between 1867 and the First World War the problem of Austria-Hungary was the elementary one of existence. It has been said, and not without some justice, that if the Danubian Monarchy had not existed it should have been invented. The Habsburg state had served an important function in Europe; it may have contained the possibility of a solution in miniature of the problem that is the diversity of all Europe along lines other than the crude application of either self-determination or the mere suppression of certain nationalities by others. There were those in Austria-Hungary who envisaged the alternative of union in diversity, but however sane and attractive such a prospect might be, the fact remains that Austria-Hungary was the one major state in Europe that was not a national state. In view of the strength and success of the nineteenth-century wave of nationalism, the question simply was, could such an organism continue to exist? It was out of the stresses inherent in this situation that was to arise the immediate occasion for the explosion of 1914.

The vast domain of the tsars was undoubtedly one of the Great Powers of Europe, though the question of the extent to which its inner composition and structure made it European or not could be argued. Its physical extent and that of its resources, both human and inanimate, made up in part at least for the backwardness of its development. De Tocqueville, for one, had already had surprisingly prescient vision of the power that Russia was to achieve in our day; others might be cited. In a limited and concrete sense the paramount problem of Russia remained what it had been for two centuries, that of access to the open seas of the world, with the curious result that this enormous mass of land, much of which was still virgin, hence offered ample scope for the use of its energies at home, showed strong tendencies to territorial expansion. But the related aspect of this endeavor, that also went back to

Peter the Great, was the not less important one of adaptation to the more modern, progressive, and efficient ways of the West. In view of the constitutional structure of Russia, whether this adaptation could or could not take place without political domestic upheaval became an increasingly relevant question for the future of the state. Here too the First World War was to supply the answer to what, before 1914, was a debatable issue.

The characterization of the Benjamin among the nations rather befits Italy. Certainly at the bottom of the list of Great Powers, to the point that there were always those who questioned whether she really belonged in that category, she was nevertheless counted in it. Her problem was similar in a way to that of Germany; like Germany a late arrival, Italy wished to find her place under the sun among nations. Weak and poor, and weak because poor, there could be little question on her part of initiating or directing policy in the way that Germany could and did; her tendency was to seek adaptation, to fit or insinuate herself into the issues and differences arising among other Powers. A balance of power, preferably a delicate one, was the asset that she could best exploit and that at times magnified her importance beyond its own intrinsic merit. The peculiarity of the Roman situation gave for a time at least special importance to the Roman question, resolved after a fashion only in 1870.

This completes the roster of the Great Powers. Whatever question there might be about the rating of Italian power, there could be none about that of the empire of the Osmanlis. The history and extent of the Ottoman Empire placed it nevertheless in a unique category, different from that of the so-called small Powers. To a degree, though in more urgent fashion, its problem, like Austria-Hungary's, was the basic one of existence. If we think of Turkey in Europe alone, the process of disintegration had, by 1870, already gone a considerable distance. In its inability to rejuvenate itself through effective reform, the Ottoman state had adopted the inglorious policy of insuring its own survival through the encouragement and exploitation of the differences among the major Powers over the issue of its ultimate fate and of the distribution of its inheritance in the event of its demise. In the practice of this policy not a little skill was acquired by the Turks.

Given the condition of the Ottoman state, it followed that the politics of the Christian communities of the Balkans, whether already free or in hope of achieving that state, assumed unusual importance on the international scene of Europe.

Such were the components of the Concert of Europe. It may not be amiss to point out, especially in view of the sudden and cataclysmic change that was to follow it, that the half-century before 1914 constitutes the apogee of Europe. The process initiated some four centuries earlier was now reaching its climax and Europe was completing the conquest of the planet. Not merely in crude physical terms of superior military power—although this, too, was happening—but in the broader sense that, whether by imposition or willing imitation, the ways, the thought, the institutions of Europe, political, economic, and social, were spreading over the surface of the earth; in Europe lay the powerhouse of the planet. Of this, Europe, collectively and in her individual components, was at once conscious and proud, and she was also confident in the sense of her destiny. The saying may occur to some that pride goeth before a fall.

III. The Sources of Information

Having sketched the broad lines of the principal preoccupations that presided over the direction of the various members of the European community, the concrete and detailed story of the relations of the Powers may be begun. Yet, before entering the telling of that story, another should be recorded, a unique tale that has to do with the sources of our knowledge of the record and how these came to be available.

The records of the diplomacy of the period under consideration are fuller than those of any other, and this state of affairs may be credited to the operation of the democratic factor mentioned in the foregoing pages. This is how it came about. The war that broke out in the summer of 1914 turned out to be a peoples' war in a way that no earlier conflict had been. From the outset, millions were mobilized in the various belligerent countries and the passage of time only increased the demands on the nations' resources, human no less than material. From the outset also efforts were made by all the warring governments to present their position, to their own and to outside opinion, as the morally justified one of defense. The belligerent masses largely accepted this view which the insatiable demands of the conflict made it more than ever necessary to sustain.

The initial publications of selections of diplomatic documents were followed by a steady stream of propaganda intended to bolster the morale and insure the loyalty of the masses. But the scant and highly edited documentary selections that went into the various colored books of 1914 were of little assistance to the historian.

Then something unexpected happened. The year 1917 witnessed the intervention of the United States in the war and the withdrawal of Russia. From the standpoint of the development under consideration, both events operated largely to the same purpose, but the effects of the Russian Revolution came first in the form of the disclosure of secret agreements and other diplomatic exchanges. This was done by the Bolsheviks with a view to establishing the common wickedness of all capitalist states, exploiters of the people whom they deceived and led to the point of slaughter for the benefit of their masters. The Bolshevik disclosures were undeniably awkward.

America was not involved in the secret diplomacy of the belligerents of which it took a disapproving view. Such practices were the denial of the democratic principle, the right of peoples to govern themselves, of which knowledge of their governments' commitments was an obvious corollary. When President Wilson formulated the charter of the Fourteen Points, the first among them was a condemnation of secret diplomacy and it spoke of "open covenants, openly arrived at." More generally, the effect of the American intervention and of the leadership that America assumed of the allied cause was greatly to increase the emphasis on the moral aspects of the struggle—justice, democracy, and self-determination. For a brief moment Wilson and Lenin were rival poles of attraction on which were focused the hopes of great masses of men, and for a moment also the two prophets seemed to assert gospels that had not a little in common. This was passing illusion, but an important residue was left of which the governments had to take account in their calculations.

When it came to making the peace that followed the allied victory, made possible by the American intervention, the American role was inevitably of overwhelming importance. The result was at once interesting and unprecedented. Former conflicts—the Franco-Prussian War, for instance—commonly ended in territorial amputation and financial indemnity for the loser: the fact of defeat was simple and sufficient justification for this outcome. But the First World War was different: justice, not the verdict of superior force, was the proclaimed purpose of the peacemakers assembled in Paris in 1919. How to reconcile this justice—no war indemnity, for instance—with the righteous expectation that the damage of war would be made good by the defeated enemy was the problem that confronted the peacemakers. It is, of course, the part of justice to mete out punishment for wrong and to provide compensation for its victims.

This is in fact what provided a resolution of the difficulty. Its most vivid and concrete expression is to be found in Article 231 of the Treaty of Versailles. That article, which opens the section of that treaty that bears the heading Reparation—not indemnity be it noted—reads as follows: "The Allied and Associated Governments affirm, and Germany accepts, the responsibility of Germany and her allies for causing all the loss and damage to which the Allied and Associated Governments and their nationals have been subjected as a consequence of the war imposed upon them by the aggression of Germany and her allies."

The point is not whether the moral judgment contained in this clause was or was not historically correct—that issue will be discussed elsewhere—but simply that here was the innovation of a moral judgment introduced into a treaty among states. The consequences of this step were enormous.[1] Those which became a part of the politics and international relations of the postwar period will be dealt with in the last section of this book. What is to be retained at this point is that Article 231 of the Treaty of Versailles was tantamount to an invitation to Germany to seek to disprove the validity of the charge leveled against her. It was the effort to do this that led to the opening of the German archives and to the publication, initiated in 1922, of the great German documentary collection, *Die Grosse Politik der Europäischen Kabinette 1871– 1914.*

Even leaving aside the question of the quality of the editorship of this publication, so vast and intricate a tale as that of the diplomacy of half a century could not but appear different from the clear and simple statement of Article 231. In self-defense, if for no other reason than to disprove the suspicion that their own record could not withstand the light of day, the victors felt compelled to

[1] The process may be said to have gone one step further after the Second World War which was followed by the Nuremberg trials held under the sponsorship of the victorious allies. After the First World War some of Germany's leaders were also indicted as war criminals, but their trial was in the end left in the hands of German courts.

undertake similar publications, until the world was flooded with a plethora of information.[2] This was a boon, if perhaps a mixed blessing, to the historian and a gold mine on which controversy could thrive. Never before—or since—had state archives been thrown wide open up to a date so close to the present.

Needless to say, controversy prospered; a German monthly came into existence with the title *Kriegsschuldfrage* (later *Berliner Monatshefte*). It could not be expected that from such a mass of material as was being made available, even when supplemented by another flood of personal memoirs, there could emerge a clear and simple verdict to which all would subscribe. But one undoubted consequence was to provide unprecedented knowledge of the period under discussion in this section.

One more consideration should be added at this point. It has just been pointed out that the opening of archives and the publication of diplomatic documents served to feed controversy, however much some of the wilder fabrications of wartime propaganda could definitely be laid to rest. But another effect was to focus the study of the entire period unduly around the issue of responsibility for the outbreak of war in 1914 instead of looking upon it as a developing story of which 1914 was only the climax.

Also, it is well to remember that history is forever being rewritten, not only or so much in the light of novel information, as under the influence of the dominant preoccupations of succeeding generations. The history of the period from 1871 to 1914 is a good case in point. That the interpretation of planned aggression and exclusive German guilt was too simple an explanation was soon apparent to all serious students of the record. This led to a revision of the war guilt thesis, and just because the emphasis had been so strong on justice, the pendulum was swung far back by the revisionist school, motivated to a great degree by the impulse to redress a wrong. That revisionism should flourish in Germany was only to be expected; but in the English-speaking world it did hardly less well. The best illustration of this in America is the work of Professor Fay, *The Origins of the World War*; a serious and painstaking work, professing to strike a balance between the initial accusation and the extreme revisionist view, it was itself a good example of revisionist literature in the broad sense, the moral emphasis of which is not far to seek.

By now the wheel has turned full cycle, after a quarter of a

---

[2] This documentation will be discussed elsewhere. At this point no more is intended than to call attention to the development and its effects.

century, just as in the case of the prevailing view of the role of armaments as a contributory factor of conflict. For a long time after the First World War the view had wide acceptance that arms are in themselves a major cause of war, a view especially attractive to the English-speaking world. Nowadays, particularly in America, the old slogan is more readily accepted *si vis pacem para bellum*, just as it was in pre-1914 Europe. In the interpretation likewise of the history of pre-1914, the course of Nazi Germany and the war that she is generally credited with having unleashed have tended to cast a backward shadow on the earlier period. A good illustration of this is to be found in the work of the English historian, A. J. P. Taylor, *The Struggle for Mastery in Europe 1848–1918*. Like Fay's, Taylor's is serious work; the competence of its author is high and his motivation doubtless unimpeachable; yet it is not unfair to say that both works are reflections of the divergent outlooks that the passing of a quarter of a century has induced. It is fitting that perhaps the best analysis of all to date should have issued from a relatively neutral quarter in the form of the masterly work of the Italian Albertini, *The Origins of the War of 1914*.

For the American student Professor Fay's work warrants special mention. Once such an undertaking has been carried out and the quality of it acknowledged, it tends to assume a position of monopoly in the field. Generations of students have been brought up on Fay, the influence of whom on the American outlook can hardly be exaggerated. Only recently, after another World War, are such works as those of Albertini and Taylor beginning to revise at the same level the revisionism of the post-First World War period. The moral of it all is a caution to the student. A substantial degree of agreement can be achieved on the score of fact, but when interpretation enters, the influence of current concern must be recognized. The activity of such a character as Poincaré, for instance, could, in the twenties, make the responsibility of France appear in the same order as the German. In the light of the course of the last two decades, his policy may be regarded as evidence of no more than clear-sighted awareness of the shortcomings of appeasement, a term now fallen upon evil days.[3]

In terms of chronology, the period from 1871 to 1914 falls into

[3] This is not to be misread as a claim on the part of the author to superior wisdom or to the advocacy of the avoidance of judgment and opinion. There will be no attempt to conceal his own interpretation and point of view, but it was thought useful to introduce the foregoing caution, especially in view of the record of the history of the particular question of the origins of the First World War.

three parts which will form the subjects of the next three chapters. Until 1890 Germany is at the center of the picture, and the combination of her power with Bismarck's skill cause the story to center around her policy and his diplomacy. With his dismissal the picture changes radically. Germany, to be sure, may be said to remain at the center of the story but in an altogether different sense; the direction of the course of events slips away from Berlin, which increasingly becomes the focus of the fears and the antagonism of others. The result is a somewhat confused and complicated period of realignment of power that opens with the formation of the Franco-Russian alliance, almost immediately after Bismarck's dismissal, and closes with the conclusion of the Anglo-French and Anglo-Russian imperial understandings. By 1907, when the last of these agreements was made, Germany begins to talk of encirclement and Europe is divided into two rival camps. The situation is not rigidly frozen, but what possibilities of relaxation existed and what efforts were made to break through the rival alignments, with a possible qualification in the Italian case, failed. Caught in the toils of mutual suspicions, armed to the teeth, as if impelled by a fatality, Europe moved to her doom.

VI The Bismarckian Period, 1871–1890

Not by speeches and resolutions but by blood and iron had the task been accomplished. It had been, beyond a doubt, a masterful performance. Having brought into being the Second Reich, Bismarck, its architect, for two decades longer was to mold the shape and guide the course of his creation. Like it or no, his competence must be acknowledged; at home and abroad his prestige naturally stood high.

The fact that it was blood and iron that had been the instruments of German unity was fraught with considerable consequences; most important, it gave the new German state a military character, extending to the whole of it the stamp of the Prussian tradition. But to Bismarck our contemporary view of the respective qualities of peace and war had little meaning. Bismarck was above all a statesman; war was not good or bad *per se*, but a tool that could be used well or poorly; so was diplomacy. War, however, always involved certain risks, and Bismarck, his purpose accomplished, now judged it the best interest of Germany to develop in peace. For the moment at least, Germany (or Bismarck) was a fully satisfied Power and it behooved her not only to remain at peace herself, but to work for the avoidance of conflict elsewhere. Bismarck was now sincerely a man of peace. To preserve both the peace and Germany's position was his purpose, which could best be achieved through a continuation of his foreign policy prior to 1870. It had been his successful diplomacy that had insured the isolation of France in the war; Germany's victory had not aroused the antagonism of others though some were critical of the terms of the peace he imposed upon France.

Since France in any case was likely to resent defeat and seek occasion for revenge, she might as well be humiliated and weakened; let her isolation continue and nothing was to be feared from her. Bismarck would therefore cultivate the friendship of all; even with France, should she decide to reconcile herself to the peace of Frankfort, he would be on good terms. But that was up to France.

I. The First *Dreikaiserbund* and the Recovery of France

Britain had been quite content to witness the defeat of a rather meddlesome France; she had no fear of Germany and Italy seemed of little account; she would continue isolated but sympathetic. It was therefore with the two Eastern empires, the Austrian and the Russian, that Bismarck's diplomacy was actively concerned. The three empires had enough in common, of what now would be called ideology, a strongly conservative outlook, to create between them a bond reminiscent of that which in 1815 Metternich had sought to weld among all the supporters of the established order. But there were also more specific and limited considerations of national interest.

The defeat of France had put the quietus on any possibility, such as had been entertained between 1867 and 1870, that France and Austria might join to block Bismarck's designs or even undo his achievements. Austria must accept her new place, and even Beust, the anti-Prussian Chancellor, though with reluctance, was coming around to the view that her future path lay in close coöperation with Germany. His displacement in 1871 by the Hungarian Andrássy, in whom anti-German feeling was absent, facilitated Bismarck's design of creating a tripartite connection.

Russian neutrality in 1870 was the fruit of earlier Bismarckian diplomacy; Bismarck thought to have repaid it by his acquiescence to the modification of the Black Sea neutralization clause, and though the feeling in Russia was that the recompense was miserly, Russo-German relations continued to be good. The chief difficulty in any tripartite arrangement was apt to stem from Austro-Russian rivalry in the Balkans, though either Austria or Russia would look askance upon a mere bilateral arrangement between the other and Germany. A Franco-Russian connection, not a likelihood at this time, was nonetheless one possibility against which Bismarck was especially anxious to guard. Success was not long in crowning his efforts. The year 1872 found Emperor William I visiting Franz Joseph in his capital, and in September both rulers were joined by Tsar Alexander II in Berlin. In May of the following year the visit of William I, accompanied by Bismarck and Moltke, to St. Petersburg was the occasion for the signing of a Russo-German military Convention whereby each state would assist the other with an army of 200,000 men in the event that it was attacked.

In June the visit of the tsar to Vienna produced a political agreement to join in consultation in the event of difference. The underwriting of this agreement by Germany in October brought into existence the first *Dreikaiserbund*. This was hardly a close alliance; the chief significance of it was its admission of the common reluctance of both Russia and Austria to assume the initiative and responsibility for a Balkan upheaval. This was wholly agreeable to Bismarck whom neither Austria nor Russia could commit to assistance against the other as in reality they would have wished.[1] The fragility of the arrangement was not long in the testing.

The French feeling about the terms of the peace needs no explanation. The 5,000,000,000-franc indemnity was deemed unduly large, but what really rankled was the territorial amputation. That particular arrangement, as noted earlier, has sometimes been described as a crime, and sometimes as worse than a crime, a blunder. The widespread German feeling that Alsace is German land is by no means devoid of historic foundation; the common Alsatian speech is to this day Germanic and the French possession of Alsace is not very old. It is, however, one of those accidents resulting from the late crystallization of German national feeling that the people of Alsace were, by 1871, essentially opposed to annexation to Germany. If the annoyance transparent in Treitschke's declaration that the Alsatians were German and should be made to know it, by force if necessary, is to a point understandable, it has also an element of irrelevancy and of naïveté. At any rate the combination of the humiliation of military defeat with a concrete grievance fed the French feeling of irreconcilability and a desire for revenge.

But, whatever French feeling may have been, French impotence and French isolation were hard realities that could not be denied in France; like it or not, they must dominate the conduct of French diplomacy, the broad purpose of which was to recover for France her lost position. Inevitably at first, domestic reconstruction, political and economic, absorbed the nation's energy; the story does not

---

[1] Andrássy was more enthusiastic than Beust about an Austro-German connection, but also less desirous of a Russian one, instead of which he would have preferred a British association.

belong in these pages of how a predominantly monarchist assembly gave birth to the Third Republic. Political disunity in France was welcome to Bismarck; as a regime in France he preferred the Republic since revanchist nationalism was largely a monopoly of the Right. This was sound reasoning which, however, made the mistake of underrating the Jacobin tradition in France.

In concrete terms, France acted wisely in fulfilling the terms of the peace. French wealth made it possible to discharge the indemnity with promptness and to secure, by 1873, the complete evacuation of the territory. For the rest French recovery was very rapid and successful, to the point of causing Bismarck some concern. Of Thiers he came to take a favorable view, but Thiers was ousted in 1873 for his premature pro-Republican statement.

In the Monarchist government that came into office Decazes was foreign minister. He was anxious to secure some success and to test the whole European situation and the position of France in Europe. Out of this came the so-called "war scare" of 1875. The nature of the new government in France and the freely expressed Catholic sympathies at the time of Bismarck's *Kulturkampf* were sufficient to create some tension out of which Decazes pretended to discover a German threat.

If Bismarck on his side had no serious thought of preventive war, he was not loath to frighten France, and the situation which had simmered during 1874 came to a head with the open discussion in the German press of the possibility of war (Bismarck disclaimed responsibility for this) and some indiscretions of Radowitz, Bismarck's special envoy in St. Petersburg, with the French ambassador in that capital. Decazes saw to it that the report came to the notice of the European chancelleries and of the (London) *Times* and succeeded thereby in creating sufficient alarm to produce British and Russian representations in Berlin. Bismarck was annoyed, especially with his Russian opposite number, Gorchakov, but kept his counsel and disclaimed aggressive intent. The episode is mainly of interest as providing a testing of the European situation: France should not be diminished further, but the *status quo* was satisfactory and ought not to be altered. The Monarchist success in France was short-lived; the forces of the Republic were to make steady gains and what Franco-German tension there had been soon relaxed. If the French Republican Left was pacific, it is well to bear in mind that, for that very reason, it was also little sympathetic to the place of the military principle in Germany. Gambetta's phrase referring to the lost provinces was apt: "think of it always, speak of it never." In any case, however, what issues were to occupy European diplomacy at this point came mainly from the East.

II. The Near Eastern Question, 1875–1878

The problem of the Sick Man of Europe is met throughout the whole nineteenth century under the two aspects of the domestic situation of the Ottoman Empire and of the struggle for emancipation of the Balkan peoples on the one hand, of the interest and activity of the Great Powers on the other. The Russian effort to break through the Straits was generally opposed by others, most determinedly by Britain; one form of Russia's attempt was to extend her influence into the Balkans, in which endeavor her most resolute opponent was Austria. Germany had no interest in the Ottoman Empire and the Balkans at this time; in Bismarck's words, these were not worth the bones of a Pomeranian grenadier. But, indirectly, German activity had notable repercussions. The defeat of Austria in 1866 had led to a drastic reorganization of the Habsburg Empire through the *Ausgleich* of the following year. This was a notable success for Hungarian nationalism which obtained a position of equality, in some respects of privilege, in the new hyphenated state of Austria-Hungary. But (German) Austrians and Magyars between them constituted a minority of the population, the largest single element of which was Slavic: Polish, Czech, and South Slav;[2] even more than the Austrian, the ruling class of Hungary, in social and political terms antiquated and semifeudal, showed little disposition to make any concessions to the various Slav nationalisms. The basic significance of the problem of nationalities for the Austro-Hungarian Empire has been mentioned, as well as the various tendencies for its solution that ranged between the extremes of complete intransigeance and of granting the Slavs equality of status.

The Franco-Prussian War, by destroying the possibility of restoring the Austrian position in Central Europe, had the effect of focusing the foreign interest of the reorganized Habsburg state more exclusively and to a greater extent than ever toward the

---

[2] Germans and Hungarians amounted to 9,000,000 each, while the Slavs were almost as numerous as both combined: 10,000,000 Czechs and Slovaks, over 4,000,000 Poles, and 3,000,000 South Slavs. There were also 3,000,000 Rumanians and 700,000 Italians.

Balkans. This fitted in, besides, with the domestic problem of the state, mainly because of the existence of Serbia. That small country had emerged to nearly complete sovereignty in a long struggle against the Turks, but it contained only a fraction of the Serbian people. The struggle would continue but its very success raised the question of the possible effects of it upon those other Serbs, more broadly all the South Slavs, still under Habsburg rule. Here also the possibilities ranged between the extremes of full emancipation of all the South Slavs, whether under Ottoman or Habsburg rule, and their complete absorption, possibly on a basis of equal partnership with the two dominant nationalities, in the Danubian Monarchy.

In any case Serbian affairs were a major concern of the foreign office in Vienna. Austro-Serbian coöperation against the Turks was not a new concept, but, especially after the *Ausgleich*, the Southern Slavs, like their Northern Czech cousins for that matter, would rather turn their eyes to Mother Russia as the great defender of Slavdom. The importance of the Pan-Slav movement has sometimes been exaggerated; to a degree it could be no more than a convenient tool and a blind for the designs of Russian expansionism; but whether in that capacity or as genuine sentiment, the fact remains that the focus of Russian policy was turned on Balkan affairs. It should be mentioned also that the divergent views of the proper implementation of Russian policy were reflected in a lack of coördination of Russian diplomacy, a phenomenon destined to occur later, as it had on earlier occasions. The appointment of General Ignatiev to the Constantinople embassy put in that post a man inclined to pursue a vigorous policy in which the element of personal initiative was large.

Andrássy's initial preference favored the preservation of the Ottoman Empire untouched, and since this was the view likewise of Alexander II and of Gorchakov, the Austro-Russian declaration of 1873 had been possible. It was, however, more in the nature of a truce than the basis of real agreement. For under the influence of military leaders, Andrássy allowed himself to become convinced of the desirability of annexing Bosnia and Herzegovina. These provinces, extreme Western outposts of Ottoman control, were placed immediately behind the thin coastal strip of Dalmatia; at the same time they completed the encirclement of much of little Serbia by Ottoman territory, while their population was predominantly akin to the Serbian. Any such annexation as contemplated by Austria would inevitably raise the Serbian problem as well as that of the Russian reaction to any alteration of the Balkan map. The other European Powers had little direct interest in the matter though Bismarck seems to have felt that such a bone of contention as Bosnia-Herzegovina could be might enhance his own arbitral position between his rival allies. The Balkan situation, more narrowly that in Bosnia-Herzegovina, besides being an obvious Turkish problem, was primarily an Austro-Russian question. What brought it to a head was domestic Ottoman conditions.

In July, 1875, rebellion broke out in Bosnia, growing out of the local conditions of abuse and maladministration familiar in the Ottoman Empire. The revolt elicited a sympathetic response in Serbia, where, however, no action was taken, and considerable interest in Vienna, but also no direct action from Austria. By the end of the year, after some attempted consular mediation had failed, feeling that the situation should not be allowed merely to drift, Andrássy outlined a minimum program of reforms that the Powers should press upon the sultan in order to pacify the provinces. The Andrássy note of December 30, 1875, was well received by the Powers with the exception of Britain. Under the leadership of Disraeli, with Derby at the foreign office, the official attitude of that country was at first one of neutral indifference which had the effect of encouraging the normal Turkish reaction of procrastinating tergiversation. Actually, Disraeli's position was not dissimilar to the earlier one of Metternich; he, too, was willing to let the trouble burn itself out beyond the pale of civilization; for the rest, he disliked the association of the three Eastern Empires which he would gladly see disrupted.

But trouble in the Ottoman Empire seemed to grow rather than abate. Moslem mobs were responsible for the murder of the French and German consuls in Salonica and rioting spread to Constantinople where, at the end of May, Sultan Abdul Aziz was found dead in circumstances that suggested to some that he might have been "suicided"; he was succeeded by his weak-minded brother, Murad V. While this was happening, an armistice proposal issued from representatives of the three Eastern Empires gathered in Berlin met a highly ungracious reception in London, and further complications occurred when, at the end of June, Serbia and Montenegro could not be restrained from going to war against Turkey. The course of British policy gave the appearance of tortuousness as a consequence of its opportunistic indecision;[3] Russia and Austria proceeded with their own plans. These were formulated in the secret convention arranged between Andrássy and Gorchakov at Reichstadt on July 8, 1876.

The Reichstadt agreement contemplated the alternative possibilities of Turkish and of Serbian victory. In the former event, maintenance of the *status quo* was to be enforced upon Turkey; in the latter, substantial changes would take place: Serbia and Montenegro would be enlarged and divide between them the Sanjak of Novibazar; Austria would acquire the major part of Bosnia and Herzegovina, and Russia would recover the Bessarabian loss of 1856. It was even contemplated that Bulgaria, Roumelia, and Albania might achieve independence and that Greece should receive compensations in Thessaly and Crete; Constantinople was to become a free city in the event of a more far-reaching collapse of Turkey. It is of interest that, whether or not the understanding was purely verbal as Andrássy later claimed, there certainly was no clear and formal definition of terms; also, that it was some months before Andrássy took Bismarck into his confidence about Reichstadt.

So far-reaching a revision of the terms of the Treaty of Paris of 1856 might have been difficult of implementation, but the fortunes of war disbarred it from consideration, for the Serbs were soundly defeated and Russian pressure alone prevented the Turkish occupation of Belgrade. Meanwhile tales were being spread in Europe of the brutal methods of repression used by the Turkish forces, regular and irregular, in Bulgaria where the rebellion had also flared up. Nowhere more than in England did these stories arouse opinion, which Gladstone's fast-selling *Bulgarian Horrors* mobilized against the "unspeakable" Turk who was not fit to remain in Europe. This to a point was awkward, for the intrusion of the factor of opinion served to confuse even further the operation and the image of British policy. However, a British proposal resulted in the meeting of a conference in Constantinople in December.

Russian skepticism of the value of such proceedings was amply

[3] Though encouraging Turkish resistance through his failure to join the other Powers, Disraeli at the beginning of June broached to the Russian ambassador, Shuvalov, the possibility of partition of the Ottoman Empire.

One of the reasons that seem to have motivated Disraeli's lack of sympathy for the insurgents was a consideration of the Irish situation, and he expressed himself very strongly on the score of Serbia's "infamous" attack.

THE BISMARCKIAN PERIOD, 1871–1890

justified. The sudden proclamation of a constitution by Midhat Pasha, the new grand vizier and leader of the party of reform, was in the tradition of Turkish devices of tergiversation; even before the Constantinople conference adjourned, a new agreement had been reached between Russia and Austria, the Budapest Convention, formally of January 15, 1877, to be supplemented by a further one on March 18. These secret understandings, Reichstadt having been superseded by events, were essentially war agreements: in return for a promise of neutrality and of opposition to collective mediation, Austria could occupy Bosnia-Herzegovina.

Russia felt now free to act. The last possibility of avoiding war disappeared with the Turkish rejection in April of the joint Protocol of the Powers drafted in London. The suitable season for military operations had arrived and Russia declared war on Turkey on April 24, 1877. The Russians had hopes of quick and complete success, which was particularly desirable in view of the fact that, by resorting to unilateral action, they were infringing their obligations under the treaty of 1856. Their confidence was such as to make them refuse a Rumanian offer of assistance, only later accepted. The possibility of British intervention existed, but the failure to achieve prompt and decisive victory gave time for second thoughts and for negotiations. Initial successes were followed by the stalemate at Plevna, the defense of which Osman Pasha was able to prolong until December. The contemplated collapse of Turkey was thereby avoided and her stock rose with her successful resistance; British opinion, though still divided, had by this time shifted considerably from pro-Balkan and anti-Turkish to pro-Turkish and anti-Russian, but Disraeli did not find among his Cabinet colleagues adequate support for his more belligerent tendencies, in addition to which he found Austria little inclined to do more than examine the situation in common with the other Powers.

Eventually Plevna fell and Turkish resistance collapsed. There was panic in Constantinople when the Russians reached the Chatalja lines at the end of January. The reaction was little less strong in London, and the British fleet, which had returned to the Straits at Besika Bay,[4] was ordered to enter them; it appeared before the Turkish capital in mid-February. The cost of victory had been high for the Russians; their forces were thoroughly exhausted and they had no desire to force the issue, which their entry into Con-

---

[4] It had been sent there in the earlier stages of the crisis but been withdrawn late in 1877.

stantinople would have raised. An armistice was concluded, followed on March 3 by peace, registered in the Treaty of San Stefano.

Deprived of active outside support, Turkey was at the mercy of Russia; the peace settlement, largely the work of Ignatiev, envisaged far-reaching rearrangements. Russia's direct gains were not considerable, consisting of some territory at the eastern end of the Black Sea—Kars, Ardahan, Bayazid, and Batum—and of the Dobrudja; this last she proposed to exchange with Rumania for the segment of Bessarabia lost in 1856.[5] But the main feature of San Stefano was the formation of a very large Bulgarian state, stretching from the Black Sea through all Macedonia, beyond the Vardar, and reaching the Aegean at Salonica. The creation of this state, to remain under Russian occupation for two years, was regarded as tantamount to the establishment of a dominant Russian influence in the Balkans, whence it could easily at any time overawe Constantinople. In addition, Serbia and Montenegro were to be enlarged and, like Rumania, be freed of the last vestiges of dependence from the Porte; Bosnia-Herzegovina was to become autonomous under Austro-Russian supervision.

This arrangement was a mistaken move on Russia's part and one devoid of subtlety or skill. Apart from the fact that the issue of the fate of Constantinople was not raised, it showed no consideration for the interests of others, more especially of Austria-Hungary. Be it on the score of the international agreement of 1856, or of the more recent ones made with Austria at Reichstadt and Budapest, Russia had clearly put herself in the position of having broken her commitments. It is some sort of reflection on the operation of Russian diplomacy that Ignatiev, who negotiated the treaty, did so in ignorance of the Austro-Russian agreements. In any case a major crisis was precipitated involving mainly, apart from Turkey, the three Powers mentioned in this story.

The Russian tactic was to isolate Britain through a fresh understanding with Austria. Appropriately, Ignatiev was sent to Vienna for that purpose, but Andrássy, holding the whip hand, asked for too high a price in exchange for a promise of Austrian neutrality in the event of Anglo-Russian conflict. An Anglo-Austrian agreement might rather have been expected in the circumstances; it was

[5] These territorial cessions were supposed to take the place of part of the war indemnity demanded by Russia. After these deductions Turkey was still liable for over 300,000,000 rubles.

in fact sought by Salisbury who, in March, had succeeded Derby at the foreign office. But Andrássy's hedging and tergiversation were such that Britain found it easier to come directly to terms with Russia in May, whereupon Andrássy, in turn fearing isolation, also came to an understanding with Britain in June. The Russian acceptance of a Congress to deal with the whole situation essentially put an end to the crisis. The Congress was to meet in Berlin, appropriate recognition of the place of Germany in the councils of Europe and of the fact that Germany was relatively neutral in the issue.

THE CONGRESS OF BERLIN

Coming twenty-two years after the last major settlement of the Near Eastern question at the Congress of Paris, the Congress of Berlin is an equally important landmark in the story of that particular issue and of the diplomacy of the European Powers as a whole. The basic lines of the settlement had been outlined in the preceding agreements involving the three Powers mainly concerned, Russia, Britain, and Austria. The result was that the business of the Congress was disposed of with expedition; the Congress lasted exactly one month, from June 13 to July 13. Nevertheless, it was not a mere formal registering of decisions for there were enough secondary points unsettled to give rise to some close discussions.

Bulgaria was the first major issue to be taken up at Berlin. By June 22, agreement was reached on the implementation of the Anglo-Russian agreement to divide the creation of San Stefano into three parts. The Turkish delegates—one of them was a Prussian by origin—protested loudly when Salisbury proposed that Bosnia-Herzegovina be turned over to Austria; Bismarck showed them scant courtesy, and in the end they yielded to the decision of Europe in this as in other matters. It may suffice to list the main results of the Congress of Berlin:

1. Most important of all, there was to be no large Bulgarian state to overawe the Balkans and the Porte, but a very much reduced Bulgaria, for which it proved difficult to secure even Sofia and Varna. South of Bulgaria, a new creation, Eastern Roumelia, was to achieve an intermediary status on the road to independence: under a Christian prince, both Europe and the Porte retained a say in its affairs. The rest of Greater Bulgaria, its Western section, Macedonia, was to remain under unqualified Turkish rule.

2. Bosnia and Herzegovina were to be "temporarily" occupied

and administered by Austria-Hungary but the sovereignty of the provinces remained vested in the sultan. The adjacent strip of territory to the southeast, the Sanjak of Novibazar, lying between Montenegro and Serbia, was to be garrisoned by Austrian forces. These arrangements were implemented in the Austro-Turkish

THE TREATY OF BERLIN
AND ITS AFTERMATH
Turkish losses to Existing Balkan States
Russian gains
Greater Bulgaria of San Stefano

agreement of April, 1879, which, however, omitted mention of the provisional character of the occupation. The matter of the Sanjak was destined to be of considerable future importance.

3. For the rest of the Balkan states there were some compensations. Serbia, who had few friends, received Nish and Pirot, and Montenegro gained Antivari. The Dobrudja-Bessarabia exchange between Rumania and Russia was effected as initially planned.

4. Britain had little direct concern in the details of Balkan frontiers. To her it was satisfactory that the status of the Straits should remain unaltered. For the rest, protection of the Mediterranean route to India was Disraeli's main concern;[6] the vision of a Russian pincers through Constantinople on one side, the Caucasus to Alexandretta on the other was perhaps exaggerated fear. Russia was able to retain her gains in Armenia. But on July 8 the Congress was apprised of the existence of a direct Anglo-Turkish agreement, concluded a month earlier, as a result of which Britain would occupy, "temporarily" also, the island of Cyprus.

The importance of the settlement of Berlin has been mentioned. Its result may be looked at from two points of view: locally, that of the Balkans proper; on a larger scale, that of the Great Powers. As to the local Balkan situation, a balance was undoubtedly maintained; but at this time the fight for independence was still the more important consideration. Disappointment was naturally greatest in Bulgaria, while the seeds of Serbo-Bulgarian enmity had been planted. Nor was Rumania content with her failure to secure Silistria. Greece was not directly involved in these affairs, but the bases were laid at Berlin for compensation to her as well. Greek irredentism was focused at this time on the mainland rather than on Crete. The result of lengthy and intricate negotiations, involving mainly France in addition to the other mentioned principals, was a Convention in May, 1881, as the result of which Greece obtained most of Thessaly and a section of Southern Epirus; Crete remained Turkish under a revised edition of the Statute of 1868, to continue a concern of the Powers. As on the later occasion of the Balkan Wars of 1912–1913, the influence of the Powers was to create as well as to settle some problems.

This was because their approach was primarily with an eye to the preservation of the equilibrium among themselves. This, in a way, was done, but the result was reached only through a Russian defeat. True as it may have been that Russia brought this outcome upon herself by the manner in which she had proceeded, the fact remains that she had fought a costly and in the end successful war, the benefits of which she had to share with others. If

[6] The building of the Suez Canal by a French company was, from the point of view of British policy, the result of an error of omission. In 1875, Disraeli had seized the opportunity of the Khedive's financial difficulties to acquire for Britain his block of shares in the Canal company. Subsequent developments in Egypt and the redressing of the British mistake will be considered later.

Austria and Britain could feel satisfied, Russia did not. One particular aspect of her dissatisfaction was the feeling that she had not received from Bismarck the support to which she was entitled. This feeling was the result of misconception, for Bismarck's contention that he had no interest of his own to promote at Berlin and meant to be no more than the "honest broker" in bringing others to agreement, was essentially correct. Yet it was one of the results of Bismarck's own activity that he now must, up to a point at least, support Austria. In any case, one of the major consequences of this episode in the Near Eastern question was the disruption of the three Emperors' League.

Had she wanted to, Austria would have obtained the consent of the Powers to the outright annexation of Bosnia-Herzegovina. She was content with the more ambiguous status, but the significance of her intrusion in the Sanjak was twofold: one purpose was to prevent the union of Serbia and Montenegro; the other, related to the first, was to keep the way open to herself toward Salonica and the Aegean. The suggestion has been made[7] that a bold policy on Austria's part might have resolved her inner contradictions and the problem of her survival; not halfway measures of occupation, but outright incorporation of all the South Slavs, those she already had, Bosnians and Serbs as well, all to be given a status of full equality as partners in a reorganized triune state. The possibility of success of such an attempt cannot be altogether dismissed; if skepticism remains warranted, it makes for interesting speculation. But the breadth of vision and boldness that this decision would have required were not to be found among the leaders of Austria-Hungary. At Berlin, Austria was content to maintain some balance, mainly on the basis of ponderable assets, with Russia. In this she was successful, but her fate was largely dependent on imponderables.

Among the major states of Europe, two have received no mention in the proceedings at Berlin; the roles of France and of Italy were essentially of effacement. This, in the case of Italy, is not very surprising; weak and without background of experience in the role of European Power, still engrossed in limited Roman and irredentist considerations, Italy was in large part content to be accepted as a Great Power. The phrase of her representative at the Congress, Corti, "clean hands," is apt description of her policy.

[7] This is the view taken, among recent writers, by Albertini. Cf. *The Origins of the War of 1914*, Vol. I, *passim.*

Corti was criticized for this at home by those who felt that Italy might have obtained something for herself at Berlin and who commented that, if clean, her hands were also empty.

France, by contrast, had a long tradition of Eastern interests; she was, for instance, the largest holder of the Ottoman debt and the application of the balance of power principle in Bulgaria, Bosnia-Herzegovina, and Cyprus might indicate some corresponding compensation for her. Both Bismarck and Salisbury considered that Tunisia would constitute such adequate compensation and they conveyed this view to Waddington, the French delegate at Berlin. However, France at this time was still recovering and in somewhat uncertain fashion feeling her way among the Powers. The whole Eastern crisis she followed with interest but her role in it was negligible. There was also the consideration that Tunis was a likely object of compensation for Italy no less than for France. Neither Bismarck nor the Italians was unaware of the possibilities contained in such a situation. In any case, in Italy as well as in France, and more markedly in Italy than in France, there was a taste of disillusion after Berlin.

III. Bismarck's New System of Alliances, 1879–1882

THE AUSTRO-GERMAN ALLIANCE OF 1879

Bismarck fully appreciated the importance of imponderables. After Berlin all the Powers were free of mutual commitments; this situation was not destined to last and Bismarck's was the hand that more than ever guided the shaping of their relations. If Russia did not agree that he had been an honest broker and felt that in the commissions issued from the Berlin settlement the German voice was none too friendly, Russian feeling was outside his control. Bismarck's own choice would have been a continuation of the tripartite connection for reasons of international policy as much as because of his conservative preference for the Eastern regimes; but the Austro-Russian difference was also beyond his control. The record of good Russo-German (or Russo-Prussian) relations was long and was almost enshrined in the aura of a desirable tradition; certainly the old emperor was deeply devoted to it. But times had changed and Bismarck felt that the new Austria—to a point his own creation—was an essential prop of German policy. Austria was, after all, a next-door neighbor in the very heart of the Continent while Russia stretched indefinitely to and beyond the borders of Europe. Also, though this seemed little probable at the time, Austria should be prevented from entering a combination with the Western Powers, Britain or France. Bismarck therefore decided that, if choice there must be, he must tie Austria to Germany.

Having come to this decision, Bismarck proceeded to put it into effect without delay; he wished to have the matter settled before the impending retirement of Andrássy from the Ballplatz. Though not sharing the more extreme Magyar outlook, Andrássy the Hungarian represented that element in the Dual Monarchy most sympathetic to a German connection. Bismarck's greatest difficulty lay in persuading his own emperor; the process is an interesting illustration of the Bismarckian method, and this time also it came to the point of his threatened resignation. In the end Bismarck had his way and the treaty of alliance was signed on October 7, 1879.

It was a simple enough instrument, the focus of which was Russia: should that country attack either partner in the alliance, the other was pledged to come to his assistance with all his strength; attack by another power (France against Germany, for instance) would call for mere benevolent neutrality of the ally, unless that Power were aided by Russia, in which case the *casus foederis* would apply. The treaty was secret, valid for five years, and renewable. It was indeed renewed and was destined to become the immovable cornerstone of German foreign policy; it lasted as long as the two Empires.

The Austro-German alliance has been the source of much debate and of widely varying estimates.[8] Since there was no direct quarrel or likely source of conflict between Russia and Germany, the alliance was tantamount to a one-way guarantee of Austria by the latter Power against the former. No doubt it served to bolster the already questionable structure that was the Habsburg state and to that extent may be regarded as an element of stability in Europe. Any alliance is a two-way relationship and inevitably implies a measure of control by either partner over the actions of the other. That the alliance was in Bismarck's eyes defensive is not open to question: Russian aggressiveness would be restrained from having to meet both Germany and Austria instead of the latter alone (the

[8] It is interesting to consider the opposite views of the Austro-German alliance expounded in Fay (*The Origins of the World War*, Vol. I, pp. 69–71) and in Taylor (*The Struggle for Mastery in Europe 1848–1918*, pp. 264 ff.).

tsar, despite the secrecy, was to be informed in the likely event of trouble); at the same time Austria would find herself alone if she were the aggressor—hence the necessity for her of German backing would operate as an element of restraint. To this extent Bismarck may be regarded as having achieved the position of arbiter between the two Balkan rivals, since in that area lay the likely cause of conflict between them. Austria remained, in fact, ever suspicious of Russian intentions, even when there was no cause for that feeling.

But the underwriting of Austria also meant that Germany might find herself involved in situations not of her making and the control of which might be outside her power. Certainly Bismarck understood, if any one ever did, that while intent may be clear, the matter of aggression versus defense in law is often clouded. It would be both unfair and idle to read 1914, or even 1909, into 1879 for all that implications existed, but perhaps another element of risk may be mentioned. Whatever one may think of Bismarck's methods and of his standards of honorability and truthfulness, that his statesmanship was outstanding is generally conceded. The alliance was a tool that he would use for certain purposes; but Bismarck was not everlasting. What would become of the tool in other, less adroit, hands?

THE DREIKAISERBUND *OF 1881*

Driven to a choice, Bismarck had selected the Dual Monarchy, to the point of entering with it into a formal alliance. But, as already mentioned, Bismarck had no quarrel with Russia, let alone aggressive intent toward her. He had been driven to his choice by the Russian reaction to Berlin, but he was willing to bide his time and let second thoughts prevail in St. Petersburg. What had Russia gained except isolation by the disruption of the tripartite connection, especially since the time was not ripe or suitable for a French or a British connection? Bismarck seems, in fact, to have calculated that his very alliance with Austria might serve to bring Russia back to him rather than further estrange her.

On the Russian side, the long tradition of German friendship continued to have determined adherents. The tsar himself was one such and so was Giers, who had succeeded Gorchakov at the foreign office. Russia was annoyed at rather than afraid of Germany; her real differences were with Austria. But those differences, in the Balkans, might not be beyond composition. Allowing for the influence of Slav affinity, Pan-Slavism was not the main directing force of Russian foreign policy. The issue of the Straits was more important and the existing status was in Russian eyes unsatisfactory. Since 1871 the Black Sea was no longer demilitarized, but the possibility of other fleets passing through the Straits at the sultan's request was highly unwelcome to Russia; it was not made less so by the British declaration at Berlin that Britain regarded the validity of her obligation to apply only to "independent decisions of the sultan," an even more elastic concept than the distinction between aggression and defense.

From the standpoint of the Straits situation, or even of the control of them, the Balkans were a means, not an end. Bismarck's idea of how to drive the Austro-Russian team in harmony was a reasonable compromise based on mutual recognition of legitimate interests: in concrete terms, divide the Balkans into two zones by a line extending southward the existing Serbo-Bulgarian frontier and let each half be the preserve in which Russia and Austria would, reciprocally, recognize the other's free hand. In Bulgaria Bismarck was quite willing to be Russian; let Austria do likewise, and, conversely, let Russia be willing to be Austrian in Serbia. These considerations prevailed, aided by the ideological affinity of the three Empires. With the assistance of Saburov, the Russian ambassador in Berlin, partisan of the Russo-German connection, Bismarck secured the signing of a new tripartite agreement on June 18, 1881. This new arrangement was more far-reaching than the earlier League of the three Emperors.

The treaty of the *Dreikaiserbund* of 1881 provided for the neutrality of the other two members in the event that the third partner should be at war with a fourth Great Power. This was to apply even to the case of a Russo-Turkish conflict, but the requirement was specified in that event of prior agreement between the three Powers. No changes should take place in European Turkey (meaning the Balkans, but not the Caucasus) save again by agreement. Russia's concern about the Straits received recognition in Article 3 of the agreement which was a rejection of the British contention; Turkey could make no exception to the principle of closure of the Straits; in the event that she should the three allied Powers would regard her "as putting herself in a state of war toward the injured party" and losing the benefits of the Treaty of Berlin guarantee of her territorial integrity.

Especially in view of later happenings, as well as because of

THE BISMARCKIAN PERIOD, 1871–1890

past events, the clause is worth recording that "Austria reserves the right to annex the provinces of Bosnia and Herzegovina at whatever moment she shall deem opportune."

It must be noted, finally, that the *Dreikaiserbund* agreement did not supersede the Austro-German alliance of 1879, so that within the partnership the possibility remained of war between Russia and the other two members: this could happen in the event that Russia failed to live up to the letter and spirit of the understanding, should she, for instance, think that unconcerted unilateral action might gain her some advantage. The very possibility however, of her having to confront her allies should be a restraining factor on her; conversely, Austria knew that she could not count on German support in the event of her aggression. In Bismarck's calculations the new alliance was intended to create stability and to strengthen the peace.[9] The value of it, like that of all such arrangements, depended in the end upon spirit rather than letter. Could and would Austria and Russia replace in their relations suspicion by trust? To what extent, for that matter, could they control the actions of their unconsulted Balkan dependents in their respective spheres? The answer—negative—was not long in coming. But, before taking up that sequel, and partly for reasons of chronology, some other matters must be dealt with first.

From the Austrian point of view, the significance of the division of the Balkans into two spheres of influence was intimately related to the domestic problems of the state. In 1878 Austria could have annexed Bosnia-Herzegovina, yet was content with the more ambiguous arrangement that has been indicated; the meaning of her occupation of the Sanjak has likewise been mentioned. If the western half of the Balkans was to be Austria's sphere, then Serbia must be a friend or at least a dependent; in no case could she be allowed to be an active enemy. On her side, Serbia in 1878 had found little of the hoped-for support from Russia that had instead shown a definite preference for Bulgaria.

In the circumstances, the Austro-Serbian alliance of June 28, 1881, may be regarded as a logical extension of the *Dreikaiserbund*. By their alliance Austria and Serbia pledged themselves to the pursuit of a policy of friendship; neither would tolerate agitation against the other. But, unlike the *Dreikaiserbund* or the Austro-

---

[9] Bismarck was so concerned with the secrecy of the treaty that he drew up the documents in his own hand and the secret was so well kept that it was not revealed until 1918.

German alliance, the Austro-Serbian was not a partnership between equals; for Serbia it implied a relationship of dependence, a near-protectorate, as expressed in the Serbian pledge that granted Austria a right of supervision over the foreign policy of her small ally. The abject letter in which Prince Milan acknowledged his subservience was the expression of a policy more personal than popular, yet one that had logic in it. This logic may be said to have been carried to its extreme conclusion with the discussion by Prince Milan in 1882 of the possibility of an Austrian occupation of Serbia following upon his abdication and that of his son Alexander, when the latter would come of age. Whatever the possibilities of this arrangement may have been—doubts on that score are permissible—Hungarian opposition to the incorporation of more Slavs into the Monarchy, result of the Hungarian fear that these might come to have a greater voice in its affairs, destroyed whatever likelihood existed of such a policy ever being attempted. The result of it all was an ambiguity, growing out of the very nature of the Austro-Hungarian state that wanted to control Serbia, yet was incapable of carrying out the full implications of its wishes.

In the same category of corollary of the *Dreikaiserbund* may be placed the Austro-Rumanian alliance of October 30, 1883, in which Germany also joined. Like the Serbian alliance, this one rested on the factor of personal predilection of the ruler (Prince Carol was a Hohenzollern) and on Rumanian discontent with Russia after Berlin. It, too, had elements of weakness, the personal factor for one, and the fact that Rumania could advance Transylvanian claims against Hungary quite as much as Bessarabian ones against Russia. The Rumanian alliance and the story of its course bears in addition a certain resemblance to another that involved a more important Power and rounded out the whole Bismarckian system.

THE TRIPLE ALLIANCE OF 1882

This is the time and place to bring up to date the role of Italy in the affairs of Europe. If Italy had viewed with mixed feelings the German victory of 1871, she had nevertheless profited from the defeat of France: Rome finally became her capital. But as there is only one Rome and one Pope, this incorporation of Rome, a minor act in terms of power, was bound to entail unique and widespread repercussions. The government of Italy had hoped that Pope Pius IX would accept the inevitable and give it the sanction of his acquiescence in a freely negotiated treaty. Italy was prepared to be generous, but in face of the uncompromising position of the Pope, there was nothing for it but to incorporate the main lines of the proposed settlement into the unilateral Law of Guarantees of 1871, a purely Italian law. The Pope was to enjoy all the prerogatives of sovereignty, save territorial possession, and this position was scrupulously observed by the Italian state.

In the immediate past it had been France who had been the defender of Papal independence. France, after 1871, had more immediately important cares than Papal sovereignty, but the influence of French Catholics might be no less after 1871 than before 1870. Internal French affairs, therefore, remained an important concern of the Italian foreign office. For Italy, as for Bismarck, Thiers, Gambetta, the Republic, the Left in general, were the preferable elements in France. The story may be summed up very briefly: nothing happened, mainly as a result of the course of the Third Republic; it was Gambetta who uttered the phrase, "clericalism, there is the enemy." But this is retrospect: during the decade of the seventies, the Roman question ever loomed large in Italian eyes when it came to relations with France.

As for Austria, that country too was Catholic and the tradition of Austro-Italian enmity was old; the very formation of Italy is one long story of a struggle against Austria. With Germany, on the other hand, there was no conflict, but rather there had been some profitable coöperation. Bismarck's *Kulturkampf* even suggested the possibility of common ground *vis-à-vis* the Papacy. However, Bismarck had little interest, at first, in any Italian connection, one reason being his very low estimate of Italian power; moreover, Bismarck's first care was the Austrian alliance, with or without Russia. Thus nothing happened for some years despite feelers and talk and even the exchange of visits by rulers. When Crispi saw Bismarck in 1877, he found him willing to consider an alliance against France but certainly not against Austria. Here also, a long story may be summed up in Bismarck's phrase, once he came to entertain the possibility of a connection: the road to Berlin lies through Vienna. It was no easy matter to find the bases of an Austro-Italian understanding. Crispi's mission to Bismarck was a failure and the defeat of MacMahon in France served to diminish Italian fears from that quarter.

From Berlin in 1878 Italy came away empty-handed and with a sense of frustration to the extent that the cry, "Down with Austria, down with Corti, long live Trento and Trieste!" was heard throughout the country. Suggestions to Italy of compensations in Albania, in Tunis, or in Tripoli, during and shortly before the Congress, evoked no interest. As to the argument that the Austrian gain was a favorable development for Italy because it increased the likelihood of compensation in the *Irredenta*, it cannot be taken very seriously.

But the French reacted otherwise to Berlin. Inactive at the Congress from which they also came back empty-handed, three years later, in May, 1881, they established a protectorate over Tunisia.[10] The French occupation of Tunis came to Italy as a shock; it caused the fall of Cairoli whose unpreparedness for the event was somewhat less than warranted. What in some ways was worse was the isolation in which Italy found herself: neither Britain nor Germany showed any inclination to object, but both instead supported France.

This event, added to the latent concern over the Roman question, caused Italy to renew her efforts to escape from her isolation. She took the road to Berlin via Vienna and her wishes were this time rewarded, though agreement was especially difficult to reach between Rome and Vienna, where, on May 20, 1882, the first treaty of the Triple Alliance was signed. By this treaty Germany and Austria pledged themselves to go to Italy's assistance in the event of French aggression against her. The *casus foederis* would arise for all three members if one of them were attacked and found itself at war with two or more Great Powers; benevolent neutrality at least was to be observed by the other two members if the third ally had to make war on a Great Power that threatened it. In the event of a threat to the peace, the three allies would consult on necessary military measures. The treaty had a five-year duration and was to be secret and renewable.

For Germany and Austria, the main significance of the treaty was the neutralization of Italy; for this they were willing to pay the price of a guarantee against a French attack, not a very likely possibility. As to Italy, apart from this concrete asset, perhaps more imagined than real, she was no longer isolated, and though she failed to obtain the territorial guarantee that she would have liked, the Roman question was in effect removed from the international domain. It has been said with some justification that Italy and Austria must be allies or enemies, and could not in any case remain

[10] More will be said presently about the Tunisian episode. See below, pp. 186–187.

merely indifferent to each other. The alliance did not put an end to Italian irredentism, but, officially at least, irredentism must be put on ice. To a degree, the alliance had the effect of emphasizing the domestic division of the country into two camps that 1914 was to find less than ever reconciled. The so-called Right, heirs of Cavour, claimed the inheritance of the *Risorgimento;* but in broad terms it was the conservative elements in Italy that became the main supporters of the connection with the kindred conservative empires of Central Europe; by contrast, the Left, heir of the Mazzinian tradition, remained more sympathetic to liberal Republican France and increasingly identified itself with the irredentist, anti-Austrian tendency.[11]

It should be mentioned finally that Italy insisted on a declaration in connection with the treaty, though not incorporated in it, to the effect that the alliance could not "in any case be regarded as being directed against England." To this neither of her allies objected, but it was a significant enunciation of one cardinal principle of Italian foreign policy: her geography and British naval superiority forbade Italy from ever entertaining the possibility of being in a conflict on the side opposite Britain. It was a principle that served Italy well so long as she adhered to it.

At the beginning of the decade of the eighties it thus appeared that a whole network of connections had been established, the center of which was in Berlin and the threads of which were mainly in Bismarck's hands: the Triple Alliance and the *Dreikaiserbund*, supplemented by the minor Rumanian alliance and the Austro-Serb. Britain lived still in splendid isolation but her relations with Germany were friendly; what thought there may have been of a formal connection in 1879 came to nothing, but to Bismarck's inquiry while he was negotiating with Andrássy of what Britain would do in the event of a Russo-German conflict growing out of German support of Britain's and Austria's policy in the Ottoman Empire, Disraeli had replied that Britain would, in that event, keep France quiet.

Even with France, for that matter, tension was considerably relaxed during the decade that followed the war scare of 1875. Domestic French developments account for this in part; but one contributory factor was the diversion of French interest into other

---

[11] The Crispian episode, as will be indicated later, constitutes an important qualification to this statement, though it does not invalidate the general tendency of Italian liberalism.

channels, a diversion welcome to Bismarck and which he gladly encouraged. Just as in Bulgaria Bismarck was willing to be Russian, so in France he could be both imperialistic and republican.

Before resuming the main thread of the story centering in Europe proper, other developments must receive some attention.

IV. Beginnings of the New Imperialism

MEDITERRANEAN DEVELOPMENTS: TUNISIA AND EGYPT

It has been mentioned that during the first half of the nineteenth century the European urge to imperial expansion was at a relatively low ebb. The Mediterranean area, where the entire North African coast except Morocco, the eastern extremity, and the Balkans were all part of the Ottoman Empire, falls in a separate intermediate category, partaking at once of the strictly European and of the colonial. Its location and the internal conditions of the Turkish state made it an important focus of European conflicts. The competition before 1870 of the two chief Mediterranean rivals, Britain and France, has been traced in the first part of this book. By 1870 the French were firmly established in Algeria. But in many respects the whole western half of North Africa, from Carthage to Casablanca, constitutes a unit. French interest and activity in Morocco were to reach a climax at the turn of the century. To the east, Tunisian matters commanded greater urgency.

On the internal conditions of Tunisia it is unnecessary to dwell: a backward state, inefficiently managed, it was natural ground for the extension of European control. Tunisia was the meeting place of the interests of three major European Powers. The simple fact of Algerian contiguity sufficiently explains the French interest; to a point it was a negative interest in that France would not like to see another influence established in Tunisia. The Italian interest stemmed in considerable measure from simple geographic reasons. A look at the map suffices to show the continuity from Sicily to Tunisia, similar lands in many respects. If Italy was ever going to play the role of major Power and expand overseas, Tunisia was the logical step for her to take; her establishment there would, moreover, give her the strategic command of the straits at the mid-point of the whole Mediterranean between Gibraltar and Suez. Even before complete unification, Italy had developed economic interests in Tunisia where Italian settlers constituted the most numerous alien group. The British interest was essentially strategic. Britain was established at Malta and was France's traditional rival.[12] But with the appearance of a united Italy and the defeat of France by Germany, Britain came to feel that it might be preferable to have two different Powers rather than a single one in control of opposite sides of the Sicilian straits. At the Congress of Berlin Britain had indicated her willingness to see a French establishment in Tunis; Bismarck took the same view for reasons already indicated. A French conquest of Tunisia could, in addition, serve to raise an issue between France and Italy. Balance of power considerations would cause Britain as well as Germany to contemplate such a prospect with equanimity.

All this background was familiar in France as well as in Italy, and neither country reacted immediately to the suggestions made to her at Berlin, but Franco-Italian rivalry in Tunisia, in the form of competition for the acquisition of the Tunis–La Goulette railway stretch, of the activity of the Italian consul in Tunis, began to take on sharper edge. When the French cut the Gordian knot in 1881, using the pretext of border raids to send an expeditionary force and then establish a protectorate by the Treaty of Bardo in May of that year, Bismarck's behavior may be described as correct and loyal. Britain hesitated at first, but Gladstone felt that her own occupation of Cyprus gave her poor grounds for objection and he, too, acquiesced. Italy was disgruntled, turned to the Central Powers for an alliance, but clearly she could hardly entertain any thought of undoing the *fait accompli*, though she would not give it her sanction. The role of Tunisia was destined to be long and important in the story of Franco-Italian relations.

There was another aspect of the matter of possibly far-reaching consequences. Division was sharp in France on the score of the desirability of the Tunisian adventure, small though it was, for a larger issue of principle and policy was involved: should France concentrate on rebuilding her strength at home with an eye to the German danger, the lost provinces, and possible *revanche;* or should she, to a point accepting Bismarck's view, if not wholly forget, at least seek compensation elsewhere? That last motivation, as well as considerations of prestige, power, and glory, had greater relevance in the French case where, owing to

---

[12] An important consideration was the possible establishment of a naval base in Tunisia, which the French eventually built at Bizerte.

slower growth than in Britain or Germany, the economic motivation for imperial expansion was weaker. The debate on colonialism was never resolved in France, but, through alternations of emphasis, a steady program of imperial expansion was carried out by the Third Republic. The enterprise was highly successful since it made France again a large imperial Power, second to Britain alone. The establishment of the Tunisian protectorate marks the beginning of this development.

France also had an interest in Egypt, rather more important than the Tunisian, and the whole nineteenth-century story of Egypt may be written as one of Franco-British competition. On the very eve of the Franco-Prussian War, in 1869, the Suez Canal, a French undertaking, had been opened. Despite some British opposition, the project had been carried out successfully and what skepticism there was about the economic soundness of the scheme was soon dispelled by its indisputable success. French interest in Egypt proper may have been larger than British, but in terms of empire the significance of Egypt had ever loomed large, at least since the first Napoleon's expedition. The opening of the Canal emphasized and magnified the imperial importance of Egypt in strategic no less than in economic terms; Britain became by far the largest user of the Canal. From the British point of view, an opportunity had been allowed to slip.

The possibility might of course be considered of a British establishment in Egypt in connection with a general partition of the Ottoman Empire. The Russians at Constantinople and the British at Suez seemed to Bismarck a possible solution, but this ran counter to the position steadily adhered to by Britain that all such partition schemes would raise insoluble divergences among the Powers, hence could not be entertained. Undoubtedly a British seizure of Egypt would have raised a major difference with France. To a small degree Disraeli was able to retrieve the situation through his purchase of the Khedive's block of shares in the Canal Company in 1875, but this only gave Britain some voice in the affairs of the Company.

Egypt, like Tunis, was endowed—or saddled—with a ruler whose financial management was less than efficient;[13] in 1876 Khe-

---

[13] The usurious loans obtained by such rulers from European countries had the effect of involving these rulers in a vicious and deepening circle of debt and thus became one of the standard means through which initial penetration could lead to eventual political control.

dive Ismail was again in difficulty over interest payment on his debt. The French being determined to protect their interest, and Salisbury being unwilling either "to renounce or monopolize," the only solution was "sharing"; joint Anglo-French control of Egyptian finance in the form of the creation of the *Caisse de la dette publique* was the result, and Ismail's recalcitrance led to his substitution by Tewfik on orders of the still nominal suzerain of Egypt, the sultan, prodded into this action by Anglo-French pressure. This joint policy was not, however, the result of agreement, but rather of the fact that in face of the French refusal to restore Turkish authority in Egypt Britain preferred to go along with France instead of letting her act alone in Egypt. Such a state of affairs was wholly satisfactory to Bismarck, whose main interest in the matter was that Egypt should continue as a bone of contention between Britain and France.

In 1880 Gladstone succeeded Disraeli in Britain. His personal inclination and a variety of problems, ranging from Ireland to India via the Transvaal, made British reluctance to take forcible action in Egypt greater than ever, despite the fact that confusion and discontent were making the situation in that country one of near anarchy. To complicate matters even further, a nationalist movement of sorts, whose chief support was among army officers and Moslem intellectuals, had made its appearance in Egypt and was assuming an increasingly antiforeign orientation. On the European side, negotiations between Paris and London were not facilitated by the displacement of Gambetta by Freycinet in January, 1882, with a resultant discontinuity of policy on France's part.

Those were not the days, however, when European Powers or their nationals could with impunity be threatened. British and French naval forces appeared before Alexandria, and when riots in June resulted in the killing of some Europeans, the British fleet bombarded the forts. But at this point the French squadron withdrew, Freycinet being overthrown in the French Parliament when he proposed joint intervention. Britain was now left alone.[14] A British land force thoroughly defeated the Egyptian army in September and Arabi Pasha, leader of the army group, was eliminated as an active force.

Here was a somewhat curious situation. The saying that the

[14] For the sake of avoiding unilateral intervention, Gladstone tried to induce the Italians to join the British if the French would not, but the Italians also refused participation.

British Empire was built in a fit of absent-mindedness often evokes a smile of incredulity, yet here was an example of the process in operation. Things had developed without organized plan or deliberate intention and Gladstone was anything but happy at the turn of events; he kept insisting—and meant it—that the British occupation would momentarily cease, a statement reiterated with frequency over the passing decades. But clearly, order must first be restored; having become involved in reëstablishing the functioning of disorganized Egyptian finances, the tale became one of deepening involvement instead of withdrawal. The story of this growth of British interest along the Nile is an outstanding chapter of the new imperialism which was destined to have increasingly important repercussions on the relations of the states of Europe among themselves.

As far as Egypt was concerned, the British position continued to remain ambiguous. The everlasting temporariness of British occupation made Britain, to a point, a hostage. France was understandably irked at feeling herself displaced, which in effect she was; yet her rights were not altered any more than those of others and it was always possible to create embarrassment for Britain in Egypt. Bismarck was not blind to this result, but in view of her past history, Egypt continued to be primarily a source of Anglo-French irritation. As to Egypt herself, an excellent job of financial restoration was done by Sir Evelyn Baring (later to become Lord Cromer) that was equally profitable to all. For the better part of two decades the French were always ready to use so convenient a source of diplomatic embarrassment to England. Clearly, there was no question of France resorting to force in order to oust Britain from Egypt, though when the two countries found themselves on the verge of war in 1898, it was over the control of the Nile. Up that river the British moved, always bent upon keeping or restoring order, until by 1885 they were fighting in the Sudan, where the policy of reluctant involvement supported by insufficient means of action resulted in a momentary setback for them.

IMPERIALISM IN ASIA AND ELSEWHERE IN AFRICA

Not around the Mediterranean alone was the imperial interest of Europe manifesting itself; the tentacles of European power were reaching out over the entire face of the planet. This expansive force was enormous; in vivid and concrete terms its effects may be seen by comparing the map of Africa in 1880, for

example, with that of 1900. During the period until 1890, however, there was still ample room for all, with the consequence
that the bases were laid at this time for further penetration and
expansion and for the eventual meeting and clash of rival imperial
interests. It will be useful, if only sketchily, to enumerate the
main foci of the initial phase of this European expansion.

If Gladstone was a reluctant imperialist, the very existence of
Britain had for so long been geared to her Empire that even he
could not withstand the expansive force of the British imperial
tradition. The case of Egypt has just been mentioned. The renewed expansion was not the result of organized and conscious
planning by the government, but rather of the activity of groups
of dedicated individuals; some of it was the work of chartered
companies of the old type. In Africa, during the eighties, the
foundations were laid of British Somaliland (1884), Nigeria (1886),
and British East Africa (1889), while the Cape Colony was an
obvious base for northern expansion.

Asia was of even greater importance. In India, the largest British interest, the old Company had been superseded by the British
state in 1858, and one may speak of a more clearly organized
direction of policy. To the east and west the tendency was also
to expand, partly for purposes of defensive security. A mission
had gone into Afghanistan in 1879 but trouble persisted on the
Northwest Frontier, leading to armed intervention until relative
stability was achieved in 1885. The same year saw the establishment of the protectorate of Burma on the opposite side of India.

In the Pacific, too, British influence was extending its reach.
An establishment in New Guinea (1883) and in North Borneo
(1888) followed an earlier one in the Fiji Islands (1874), while
a condominium with France was set up in the New Hebrides in
1887. The internal evolution of the British Empire and the trend
of this evolution need not concern us at this point and in this
connection.

Imperial development had less *raison d'être* for France. But
the movement, launched in 1881, despite the Egyptian events of
the following year, on the whole continued. In the French case
also, the work of imperial expansion was done by a handful of
men, though by contrast with the British, the military role is
more conspicuous in the French case. There were also conscious
imperialists in the government, such as Jules Ferry, the most
notable, during the decade of the eighties. From the North African base of Algeria and from the old Senegalese possession, from

new establishments on the Ivory Coast and in Dahomey, French influence converged toward Lake Chad, the Niger, and the equatorial Congo, while it was also penetrating the island of Madagascar.

In farther Asia the Annamese protectorate, established in 1874, was a new base of expansion. Though Ferry came to grief in Tonkin, where the French met temporary setbacks that caused his downfall, the French hold on that territory was made good after war with China and the Treaty of Tientsin in 1884. The various segments of the Southeastern extremity of Asia could be consolidated into the dependency of Indochina.

Russian imperialism has inevitably a character different from either the British or the French because of the contiguity of the lands into which it flows, whereas the former are of necessity directed overseas. The growth of Russia, ever reaching out for the open seas, rather bears some resemblance to the American, taking the form of an expansion of the initial core; it was imperial, none the less. In addition, the urge of Russian expansion has shown a general tendency to concentrate its pressure in a particular direction at a time. The setback of 1878 was followed by an intensified and more vigorous pressure in Central Asia; Persia and the back door of India, Afghanistan, were the objects of this renewed Russian interest, as well as Turkestan, concerning which treaties were made with China in 1879 and 1881.

In their expansion, Britain, France, and Russia had old traditions to fall back upon. Save in the Balkans, where her interest was as much a matter of purely European equilibrium, Austria-Hungary cannot be regarded as an imperial Power. But Germany and Italy were newcomers on the scene. After 1871, Bismarck took the position that Germany was a contented Power, with ample scope for her activity in Europe where her interests should remain confined. He was willing to recognize the prior imperial claims of Britain, France, and Russia, feeling that imperial activity would constitute for Germany a diversion of strength and a potential source of unnecessary conflicts. That a colonial party should make its appearance in Germany is perhaps not surprising if one thinks of the astonishingly rapid growth of that country and of that component of imperialism that is economic. Bismarck at first looked askance at the prospect of overseas expansion, but eventually accepted it for two reasons: domestic pressure and the opportunities which it offered to his European diplomacy. From about 1884 Africa was an object of Germany's colonial interest: East Africa, Southwest Africa, the Cameroons, and Togoland were the four places on that continent where German colonies became established, while Germany also made her appearance in the Pacific and developed substantial economic interests in the Far East. Despite Bismarck's earlier observation about the value to him of the Ottoman Empire, the end of the decade of the eighties also witnessed the beginning of direct German interest in that quarter.

Italy did not have the justification of power and economic growth that Germany could advance for imperial activity; the argument of population pressure is essentially devoid of validity. But she, too, albeit in a modest way, began to share in the imperial race. As Mancini put it some time after the Tunisian disillusion, "The keys to the Mediterranean lie in the Red Sea." Beginning in 1882, at Assab, on that sea, then at Massowa in 1885, the foundation of the Eritrean colony was planted; a little later, in 1889, Italy established herself in Somaliland.

The Dutch and the Portuguese had remnants of former empires. Small Powers, they were not engaged in the new colonial expansion, their possessions, especially the Portuguese, being preserved to them rather as the result of rivalry and balance among the other participants. But one special instance of colonial activity must be mentioned. Out of the Brussels Geographic Congress in 1876 and of Stanley's African explorations grew the Congo International Association and eventually a large private undertaking of which King Leopold of the Belgians was head. It was in order to regulate differences growing out of this situation specifically with Portugal, that a colonial conference met in Berlin from November, 1884, to February, 1885. As part of its activity this gathering endeavored to put some order in the process of colonial expansion, dealing with such issues as the effectiveness of occupation, claims to the hinterland deriving from coastal possession, the obligation of notification to others; its decisions were registered in the Act of Berlin of 1885. Out of the conference also grew the recognition of the Independent State of the Congo, whose frontiers were fixed and the government of which was entrusted to King Leopold personally, not to Belgium.[15] One

[15] The Berlin conference decreed the open door for the Congo, but a subsequent meeting at Brussels in 1889 allowed the imposition of tariffs. The decision of 1885 was the origin of the Belgian Congo. When in financial

aftermath of the Berlin colonial conference was an intensification of the race for empire.

It has also been pointed out that in the early stages of this competition there was room for all, hence, relatively speaking, a minimum of friction among the colonial Powers. But the awareness of potential conflict was present. Britain, by far the first imperial Power, claimed no monopolistic right to empire, but she would naturally resist encroachment on her established positions by others; it must be pointed out, however, that the requirements of security automatically tend to point to ever-widening circles of control. Also, Anglo-French and Anglo-Russian imperial rivalries were old. There was a near Anglo-Russian crisis following the Russian defeat of the Afghans at Pendjeh in 1885. To the east of India, Britain in Burma and France in Indochina were surrounding still independent Siam. Britain and France met in Africa in a variety of places besides Egypt.

Bismarck was less interested in colonies for Germany for their own sake than in the consequences of colonial activity on the relations and alignments of the Powers in Europe. Russia's Central Asian expansion was encouraged by the existence of the *Dreikaiserbund;* to Bismarck this Russian activity had the double advantage of diverting Russian interest from the region of possible conflict with Austria, the Balkans, to one where it would meet British opposition. Similarly in the case of France, Bismarck was favorable to an imperial activity that could divert France's strength and attention away from the Rhine while at the same time possibly embroiling her with Britain. Considerations of equilibrium again were responsible for Britain's sympathy for Italy's Red Sea interest since France was Britain's chief opponent in Egypt.

But, to repeat, these conflicts of imperial character were in the main more potential than actual before 1890. It was in Europe proper that the main focus of European diplomacy lay and to the European scene we must return.

V. The End of the Bismarckian System

FRANCE AND BULGARIA

In Bismarck's courting of both Russia and France might be seen the seed of a continental league which could only be anti-

---

difficulties in 1890, King Leopold borrowed 25,000,000 francs from the Belgian state which was, in return, to inherit the Congo, and did.

British in its orientation and the formation of which, should it seem to materialize, Britain was bound to seek to prevent. But this did not prove necessary, for the differences among the continental Powers were sufficient to prevent their union. These differences had two main foci.

Franco-German relations had indeed improved for a time, but if the gulf dug between the two countries by Bismarck himself in 1871 were ever to be bridged, much time would have to pass. Relations could be correct, and even to a point friendly, but the one thing Bismarck required, France's willing acceptance of the *fait accompli*, was precisely the one that was beyond realization. The situation is perhaps best summed up in the words of the French ambassador in Berlin reporting to Ferry in 1884: "At the beginning of our discussions I specified with Count Hatzfeldt and with the Chancellor himself that neither Alsace nor Lorraine should ever be a question between us, that here was a domain reserved on both sides where we ought to be forbidden to penetrate. . . . I shall never speak of Alsace, I have said; and on your part, if you sincerely desire an understanding with us on various points, avoid drawing the sword over our wound, because the French nation will not remain in control of her feelings."[16] Even when relations were at their best, at the official level, the hope of *revanche* was kept alive in France; it seemed to increase during the early part of the decade if one is to judge by the activities of the *Ligue des Patriotes*, of Déroulède, and of sections of the French press. Following the fall of Jules Ferry in May, 1885, the nationalist fever that seemed to have seized the country was strongly reflected in the elections of the following October. The movement had, moreover, found a symbolic standard-bearer in the person of General Boulanger, a dashing figure on horseback, but, as the event was to prove, little more than that. Though mostly froth, the agitation seemed for a time impressive; General Boulanger became war minister in May, 1886. The leaders of the Third Republic were sane and sober men, solid bourgeois little attracted by the prospect of adventure, and indeed the German ambassador appraised the agitation at its true, mostly superficial, worth. However, the past French record was not devoid of adventures; partly by way of authentic precaution, partly because it suited his book in other respects, Bismarck ostensibly attached a fair amount of importance to the Boulanger episode in France.

[16] De Courcel to Ferry, December 3, 1884. Cited in Fay, *op. cit.*, p. 100.

But more important, after all, in the Bismarckian system were affairs in the East. There, the revived *Dreikaiserbund* of 1881 was, after passing hesitation, renewed in 1884. But the meeting of the three emperors at Skiernewice in September was largely a disappointment, leading to no concrete results. The basic flaw in the *Dreikaiserbund* lay in the Austro-Russian relationship and the persisting mutual suspicion that prevailed in it. This in turn may be regarded as owing to the fact that, for reasons of her own internal nature and problems, Austria-Hungary could never make up her mind to an extension of herself in the Balkans; as a consequence, Austria, unlike Bismarck, was unwilling to be Russian in Bulgaria but instead sought to minimize and check the influence of Russia in the eastern half of the Peninsula. Bismarck's dividing line did not remain uncrossed and his Balkan policy, hence the *Dreikaiserbund*, was destined to be a failure.

In actual fact, and quite apart from Austrian opposition, Russia was having troubles of her own in Bulgaria. From the Bulgarian point of view in general, the settlement of 1878 was a source of deep disappointment at the failure to bring Greater Bulgaria into existence; the degree of control that Russia could exercise over Bulgaria was limited and her occupation, though brief, had been less than popular. In addition, we may observe again in this region and at this time a manifestation of that recurrent Russian failing, lack of coördination of policy. The divergence between the military and the diplomats became a factor in Bulgarian politics in which it was exploited for purposes of independent action. Thus, Prince Alexander of Battenberg, though Russia's choice, came to incur the displeasure of Tsar Alexander III.

The actual crisis opened with an outbreak in Eastern Roumelia on September 18, 1885, followed the next day by Prince Alexander's proclamation of the union of that province with Bulgaria. Turkish intervention to maintain the settlement of Berlin might have resolved the issue, but Turkey was instead content to appeal to the Powers. Meanwhile a new complication arose from the Serbian claim to compensation for the enlargement of Bulgaria, the Serbian declaration of war in November, and the prompt Bulgarian defeat of Serbia from the consequences of which Serbia was saved by Austrian intervention alone. Bismarck, at this point, made use of the influence which derived from the Austro-German alliance of 1879 to exert a restraining hand by clearly indicating to Austria that a conflict with Russia arising out of Austrian armed intervention would not find Germany at her side; the alliance intended as an instrument of stability and peace was used to serve these ends on this occasion. But the recrudescence of Austro-Russian distrust was outside his control.

Nevertheless, the first crisis seemed to have been surmounted through the acceptance by the Powers in April, 1886, of the compromise solution of a personal union of Bulgaria and Eastern Roumelia. But new complications ensued from the nature of Russo-Bulgarian relations: in August, a group of pro-Russian officers kidnapped Prince Alexander who was forced to leave. He contrived to return in September, whereupon pressure from the tsar resulted in his abdication. In November relations were broken between the two countries. If this was a prelude to armed Russian intervention, as was suspected in Vienna, the question was raised anew of what action Vienna should decide to take.

Neither Bismarck nor Britain, where Salisbury was again in office, wanted war; but neither wanted to incur Russian displeasure alone and therefore hoped that the other would be first to take on the onus of restraining Russia through indicating its support of Austria. This in turn raised the question of the French attitude. Would France use the occasion, by giving her support to Russia, to open other issues, and if so, what issues? Would she turn against Britain or Germany? Between those two countries an Alphonse and Gaston situation developed through the hinted possibility that either might restrain France against the other. Actually, French policy was highly cautious, for all that these events took place in the midst of the nationalistic Boulangist agitation. Nevertheless, real or supposed French danger was Bismarck's main argument in support of the new army bill passed by the Reichstag in March, 1887.[17]

THE TRIPLE ALLIANCE AND THE MEDITERRANEAN AGREEMENTS

What precedes makes it appear that the year 1887 opened under clouded and uncertain prospects. The complex relationships involved in intricate issues gave ample scope for diplomatic activity, which was intense during that year. The fact that 1887

[17] The bill was first presented to the Reichstag in November, 1886. After it was rejected, the Reichstag was dissolved and the ensuing election gave Bismarck the desired majority. Bismarck showed annoyance at Münster, his ambassador in Paris, for the latter's reports playing down the importance of the French nationalist agitation.

was also a year of economic crisis did not, needless to say, serve to alleviate tensions.

The adumbration, or in some quarters the fear, of a Franco-Russian connection was balanced by the possibility of an Anglo-German one. In the stalemate of fencing for position Italy became the center of considerable activity, behind much of which the directing guidance of Bismarck's hand is to be found. Since 1882 Italy was a member of the Triple Alliance, but that association had given less than satisfaction to its members. Austria was irked by continuing manifestations of Italian Irredentism and Bismarck for his part feared that Italy was interested in making use of the support of the alliance for aggressive purposes and imperial adventures in which he had no wish to see Germany entangled. On her side Italy felt that she had derived little benefit from the alliance, the renewal of which seemed doubtful for a time; Robilant's inquiries in 1885 met with a cold reception and the matter was dropped for the moment.

But as the date of expiration of the treaty approached the situation had changed considerably. From Bismarck's point of view both France and the Balkans were centers of uncertainty, especially as Robilant had dangled before him the possibility of a Franco-Italian connection. The result of this state of affairs was that not only was the alliance renewed, on February 20, 1887, but this was done largely on Italy's own terms. The new alliance of 1887 consisted of three instruments, the original treaty of 1882, to which were added separate Italo-German and Italo-Austrian treaties. From Germany, Italy gained the desired promise of support for her colonial ambitions: the *casus foederis* would arise in the event that Italy should find herself at war with France as a consequence of French action in Tripoli or Morocco; also, in the event of war, Germany would not object to Italian claims against France proper; in obvious though not stated terms this meant Corsica, Nice, and Savoy. This was undoubtedly going rather beyond the letter and the spirit of the earlier alliance, clearly defensive in character, even though Bismarck had no qualms about reassuring France that he had no intention of supporting Italian colonial ambitions.

With the Austrian Kálnoky negotiations were difficult and Bismarck had to exert some pressure on his Austrian ally. The chief significance of the Austro-Italian treaty lay in the following part of its first Article, destined to have considerable later importance. It read as follows:

> If, in the course of events, the maintenance of the *status quo* in the regions of the Balkans or of the Ottoman coasts and islands in the Adriatic and in the Aegean Sea should become impossible, and if, whether in consequence of the action of a Third Power or otherwise, Austria-Hungary or Italy should find themselves under the necessity of modifying it by a temporary or permanent occupation on their part, this occupation shall take place only after a previous agreement between the two Powers aforesaid, based upon the principle of reciprocal compensation for any advantage, territorial or otherwise, which each of them might obtain beyond the present *status quo* and giving satisfaction to the interests and well founded claims of the two parties.

What, in effect, this meant was that Italy had secured from Austria the recognition of a position of equality in the Balkans. From the Italian point of view this was clear gain, though for Austria it meant that an added complication and encumbrance had been introduced into the operation of her Balkan policy. The treaties of 1887 constitute an important landmark in the development of Italian foreign policy, a staking out of claims in regions of prime concern to her; they may also be regarded as a recognition by others of enhanced Italian power, but most of all of the skillful Italian use of the balance of power, albeit for not unreasonable aims.

Thus, it appears that in the context of Europe as a whole Bismarck and Kálnoky were willing to pay a price to preserve the Italian alliance, hence indirectly their own positions. Interestingly, the treaties of 1887 were not accompanied by a renewal of the Mancini declaration of 1882,[18] a fact which may be related to the highly cordial state of relations between Britain and all three members of the Triple Alliance at this time. The renewal of February 20 was in fact preceded by a week (February 12) by the signature of the first so-called "Mediterranean agreement" between Britain and Italy. Bismarck had deftly fostered this agreement and it was Salisbury who first suggested it to Italy. It came to nothing more in the end than an innocuous declaration of the common desire to maintain the *status quo* in the Mediterranean and to coöperate to that end; Bismarck and Italy would have liked a stronger statement but Britain would not commit herself

[18] This was the statement, insisted upon by Mancini, that the alliance would, in no event, operate against Britain.

further at this point;[19] as Salisbury put it to Queen Victoria: "It is as close an alliance as the Parliamentary character of our institutions will permit." A similar exchange, with particular reference to the Aegean and the Black Sea, though not specifically mentioning the Balkans, took place between Salisbury and Kálnoky on March 24; even Spain was brought into the picture through an agreement with Italy on May 4.

Rome thus appears as the meeting point of two axes, the Triple Alliance and the Mediterranean. Though Germany was directly involved in the first combination only, Bismarck had had a hand in the shaping of both arrangements and the Mediterranean agreements have sometimes been presented as the crowning climax of his diplomacy. Ostensibly, Britain had gone some distance in associating herself with the Powers of the Triple Alliance with whom her relations were indeed good. It will also appear that from these various combinations two Powers were excluded, Russia and France. Yet this appearance was, to a degree, misleading and superficial. Britain and France had differences in Egypt but there seemed to be little likelihood of an open conflict on that score and Britain had little to fear from France with whom Salisbury, despite superficial annoyance, was not loath to contemplate accommodation.

Even between France and Germany the situation was better than surface appearance might seem to indicate. Friction existed, to be sure, which the Schnaebele incident[20] and the Boulangist agitation kept alive. But in May, 1887, the handsome General was dropped from the government and, though the first reaction to this was an increase of his popularity, the determination of the leaders of the Republic effectively disposed of this apparent danger.[21] Nevertheless, while a seeming danger existed, it was more than ever desirable to keep France isolated. This Bismarck did successfully. The one possible flaw in his system was the isolation

[19] Robilant had proposed that the agreement include a promise of mutual support in the event of war with France, but, despite Bismarck's arguments, Salisbury refused to bind Britain to so definite a commitment.

[20] In April, 1887, Schnaebele, a minor French police official, was arrested on German soil whither he had gone on business by invitation. A great outcry was raised by the French press, but, upon ascertaining the facts, Bismarck ordered his release and offered a near apology.

[21] Boulanger was elected to the Chamber by several constituencies in 1888 and 1889. There was talk of a *coup d'état*, but Boulanger was not made of the necessary stuff. When expected to lead a march on the Elysée he disappeared instead. The movement could not survive the awkwardness and ridicule of his flight to Brussels and the election of 1889 was an endorsement of the Republic.

of Russia with the consequent possibility of a Franco-Russian connection, raising the specter of the war on two fronts. Of such a connection there were advocates in both Russia and France.

BISMARCK AND RUSSIA: THE REINSURANCE TREATY

The second breakdown of the *Dreikaiserbund* as a result of the Balkan complications of 1885 was beyond Bismarck's power to prevent. The issue for that matter was not yet resolved in 1887 and to rebuild once more the tripartite association was not in the domain of the possible. But since there was no direct German quarrel with Russia, some Russo-German connection might be contrived; it too had partisans in both Russia and Germany. However, since Bismarck regarded the Austrian alliance as a fixed point, in view of the state of Austro-Russian relations, the problem was how to reconcile the seemingly irreconcilable. The answer was the so-called "Reinsurance Treaty" of June 18, 1887.

The manner in which Bismarck reconciled his Austrian alliance with his desire to guard against a Franco-Russian coalition found expression in the undertaking that Germany and Russia would each maintain a benevolent neutrality in the event that the other found itself at war with a third Great Power, with the qualification that this provision did not apply to an aggressive war of Russia against Austria or of Germany against France. Allowing that "aggression" is open to interpretation, this was the price that Bismarck had to pay: it was within his control whether or not to attack France—this he had no intention of doing for all his playing up of the French danger—and Russia was forewarned in unambiguous terms that an attack by her against Austria meant that she would have to face Germany as well; capable of appreciating that even frankness can be of use in negotiations, during the course of these Bismarck had recourse to the rather sensational gesture of showing to Shuvalov, the Russian ambassador, the text of the treaty of 1879. For that matter Russia was more interested in the Straits and the Balkans than in defending France. The legitimacy of Russia's preponderant influence in Bulgaria and in Eastern Roumelia was recognized by Bismarck (Article 2) who went even further by promising, in an additional protocol, German neutrality, and even moral and diplomatic support, "if H. M. the Emperor of Russia finds himself compelled to defend the entrance to the Black Sea in order to safeguard his interests." In simple language, Germany would not oppose Russian control of Constantinople and the Straits.

The Reinsurance Treaty was not an instrument of aggression and may rather be viewed as an additional device to preserve equilibrium and peace; like the Mediterranean agreements, and in combination with them, it has sometimes been regarded as the great masterpiece and crowning accomplishment of Bismarckian diplomacy. The secrecy of it was highly guarded—it would have made strange reading in London or in Vienna. For all that in strict logic and law the Reinsurance Treaty was not inconsistent with Germany's other commitments, the matter of intent becomes at this point of paramount importance. The Reinsurance Treaty has also been described as a breach of faith, mainly toward Austria; but if breach of faith or double-dealing act, it was so rather toward Russia than Austria. That, in the circumstances, the arrangement was a skillful device to reconcile the hardly reconcilable may be granted, but it may also be characterized as a tortuous piece of diplomacy, a tightrope walking act, the chief aspect of which was its fragility. Politics is the art of the possible and, like diplomacy, concerns itself with the immediate; but it cannot escape the consequences of the direction it imparts to the course of events.

The ink was barely dry on the signature of the Reinsurance Treaty when the unresolved Bulgarian situation flared up again. The choice in July of Ferdinand of Saxe-Coburg as ruler by the Bulgarian Assembly aroused anew Russian suspicion of Vienna no less than of Berlin and seemed likely to precipitate Russian intervention. If Bismarck would not side with Russia against Austria in the matter of the Bulgarian prince, he did unquestionably make it clear to Austria that he would not support her in a conflict at this point. His problem was how to produce sufficient force to restrain possible Russian action; having just stated his own willingness to allow Russian designs freedom of scope, even support, others must do the task.

Italy seemed a suitable and willing tool. Following the mild compromiser Depretis, Crispi had become Prime Minister, in charge of the foreign office as well, in August, 1887. Crispi belonged to the Left and had been active in the making of Italy, though he belonged rather to the flamboyant Garibaldian tradition than to that of the quieter statesmanship of Cavour. Not devoid of ability, and even less of energy, he was given to dreams of grandeur for Italy; the French epithet *brouillon* befits some of his activity. A strong personality, like other liberals in opposition, his tendency once in power was toward the authoritarian. Crispi also was strongly, and in large measure unwarrantedly, highly suspicious of French intentions toward Italy.

When Crispi went to see Bismarck at Friedrichsruhe in October, the latter found little difficulty in making him serve his purpose. It was perhaps somewhat surprising to find the Italian patriot offering the Austrian ambassador Italian military assistance against Russia; Bismarck was satisfied to use Italy as the instrument of a strengthened Mediterranean axis joining Britain and Austria. This was the meaning of the exchange of notes between the Austrian ambassador in London and Salisbury on December 12, subscribed to by Italy and sometimes called the second Mediterranean agreement. Here was a characteristic illustration of Bismarckian technique: while assuring Russia of his support of her desires, with his left hand he was encouraging others to resist these same Russian ambitions; this would make his Reinsurance commitment innocuous and safe and is the reason why his policy toward Russia has been charged with tortuousness and disingenuousness.[22] Yet in their different ways both Germany and Britain wanted the same thing in the East: peace and the *status quo;* satisfied that Russia alone was powerless and would not initiate aggression, Bismarck would restrain his allies. His own military, willing to contemplate a preventive war against Russia, he squelched; the Austrian effort to clarify the conditions of such a war yielded no more than publication, on February 3, 1888, of the Austro-German treaty.[23]

THE END OF BISMARCK'S "REIGN"

As to Italy, Crispi was much concerned with France and was therefore desirous of strengthening the Triple Alliance. In January, 1888, an Italo-German convention specified the conditions of military action: Italy's main effort would be along the Alps

---

[22] Salisbury's objection to notification of the agreement to Turkey, whose resistance to Russia it was intended to bolster, is an indication of Britain's hedging policy.

[23] Austria obtained the suppression, in the publication, of the time limit of the treaty with the result of conveying to others the impression of the permanency of the alliance, a condition she had endeavored to obtain but which Bismarck had resisted.

and she would send some forces on the Rhine. With Austria he failed to make arrangements for military and naval coöperation. Crispi's suspicion and dislike of France were cordially reciprocated. French attempts at pressure merely stiffened Italian resistance and the relations between the two countries entered a highly unsatisfactory phase of which the outbreak of a tariff war in 1888 was one manifestation.

At the opening of the year 1888 the picture of European relations may be summarized in the words of A. J. P. Taylor: "The balance which Bismarck had created at the beginning of 1888 was a curious one. Russia received diplomatic support at Constantinople from France and Germany, and was opposed there by the three Powers of the Mediterranean entente; on the other hand, Salisbury, not Bismarck, restrained this entente from turning against France."[24] Such a state of affairs constituted a highly unstable equilibrium wherein Bismarck might find ample scope for his tightrope walking abilities. But the question could fairly be raised, for how long?

The year 1888 might in fact be taken as the one during which the new orientation began to shape itself. Bismarck and Emperor William were both old men. On March 9 the Emperor died. His successor, Frederick, survived him for a bare three months, whereupon, in July, the German throne was mounted by the man destined to be the last German Kaiser, William II. The new Emperor was a curious figure, in many ways an apt, if unfortunate, representative of the new Germany, a Germany that Bismarck himself had done so much to bring into existence and mold. It was a Germany conscious of her success and of her growing power, one also that displayed some of the characteristics that commonly attend too rapid an ascent: impatient of recognition, unduly conscious of having earned a place that older, longer established Powers, seemed slow in granting adequate acknowledgment; hence highly sensitive and "touchy," ready to see slights where none were intended. Such a Germany was in need more than ever of the steadying hand of a Bismarck who, whatever one may think of the man and his methods, did undeniably possess a strong sense of reality.

But William II was very conscious of his own position within the German system no less than of the place of Germany among the Powers. In modern parlance some would say that he, like Germany, was afflicted by an inferiority complex. In addition to

[24] Taylor, *op. cit.*, p. 325.

this, William II was highly erratic, to the point that there were those in later years who came to question his sanity. A clash of personalities between the young emperor and his old, by now crotchety, chancellor, was the least that could be expected. Bismarck, in fact and quite rightly, though respectful of the monarchical institution, had become accustomed to making his own decisions, in which activity the old emperor had, very sensibly, given him an increasingly free hand.

William II had his own ideas on policy, foreign no less than domestic; they were often rather "half baked" and leaning toward the sensational. Under these conditions Bismarck carried on for a time, but control was slipping out of his hands. The great difficulty lay on the Russian side. Impressionable and lacking self-control, the Kaiser was very free with his speech. Not overmuch importance should be attached to his statement to Francis Joseph on the occasion of the latter's visit to Berlin in August 1889 that an Austrian mobilization, for whatever reasons, would be followed immediately by a German. His ostentatious visit to the sultan in November of the same year, appropriate manifestation as it was of Germany's direct and growing interest in the Ottoman Empire, nonetheless augured ill for the future of Russo-German cooperation; Tsar Alexander's visit to Berlin in October had been less than successful. All this did not represent an organized and consciously thought out anti-Russian orientation, rather the failure to think out the implications of one's acts.

If Russian friendship were to be lost, a closer connection with Britain might be a logical alternative. But nothing came of the approaches of Bismarck to Salisbury in January, 1889, with a view to an alliance directed against France. There was as yet in Britain no appreciable fear or suspicion of Germany. On the contrary, the feeling had been gaining ground of too great a British dependence on others—*vide* the Mediterranean agreements—a dependence due, however, not to British weakness but rather to the existing state of British armaments. This could be remedied; a Naval Defence Act was passed in March, 1889, to secure the independence of British policy, another aspect of which was the adoption of the two-power standard.[25]

It was during this very period that minor additional sources of friction developed between Russia and Germany: Russian land

---

[25] The two-power standard meant the decision on Britain's part to maintain a navy as large as the combined navies of the two naval Powers next in line of importance.

legislation annoying to the latter, Russian financial difficulties in Berlin irritating to the former. In October, 1888, the first Russian loan of 500,000,000 francs was very successfully floated in Paris;[26] the first of a long series, it was shortly followed, in January, 1889, by a substantial Russian order for rifles in France while Russian Grand Dukes were made welcome in Paris. A Russian loan in Paris and even an order for arms are not to be equated with an alliance. But the trend of things gave particular importance to the fate of the three-year Reinsurance Treaty of 1887. It was in March, 1890, that the formal break took place between Bismarck and Kaiser William II. The occasion for it was a domestic issue, but one of its consequences was the German refusal to extend the Reinsurance Treaty.[27] Even then the situation, from the German point of view, was by no means irretrievable, but since, instead of being redressed, the drift of things continued in the same direction, the dismissal of Bismarck constitutes a convenient landmark and an important turning point in the story of the affairs of Europe.

Up to that point, Germany, under his guidance, had been at the center of the story, to a large extent, though not exclusively, in the capacity of director of the course of relationships and events. That Bismarck was a master of statecraft may be granted, especially of that statecraft that deals with the immediate and provisional—how far the future can be planned is forever a question—but he also did things and set in motion forces that served to shape the future as well as dealing with the present. Peace he strove to maintain, though the fact must be borne in mind that his task was made easier by the predominance of power that he could command; if only an Austro-Russian clash could be prevented, he had sufficient power at his disposal to discourage any would-be disturber of that peace. After him Germany continues to remain at the center of the relations of Europe; but, partly because there was no Bismarck, partly because of the operation of some of the very forces that he had helped release—how Bismarck would have dealt with them makes for interesting speculation—she remains the central factor in Europe in an entirely different capacity, increasingly the object of hostile reaction from others. With that tale we may now proceed.

---

[26] The tariff war with Italy had, among other effects, that of stopping the flow to that country of French capital which was, as a consequence, available for investment elsewhere.

[27] The reasons for this decision will be discussed in the next chapter.

VII *The Realignment of Power, 1890-1904*

On the score of what action to take with respect to the Re-insurance Treaty, the governing opinion of Germany was divided. Bismarck's successor was Caprivi, a man of military background, whose competence in the domain of foreign affairs, like that of his secretary of state in that department, Marschall, is perhaps best expressed in the French quip that he was *étranger aux affaires*. The views of the permanent officials of the foreign office would, in the circumstances, carry greater weight. Thus it happened that the advice of Friedrich von Holstein became of considerable importance in shaping the future course of Germany from this time until his retirement in 1906. Holstein has often been called the evil genius of Germany; this description is fitting in the sense that his tenure of office and his influence are associated with policies that turned out to be disastrous. Yet Holstein has been to a degree maligned;[1] the reasons he advanced against the renewal of the Reinsurance Treaty—its ambiguity, its possible effect on relations with Austria should it come to be known—were not devoid of cogency. The Kaiser in the end allowed his initial preference to be overcome and the treaty was allowed to lapse.

But if the reasons for this decision had validity, in view of the fact that the treaty had been in existence, the German refusal to continue the arrangement could not but assume the significance of a change in the orientation of German policy, especially since, on the Russian side, Giers in particular was anxious to renew the treaty. In Russian eyes the German decision was bound to appear less than friendly. Yet nothing need be irrevocably lost; the broken wire to St. Petersburg might be mended, as it had been before,

---

[1] The Holstein papers have been published but do not seem to be very revealing. Norman Rich and M. H. Fisher (eds.), *The Holstein Papers*, 2 Vols., Cambridge (England), The University Press, 1955-1957.

after 1878 and after 1885, for instance. The tradition of Russo-German friendship had old roots and, on both sides, many were partisans of its continuance. The period that begins with the fall of Bismarck is one of readjustment in the relations of power, one during which fluidity characterizes these relations that had the possibility of evolving in a variety of divergent directions. It took some fifteen years before a new pattern emerged, when, in place of the Bismarckian system in which Berlin stood at the center of all connections, Europe became divided into two increasingly rival and fairly evenly balanced camps.

The period is characterized by the continued economic growth of Europe, a process which absorbed much of the energy of her nations and acted as a safety valve; but this continued growth also had the effect of creating new or increasing old frictions among the European Powers, mainly out of their imperial expansion. In 1890 the Triple Alliance was a solid structure, but Russia, Britain, and France were essentially unattached. This isolation was still considered largely satisfactory by Britain, but less so by either Russia or France, especially the latter, kept in that state for twenty years by Bismarckian diplomacy but ever anxious to escape from it. Between either of these last two countries and Britain sources of frictions were old and well established, and it was one of the basic assumptions of German foreign policy that these differences were beyond composition. The ensuing story might be told around the theme of how the fallacy of German assumptions was proved.

I. The Franco-Russian Alliance

Between Russia and France there were no major points of either contact or difference, save to a minor degree the Near East; yet in this case also the assumption was made by Germany in 1890 that France and Russia would not come together. If the assumption were correct, it would then be safe to sever the German connection with Russia. The first major development of the nineties was the formation of the Franco-Russian alliance, the first important breach in the Bismarckian system.

The German assumption could indeed be defended. It takes a common interest in order to build an alliance; wherein lay the common interest between Russia and France? Russian interest was at the Straits and in farther Asia; France was indifferent to the second and, if anything, inimical to the first, and certainly France had no wish of involvement for the sake of such interests. Moreover, as between Germany and Russia, though relations may have deteriorated, there was little apparent cause for direct conflict. It was otherwise with France where suspicion of Germany persisted as well as the hope, remote but real, of recovery of the lost provinces. But this French interest left Russia totally unmoved and Russia on her side had certainly no wish to go to war for the sake of Alsace-Lorraine. Unless it were for purposes of general aggression, the real binder of a Franco-Russian connection could only be common fear of Germany. Nor should what we now call "ideological divergence" be ignored. It is well to remember that, in the nineties, France was the only republic among the major states of Europe; among crowned heads, most of all for the tsar, a republic was less than respectable and in itself suspect; France was the country which, though ruled by staid bourgeois, gave free scope to the voicing of subversive ideas, in religion no less than in politics, the haven whither political malcontents of all ilk found shelter and welcome. Godless Marianne and Holy Russia stood at the opposite poles of belief.

If Germany had cut the wire to St. Petersburg, her relations with London and Paris assumed all the greater importance. With the former they were satisfactory as seemed to be borne out by the conclusion on July 1, 1890, of a treaty as a result of which, in exchange for the acquisition of the island of Helgoland, Germany yielded Zanzibar to Britain. This amicable *quid pro quo* aroused in Russia suspicion of a more far-reaching Anglo-German understanding.

There was more to feed the suspicion. In Italy, the mercurial Crispi was strongly anti-French and correspondingly devoted to the Central European association. Already in 1890 he began to discuss renewal of the Triple Alliance. His aim was to consolidate into a single one the three treaties of 1887 in order to include Austria in the German guarantee against France and Germany in the Austrian guarantee in the Balkans. In this attempt he failed at first; after his fall on January 31, 1891, his successor Rudinì was regarded as a francophile. But the French hope of detaching Italy from the Triple Alliance, translated into a policy of pressure, rather served to facilitate the renewal of the alliance

on May 6.[2] The three treaties were merged, with minor alterations, and, in addition, in the event of the impossibility of maintaining the North African *status quo*, the following clause was
introduced:

> Germany engages, after a formal and previous agreement, to sup-
> port Italy in any action in the form of occupation or other taking of
> guarantee which the latter should undertake in the same regions [Cyre-
> naica, Tripolitania, and Tunisia] with a view to an interest of equilib-
> rium and of legitimate compensation. It is understood that in such an
> eventuality the two Powers would seek to place themselves in agree-
> ment with England. (Article 9)

An additional protocol spoke of "the accession of England
being already acquired, in principle, to the stipulations of the
Treaty" as far as territory of the Ottoman Empire proper was
concerned and of the extension of this British agreement to cover
North African territories as well, not excluding Morocco. This
statement was not altogether warranted by the facts. Britain, to
be sure, was coöperating with Italy in the Red Sea and around
Abyssinia, and her relations were good with all three members
of the Triple Alliance, yet she showed no desire to renew or
extend the Mediterranean agreements of 1887.[3]

Nevertheless, Rudinì's speech in the Italian Parliament on
June 29, 1891, conveyed the impression of British association with
the Triple Alliance; in Russia no less than in France this was cause
for concern. William II was by no means inimical to France, in
many ways rather the opposite, as shown by gestures on his part
intended to be pleasing; yet in 1891 the proposed visit to Paris of
his mother, the Empress Frederika, aroused such a storm in France
that it had to be cut short; a small thing in itself, but of considerable significance as indicative of the fact that the old suspicion of
Germany persisted on the French side.

The French desire for a Russian connection was greater than
the reverse. In spite of loans and the sale of arms, in spite of the fall
of Bismarck and the failure to renew the Reinsurance Treaty, in
1890 French advances met with little response from Russia. That
was one reason for trying the Italian card, but that, too, was a
failure. But the picture began to change in 1891 when the accumulation of events was bearing fruit in Russia. Contacts were at two

---

[2] This renewal of the Triple Alliance was in turn influenced by the Franco-
Russian rapprochement in process of taking place.

[3] This was the gist of Salisbury's reply to Crispi on August 4, 1890, warning
against an Italian occupation of Tripoli without French provocation.

levels, military and political. The first were in the form of discussions between General Boisdeffre, who was attending Russian maneuvers, and the Russian Chief of Staff, General Obruchev; they were tentative and exploratory. Their political counterpart was not very far-reaching. It took some difficult negotiating[4] before agreement was reached on the text of an exchange of letters on August 27, 1891, which provided as follows:

1. In order to define and consecrate the cordial understanding which unites them, and in their desire to contribute with one accord to the maintenance of peace, which is the object of their sincerest wishes, the two Governments declare that *they will confer on every question of a nature to threaten the general peace.*

2. In case this peace should actually be in danger, and especially in case one of the two parties should be threatened by aggression, the two parties *agree to come to an understanding* on the measures which the realization of that eventuality would make it necessary for both Governments to adopt immediately and simultaneously.[5]

This was no more than an agreement to come to an agreement, if and when danger should materialize; the plant of Franco-Russian association was still a tender growth. There were, to be sure, factors pointing to a general climate of growing friendliness; the visit of a French fleet to Kronstadt at the tsar's invitation in the summer of 1891 was outward manifestation and open notice to all of changing conditions. Some aspects of this visit deserve humorous treatment, such as the picture of the tsar standing at attention while the revolutionary anthem of the godless republic was being played—the ban on the playing of it in Russia was temporarily lifted—yet this gave the gesture all the greater significance.

Giers could be counted on to recall the virtues of the German connection, but German policy gave him little assistance, a fact that made it possible for French diplomacy during the year following the exchange of August, 1891, to score an important success. This took the form of a military convention which had the effect of clarifying the German focus of the Franco-Russian association while minimizing the possible aspects of it inimical to Britain.

Again negotiations were protracted and the opposition of

[4] It took considerable pressure on the part of Tsar Alexander III, assisted by his ambassador in Paris, Mohrenheim, to obtain Giers' agreement, one difficulty being that of finding a formula that would reconcile Giers' view of a Franco-Russian understanding as primarily directed against Britain with the essentially anti-German French interpretation of any such agreement.

[5] The italics are the author's.

Giers, by now a sick man, had to be overcome. General Bois-deffre went again to Russia in 1892 and finally, on August 27, the draft of a military convention, signed by the two Chiefs of Staff, himself and Obruchev, received the tsar's approval. This document provided that in the event of a German attack against France, or an Italian attack supported by Germany, Russia would employ all her available forces to fight Germany; conversely, a German attack against Russia, or an Austrian attack supported by Germany, would involve a similar obligation for France. In addition, mobilization by one or more members of the Triple Alliance would entail mobilization by France and Russia without further or prior consultation. "All the available forces" was more specifically defined by the provision that "the forces available which must be employed against Germany shall be for France, 1,300,000 men; for Russia, from 700,000 to 800,000 men. These forces shall begin complete action with all speed, so that Germany will have to fight at the same time in the east and in the west." Finally, there was the interesting provision that the duration of the convention was to be the same as that of the Triple Alliance. Its terms were to be secret.

This Franco-Russian agreement is a major landmark in the story of European relations. From the standpoint of numbers two fairly equal groups of armies, about 3,000,000 in each camp, could now confront each other. The agreement was unquestionably defensive in intent, a response to the Triple Alliance. For both Powers it meant escape from isolation, in which respect it had greater importance for France than for Russia. It was a French success, partly the reward of patience and skill, especially since the German focus alone appears in its provisions; this is all the more significant since it was France who was the demandant and to whom Germany was the more real danger, a fact reflected in turn in the larger French military contribution despite a population that was about one-third the size of Russia's. What support Russia might obtain from France in other quarters would depend, not upon the terms of the alliance, but upon the general value that France would place upon Russian friendship. That the alliance would serve to regain Alsace-Lorraine for France did not seem likely, save perhaps in connection with a general conflict growing out of other issues. Russia might indeed lose interest in the French connection, but that would essentially depend upon decisions made in Berlin. Germany continued to be the focus of European diplomacy, a potentially great force of change, but one against which, for that very reason, others might wish to guard.

To a degree, a vicious circle was now already being entered. The first German reaction to the initial stages of the Franco-Russian association was rather to minimize its importance, but things were different in 1892. In dealing with the Russians the French had stressed the German danger. It was in the summer of 1892 that there took place in Germany the appointment of Schlieffen to succeed Waldersee at the head of the General Staff. This meant the adoption of a new strategy to deal with the war on two fronts: geography pointed to the desirability of crushing France through a quick massive blow. This in turn necessitated an increased military establishment which was provided for in the military law of November, 1892. The decision was a technical one, but its political implications could not be escaped.[6] Interestingly, by contrast with 1887, when Bismarck had stressed the French danger, Caprivi now sought votes in the Reichstag by playing up the Russian, though France was the main focus of military preparations.

The Franco-Russian military convention of 1892 still needed the formal approval of the tsar and of the French government in order to make it a binding commitment. It took a year and a half before the last obstacles were overcome. On the Russian side the tsar still entertained some reservations *vis-à-vis* the republic where the Panama scandal in 1892 seemed to confirm his opinion of the regime and of its politicians;[7] the German army law and the firm stand that France took toward Britain over Siam[8] helped overcome his doubts. On the French side the question was how to avoid the intrusion of Parliament, whose consent was needed for the ratification of a treaty; but the requirement of secrecy alone made that a clear impossibility. The French constitutional difficulty was circumvented by taking the position that neither the exchange of notes of 1891 nor the Military Convention of 1892 was, strictly speaking, a formal treaty and that an exchange of letters between the foreign ministers would suffice to give the Convention the force of a treaty commitment.

[6] This decision is not to be confused with the specific plan of campaign, known as the Schlieffen Plan, designed to achieve the result of crushing France before Russian forces could effectively come into action. The Schlieffen Plan dates from the end of the nineteenth century.

[7] Irregularities in the financing of the building of the Panama Canal were disclosed that involved a large number of deputies. The scandal shook the regime but it blew over fairly shortly.

[8] More will be said about this presently, see below, p. 219.

In October, 1893, a Russian squadron visited the French Mediterranean base of Toulon, repaying the French visit to Kronstadt of two years earlier. The choice of Toulon and the talk of a permanent Russian force in the Mediterranean pointed to the possible anti-British content of the Franco-Russian association,[9] a possibility that was indeed of interest to Russia. The French, however, would not alter the terms of the Military Convention, and on January 4, 1894, the Franco-Russian exchange of letters brought into existence what, despite the speciousness of the French position where the role of Parliament was concerned, is usually, and on the whole properly, referred to as the Franco-Russian alliance.

II. Imperial Rivalries and the Isolation of Britain

The validity of one German assumption had been disproved. Yet Germany drew comfort from the thought that the anti-British content of the Franco-Russian alliance might serve to bring Britain into the camp of the Triple Alliance. In retrospect one may observe the roots of such developments as the basic reluctance of Britain and France to become involved in open conflict with each other, leading first to a composition of differences, then active coöperation of these two Powers, and credit this to the fundamental fact that both were increasingly Powers on the defensive, the position of both being threatened by new claimants to a place under the sun; but this result was only reached by a highly tortuous path, and while the story unfolded its outcome seemed far from clear, let alone inevitable. To contemporaries, Anglo-French and Anglo-Russian rivalries were well-established traditions that could easily seem to fall in the category of the unchangeable; such they appeared in Berlin. Another consideration is that the formation of the Franco-Russian alliance established an equilibrium in Europe independently of Britain. In fact, the addition of Britain to either camp would have tended to upset this equilibrium; and this, in turn, may be regarded as fitting well with the traditional isolation of Britain. There was in Britain no desire for entanglements, but the fact that British interests were world-wide brought Britain into close contact with all other imperialisms, while the consciousness of deficiency in her naval establishment made

---

[9] An Anglo-Italian naval meeting at Taranto may be regarded as a reply to the Russian visit at Toulon.

her begin to question the merits of an isolation that could no longer be called splendid.

The story is an intricate one and for simplicity of presentation it will be easiest to deal with it in separate spheres of action. The African scene may be considered first.

EUROPEAN RIVALRIES IN AFRICA

This was the age of imperial dreams on a grandiose scale. But if there were in Britain great empire builders, such men as Cecil

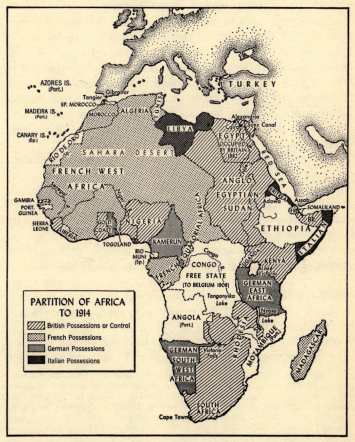

Rhodes, the policy of Britain was rather conditioned by the necessity to maintain and defend established positions, a necessity which by itself led to expansion, out of which could eventually be formulated consciously such a design as that of a Cape to Cairo connection. The British position in Egypt was secure, in the sense that no one seriously thought of ousting Britain; yet it remained vulnerable in default of clear title since Egypt was still nominally Ottoman territory. The Franco-Russian alliance, for all the anti-British character that the Russians would have liked to give it, never led to serious Russian support of France in Egypt nor French backing of Russia at the Straits. But Egypt meant the Nile, stretching into the very heart of Africa, hence the issue of recognition of a British interest in the upper reaches of that river.

The establishment of the Congo state and the Anglo-German agreement of 1890 stabilized the situation in the region of the sources of the White Nile. On the Red Sea side, Italy's East African ambitions have been mentioned[10] as well as the fact that Britain was sympathetic to Italian imperialism in those regions. As a logical counterpart of this France tended to support Abyssinia; her influence in that quarter was enhanced by the opening of the Djibouti–Addis Ababa railway in 1894. But to the west the situation remained open to the penetration of French influence; France did not recognize the British claim to the Sudan. Negotiations between the British and King Leopold of the Belgians looked to the northern extension of the Congo in exchange for the lease to Britain of a strip of the Congo. To this arrangement the French objected[11] and were at first supported by the Germans. Though meant by Germany as a tactical move, the Franco-German conjunction, even if passing, was cause of second thoughts about isolation in Britain. The matter of the lease was dropped as the result of French pressure on King Leopold and the French seemed determined to push their advantage. Despite a public British statement in March, 1895, that a French expedition to the Upper Nile would be considered "an unfriendly act," it was in November of that year that the French foreign minister, Hanotaux, decided upon the sending of precisely such an expedition. In France, too, there were

[10] From her establishment in Eritrea Italy participated actively in the domestic politics of Abyssinia, an independent state whose level of political evolution may, by European standards, be properly described as medieval. In 1889, Italy concluded with the Negus Menelik the Treaty of Uccialli, which she sought to interpret as tantamount to a protectorate. A dispute arose over the Italian and Amharic texts of the treaty, the Italian interpretation of which the Negus refused to accept.

[11] On the plea that the territory was either Ottoman or ownerless, while the British could not use the argument of territorial occupation. The British lease of Congolese territory would have served to establish the continuity with British-controlled territory to the north and south.

those who entertained the grandiose project of French control across the width of Africa from west to east.

It was the turn from 1895 to 1896 that brought South Africa into the picture of European relations. The main significance for Britain of the Cape Colony was strategic; the opening of the Suez Canal had naturally made the Mediterranean the logical route to the East, but the Canal was vulnerable. The story of the north-ward growth of Cape Colony and of the republics established by the Dutch settlers moving away from the Cape need not be con-sidered here. During the eighties the discovery of important gold deposits in the Transvaal confronted the Boers with new prob-lems in the form, among others, of an influx of *uitlanders*. The course of events in South Africa may be regarded as an instance of the inevitable encroachment of the expanding, industrial West upon less developed regions; but the presence in South Africa of earlier white settlers instead of merely "natives" gave it a peculiar twist. The conflict, long maturing, came to a head in the second half of the nineties; it was dramatized by the presence of two strong personalities: Cecil Rhodes, empire building financier, on one side; President Kruger of the Transvaal, dour and intransi-geant, on the other. Out of this situation grew a somewhat sordid intrigue and the so-called Jameson Raid at the close of 1895.[12] The raid was a failure, but what gave it European significance was the startling telegram sent on January 3, 1896, by Kaiser William II to President Kruger while at the same time the German government suggested that the status of the Transvaal be dealt with by an in-ternational conference. The spectacular move that was the Kruger telegram has often been described as a typical *coup de tête* of the Kaiser. Granting that it was in character, the fact is that it was part of a well-thought-out move of German diplomacy. Germany had some interests in South Africa—her own possession of South-west Africa and an eyeing of the Portuguese holdings—but the idea of possible German assistance to the Boers *against* Britain was simply ludicrous. The intention was rather to bring home to England the fact of her isolation, from which the conclusion should follow that Britain had better escape from this condition through a firmer connection with the Triple Alliance. The pol-

---

[12] This was a filibustering expedition that was to be synchronized with a rising in the Transvaal. But the latter failed to materialize with the result that Dr. Jameson's attempt on Johannesburg was an abortive one, whereupon he was conveniently disowned by the British authorities.

icy of browbeating others into friendship is no German monopoly, though it recurs with surprising frequency in the German diplomacy of the two decades before the first World War. The fact of isolation was indeed brought home to Britain, but if there were those who were concerned over it, Britain could not be so easily coerced. The general British reaction was one of intense annoyance that did not help Anglo-German relations.[13]

Interestingly, there was reciprocal resentment in Germany that was of use to those who thought that German power, naval power in particular, should be built to a point where it could be a significant counter in the diplomatic game. Germany had indeed embarked on the *neue Kurs*, and here also no more suitable exponent of this orientation could have been imagined than the Kaiser himself, with his fondness for ships and his dreams of *Weltpolitik*. This new aspect of German policy may be regarded as no more than the expression of the surprisingly rapid and successful growth of Germany; it was no more than natural in the circumstances that Germany should emulate others on the imperial path. For Germany the period was transitional and no clear decision was made on whether she should embark upon empire building as an end in itself or whether imperial issues should be looked upon as secondary in themselves but of significance and use as counters on the checkerboard of European relations.

To match the large British and French African dreams, each of which embraced a good half of the continent, the view was to appear in Germany that from the existing German establishments, converging upon the Congo, a huge block could be consolidated that would cover the bulk of Central Africa. But this was fancy rather than sober diplomacy; in 1896 Germany had no thought of seriously challenging Britain in Africa.

If the chief hope of German diplomacy at this point was to secure a British connection *in Europe*, pressure could also be brought to bear upon Britain through the prospect of a Continental League. Here also two avenues were open. Though such a prospect would appeal to the Kaiser's imagination and sense of the dramatic, the unlikely project was not too seriously pursued; should it materialize, however, a Continental League led by Germany would be an eminently satisfactory development which

---

[13] The pressure of successful German competition was making itself felt at this time. It was in 1896 that there appeared in England a book entitled *Made in Germany*, which created a minor sensation.

would, in addition, have the merit that Britain could then be safely ignored or challenged. But the prospect of a British connection, more or less on Germany's terms, was the more seriously pursued.

DEVELOPMENTS IN THE FAR EAST

Almost on the opposite side of the planet from South Africa, in the Far East, these same years, 1894–1895, offered scope for the exercise of European diplomacy. Of established interests in the Far East the British and the Russian were the principal. The meeting of British and French influence in Siam had led to a minor crisis in 1893,[14] on the whole composed without too great difficulty: Siam retained her independence as a buffer between British Burma and French Indochina. The British interest in China proper was essentially commercial, the Russian aimed at physical expansion as well; this is the time during which Russia had undertaken the construction of the Trans-Siberian railway: prospects of unlimited extension of control in the Far East may be seen as the Russian counterpart of the African dreams of other Powers. In more limited terms, Manchuria and Korea were the specific points of Russian interest.

But in the Far East a novel and unexpected factor intruded. The record of the transformation of Japan is both unique and impressive; during the period before 1914 Japan offers the sole example of a non-Western state successfully adopting and adapting the ways of the West. Her economic development went along with her military and naval; insufficiently noticed, Japan had, by the nineties, successfully mastered the European ways of power; she likewise began to evince the characteristic European tendency to imperial expansion. Weak and chaotic China was the obvious ground where Japanese expansion could take place, and Japan was not unaware of the Russian tendency toward eastern expansion. Another decade was to elapse before the two would meet in open clash; meanwhile, in September, 1894, Japan went to war with China. This first demonstration of Japan's imitation of Western imperialism resulted in the easy defeat of China on whom Japan imposed the Treaty of Shimonoseki in April, 1895, which secured for Japan Port Arthur and the Liaotung Peninsula, while Korea became independent.

[14] On that occasion, too, Germany gave signs of supporting France and, interestingly, what was regarded as the weakness of Britain's behavior caused British stock to fall in Berlin.

Neither Germany nor France had very substantial interests in this part of the world, but Germany was highly favorable to Russia's Far Eastern involvement which would divert her from the Balkans, while France had just become Russia's ally. It would be awkward for France to find Germany the chief supporter of Russia in that country's determination to oppose Japanese expansion.[15] The result was something in the nature of a Franco-German competition for Russian favor and the momentary union of the three Powers in putting joint pressure on Japan, forcing her to yield back some of her gains to China. Here was the Continental League in action, or such it could be made to appear in London, Britain being the only one among the interested Powers not to participate in the Far Eastern arrangements. Actually, the combination was wholly artificial; when tested it was destined to founder on the perennial obstacle of the fundamental difference that the Franco-Prussian War had created.

MEDITERRANEAN PROBLEMS

One reason for the passivity of Britain in the Far East was British doubts about the viability of China. Similar doubts had long been entertained about the Ottoman Empire. Near Eastern affairs had been relatively quiescent for some years, but the perennial of Turkish maladministration threatened to reopen the problem of the fate of the Ottoman Empire. Christian revolts, especially Armenian, which the Turks met with the time-worn device of massacres, aroused considerable indignation in Europe. Yet Britain alone seemed willing to interfere. Salisbury had returned to office in June, 1895, and toyed with the possibility of a radical solution of the Near Eastern problem through the complete partition of the Ottoman Empire. The scheme foundered on the usual inability of the Powers to agree on fair shares; the British scheme in fact did little more than arouse the suspicion of others, not least of Russia which, in both 1895 and 1896, threatened direct action at the Straits. The plan, a feeler rather than a serious proposal, was abandoned.

But Christian revolts kept flaring up. It was the turn of Crete in May, 1896, and Greek support of the Cretans resulted in a Turkish declaration of war against Greece in April, 1897. To the Powers this was an embarrassment rather than an opportunity for

[15] Considerations of the same nature and Russian pressure induced France to be represented at the opening ceremonies of the Kiel Canal in June, 1895.

individual advantage. The defeat of the Greeks eased the situation for them and offered an occasion for their coöperation in preventing punishment for Greece, while Cretan emancipation advanced another step through the autonomy that was secured for the island in July, 1898.[16]

In Macedonia, too, disturbances arose whose locale made them of especial interest to Austria. In that country, Kálnoky's long tenure, going back to 1881, had come to an end with the advent of Goluchowski in his place in May, 1895. Personally, Goluchowski was not aggressively disposed; of Polish origin, his inclination was not pro-Russian; his policy, therefore, was one of opposition to Russian designs, while the Magyar influence remained inimical to Austrian territorial expansion in the Balkans. It was logical, in the circumstances, for him to seek closer ties with Berlin and with London. But in the former capital Hohenlohe[17] would not further clarify the conditions of the *casus foederis*, while London was evasive; if anything, Salisbury showed signs of withdrawing from the Anglo-Austro-Italian coöperation initiated in 1887.[18] But the fact that Russia was not at this time seriously interested in Balkan possibilities as Lobanov, the Russian foreign minister who had succeeded Giers, indicated during a visit in Vienna in August, 1896, opened the door to a direct Austro-Russian understanding that was reached in May, 1897, and the effect of which has properly been described as "putting the Balkans on ice." The agreement, like other Austro-Russian agreements, was not devoid of ambiguity. Goluchowski laid down the principle of Russian recognition of the Austrian right to annex Bosnia-Herzegovina and the Sanjak, of the creation of an independent Principality of Albania, and of equal partition of the rest of the Balkans; however, the Russian reply, by Muraviev, added to these terms reservations that were tantamount to denial.

Peace nevertheless continued to prevail in the Balkans, save for the brief Greco-Turkish interlude, but the real reason for it was

[16] Coöperation was actually less than complete and in the end a combination of British, French, Russian, and Italian fleets was stationed around Crete, the German and Austrian having refused to join the others. Germany's behavior, in this as in the Armenian case, was conditioned by her attempt to establish her influence in the Ottoman Empire, hence her courting of the sultan.

[17] Hohenlohe succeeded Caprivi as Chancellor in November, 1894, which date also saw the accession to the throne of Tsar Nicholas II.

[18] Italian stock on the international market had inevitably gone down as a consequence of the setback of 1896 which was followed by a policy of retrenchment on Italy's part.

the fact that Russian interest was at this time focused on the Far East; in addition to which Germany exerted a restraining influence on Austria, as did France where Russia was concerned.[19]

One of the difficulties in the way of agreement on schemes for Ottoman partition was the question of Egypt. Britain was now well established in that region and any French demand for her withdrawal could hardly be entertained in London. Mention has already been made of the ramifications into farther Africa of the British involvement in Egypt. When Hanotaux, the French Foreign Minister, decided in November, 1895, to send an expedition across Africa, his motive was not so much to challenge Britain on the Nile as to exert pressure, which might lead to an international consideration of the Egyptian problem. It has also been pointed out that in the Anglo-French imperial contest, Italy was regarded by Britain as a useful pawn. But Italy looked at the situation from her own point of view and had her own designs.

Among Italian statesmen Crispi was the chief exponent of an active imperialism. On his return to power in 1893 he resumed the pursuit of his policy when previously in office. The outcome of it was war with Abyssinia which provided one of the relatively rare occasions when Europeans suffered defeat at the hands of native forces. The battle of Adowa on March 1, 1896, is a landmark in the story of the development of Italy. The aftermath was interesting, for instead of reacting with the determination to avenge the humiliation, the result was an outburst of anger, mainly directed against Crispi, whose government had to resign and whose personal political life the incident brought to a close. For it was little more than an incident and the Italian defeat was rather the result of poor management than a true measure of Italian power. Yet power consists of will as well as of material means; allowing for the limitation of those means, the judgment is not unwarranted that Italy lacked the power for the pursuit of imperial designs. The rating of Italian power on the European market consequently suffered a severe setback. Having abandoned for the time their colonial ambitions in East Africa, the Italians withdrew into

[19] A Russian scheme, often referred to as "the Nelidov Plan," from the name of the Russian ambassador in Constantinople who sponsored it, for seizure of the Straits in December, 1896, met definite opposition from the French foreign minister, Hanotaux, and was thereupon abandoned. This is an interesting instance of the role of French money. The Russian finance minister, Witte, was anxious to secure French capital for his Far Eastern development schemes and threw the weight of his influence against any Russian action at the Straits in the absence of full French support.

their existing holdings. This meant that their value as a counter to possible French ambitions toward the Sudan was destroyed and that Britain had to look after the matter herself; the British decision to reconquer the Sudan dates from March, 1896.

The Italians on their side felt deceived. They had expected greater British assistance, and Crispi had also complained of the uselessness to Italy of her membership in the Triple Alliance, even hinting at times at the possibility that Italy might come to terms with France and join the opposite camp. On the British no less than on the German side there was some tendency to look upon Italian tactics as in the nature of blackmail. Rudinì, who succeeded Crispi, was in a weak position to obtain more favorable terms for Italy if the Triple Alliance, due for renewal at this time, were to continue in effect. His efforts to revive the Mancini declaration of 1882 were curtly turned down by Germany and the alliance was allowed to continue unchanged. No less important, the fall of Crispi marks the beginning of a new orientation of Italian policy that was to find expression in a few years in a complete change of Italy's relations with France. But this will be better dealt with after some other developments have been considered first.

III. Fashoda: The Anglo-French Showdown

The dramatic encounter that brought Britain and France face to face on the Nile was less the result of plan than a manifestation of forces which once unleashed proceeded on their own momentum. Once the decision had been made in Britain to have Kitchener reconquer the Sudan, abandoned after the setbacks of a decade earlier, and once Captain Marchand had been ordered to set out from Gabon and march toward the Nile, an Anglo-French clash may be called inevitable. But Gabon and the Nile are far apart; it took the better part of two years before the open clash occurred. At the beginning of September, 1898, Marchand raised the French flag on the Nile at Fashoda where Kitchener, having just defeated the dervishes, found him established. No more picturesque and apt illustration could be cited of the far-reaching tentacles of the imperialism of Europe, stemming respectively from London and from Paris, physically meeting at Fashoda in the form of two handfuls of men. Kitchener summoned Marchand to withdraw, which the latter, in the absence of instructions, refused to do. Inadvertently, in a way, the Anglo-French crisis was opened, for both Britain and France had set forces in motion with little preparation for dealing with the situation that their encounter had created. Now that they had met, the resolution of the conflict was far more difficult for its having been brought out in the open.

The British position was simple: Britain must have control of the Nile; the choice was therefore France's whether to fight or yield. In France, Delcassé had been at the foreign office since June. Delcassé's place in the diplomacy of Europe is large and his tenure of the foreign office is the longest on record of the Third Republic, from June, 1898, to June, 1905. But in the particular matter at hand he had merely allowed matters to drift and was now caught largely unprepared. France soon found out the extent of her isolation; Russia and Germany, each for her own and different reasons, saw an Anglo-French clash without reluctance. If it came to considering an isolated conflict between the two countries, then British naval superiority furnished a ready answer. Delcassé wanted negotiation, not war, but the uncompromising attitude of Britain made it difficult to find a face-saving solution, and for a moment the tension was acute and war seemed even probable. Quite wisely in the end, especially in retrospect, on November 4 Delcassé decided to yield and to accept the inevitable humiliation that went with the French surrender.[20] The significance of this decision is difficult to overestimate: if it would be unwarranted to read into it the Entente of six years later, it is nevertheless one of the two chief factors that made that understanding possible, the other being German policy and tactics. Nor can one resist the temptation to speculate upon the factor of "inevitability" in historical development. Had it come to the test of arms on this particular occasion, we should now be explaining how, in the light of the centuries-old record of Anglo-French conflict, this was but one more logical and natural episode. Such did the clash appear at the time, in Germany for instance, and, understandably, on the French side feeling ran high.

Considerable time was to elapse before Delcassé was to embark, deliberately and consciously, on the attempt to settle differences with Britain. But one thing was clear at this point: France certainly could not afford the enmity of both Britain and Germany. Treading softly with Germany, Delcassé sent to Britain

[20] This was the time when France was bitterly divided over the Dreyfus affair, an episode that served to undervalue the impression of French power outside France.

Paul Cambon, an anglophile, whose long tenure of the London embassy was also destined to have important consequences. Britain, for that matter, having clearly won her point, had no desire to push her advantage to unreasonable lengths; in March, 1899, an Anglo-French agreement delimited the respective spheres of influence of the two countries in North Africa and around the Nile.[21] Having yielded on the Upper Nile, it was a logical next step for France to cease opposing Britain in Egypt, but neither Delcassé nor French opinion was yet quite ready for the drawing of this conclusion.

The episode could be regarded as a vindication of Britain's traditional isolation: single-handed she had had her way. But British commitments were world-wide; commercially, the Far East was of greater importance than the Upper Nile. But if the British share of the China trade was very large, others had been increasingly intruding into that preserve. The successful emergence of Japan has been mentioned, which Russia, after Shimonoseki and with French and German support, had in part contained. Russia's Far Eastern dreams were also on a grandiose scale, comparable to those in the Near East, which found occasional expression in the attempt to bring the Ottoman Empire in its entirety under Russian protection. In May, 1896, a Russo-Chinese defensive alliance, directed against Japan, was concluded.

But Germany here also appears upon the scene as a newcomer and intruder in her own right and for the furtherance of her own interests, commercial no less than political. The murder of some missionaries was easy pretext for the seizure, then long-term lease, of Kiao-chow in November, 1897. At the opposite ends of Asia, the Ottoman and the Celestial Empires presented the similarity of decadence raising the question of their ability to survive. In both cases, Britain preferred to maintain their integrity, but the Far Eastern situation was becoming more complicated from the multiplication of interests, Japanese and German, in addition to Russian and British.[22] The classical approach of splendid isolation might be less suitable than that of combination with others. March, 1898, saw the granting of an Anglo-German loan to China as well

[21] This agreement was a source of concern and annoyance to Italy, who feared that it might be interpreted as British recognition of French claims to Tripoli, despite Salisbury's somewhat casuistic denials.

[22] The French stake in China proper was relatively secondary, French interest in the Far East being centered in Indochina, but the United States had a considerable interest in China and the China trade. The American position was of insisting on equality of opportunity and of opposing the division of China into spheres of influence by others.

as the leasing of Port Arthur to Russia; this was promptly followed by the lease to Britain of Wei-hai-wei, the significance of which, at the opposite side of the Gulf of Pechili from Port Arthur, was in large part strategic. France, not to be left behind others, also secured a concession in Kwang-chow-wan.

IV. Britain Reconsiders Isolation

BRITAIN AND GERMANY 1898-1901

It has been said that the German lease of Kiao-chow was for the purpose of establishing a coaling station for the needs of a non-existent navy which it therefore became necessary to create. This is a quip only in part. It was in July, 1897, that Bülow took charge of the German foreign office; three years later he succeeded Hohenlohe in the Chancellorship. In that office, which he filled for nearly a decade, Bülow's influence on the affairs of Germany and of Europe was to be very considerable. Bülow was a cultivated European, married in romantic circumstances to an Italian wife, fond of his Italian villa in Rome, and devoid of neither intelligence nor charm; but apart from an excellent opinion of himself and much vanity, Bülow also evinced that characteristic that the Italian word *prepotenza*[23] best describes. The conjunction of Bülow and Kaiser William II, with Holstein in the permanent background ready to add his advice, may well be regarded as disastrous in the end, no less for Europe than for Germany. For all that they differed on specific issues, the Kaiser and Bülow both stood for the new Germany, the Germany of the *neue Kurs* and of *Weltpolitik*. The advent of Bülow may be taken, in fact, to mark the clear embarking by Germany on the conscious course of world power; exploiting existing imperial differences, German power, in Bülow's phrase to the Kaiser, could be in the position of *arbiter mundi*. Even better, if also more dangerous, expression of this state of affairs, was the advent to power of Tirpitz, the father of the German navy. The Kaiser's, one is tempted to say juvenile, enthusiasm was readily aroused by the prospect of a powerful German navy; *Weltpolitik* demanded such a tool, and with his supreme gift for diplomatic blundering and unintended humor, it was he who uttered the dictum that "our future lies on the water."[24]

[23] "Overbearingness" is as close an equivalent as may be given in English.
[24] On September 23, 1898, in connection with the presentation of the first German navy bill.

What purpose could a German navy serve? The exponents of navalism in Germany had no specific aggressive intent, against Britain or anyone else; the navy was to be a tool of power and an instrument of diplomacy. Clearly, the one Power which above all would take notice of, and possible alarm at, German naval plans was Britain, traditional mistress of the seas, by now committed to the two-power standard. Ships are costly and relatively slow to build; it would be years before a German navy could offer any kind of challenge to Britain's. During those years Britain might take sufficient alarm to be driven to take action to nip the danger in the bud. The possibility was faced by the proponents of a German navy; their reasoning and ultimate decision were based on two assumptions, one correct and one false: the first, that Britain would not take the initiative of aggression, hence that it was safe to proceed with the building of a "risk navy"; the other, that the British would be cowed into greater amenableness by the existence of a threat. It took time for all this to develop and the importance of Anglo-German naval rivalry will only appear somewhat later, but the advent of Tirpitz and the passage in 1898 of the first German naval law designed to implement his program were the planting of dragon's teeth, which is the reason for introducing the issue at this point.

The figure of Bülow in Germany may, in some respects, be matched by that of Joseph Chamberlain in Britain. Able, restless, and not overscupulous in his methods, Chamberlain had, over the years, moved across the political spectrum from his initial liberal outlook until he came to place great stress on the significance of the Empire for Britain. He had shared in South African intrigues (preparations for the Jameson raid) and despite his position as colonial secretary, his influence in the Cabinet rivaled the Prime Minister's. On the score of the virtues of isolation and of the desirability of seeking a connection, and with whom, opinion in the Cabinet was divided. Chamberlain, open to a degree to the influence of racial conceptions, leaned toward a connection with the kindred Teutons of Germany rather than with Latins or Slavs;[25] for that matter, if

[25] Not to be confused with Houston Stewart Chamberlain, whose *Foundations of the Nineteenth Century*, originally published in German in 1899, created a considerable stir. The influence of the racial myth, one of those imponderables the weight of which is difficult of precise measurement, cannot be wholly ignored. The creation by Cecil Rhodes of the scholarships that bear his name is one interesting expression of it, and the appeal of the prospect of an Anglo-German-American association is likewise one of its manifestations.

Britain were to enter into association with a Continental Power, there was history to point to a long record of friendly relations with Prussia, while conflict constituted the essence of the story of relations with Russia and with France.

At any rate, Chamberlain was given *carte blanche* to try his scheme of a German alliance. With perhaps more directness than diplomacy he made the proposal of a defensive alliance to the German ambassador, Count Hatzfeldt, on March 29, 1898. A public treaty could be ratified by Parliament, but that would not prevent the inclusion of secret clauses; it was also hinted to Hatzfeldt that in the event of failure Britain might turn to France or Russia. Apart from the fact that the climate of opinion was not too favorable in either country to the conclusion of an alliance at this particular moment, this is one occasion when the phrase "perfidious Albion" warrants mention. There was suspicion of British motives on Bülow's part as well as the rooted conviction that an Anglo-French or an Anglo-Russian connection was not in the domain of the possible, hence that if an alliance were to be made with Britain it was safe to hold the bid high.[26] But there were reservations in England as well, on Salisbury's part for instance, and certainly no disposition to make "enormous" or "amazing" offers to anyone. Consequently, nothing came of Chamberlain's attempt save an Anglo-German agreement on August 30 that dealt with the possible partition of Portugal's South African colonies, a scheme which in the end provoked further suspicion.[27]

Britain's interest in the possible fate of the Portuguese colonies stemmed from her own South African involvements. In 1897 Milner had been appointed High Commissioner in South Africa, and the following year saw the reëlection of President Kruger in the Transvaal. Kruger was making bellicose preparations (hence the Treaty of Windsor, whereby Portugal undertook not to allow the passage of war supplies to the Boers), and negotiations between himself and Milner were not helped by the latter's intransigeance. By 1899, with the Anglo-French clash over Fashoda liquidated,

[26] On the score of duplicity, it is worth mentioning that the Kaiser took it upon himself to inform the tsar of the British proposal, crudely asking, "what can you offer me?" if he refused the British advance. The bait did not prove effective, and the tsar's reply, referring to "amazing" British offers to Russia, confirmed the German suspicion of British perfidy.

[27] The scheme was predicated on Portugal's financial difficulties and the granting to her of a loan. Portugal was able, however, to dispense with Anglo-German assistance, and a year later the so-called Treaty of Windsor (October 14, 1899) confirmed Britain's support of Portugal and the integrity of her empire. Understandably, this having taken place unbeknown to Germany, it was taken in that country as further evidence of British duplicity.

Chamberlain was prepared for war with the Boers, which Kruger's ultimatum in October unleashed.

Of the Boer War itself little need be said here. The British did not realize the magnitude of the undertaking and the first stages of the war were marked by reverses for them. But the effect of these on imperial Britain was the opposite of what that of Adowa had been on Italy three years earlier; undoubtedly, if Britain had the will, she had the means to subdue the brave but puny Boer republics. The tide of war turned in February, 1900, with the freeing of Ladysmith and Kimberley; the Boer territory was overrun and its annexation proclaimed in October. Guerrilla fighting, attended by considerable brutality, delayed until 1902 the pacification of the country and the making of the formal Treaty of Vereeniging in May of that year. Britain, once more, as on the Nile, had had her way, but the repercussions of the episode were considerable.

Two things were brought out: the weakness of British military power in being and a remarkable outburst of anti-British feeling that was nearly world-wide. German opinion did not differ from others, but the Kaiser seemed to have learned the lesson of the Kruger telegram. His visit to Britain with Bülow in November, 1899, was the occasion for the renewal of discussions with Chamberlain, who this time brought out the idea of an association that would include the United States as well as Britain and Germany.[28] Perhaps misunderstanding the warmth of Bülow's response to his advances, Chamberlain committed himself publicly in his famous speech at Leicester on November 30 in which, having mentioned the affinity between the Teutonic and the Anglo-Saxon peoples, he went on to hold up the prospect of "a new Triple Alliance between the Teutonic race and the two great branches of the Anglo-Saxon race." Bülow's response, in the course of a speech in the Reichstag on December 11, was more than disappointing; it was a rude rebuff that could not but arouse resentment, all the more that the occasion for it was the advocacy of a new German navy bill.

Once again Bülow had missed an opportunity, though this is understandable enough in the light of the international circumstances and of the pro-Boer state of opinion in Germany. Germany in fact toyed again with the perennial of a Continental League for which friction with Britain over the seizure of German ships gave

[28] In view of subsequent developments, some of them of current import, it is interesting to speculate on what the course of events might have been had an association of Britain, Germany, and the United States become a reality at this time. The power of such a combination, especially if Japan be added to it, certainly would have been very great, not to say overwhelming.

occasion. But what discussion there was of such a possibility soon ran into the usual impasse of the German requirement—and the usual French refusal—of a guarantee of European possessions. But if the League failed to materialize, its alternative purpose of frightening Britain into paying a higher price for German friendship was no more successful. The one concrete result for Germany was the passage of the second navy bill.

One more attempt was to be made, in 1901, at forming an Anglo-German alliance; the occasion for it arose in a different quarter. In the Far East, the year 1898 had seen what looked like the beginning of the partition of China by the Powers. Like Turkey, China was unable to withstand the pressures of the outside world and resentful of its encroachments. Contempt for the foreign barbarians could achieve little against their more efficient guns. The so-called Boxer rising was essentially an outburst of obscurantist impotence. Some Europeans, traders and missionaries, could be killed and legations besieged, but those were not the days when Europe would meekly submit to such outrages, and the fact that the German minister was one of the victims put Germany in the forefront of the avengers. An international European expedition, under the command of the German, Marshal Waldersee, duly restored European prestige and went some distance in justifying the Chinese view of Europeans.[29] It gave the Kaiser occasion to ride another one of his pet hobbies, the Yellow Peril, and to extol to the departing German contingent the virtues of a policy of frightfulness.

But this outward appearance of European coöperation hardly concealed the truer reality of deep-seated differences. A three-cornered contest involving the relations between Britain, Germany and Russia ensued which, after intricate maneuvering, produced an Anglo-German Yangtse agreement in October, 1900, ostensibly purporting to preserve the integrity of China and the maintenance of the Open Door policy in that country.[30] From the British stand-

[29] The Chinese outbreak, for all that it had the sympathy of the Dowager Empress, could hardly be said to represent enlightened civilization. The penetration of Western influence in China continued to be attended by confusion and chaos and another half century was to elapse before a government was to arise—the present regime—that could achieve at least effective control and the establishment of order.

[30] The American interest in the Far East, and therefore in the activity of the European Powers in that part of the world, had led to the sending by Secretary of State John Hay, in September, 1899, of a note wherein was stated the so-called Open Door policy advocated by the United States.

point, this was an instrument designed to contain Russian expansion and bears some similarity to the earlier Mediterranean agreements which had a comparable purpose at the western extremity of Russia and of Asia.

The first month of the year 1901 saw the end of the long reign of Queen Victoria; her passing brought the Kaiser to England and was the occasion for the last attempt at the formation of an Anglo-German alliance, still sponsored by the same Chamberlain who thought this time that Japan might also be brought into the combination. Negotiations dragged on through the year and the prospect of their success was never very bright. There was reticence on the British side;[31] Lansdowne, who had succeeded Salisbury at the foreign office in December, 1900, though willing, was not enthusiastic, and Chamberlain himself was inclined toward caution from having had his fingers burned on the earlier occasion.

On the German side there was continued misjudgment of the British position. Bülow and Holstein felt, unwarrantedly, that Germany was in the position of *arbiter mundi*, hence able to extract her own price from Britain; the result was an attempt to force Britain into joining the Triple Alliance. This Britain would not do, and the German view of the Yangtse agreement, revealed in Bülow's statement in the Reichstag on March 15 that it was not concerned with Manchuria, was a disappointment to the British who felt that it had been robbed of its meaning; in the Far East also Germany acted as if she were in a position to arbitrate between rival contenders. This last attempt at an Anglo-German connection met the same fate as its two predecessors and ended on a sour note of recriminations between Chamberlain and Bülow.[32] In actual fact, Britain had greater freedom to choose than Germany now that her hands were free both on the Nile and in South Africa.

[31] The British position had been aptly stated in a memorandum of Lord Salisbury of May 29, 1901. "The British Government," wrote Salisbury, "cannot undertake to declare war, for any purpose, unless it is a purpose of which the electors of this country would approve. If the Government promised to declare war for any object which did not commend itself to public opinion, the promise would be repudiated, and the Government would be turned out. I do not see how, in common honesty, we could invite other nations to rely upon our aid in a struggle which must be formidable and probably supreme when we have no means whatever of knowing what may be the humour of our people in circumstances that cannot be foreseen." (Quoted by Albertini, *op. cit.*, Vol. I, p. 115.)

[32] In a speech at Edinburgh on October 25, 1901, Chamberlain took strong exception to the criticism of Britain's conduct in the South African war, comparing it to the behavior of other nations. This in turn evoked a sharp retort from Bülow in the Reichstag on January 8, 1902.

THE ANGLO-JAPANESE ALLIANCE

The Russian advance in the Far East was of no less concern to Japan than to Britain. There are two ways to meet such situations, outright opposition or accommodation. Japan, who had no thought at first that she might successfully meet Russia in open clash, was willing to consider the second, but the Russian tactics of dilatoriness turned Japan toward the possibility of coöperation with Britain on the basis of their common interest in the containing of Russia. After the failure of the German connection, Britain was willing to consider this alternative; negotiations during the second half of 1901 led to the signature, on January 30, 1902, of a treaty of alliance between the two countries.

The treaty provided for the neutrality of either participant in the event of the other being involved in war with one other Power, the *casus foederis* applying to the case where he would be at war with more than one enemy. The significance of the alliance lay in this: for what was essentially the price of Korea, Britain had insured herself against the possibility of a Russo-Japanese combination. In the event of war between Japan and Russia, the threat of British intervention—the treaty was made public—would prevent France from going to the assistance of her ally. This was a fair *quid pro quo;* what gives it special interest is the fact that it constituted for Britain the first formal departure from the time-honored principle of isolation during peacetime. At the same time it should be noted that isolation was thought of in Britain as primarily a European policy; the alliance with Japan could therefore be said to confirm, in a sense, the tradition of isolation since the focus of it was obviously Chinese and it tended in fact to increase the independence of Britain in Europe.

V. Emergence of a New Alignment of Power

ITALY ON THE FENCE

Germany refused to take alarm at the Anglo-Japanese alliance, preferring to see in it added possibilities of Anglo-Russian difference. In a different quarter, within the by now long-established Triple Alliance, the situation was gradually changing; the development in question grew for the main part out of the evolution of the Italian position. The vicious circle of strict adherence to the Triple Alliance and bad relations with France had been characteristic of the period of Crispine dominance. Even Crispi had been disappointed by the lack of support that his allies gave to Italian imperial ambitions; the Adowa disaster, fruit of his reckless policy, and his consequent fall mark an important turning point in the course of Italian foreign policy. For the time being colonial designs were to be left strictly alone and his successor Rudinì was reputed a francophile. This did not mean abandoning the Triple Alliance connection which Rudinì himself renewed in May, 1896. But 1896 also witnessed a turn in Franco-Italian relations. France was established in Tunis as Britain was in Egypt, and the French attitude toward Britain in Egypt was comparable to the Italian position in regard to France in Tunis, amounting in both cases to a policy of irksome, but essentially ineffective, pinpricks. A Franco-Italian convention was made that granted certain privileges to Italians in Tunisia, as well as some commercial advantages, and was tantamount to an Italian recognition of the French protectorate. The tariff war that went back to 1888, and had on the whole proved more injurious to the Italian than to the French economy, was also finally liquidated with the conclusion of a commercial treaty in 1898. These were essentially negative acts, but they served to effect the transition from definitely inimical to eventually friendly relations.

One consideration ever of prime importance to Italy was the position of Britain. That country had extricated herself from even the modest commitment of the Mediterranean agreements, but Anglo-French relations struck a low point in 1898. However, the sequel to Fashoda was the Anglo-French Convention of March, 1899, suspected and resented in Italy; but Italy obtained from France a declaration of disinterestedness to the east of Tunisia.

In Rome France was represented by one of her ablest ambassadors, Camille Barrère, whose role during this period is comparable to that of Paul Cambon in London. Barrère conducted a long and patient negotiation with the Italian foreign minister, Visconti Venosta, the outcome of which was the exchange of letters that took place beween them in December, 1900. The essence of this exchange was a reciprocal declaration of Italian *désintéressement* in Morocco, of French in Libya.[33] This development constituted an important modification of the Mediterranean alignment since

[33] The letters were written in December, 1900, but the formal exchange took place on January 4, 1901. The *quid pro quo* was not, strictly speaking, complete, for the French negative *désintéressement* was given in exchange for a positive Italian recognition of French interest in Morocco.

France was no longer isolated in that sea; the value of the German guarantee to Italy in the event of a clash with France over North African interests was largely voided of its meaning. No less important than the agreement itself was the altered atmosphere that made its conclusion possible; amid an exchange of amenities (official visits, decorations bestowed) the plant of Franco-Italian rapprochement continued to prosper.

This new turn of events could not but be a source of concern to Germany. Yet, even Prinetti's disclosure in Parliament, in December, 1901, of the existence of the Franco-Italian exchange was countered by Bülow with urbane good grace and the *tour de valse* simile.[34] Unable to prevent these happenings, it was indeed the part of wisdom to *faire bonne figure au mauvais jeu*, but Bülow's earlier comment, reported by Barrère, that "Italy will have to decide soon to make her choice between matrimony and concubinage," is more accurate expression of his correct assessment of the state of affairs.

In Italy Prinetti had succeeded Visconti Venosta at the foreign office. Inexperienced in diplomacy, yet active and desirous to achieve some personal success, he allowed the Italian position to drift into yet deeper ambiguity. Two things were done, almost simultaneously, in June, 1902: on the 28th the Triple Alliance was renewed, the military convention going back to 1888 being, however, allowed to lapse; on the 30th there took place a new exchange of notes between Prinetti and Barrère.

The ultimate aim of French policy was to detach, if possible, Italy from the Triple Alliance; failing this, to find out with precision the nature of that tripartite connection. Prinetti's reassurances that it was devoid of aggressive intent toward France naturally gave little satisfaction to either Barrère or Delcassé; the exchange of June 30 is a measure of their success. The heart of this interesting document is worth quoting; it stated as follows:[35]

In the case that France [Italy] were to be the object of a direct or indirect aggression on the part of one or more Powers, Italy [France] will maintain strict neutrality.

[34] In a Reichstag speech Bülow had recourse to the illustration of the civilized and wise man who, noticing that his wife is dancing an extra dance with another man, will look the other way rather than make an issue of it, confident in the ultimate faithfulness of his spouse.

[35] The date of this exchange is often given as November 1. June 30 is the correct date, but in deference to the understandable awkwardness felt in Italy at the simultaneity of the two commitments, the original letter was destroyed and replaced by another bearing the later date.

The same will happen if France [Italy], in consequence of direct provocation, should find herself compelled in defense of her honor and her security to take the initiative in the declaration of war. In this event, the Government of the Republic [the Royal Government] shall have the duty to give previous information of its intention to H.M. Government [the Government of the Republic], thus permitting the latter to take cognizance that it is a case of direct provocation.

It is difficult enough in many cases to reach a clear decision on the matter of aggression; the "defense of security" opens still looser possibilities; to introduce the concept of "honor" well-nigh removes all restraint. The Italian commitment to France was therefore very elastic in nature; it simply meant that, in the test, Italy would be judge of the merits of the case, and the ambiguity was compounded by the fact that Italy remained a member of the Triple Alliance. Much ink has been spilled over the issue of the consistency, or lack of it, of these simultaneous Italian commitments. In a strict sense their consistency may be granted since they were both defensive; it has even been said that the straddling position taken by Italy was a clearer expression of her true intent and interest and put her in a stronger position to restrain aggression wherever it might originate. But this is rather casuistry since neither side knew in advance the precise meaning of his commitment to the other. In simpler and also truer terms, Italy was placing herself on the fence between possible rivals and, as was later pointed out quite soundly by Poincaré, no one could rely with assurance on what Italy would do—probably whatever she thought her interest might dictate in the circumstances of the moment.

But, in view of the fact that hitherto Italy had formally been aligned with one camp, the Franco-Italian exchange marked an important turning. Gone were the days when the overwhelming preponderance of power was controlled in Berlin, and France stood in complete isolation. From the limited standpoint of national interest it may also be said that Italy, weakest among the Powers, and always highly sensitive to the shifts in the relationships of power, was seeking reinsurance for herself and accurately reflecting the uncertain trends of the day.

FRANCE, GERMANY, AND RUSSIA

The entire decade of the nineties appears in retrospect as a period of groping for readjustment in the relations among the Great Powers of Europe. The repercussions of imperial growth, in full bloom at this time, to a degree drew away from the confines of Europe the attention and energy of the Powers and correspondingly acted as a safety valve, but they also had the effect of raising novel issues or giving a new slant to older rivalries. The consequence was a fumbling search for new alignments, often in response to unexpected developments, which makes the story of the diplomacy of the period intricate and confused. To what extent men directed events or were controlled by them may often be debated.

In the free-for-all of reshuffle it was only natural that long-standing traditions should raise the possibility of an Anglo-German alliance; the failure to achieve this connection may well be regarded as the single most important development of the period. Once this had failed, new possibilities were opened and the initial years of the century saw the shaping of an entirely new orientation. In retrospect and taking the broad view it may also be said that basic similarities in their position tended to align together in a fundamental sense what may already at this time be called the Powers of conservation, the "haves" as the expression came to be; though never a formal alliance, the Franco-British connection was in the test to prove stronger and more durable than many formal alliances.

The story of the final stages of the transformation may be told from the standpoint of any one of the major Powers, but, taking Europe as a whole, it may not be unfair to situate France at the center of this particular tale. One characteristic which the preceding pages have brought out is the hesitancy of both British and German diplomacy, in the last analysis equally reluctant to commit themselves to irrevocable courses. France with less power had less choice and her diplomacy strove to procure for her the assistance of others wherever it might be found. The quality of French diplomacy at the turn of the century was high; for all that has been said about the political instability of the Third Republic, the permanency of the triumvirate of Delcassé at the foreign office, Paul Cambon in London, and Barrère in Rome gave to French foreign policy a great steadiness of direction, while the ability of these men had not a little to do with the successes of French diplomacy during this period.

The brilliant work of Barrère in Rome has been described. But this success, if useful, was in large measure negative, because of the nature of the Italian commitment and because also of the limitations of Italian power. When Delcassé came to the Quai d'Orsay in 1898, almost his first experience was a harsh lesson in the limitations of French power; largely unprepared, he wisely yielded at Fashoda. But the lesson was taken to heart. On the score of his plans there is controversy; the view that he began immediately and consciously to prepare the ground for an Anglo-French alliance seems hardly warranted. In 1899 such a connection would in fact appear highly improbable; it seemed more reasonable to survey the Continent for possible assistance.

Germany was not to be excluded *a priori* by France any more than the reverse. But what explorations were made in this direction invariably came up against the result of the war of 1870: Germany always sought to extract from France a formal acceptance of the new frontier, the very thing that no French government could afford to do, even if it had wanted to. Therein lay the great German blunder of 1871. Russia alone remained, with whom indeed France was already formally allied. But Russia was at this time more interested in the Far East and the alliance had certainly been of no use to France at Fashoda; Russia and France seemed more likely to find sources of difference with Britain than with Germany.

Out of these circumstances grew a modification of the original terms of the Franco-Russian alliance. On the occasion of Delcassé's visit to Russia, he and Muraviev exchanged letters on August 9, 1899, the import of which was that, instead of being confined to "the maintenance of peace," the scope of the alliance was enlarged, or rather sharpened, to "the maintenance of equilibrium" among European forces. In addition, the duration of the military convention, originally established as the same as that of the Triple Alliance, was now made indefinite. In simple terms this meant that, in exchange for French support of Russia's Balkan policy, Russia would take into account France's claim on the Rhine; neither question was urgent at the time. The following year, in July, the Chiefs of Staff of the two countries considered the possible bases of military coöperation in the event of war against Britain; another visit of Delcassé to St. Petersburg in 1901 resulted in a new exchange between himself and Lamsdorf, in May, which ratified the military decisions. This did not mean that France was planning to attack Germany, or Russia Austria, or that either or both were preparing for aggression against Britain, but undoubtedly the scope of the alliance had been broadened.[36]

---

[36] Here again French money played a role, the French insisting that their loans be used in part for the construction by Russia of railways of strategic importance.

France was the prime mover in seeking the extension of the Russian alliance. One of the minor causes contributory to the tsar's willingness to entertain the changed provisions of the alliance was his annoyance with Germany's behavior at The Hague. Pacifism and disarmament can hardly be said to have been dominant traits of this period, though not a little discussion of them was taking place. The tsar's unexpected proposal, in August, 1898, that the Powers meet to discuss the limitation of armaments was cause for general surprise and, in some cases, for alarm. But since no one will openly espouse the cause of sin, a meeting took place at The Hague from May to July, 1899. The discussions were lengthy and learned but the results were small,[37] and the meeting served as a demonstration of needlessly clumsy German diplomacy: Germany, instead of quietly agreeing with others (France, for example, who took much the same view of the proceedings) on how to emasculate any decisions, quite needlessly cast herself in a role of stubborn and solitary opposition, thereby giving support to the view that German methods and intentions were fundamentally aggressive.

More concrete were affairs in the Ottoman Empire where Germany was a relative newcomer. With the passing of Bismarck, his comment about the lack of German interest in the Near East began to lose its validity; the decade of the nineties saw the beginning of German economic interest in Turkey which took the concrete form, among others, of railway building activity in Asia Minor. Railway building, diplomacy, and strategy are apt to be closely related in colonial or semicolonial regions. Starting from small beginnings as early as 1893, a German company obtained, in the spring of 1899, the concession for the grandiose scheme that, joining Constantinople to Baghdad, is usually known as the Berlin-Baghdad railway project.

The Kaiser was visiting the sultan in October, 1898, and in Damascus found occasion for one of his colorful speeches, taking the pose of protector of the world of Islam. By contrast with other Powers, Germany, having had little contact with Islam and not possessed of Moslem-inhabited colonies, was in a relatively advantageous position to cultivate the sultan's friendship. The German concession was at first viewed with favor by Britain, who saw in it a possible diversion of German interest, and by France, who seemed

---

[37] This first Hague Conference on the limitation of armaments yielded nothing more than a limited agreement on arbitration.

content to share in the investment. But Russia was suspicious and opposed. The Baghdad railway project was the beginning of a long and involved tale; it is mentioned at this point because of its role in Russo-German relations; it was an appropriate symbol of Germany's own interest in the Near East, which was destined to grow and take on an increasingly political color.[38]

THE REORIENTATION OF SERBIA

For the rest, the Near Eastern situation was relatively quiescent at the turn of the century; the Balkans were "on ice." The domestic troubles of the Ottoman Empire, arising from the discontent of its Christian subjects, were mainly at this time centered in Macedonia. Bulgaria was naturally involved in any Macedonian situation and there were fears that she might be at war in the spring of 1903. Neither Goluchowski nor Lamsdorf had at this time any wish other than to maintain the *status quo*, and the Powers had already accepted their proposed joint recommendations for reform to the sultan. Later in the year, in October, while the Austrian emperor and the tsar were meeting at Mürzsteg, their foreign ministers elaborated a further detailed program of reforms which was presented to the sultan and notified to the Powers.[39] The chief significance of all this was the fact of Austro-Russian co-operation, a condition that on the whole continued to obtain so long as Russia's interest remained focused on the Far East and until she came to grief in that quarter.

But before resuming the main thread of the story, mention must be made of another development in the Balkans in the same year, 1903; of small dimensions in itself, the ultimate consequences of this episode were destined to be considerable. It is a tale of Balkan intrigue at its darkest. After the settlement of Berlin, Serbia under Prince—then King—Milan had become a thorough dependent of Austria. Despite the unpopularity of this policy, King Milan continued to adhere to it; his son Alexander, who succeeded to the

[38] The definitive convention was finally signed in March, 1903. Until 1914 the Baghdad railway scheme was an object of diplomatic negotiations between the Powers. Partly because the engineering difficulties of the project turned out to be greater than expected, developments were slow and gave rise to a minimum of international friction. But the political influence of Germany in the Ottoman Empire continued to grow until the conclusion of an alliance with Turkey in August, 1914.

[39] The Mürzsteg program gave Austria and Russia considerable rights of interference and a privileged position in the Balkans. It is of interest that Italy was deliberately excluded from participation, a fact which is in turn a reflection of the state of relations in the Triple Alliance.

throne upon Milan's abdication in 1889, did not in 1895 renew the Austrian alliance, but Milan's influence was sufficient while he lived, until 1901, to prevent a complete Russian orientation of Serbian policy.

At this point personal complications intruded in the form of Alexander's abuse of his own power—the constitution was suspended in 1903—on top of his unpopular marriage to his mistress; the two facts were not unrelated, for Queen Draga's family were active in political intrigue. The outcome of this situation was that, during the night of June 10–11, 1903, a group of army officers, who had decided to take matters in their own hands, entered the royal apartments and brutally murdered the occupants;[40] several ministers and the Queen's brother were also victims of the massacre. The pages of Serbia's nineteenth-century history are bespattered by the blood feud between the two rival families that led her to independence; the murder of King Alexander was the occasion for the last change in dynasty. The Obrenović king having been eliminated, the head of the Karageorgević house was called upon to rule. Prince Peter was a quiet, scholarly man, but not unnaturally, though wrongly, widely suspected of being a party to happenings of which he emerged as the beneficiary. His beginnings were difficult, but order was eventually restored, the liberal constitution of 1889 was reinstated, and the main result of the change was the advent to power of the Radical party under the leadership of Pašić. The chief significance of this was that henceforth Serbia was in the Russian camp, and the consequences of the change, once Russia was to return to an active policy in the Balkans, will appear in the following chapter.

THE ANGLO-FRENCH ENTENTE OF 1904

But far the most important development of this time had to do with Anglo-French relations in the following year. On the French side, Delcassé was steadily directing French policy with a view to strengthening the international position of his country. One thing that Delcassé was bent upon doing was the furthering of France's imperial expansion. France's position in Egypt was clearly irre-

---

[40] It is of interest that two of the participants in the murder, Captain Dimitrievič and Lieutenant Tankosić, were to be involved in the Sarajevo plot in 1914. It is also interesting that the widespread indignation to which the gruesome episode gave rise was not shared by the governments of Austria and of Russia, who sent instead congratulations to the new king and to whom the assassination does not seem to have come as a surprise.

trievable, and the passage of time could only confirm and strengthen the British hold on the Nile; but at the opposite end of Africa the Moroccan Sultanate made an attractive prize. Morocco was a state, in some respects reminiscent of Turkey and of China, in which the government, such as it was, was incapable of effective operation, a fact which fated Morocco to fall under outside control. Surrounded as it was by French possessions, it was but natural that its acquisition should appear as the obvious rounding out of France's African Empire. But if in the context of the imperialism of the day Morocco may be said to have legitimately "belonged" to France, this did not mean that France could simply expect to oust other European interests from Morocco. The only thing to do was to conclude some bargains, of which the Franco-Italian *quid pro quo* of 1900 could be taken as a model. However, it takes two to make a bargain; but this was a time when a variety of circumstances made possible the achievement of an Anglo-French understanding.

Queen Victoria had died in January, 1901, and had been succeeded by her son, Edward VII. Too much has often been made of the francophile inclination of the new British ruler;[41] the fact remains that, especially at a time when there was still much talk and feeling about Anglo-Saxon and Teuton affinity, King Edward represented that tendency in England that looked upon France and things French with sympathy instead of with innate suspicion.

Of greater importance was the failure of the third British approach to Germany; the Cabinet had always been divided on that issue and, naturally, Chamberlain's stock went down with his failure, which opened the field to alternative possibilities; Chamberlain himself, for that matter, had hinted at the existence of these to the Germans who, however, declined to attach importance to the caution. Moreover, this failure must be seen in the context of German naval policy, even though naval rivalry had not been an object of the Anglo-German discussions. An understanding with Germany was the British way to avoid the cost of naval competition and the possible threat of a rival naval establishment; the German plan of a "risk" navy for purposes of pressure, if understood at all, had in England the opposite effect to that intended. If Germany, in fact, were to embark on a program that could become a threat to Britain, then the objections to French naval bases in the vicinity of Gibraltar would be transferred to Germany, should

---

[41] The last British effort to reach an understanding with Germany took place during the first year of his reign.

the latter in turn show signs of entertaining designs of her own in Morocco. An understanding with France might, on the other hand, serve to neutralize that country even more effectively as an ally of Russia in the Far East. Nor should it be forgotten that all the while Britain had been growing increasingly sensitive to the encroaching success of German economic competition.[42]

Morocco had become the focus of Delcassé's policy and it was shortly after the Franco-Italian exchange of June, 1902 (in the following August), that the first approaches were made to Lansdowne. The response was not unfavorable, and the patient work of Cambon in London was supplemented by laying the public basis of a rapprochement between the two countries. The official visit of King Edward to Paris in 1903 was a delicate operation that the tact and deftness of the British ruler turned into a marked success; the return visit of President Loubet to London, in July, was equally successful.

In view of the long background of Anglo-French relations in the imperial field, it is not surprising that negotiations should have been protracted. Agreement was finally reached, however, and the documents that were signed on April 8, 1904, mark the birth of the so-called *Entente Cordiale*.[43] These instruments consisted of a public convention, two declarations, and some secret articles. The convention dealt with relatively minor issues scattered over the world, Newfoundland fishing rights going back to the Treaty of Utrecht of 1713, African and Oceanic compensations; small as they were,[44] they had significance as indication of a desire on both sides to liquidate *all* outstanding colonial differences. But the heart of the agreement was in North Africa. France decided to abandon her futile policy of pinpricks and to cut her losses in Egypt where she gave Britain a free hand, giving up the fiction that Britain could be made to set a terminal date to her occupation. The *quid pro quo* for this concession was Article II of the declaration which stated that

. . . His Britannic Majesty's Government recognize that it appertains to France, more particularly as a Power whose dominions are coterminous for a great distance with those of Morocco, to preserve order in that country, and to provide assistance for all administrative,

---

[42] However, this consideration was, then as later, two-edged, for Germany was at the same time Britain's first rival and first customer.

[43] A treaty of arbitration had already been concluded on October 14, 1903.

[44] Interestingly, it was the issue of fishing rights that proved the most difficult of resolution. Sensibly, Delcassé decided to yield on this point in order to achieve his larger purpose.

economic, financial and military reforms which it may require. They declare that they will not obstruct the action taken by France for this purpose, provided that such action shall leave intact the rights which Great Britain enjoys in Morocco. . . .

Provision was also made for Spanish interest in Morocco and, not least important, the secret articles envisaged the possibility of an actual partition of Morocco between France and Spain.

There has seldom been cause to mention Spain in this story for the simple reason that Spain was not a Great Power, a fact which, in combination with her geographic position, kept her outside the stream of development of European and world politics. But in the one case of Morocco, especially since Britain was established at Gibraltar, Spanish interest had to be taken into account. Moreover, it suited the British book that no other major Power should control the African side of the Strait. It was therefore a logical corollary of the Anglo-French agreement that France and Spain should likewise agree on the division of their respective shares of Morocco; this they did in the convention of October 3, 1904, whereby Spain endorsed the Anglo-French agreement of April, and whose secret provisions delimited the respective French and Spanish zones in the event of Moroccan partition.

The formation of the *Entente Cordiale* is indeed a historic event. Yet, to a degree, the phrase is a misnomer. This was not an alliance, let alone an instrument of aggression, but essentially a negative act, the liquidation of outstanding disputes. It is highly significant that the chief imperial Powers should agree to compose all their imperial differences. But, especially on the British side, there was no thought at first beyond the negative aspect of the agreement; and one may also read in it the expression of the fact that Britain no longer considered France a serious menace. Without clear consciousness of it, it may even be said that the fundamentally defensive position of the two countries was bringing them together. Of relative weakness, France had greater awareness than Britain, and it is a credit to French diplomacy that, by contrast with German in dealing with Britain, it knew how to be moderate and patient, that it would be content with a limited colonial agreement, not seeking to extract from Britain political commitments *in Europe*. This quality of suppleness, especially where Britain was concerned, French diplomacy continued to display; it was to bear valuable fruit in time, though it was much assisted in its task by the unfolding of German policy, which in a sense, remains the focus of the story of the remaining decade until 1914.

VIII

The Road to War, 1904-1914

I. Germany and the Anglo-French Entente

It was shortly after the conclusion of the Anglo-French agreement that Kühlmann, the German minister in Tangier, commented that "The Egyptian question is dead, but the Moroccan question is very much alive." The observation was most apt and the year 1905 was to find Morocco at the center of the affairs of Europe. But Paul Cambon also observed that "Without the war in the Far East which made for reflection on both sides of the Channel and inspired in all a desire to limit the conflict, our agreements would not have been possible." There is a close connection between Manchuria and Morocco.

THE RUSSO-JAPANESE WAR

During the opening years of the century the Balkans were "on ice" largely because Russian interest was focused on the Far East. One consequence of the Boxer rebellion had been the Russian occupation of Manchuria; in April, 1902, a Sino-Russian agreement provided for the evacuation of the Russian forces, but the application of it led to further difficulties. Within Russia herself there were two distinct currents: one, led by Witte and the financial interests, put the stress on economic penetration that could be pursued through political agreement; the other, associated with the name of Berobrazov, had more far-reaching aims that went the length of absorbing Korea.

As between Russia on one side, Japan and Britain on the other, the status of Manchuria was negotiable. But the dismissal of Witte in August, 1903, from his post at the ministry of finance, by removing his restraining influence, left the field open in Russia to the advocates of more forcible methods. In the midst of intrigues aimed at the surreptitious penetration of Korea, negotiations between Japan and Russia seemed to be proceeding under unfavorable auspices, until the Japanese became convinced of their futility. With ruthless logic, if dubious ethics, the Japanese thought to secure the advantage of surprise by an attack on Port Arthur on February 8, 1904, dispensing with the formality of an ultimatum or a declaration of war. Many thought the contest unequal and the Russian contempt for "the little yellow men" justified. But the Japanese turned out to have been proficient students of the Western ways of power. In addition, they enjoyed certain advantages, in the form of proximity and control of the sea, that they put to good use against the corresponding drawbacks that hampered Russian operations— 5,000 miles of uncompleted single-track Trans-Siberian railway. The war was no Abyssinian affair, or even Boer War, but the encounter of very large modern armies. Port Arthur, besieged, surrendered in January, 1905; meanwhile, the battles of the Yalu in May, of Liao-Yang in August, and finally of Mukden in February–March, 1905, clearly established the superior quality of the Japanese military machine.

In an effort to counter the Japanese advantage on the sea the Russians indulged in a romantic gesture: since their Black Sea fleet was immobilized by international conventions, they chose to send their Baltic squadron halfway around the world to Far Eastern waters. The battle of Tsushima Strait in May, 1905, was the maritime counterpart of Japan's victories on land. By this time Russia was further hampered by the outbreak of revolution at home, while Japan was beginning to feel the financial strain of the war, and the proffered mediation of the United States led to the restoration of peace with the conclusion of the Treaty of Portsmouth (New Hampshire) on September 5, 1905.[1] Japan had successfully met the final test of power, armed conflict; she was beyond question a Great Power and, naturally, her success greatly enhanced her prestige, all the more that this was the first occasion in modern times when a non-European Power had successfully met the full force of a European.

But of more interest are the European repercussions of the Russo-Japanese War. Britain was Japan's ally as France was Russia's, and from Delcassé's point of view the outbreak of hostilities in

---

[1] Russia ceded to Japan the southern half of the island of Sakhalin and transferred to Japan the lease of the Liaotung Peninsula. She also agreed not to oppose any Japanese action in Korea, while Manchuria was to be evacuated by both Powers and returned to China.

the Far East was most embarrassing. Both Britain and France, however, shared the desire to circumscribe the sphere of conflict; the Anglo-French agreement in April was expression of this wish. To Germany, the war seemed an opportunity, confirmation of her basic assumption of ineradicable Anglo-Russian difference that the Franco-Russian alliance might help turn into Anglo-French. Though not desirous of involvement herself, Germany wished to pose as Russia's only friend—was France not flirting with Britain? —and at no cost to herself to capitalize on the providential occasion.

The Dogger Bank affair seemed calculated to make her wishes prosper. That the Russian fleet, sailing through the North Sea in October, should have mistaken harmless British trawlers for Japanese men-of-war and opened fire on them may seem peculiar; it has been suggested that vodka can blur the vision no less than the wits. In any case the incident was highly awkward. But Russia had her hands full. Britain had no wish for war, and France naturally sought to pour oil on the troubled waters between her ally and her newly found friend; the issue was amicably adjusted.

Nevertheless the heightened possibility of conflict seemed suitable occasion for a German offer of alliance to Russia that would involve joint action in the event of attack by a European Power. Also, France was to be reminded of her obligations to Russia under the existing alliance.[2] The German calculation was this: either France would be dragged into a Russo-German combination, and the will-o'-the-wisp of the Continental League thereby become reality, or the Franco-Russian alliance would be broken. The calculation was too simple and negotiations broke down over the issue of whether France should be consulted first, as the Russians wished, or faced with a *fait accompli*, as the Germans proposed.

THE FIRST MOROCCAN CRISIS

Germany was thus unable to turn to advantage the Far Eastern opportunity; but other material was at hand. Bülow, in the Reichstag in April, took the position of welcoming the Anglo-French understanding as a contribution to peace. This was politic, but did not really conceal the inevitable German reaction of concern and annoyance. Germany, among other things, wished to discover the precise nature of the Entente and for this purpose Morocco was a ready-made occasion. Even if one granted that Morocco logically

---

[2] The terms of the alliance, mainly directed against herself, and not to the Far East, were unknown to Germany.

"belonged" to France, this could not be translated into a French claim to the mere surrender by others of existing interests and rights. Such indeed was not the French view, as the agreements with Italy and Britain, fair and reasonable *quid pro quos*, had shown. Germany was the one other Power with appreciable Moroccan interests; a similar Franco-German *quid pro quo* would have seemed an appropriate solution.

The curious thing is that such was basically the view held both in Paris and Berlin. But Delcassé thought to strengthen his hand by making the afore-mentioned agreements *before* dealing with Germany; Bülow thought that by threats he could instill fear and thus accomplish the twin purposes of testing—possibly disrupting—the newly formed Entente and ultimately extracting a higher price for Morocco. On both sides there was gambling and the duel between the two men and the two countries is the essence of the first Moroccan crisis.

Little was done at first by Germany besides considering the matter and deciding that something would have to be done; Far Eastern developments seemed to hold greater possibilities, but with the failure of the Russian alliance scheme, Morocco became the main fulcrum of German operation in the year 1905.[3] Curiously enough, the Kaiser and Bülow, then and later, were at odds on the score of the use to be made of the Moroccan question. That France would seek to penetrate, eventually "Tunisify," Morocco was reasonable expectation; but Morocco was ostensibly equally open to all in accordance with the Madrid Convention of 1880. Germany would, therefore, at first encourage the Moroccan sultan to resist French encroachment.

This policy received spectacular implementation in the form of a visit paid by the German Kaiser to the Moroccan sultan at Tangier, notice to the world at large that Germany would only deal with the Moroccan ruler, hence by implication refuse to recognize any special French claims.[4] The gesture was followed by Bülow's

---

[3] It is useful to bear in mind the chronology of developments. The Russo-Japanese War broke out in February, 1904, the Anglo-French Entente dates of April, the Dogger Bank incident took place in October, and the Russo-German discussions in October–November; the Kaiser's visit to Tangier was in March, 1905, Delcassé's fall occurred in June, the Björkö episode in July, and the final Franco-German agreement in September, 1905.

[4] The Kaiser was opposed to making the visit and his hand was forced through a public announcement of it in the *Kölnische Zeitung*. He could hardly withdraw after this, lest, as Bülow pointed out, a change of plans be interpreted as due to French pressure, hence tantamount to a French diplomatic victory.

proposal of an international conference of all the signatories of the Treaty of Madrid in order to review the Moroccan situation. The calculation was that Austria and Italy would support their German ally, that Russia would be friendly, that Britain and Spain could use the occasion to extricate themselves from any commitments to France, and that the United States would support the Open Door policy in Morocco; France would therefore be isolated and Germany secure a diplomatic victory, more important in Bülow's eyes than specific Moroccan advantages.

Delcassé's whole Moroccan policy had, on the other hand, been based on the making of bilateral agreements; an international conference might easily spoil his tactics. Thus, the holding of a conference became the central issue, but in the face of Bülow's deliberate sphinx-like attitude France was at a disadvantage in her attempted approaches to Germany. On the score of Morocco itself French opinion was divided; but it was undoubtedly opposed to war in Europe for the sake of Morocco. One of the frequent changes of government in France brought Rouvier to the Premiership while Delcassé was left in his usual post. Apart from the fact that the two men disliked each other, they also stood for opposite policies: Rouvier, fearful of German threats, hence in favor of yielding; Delcassé, relying to an unwarranted degree on British support in the event of an open clash, insisting that Germany was bluffing, hence in favor of uncompromising resistance.[5] It finally came to a showdown between the two men at a Cabinet meeting on June 6; Delcassé found himself completely alone in his advocacy of intransigeance and as a consequence did the only possible thing, that is, resigned.

Here was a great diplomatic victory for Germany no less than for Bülow personally: the German chancellor had forced the resignation of the French foreign minister. Such victories are dangerous, and Bülow was not the man to exploit his triumph with the subtlety of effacement. Instead of coming easily to terms with Rouvier—even for a good price—as the latter expected, he sought unwisely to push his advantage, in the end destroying the fruits of his own victory. In the lengthy and difficult negotiations that followed the fall of Delcassé, which incidentally had made a most

[5] To a degree, Paul Cambon's reports from London may have misled Delcassé. Rouvier took the unusual step of establishing contacts with the Germans behind the back of his foreign minister, a move obviously calculated to harden the German position.

deplorable impression in England, that country was led to give France greater support than planned in resisting apparent German aggressiveness. In France, also, it was one thing to oppose Delcassé's rashness, it was quite another to submit to German interference and pressure. Bülow's policy of the mailed fist and saber rattling was beginning to bear its unintended fruit.[6]

A curious diversion occurred at this juncture. While the Kaiser, ever fond of travel, was cruising on the *Hohenzollern* in the Baltic, he had a meeting with the tsar at Björkö. The two rulers were on personally friendly terms and the Kaiser used the occasion, enlarging on British perfidy and French weakness, to revive the idea of the proposed Russo-German alliance of the preceding autumn: France, after her diplomatic defeat at German hands, would easily be dragged into the combination and the Kaiser's Continental League would finally become reality. The dream was short-lived and foundered on the usual rock of French objection when Russian second thoughts brought up the usual suggestion of French agreement *prior* to the conclusion of the treaty. The episode is not of very great importance and its main significance is perhaps psychological. To believe that the moment when France had just been humiliated was the most propitious time to obtain her friendship reveals obtuseness in a high degree. The Kaiser's mercurial and erratic personality stands here revealed in full light; his glowing account of the Björkö meeting, and even more his abject telegram to Bülow when the latter threatened resignation, make for interesting, if somewhat uncomfortable, reading.

For the Continental League idea was no part of Bülow's policy; in a different direction, he was at odds with Holstein on how to handle the Moroccan question. A certain lack of coördination in German policy stands here revealed. In any case, however, the Björkö flurry over, Morocco was again at the center of the stage. Bülow had his way when Rouvier finally consented at the end of September to the holding of an international conference at Algeciras, the invitations for which were issued by the Sultan of Morocco.

ALGECIRAS AND THE AFTERMATH OF THE MOROCCAN CRISIS

When the Powers met at Algeciras in January, 1906, the bases of agreement between France and Germany were still open to

---

[6] The Kaiser's choice of this occasion to bestow upon Bülow the title of prince was a prime example of less than tactful procedure.

dispute, the focus of which came to be the control of Moroccan finances and the organization of an international police. There was deadlock in February, but the same tactics of intransigeance to which Germany continued to adhere had the effect of placing her in turn in isolation until she yielded to a compromise of Austrian origin at the end of March.[7] The final Act of Algeciras was signed on April 7, 1906.

Taken by itself, the Moroccan settlement represented a compromise, a stage in the development of the Moroccan question rather than a final closing of the issue. The very fact that there had been an international conference was reassertion of the international status of Morocco and the policy of the Open Door was maintained. To this extent Germany had gained her objective and, from the French point of view, Morocco remained subject to international interference. At the same time, the French mortgage on Morocco was also strengthened by the international recognition of France's special interest, particularly in the matter of the preservation of order in the country; France, together with Spain, was to be in charge of the sultan's police. It was to be expected that the preservation of order in Morocco would give rise to further problems; what would happen at that point would largely depend on the state of the relations among the Great Powers of Europe, mainly France and Germany. A further compromise, some fair *quid pro quo*, might lead to the quiet liquidation of the issue through the establishment of some form of French control, or the letter of the law might be used to test anew and further the state of European relationships. It took another five years before things were to happen in an interesting and curious repetition of the crisis of 1905.

Within its own confines Morocco was no more than another imperial problem. What gave it far greater importance was the fact that it was the occasion for a major European crisis. No one wanted war over Morocco, yet there was talk and fear of the possibility of conflict. This was largely because of the tactics of German diplomacy: it suited Bülow's book for a time to let the impression be spread abroad—in fact to foster the impression—that Germany might go to war. In this he was far too successful. He did frighten the French into jettisoning Delcassé, but in the process

[7] This was the occasion for the departure of Holstein from his position in the German foreign office. A Cabinet crisis in France in March did not affect the proceedings of the conference.

of achieving this Pyrrhic victory he produced a very strong British reaction. The new government that came into office in England in December, 1905, had no belligerent intentions, being more concerned with issues of domestic reform; yet Grey soon found himself driven to giving France far greater support *against* Germany than ever contemplated when the agreement of April, 1904, was concluded. It was he who, on the eve of the Algeciras conference, on January 3, 1906, cautioned Metternich, the German ambassador, that "The British people would not tolerate France's being involved in a war with Germany because of the Anglo-French agreement and in that case any English government, whether Conservative or Liberal, would be forced to help France."

France was no less than Germany anxious to know the precise nature of the British position, and the discussions between Lansdowne and Cambon, interrupted by the fall of Delcassé, were taken up again with Grey. It was on January 31 that Grey took the decision to authorize discussions between the British and French general staffs. In such fashion had begun, fifteen years earlier, the Franco-Russian connection. Yet, in view of the fact that British power was almost exclusively naval, and that, as was said, the British navy does not run on wheels, the purely military value of a British commitment could not be very great. Nor was it taken with too much seriousness by the French, or by the Germans, for that matter; the significance of it was political and in that sense it was very considerable. Grey was a well-intentioned and peace-loving man, though the clarity of his thought and his perception of its implications may be called deficient. Somewhat unconsciously perhaps, he was following the traditional British policy of preserving the European balance of power. Since there was, or was thought to be, some threat to the peace and the balance, and that threat seemed to come from Germany, it was the weaker party, France, who must receive assistance.

In this context, the specific details of the Moroccan question, the rights and wrongs of it, became secondary and vanished into the larger issue of the power relationships of Europe. Characteristically also, and in the consistent tradition of the operation of British policy, the decision was made to meet the situation of the moment, without thought of long-term policy planning and commitment such as the existing formal alliances implied. In retrospect, this was a momentous decision, the thin end of the wedge of increasing British involvement in Continental affairs, the ultimate logical outcome of which was the declaration of war of August 5, 1914. This is perhaps the place to raise the question of the respective merits of long-term planning versus improvisation and muddling through. It is worth mentioning also that there was a minimum of discussion in the British Cabinet of the decisions that were made.[8]

For Germany likewise Morocco was in itself a secondary matter, rather the occasion and pretext to deal with the larger issues of power. Bülow had set out to test the precise nature of the Entente; the irony of the outcome was that, in the process of testing it, he had succeeded in altering its nature and made it from the start a far stronger association than French diplomacy unassisted would have been able to contrive. It was in the nature of a shock to Germany to realize, not only the nature of the British reaction, but the extent of her diplomatic isolation. If Russia had little interest in and less enthusiasm for France's Moroccan policy, she also felt in her weakness that adherence to the French alliance was a safer card than the dependence that a German alliance might entail for her. Spain had come to terms with France, with the blessing of England; her disgruntlement at the nature of the agreement "forced" upon her was not sufficient to make her a willing pawn of German calculations, destined to be deceived in that quarter also. Even allied Italy, embarrassed though she was and striving to mediate differences, in the end lived up to her commitment of 1900 to France where Morocco was concerned; there was understandable anger at Italy in the German camp. Germany was thus left with her one dependable ally, Austria, and even Austria had endeavored to mitigate German intransigeance.

It would be quite unwarranted to speak at this point either of calculated and conscious intent of aggression by Germany, or of a similarly calculated and conscious combination of others directed against Germany. But a condition had arisen where a common impression was being spread and shared increasingly by others, more as a consequence of the tactics than of the actual designs of German diplomacy, the repercussions of which were a combination of anger and concern in Germany over the fact of her isolation. Yet Germany felt strong; the instinctive reactions of frustrated

[8] On January 31, 1906, Grey sent to Bertie, the British Ambassador in Paris, an interesting account of his conversations with Cambon, in which he pointed to the difficulty of enlarging the commitment of the Entente without bringing in the whole Cabinet and Parliament, but indicated also that the force of circumstances might bring England and France together more effectively than formal commitments.

strength can be dangerous. The task of German diplomacy was a delicate one that called for rather more than the usual skill, certainly more than Bülow and the Kaiser possessed.

II. The Triple Entente

ANGLO-GERMAN NAVAL RIVALRY

A decade had nearly passed since Germany had launched the program that was to place her future on the seas. The proposed German navy, as mentioned earlier, was not intended as a deliberate instrument of aggression but rather as a tool of diplomacy, fitting the view of that activity as the pursuit in peace of the same objectives that war seeks to attain by force. The German navy was aimed at England in the sense that its very existence would cause that country to show greater consideration and deference in her dealings with the German power. All this was obvious to Britain and was one of the reasons for British opposition to the possible establishment of a German base on the Moroccan coast. It was in 1904 that Britain reorganized the distribution of her fleet with a view to the creation of a strong force in the North Sea. British sensitivity to Germany's growing naval power was no less than could be expected and there were those in Germany who feared that Britain might decide to nip the German danger in the bud with a twentieth-century version of the Copenhagen performance of Napoleon's day. Such views indeed were also to be found in England where they appealed to no less a personage than the First Lord of the Admiralty, Sir John Fisher.[9] Germany elected to run the risk and from her point of view the assumption was sound that Britain would not resort to preventive war. However, Britain sought to increase the margin of her strength with the launching of a new type of ship, the Dreadnought,[10] while Germany in 1906 enacted yet another navy law.

Limited considerations of naval power and broader ones of general policy were competently analyzed and reviewed in an important paper written by Sir Eyre Crowe, Senior Clerk of the

[9] In political terms, Sir John Fisher may be regarded as the counterpart of Tirpitz, though a more genial personality. The important difference lay not so much in the personalities of the two men as in the institutions of the two countries.

[10] This was a two-edged weapon for, if the Dreadnought rendered the old navies obsolete, it gave Germany an advantage since she could also embark in the Dreadnought competition less handicapped than Britain by the prior investment in older categories.

Foreign Office, under the title, *Memorandum on the present state of British relations with France and Germany*, dated January 1, 1907.

The danger of a general combination against Britain's naval supremacy, wrote Crowe, can in practice only be averted on condition that the national policy of the insular and naval state is so directed as to harmonize with the general desires and ideals common to all mankind. . . . Now the first interest of all countries is the preservation of national independence. It follows that England, more than any other non-insular Power, has a direct and positive interest in the maintenance of the independence of nations, and therefore must be the natural enemy of any country threatening the independence of the others, and the natural protector of the weaker communities. . . . It has been well said that every country, if it had the option, would, of course, prefer for itself the power of supremacy at sea, but that, this choice being excluded, it would rather see England hold that position than any other State.

This analysis led to the conclusion that

A German maritime supremacy must be acknowledged to be incompatible with the existence of the British Empire, and even if that Empire disappeared, the union of the greatest military with the greatest naval power in one State would compel the world to combine for the riddance of such an incubus.[11]

Thus the issue of Anglo-German naval rivalry was perhaps the single most important one in the background of the second conference that met at The Hague on June 15, 1907, presumably to resume and extend the work of the meeting of 1899. The work of the second Hague Conference need not detain us here, mainly because of its barrenness. Clearly, once the creation of a large German navy was posed as a fixed point, it made little sense for Germany to discuss limitation midway in the course of her program, for this would have been tantamount to modification or surrender of her ultimate goal. The only question that could be raised with relevance was the more fundamental one, what was the purpose and aim of German armament? Not that Germany was alone in viewing with suspicion the subject of limitation of arms, but on this occasion again she put herself in the position of chief obstacle to discussion of the question and, quite unnecessarily, went beyond this to opposition to the compulsory arbitration of disputes.

[11] This document may be found in *British Documents on the Origins of the War, 1898–1914*, Vol. III, pp. 397–420. It is quoted in Albertini, *The Origins of the War of 1914*, Vol. I, p. 185.

This may well be regarded as the result of poor diplomacy, as much as, if not more than, of evil intent. Seen against the background of Morocco and Algeciras, in the context of the glorification of the military characteristic of Wilhelmine Germany, it furnished ample food for thought to other foreign offices and helped confirm the view increasingly widespread, not least among those that may broadly be labeled as liberal, that at the very least Germany was determined to have her way and be the sole decider of her right, willfully blind to that of others. Fear and suspicion are the best breeders of themselves; the vicious circle had already been entered into of such fears, more concretely of rival armaments, which the passing of time would render it ever more difficult to break.

THE ANGLO-RUSSIAN AGREEMENT

It has been pointed out that German foreign policy had, ever since 1890, operated under the sign of certain false assumptions which had already led to unwelcome surprises for Germany. Yet this was not the end of her disillusions. One of these cardinal assumptions of German policy had been that, like the Anglo-French, the Anglo-Russian difference was beyond hope of composition. It was during the very time of the meeting of the Hague conference that the Triple Entente came into existence. As a consequence of her defeat in the Far East at the hands of Japan and of the domestic repercussions of the war, Russia was weak and for some years would remain relatively impotent in the councils of power, until she had at least reorganized her domestic structure, more specifically restored her military establishment. The Japanese war had not produced either the Continental League or a shift in the European alliances. But France, too, had suffered a setback in the standing of her power when Delcassé had fallen under German pressure. The balance between the Triple and the Dual alliances seemed tipping in favor of the former.[12] Britain could restore that balance and her unexpectedly strong support of France may be regarded as in effect a redressing of the equilibrium of power.

[12] Italy's behavior at Algeciras had caused much irritation in Germany, but the very fact of Germany's isolation made it imperative not to let Italy drift away from the Triple Alliance. On the Italian side there was a measure of embarrassment and Tittoni, the foreign minister, did not seek to exploit the situation to his advantage as he might have. The result was the tacit renewal of the alliance without change in July, 1907.

Such a relationship of power in Europe was favorable to a rapprochement between Britain and Russia, a consummation naturally greatly desired by France. In the Far East, the setback suffered by the more irresponsible Russian aspects of the attempt at expansion left the field open to the more conciliatory tendency. Japan, on her side, if victorious, had found the war an exhausting performance. The consequence of these events and tendencies is the background of negotiations between Russia and Japan on one side, Russia and Britain on the other. A French loan to Japan assisting, Japan and Russia concluded an agreement on July 30, 1907, on the basis of the mutual recognition of their established positions in the Far East. Their pious public declaration upholding the principle of the Open Door in China was meant to conceal the more solid substance of the secret terms that provided for a division of Manchuria between them. For the moment at least the Far Eastern situation was stabilized.

Anglo-Russian negotiations encountered some of the same difficulties that had delayed the conclusion of the Franco-Russian alliance. Just as the tsar and the conservative forces in Russia found more congenial a regime like the Kaiser's than Britain's parliamentary democracy, so likewise the liberal forces in Britain were outraged by the display of Russian racial persecution and by the tsar's high-handed dealing with the Duma that fear had extracted from him. The Liberal Prime Minister, Campbell-Bannerman, with more forthrightness than diplomacy, made no secret of his own feelings. But Grey and King Edward were both in favor of a Russian agreement and, correspondingly in Russia, Izvolsky, who had superseded Lamsdorf at the Foreign Office in April, 1906, was an advocate of an understanding with Britain.

On August 31, 1907, an Anglo-Russian agreement was finally signed. Across the width of Asia, from Constantinople to Peking, the influences of Britain and of Russia had for long met and clashed. On the score of the everlasting issue of the Straits, Britain was not amenable to concession; the status of the Straits was therefore left unchanged under existing international arrangements. Since the Far East was also stabilized, the Anglo-Russian agreement dealt mainly with the approaches to India, in Tibet, Afghanistan, and Persia, for all of which the guiding principle was that of the erection of a barrier of buffer regions. Neither Britain nor Russia would seek to penetrate Tibet, the suzerainty of which was acknowledged to be Chinese.[13] Afghanistan was recognized by Russia as essentially a British preserve; Russian representation was withdrawn from it while Britain promised to refrain from its annexation. But the heart of the Anglo-Russian agreement lay in Persia, which was divided into three zones, after the customary recognition of her integrity and independence: two spheres of influence, Russian and British, in the north and south respectively, separated by a neutral zone in the center.

The similarity may be seen in the treatment of Manchuria, Persia, and Morocco, all typical illustrations of the meeting of rival European imperial influences. In passing, it may be pointed out that the wishes of Moroccans, Persians, and Manchurians were never taken into consideration by the Powers of Europe; by the standards of a later day, our own, this is often regarded as indication of deficient moral sense. But for the time with which we are concerned such an approach is largely irrelevant; Europe was dealing with decadent societies and states, largely incapable of fulfilling that first and most elementary requirement of a modern state, the providing of internal order and justice; it would be idle to deny that, on balance, European control meant that these states and their inhabitants were introduced to a higher level of organization. From the standpoint of European power, these imperial arrangements were essentially reasonable and fair compromises between rival interests.

But to return to the Anglo-Russian agreement of August, 1907, it was the instrument that put the seal on the combination known as the Triple Entente. This grouping of Britain, France, and Russia was not a solid bloc with commitments clearly defined in a treaty such as that of the Triple Alliance. It consisted instead of three separate and distinct bilateral instruments, one alliance, the Franco-Russian, and two agreements dealing exclusively with extra-European matters, understandings that were largely negative in their initial intent. The Anglo-French agreement of 1904 was in spirit what it purported ostensibly to be, a liquidation of Anglo-French differences, and if German policy was part of its background, it was not directed *against* Germany, though subsequent German actions almost immediately deflected it from its original

[13] In 1904 Sir Francis Younghusband had penetrated into Tibet and forced a treaty upon the Dalai Lama, as a result of which Britain enjoyed a certain degree of influence in that region.

direction. Even less anti-German in motivation was the agreement of 1907, dealing as it did with regions where German interest was wholly nonexistent.[14] The view nonetheless is warranted that Europe was becoming divided into two opposite and rival camps. For one thing, the bare fact of an Anglo-Russian understanding, disproving as it did yet another of the fundamental assumptions of German foreign policy, could not fail to impress the directors of that policy. This is the time when Germany began to conjure up the myth of *Einkreisung*. A myth it was if taken in the sense of conscious objective on the part of the Triple Entente Powers, though the fact could not be denied that these Powers were being drawn increasingly together. As determinants of human decisions and actions, myths are sometimes more real forces than objective reality.

And this also must be said, that in considerable measure the interests of the members of the Triple Entente diverged. France's interest in Russia's Far and Near Eastern ambitions was about equal to Russia's interest in the French recovery of Alsace-Lorraine: each country was mainly concerned with not becoming involved for the sake of the other. Britain's main single source of difference with Germany was that country's naval expansion, and Britain would gladly compromise that issue at any time that Germany would be content with what Britain considered legitimate and moderate ambitions on the seas. Russia had no real quarrel with Germany, and the current remained strong in Russia that would elect understanding if possible. Perhaps the Franco-German difference over Alsace-Lorraine was the issue most recalcitrant to composition; yet if France would never officially and formally forgive and forget, the mere passage of time could not but soften the rankling of French resentment. A new generation had grown up in France to whom the Franco-Prussian war was hearsay and school history rather than personal experience. The Republic was definitely established in France; its chief concern during the two decades that enclose the turn of the century was the curbing, first of the army, then of the Church. The prevailing temper of opinion was strongly antimilitaristic in France. It was Morocco, not Alsace, that brought a crisis in 1905. But yet again, if Delcassé had been alone in the showdown, the tactics of Bülow were

[14] Asia Minor with the Berlin-Baghdad railway scheme was the nearest approximation to such a point of contact.

calculated to justify those in France who upheld the view of an aggressive, militaristic Germany, given to negotiations through saber rattling and banging of the fist upon the table. Those in France who had little love for militarism at home would find even less attraction in the same product across the Rhine. The Jacobin tradition was still reality in France.

The foregoing explains why, in 1907, the condition of Europe still had in it much that was fluid and contained possibilities of shifting alignments. It also shows the extent to which Germany was at the center of the stage and, by indirection at least, the chief determinant of Europe's course. In the end, the more formal combination that was the Triple Alliance proved less solid than the much looser aggregation of the Triple Entente; fundamental community of interest is a stronger binder than formal commitments. Germany, her power, her deeds, and most of all the view that others took of her, was that binder.

III. The Bosnian Annexation Crisis

BACKGROUND AND PREPARATION OF THE CRISIS

The state of European relations was tested and brought out by the next crisis in which Europe found herself involved in 1908 and 1909. The Bosnian annexation crisis, to which Germany was initially extraneous, in the end vastly contributed to the estrangement between herself and Russia; to a remarkable degree it was a rehearsal of 1914.

For a decade, since 1897, the Balkans had been "on ice" while Russia concentrated her efforts in Asia. Her failure in the Far East had been followed by a process of consolidation through Asia, of which the Russo-Japanese and the Anglo-Russian agreements were the expressions. Following the traditional rhythm of oscillation between East and West, Russian interest was now to turn again toward Europe. The fact of Russian weakness, of its probable persistence for some years, has been mentioned; but in September, 1906, the direction of Russia's foreign affairs had come into the hands of Izvolsky, a man whose restless ambition caused him to look abroad for some sensational achievement. The agreements of 1907 were his work; having through them secured his rear, he turned to the perennial of the opening of the Straits. The rash suggestions that he made were decisively turned down in the

Russian Council of Ministers at the beginning of 1908,[15] but Izvolsky's reaction was, rather than to abandon his project, to pursue its achievement through diplomatic means.

The accession to power of Izvolsky in Russia was simultaneous
with the corresponding rise of Aehrenthal in Vienna. Like Izvolsky, Aehrenthal was an ambitious man, able and shrewd, but also
ruthless and unscrupulous. Aehrenthal considered that Austria's
recent role in Europe had been one of undue effacement and was
desirous of restoring her standing and prestige among the Powers
through the pursuit of a more active policy. This meant activity
in the Balkans where Austrian interests were likely to meet Russian, but whether on a basis of friendly compromise or clash was
not predetermined. The advent of the combination of Aehrenthal
and Izvolsky in replacement of that of Goluchowski and Lamsdorf
was to have not a little influence on the course of European events.
In any case the Balkans were about to be taken off the ice.

But Balkan policy for Austria bore an especially close relation to domestic affairs. The passage of time did not render less
acute the problem of the Slav population of the Dual Monarchy;
the divergent approaches of conciliation and thoroughgoing suppression, the latter mainly associated with the Magyar element,
still plagued Austria-Hungary. Among the Slavic subjects of the
Habsburgs the most restive were the South Slavs, whose contiguity to Serbia caused that small country to assume unusual importance in the eyes of the Ballplatz. The changed orientation
of Serbia, especially after the coup of 1903, has also been mentioned. Pašić, the Radical leader and dominant personality of Serbian politics, who was both Prime Minister and foreign minister
in 1904, spoke of Serbia's role in South Slavdom as comparable
to that of Piedmont in the formation of Italy. There were those
in Austria who felt that such a danger would be best warded off
by reconciling the South Slavs of the Monarchy through placing
them in a position of equality with the currently dominant nationalities.[16] This would serve to thwart any separatist tendency on
their part and might even eventually lead to the complete incor-

[15] In February. Izvolsky's scheme would have entailed Anglo-Russian action
at the Straits, surely a fanciful reading of the agreement with England of the
preceding August.

[16] Thus, in October, 1905, a group of forty Croatian members of the Hungarian
Parliament passed the so-called Fiume resolution that looked to the restoration of
the Kingdom of Croatia, Dalmatia, and Slavonia, though not its secession from
the Habsburg crown. Shortly thereafter, this resolution was endorsed by
Serbian representatives meeting in Zara.

poration of Serbia herself. But the annexation of Serbia was also advocated from the diametrically opposite motive of thorough suppression. This latter approach was congenial to such a man as Conrad von Hötzendorff, Chief of Staff since 1906, who would have been content with the simple destruction of Serbia.[17]

Aehrenthal was not at first anti-Russian, but rather inclined to coöperate with that country, and he was also willing to acknowledge the failure of the policy of coercion applied to Serbia,[18] but he could not overcome the influence of the traditional reactionary Magyar outlook. In any case, and whatever course might be adopted, Bosnia-Herzegovina became the focus of his policy. In these provinces, incorporated into the Empire in all save formal title since 1878, Austria had provided good administration; but, politically, she had adhered to her usual policy of *divide et impera*, favoring the substantial Moslem element at the expense of the Orthodox. The population of these provinces, whether Orthodox, Moslem, or Catholic, was in nationality akin to the Serbs; looked at from Serbia, the provinces were a focus of irredentism which, if successful there, might spread its influence to the South Slavs of the Empire proper.

Out of this situation and these considerations the idea began to crystallize in Aehrenthal's mind that the status of Bosnia-Herzegovina should be clarified through its outright incorporation into the Monarchy. Annexation of the provinces would have the effect of putting an end to any Serbian hopes; if the South Slavs in Austria became reconciled to their membership in the Empire, the fact of their greater numbers might create a force of sufficient attraction that would make possible the absorption of the smaller Serbian group as well.

It was at the end of 1907 that the issue of Bosnia-Herzegovina was made by Aehrenthal the main concern of his policy and was

---

[17] Hötzendorff has often been painted in unattractive colors. That he was ruthless and insensitive may be granted, but he must also be granted consistency of thought, willingness to face issues, and courage to accept the consequences of his own policies. A measure of these qualities may be gathered from his advocacy of preventive war against Austria's ally, Italy, whose loyalty he, with good reason, doubted; having espoused this view, he thought that the distress caused by the Messina earthquake constituted a particularly suitable occasion to launch a preventive attack.

[18] Austro-Serbian antagonism resulted in the failure, in 1906, to renew the commercial treaty between the two countries. Austria thought to put pressure on Serbia by closing her own market to Serbian products. This so-called "Pig War" embittered Serbian feeling, but Serbia was able to readjust her trade, not least by substituting the German for the Austrian market.

considered in the Council of Joint Ministers. But annexation would entail a modification of the Treaty of Berlin, whose signatories must therefore give their consent. It seems to have been Aehrenthal's idea that Austria could offer as a *quid pro quo* the evacuation of the Sanjak by herself. With this in mind, it would be useful to enhance the value of this last concession; the importance of the Sanjak could be magnified through the proposal of building a railway through it. The Russian reaction to this last suggestion was one of annoyance and suspicion which expressed itself in the counterproposal of a railway from east to west, connecting the Danube with the Adriatic coast. However, on July 2, 1908, Izvolsky may be said to have risen to Aehrenthal's bait by taking the initiative of proposing the discussion of a *quid pro quo* that would entail Russian support of Austria's annexation of Bosnia-Herzegovina in exchange for Austrian support of Russia's wishes at the Straits. This is the specific point at which Izvolsky and Aehrenthal, Russian and Austrian policies, came into formal contact and out of which the crisis of 1908 developed.

Aehrenthal was pleased, but events had already begun to take a new turn by this time. The Ottoman Empire had continued on its uninterrupted course of decay, unreformed and unaltered throughout the period with which we have been dealing. The Berlin settlement had been the last important readjustment after which minor changes alone had occurred, though the problem of the Sick Man of Europe continued to be one of concern to the chancelleries of Europe. But now as earlier there were those, patriotic Turks, who would have restored vigor to the Ottoman state; the so-called Young Turk Movement[19] was the expression of this hope. Rejuvenation and reform in Turkey could mean one thing alone, the introduction of the ways of the West; in political terms, some sort of catching up with the French Revolution. Given the structure of the Turkish state, and the stage of development of its peoples, reform could only come about through the agency of force, and it was consequently appropriate that in

[19] This movement may be said to go back to the constitution of 1876. It consisted largely of exiles who organized their activity in Geneva, then transferred it to Paris. The movement began to show renewed activity toward the end of the century and proceeded to establish contacts with army officers, mainly in Macedonia. It was the fear of further disintegration of the Ottoman Empire that precipitated action in 1908 by the Committee Union and Progress, the active arm of the movement.

the officer corps should be found the most probable agency of action.

It was on July 6, 1908, that the standard of revolt was raised in Macedonia. The army forces sent to put it down tended instead to fraternize with the insurgents, and Sultan Abdul Hamid, deciding that opposition was futile, yielded to the demands of the Young Turks by restoring, on July 24, the constitution momentarily granted in 1876, which thus became the Turkish constitution of 1908. In the Ottoman Empire proper the immediate result was astounding. Emulating the secular West, the Young Turks would only recognize equal Ottoman subjects: the regular army, *comitadji*, leaders of the Orthodox Christians, joined in an enthusiastic love fest of seemingly authentic brotherhood; elections were held in August-September for a lower house in which some forty Christians and a few Jews were returned out of 278 members, and the government in Constantinople was dominated by the Committee Union and Progress.

Revolutions, as distinct from *coups d'état*, are not so easily made. The manifestations of Christian and Moslem love under the banner of *égalité* were short-lived. The Young Turks may have imported secularism from the West, but nationalism, too, is a Western product; from the point of view of non-Turks, efficient efforts at Turkification might be even less attractive than sporadic religious persecution under an inefficient and corrupt, but also largely indifferent, administration. That aspect of domestic Ottoman affairs need not detain us here.

The extent to which some at least of the Chancelleries of Europe allowed themselves to become hopeful of real change in Turkey may seem surprising. In Vienna, Aehrenthal saw in it an argument for proceeding without delay with the intended annexation of Bosnia-Herzegovina: the title to those provinces was after all still Turkish, the Austrian occupation though now thirty years old was "temporary," and the Young Turks were highly nationalistic; it might be wise to shut the door on the raising of awkward issues. An interesting memorandum of his, drawn up in August for the Joint Ministers, dealt at length with the Sanjak and argued its unimportance in view of the fact that the real aim of Austrian policy should be the destruction of Serbia, an outcome to be achieved in coöperation with Bulgaria.

Aehrenthal, if rash, was determined and not devoid of skill

and guile in the pursuit of his aim. With Schoen and Tittoni, the German and Italian foreign ministers, whom he saw at this time he was somewhat less than open; Izvolsky was his principal concern. The two met at Buchlau in Bohemia on September 15 and there indulged in an interesting repetition of the performance of 1876. Between Austria and Russia no careful agreement was drawn up; what understanding was made, not surprisingly therefore, turned out to be misunderstanding and source of recrimination; understandably also the versions of the two principals were at variance. Izvolsky was amenable to the annexation of Bosnia-Herzegovina in exchange for Aehrenthal's support of his policy at the Straits. He seems to have been careless, to say the least, both in failing to secure a firm commitment from Aehrenthal in this last respect and also in failing to obtain precise knowledge of the manner in which the annexation was to be brought about. In his own mind he seems to have considered that the matter would need the prior assent of the Powers. That Aehrenthal was disingenuous seems clear, but Izvolsky had no one but himself to blame for the disillusion that was to be his when he found out that Aehrenthal was proceeding on the assumption that, in the matter of securing the approval of the Powers for his plans, the Russian assent had already been given.

THE ANNEXATION AND ITS CONSEQUENCES

From the meeting with Aehrenthal, Izvolsky set about a tour of Europe with a view, as he thought, to obtaining the consent of the Powers to his plans. Great were his shock and indignation when, on his way to Paris, he learned that Austria-Hungary had proclaimed the annexation of Bosnia and Herzegovina on October 5. But he was doomed to greater disappointment when he found that neither Paris nor London was anxious to give him much support; his plea in Berlin for German backing of a European conference found no response; even at home his policy was looked upon askance.

Like Russia in 1870, Austria now had by unilateral action violated an international agreement, the Treaty of Berlin of 1878. The step of formal annexation had been taken deliberately to close the door to retreat, but the matter was properly the concern of the Powers; as in the case of Morocco three years earlier, the question of a conference therefore became the central issue around which the crisis unfolded. It was natural that the Entente

Powers should favor the device of a conference, but Austria would have none of it and Aehrenthal put pressure on Izvolsky with the threat of public revelations which doubtless would have been embarrassing. The focus of Austrian interest lay in the Balkans, particularly Serbia, rather than in a wish to humiliate either Izvolsky or Russia, but Germany, specifically Bülow, perceived the opportunity of procuring a diplomatic victory at the expense of the latter.[20] This could best be achieved by giving staunch support to Austria; as he put it to Aehrenthal: "I shall regard whatever decision you come to as the appropriate one." His calculation proved correct that intransigeance on Germany's part would frighten France into restraining Russia, and the crisis was still unresolved at the opening of the year 1909. Negotiations around the issue of a conference continued, but Austria would accept it only on the prior agreement of acquiescence by the Powers to registration of the *fait accompli*. In order to induce Russia to yield, Germany sent that country a note in March that has often been described as an ultimatum. It was not formally such though Izvolsky was asked to give a yes or no answer to the annexation, failing which Germany "would let events take their course."

There was nothing for it but to yield. When that result had been secured, a face-saving solution was contrived out of the Turkish situation. Since formal title to Bosnia and Herzegovina was still Turkish, a direct Austro-Turkish agreement provided for the transfer of sovereignty from the Ottoman state to the Austrian;[21] to this bilateral agreement the Powers gave their assent, thereby maintaining the fiction that legality had been preserved. In this manner the crisis was solved and peace assured.

But the aftermath of consequences that the episode left in its train was considerable. The most significant aspect of it was that it had served as a test between the Central Powers and the Entente. The outcome was undoubtedly a clear victory for the former, though Bülow was too sanguine in his conclusion that the British, and even more the French, failure to give Russia support meant that he had broken the ring of the encirclement of Germany. Russia was indeed disappointed at the absence of British and French support, but her resentment and bitterness were natu-

[20] Bülow was motivated in part by resentment against Russia for her agreement with Britain of the preceding year.

[21] There was, in addition, a money payment by Austria to Turkey in indemnification of state property acquired.

rally directed toward the Central Powers, and most of all toward Germany, whose uncompromising attitude had insured the victory of Austria. This behavior of Germany may be said to have strengthened the bonds of her alliance with Austria, by contrast with the weak behavior of the Entente. The exchanges that took place during this period between the Chiefs of Staff, Conrad and Moltke, considering the implementation of military operations in the event of general war, if they fell within the legitimate province of the military, also put added stress on that aspect of the alliance, the tone of which was now considerably altered from that of its initial intent. Bismarck had opposed the conclusion of a military convention with Austria; as he had put it in 1887: "In order not to obscure the clear delimitation, at present existing, of the *casus foederis* we must not encourage the temptations, to which the Austrians are prone, to exploit the situation in order to use the armed forces of Germany for the benefit of Hungarian and Catholic ambitions in the Balkans. . . . For us, Balkan questions can in no case be a motive for war."[22]

To be sure, it was Bülow's own choice to support Austria to the extent that he did, but his decision followed upon the Austrian initiative in the affair. Instead of the alliance being used, as was Bismarck's intention, to reinforce the peace and restrain Austria from adventures, the relationship had in a measure been reversed, Austria now taking the lead of action. Bülow's behavior had been motivated by his view of the whole complex of European relationships, which is why the annexation of Bosnia-Herzegovina, a small enough matter in itself, gave rise to a major European crisis, and why in the eyes of others Germany loomed larger and more dangerous than Austria. Once again, in St. Petersburg, in Paris, and in London a bad aftertaste was left of what appeared like German saber rattling technique.

But the larger aspect of Great Power relationships should not obscure the smaller, but no less dangerous, local issues in the Balkans, nor the impact of domestic issues on foreign policy. Austria, or Aehrenthal, was largely motivated in these matters by concern over the internal problem of disparate nationalities. It was in 1909 that there occurred both the Friedjung and the Zagreb trials.[23] To implicate the South Slavs of the monarchy in charges

---

[22] Quoted in Albertini, *op. cit.*, Vol. I, p. 271.
[23] The Friedjung trial grew out of an article in the *Neue Freie Presse* (March 25, 1909) by the historian Friedjung wherein, on the strength of documents fur-

of treasonable activity, and to do so on the basis of forgeries that were revealed as such in trial, in addition to creating a major scandal, could only redound to the discredit of the government; it served to exacerbate the discontent of the South Slavs, more than ever therefore amenable to the thought that their free Serbian cousins might play the role for them that nineteenth-century Piedmont had played for Italy. The annexation of Bosnia-Herzegovina closed the door to any hopes of union of those provinces with Serbia; it did not serve to destroy the South Slav nationalist feeling which instead was driven to look to violence and illegality as a last resort.

Serbian feeling, at all levels, was highly incensed over the annexation. But in the absence of Russian support it would have been mere folly for Serbia to precipitate an open conflict with her neighbor. Instead of this, she yielded to the Concert of Europe which had become the agent of Austria's success. On March 30, the Serbian government subscribed to the following statement:

> Serbia recognizes that she has not been injured in her right by the *fait accompli* created in Bosnia-Herzegovina and that consequently she will conform to such decisions as the Powers shall take in regard to Article 25 of the Treaty of Berlin. Submitting to the advice of the Great Powers, Serbia undertakes already now to abandon the attitude of protest and opposition which she has maintained in regard to the annexation since last autumn and undertakes further to change the course of her present policy towards Austria-Hungary to live henceforward with the latter on a footing of good-neighbourliness.[24]

This untrue statement may be regarded as a measure of the Austrian success, but there was danger in allowing Serbia to continue in independent existence while humiliating and antagonizing her.[25] If the Austro-German bond had been strengthened during

---

nished him by the foreign office, accusations were made against Serbia in connivance with whom members of the Serbo-Croat coalition were accused of working. These charges led to a libel action by members of the coalition and to the exposure of the fraudulent foreign office documentation.

The Zagreb trial, also in 1909, was the trial of a group of Serbs, subjects of the monarchy, accused of high treason for conducting Pan-Serb propaganda. Here also the documentary bases of the charge were shown to be forgeries. The court's finding of guilt merely created a scandal of European dimensions and the sentences were eventually quashed by a higher court.

[24] British Documents, cited above, Vol. V, p. 782. Quoted in Albertini, *op. cit.*, Vol. I, p. 291.

[25] In connection with the annexation of Bosnia-Herzegovina Austria relinquished the Sanjak. There was an element of inconsistency in antagonizing Serbia and cutting off her hopes in Bosnia-Herzegovina while at the same time removing a barrier between her and Montenegro that the Austrian occupation of the Sanjak had constituted.

this episode, the same was not the case of the Triple Alliance as a whole. Under the terms of the alliance, Italy would have been entitled to some compensation for such a change as the annexation entailed. She received none, and though the management of her policy under Tittoni was less than skillful, she was understandably disgruntled. It was in October, 1909, that Tittoni and Izvolsky concluded the Racconigi agreement under the common motivation of forestalling a recurrence of unilateral Austrian action in the Balkans: declaring their similar interest in the preservation of the Balkan *status quo*, they expressed in addition reciprocal sympathy for their respective wishes, Russian at the Straits, Italian in Tripoli. This was Italy's second *tour de valse* outside the circle of her formal allies.

THE SEEMING RELAXATION OF TENSIONS

Some of the unfavorable consequences of the Bosnian annexation crisis did not escape Germany, who set about procuring some relaxation of the existing tensions. This effort had little success in the end, but for a while, some two years, the European atmosphere appeared somewhat less somber. It was shortly after the formal Austrian announcement of the annexation, at the end of October, 1908, that the *Daily Telegraph* incident[26] cast a new cloud over Anglo-German relations. It was a poor climate for negotiations to prosper on the by now long-standing issue of naval rivalry. England was increasingly alarmed at the fast-developing German building program; from the German point of view some form of understanding with England would have been all the more desirable, but the familiar difficulty growing out of the British reluctance to undertake political commitments continued

---

[26] This incident grew out of an interview with the Kaiser published in the *Daily Telegraph* on October 28. The Kaiser, during the interview, acknowledged the unfriendliness of German feeling toward England and sought to explain his own good will, as evidence of which he cited the services he had rendered England during the Boer War (a proposed plan of campaign he had communicated to Queen Victoria and his refusal to join France and Russia in mediation). The publication of the interview was the result of a comedy of errors—bad coördination in the German handling of the dispatch—but the effect of it was an international sensation.

In Germany it gave rise to sharp criticism of the Kaiser as an irresponsible chatterbox and William II had to eat humble pie. He begged Bülow to withhold his proffered resignation and promised better behavior in future. Bülow's failure to defend William II in the Reichstag in turn annoyed the latter and relations between them were thereafter much cooler.

to prove an insuperable stumbling block. Despite the opportunity offered by the visit of King Edward VII to Berlin in February, 1909, this time again nothing came of the discussions.

Bülow had somewhat better success with France. An incident at Casablanca in Morocco in September, 1908, growing out of the desertion of some Germans from the French Foreign Legion, instead of leading to renewed friction was composed with relative ease through the willingness of both sides to accept the verdict of the Hague Tribunal to which the matter was submitted. More important were the discussions that eventually led to the agreement of February, 1909: both countries seemed willing to recognize one another's interests and to make an effort to collaborate in the economic development of Morocco. The ensuing period of relaxation was short-lived, and with the reassertion of economic rivalry within two years Morocco was to be the object of another major European crisis, while the affairs of eastern Europe, following the flare-up of 1908–1909 were relatively quiescent.

During the interval Bülow's tenure came to an end. Increasingly estranged from the Kaiser since the *Daily Telegraph* episode, differing from the Kaiser as well as from Tirpitz in the matter of naval policy, Bülow tendered his resignation in June, 1909.[27] Perhaps to his surprise it was accepted, for the chancellor held in no mean esteem his own abilities, though toward the end he seems to have become aware of the cost of his apparent successes which had gone a long way toward fostering distrust of Germany abroad. His tenure of office was a highly important period and his record has thus been summed up by a recent writer:

He had made no attempt to moderate the policy of Austria, either in the Near East or towards the Italians under Austrian rule. On the contrary, he had fomented Austro-Italian friction in order to prevent the two countries from coming to an understanding which might render them less appreciative of the benefits of the Triple Alliance and less submissive to the predominance of Berlin in the alliance. In the European field his record is no more satisfactory. It was during his Chancellorship and by his action that Germany laid the foundations of the situation from which, in 1914, arose the First World War.[28]

The succession of Bülow went to a man of highly contrasting temper. There was no arrogant self-complacency in Bethmann-

[27] The occasion was the defeat in the Reichstag of a bill on death duties.
[28] Albertini, *op. cit.*, Vol. I, p. 321.

Hollweg, but retiring quiet instead; there was also timidity and indecision. This gave all the more scope to the influence of Kider-len-Waechter who, shortly after Bethmann assumed the chancellorship, was put in charge of the foreign office. Not lacking in intelligence and wit that was sometimes too sharp[29]—Bülow he called "the Eel" and Bethmann "the Earthworm"—his influence on the direction of German policy was to be considerable. The time was especially delicate, for three of the basic assumptions of that policy had been proved false by the formation in succession of the Franco-Russian, Anglo-French, and Anglo-Russian connections, which in their turn gave rise to the German fear of *Einkreisung*. Bülow had only made matters worse with his Moroccan and Balkan policies, which served to give reality to German fears. To cultivate any possible source of difference between the members of the Triple Entente was obviously a German interest.

Despite the bad aftertaste of the Bosnian crisis, there was some relaxation in Franco-German relations. The Moroccan agreement of 1909 seemed to offer the hope that this particular bone of contention had been buried, and the tendency that was favorable to collaboration had representatives in France. With Russia, too, there seemed to be reasons for hope. Those were not lacking in Russia who favored a German orientation of that country's policy; here also, despite the annexation, the tendency was strong to put much of the blame on Izvolsky's bungling. Moreover, the Anglo-Russian agreement turned out in some respects to be not altogether satisfactory; it was felt in Britain that Russia was taking advantage of it in the Far East no less than in Persia. In September, 1910, Izvolsky was transferred to the coveted Paris Embassy and his place in St. Petersburg was taken by Sazonov, a man less mercurial though one, like Bethmann, lacking resolution and strength. Almost immediately, he and the tsar went to Germany on a visit. This augured well for Germany, but the Russians talked Near East—Persia and the Baghdad railway—while Kiderlen was mainly interested in separating Russia from Britain; as he put it to the German ambassador in St. Petersburg, "the Russian assurance concerning relations with England is the alpha and omega for me of the whole agreement." Sazonov declined to walk into the

---

[29] His lack of reticence had interfered with his advancement. He was in charge of the Bucharest Embassy from 1900 to 1910, except for an interval at the foreign office during Schoen's illness in 1908–1909. It was he who was essentially responsible for the "ultimatum" to Russia in March, 1909, as well as for the Moroccan agreement with France in February.

German trap and the Russian visit remained barren of concrete results.

This was also the time when German naval building threatened to create a sharp issue with Britain. The efforts of Bülow during the last months of his tenure of office have been mentioned. The acceleration of building in the autumn of 1908 had made a bad impression in England where the issue of naval power was aired in public debate, creating a shift away from the previously prevailing orientation of sympathy for Germany; the slogan of the day, "We want eight and we won't wait," is reflection of this changing temper.[30] In this matter, Bethmann, like Bülow, was aware of the dangers of naval competition with Britain, but Tirpitz remained unconvinced and the Kaiser was always highly sensitive, and unwarrantedly suspicious, on the subject of German naval power, on occasion giving immoderate expression to his feelings. In this issue of naval power German policy had impaled itself on the horns of a dilemma: it was willing to consider a limitation, or slowing down, of its program only in exchange for a political agreement, essentially a British promise of neutrality in the event of conflict; at the same time, the growth of German naval power was the very thing that made Britain all the more reluctant to undertake such a commitment.

It made the British feel that it was all the more essential that they do not loosen their connection with the French and the Russians, even though there was annoyance at the tendency, especially of the latter, to take advantage of the newly made agreements. As Grey put it, "An entente with Germany such as M. Kiderlen sketches would serve to establish German hegemony in Europe and would not last long after it had served that purpose." In so far as there was expectation in some German quarters that Britain might be "frightened" into concessions and agreement, this can only be called a crude psychological blunder, of which not a few samples are to be found in the direction of German policy during this period, a gross misunderstanding of the British temper. In this atmosphere, the negotiations that went on for two years, from Bethmann's accession to the middle of 1911, were therefore fated to sterility: where Germany kept asking for a political commitment as the price of naval agreement, Britain kept reiterating her demand for unconditional agreement *prior*

[30] This referred to the British determination to outmatch the naval building program that had been laid down in Germany.

to the discussion of political considerations. The discussion did not end at this point, but for a time was interrupted by the diversion of a new crisis, once more over Morocco.

IV. The Second Moroccan Crisis and Its Aftermath

THE AGADIR CRISIS

The second Moroccan crisis, or Agadir crisis, in 1911, was in many respects a curious repetition of the affair of six years earlier. But there were also differences in the atmosphere of 1911 compared with that of 1905. From the German point of view there was much to be said for reconciliation with France, the real hinge of the Entente; Kiderlen regarded Morocco as the agency through which his policy might be implemented. The agreement of 1909 opened the possibility of economic coöperation between the two countries. But an involved tale of intra-French and intra-German differences no less than the Franco-German aspect of the matter rendered the prospect barren. Meantime, the internal affairs of Morocco followed a not unexpected course of disorder until, in May, 1911, a French force moved to occupy Fez. The fundamentals of the problem were relatively simple. The French, in occupying Fez, had acted quite correctly *vis-à-vis* the signatories of the Act of Algeciras. But, as Kiderlen saw it, the occupation was but a step on the road that was leading to the complete absorption of Morocco by France. This seemed to him a natural development. The only question was to extract the best possible price for Germany's consent. His policy therefore was to let the French become involved, then raise the issue of compensations.[31] Like Bülow in 1905, he would play the sphinx at first; but beyond this, again like Bülow, he assumed that frightening the French would make them more amenable in negotiation. In this lay the fundamental vice of his calculations.

The operation of his policy was at once crude and simple: on July 1, the *Panther*, a German gunboat, appeared in Agadir, ostensibly for the same purpose that had brought the French into Fez. From this act, in Kiderlen's own words, the thumping of the table, intended to convey the impression of a German assertion to

---

[31] Kiderlen's policy was clearly laid out in a long memorandum, drawn up in May, in which the whole Moroccan situation was closely analyzed.

equality of position with France in Morocco, derives the name of the crisis. To a point, Kiderlen's calculations were successful; the Russian reaction toward France was to pay her back in the same coin that France had used in the Bosnian affair: Russian opinion would have difficulty in seeing a sufficient cause for European conflict in such a colonial dispute. Better still, in France, Caillaux became Prime Minister on the very day of the appearance of the *Panther* in Agadir. Caillaux was not Delcassé;[32] he represented instead that current in France that viewed the Russian alliance with suspicion and favored in its place an understanding with Germany. He was fully prepared to negotiate—a *quid pro quo* could be evolved between Morocco and the Baghdad railway—and even the Agadir coup did not unduly alarm him, though it had the effect of making his position—like Rouvier's in 1905—more difficult in France.

Already in June, Kiderlen had indicated that he expected France to pay some price for Germany's consent, though the sphinx would give no indication of what the price might be; as he put it to Cambon on the 21st, "bring us something back from Paris." The German wish for compensation was wholly understandable, and the desire to secure the best possible price wholly legitimate defense of German interest; only the manner of procedure was disastrously clumsy. Back in Berlin from his visit to Paris, Cambon was having great difficulty in finding the extent of German expectations, until on July 15 Kiderlen pointed on a map to the entire French Congo. The shock to Cambon was great, but, despite the Kaiser's opposition and dislike of the whole affair—again as in 1905—Kiderlen still adhered to his belief in the strong method.

British counsels were by no means united on the issue, and this presumably constituted another asset for Kiderlen. Britain had no objection to some colonial exchange between France and Germany, but Kiderlen's unreasonable demand for the Congo, even though a mere bargaining move, was put to good use by the French. There followed Lloyd George's Mansion House speech on July 21; whatever may have been the precise intent of the

[32] The foreign minister was de Selves who, however, was not a strong personality, with the consequence that Caillaux remained the chief director of French policy. Negotiations, however, had to be conducted through the foreign office, and, curious parallel to 1905 on the French side, Caillaux resorted to direct and secret negotiations with the Germans behind the back of his own foreign minister.

speech,[33] it was taken as a threat to Germany and had the effect of encouraging French resistance and of turning a Franco-German into an Anglo-German dispute. There were naval preparations in Britain and the specter of war was raised.

Kiderlen had never meant more than bluff, and the outcome was a Franco-German agreement,[34] finally signed on November 4, as a result of which the crisis was resolved. Germany accepted the establishment of a French protectorate in Morocco, in exchange for which she received two substantial strips of territory from the French Congo. To make the deal more palatable in France, Germany in turn ceded a strip of land next to Lake Chad, so that the arrangement could ostensibly be presented as an exchange of territories.

Taken in isolation, the agreement of November, 1911, may be regarded as one more in the long list of colonial compromises contrived among the imperial Powers of Europe. In the context of the imperial activity of the day, the French claim to Morocco may be called both legitimate and reasonable; but this also meant that reasonable compensation should be given to those who had equally legitimate interests in Morocco. This was what France had done from 1900 to 1904 where Italy, Britain, and Spain were concerned, leaving Germany alone to be dealt with. Germany was quite reconciled to the French possession of Morocco, but she wanted a price and the best price that could be had. Strengthened by the prior consent of others, France was at first inclined to exploit her position, until Caillaux came, who was anxious for understanding; on her side Germany twice thought that saber rattling and threats were the most suitable tactics to use. Thus Morocco was the cause of two European crises; but in the end agreement was reached that may be viewed as a not unfair compromise, at least in its own limited terms. Morocco disappeared as an issue of European international politics and the French Protectorate was established in March, 1912.

But the crisis that the *Panther* had set in motion left the climate of Europe beclouded. Not least significant was the effect

---

[33] A. J. P. Taylor takes the position that it was merely intended as a warning that Britain could not be ignored in any partition of Morocco (Taylor, *The Struggle for Mastery in Europe 1848–1918*, p. 471). The fact remains that the Mansion House speech came after a French request for support.

[34] A further contributory factor to agreement was a financial crisis in Berlin to which France was not extraneous, one more manifestation of the role of French finance during this period.

on domestic opinions. That the agreement was criticized in both France and Germany may be taken as evidence of its essential reasonableness. But Caillaux did not long survive it; his ministry was overthrown in January, 1912, and his succession went to Poincaré. No better symbol could be found of the changing temper of France. Poincaré was a man of upright character and strong resolve, endowed with no little ability; living embodiment of the bourgeois virtues of France, with both their limitations and their strength, devoted to the lay Republic, Poincaré stands out among the statesmen of the immediate prewar period, and his influence on the course of events of that time was considerable. Where Germany was concerned his views were both clear and simple: Germany was *the* enemy on whom a watchful eye should forever be kept from the border of his native Lorraine. Poincaré was the living expression of the *réveil national* of France which on his side he did all in his power to nurture.

In Germany, correspondingly, much had been said about Morocco since the crisis of 1905, until the name had penetrated the popular consciousness in which it had given rise to unwarranted expectations. Both Kiderlen and Bethmann were widely criticized for the agreement, in the country no less than in the Reichstag. Yet from his point of view Tirpitz could turn it all to good account, extracting added credits for his navy, which were matched by larger appropriations for the army. This was, to say the least, an odd and unexpected outcome of Bethmann's efforts to obtain relaxation of the tensions of Europe.

THE TRIPOLITAN WAR

It was just over a month (September 28) before the signature of the Franco-German agreement, formal closing of the Agadir crisis, that an ultimatum went from Italy to Turkey, followed immediately by a declaration of war. The concrete issue lay in the vilayets of Tripoli and Cyrenaica where Italy complained of the treatment of her interests at Turkish hands. The complaint was not devoid of foundation, for on the Turkish side there was equally founded suspicion of Italian designs on the southern shore of the Mediterranean. What prompted Italy to act at this juncture was domestic as well as foreign considerations. In Italy, too, nationalism of the more aggressive variety had witnessed a revival; it is significant that it should have fallen to Giolitti, himself neither a nationalist nor an imperialist, to launch the Tripolitan adventure.

But the foreign situation was even more important. Tripoli—later Libya—was the last unpreëmpted segment of North African territory. If there is basis for the charge that the Moroccan crises grew out of France's failure to make adequate diplomatic preparations—since the consent of all but Germany had been obtained, or purchased—the same may not be said of Italy in Tripoli. At one time or another, all the Powers had expressed their acquiescence to an Italian establishment in Tripoli; Italy was, therefore, where Europe was concerned, in possession of a blank check. With the closing of the Moroccan chapter and the general intensification of Mediterranean rivalries—Italy was concerned over the growing German interest, even in Tripoli—she felt that the time was ripe for the collection of her check lest some of the signatories pretext altered conditions to review their consent. The Italo-Turkish War was a source of annoyance to all the Powers: it was an extension of the Moroccan disturbance and, most of all, it raised the unwelcome possibility of a reopening of the Near Eastern question.

Of the military aspect of the war in Tripoli it will suffice to say that the undertaking proved somewhat more onerous than anticipated in Italy; this was no repetition, however, of Crispi's ill-prepared Abyssinian adventure. Willing to make the necessary additional effort, Italian power was sufficient and Italy in the end had her way. With a view to closing the door to complicating outside interventions, Italy created a *fait accompli* by proclaiming the annexation of the two vilayets on November 5. The international and diplomatic aspects of the matter are the more interesting in the present context.

Among the Entente Powers, Russia alone seemed to be sympathetic to the Italian enterprise. France was reserved, not having yet proceeded with the establishment of her own protectorate over Morocco, but the incidents of the *Carthage* and the *Manouba* in January, 1912, gave rise to considerable feeling and altered the tone of Franco-Italian relations.[35] The only reason for the British failure to voice stronger dislike was the fear of antagonizing Italy.

---

[35] These were two French ships that were stopped by the Italians on suspicion that they were conveying assistance to the Turks in Tripoli. The incident, though eventually composed, gave rise to very sharp French protests and to corresponding Italian resentment.

But friction was greater with Italy's own formal allies. Like Britain, Germany was annoyed and fearful of antagonizing Italy; but in view of her own growing interest in the Ottoman Empire and of the influence that she was seeking to establish in it, Germany could not but dislike intensely an open conflict between an existing and a prospective ally. Sharpest of all was the Austrian reaction. The formal terms of the alliance were used to restrain Italy from taking action in the Balkans, and Conrad went the length of again advocating war with Italy, for which he was dismissed from his post.

As local resistance continued in Tripoli, Italy turned to the Aegean. Ostensibly in preparation for action at the Straits, she proceeded, in April–May, 1912, to the occupation of a number of islands that came to be known as the Dodecanese group. This naturally increased the fears of the Powers and their protests against extension of the field of hostilities. Amid much diplomatic activity, it was eventually the threat of local Balkan complications that brought the Turks to terms. At Ouchy, in October, 1912, the Porte agreed to the cession of sovereignty and to the withdrawal of its troops from Libya; pending fulfilment of this last provision the Italians would remain in occupation of the Dodecanese Islands. Thus was closed another chapter in the story of Europe's imperial activity; Italy added one item to her collection of deserts and the initially temporary occupation of the Dodecanese was not to terminate until 1946. The episode, in itself minor, had served to test the balance and the tensions of Europe.

BRITAIN, GERMANY, AND FRANCE: NAVAL ARRANGEMENTS

The Tripolitan War did not interrupt the negotiations centering around the issue of Anglo-German naval rivalry. The Moroccan aftermath of tension between the two countries and the German decision to increase armaments have been mentioned. In spite of this, there were those, both in England and Germany, who would not yet abandon the hope of agreement. Albert Ballin, director of the Hamburg-Amerika Line and close to the Kaiser, and Sir Ernest Cassel in Britain had for some time endeavored to bring the political leaders together. Eventually, Cassel went to Berlin with a British memorandum that became the basis of renewed discussions at the end of January, 1912. These seemed to prosper to the point of warranting the visit to Germany, in February, of Haldane, the British secretary for war and himself of liberal imperialist orientation.

Discussions took place in a generally frank and friendly atmosphere, until Bethmann-Hollweg, in accordance with the unchanging German wish for a political agreement, suggested among other things the following formula:

1. Neither of the two parties shall enter into a combination directed against the other. They expressly declare that they are not bound by any settlement of such a kind.
2. If one of the High Contracting Parties comes to find itself involved in a war against one or more Powers, the other of the High Contracting Parties shall observe at least benevolent neutrality towards that Power, and shall use all its efforts for the localization of the conflict.

On the one hand the Germans maintained that the proposed new naval law, the *Novelle*, must be enacted, though some concession on the rate of building would be possible. Grey, on his side, went as far as proposing the formula:

England will make no unprovoked attack upon Germany and pursue no aggressive policy towards her. Aggression upon Germany is not the subject and forms no part of any Treaty understanding or combination to which England is now a party nor will she become a party to anything that has such an object.

This represented the extreme limit of British concession and the influence of what may be labeled the pro-German group in the Cabinet. It did not, however, completely tie Britain's hands in the event of a German aggression and in the end proved unacceptable to Germany, while on the British side there was opposition to making an agreement concurrently with an intensified naval competition. For these reasons, the Haldane mission, like preceding attempts, was a failure. Interestingly enough, this failure and the enactment of the *Novelle* were not followed by recriminations, but rather by an improved, perhaps because clearer, atmosphere of Anglo-German relations.

Needless to say, these negotiations had been followed with considerable anxiety in Paris where their failure was seen with much relief. Poincaré was no less anxious than Bethmann to secure a clearer British commitment, but in this effort met with little more success than the Germans, despite some support in England for changing the Entente into a clear alliance. But the logic of

events could not but prod England in the direction of closer cooperation with France. It was the year 1912 that witnessed the
rearrangement of the British and French fleets; the former, withdrawing from Malta, would concentrate in home waters and at
Gibraltar, while the latter, withdrawing from Brest, concentrated
at Toulon.

It was a logical enough arrangement to divide responsibility
in this fashion, the French to look after their own as well as
British interests in the Mediterranean, while the British looked
after both in the Atlantic. But this implied community of interest
the British were reluctant to acknowledge formally. The most
that could be done, under Cambon's patient but persistent prodding, was the ambiguous declaration contained in the letter written
to him by Grey on November 12. It is worth quoting as the
best description both of where England stood and of the manner
of procedure of British diplomacy:

> From time to time [wrote Grey], in recent years the French and
> British naval and military experts have consulted together. It has always
> been understood that *such consultation does not restrict the freedom
> of either Government to decide at any future time whether or not to
> assist the other by armed force.* We have agreed that consultation be-
> tween experts is not, and ought not to be regarded as, an engagement
> that commits either Government to action in a contingency that has
> not arisen and may never arise. The disposition, for instance, of the
> French and British fleets respectively at the present moment is not
> based upon an engagement to coöperate in war.
>
> You have, however, pointed out that, *if either Government had
> grave reason to expect an unprovoked attack by a third Power, it might
> become essential to know whether it could in that event depend upon
> the armed assistance of the other.*
>
> I agree that, if either Government had grave reason to expect an
> unprovoked attack by a Third Power, or something that threatened
> the general peace, *it should immediately discuss* with the other whether
> both Governments should act together to prevent aggression and to
> preserve peace, and, if so, *what measures they would be prepared to
> take in common.* If these measures involved action, the plans of the
> General Staffs would at once be taken into consideration, and the Gov-
> ernments would then decide what effect should be given to them.[36]

Such was the extent of definition of the Anglo-French relationship to which Grey would consent. Even the staff discussions
were not known to the entire Cabinet and one may here observe

[36] Quoted in Fay, *The Origins of the World War*, Vol. I, pp. 322–323. Italics
are the author's.

another step in the gradual, though reluctant, involvement of Britain. It ran against the grain of the British tradition and mind to make definite calculations on the basis of a contingency that "may never arise." But that it might arise could hardly be denied; if and when, *discussion* should take place, prior to deciding "what effect should be given" to hypothetical plans. From the French point of view this was meager satisfaction and it is to the credit of the suppleness of French diplomacy that it would be content with Grey's statement rather than insist on more.

But what really counted was the drift of events and the fundamental facts of the situation. In the light of past experience Britain's tergiversation and fumbling are altogether understandable; Britain was interested in maintaining the balance of power and preserving the peace as being those conditions most suitable to her own interest. Her hesitation we shall see persisting into August, 1914. Only in retrospect has it become clear, and by the British themselves acknowledged, that the uncertainty about their action, which they were only too successful in conveying to others, was in the end no service either to themselves or to the cause of peace. In effect, and albeit in different degrees, Britain and France, *vis-à-vis* the rest of the world, were both in a similar position of Powers essentially satisfied, in relative decline, hence basically more likely to suffer than to gain from far-reaching readjustments. This is, however, largely the wisdom of after the event.[37]

V. The Near Eastern Question Again

THE BALKAN WARS

From the time of the second Moroccan crisis the tempo of European tensions shows an accelerating tendency. The connection between Morocco and Tripoli was close. If the Italo-Turkish War, a matter in itself of not overwhelming importance, had been so universally unpopular it was because it touched the highly sensitive spot that was the Ottoman Empire. That war and the wars in the Balkans in 1912–1913 are also intimately related.

In August, 1912, Poincaré, at the time Prime Minister of France,

[37] Other naval developments of this time included a Franco-Russian naval convention of July 16, 1912, that looked to closer coöperation of the naval forces of the two countries, in particular the development of the French naval base of Bizerte in Tunisia, and in general pointed to a division of labor among the navies of the Entente Powers: Britain in the North Sea, France in the Mediterranean, Russia in the Baltic and Black Seas.

paid a visit to Russia. He was on that occasion apprised, and somewhat shocked to be apprised, of some of the results of Russian
diplomatic activity. It is an interesting aspect of that activity that
it has often been characterized—witness Ignatiev in Constantinople
in 1878 or Izvolsky at Buchlau in 1908—by a surprising lack of
coördination. Russia was not at this time especially concerned with

THE BALKAN WARS,
1912 - 1913

- Bulgarian gains from Turkey
- Serbian gains from Turkey
- Montenegrin gains from Turkey
- Greek gains from Turkey
- Rumanian gains from Bulgaria

extending her influence in the Balkans, but rather with the status
of the Straits. Their closure by the Turks for a short period,
when the prospect of Italian action was threatening, sharply
brought home to Russia the disadvantage of her position.[38] This

[38] The importance of the grain export trade and of Western imports in connection with the development of industry in the Ukraine emphasized the desirability of unimpeded freedom of passage through the Straits.

was in 1912, and as early as 1911, Izvolsky in Paris and Charykov in Constantinople, acting largely on their own initiatives, had sought to enlist French support in one case, Turkish acquiescence in the other, for some change in the status of the Straits. These efforts were stillborn, but the Russian ministers in Belgrade and in Sofia, Hartwig and Nekludov respectively, were very active in promoting schemes of Balkan reorganization. They, too, were acting on their own initiatives rather than on the basis of clear instructions from St. Petersburg. Their efforts, Hartwig's especially, met with surprising success when on March 13, 1912, a Serbo-Bulgarian alliance was concluded.

The clear intent of the arrangement may be described as the satisfaction of the irredentism of the two countries at the expense of Turkey. The partition of Macedonia was agreed upon on the basis of Serbian and Bulgarian zones, in the north and south respectively, between which a "contested zone" would be allotted in accordance with the arbitral decision of the tsar who was to be informed of the whole arrangement.[39] Apparently, Sazonov did not fully grasp the import of the Serbo-Bulgarian alliance, for, though not desirous of war, he professed to be wholly satisfied with it. Poincaré's vision was clearer when he was informed on the occasion of his Russian visit; he remonstrated with his ally for the ignorance in which France had been kept of so important a development. He, too, did not want war, of either Balkan or more general dimensions, but, in keeping with his broad policy of firmness and of strengthening the Russian alliance, he went on to assure the Russians of the dependability of French support.

Poincaré's misgivings were entirely founded: the initial agreement of March had been supplemented by subsequent and more precise military arrangements, and, in May, the Balkan League came into existence with the conclusion of a Greco-Bulgarian understanding, a consummation toward which Venizelos had been striving for some time. The rising discontent in the Ottoman section of the Balkans, result of the nationalistic policies of the Young

[39] Bulgaria held that Macedonia properly belonged to herself, but she accepted the compromise in the hope of gains in Thrace; on her side, Serbia hoped to extend herself toward the Adriatic. Serbia and Bulgaria had thus a common interest in the liberation of Turkish-held territory, but Serbian irredentism was directed as much, in fact rather more, toward Austria-Hungary as toward the Ottoman Empire. Although no Bulgarian interest was at stake in the former direction, it was the Serbian hope that coöperation with Bulgaria might eventually be extended to it.

Turks after the initial and short-lived fraternization of 1908, and the fact that Turkey was currently involved in war with Italy, made the Balkans fully ripe for an explosion.

Interestingly, the effect of Poincaré's Russian visit was not so much to encourage Russian agressiveness as to bring Sazonov to full realization of the danger. Nor were the Central Powers at this time interested in more than the preservation of peace.[40] Germany, to be sure, would give Austria support, much as France would Russia, but on the broad basis of the necessity of maintaining the bonds of the alliance, rather than with a view to specific results. In Austria, Berchtold, who had succeeded Aehrenthal at the beginning of the year upon the latter's death, was not inclined to strong initiative; for the central problem of the Monarchy he had no solution. The result of these circumstances was what may be described as the last successful operation of the Concert of Europe in the face of a major crisis.

In August, Berchtold approached the Powers with a view to joint action in Constantinople. Though his particular proposals were not acceptable to Russia, negotiations went on during the summer, until a French proposal,[41] on October 4, that the Powers undertake to oppose any change in the territorial *status quo* of European Turkey became the basis of a *démarche* that rallied the consent of all. Appropriately enough, Russia and Austria, the two Great Powers most immediately concerned with Balkan matters, were entrusted with conveying the joint will of Europe to the Balkan states. It was too late; the Austro-Russian note was not in time to prevent the opening gun of a Montenegrin declaration of war against Turkey on October 8, shortly to be followed by that of the Balkan League.

The fact of war ever introduces an incalculable element and the course of the conflict was source of surprise in all quarters. The month was hardly out before the Turkish armies were everywhere defeated in the field; only in besieged Janina, Monastir, and Adrianople did resistance continue, while the Bulgarians were held at the Chataldja lines, within sight of Constantinople. On December 3 an armistice was concluded by all save the Greeks that pledged the belligerents to remain on their positions. Turkey

[40] Because she was herself at war with Turkey, Italy rather welcomed the prospect of Balkan complications, which in fact were useful in bringing about the termination of the Italo-Turkish War.

[41] The proposal was made by Poincaré at Sazonov's urging and it had the agreement of Germany.

had, in effect, save for the Straits, been evicted from Europe.

Europe was not prepared for this outcome; but neither were her members prepared for conflict among themselves, which the Bulgarian failure to capture Constantinople made it easier to avoid. In London, on December 16, a peace conference met, or rather one should say two meetings began that were to run parallel, one of the Balkan states, another of the ambassadors of the Great Powers. Clearly, Turkey-in-Europe could not be restored, and between the Turks and the Balkan allies agreement seemed reached at the end of January. Its final conclusion was delayed by what is sometimes called the Second Balkan War, a futile flare-up of Turkish resistance.[42] The Turks eventually had to agree to the cession of all Turkish territory in Europe west of the Enos-Midia line, and peace was signed in London on May 30, 1913.

But peace was not yet restored to the Balkans. During the early stages of the conflict, Austria had remained inactive, allowing the junction of Montenegrin and Serbian forces to take place in the Sanjak, abandoned by her in 1908. In view of the Austrian opposition to Serbian nationalism, it was perhaps too late in any case to embark on a policy of conciliation and friendship; at any rate it was not done, but instead the focus of Austrian policy became the prevention of Serbia's access to the sea. The creation of an Albanian state would accomplish this purpose, in securing which Austria had the support of Italy, opposed for her own reasons to a South Slav aggrandizement along the Adriatic.[43] As between the Great Powers, though Russia did not give Serbia any substantial support, there was, nevertheless, a new issue that gave rise to protracted negotiations. It is an interesting consideration that the two principals, Russia and Austria, seemed more amenable to compromise than their respective seconds, France and Germany.[44]

[42] In Constantinople, the Young Turks, unwilling to accept the cession of Adrianople, overthrew the government of Kiamil Pasha. Hostilities were resumed as a consequence, but had little effect. In February–March, the Greeks succeeded in capturing Janina and the Bulgarians Adrianople, but they were unable to break through the Chataldja lines.

[43] There was, beyond a doubt, such a thing as Albanians. Whether a population of some one million, divided religiously between Moslem, Orthodox, and Catholic, and in the stage of political and economic development that was Albania's, constituted the material for a viable state is another question.

[44] In France, Poincaré became President of the Republic in January, 1913, but he continued in that post to exercise considerable influence on the direction of foreign policy. His support of Russia was far-reaching and the appoint-

But as between the Balkan states, the Austrian pressure on Serbia had the effect of making that country turn elsewhere for compensation. This meant reopening the Macedonian issue, which Bulgaria saw no reason for doing.[45] Having come into difficulties with Greece as well over the possession of Salonika, Bulgaria, foolishly as it turned out, took, without warning, the initiative of hostilities against her former Serb and Greek allies. Thus, on June 29, 1913, was begun the Third Balkan War.

This war was even shorter than the first. Seizing the opportunity, the Turks reëntered the fray, recovering Adrianople; even the Rumanians, who had been watching uneasily the gains of all the other Balkan states, moved against Bulgaria. Within three weeks Bulgaria was at the mercy of an unequal combination; an armistice was concluded at the end of July, and peace was promptly reëstablished by the Treaty of Bucharest of August 13, 1913.

Given the circumstances, Bulgaria had to foot the bill and pay the price of her mistake. Turkey regained Adrianople, but, save for this improvement, she remained in full control of no more than the Straits. Thus, apart from the still important fact that the Straits remained Turkish, the Balkan aspect of the Eastern Question, where Turkey was concerned, was finally and conclusively solved: the Ottoman Empire was no longer a European state.

Rumania obtained possession of the Southern Dobrudja and Bulgaria was evicted from hoped-for Macedonia, which was divided between Serbs and Greeks. The matter of Bulgaria's access to the Aegean gave rise to some difficulty in connection with the

---

ment of Delcassé to the St. Petersburg embassy was in the nature of a sensation. It is largely out of the events of this period that grew the war-mongering charge subsequently leveled at Poincaré.

As to Germany, she has often been presented as exercising a restraining influence on Austria. Actually, Germany took a position toward Austria not very dissimilar to that of France toward Russia. The legend of Germany's restraining influence was mainly fostered in Austria as a convenient alibi for her own inaction.

[45] The situation was complicated by the fact that, during the war, the Bulgarians had concentrated their effort in the east, with the consequence that all of Macedonia, their share included, had been occupied by the Serbs who now refused to evacuate any of it, their purpose being to secure the Vardar Valley and access to the Salonika outlet. One reason for the disastrous Bulgarian behavior seems to have been the mistaken calculation on the part of King Ferdinand that Austria would use the opportunity to attack Serbia. Whatever basis there may have been for this expectation—the idea was not a strange one in Vienna—it was not seriously entertained and certainly no adequate diplomatic preparations had been made by Sofia.

ultimate ownership of Kavala, currently under Greek occupation. This issue was the occasion for a curious manifestation of Great Power relationships; with an eye to future developments, both Russia and Austria, desirous of bringing Bulgaria into their respective camps, favored the Bulgarian claim; conversely, and for similar reasons, France and Germany, courting Greece, supported the Greek demand. In the end Kavala went to Greece. Germany, not informed of the Austrian calculation, accepted from the first the arrangements made at Bucharest, which registered an Austrian setback.

The Treaty of Bucharest thus settled the situation in the eastern half of the Balkans. It may be noted at this point that it was a settlement essentially contrived among the Balkan states themselves, to a degree, therefore, an assertion by them of independence from Great Power tutelage; also, it was destined to be a settlement which, apart from minor modifications, was to prove remarkably durable.

EUROPEAN RELATIONS AFTER THE BALKAN WARS

But it was otherwise in the West. In that quarter, Austria was all the more anxious to confirm her prior success in an effort to compensate for the setback of Bucharest. The issue naturally turned into an Austro-Serbian dispute. The conference of ambassadors in London had decided to create an Albanian state, for the purpose of establishing the frontiers of which two commissions were set up. The task of settling the frontier between Albania and Greece was not to be completed until after the first World War—if then, but agreement had been reached in 1913 over the Serbo-Albanian frontier.[46] Yet, following local disturbances, the Serbs were back in Albania in September, 1913. This prompted Austria to action, or rather to seeming action. There was again discussion in Vienna of the desirability of settling scores with Serbia, of teaching her a lesson; this went the length of an ultimatum on October 18. The step was generally disapproved by the Powers, including Italy, though William II was enthusiastically in favor of supporting his ally; in any case, the prompt withdrawal of the Serbs removed the possibility of conflict and the issue was closed.

The settlement of 1913 in the Balkans closed a chapter in the

---

[46] It had taken considerable pressure, and even a joint naval demonstration by the Powers, to secure the evacuation of northern Albania by Serb and Montenegrin troops.

troubled tale of the Balkan peoples, but it did not settle all differences. Bulgaria was understandably disgruntled and Serbia remained deeply resentful toward her northern neighbor which, on
its side, was equally dissatisfied. Serbian irredentism was to have
henceforth but one focus and more than ever the very existence
of Serbia was considered a threat by Austria. It was now too
late for schemes of tripartite reorganization of the Dual Monarchy; these were viewed with no less suspicion by the ruling elements within, the Hungarian especially, than by the more intransigeant Slav elements within as well as without. Austrian policy,
and behind that the German, would henceforth seek to play the
Bulgarian card in the Balkans.

Among the Great Powers the Balkan explosion of 1912–1913
had given rise to a relative minimum of friction. The crisis was far
less acute than that produced by the Bosnian annexation. After the
Balkan wars the relations of Europe stood poised in delicate balance and uncertain orientation. Between Germany and Britain,
the failure of the Haldane mission of 1912 had not left an aftermath of bitterness; the naval competition went on, but Britain,
though regretting its cost, felt confidence in her ability to maintain the edge of her advantage at sea. Britain was much concerned
with matters domestic, the war on poverty, constitutional change
enacted in the Parliament bill, and the sharp tension generated by
the Irish question. Among the members of the Liberal government, the Radical wing especially, not a few were sympathetically
inclined toward Germany. In this atmosphere it was possible, in
June, 1913, to resume discussion of the long-standing possibility of
the eventual partition of the Portuguese colonies and to reach tentative agreement on that subject. British "reasonableness" acknowledged the validity of Germany's much touted claim to a
place under the sun—so long as some third party would provide
the wherewithal. Even the much debated Baghdad railway problem seemed by way of solution, as will be indicated presently.

Such amicable dealings caused some alarm in France, whose
relations with Germany had not improved of late. The forces of
the Left were strong in France; the Republic had won the bitter
struggle with the army and with the Church; the Socialists were
making progress and Jaurès entertained hopeful feelings of broth-
erliness toward the Social Democrats across the Rhine. There had
been not a little criticism in France of the government's Moroccan
policy, but the manner of operation of German diplomacy had

left a trail of distrust. The election of Poincaré to the Presidency in January, 1913, was a triumph of the *réveil national*, the focus of whose attention lay in the eastern provinces.[47] Though much debated, the restoration of the three-year term of military service, in place of the two-year law, was enacted; through it, France hoped to compensate for the deficiency of her manpower *vis-à-vis* Germany. Logically enough, France made use of Russia's need of capital for that country's industrial expansion; to get new loans Russia must promise to enlarge her standing army and to proceed with the construction of strategic railways. Germany, too, enlarged her military establishment and the armaments race continued, on land no less than on the sea. This did not mean that Poincaré or the Kaiser actively wanted war; but they were firm believers in the old adage, now honored again after a temporary lapse, *si vis pacem para bellum*.

In the midst of divergent indications, Italian policy well reflected the prevailing uncertainties of established alignments. Italy had supported Austria in procuring the establishment of Albania, but the two countries no longer saw eye to eye thereafter and Albania became a bone of contention between their rival influences, Austria regarding her ally as an intruder in the eastern Adriatic. The dormant irredentist issue had a flare-up in 1913.[48] Nevertheless, it was in June, 1913, that a naval agreement provided for the coöperation of the Austrian and Italian fleets, almost simultaneously with the conclusion of agreements of the general staffs of the Triple Alliance. But the ambivalence of Italian policy is well illustrated by the fact that, in 1914, when war broke out, Italy was engaged in negotiations with both Britain and France in regard to the Mediterranean situation.

UNRESOLVED EASTERN ISSUES

All things considered, the situation in the East remained the more delicate and fraught with danger. Perhaps the most significant new development in that quarter over the preceding twenty years had been the intrusion of Germany's own interest. In the days of the Berlin Congress, Bismarck could be the "honest bro-

[47] At Saverne, in Alsace, there occurred a manifestation of military arrogance at its worst when a German officer struck a lame cobbler and insulted Alsatian recruits, with the consequence of creating local friction and strong resentment in French opinion.

[48] There was considerable resentment in Italy at the Hohenlohe decrees which had resulted in the dismissal of Italian employees in the Commune of Trieste.

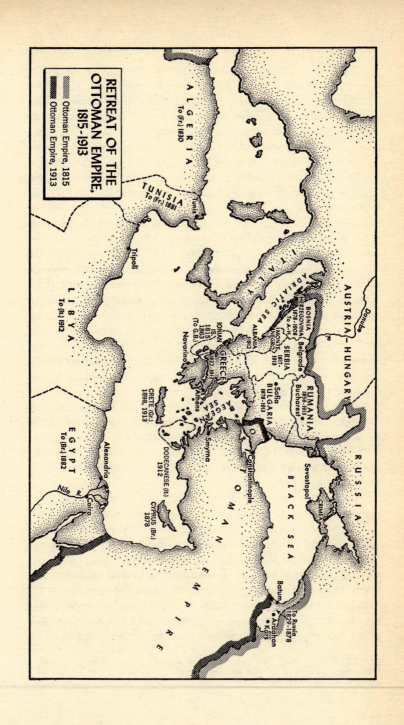

RETREAT OF THE
OTTOMAN EMPIRE,
1815-1913

Ottoman Empire, 1815
Ottoman Empire, 1913

ALGERIA
To (Fr.) 1830

TUNISIA
To (Fr.) 1881

Tunis

Tripoli

LIBYA
To (It.) 1912

EGYPT
To (Br.) 1882

Alexandria

Nile R.

Cairo

ITALY

ADRIATIC SEA

BOSNIA
HERZEGOVINA
1878-1908
To A-H.

MONTE-
NEGRO
1817-
1912

ALBANIA
1912

SERBIA
1856-1913

Belgrade

AUSTRIA-HUNGARY

Danube

IONIAN
IS.
1815
1863
(to G.B.)

GREECE
1832-1913

Navarino

CRETE (Gr.)
1898, 1913

Athens

AEGEAN SEA

Smyrna

DODECANESE (It.)
1912

CYPRUS (Br.)
1878

BULGARIA
1878-1913

Sofia

RUMANIA
1856-1913

Bucharest

Constantinople

OTTOMAN EMPIRE

BLACK SEA

Sevastopol

CRIMEA

RUSSIA

Batum

To Russia
1878-1878

Ardahan

Kars

ker," but the expansion of German activity throughout the world did not leave the Eastern Mediterranean untouched. The visits that Germany's first traveling salesman, William II, paid to that area were outward manifestations of this new German interest, as well as notice to the world that henceforth Germany would claim a say, in her own right and not merely as Austria's ally and second, in the affairs of the Ottoman Empire.

This German interest was at first essentially economic. It differed in this respect from the Austrian, for, bypassing the Balkans, it asserted itself at once in Asia Minor, where its most concrete manifestation took the form of railway building, which began as early as 1893. By the end of the century, a German company was laying more grandiose plans for linking the Turkish capital with the Persian Gulf. Despite the early German disclaimers, a project of this nature could not long help becoming a political issue. The German interest in Asia Minor was at first welcomed by the British, who saw in it a possible diversion of Germany away from South Africa, no less than by the French, who thought of it as bolstering the Ottoman Empire and offered to share in the financing of the railway scheme. The Russians alone sought to extract political advantage from the project, bargaining their consent for German support at the Straits; but they were unwilling to pay the additional German price of guarantee of the Franco-German frontier, and the negotiations remained sterile.[49] The German company obtained its concession in November, 1899, and went on with the undertaking which, however, for technical reasons, proved much more difficult and slow of realization than had been thought would be the case.

The matter remained dormant for a time, and in the end proved amenable to compromise. The process was a lengthy one and was accompanied by protracted and involved negotiations which make it an excellent occasion for observing the intricacy of the relations of the Powers, no less than the divergence within individual countries between financial interests and opinion. To reach the Persian Gulf was inevitably to touch a sensitive point of British imperial interest, especially in the context of Anglo-German naval rivalry; the press and opinion in Britain were less inclined to compromise than British bankers. But then again, Ger-

[49] The Russians were able to conclude an agreement with Turkey, in April, 1900, which gave them a right of veto on railway building in the regions adjacent to the Black Sea.

many in Asia Minor, and beyond that in Persia, could be a useful counter to Russia with whom friction continued in that quarter despite the 1907 agreement. In a different direction Britain felt that France must be taken into account. If the French commercial interest in the Ottoman Empire was smaller than the British, France was by far the largest holder (60 percent) of the Ottoman debt. France stood to be the loser by any Anglo-German agreement that might be a prelude to a partition of the Ottoman Empire.

But this French interest was becoming secondary to the increasing French financial stake in Russia, whose wishes, for other reasons as well, must be considered. In France, as in Britain, the position of the government altered in response to the shifting dominant trend: Delcassé and Caillaux took different views of the matter. And between Russia and Germany the Persian counter offered some of the same possibilities, in reverse, that it held in Anglo-Russian relations. Out of all this came a solution, worked out in a series of agreements in 1913–1914; their main effect was the German undertaking not to proceed beyond Baghdad, leaving the section of the line from there to the Persian Gulf under British control, while the participating shares of various national interests were likewise agreed upon.

The Baghdad railway question has been cited as an illustration of the fact that the Powers were capable of adjusting their rival interests in reasonable fashion, and also as evidence of relaxation of tension between them on the very eve of the clash of 1914. But that particular issue was by this time a relatively secondary aspect of the larger perennial of the survival of the domain of the sultan. The Balkan wars of 1912–1913 had given renewed point to the problem. On balance, Russia and France had greater cause for satisfaction in the outcome than had the Central Powers, and the military performance of Turkey was to a point a setback to the prestige of German arms. In the Balkans proper, the Balkan states had come to stay. Both Bulgaria and Turkey in the end emerged in defeat; out of Bulgaria's leanings toward Austria, in combination with the German influence in Constantinople, added to the fact that Rumania was still allied to the Central Powers, might not a combination be contrived that would give Berlin-Baghdad political reality and establish Austro-German influence in a dominant position over the entire Balkan peninsula?

The prospect, if attractive, would not be easy of realization.

But it was the sort of large scheme that appealed to William II; the Balkans were the heart of the discussions that he and Franz Ferdinand, the heir to the Austrian throne, held at the latter's castle of Konopischt, in Bohemia, in October, 1913, prior to the Kaiser's visit to the old emperor himself at Schönbrunn. Bulgaria was the pivot of Berchtold's policy, but mainly in the negative sense of preventing a renewal of the Balkan League. One difficulty lay in the state of relations between Bulgaria and Rumania after the Treaty of Bucharest; another lay in the relations between the latter country and Austria, or more precisely Hungary. Franz Ferdinand himself would have given some satisfaction to the legitimate enough Rumanian grievance in Transylvania,[50] just as he would have tried to reconcile the South Slavs to their acceptance of the Habsburg crown. The danger to be forestalled, apart from the Balkan League possibility, was that of a combination of Russia with Rumania, Serbia, and Montenegro. But Rumania had just been at war with Bulgaria and was on friendly terms with Serbia. This, plus her own grievances toward Austria, explains why Russia and France were having better success in Bucharest than Rumania's formal allies.[51]

In Turkey proper, the Germans were anxious to maintain their influence, specifically to restore their injured military prestige. The Turkish request, as early as May, 1913, for a German mission to reorganize the Turkish army was therefore very welcome in Berlin. The choice eventually fell on General Liman von Sanders, who, in addition to the task of army reorganization, was given the command of the Constantinople garrison. This last decision especially evoked a violent Russian reaction, for Russia, if quite willing to leave the Turks at the Straits, increasingly concerned as she was with the free passage of her trade, viewed with suspicion the establishment over them of the dominant influence

[50] Franz Ferdinand had been responsible for the appointment of Czernin as minister to Bucharest, despite violent Hungarian objections. Franz Ferdinand toyed with the vision of large concessions, even territorial, to Rumania, which then might be brought as a whole into a reorganized Habsburg state. This was the counterpart of his, and Conrad's, views on Serbia. If such a far-sighted policy ever had a possibility of success, the time for it was past, and in any case Hungarian intransigeance never gave it an opportunity of being tried.

[51] To be sure, Bessarabia constituted an obstacle between Rumania and Russia, but Rumania could hardly afford the simultaneous enmity of both her powerful neighbors. While King Carol was a genuine partisan of the Central Powers, he had to acknowledge the increasing opposition of popular sentiment, to the extent that it would be impolitic even to disclose the treaty of 1883. Czernin's mission in Bucharest was a failure and the Central Powers came to realize the small value of the Rumanian alliance.

of any other major Power. Purely economic considerations, the needs of Russia's economic development, were therefore a factor at this point, as well as the influence of the makers of arms;[52] but an interpretation of this clash primarily in economic terms would be but a misleading misinterpretation. In the delicately balanced equilibrium of European relationships of power, the value of prestige ranked high; for prestige is no empty symbol but rather the final ostensible summation of the standing of power. Of this state of affairs the Liman von Sanders affair is a good illustration.

If Germany was on this occasion making a move in the furtherance of her political influence and economic advantage, the move was not anti-Russian in calculation. But the Russians saw fit to magnify it into the threat of a Prussian garrison at Constantinople[53] and sought the help of their Entente partners, neither of whom, however, seemed unduly exercised—a British Admiral, for one thing, was in charge of reorganizing the Turkish navy. A delicate diplomatic operation ensued, designed to procure some satisfaction for Russia without causing a loss of face to Germany; by January, 1914, the solution was found in the promotion of Liman von Sanders to the rank of Field Marshal, in which exalted capacity he could not take the command of Constantinople; for the rest, the German mission went on with its appointed task.

It was a curious turn of events that Germany should, in 1914, seem to be placed *vis-à-vis* Russia in the position that had been traditionally that of the Western Powers, Britain especially. If the Kaiser's comment to Bethmann in February, "Russo-Prussian relations are dead once and for all! We have become enemies," is tinged with the melodramatic grandiloquence to which he was prone, it is nonetheless true that the *Dreikaiserbund* was indeed dead and that, in Russian eyes, not Austria alone, but Germany as well, and perhaps even more because the more powerful, was the opponent to be feared. To a degree, through the enhanced German interest in the Near East, this was an unplanned consequence of the defeat of Turkey in the Balkan Wars. The outcome of it all was, by indirection, a tightening of the Franco-Russian connection, now placed more nearly on a basis of similarity of interest; no

[52] The German firm of Krupp was anxious to secure Turkish arms contracts, just as the British had an interest in building ships for Turkey, and as the Serbs and Greeks had been equipped with French arms that were successfully tested during the Balkan Wars.

[53] To a degree this was not an altogether wild exaggeration, as the events of the second half of 1914 were to show.

longer, as twenty years ago, was France, desirous to escape isolation at almost any price, the demandant, but Russia needed France as much and perhaps more than the reverse was true. In large measure because of the mere fact of her own growth and expansion, quite as much as by plan, and because of faulty diplomacy, Germany had become the true binder of the Franco-Russian connection, just as she had made from the start the Anglo-French Entente a more intimate combination than the British intended.

That a clash should come in these circumstances may easily, in retrospect, be seen as no more than natural, not to say inevitable. Preparations for war were indeed mounting on all sides, and it is an easy game to collect quotations from the Kaiser, Conrad, Sazonov, or Lord Fisher, not to mention a bevy of others, that prove that war was expected—nay, planned; the General Staffs everywhere, singly and in combinations, were indeed making plans for war—they would have been remiss in their duty if they had not. The Cassandras were spreading their warnings abroad. The Cassandras were right, as the event was soon to prove.

Yet it is also well to remember that very few among the responsible holders of power actually wanted war—not the Kaiser himself, for all the unguarded comments and exclamation marks with which he sprinkled German state papers. By 1914 the peoples of Europe had not known war at home for two full generations; so protracted a period of peace easily produced the impression that its continuation was the normal condition, just as the gold standard, stable currencies, and freedom of travel and of speech were conditions that Europe accepted as part of the fixed, established mode of existence. Europe was strong and proud of her achievements and power; in her own eyes Europe was civilization, the benefits of which she had bestowed and was bestowing on the planet. The great civilized Powers of Europe would no longer resort to the crude test of force to settle their disputes, and the very recurrence of crises, in the end always peaceably resolved, could be used as evidence to support this opinion.

Even more—and this has special irony in 1958—the argument was heard that war among the major Powers of Europe was unthinkable, if for no other, for technical reasons alone. It was one aspect of Europe's higher civilization that her members possessed the most perfected engines of destruction that man had hitherto contrived; to use these weapons would entail the destruction of civilization; that civilized Europe should commit suicide was inconceivable. There was, or there was thought to be in Europe, peace, stability, and progress everlasting.

In retrospect, it is wholly fitting and proper to explain how and why that which did happen happened. But caution should be used lest hindsight and the climate of a later day distort the picture we try to re-create of the feeling of an earlier epoch and of the view another time had of itself. The peoples of Europe in 1914 did not and could not know that they had reached one of the great dates of their history, one that, like 1789 for instance, was irretrievably to alter the course of their destinies. If the outbreak of war in that year may be explained as but the logical outcome of long-maturing trends and forces, it may be said with equal truth that Europe in 1914 accidentally stumbled into a catastrophe from which all her members recoiled.

Part Three

THE TWENTIETH-
CENTURY
TRANSITION

IX

Introduction:
The Twentieth-
Century World

I. The Realignment of Power

When the guns were unleashed in August of 1914, a number of illusions were prevalent among the peoples of Europe. To the great mass of them, the personal experience of war was unfamiliar and for that reason they could face it even with a measure of enthusiasm while the soldiers entrained for the frontiers with flowers on their rifles. Across the Franco-German border, where the first crucial tests might be expected, *Nach Paris!* echoed *à Berlin!* and among all belligerents the expectation was widespread that the boys would be home by Christmas. Had it not been often explained that the very power of modern weapons, of which Europe was endowed with the best, rendered their use unthinkable? That prognostication belied they were now to be used, but respect for their potency lent credence to the view that their employment could not be long sustained. This last surmise was evidence of a gross underestimate of the capacity for absorbing punishment that lay in the economies and the peoples of the Powers at war.

Four Christmases were to come and go before the boys, or at least those of them still extant, could begin to come home. The consequences of so prolonged an effort were correspondingly very different from any that had been envisaged in 1914; some illusions were shattered while others were simultaneously created or fostered. Of the impact, political and social, of the war upon the peoples and of the consequences of this impact upon their relationships and upon the manner of conducting them, more will be said presently;[1] but first we may pause to consider briefly and in general

[1] See below, p. 316.

terms the effects of unexpected circumstances upon the Powers that were involved in the conflict.

It should be said at the outset that these effects were without precedent, so cataclysmic and far-reaching that the search for a new equilibrium is still proceeding unresolved after the lapse of nearly half a century; by comparison, the immediate effects of the quarter-century disturbance initiated in 1789 were relatively minor. For purposes of warfare the Central Powers enjoyed notable advantages, inner lines of communication, unity of direction, and more adequate preparation that enabled them, or at least Germany, central director of the war on their side, to put on an impressive performance. Nevertheless the judgment proved sound that unless they snatched victory with promptness, the far greater resources of the Allies, if given time to mobilize them, would in the end carry the day. However, this was only true broadly speaking and needs substantial qualification. For the judgment also proved correct, in the case of the backward tsarist Empire, that it would be impossible to sustain the demands of a modern war among the Great Powers. But just as it was not in the initial calculations that Russia would fall by the wayside, so likewise it was not initially envisaged that the United States would join the fray and turn its tide.

Victory, when it finally came, was complete, and the enemy lay prostrate and wholly at the mercy of its conquerors. But the circumstances of 1919 were vastly different from those of, say, 1814.[2] On the earlier occasion, for all the lasting suspicion of France and her revolution, France could still be and was regarded as a necessary component of Europe whose place was one of parity with others. But the things that it had been necessary to do in the course of the First World War prevented a like treatment of the defeated enemy in 1919. Two things therefore emerge as of crucial significance that were direct consequences of the war.

The first is the damage that Europe inflicted upon herself. The loss of life, appalling and great as it was, is not the most significant aspect of that damage; it was, generally speaking, absorbed and made good with comparative ease.[3] The economic loss was more

[2] On the ideological aspect of the war and the influence of that aspect, see below, pp. 311 ff.

[3] The one outstanding exception is the case of France. In addition to being very large, the French losses must be considered in the context of the demographic situation of French society, a static population, hence one with an unusually large proportion of older people. As a consequence, the effect of these losses was far greater than that of larger losses on a country like Russia, for instance, with a high reproductive capacity.

serious; it, too, was to be made good with what may seem in retrospect relative success and rapidity, but the accompanying dislocation was not so easily redressed. More will be said of that aspect, itself an important contributor to that other result of the war, the distribution and relationship of power, to which attention may be turned at this point. This last, in turn, has two faces, the intra-European and that of the position of Europe as a whole and of the individual European Powers *vis-à-vis* the outside.

Within Europe proper, or her fringes, the war brought about the downfall of four empires, no mean result in itself. Two of these, the Turkish and the Austrian, were irretrievably destroyed. This did not mean that the age-old Near Eastern question had been solved or that the issue of the fate of Central Europe had been answered, but it did place the problem of the Near East— Middle East as, with unnecessarily confusing nomenclature, it began to be called—and that of Danubia in a wholly novel context. It was otherwise with Russia and Germany; for all their territorial losses, these entities were not destroyed, but merely reduced for the moment to complete impotence. Of the former six Great Powers of Europe there remained five, and of those five only three were centers of effectively existing power. These must therefore carry the burden of the organization and functioning of Europe whose most important postwar problems bear the names Germany, Russia, and Danubia.

The power distribution that the war created in Europe was therefore a distortion that circumstances and the weight of historic tradition further compounded. For, on the one hand, Italy, a Great Power by courtesy rather than in real fact, already from the time of the 1919 peacemaking, was content to behave as a Power with limited rather than with general interests. On the other hand, Britain could contemplate the outcome in the light of superficially similar past experience: she had once more, as earlier with Spain and with France, prevented the domination of the Continent by a single Power. The thing to do, therefore, was to return to a traditional situation of balance. The view perhaps would not have been unreasonable, had there been sufficient power in Britain to implement some concrete scheme for the organization of Europe; but Britain would not face the new realities of Europe, especially those of its little known (to her) and seemingly remote Center and East. Returning to a form of imperial isolation, Britain let Europe drift.

France was thus left, and in this fact lay, in a sense, the supreme irony of all. France, unlike Italy, did not act as a Power with limited interests; she had behind her a long and impressive tradition of power and of concern with the whole Continent. The renitency of Italy and Britain served all the more to place French power in an exalted position; yet this happened at the very time when the cost of the contribution to the common victory had in effect caused France near mortal injury, had badly damaged the real bases of French power. For the most part unconsciously, France understood this and the result may be called peculiar. France proceeded to organize Europe on the simple basis of a coalition of the victors—minus Britain and Italy; yet all the while seemingly all-powerful France stood in dread fear of (momentarily) impotent Germany. Others were taken in—more than the French themselves—by this entirely false situation, as witness the widespread talk and criticism of French "hegemony" in Europe. Conceivably, a solid combination of the European victors, including Britain most of all, might have been capable either of controlling Europe through the application of sufficient force, or of leading her back gradually and peacefully to some sort of equilibrium that bore proper relation to the realities of power. For French power to carry the main burden of the organization of Europe may seem in retrospect absurd fantasy. It was. And on this wholly false basis of power relationships Europe could not be restored to stability; in this, not in the specific details of the terms of the settlements of peace, must be seen in large part the reason for the renewed breakdown of twenty years later.

Much happened in those twenty years of the "long armistice," the details of which will be retailed in the following pages. Taking the broad view, that period must be seen as an attempt at adaptation to novel circumstances, an attempt that ended in failure, partly because the new conditions were not understood, partly because the extent of change was so great that more time was needed for the transformation. The world is still in the midst of the transition, gropingly searching for a new basis of stability.

It has been pointed out that the period that preceded the outbreak of the war of 1914 is one that truly marks the apogee of Europe. That war is called the First World War and the description is quite apt; for if it was primarily European in origin and if the theater of its decision was Europe, the effects of it were indeed world-wide. Not so much, however, because of imperial readjustments that affected other continents as because of its effects on the position of Europe in the world as a whole. One aspect of this change was imperial, and here too there is not a little irony in the contrast between the seeming appearance and the less obvious reality. An illustration may bring out the point with sharpness. With the conclusion of the arrangements for the dismemberment of the Ottoman Empire, it seemed as if Britain, the chief beneficiary, had in fact realized the ambitious scheme of establishing her uninterrupted control from Egypt to Malaya. This may have seemed a glorious accomplishment, the final step in the long tale of empire building. It was indeed the last step, but in a sense other than that expected, for no sooner had it been taken than preparations for the retreat and liquidation of the proud construction got under way. For British power, like French, had in reality been diminished by the war, and for both countries the fruits of victory were ashes. It is from the First World War that must be dated the unprecedentedly sharp reversal of the process of expansion of European control over the rest of the world; the ferment began at that time to assume unmanageable proportions and has been spreading ever since in the dependent world.

Not only *vis-à-vis* this dependent world and its peoples was Europe's position to be abruptly reversed; an even more important transformation took place across the Atlantic. For all that the military contribution of the United States to the war was relatively small, that country emerged from the conflict as unquestionably the greatest Power of all. America exacted no indemnity and acquired no colonies from others, but in the most real sense she gained from the war and her power was enormously enhanced, though to be sure this was in large measure no more than making ostensible the long-existing reality of American power. Here was another drastic readjustment that because of its rapidity and sharpness was perceived by the American people even less than by outsiders. Surprised at her place in the world and disillusioned in her first experience of contact with it in her novel capacity, America sought to draw back into the irretrievably lost bliss of her past isolation.

The effect of this was added distortion in the relationships of power after 1919. Overnight so to speak, Europe, the powerhouse of the planet and to a large extent its mistress, was radically demoted. That this condition should be apprehended with clarity by Europeans, Americans, or others may indeed be more than could reasonably be expected from even wise and perceptive statesmen, let alone the broad masses of the people. The war, for victors and vanquished alike, was an unpleasant episode, and once peace was restored the overwhelming wish of all was to return to the interrupted course of normality. Despite illusions and squabblings over the making good of the damage, within a few years it did appear that this return to the interrupted course of development could be effected; for a few years following 1925 a general euphoria prevailed that made it possible for men to think of lasting peace.

This was but one more illusion, for the problem of Europe had been rather evaded than solved. Germany did receive the stamp of respectability with her admission to the League in 1926, but her most important disabilities remained after Locarno; Russia was still largely an outcast, and no real answer had been found for Danubia, while Italy was nursing a novel ideology. Moreover, this political euphoria was accompanied by, and was in part the result of, another illusion, the belief that Europe's economy and finances had been restored to equilibrium.

To this last illusion America contributed powerfully, though not by deliberate calculation; out of the problems of her own internal economy she contributed no less effectively to its destruction. The second decade after the formal restoration of peace brought out in full the fallacies on which economic relationships were based and the fact that the relations of European states among themselves had been no more adjusted than the relations of those states to the rest of the world. The troubled story of the nineteen thirties will also be considered in detail. The close of that decade, leaving exposed the failure to create a viable equilibrium of forces in Europe, showed that the 1919 settlements had established no more than a truce; once more the test of force must be resorted to. In the most authentic sense the two World Wars of our time must be seen as acts of the same drama.

But the second act, if continuation of the first, had some very different consequences. Some illusions and distortions on the score of power persist, but they are minor by comparison with those that followed the first war. The most drastic revision doubtless concerns French power, still looked upon as very great in 1939, then apparently suddenly nonexistent; in contrast, Britain's role and performance in the war gave her subsequently a large voice.[4]

---

[4] The discrepancy between the French and the German military establishments was by no means overwhelming, but the rapidity and thoroughness of the French collapse conveyed the impression that French power was almost non-

But a more accurate estimate would see in the very cost of victory to Britain a situation not very dissimilar from that of the injury that the cost of the earlier victory did to France. Germany once again put on an impressive military performance; her fall was all the greater. Whatever differences exist between British, French, and German power, these remain, by comparison with the outside, in the category of nuances, and the component states of Europe have all been so drastically demoted that perhaps the only question to be raised in regard to their power is whether the estimate of their weakness is not now erring in reverse exaggeration.[5]

However that may be, no question can exist about the extraordinary degree of the demotion of all the former Great Powers of Europe. Again this has two aspects. One is in regard to empire and affects most of all Britain and France, whose imperial positions have been, since the Second World War, undergoing a process of rapid liquidation.[6] The other has to do with the clear emergence of Powers in an entirely different category. That the United States emerged from the first war as far the greatest Power in the world is clear. To a degree, however, the American reluctance to accept the full implications of American power, distorted, minimized, and concealed its true significance and measure. But such denial of reality could not be persisted in forever; it had itself been one of the contributory causes of the renewed outbreak of war in 1939. It took two years thereafter to explode the wishful thinking of American isolationism, but ever since America, albeit with wistful backward glances toward a simpler and happier past, has accepted the recognition of her place of power. America emerged enormously enhanced from the second war, in absolute as well as in relative terms. An operation like the Marshall Plan, whether

---

existent. Thus, the purely military aspect of the war had the effect of creating a distorted picture of the true measure of power. Conversely, Britain after Dunkirk was mainly saved by the fortunate accident of her island position. She was, however, as a consequence able to continue the struggle, thereby creating an impression of power greater than really existed.

[5] There has been considerable discussion of the desirability for Europe to unite. No doubt the collectivity of the demoted Powers of Europe, or even of some of them, would command very considerable power, perhaps sufficient to constitute a third force in a category with the two superpowers.

[6] Some of the liquidation of the British structure has proceeded in orderly fashion to the extent that reorganization might seem a better word than liquidation to describe the process. The case of India is the best illustration of this. France, by contrast, has not succeeded in effecting such peaceful readjustments. But whether, in the final reckoning, the comparison between the British and the French cases will have to stress contrast or similarity is a question that the future alone can decide.

one see its motivation as primarily humanitarian or hard-headed self-interest—it was both rather than either alone—is a measure of the relative place of the United States and Europe. Already from the time of the First World War in actual fact, more obviously from the time of the Second, there is no sense in speaking of European affairs without taking the United States into consideration.

The second war brought about further clarification of the relative power position of states by giving the sanction of formal recognition to the concealed reality of Russian power. From this standpoint of power, and whatever one may think of the merits of the Soviet system and of the quality of its methods, it cannot be denied that the Soviet experiment has been successful in building up Russian power to a position commensurate with Russian potential. The Soviet Union and the United States are commonly described as "superpowers," a wholly adequate characterization, for indeed they are in a category by themselves. The fact is enlightening that, between the two World Wars, the permanent members of the Council of the League were all European Powers, with the exception of Japan, whereas of the five corresponding positions in the Security Council of the United Nations, two are filled by wholly non-European powers, America and China.[7] This last situation throws further light on the true state of things. Outside of the two superpowers, the other three members of the Security Council, Great Britain, France, and China, are clearly in a different category; in their place of ostensible parity must be seen an expression of historic tradition combined with transitional adaptation to the changing reality of power. Allowing for the difference in the current power standing of Britain and France, both are essentially declining Powers whose role has for so long been so great that, demoted as they may be, their place is still substantial; in reverse fashion, China, long impotent and still possessed of relatively little power, is a nation that seems on the ascendant and contains possibilities of very great magnitude. The present world may not be a very pleasant one, just because it is going through so rapid and violent a transition, but, if one grant that the acknowledgment of reality is a desirable condition, the recognition of

[7] Technically, it is Nationalist China, reduced to the control of Formosa, which has permanent representation in the Security Council. This, however, may be regarded as a passing anomaly, pending the time when the mainland of China, under whatever dispensation, will obtain possession of the Chinese seat in the Council.

power relationships and standing may be said to be a healthier situation than the wholly false condition that prevailed after the First World War.

One more thing may be said at this point. After a fairly brief interlude of more or less easy collaboration induced by the common purpose of war, the two superpowers found themselves engaged in bitter rivalry. This is the dominant fact of the present, a condition that may be expected to be of some duration. Between them, however, these two Powers encompass but a fraction of the planet; but the rest of the world has no unity and its problem has been to accommodate itself to the all-pervading contest. Much of it has gravitated into the orbit of one or the other of the superpowers while some of it is seeking the uneasy independence of neutrality.

Europe herself is cleft in two. Because of her still vast potential of resources and skills she has been a coveted prize. That part of her associated with the Soviet Union has been in a position of close supervision from Moscow, though not formally incorporated into the Soviet empire; most of the rest of Europe, though enjoying traditional democratic freedoms, has in effect been severely limited in the direction of its policies by the *de facto* ultimate dependence on American power for the preservation of its independence. So drastic a readjustment in so short a time on the part of Great Powers that but yesterday were masters of the earth is without precedent and of itself creates great stresses and strains in the inevitable necessity of adaptation.

In such circumstances, that the expression "cold war" aptly describes, the main contestants remain armed to the teeth, each standing in fear and suspicion of the other, each convinced that any diminution of its strength would be mere invitation to attack. The dream of universal peace and disarmament, characteristic of the post-1919 period, appears like a remote utopia, and correspondingly, by contrast with the popular view of that time that armaments are a prime cause of conflict, the maxim honored before 1914, *si vis pacem para bellum,* has regained its former standing. The existence of arms can be dangerous, but their absence is no guarantee of peace; neither view has validity that is universal, and what matters is the circumstances of any particular moment. In any case, an equilibrium of forces, the old balance of power, with few or many arms, is the more relevant condition.

If the bitter experience of two major conflicts in the span of one generation has been conducive to a more realistic approach toward the facts of power, hopes and illusions still exist. The dream of universal lasting peace that prevailed for a while after the First World War and found expression in the League of Nations was shattered in considerable measure because of the unwillingness or failure to acknowledge these facts of power which it was sought to curb with paper covenants. Incapable of either enforcing the maintenance of the *status quo* or of managing peaceful modification of it, the League died. States still insist on calling themselves sovereign, but the attempt to establish a rule of law among them also persists; the United Nations is a close replica of the Genevan institution. But like its predecessor, it is no more than the collectivity of its members and has no independent power of its own, save the frail reed of world opinion. A rule of law among sovereigns remains in the last analysis a contradiction. One consequence of this is the legalized fiction of the equality of states. Fictions are not necessarily devoid of utility in the operation of politics, as witness the success of the underlying egalitarian assumption in (some, at least) democratic states. But a fiction too far divorced from reality may in itself constitute a danger by diverting men's thoughts and attention away from the hard facts of power and of life. In this lies one of the great posers of the present, the fate and role of the world institution. The United Nations is far more universal in its composition than the League ever was; if this has some advantage, the fact remains that it lacks a common basis of agreement, its members do not speak the same political language.[8]

II. The Underlying Forces of Change

This failure of a common medium of communication—words can be used to conceal, distort, and mislead as well as to produce agreement and understanding—is itself a consequence and the expression of the great upheaval of our century. If power lies at the root of the relations among states, there has already been occasion to point out that this power is the result of a number of components and that it operates in the context of large forces that dominate the course of change. It is appropriate to

[8] The United Nations has been able to deal with some important situations, the Korean for instance. Like the League, it may be capable of absorbing some failures and still survive in usefulness. But, as with the League, the test will lie in its ability, or failure, to settle Great Power disputes.

make some further reference to these and to their current shape in this introductory chapter, prior to undertaking a more detailed account of the diplomacy of our time.

Whether one take the view that the war of 1914 was an accident or the logical product of forces long at work, there can be little question that it marked the end of an epoch. Unfortunate though they may be, wars are great agents of change; they promote revolutions as much as they can be occasioned by them. The First World War served to accelerate some trends at work during the nineteenth century, but it also introduced novel tendencies while distorting those that already existed.

The effects of the economic development of Europe, especially during the second part of the nineteenth century, on the relations of her members as well as on the position of Europe *vis-à-vis* the outside have been observed in the second part of this book. For all the physical damage that the war produced, it amounted to no more than a setback in a continuing process. Technological progress since the first war has been proceeding at an accelerating pace. But what is of considerable importance in this respect is the diminished place of Europe and the inability to recover from the dislocations that the war induced. This is best seen in the case of Great Britain, originator of industry, whose existence had become adjusted to an almost exclusively industrial economy. Britain's place of primacy was already being challenged before 1914; after 1919 Britain never fully recovered her place, struggling between semiprosperity and half-depression. Her return to gold in 1925 she could not long sustain, and the drain of another war has increased the precariousness of her economic equilibrium.[9] The United States, by contrast, developed its production with enormous strides, but in its case maladjustment is no less real. The system, already practiced between the two wars, and much emphasized after the second, of subsidizing the sale of American products abroad through loans and outright gifts, if it has served a useful purpose and not proved injurious to the American economy itself, hardly seems a stable device of permanent validity.

If the production and exchange of goods have risen vastly since the First World War and if industry has tended to spread over new regions of the earth, the effects of these developments

[9] There have been, since the war, several instances that have demonstrated the fragility of the British economy. The everlasting struggle to maintain adequate foreign balances is the most permanent manifestation of the British difficulty.

have been very uneven. Certainly in America, and in Europe to a lesser extent, the improvement of productivity has made for a rising standard of living, but the increase of productivity must be noted in relation to the growing numbers ready to share its benefits. The population growth of Europe continued at a slowing rate after the first war, until predictions of stability of numbers, following the earlier French pattern, were common. The trend has been reversed after the second war. The long-term consequence of this and the persistence of the trend remain uncertain factors, but many areas of the world have found the pressure of numbers outpacing the growth of their resources and production, until a flourishing literature has developed which is restoring to a place of honor the earlier Malthusian view.

The elementary problem of feeding the world's population has come to concern many to whom it increasingly appears that Europe's nineteenth-century experience in becoming the workshop of the world while drawing upon its still vast and undeveloped spaces may have been a unique situation rather than a repeatable pattern. The world is unevenly filled: America and Russia could sustain far larger populations than their present ones, but most of Asia and some parts of Europe have reached the point of explosive pressures. In this elementary and fundamental fact of the pressure of numbers and in the differential of pressure among various parts of the earth lie one of the great problems of the future, one by comparison with which other issues may dwindle into relative insignificance. The problem, however, has not yet reached the point of prime concern of most diplomacy.

Numbers alone have but distant relation to power, as witness the relative ineffectiveness to date of the vast masses of Asia. Here mention must be made of weapons, in which respect the Second World War has brought about a true revolution. The process, to be sure, is but a continuation of scientific and technological development initiated long ago, but the degree of change is such as to have become qualitative, while the rate of it itself makes obsolence a major problem. The argument that weapons are too powerful to envisage their use dates from before 1914. Two wars have proved its fallacy but not necessarily destroyed its validity, for the recent contributions of nuclear physics have made the prospect of the wholesale destruction of mankind an entirely literal possibility rather than a mere point of rhetoric. Whether universal peace will be the child of universal terror remains to be seen; it is presuming much of the sanity of mankind for all that the saying is old that fear is the beginning of wisdom.

Meanwhile, curious and unprecedented situations have developed. The monopoly of atomic weapons at the end of the Second World War enabled the United States to disband in great part its military establishment while retaining the possibility of standing off an aggression. That monopoly is now gone: Russia has atomic weapons, Britain has produced some samples, and it may confidently be expected that others will in time follow suit. This raises the problem of whether any war must be a major war among Great Powers using the full panoply of their armor, or whether and how far little "classical" wars may be permitted to occur. To put it in crude and simplified fashion: ought atom bombs to have been used at Dien Bien Phu? or should a Communist regime appear in Saigon or Beirut must atom bombs instantly be dropped on Moscow? Such considerations have become the stuff of the thoughts of the foreign offices and the diplomats of our day.

The power of liberal and democratic ideas during the nineteenth century is well known; it had come to be taken for granted that the pattern of the West was the inevitable model that all would imitate and the First World War was to make the world safe for democracy. Without espousing a crude materialistic view, it may be granted that much of this development was rooted in the scientific, technological, and economic growth of the nineteenth century. If man could understand, and through his understanding subjugate to his use, the forces of nature, the path of unlimited progress lay open before him. With a rising standard of living, the spread of education, literacy, and the popular press, the vision began to seem attainable of a state where all men—not only the rulers of society, whether divinely or self-appointed—could share in the things of this earth and in the management of their affairs. The tide of scientific and economic progress has continued to flow in our century, at an accelerated pace, in fact, but the impact of it has been channeled, or distorted, into unexpected paths. In this respect it may be said that the first war, the great depression, the Soviet experiment and the American example all acted to much the same effect. This judgment needs some explanation.

Here again 1914 marks the great turning point and the break in a development the course of which had come to seem firmly established. Just because the first war made such demands on the peoples it was thought necessary to hold up to them the prospect of a much improved future after its termination. Lloyd George's "world fit for heroes to live in" was apt phrasing, if also not a little dangerous. In 1919 there were great expectations among the masses of the people and not a little social unrest abroad. It was in America and in Russia, whence appropriately had come the rival Messiahs of the future, Wilson and Lenin, that was given verbal expression to these hopes of the mass and to the expected shape of that future. While the older, stronger and richer victorious states, America, Britain, and France, retained unaltered their existing political institutions, elsewhere a rash of democratic regimes made its appearance.[10] The passage of three decades has shown that things were not so easy and simple. The older democracies had had experience in the operation of a system that had grown up in them as a native plant; there is no magic in the word "democracy," any more than in "constitution," as disillusioned early nineteenth-century liberals had discovered.

Yet the people could not be denied and the clock of time be turned back to the pristine simplicity of Metternich's *ancien régime*. The results have been unexpected and interesting, a valuable if costly lesson in political philosophy. In 1917 Russia had broken under the strain of an effort that her backwardness could not sustain. The advent of communism in Russia was, by the Marxist book itself, a deviation from the proper course of evolution;[11] dedicated as they may have been to the ultimate abolition of the exploitation of man by man and to the establishment of the ideal egalitarian society, the Bolsheviks soon discovered the dead weight of the uneducated, politically or otherwise, Russian mass. But that problem was easily solved, for the dictatorship of the proletariat, meaning the rule of its self-appointed benefactors, could insert itself without difficulty into the Russian autocratic tradition.

[10] Despite the ideological attraction of the Russian Revolution, which caused not a little concern to other governments, Russia herself was too weak to be able to offer material assistance to revolutionary movements elsewhere. Her own survival was all that she could manage and the only instance of a Communist regime outside Russia at this time was the short-lived Hungarian experiment of Bela Kun which soon succumbed to combined domestic opposition and external pressures.

[11] The future significance of this state of affairs was to be very considerable, for the consequence of the revolution occurring in Russia *before* the existence of a large and politically conscious proletariat was a distortion of the supposedly proper sequence of development. Instead of being the product of a stage of economic development, the Russian Revolution had to create industry and the proletariat. This was done, but only at the cost of the maintenance of rigid controls which, after forty years, instead of being relaxed show signs of having become an essential aspect of the Soviet system.

Nevertheless, the widespread popularity and knowledge of the Socialist idea caused the Russian Revolution to have considerable impact on and attraction for large sections of the industrial proletariat of Europe. Europe survived the threat and the fear of the Red bogey, but as early as 1922 another form of response appeared in Italy that Germany was to follow ten years later. This is not the place to examine the nature of these movements. But what is significant is the fact that in no case were the people deprived of their ostensible right to rule themselves, the franchise, which they were on the contrary encouraged, sometimes coerced, to use. Fascism and Nazism must be seen as results of a form of adaptation to circumstances; they provided, or at least attempted to provide, a solution to the dilemma of how to give the masses the apparent and ostensible trappings of self-government while in effect holding them under controls more reminiscent of oriental despotisms than of a Napoleon or Louis XIV. That the free spirit of man may reëmerge in time and succeed in procuring an ordering of his governance that will reconcile freedom and organization one may hope and desire; the future will provide the answer to this question, but it can hardly be gainsaid that in our transitional period vast masses of men have been subjected to a variety of systems of which the term totalitarian best describes the common denominator. Many, even among confirmed believers in democratic rule, would now grant that such systems may, for a time at least, be better suited—if not the only possible solution—to the governing of large sections of mankind.

These totalitarian systems have displayed great skill in the operation of the necessary controls that range all the way from coercion of the most brutal and ruthless sort to the use of education, indoctrination, and propaganda; these techniques, not wholly extraneous to the advertising art, are based in large degree on the use—and abuse—of that other art often called "science" that is psychology. It all adds up to an enormously enhanced power of all states, whether totalitarian or free, which must be seen as a response to the combined effects of increasing numbers and of the growing complexities of our technical age.

War itself is a promoter and accelerator of this tendency. In this respect the first war was a novel experience; during its course it was found necessary to create all manner of agencies to deal with concrete technical problems, be they shipping, supplies, or the relation of currencies. This was inimical to the Western spirit

of freedom and free enterprise and many controls were abolished
—too soon, in some cases—after the war, but many others remained or had to be reinstated. To the economic ills that visited
mankind ten years after the war no answer could be found other
than the assumption by the state of vastly enlarged responsibilities.
Mouthings about political freedom, however sincerely meant, are
apt to have a hollow ring for bellies that are hollow. The institution of the New Deal in America, wealthiest land of all and home
par excellence of free enterprise, is perhaps the most significant instance of this trend. From devices that were brought into use in
the expectation or hope of temporariness there has been no retreat;
another world war has enlarged their scope and strengthened their
hold until the welfare state is well nigh taken for granted. A measure of the potency of this trend may be seen in the fact that, in
an American or British election, conservatives, instead of attacking
the all-pervading state, have largely veered to the contention that
they could operate the controls more efficiently than those who
instituted them from conviction.

Seen in this light, there is not a little in common between the
free world and the totalitarian; but there are also profound differences that are best put under the label, "ideology." However much
distorted and perverted in practice away from its original professed intent, the Russian Revolution has radically altered the supposedly established course of political evolution. Fascism and Nazism are gone but the totalitarians speak a common language
which, as mentioned before, is other than that of the rest of the
world. In this respect, the two sides have little in common besides
the language of power, and if this in a sense constitutes a clarification, it also makes accommodation more difficult.

It is also customary to rate nationalism as one of the dominant
forces of the nineteenth century, which indeed it was. The First
World War was the occasion for an orgy of nationalistic aberration and its conclusion brought about in Europe the most thoroughgoing application of the sanctified principle of self-determination. Socialism was by its nature anti- and supranational. It was
another discovery of the postwar era that the two antagonistic
tendencies could be fused in practice; this dubious contribution of
the Fascists and the Nazis was also a response and adaptation to
changed and unforeseen circumstances, but even communism has
taken on an increasingly national color; the post-1919 forecasts

that nationalism had seen its heyday have also been belied. A factor of confusion is thereby introduced into the relations of states, for the appeal of an ideology purporting to be of universal application has been annexed to the enhancement of the power of a particular state. The difference is hard to perceive between the aims of the state of the tsars and those of its successor, but a new tool has been put to good use, of far wider applicability than the limited scope of pan-Slavism could ever provide.

Moreover, the nationalistic virus, of which the native home is undoubtedly European, has been exported with the most outstanding success. It is after the first war, and even more after the second, that the revolt of the dependent world has become increasingly vocal and currently successful. This new development, too, has been full of awkwardness and complicating confusion. The imperial Powers of the West have been forced to retreat, and in so far as they had been extolling the civilizing aspect of their activity whose aim was to lead their dependents to the point of self-government, their professions of faith have been severely challenged and the charge of disingenuousness, with varying degrees of justification, has often been made. With far greater disingenuousness, the Soviet state has found the espousal of the revolt of the dependent peoples a most useful and potent tool in its struggle against all "imperialist" states, for it itself has been in Europe rather more ruthlessly imperialistic than its professed enemies. This situation has placed the United States in the most awkward of dilemmas; from the memory of its own origins in anti-British revolt, though not perhaps with the fullest consistency, the temper of American opinion tends to be *a priori* sympathetic to any and all movements that call themselves anti-imperial. Yet at the same time the nature of its own domestic system, in combination with the interests of its defense, has brought the United States into closest association with the very same imperial Powers of Western Europe. The latent contradiction has not been resolved. It is easy enough to assert the principle that any people is entitled to its independence if it wishes to have it. To point out that there are shades and degrees in the qualification for self-rule is invidious and easily identified with the cloak of hypocrisy; yet the consideration is relevant and in this matter as in most, shades of gray are more important than rarely encountered blacks and whites.

As ever, when large ideas seize the minds of men, there will be those for whom these will command first allegiance. From the point of view of the state this may be treason and can be dealt with as such. But treason of this sort and on this scale is different from the simpler kind motivated by the desire for pecuniary gain, for instance; it often stems from high motive and principle. Our time has had to deal with subversion, fifth columns, and indirect aggression, all fundamental realities, but conditions very awkward to cope with under the rules of classical diplomacy.

THE CONDUCT OF RELATIONS AMONG STATES

These then are some of the basic features that have characterized the twentieth-century world. Brief mention has been made of them for the reason that states conduct their relations against this broad but fundamental background. To repeat, the single most important element of all is what may be labeled the rising of the mass; if this phenomenon is no more than the consequence of a long-operating nineteenth-century trend, its accelerating manifestations have produced unforeseen results, of which totalitarianism is one. There has been occasion to mention the problem of conducting foreign policy when the mass has to be taken into calculations. The totalitarians have offered one solution which consists in coercing the mass if necessary, but preferably securing its consent through various devices that may be put together as "bamboozling." The success of their methods may be called distressing, but the fact remains that it has given them great freedom in the conduct of foreign policy. So startling a contrivance as the Nazi-Soviet Pact of 1939 created no domestic difficulties for either of its makers.

How to operate foreign policy in a democratic milieu is a wholly different matter. A measure of "bamboozling" doubtless also takes place in a democratic state, but the freedom of speech and the press and the existence of authentic representative institutions put severe fetters upon it. It was because of the supposedly nefarious manner in which diplomacy had functioned before 1914 that the first of Wilson's Fourteen Points declared itself in favor of "open covenants, openly arrived at." The limitations of any attempt to conduct negotiations *coram populo*, the crude and naïve interpretation that people and the press initially read into the statement, were not long in appearing. Nevertheless, a significant residue was left and a marked change ensued in the manner of conducting the relations of states after the First World War. The foreign minister in a democracy, holding political office, is more responsible to opinion and Parliaments than permanent civil servants. The prevalent suspicion of arcane diplomacy, in combination with technological change that made transportation and communication far easier than it had been hitherto, resulted in the popularity of diplomacy by conference. Conferences there had been in the past, but they were relatively rare and reserved for important occasions, the current business of states being transacted by ambassadors while the foreign minister resided in his homeland. The ambassadorial position has lost much of its importance, while foreign ministers have been leading a peripatetic existence to meet their counterparts on numerous occasions. With the further progress in means of communication, both physical and ethereal, the ultimate point has been reached where in virtually a matter of hours any point of the planet may now be reached from any other point.

The consequences of this have been varied. Foreign ministers are apt to come and go with greater facility than permanent representatives. Also, it was thought to be a virtue that heads of the foreign services should establish direct and personal contacts among themselves, while the age of the mass man was conducive to informality of contact, by contrast with a supposedly outmoded punctilio. But the widespread publicity that accompanies the transaction of international business has introduced considerable limitations in the conduct of negotiations. Speeches and statements that are to receive immediate publicity are apt to be made primarily with an eye to their effect on opinions, both domestic and foreign. This development is not wholly new, but the extent of the practice is.

Concurrently, there has been a considerable lowering of tone until the use of the expressions "market place" or "gutter" diplomacy seems wholly warranted. For this change the totalitarians deserve most of the credit. Hitler often used the public rostrum to make highly important announcements of policy that he was wont to couch in crude and most offensive language, but the self-appointed leaders of the world proletariat have seen no reason to refrain from verbal vituperation. Even the more sedate and gentlemanly representatives of the democratic states, if generally refraining from the resort to outright insults, have had recourse to language the forthrightness of which would in days gone by have been cause for major crises. In this state of affairs must be seen a manifestation of the world-wide tendency toward proletarianization; what gains this represents for diplomacy are somewhat difficult to perceive, but it must be acknowledged as the manner in which the affairs of states are now conducted.

The wish and the desire for publicity have been the cause for an enormous quantity of state papers becoming available, either from the time of their drafting or very shortly thereafter, while those responsible for the conduct of international affairs have to a very large degree shed the discretion and reticence that used to be regarded as good taste until a lapse of time had passed. We have currently at our disposal enormously vaster sources of information than used to be the case before 1914, but the effect of this has been not only or so much greater knowledge as distorted and unbalanced knowledge. For much remains concealed, especially by the totalitarians again; there is not a little irony in the fact that the process of revealing state papers was initiated in Russia and in Germany in connection with the First World War, when one considers the methods of secrecy that were used by the Nazi foreign office and that still prevail in the Kremlin.[12]

The impact of technological change on international relations and on the conduct of diplomacy must be stressed. This aspect of things is not peculiar to the twentieth century, but what is new is the degree and rate of change that result in conditions truly unprecedented.

The 1914 argument that the destructive power of weapons was in itself a guarantee of peace has an ironic flavor in 1958; the world has survived two World Wars. Yet it is heard again in our time, with added point, for no longer civilization alone but mankind itself, in the most literal sense, stands in danger of obliteration; war we are told is obsolete. Whatever the future may disclose on that score, important changes are currently taking place. For one, the vanishing factor of time in the delivery of engines of destruction may, in some circumstances, deny the validity of the time-honored device of consultation while greatly altering the location of the responsibility for decision. But, for the longer term, perhaps the most significant change lies in the increasingly apparent limitation of the prerogative of sovereignty, to a degree for all, but most markedly for the former Great Powers of Europe.

The response to this effect of technological developments has

[12] Much documentation about Nazi and Soviet foreign policy has become available as a result of the seizure of the German archives, the Nuremberg trials, and the publication by the Allies of the content of these archives. But the operation of the policy of Communist states continues to be shrouded in considerable secrecy.

already been considerable and it holds marked possibilities of further change. The necessities of the First World War had compelled the Allies to set up international agencies endowed with extensive powers; more of this occurred in the Second World War and its immediate aftermath. Such agencies as UNRRA and OEEC establish at least *de facto* limitations on the unfettered freedom of decision of their members. Organizations like the European Coal and Steel Community imply the inevitable surrender of a measure at least of sovereignty, and even NATO differs from the old-fashioned type of military alliance. Within this last named grouping of states the demand has been growing louder for political coördination which would have the effect of giving all a voice in many of the affairs of each. These may be seen as illustrations of hesitant steps in the direction of integration of formerly unqualifiedly sovereign entities into larger wholes. Fumbling as they may be so far, and inevitably subject to much resistance, of the general direction of change there can be little question.

Much of what precedes does not concern Europe in any special or exclusive way. In this must be seen a reflection of the fact that since the First World War, and even more after the Second, Europe no longer stands as the central director of world affairs that she was until 1914. It is little exaggeration to say that Europe has become an appendage of the two superpowers of our day, and since the First World War it has become totally impossible to speak of Europe except in a world-wide context. Nevertheless, Europe in her totality still contains vast resources of power, be it in population, material assets, or skills. But if there has been talk of a United Europe, the idea so far has been conspicuous by its lack of effective results. The hand of history lies heavy upon Europe and the current process of readjustment and adaptation to circumstances which have altered with such rapidity and in so drastic fashion creates enormous strains. One form of these is malcontent, disillusion, and hopelessness, the common malady of Europe.[13] Britain and France may contemplate in wistfulness

[13] This malady may seem most conspicuous in the French milieu. That is because of some outward—not to say superficial—manifestations of the operation of the French body politic and of the French fondness and respect for ideas and the discussion of them; in perhaps varying degrees, the malady is common to all of at least the free peoples of Europe. In America, where the effects of the war have on the whole been the opposite of what they have been in Western Europe, the nineteenth-century optimism and confidence in progress remain quite strong; but even in America there are substantial indications of questioning and doubt, best revealed in the nature of her more serious literature and in the writings of her thinkers.

their past proud record of power, Germany may regret that she never had the opportunity to which her capacities entitled her— she herself botched it—while the Mussolinian dream of power reminds one of the fable of the bull and the frog. In face of the outside all stand sadly diminished and demoted.

It is an easy exercise to devise rational and reasonable solutions for the world's ills. In the long term, clearly it would be beneficial for the states of Europe to develop some form of union. Europe's need of the petroleum resources of the Middle East could be the source of the mutually most profitable association, and the Arab world could benefit immensely from the use—if not the exploitation—of the vastly greater modernity and competence of Israel. All such considerations are largely irrelevant. The world remains divided into states, states that insist on calling themselves sovereign, however in fact a sham that contention may be; and peoples are less moved by reason than by dark forces stirring in their consciousness or beneath the surface of it. This must ever be borne in mind as we proceed to examine in some detail the operation of the state of Europe during the Age of the Great Transition, the gates of which Europe opened in 1914.

X

The First World War
and the
Ensuing Settlements

I. The July Crisis

THE SARAJEVO ASSASSINATION

Had the heir to the British throne elected to visit Dublin on St. Patrick's day of 1916, the gesture would have been regarded as a manifestation of insensitive bad taste, unless it were deliberately intended as an especially effective way of proclaiming Britain's determination to refuse compromise and concessions. At the very least one would have expected unusually alert police precautions lest some hotheaded Irishman choose the occasion to vent his feelings with a pistol shot or a bomb. It was no less rash of Archduke Franz Ferdinand to visit the capital of Bosnia on the 28th of June, Vidovdan, anniversary of the battle of Kossovo.[1] There had indeed been warnings against his visit but no extraordinary precautions were taken to insure his safety.

To be sure, within the Dual Monarchy, Franz Ferdinand's name was associated with the pro-Slav tendency of trialism. But too much time had passed during which Serbian and South Slav feeling had become increasingly exacerbated; the Archduke's views made him all the more hated and feared by the more intransigeant South Slav nationalists, those who would not be content with anything short of complete independence. It was just such a group of enthusiasts who, with assistance from across the border,[2] plotted

---

[1] The battle of Kossovo occurred in 1386. The subsequent eclipse of Serbia and her long subjugation to Turkish rule had made the tale of Kossovo a South Slav folk epic and the anniversary of it a day of national mourning. By 1914 Serbia existed again in independence, but the liberation of the South Slavs was still far from complete.

[2] The *Narodna Obrana* (national defense), dating from the 1908 crisis, was dedicated to keeping alive irredentist, especially anti-Austrian, agitation but was not an advocate of terroristic methods. The *Black Hand* (Union or Death) was

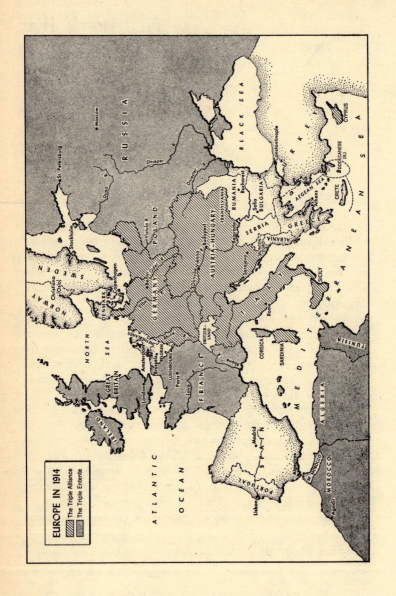

the assassination of Franz Ferdinand. They were raw youths, even unpracticed in the use of arms, and for the most part their courage failed them in the test. The accident of bad coördination in arrangements,[3] causing the driver of the Archduke's automobile to stop in order to retrieve a mistake, gave one of them, Princip, an opportunity to fire virtually point blank at a sitting target. Both Franz Ferdinand and his wife were killed. The deed was brutal murder, yet in all fairness not murder of the common kind, for an idealism of sorts, albeit only nationalistic, was its motivation. Sober citizens eschew and condemn violence; yet the fact must be faced that terroristic tactics can be warranted on occasion, in the sense at least that they sometimes succeed in accomplishing ends that are widely desired. The youths whose irresponsible ideal was a union in freedom of the South Slavs, be it at the incidental cost of a Europe in ruins, succeeded in their purpose. "The shot heard round the world" fits Sarajevo rather better than the original occasion of the phrase.

FROM THE ASSASSINATION TO THE AUSTRIAN ULTIMATUM TO SERBIA

Political assassination, in the Balkans especially, need not be the cause of very far-reaching repercussions. But this one set in motion a train of events whose ultimate effect was the collapse of the house of Europe as it had functioned in peace for nearly half a century. This consequence was the outcome of existing conditions which have been dwelt upon in earlier pages. Most important was the state of affairs in Austria-Hungary, the growing tensions which were a threat to the very existence of the state. Against the background of the aftermath of the Bosnian annexation crisis and the recent Balkan Wars, the consequences of Sarajevo are fully understandable.

The first point in the story is the decision by Austria, more specifically by Berchtold, that scores must be settled with Serbia once and for all, a decision in which Hötzendorff concurred; in

---

not averse to such and in actual fact there was overlapping membership between the two groups; the latter made use of contacts available to it through the former in establishing secret connections across the border from Serbia into Bosnia-Herzegovina. It is out of this connection between the two societies that considerable confusion has arisen in the discussion of the prime location of Serbian responsibility.

[3] An earlier attempt, in the form of a bomb, which had injured some of the party but not the Archduke, had caused a change to be made in his planned return route from the Konak.

324 A DIPLOMATIC HISTORY OF EUROPE SINCE THE CONGRESS OF VIENNA

concrete terms Austria must go to war with Serbia and crush her. But this decision implied at once complications no less domestic than foreign. At home, Tisza, the Hungarian Premier, was opposed to war: there were too many Slavs in the Monarchy as it was. It took about two weeks to overcome his objections, and this was only done through Berchtold's assurance—that he did not intend to keep—that no annexation would occur and by his playing the card of full German support.

But however true it might be that the very existence of Serbia constituted a threat to Austria, something more concrete was needed to justify an Austrian attack on Serbia in the eyes of the rest of Europe. This, too, made for delay while an investigation was being conducted in Sarajevo. That the assassins had Serbian connections was easily established, but there was a long distance between this fact and the clear implication of the Serbian government in responsibility greater than possible negligence.[4] The formal weakness of the Austrian case against Serbia gave, therefore, added importance to the attitude of the other Powers of Europe.

Even apart from this, Berchtold had from the very beginning sought to discover the position of his German ally. Adding to a memorandum of his of June 24 that dealt with the Balkan situation the consideration that Serbia was to be blamed for the assassination, he drew the conclusion that "Serbia must be eliminated as a power in the Balkans." With this Kaiser William II fully agreed on July 5, and Szögyény, the Austrian representative in Berlin, was also able to report Bethmann's concurrence. This episode is usually described as Germany's "blank check" to Austria; what it meant was that Germany was in effect surrendering to Austria the initiative of decision, decision in the taking of which the unconditional assurance of German support was a capital factor. Levity in such a degree almost warrants the description of criminal.[5] The German ambassador in Vienna, Tschirschky, used to the full his own influence to sustain Austria on the path of drastic action.

[4] From the Austrian point of view the results of the investigation were unsatisfactory, which is the reason for the Austrian refusal to submit them to the Powers. Later revelations about the extent of involvement in the plot of persons in high position in the Serbian government have no bearing on the Austrian decision of July, 1914.

[5] Yet at this stage it was no more than irresponsible levity. It is out of this that grew the legend of the Potsdam Council in which Germany was supposed to have taken the decision of war. There was no such thing as a Crown Council at this time, but merely a series of separate consultations which did, however, have the effect of governmental decision.

The question that arises at this point is whether a solid Austro-German combination would induce Russia, as in 1909, to recoil before the test of force, thereby enabling Austria to have her way with Serbia. And behind Russia there stood France for whom therefore a similar question arose in regard to the degree of her support of Russia. Long before Sarajevo an official French state visit to Russia had been planned for this time. Despite the stir caused by the assassination it was decided to proceed with the visit lest to abandon it create undue alarm in opinion—just as the Kaiser decided to proceed with his projected northern cruise. No one thought at this stage that general war was imminent. Thus it happened that Poincaré, the French President, and the French foreign minister, Viviani, were in Russia from July 20 to 22. The consequences of this were two, of divergent effect. On the one hand the government in Paris was relatively disorganized, with the result that French diplomacy did not play a very active role at first; on the other, Poincaré, in keeping with his consistent views, used his presence in St. Petersburg to bolster the Russian determination through his assurance of French support, even indicating this clearly to the Austrian ambassador to Russia. As we should put it now, Poincaré did not believe in appeasement.

When the French departed from Russia no irretrievable move had yet been made ostensibly by anyone. But the Austrian decision had been taken, which was made known, on July 23, in the form of an ultimatum to Serbia.[6] This ultimatum had been carefully designed in the hope that its demands would prove unacceptable. There was indeed alarm in Belgrade and frantic efforts, first to gather together the ministers dispersed through the country on account of the impending elections, then to elaborate an answer.[7] This answer was a skillful one. It was so worded as to convey the impression of extreme conciliatoriness, and those Austrian demands alone which constituted a clear infringement of Serbian sovereignty were not accepted; even in the case of these demands Serbia pro-

[6] The reason for the date was the calculation that the absence of the French government on its way back from Russia to France, a five-day journey, would make it difficult for France to act effectively. At the same time, the lapse of nearly four weeks between the assassination and the ultimatum robbed Austria of much of the psychological asset of the impact of indignation and sympathy caused by the former event.

[7] On July 10, Hartwig, the Russian Minister in Belgrade, who had played such an important role in Serbian affairs, died in dramatic circumstances, victim of a heart attack, in the home of the Austrian minister whom he was visiting. The removal of Hartwig deprived the Serbian government of his influence and had a certain disorienting effect.

posed, if Austria did not consider her reply satisfactory, that the matter be submitted to the Hague tribunal or to the Powers. On outside opinion the Serbian reply made an excellent impression, even the German Emperor regarding it as an outstanding success for Austria. Following his instructions, however, the Austrian minister in Belgrade, in the failure of unqualified Serb acceptance, immediately departed from his post.

FROM THE AUSTRIAN ULTIMATUM TO THE OUTBREAK OF GENERAL WAR

The Austrian ultimatum produced a marked Russian reaction. Russia let it be known that she would not passively allow Serbia to be destroyed. Thus the initial Austro-Serbian conflict was enlarged and altered into a more dangerous Austro-Russian one. A situation of this sort was by no means unprecedented, and Britain, least involved of the Powers either through direct Balkan interests or formal alliances, put forward the suggestion of an international conference. The German response to this was unfavorable, Germany insisting on localization of the conflict, while Austria, burning her bridges with the creation of a *fait accompli*, formally declared war on Serbia on July 28. This was the first in the list of such declarations.

Even this step was perhaps not irretrievable, for the Austrian forces were not ready for action, but it had the effect of making more acute and broadening the conflict. In order to make her position clear, on the 29th Russia resorted to the proclamation of partial mobilization, directed against Austria alone. Having gone the length of a declaration of war, clearly Austria could not simply withdraw it. However, Germany seemed at first to accept the Russian view that partial mobilization was not directed against her, and this made possible consideration of the so-called "Halt in Belgrade" scheme: Austria would occupy Belgrade but pursue no further operations, thus giving a last chance for diplomacy to find some compromise.

But ambiguity and confusion occurred at this point in both Germany and Russia. In the former country some of the leaders became at last aware of the initial levity of Germany's behavior. Bethmann for one was thoroughly alarmed, not to say in a state of panic. It was too late, however, to restrain, let alone abandon, Austria; in addition, the danger of Russian mobilization was fully realized in view of the German plan of military action in which the factor of speed was such a large component. Germany therefore essentially let matters take their course, endeavoring to pursue the fundamentally contradictory aims of assuring Austria of continued support *and* encouraging the British efforts at compromise.[8] On the Russian side it was recognized that, as the military had pointed out, partial mobilization was a risky move that would throw total mobilization into confusion, should the latter have to come into effect. Ever weak, the tsar was torn and vacillating; on the 29th he agreed to general mobilization which, however, was not yet officially proclaimed.

The technical significance of mobilizations must be stressed. Mobilization is a vast and complex operation that can, once launched, hardly be stopped in its tracks. Inevitably, it has the consequence of giving high priority to purely military factors, hence of automatically impeding the operation of diplomacy. The German plan for war, should it come to that, conditioned in the last analysis by considerations of geography, did not permit the Russian advantage of prior mobilization. When Russian mobilization was ordered on the 31st the German response was an ultimatum. Since no answer to this last was forthcoming, on August 1 Germany proclaimed her own general mobilization, followed the same day by a declaration of war against Russia. Thus the Austro-Serbian conflict had the first effect among the Great Powers of producing a Russo-German war.

In France, too, there had been hesitancy and confusion owing to the special situation of the absence of much of the government. The French role in the crisis was therefore relatively minor, save for the important assurances given to the Russians by Poincaré in St. Petersburg.[9] He was back in Paris on July 29; he, too, was torn by the dilemma, as he put it, of saving both the peace and the alliance.[10] However, on the 31st, an ultimatum was received from Germany asking what position France would take in the

[8] One may speak at this point of a genuine lack of coördination in German policy. Apart from the broad differences of approach between the military and the diplomats, even among the latter there was a lack of uniform direction. Bethmann's own actions lacked consistency, and some of this confusion was conveyed to Vienna where it created in turn confusion and puzzlement.

[9] As a result of the travels of the French government the role of Paléologue, the French ambassador in St. Petersburg, assumed unusual importance. He acted with considerable independence and his activity is somewhat comparable to that of Tschirschky in Vienna in strengthening the bonds of the alliances at this crucial juncture.

[10] On July 30, Viviani sent a telegram to Russia advising holding up general mobilization. The message was too late to alter the course of events.

event of a Russo-German conflict. It was an essentially superfluous gesture;[11] France replied that she would follow the dictates of her interest, and, like Germany, decreed mobilization on August 1. On the 3d, Germany issued a declaration of war against France.

During the last days of July the situation may be said to have passed out of control from the hands of the foreign offices and the diplomats into those of the military. Allowing that 1914 was not 1958, or even 1939, nevertheless mobility was sufficient to give the factor of time and the initiative of action considerable importance. This was especially the case where Germany was concerned, for her solution of the problem of the war on two fronts was the elimination of one of them, logically the western, since French mobilization would be much more rapid than Russian, in time to concentrate against the eastern threat. This was the strategy reflected in the Schlieffen Plan: to give the German mass the full effect of speed, the delay that French border fortifications would involve could be avoided by turning them, moving through relatively undefended Belgium into northern France.

But this approach encountered the difficulty that Belgium was a neutral state, under guarantee, since her creation, of the Powers, Germany among them. Germany had decided that in the face of such a situation necessity must be the higher law. On August 2 an ultimatum, demanding free passage, was sent to Brussels. If passage were granted, Germany would make good what damage might ensue to Belgium, but in the event of refusal Belgium must take the consequences. Belgium refused to be a party to the violation of her neutral status, an act that Germany therefore committed unilaterally on August 4.

Throughout the crisis Britain had striven to save the peace. When war was first unleashed among the Great Powers she was faced with a major decision. Formal commitments she had none though moral obligations may be said to have existed. Such as they were, these were but the expression of the fact that the gradual involvement of Britain in the Entente, especially with France, was merely her reaction to the growing German power, a reaction expressive of the traditional British tendency to maintain the European balance untipped. Could Britain run the risk of a German

---

[11] There was little expectation in Germany by this time that France would agree to remain neutral. Had she done so, Germany was prepared to ask for the surrender for the duration of the war of the French border fortifications, clearly an absurd condition.

success? was the question that now demanded an answer. Despite the awkwardness of unrevealed preparations that must now be brought into the light of day, and differences that led to resignations from the Cabinet, the decision was made for war. The German violation of Belgium intervened at this point and greatly simplified the issue for Britain. It was the needed catalytic to arouse opinion which could now enter the conflict in defense of long-recognized British interest—control of the Channel coast—as well as in defense of the sanctity of written obligations—the common guarantee of Belgium. The British declaration of war on Germany took place on August 5.

No mention so far has been made of Italy, a member of the Triple Alliance, renewed for the last time in 1912. Rightly suspecting that, if consulted, Italy would oppose Austrian action against Serbia, Berchtold had carefully kept Italy uninformed of his plans. On August 3 Italy proclaimed her neutrality on the plea that the Austrian behavior violated both the letter and the spirit of the defensive alliance. Rumania, another ally of the Central Powers, adopted a similar position. By August 5 general war had broken out in Europe that involved all the Great Powers save one, Italy, and in addition two small ones, Serbia and Belgium. For the time being diplomacy must yield to the language of force.

THE ISSUE OF RESPONSIBILITY

Wars have occurred before and since the First World War. But the peculiar circumstances of that conflict, as pointed out earlier,[12] gave the issue of responsibility for its outbreak an unprecedented importance and have caused it to overflow the bounds of historic controversy into the domain of practical politics. For that reason, it is desirable to look briefly at this question in the light of the events just described.

The Sarajevo murder is the opening gun, followed by the next step in the form of Austria's decision to settle scores with Serbia. The Austrian fear of Serbia had substantial foundation, and Serbia had indeed been lax in allowing secret societies and plotting to flourish on her soil that involved personalities in high office. But the result of the Austrian investigation was essentially negative at the time and the Austrian decision was largely independent of it, stemming rather from the domestic problem of the Dual Monarchy and the view that it could be revivified by such action. However,

[12] See above, pp. 157 ff.

in the light of the recent past, Austria could not help but consider the probable Russian reaction, hence her logical consultation of Germany. The German answer was the "blank check" of July 5–6. All evidence points to the conclusion that this was not the result of careful calculation and a deliberate design to precipitate war, but rather of an unthinking wish to repeat the performance of 1909 by frightening Russia and France into acquiescence to a localized conflict and with a view to retrieving the diplomatic setback of the Balkan Wars. The extraordinary levity that prompted the German decision places Germany squarely at the center of the issue of responsibility. For not dissimilar reasons, Russia took the position that she would not allow the detruction of Serbia, and her position was made clear through the step of partial mobilization.

Time passed that left both Austria and Germany unmoved in their purpose. Not until the eleventh hour did the realization come to Germany of the seriousness of the situation. If the military were undisturbed by the prospect of war, the Kaiser and Bethmann recoiled from it. But, having failed to respond to the first British proposal of mediation, they found themselves caught in the coils of their own initial action. Faced with the dilemma of saving the peace or supporting Austria, they gave priority to the second alternative, accepting the consequences of this decision, or perhaps better, allowing them to unfold. In the last stages, at the end of July, the principal German preoccupation was to give Austria the feeling of continued support while conveying to others the impression that Germany was not rejecting conciliation. This led to ambiguity and uncomfortable squirmings that caused Berchtold to ask who made decisions in Berlin.

The peculiar situation of the French government made action by it difficult, a fact taken into full consideration in Vienna. But Poincaré's presence in St. Petersburg was important in bolstering Russian determination. These circumstances gave added importance to the role of Paléologue, the French ambassador, whose activity, comparable to that of Tschirschky in Vienna, may be said with both men to have gone beyond the proper bounds of their function. In dealing with his own dilemma, the decisive factor for Poincaré was the rejection of appeasement.

The special position of Britain has been mentioned, and the British mistakes are grievous, for all that they are sins of omission. Grey's good intentions are not open to question and his reluctance to take a definite position lest he thereby unduly encourage either side in its intransigeance is understandable. But it was a misunderstanding of the situation nonetheless to convey the impression that Britain was indifferent to the purely Austro-Serbian quarrel. To accept the thesis of localization was to espouse in effect the Austro-German view, and to encourage the German hope of British neutrality was calculated in turn to encourage Germany to face the possibility of war with greater confidence. In the circumstances, it was to mislead Germany, even though this does not exonerate the false German reading of the British attitude.

Of the German violation of Belgium little need be said. This was 1914, not the era of Hitler and after, and international obligations had meaning. Even Germany did not attempt to justify her action save on the plea of the higher law of necessity, and the famous "scrap of paper" phrase of the German Chancellor is inexcusable by any standards, even those of intelligent craftiness.

Yet with all this it remains true that the vast majority of the responsible statesmen of Europe did not deliberately and consciously want a general war. They took certain positions as the result largely of past background and experience; once they had taken these positions, they acted according to their varying capabilities, often limited, caught in a stream they were unable to control.[13] Of course war could have been avoided by either side retreating, but this observation, if true, has little significant content.

Nevertheless, the issue of responsibility has relevance. If seen in terms of long-range factors, it implies judgment on the whole course of events during the preceding half-century. Here the rate of German growth, combined with the ineptitude of German diplomacy after Bismarck, would seem to be the central factor. When it comes to the limited sphere of the July crisis alone, this ineptitude was combined with initial frivolity, and for all that the crude explanation of plots has long since been exploded and that responsibility remains allottable to a variety of individuals in a variety of nations, it does not seem unfair to say that the leaders of Germany remain at the center of the story.

Our views of these events have varied and the issue will remain controversial. The wartime view, prevalent in the allied countries,

[13] One factor which often receives little attention but is of considerable importance is the simple one of the pressure of work and of physical fatigue. The foreign offices were operating on a twenty-four hour basis and their heads were in a state of exhaustion from overwork and lack of sleep, a condition highly inimical to the making of pondered decisions.

of exclusive and willful German aggression, was not long tenable. Just because it was so crude and based on incomplete and false evidence, a reaction ensued that had marked success, especially in the English-speaking world. The revisionist school expressed not only the results of honest and serious historical scholarship, but also the promptings of a guilty conscience. The pendulum has been swinging back for some time, though the wheel will never come full circle, and a summing quotation seems apt:

. . . To attribute the responsibility for making war in July 1914 to the Central Powers is not to deliver judgement on the conditions which drove Austria to war with Serbia and led Germany to support Austria. To state that Austria and Germany acted as they did . . . is not to assert that from their own point of view they had not good reasons for seeking to change a state of affairs injurious directly to Austria and indirectly to Germany. The same holds good in respect of France and Russia. These two Powers manifested no great fear of the tempest that was being unloosed. Nay, they seemed almost ready to welcome it in certain conditions, hoping perhaps that its end might turn out to their advantage. The fact is that the question of the origins of the war is an entirely different one from that of the rights and wrongs of the war. . . . All that we can affirm . . . is that even if one or both of the Central Powers had sufficient reasons for starting a war, it would have been a wrong decision on their part to do so in conditions unfavourable to themselves, throwing the world into chaos only to bring about their own defeat and ruin.[14]

THE INITIAL STAGES OF THE WAR

The Central Powers did not know that they were bringing about their own defeat and ruin. Allowing for the frivolity of their behavior, one aspect of which was their miscalculation where Britain was concerned, even this last mistake need not be fatal to them. The observation was not new that the British fleet could be of little assistance in the defense of Paris. With war generalized, the initial dispute receded into the background; the crushing of Serbia would have to wait until more important matters were settled, and the bulk of the Austrian forces were directed toward the Russian frontier. But in view of her physical expanse and of her economic backwardness, of which relatively scant communications were one aspect, Russia could not mobilize as rapidly as the rest of the Continental belligerents. The German plan for the war, as mentioned earlier, consisted of a holding operation in the East while

[14] Luigi Albertini, *The Origins of the War of 1914*, Oxford University Press, 1952–1953, Vol. II, pp. 136–137.

using the assets of mass and speed to destroy the French army. The situation in the West was therefore crucial.

The French wisely declined to be entrapped into considerations of the priority of necessity over law;[15] less wisely, they did not take adequate measures to have large forces on their Belgian frontier, for all that the German action taking the form that it did had long been contemplated by them. Belgian resistance could hardly hope to stop the German war machine; nevertheless it was useful in causing some delay. However, the Germans overcame this resistance and achieved further success in their first encounter with substantial French forces; this enabled their own to march in rapid strides toward Paris. The French government moved to Bordeaux, but the discussion of whether to withdraw behind the Loire or make a stand for Paris resulted in a decision for the latter course. The month of August was high drama. Despite their losses the French forces were not disorganized, while the German, despite their successes, had to cope with lengthening lines of communication. The French stand on the Marne, at the beginning of September, was successful and the Germans fell back, but only a certain distance, for the French drive in turn lacked the power to engage in sustained pursuit.

The momentary equilibrium reached in northern France led to an attempt by either force to outflank the other, the "race to the sea," which ended at the Channel. Thus the war of movement very early became transformed into a war of siege. From the North Sea, across a minute corner of Belgium, through northern France and along the Franco-German frontier to Switzerland, a solid front of some four hundred miles was established. At mounting cost that reached staggering proportions, it was maintained with but relatively minor changes for the better part of four years. The Germans were in control of substantial and valuable enemy resources, but they had failed of their essential purpose, the destruction of the enemy, hence must adjust themselves to the war on two fronts.

Meanwhile in the East a similar situation developed. The Russians were able to take action earlier than had been expected, thereby relieving in some measure the German pressure in the West. But sufficient German forces were assembled to inflict upon

---

[15] With a view to establishing clearly the defensive position of France in the eyes of the outside world, on July 30 the French government had ordered French troops to withdraw from a 10-kilometer zone away from the frontier.

them among the Masurian Lakes a major defeat that laid the basis for the fame of General von Hindenburg. In the East also a stalemate ensued, roughly along the line of Russia's western frontier from the Baltic to the Rumanian border. The early predictions of the impossibility of a long war, for technical, if for no other reasons, were belied, and preparations had to be made by all for a conflict of indefinite duration.

The view that war is an instrument of progress has had not a few adherents. It is largely unpopular at present, but that war is a great promoter and accelerator of change, economic and social, no less than political and technological, can hardly be gainsaid. That is not the least significant aspect of it, yet one with which we are not concerned at this point. But the stalemate established in 1914 meant that both sides must seek to increase their strength to overcome the opponent's. This meant two things: on the one hand, a greater use and mobilization of their own domestic resources, both material and human; on the other, the effort to secure additional assistance from hitherto neutral quarters. It is this last aspect of things with which we must now deal.

II. The Diplomacy of the War

THE DIPLOMACY OF POWER (1914–1917)

Each side at first, quite naturally, expected victory, with this qualification that the geographically more favorably situated and militarily better prepared Central Powers might achieve this result with promptness, while it was unlikely to come to the dispersed and less well prepared Allies—the Russian army was still in process of reconstruction and Britain had virtually no effective force on land. The peoples in all belligerent countries generally entered the fray with enthusiasm. An Allied victory would give the French their lost provinces and insure Russia's dominance in the Balkans and possibly at the Straits, while presumably ridding Britain of the German threat, specifically of its naval aspect; victory for the Central Powers would insure the continuance of a revivified Austria-Hungary, more broadly it would mean German dominance of the European Continent, plus doubtless some imperial advantages. No one envisaged at first a mere continuation of the equilibrium and of the *status quo* of July, 1914.

Japan had an alliance with Britain, under the terms of which she had no obligation to go to war in the existing circumstances.

But Japan thought the occasion auspicious for taking over Germany's Far Eastern position and interests; with this purpose in view she entered the war on August 23. The British were not unduly enthusiastic but could do little other than acquiesce in an intervention that was of little use to the Allied cause since Japanese aims and activity remained exclusively Far Eastern. Not until the final settling of accounts was the Japanese intervention to give rise to a difficult issue.

The conflict was still essentially European and the belligerents at first had no well defined aims other than the achievement of victory.[16] Their policy was shaped in large part by the necessities of war and the arrangements that they came to make in the course of its prosecution. Italy, the Balkan states save Serbia, and the Ottoman Empire were all neutral; they became the natural foci of the belligerents' diplomacy. Sazonov's mind was fertile of schemes for the eastern half of the Mediterranean, schemes which, however, may be said to have got in each other's way: the interests of Bulgaria and Serbia in one case, of Serbia and Italy in another, were not easy to reconcile. For that matter, it could hardly be expected that the neutrals would care to commit themselves before the result of the first test of arms was apparent. The first concrete diplomatic developments occurred in the Ottoman Empire.

In that state German influence had been making notable progress before 1914. As early as August 2 it secured the asset of a formal alliance with Turkey. Nevertheless, Turkish opinion was divided, and if there was little response to Russian offers of a guarantee of Ottoman integrity, not all in Turkey wished to enter the war. Germany did not hesitate to exert pressure: Liman von Sanders was largely in control of the army, and the German cruisers *Goeben* and *Breslau*, escaping from the Mediterranean into the Sea of Marmora, were used to give Turkey the final push.[17] When, on their own initiative, they entered the Black Sea at the end of October and went on to bombard Odessa, the Entente Powers broke relations with Turkey and declared war on her.

In retrospect this action may be taken as the death warrant of the Ottoman Empire; its consequences, destined to be enormous, and not for Turkey alone, have not yet been worked out in full.

[16] On September 5, 1914, Great Britain, France, and Russia undertook a mutual commitment not to make separate peace.

[17] These ships were formally sold to Turkey but continued to operate with their German crews and commanders. The Straits were closed by the Turks on September 26.

But one of the more immediate of these consequences was the definite cutting off of communications between Russia and her Western allies.[18] In 1914 Russia was already beginning to experience difficulties in supplying her armies with adequate matériel. Out of this situation it was only natural that the idea should occur of reëstablishing contact with Russia by forcing open the Straits.

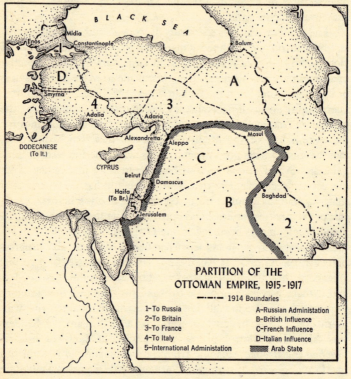

PARTITION OF THE
OTTOMAN EMPIRE, 1915-1917

—·—·— 1914 Boundaries

1-To Russia
2-To Britain
3-To France
4-To Italy
5-International Administration

A-Russian Administration
B-British Influence
C-French Influence
D-Italian Influence
//// Arab State

The Russians could offer little assistance and the French had their hands more than full on their home ground; the expedition to the Dardanelles, when it was finally agreed upon, was therefore primarily, though not exclusively, a British undertaking.

But this itself aroused traditional Russian suspicion; even Greek assistance that the British would have gladly enlisted was looked at askance in St. Petersburg. There were long and difficult negotiations among the Allies that resulted in a rather startling agreement

[18] The avenues of access to Russia from the north and through Persia, that were developed during the Second World War, were of little avail in the First.

at the beginning of March, 1915: as the price of Russian agreement, the British and the French consented to outright Russian possession of the Straits after the war. They felt they had to pay this price in order to insure Russian allegiance to the common cause, for the suspicion, not wholly devoid of foundation, never completely died out in the West that Russia might find some separate accommodation with the enemy. If the concept of forcing the Straits was basically sound, the implementation of it was not successful. Discouraged sooner perhaps than they need have been, the Western forces after a time abandoned the attempt.[19]

Since we are dealing with the Ottoman Empire it will be convenient to anticipate the order of chronological developments in other quarters in order to follow their unfolding in this. The decision in regard to the Straits and the fact that the discussion was reduced to three Powers led to a solution of the long-standing issue of the fate of the Sick Man of Europe, the division of whose inheritance was finally agreed upon. The circumstances of the war made it natural that the prosecution of it against the Ottoman Empire should be primarily in British hands; the forces used were drawn largely from Britain and from her overseas dominions and possessions, Australia, New Zealand, and India, which operated on the periphery of the Ottoman Empire, at Suez and in the Persian Gulf.[20] They met at first with varying success, but the fact was put to advantage that much of the sultan's domain was Arab land and that among Arab chieftains and sheiks opposition to Turkish rule existed.[21] From London, through Cairo, and from the seat of government in India, in Simla, but mainly from Cairo, negotiations were conducted which led in 1915 to an agreement between the British and Sherif Hussein of Mecca whereby the British would support an Arab movement for independence. The northern boundary of Arab territory lay roughly along the present southern border of Turkey.

But the French had long-standing interests in the Levant. These they insisted should be taken into consideration, with the consequence that the Sykes-Picot agreement in March, 1916, between

[19] The transfer of the Dardanelles expeditionary force to Salonica in October, 1915, had implications for the Balkan situation which will be dealt with presently. See below, pp. 340–341.

[20] In December, 1914, Britain proclaimed the formal establishment of her protectorate in Egypt.

[21] It is permissible to speak of Arab nationalism in this connection though it is well to bear in mind that much of Arab politics was a matter of personal and dynastic rivalries.

338 A DIPLOMATIC HISTORY OF EUROPE SINCE THE CONGRESS OF VIENNA

the British and themselves, acknowledged their future position in Syria. This understanding was, later in the year, underwritten by Russia, which also secured a claim in Asia Minor in this connection.

The Italians had also for some time been eying Asia Minor, off the coast of which they had held a foothold since 1912 in the Dodecanese Islands.[22] The arrangements just mentioned, despite the fact that the Italians had joined the Allies in 1915, were made without their participation or knowledge. But they, too, began to assert their claims which were given recognition in April, 1917, in the agreement of St. Jean de Maurienne among themselves, the British, and the French.[23]

One more item must be mentioned to complete this roster. Without going into the nature, origin, and background of the Zionist movement, the home of which lay mainly in Central Europe, it may suffice to say that the Allies endeavored to annex this movement to their cause. This they did in the form of a British statement, the famous Balfour declaration of November, 1917, which advocated the establishment of a "national home" for the Jews in Palestine.

The sum total of this elaborate network of understandings and agreements was that the Ottoman Empire would cease to exist. In its place would arise a separate Arab world in which, however, Britain and France had carved out definite zones of predominant influence, while a corner was in some form to be set aside for the Jews. In addition, the rest of the Empire, apart from the Straits allotted to Russia in 1915, was divided into four sections: a Russian sphere south of the Caucasus, abutting on a French one, Cilicia, that was in turn adjacent in the south to the French portion of the Arab world; next to the French sphere, to the west, roughly the southern half of the remaining part of Anatolia, including the city of Smyrna, was to be the Italian share. The northern half of Anatolia alone was to remain unreservedly Turkish. It will be noted that, while these commitments were not in a strict legal sense contradictory, to speak of their consistency was to skate on thin ice: this was especially the case of the Arab and French claims in Syria and of those of the Arabs and Jews in Palestine. Britain was the connecting link between all these arrangements; as Balfour put it later, the necessities of war sometimes induce one to under-

---

[22] The intervention of Italy will be dealt with presently. See below, p. 339.
[23] This understanding was subject to Russian agreement, but this, owing to the Russian events of 1917, was never forthcoming.

take commitments that one would otherwise prefer not to have made.

The disposition of the Ottoman Empire was but one of the objects of diplomatic activity during the two years from 1915 to 1917. There were others, which we must now go back to trace. The first in point of time concerned Italy. As previously stated, Italy rested her case for neutrality in August, 1914, on the terms of the treaty of the Triple Alliance. Her case was sound in law, but her decision clearly implied a broader judgment of the best defense of Italian interest. Clearly, also, it was henceforth out of the question that Italy should join her allies in the war; the issue therefore became from the beginning one between continued neutrality and participation on the side of the Entente. Some efforts from that camp, mainly of Russian source, to bring Italy into the war at once had no results; if nothing else, Italy would hardly commit herself while the outcome of the initial battles of the war was in suspense. There were in Italy partisans of both courses, and the debate waxed increasingly hot between neutralists and interventionists. The foreign minister, San Giuliano, was by personal inclination sympathetic to the Central Powers, and so was his successor, Sonnino;[24] but the Prime Minister, Salandra, and the government fairly early came to the conclusion that in all likelihood Italy would eventually join the Allies. The problem, from the Italian point of view, was how to secure the greatest possible benefits from the war situation.

Negotiations were carried on in Vienna with a view to obtaining a price for continued neutrality. Italy wanted territorial cessions—the *irredenta*—which Austria was understandably reluctant to make; where the Italians said Trento and Trieste the Austrians, feigning not to have heard, replied Valona. Germany sought to mediate, urging concessions on Vienna, but even Bülow's personal intervention in Rome had no success. The negotiation dragged on into the spring of 1915; Austria did make concessions, but it was a case of too little and too late, and the Italian demand for immediate cession was an added obstacle to agreement.

The Italians were at the same time conducting negotiations with the Entente, mainly through London. Their demands, which ran athwart South Slav desires, were principally opposed by Russia, but a compromise was eventually reached which was em-

[24] San Giuliano died in October, 1914, and was succeeded by Sonnino after a brief interim during which the Prime Minister, Salandra, held the foreign office.

bodied in the Treaty of London of April 26, 1915.[25] Italy went on to denounce the alliance and proceeded to declare war on her former allies in May.[26] In exchange for her participation in the war, she was promised by the Entente Powers certain concrete advantages. These were tantamount to making the Adriatic an Italian lake;[27] more loosely, Italy was promised some "adequate" colonial compensations, which were in part spelled out in the St. Jean de Maurienne agreement of 1917, previously mentioned. This outcome was a logical and consistent step in the unfolding of Italy's foreign policy: making good use of the balance of power, the enhanced position that the war gave to her neutrality enabled her to obtain a high, though not an altogether unreasonable, price. Her control of the Adriatic laid the bases of her future influence in the Balkans, and Sonnino's concentration on Asia Minor was, in the context of the time, likewise sound.

The calculation that the stalemate of 1915 could be broken by the weight of Italian power—the Italian intervention was, logically, to be coördinated with a Russian offensive, a plan that went awry—proved wrong. The Central Powers were able to muster sufficient forces to man the new front that was established from Switzerland to the Adriatic. The theater of war had merely been enlarged, and the next significant military development was the result of a success of the diplomacy of the Central Powers.

Just as the Allies had an advantage in dealing with Italy in that they could freely dispose of enemy territory, it was correspondingly easier for the Central Powers to give satisfaction to Bulgarian desires in Macedonia. In September, 1915, King Ferdinand, despite parliamentary opposition—note the Italian parallel—entered into an agreement with them as a result of which Bulgaria joined them in the war, on October 5. The Allied forces in Salonica were not

---

[25] It is of interest that it was on March 4 that the British foreign office received two important documents, the Russian memorandum containing the Russian demand for the Straits and that which embodied the formal Italian demands.

[26] The last phase of Italian neutrality was complicated by the fact that Giolitti, who controlled the majority in Parliament, was a neutralist. Parliament—and Giolitti—therefore had to be maneuvered into acquiescence. The maneuver was skillful, but the result was that Italy did not enter and participate in the war as a united country; the future consequences of this situation on the course of Italian affairs were to be very considerable.

[27] Russian opposition caused Italy to relinquish her demand for the whole of Dalmatia, the northern half of which was alone to be hers. Likewise, she would not have Cattaro, but her foothold in Albania would give her control of the entrance to the Adriatic. In December, 1914, Italy had already sent an expeditionary force to Valona, a move pleasing to none of the belligerents but in which the necessities of war caused all to acquiesce.

ready for action and Greece did not intervene as the Allies had hoped; caught in a pincers Serbia was quickly overrun. Bulgarian force alone was not a very great asset, but the immediate outcome had two effects: it was a marked setback, diplomatically, for the Allies and a corresponding asset for the Austro-Germans; also, as a result of the destruction of Serbia, the Central Powers—perhaps one should say Germany, since the direction of the whole war was to such a large degree in her hands—were in control of unbroken territory extending from the North Sea to the Persian Gulf; here was Berlin-Baghdad in a new guise.[28]

By the end of 1915 the war map was highly favorable to the Central Powers. If the western and the Italian fronts had remained essentially stabilized, in the East the Russians had been pushed back to a line that deprived them of all of Poland. Germany then returned to a variation of her initial plan, the destruction of the Western forces. The attack on Verdun was a failure; for some months the Germans and the French inflicted upon each other staggering losses that represented the war of attrition at its most appalling. The subsequent battle of the Somme, an Anglo-German episode, was essentially of a similar nature.

But in the year 1916 the Russians were able to mount an offensive that brought them to the Carpathians and this momentary success had the effect of bringing Rumania into the war. Ever since the beginning the Rumanians had been biding their time, waiting for a propitious moment; the Russian success caused them to fear that they might be too late and, in August, the Allies having accepted the Rumanian terms—the acquisition of Transylvania, Bukowina, and the Banat—Rumania, like Italy earlier, entered the war against her ex-allies. Actually, she was too late;[29] an initial advance into Transylvania soon turned into retreat. By the end of the year the Austro-Germans had overrun Rumania, whose intervention thus turned to their advantage since Rumanian resources were now at their complete disposal.

[28] The remnants of the Serbian forces made an epic escape through Albania in the dead of winter; they were settled for a time on the island of Corfu, whence the Greeks would not allow them to be transported to Salonica. Eventually, they were taken there to join the Anglo-French expeditionary force. On the score of the disposition of that army there were Anglo-French differences that resulted in a compromise whereby the force was neither withdrawn nor reinforced. In the Balkans the French interest was more active than the British, by contrast with the Straits, and the Salonica corps was placed under French command.
[29] The Russian offensive had spent itself by this time and the planned assistance of the Salonica army failed to materialize.

One more Balkan state was to be involved in the war. Greece was divided in her sympathies; Venizelos and King Constantine, brother-in-law of the Kaiser, led the opposing tendencies, pro-Allies and pro-Central Powers respectively. On two occasions, in 1915, Venizelos had been on the verge of a successful negotiation that would have brought Greek intervention. The King dismissed him, and not until June, 1917, after forcible pressure by the Allies, was Greece propelled into the war.[30]

THE DIPLOMACY OF IDEOLOGY

WAR AIMS AND PEACE PROPOSALS. Initially, all the belligerents had had one simple aim, victory, but the prolongation of the war and its accumulating cost, with no clear end in sight, gave increasing point to the question, What are we fighting for and how is it to be achieved? and even to the consideration of the possibility of finding some compromise acceptable to all. The necessities of the war itself to a degree tended to shape its course, and the various treaties and understandings made by the belligerents constituted what may be regarded as so many mortgages on the future peace. These were more numerous and involved on the Allied side, for the reasons that the Allies were more numerous and that there was among them considerable divergence of interests. Between Germany and Austria there were no such important differences, save to some degree in the case of Poland.

What the clear victory of either side would mean assumed considerable importance for all, and not for the belligerents alone. The United States was far removed from the conflict, but the comment is of interest, made by Colonel House as early as August, 1914, that "If the Allies win, it means largely the domination of Russia on the Continent of Europe; and if Germany wins, it means the unspeakable tyranny of militarism for generations to come."[31] House's judgment may be put side by side with the observation of Pilsudski, viewing a narrower horizon, the liberation of Poland: "Germany must first defeat Russia and must then be herself defeated by the western Powers."[32] This last contains in germ what

[30] The Near East continued to remain a theater of intra-allied rivalries. Greece and Serbia could constitute a counterweight to Italy which, reciprocally, was not favorable to Greek intervention and always viewed the Serbs with suspicion.
[31] The Intimate Papers of Colonel House, arranged as a narrative by Charles Seymour, Boston, Houghton Mifflin, 1926–1928, Vol. I, p. 291.
[32] Quoted in A. J. P. Taylor, The Struggle for Mastery in Europe, New York, Macmillan, 1954, p. 554.

came to be the ideology of the war and the peace, self-determination and democracy.

The above-mentioned commitments may be viewed as representing essentially the operation of the factor of power, establishing an equilibrium among rival components. The need to induce peoples to continue in their acceptance of the sacrifices demanded of them put a premium on factors other than that of crude power, ideologies laden with moral content. And this became an increasingly important aspect of the struggle, which introduced into it and into the settlements that were to follow a fatal element of ambiguity. From its detachment and distance the United States was in a good position to view the conflict with a minimum of passion and to think in terms of reasonable compromise. Colonel House was in Europe in the spring of 1915 and again in the winter of 1915–1916, only to discover that no basis of compromise yet existed.

By the end of 1916 the war had exacted high toll from all belligerents. Allied resources were undoubtedly far larger than those of the Central Powers, but the war situation seemed highly favorable to the latter as a mere glance at the map will show. On the other hand it was not clear how they would break their opponents' will to resist. A new government had just been organized in Britain, under the leadership of Lloyd George who represented the war *à outrance*. Capitalizing on her latest Rumanian success, Germany announced in December a willingness to negotiate, without however offering a more concrete basis than the extolling of German victories. Since the physical assets were all in German hands and it was hardly to be thought that they would merely be surrendered, while the Allies had no intention of recognizing any of their territorial losses, but instead had claims of their own against the Central Powers, there was clearly no basis for any meeting of minds. The Allies declined an offer which, in effect, rather than being seriously intended was designed to test their determination while gaining Germany some advantage *vis-à-vis* world opinion.

At this same time President Wilson called upon the belligerents to give an indication of their war aims. In this the Central Powers were at a disadvantage since they did not propose to relinquish some at least of their gains;[33] it was their turn to decline. The Al-

[33] In April, 1917, discussions between Bethmann-Hollweg and the military leaders, Hindenburg and Ludendorff, resulted in establishing the conditions of

lies on the other hand could and did answer the American proposal, formulating on January 10, 1917, the first definite statement of their purpose. They asked for restoration; but beyond restoration they espoused the principle of nationality. Whether that principle be good or evil, it represents in any case one of the great historic forces of modern times; it is a simple fact that there were alien minorities under German rule, while, in addition, the complete application of self-determination would imply the destruction of that collection of minorities, the Habsburg Empire, and could be used as well for the destruction of the Ottoman. On the basis of the exchanges that took place at the turn from 1916 to 1917 it appears that the war was being put on a plane of ideology and principle, hence was far less amenable to compromise than a simple contest of power, the very essence of which is equilibrium and adjustment.

To the advantage that the espousal of self-determination presented to the Allied cause there was one important qualification, the Russian, in its most concrete form the Polish question. As in the eighteenth century, at the time of her partitions, Poland was the concern of her three neighbors. However, since 1915, Poland had been under effective Austro-German control. What to do with Poland was a poser, for, apart from certain Austro-German differences on her score, the thought was ever entertained by the Central Powers of a separate Russian peace. During 1916, in fact, that possibility was foremost in Bethmann's mind, but eventually he accepted the idea of a reconstituted Poland under Austro-German auspices.[34] On November 5, 1916, the German and the Austrian emperors issued a proclamation to the Polish people, promising them the creation of an independent Polish state. This, for the time being at least, inevitably closed the door on any

---

peace that would be acceptable to Germany. These involved substantial acquisitions in Eastern Europe for both Germany and Austria-Hungary; in the West, Germany would retain some form of effective control of Belgium and she would annex the French coal region of Briey-Longwy, allowing for possible minor frontier rectifications in southern Alsace. The measure of control of the military over the civilian government must be stressed in the case of Germany.

[34] The motivation for this was in part purely military. Ludendorff thought that he might recruit substantial manpower in Poland to compensate for the heavy German losses, but German efforts to that end yielded but meager results. That Germany would have relinquished effective control of Poland in the event of victory may well be doubted; it was not long before Pilsudski, partisan of collaboration with the Central Powers, who had organized a Polish legion to fight against the Russians, fell out with his German sponsors and was imprisoned by them. The attitude of Polish nationalism toward Russia and Germany is aptly summed up in the above quoted comment of the same Pilsudski (p. 342).

prospect of separate Russian peace. But the military, in a dominant position in Germany, still thought a clear victory could be theirs and they overrode the timid Bethmann.

The Western Allies would have liked to be able to give the Poles promises of freedom; instead of this, their never fully laid to rest fears of Russian defection in the form of a separate peace, caused them to show special deference to Russian wishes. It was in February, 1917, on the occasion of an interallied discussion in Petrograd, that a Franco-Russian agreement was made, the essence of which was Russian agreement to France having a free hand on the Rhine in exchange for a similar French consent to a Russian free hand in the East; what this meant in effect was that Russia might incorporate all of Poland.[35] This represented, as far as Eastern Europe was concerned, the abandonment of a long-standing French tradition.

The remarkable military performance of the Central Powers was due in large measure to the fact that the direction of the war was centralized in German hands to a degree that had no counterpart among the Allies. But the Austro-German association was not free of weaknesses, mainly in the Austro-Hungarian partner of the combination. The death of the old emperor, Franz Joseph, in November, 1916, was in more senses than one the end of an era. Charles I, his successor, was not unresponsive to the possibility of novel prospects for his state and was less irrevocably wedded to the German connection. Out of his personal inclination and of the growing stresses to which the war subjected the Danubian Monarchy came the so-called Austrian peace offer. The Austrian calculation seems to have been that if a basis of agreement could be found with the Allies, an Austrian threat of desertion might in turn induce Germany to negotiate. The negotiations were conducted through the intermediary of Charles's brother-in-law, Prince Sixte of Bourbon-Parma, currently an officer in the Belgian army, who conveyed the Austrian proposals to the French government. The details of this offer and of the negotiations need not detain us here for they were foredoomed to failure. The French and the British were indeed highly interested at first, but they saw in the scheme mainly a hope of weakening their chief enemy, Ger-

---

[35] Like other wartime agreements this one was secret. It was largely the work of the French delegate, Doumergue, acting on his own initiative; it caused considerable qualms in Paris, but, owing to the precarious military situation, the French government decided to underwrite it in March.

346 A DIPLOMATIC HISTORY OF EUROPE SINCE THE CONGRESS OF VIENNA

many; when it came to taking account of Russian and Italian interests, the possibility of agreement quickly evaporated and the final outcome was mere recriminations, both between the French and the Austrians and also between the latter and their German ally; Emperor Charles had to go to Canossa and the net result was a tightening of the German hold upon Austria.

No more than mention need be made of the Vatican's "peace note" of August, 1917, which essentially proposed a return to the *status quo ante*. For one thing it was so handled as to give rise to the suspicion, especially in France, of being a pro-German move. Since neither side was really prepared to contemplate such a basis for peace it was a futile gesture.

War weariness, however, affected all in 1917, but if its effects were far-reaching in Austria and in Russia, the will to fight was still dominant in Germany and among the Western Allies. In Germany the resignation of Bethmann, willing to toy at least with the prospect of compromise, was forced by the military. Even the revival of international socialism,[36] recovering from the blow of 1914, and leaning toward the advocacy of a peace without indemnities or annexations, and the mutinies that endangered the French army during the summer of 1917 did not prevent those who favored the prosecution of the war to ultimate victory from retaining control. The advent of Lloyd George to the Prime Ministership in Britain has been mentioned. In France, after a difficult passage, the end of the year 1917 saw the rise of Clemenceau to a similar position; he was the most authentic incarnation of the French will to victory.

The net result of the activity just rehearsed of the year 1917 was to put greater stress on the ideological aspects of the conflict. But this effect was enormously enhanced by events that took place, one on the fringes of, the other far away from the confines of Europe, events which were to alter considerably the nature of the war. Both were born out of the conflict, but for the longer term they were destined to dominate the shape of the future.

THE RUSSIAN REVOLUTION AND THE DEFECTION OF RUSSIA. With the revolutions that engulfed Russia in the year 1917, as primarily Russian events, we need not be concerned; that aspect alone of their course will be retained which influenced the conflict. It may

[36] Socialists from the belligerent countries met in Switzerland, at Kienthal and at Zimmerwald, in 1915. They were to meet in Stockholm, after the first revolution in Russia, but were prevented from attending by their governments, save in the case of the Russians and the Germans.

suffice to say that the domestic conditions of Russia, her economic backwardness in combination with the institutions of the Russian state and with the quality of Russian management, all taken in the context of the Russian historic experience, resulted in the collapse of the existing system of Russia. What may broadly be called the German orientation in Russia, meaning the view that a German connection rather than one with the Western states was the more desirable, always continued to have spokesmen in Russia, some of them in high places, even after the war had broken out, just as the pro-Russian current ever had representatives in Germany. As a consequence, Western doubts of Russian loyalty persisted, which Russia had turned into assets in the form of the Straits agreement of 1915 and the one with France of February, 1917. From the German point of view, peace with Russia would be a step toward total victory, just as in the Allied view peace with Austria could mainly serve as a device that would assist in the defeat of Germany.

The first revolution in Russia took place in March, 1917. The tsar abdicated and the path was embarked upon that seemed at first as though it might lead Russia to the point reached by the West in its political development, making her a bourgeois parliamentary democracy. To her allies the change was at first not unwelcome: it would strengthen their moral case and might even provide a solution for the Polish problem. A revolution is always a delicate operation, the terminal effect of which is ever uncertain; to launch one in the midst of war is doubly so. In the Russian case an ambiguity appeared almost from the beginning: the Russian people in their mass were not deeply versed in political ideology, Marxist or other; but also in their mass they were intensely weary of a war fought with inadequate means that meant appalling suffering and slaughter for reasons hardly clear to them. The later slogan, "land, peace, and bread," they could understand, and the declared intention of the Provisional Government to continue the war provided ammunition to those of more radical inclination. This, combined with a measure of ineptitude and lack of resolution on the part of this same Provisional Government, gave the Bolsheviks their chance. At the beginning of November—October in the Julian calendar of Russia—they succeeded in seizing power[37] in Petrograd.

[37] Lenin, who was destined to play such a large role of leadership in these events, was in Switzerland when revolution first took place in Russia. The problem of his reaching Russia was solved by the willingness of the Germans to convey him thither. This was the result of an interesting gamble: on the German side the belief that revolution in Russia would result in the military defeat of that

In the early days of the first revolution, Miliukov, the foreign minister, had taken the position that Russia would continue in the war while insisting on the validity of the agreements, such as those dealing with the Straits, to which the tsarist government had been a party.[38] The Bolsheviks had other views. Consistently with their Marxist belief, they saw the war as merely an example of the numerous conflicts to which the imperialism of capitalist states is fated. The war among nations was senseless; whatever quarrel there was was not among peoples but between the exploited and their capitalist exploiters. With complete catholicity of taste they appealed to all peoples alike, ex-friend and foe, to change the war of states into a war of classes, emulating the Russian example. The appeal of their call to the weary masses of Europe, many of them long familiar with the Marxist outlook, was no little cause of concern to the governments of all the belligerents. At the time, however, no other country followed suit and all the other belligerents contrived to ride out the storm of 1917.

The Russian revolution created none the less an awkward situation, for the Allies especially, for in the process of proving their contention about the imperialistic nature of the war, the Bolsheviks made public the various secret agreements that have been mentioned and to which the tsarist government had been a party. This challenge had the effect of putting considerable pressure on Russia's ex-allies further to clarify the purpose of the struggle, their war aims, in an effort to place these in a more favorable light. The leadership of this endeavor, logically enough, fell into other hands, the American, and with it we shall deal presently. But at this point it may be noted that great popularity attached to the concept that competition for power and concrete interests was evil, that moral ends alone could justify the struggle. Power indeed may be corrupt and evil, as has often been said, but the mixture of power and principle is an unholy brew, a combination the effects of which are most awkward to manage. Not the least interesting aspect of the war at the turn from the year 1917 to 1918 is the fact that the revolution in Russia and the influence of the United States worked at the time to much the same effect.

It is convenient to complete at this point the Russian chapter of

---

country; on Lenin's side the conviction that this result was unimportant since revolution, once successful in Russia, would in turn sweep Germany.

[38] An attempt was indeed made to launch a Russian offensive during the summer. The failure of that offensive served to precipitate the October revolution.

the war. Whatever others might do, the new Bolshevik government of Russia would withdraw from the war. In December it concluded an armistice which was followed by negotiations that lasted through the winter. The Central Powers found some difficulty in dealing with the representatives of the new Russian regime, who for a time resorted to tactics of tergiversation. Confronted at last with a renewed German threat, and still in the belief that universal revolution would soon come, that meantime it was most important to save the revolution in its Russian home, on March 3, 1918, the Bolsheviks accepted the dictated peace of Brest-Litovsk. Russia renounced all Poland and the Baltic region, while the Ukraine, with whom the Central Powers made a separate peace, emerged as a distinct entity.[39] The first phase of Pilsudski's program had been accomplished.

The unexpected fortunes of war had thus in a way realized the initial German plan for dealing with the war on two fronts by getting rid of one of these; but it was the eastern front that had collapsed and it had taken more than three years to achieve this result.[40] However that might be, here was undoubtedly a very major German victory that might compensate for her losses. Life was becoming hard in Germany, suffering from numerous shortages, not least of food, but hope of complete victory was still entertained by her military leaders. This hope indeed, had it not been for the effect of the other great event of the year 1917, almost simultaneous with the first revolution in Russia, was not perhaps altogether devoid of foundation.

THE INTERVENTION OF THE UNITED STATES. We must now go back a little in time. The outbreak of war in 1914 had come as a shock to America, but there seemed to be no cause for the United States to take a share in the affairs of Europe, save perhaps, as in the case of the Russo-Japanese War, to proffer, at the appropriate time, mediatory service. The exploratory European journeys of Wilson's *alter ego*, Colonel House, have been mentioned and the view that he took of the possible outcome of the conflict.[41] But

[39] In the circumstances, Rumania also decided to make peace by the Treaty of Bucharest of May 7, 1918.

[40] In passing, the effect cannot be overemphasized of the fact that, from the point of view of the Allies, Russia defected from the common struggle and did so in a particularly obnoxious manner, not pleading so much the inevitable necessity of her weakness as emphasizing the ideological aspect and denouncing her former allies. This situation was a heavy mortgage on the future relations of Russia.

[41] See above, p. 342.

one specific American point of contact with the war, however, soon appeared as a consequence of developments on the seas.

The Allies had clear command of the seas with their superior fleets[42] which they used to blockade the Central Powers. Out of these blockade operations there developed some controversy and friction between the Allies and the neutrals over the general issue of the rights of the latter in trading with the Central Powers, the Allies acting arbitrarily in the matter of deciding what articles of trade were contraband. The German reply to this situation was the resort to the use of the submarine, which inevitably put Germany at a disadvantage *vis-à-vis* the neutrals: the propriety of seizing a cargo may be argued in court or through diplomacy and be adjudicated; a sunken ship, and especially the lives of her crew and passengers, are irretrievable. But, because of its very nature, the fragile submarine must attack surreptitiously or not at all. In this case also, as in the case of Belgium, Germany took the position that necessity is the higher law: the victor can at least dictate the peace and disregard the verdict of history, which it may even possibly write.

As early as February, 1915, Germany declared British waters a zone in which ships, enemy and even neutral, were liable to sinking. This was intended as a means to bring about some relaxation of the Allied blockade, and Germany, when confronted with neutral, mainly American, objections relaxed her threat. But as victory continued to elude her arms and her domestic economic situation worsened she once more decided to make full use of the submarine arm. The German decision to resort to unrestricted submarine warfare dates from January, 1917; it was made public on the 31st.[43] It produced a frontal collision with the United States. The German attempt to induce sabotage in America and to involve Mexico[44] may be seen as another manifestation of the

[42] The Germans used some surface raiders, especially in the early stages of the war, but the only naval engagement of any consequence was the battle of Jutland, in May, 1916, an encounter that was essentially inconclusive.

[43] Along with the German note of January 31 went a secret letter to House that indicated the bases on which Germany would entertain negotiations for peace. These German conditions seemed preposterous to Wilson and served further to antagonize him. (Cf. Taylor, *op. cit.*, p. 557.)

[44] After the German decision to resort to unrestricted submarine warfare, in the expectation that the United States would be brought into the war as a consequence, the German foreign minister, Zimmermann, sent a note to the German minister in Mexico instructing him to seek to involve both that country and Japan in war against the United States, holding up to Mexico the prospect of recovering some of the nineteenth-century territorial losses.

clumsiness that had characterized German diplomacy before the war; it played into the hands of the Allies, naturally anxious to enlist the United States on their side. Having previously broken off relations, and failing to obtain satisfaction, on April 6, 1917, the United States declared war upon Germany.

America was unprepared for war—her purely military contribution was in fact never very large compared with that of the other belligerents—but the effect of her participation was enormous. All sorts of problems, financing and supplies, were automatically solved for the Allies; should the war be prolonged considerably, American manpower could participate in large numbers. In any case, the prospect of the unlimited reservoir of American resources gave the wavering morale of the Allies a boost that made it possible to absorb the shock of the Russian defection for which the American asset was more than compensation.

The issue of the intervention of the United States in the First World War has been the object of much debate and recrimination in America. That aspect of the matter is no concern of this story. It may suffice to say that, in the limited and immediate sense, America went to war over the issue of submarine warfare and the rights of neutrals at sea; from a larger point of view, the consideration must be borne in mind of the long-term significance for the United States, as for other initial neutrals (Italy, for example) of a German victory in Europe. If the traditional and familiar aspect of British policy that caused Britain to oppose the dominance of the continent of Europe by any one Power cannot be said at this time to have been common property of the American popular consciousness, in retrospect it does not seem unfair to say that, in the deficiency of British power, the American declaration of war was the specific act whereby America became heir to one large and fundamental aspect of British policy. More immediately and concretely, the American intervention may fairly be regarded as an act in defense of American interest.[45]

But if the United States joined in the common enterprise designed to prevent a German domination of Europe, its position remained distinct in some respects. The power of the United States was bound to give the newcomer a very large, if not a dominant,

[45] This is equally true whether interest be taken in the broad sense of long-range political considerations just mentioned, or in the narrower sense of interests immediately deriving from the war, be these the safety or private loans, or the prosperity of industry, labor, and agriculture.

voice in Allied councils. Moreover, the United States had no such specific and concrete interests as found expression in the desire for bits of territory, be they European or colonial; the United States was no party to any of the wartime agreements that have been enumerated before: as some would put it, American hands, by contrast with European, were clean.[46] This situation contained the seeds of troubles that would materialize at the peace, but for the moment it put the United States in an excellent position to emphasize the ideological aspect of the war: America was seeking no concrete advantage for herself, but fought instead for the establishment of universal justice and peace.

The role of spokesman for the New Order was highly congenial to President Wilson. His endeavor to obtain from the belligerents some concrete statement of their war aims at the turn from 1916 to 1917 has been mentioned as well as the response to that attempt.[47] It has also been mentioned that one effect of direct American participation in the war was, if not to change completely, at least greatly to emphasize, the ideological aspect of the struggle. Apart from the fact that no one will publicly take the role of advocating sin, the general appeal to such abstractions as justice and peace elicited a very powerful and authentic response at the popular level; the war on the side of the Allies increasingly took on the aspect of a crusade, of which the slogans "to make the world safe for democracy" and "the war to end wars" were adequate expressions. If the latter expressed a universal longing, the former summed up a historic trend as well.

Such a state of affairs is apt to complicate the task of diplomacy, the essence of which is compromise based upon an adjustment of the balance of forces. Ideological conflicts have ever proved more recalcitrant to composition than mere contests of power, for by its nature principle is refractory to compromise. America, like the other Allies, made preparations for the future peace; in her case, a long story may be summed up by saying that the outcome was the statement of the American program for peace that was enunciated by President Wilson in his speech to Congress on January 8,

[46] There was clear awareness of the special position of the United States which found expression in the American refusal to become an "allied" Power; the United States ever remained an "associated" Power. Wilson's attitude toward the Allies' wartime commitments was a rather cavalier one that amounted essentially to brushing them aside.

[47] See above, pp. 343–344.

1918, and that came to be known as the Fourteen Points.[48] It is of interest to note that three days earlier Lloyd George had made in the House of Commons a comparable and not very dissimilar statement of the British war aims, largely in response to the pressure generated by the world-wide appeals issuing from Russia. The fact that Lloyd George's program was largely obscured and superseded by Wilson's is adequate expression of the universally recognized American role of leadership. In view of their historic importance the Fourteen Points are worth recalling. They provided as follows:

    I. Open covenants of peace openly arrived at, after which there shall be no private international understandings of any kind, but diplomacy shall proceed always frankly and in the public view.

    II. Absolute freedom of navigation upon the seas outside territorial waters alike in peace and in war, except as the seas may be closed in whole or in part by international action or the enforcement of international covenants.

    III. The removal, so far as possible, of all economic barriers and the establishment of an equality of trade conditions among all the nations consenting to the peace and associating themselves for its maintenance.

    IV. Adequate guarantees given and taken that national armaments will be reduced to the lowest point consistent with domestic safety.

    V. A free, open-minded and absolutely impartial adjustment of all colonial claims based upon a strict observance of the principle that in determining all such questions of sovereignty the interests of the populations concerned must have equal weight with the equitable claims of the government whose title is to be determined.

    VI. The evacuation of all Russian territory, and such a settlement of all questions affecting Russia as will secure the best and freest coöperation of the other nations of the world in obtaining for her an unhampered and unembarrassed opportunity for the independent determination of her own political development and national policy, and assure her of a sincere welcome into the society of free nations under institutions of her own choosing; and, more than a welcome, assistance also of every kind that she may need and may herself desire. The treatment accorded Russia by her sister nations in the months to come will be the acid test

---

[48] The bulk of this program was the result of much careful work and study by a group of technicians, lawyers, historians, economists, etc., who dubbed themselves *The Inquiry*, gathered together by House. The product of their activity, passed on to House and by him to Wilson, became the origin of much of the Fourteen Points

of their good-will, of their comprehension of her needs as distinguished from their own interests, and of their intelligent and unselfish sympathy.

VII. Belgium, the whole world will agree must be evacuated and restored, without any attempt to limit the sovereignty which she enjoys in common with all other free nations. No other single act will serve as this will serve to restore confidence among the nations in the laws which they have themselves set and determined for the government of their relations with one another. Without this healing act the whole structure and validity of international law is forever impaired.

VIII. All French territory should be freed and the invaded portions restored, and the wrong done to France by Prussia in 1871 in the matter of Alsace-Lorraine, which has unsettled the peace of the world for nearly fifty years, should be righted, in order that peace may once more be made secure in the interest of all.

IX. A readjustment of the frontiers of Italy should be effected along clearly recognizable lines of nationality.

X. The peoples of Austria-Hungary, whose place among the nations we wish to see safeguarded and assured, should be accorded the freest opportunity of autonomous development.

XI. Rumania, Serbia and Montenegro should be evacuated; occupied territories restored; Serbia accorded free and secure access to the sea; and the relations of the several Balkan states to one another determined by friendly counsel along historically established lines of allegiance and nationality; and international guarantees of the political and economic independence and territorial integrity of the several Balkan states should be entered upon.

XII. The Turkish portions of the present Ottoman Empire should be assured a secure sovereignty, but the other nationalities which are now under Turkish rule should be assured an undoubted security of life and an absolutely unmolested opportunity of autonomous development, and the Dardanelles should be permanently opened as a free passage to the ships and commerce of all nations under international guarantees.

XIII. An independent Polish State should be erected which should include the territories inhabited by indisputably Polish populations, which should be assured a free and secure access to the sea, and whose political and economic independence and territorial integrity should be guaranteed by international covenant.

XIV. A general association of nations must be formed under specific covenants for the purpose of affording mutual guarantees of political independence and territorial integrity to great and small States alike.

The essence of this program may be put under three heads: the principle of nationality, or self-determination, was given sanction; some general provisions were designed to remedy deficiencies of past procedure (secret diplomacy was condemned and the freedom of the seas was asserted), and finally, Wilson's own and most important contribution, the rule of law, was to be substituted for that of anarchy in the relations among nations.

Here was indeed an ambitious program, one whose intent the epithet "noble" fits rather better than a later American experiment. However, this was merely a general program for the peace, at most a moral commitment, undertaken unilaterally, not a treaty among states whom it could not therefore commit, save to the extent that moral force again would induce its acceptance. This also will appear, that much at least of the Wilsonian statement could be accepted by the Allies while for the enemy it could easily spell disaster. There was little response to the Fourteen Points in the Central Powers.[49]

There matters rested for a time while the war proceeded to its ultimate outcome. The western front was the theater of decision where the Western coalition concentrated its forces. The sands were running out for Germany whose domestic difficulties were little alleviated in the failure to commandeer successfully the resources of defeated Russia largely reduced to chaos. If victory was to attend German arms it must be secured promptly since the German calculation that American forces could be prevented from reaching European soil proved to be another miscalculation. The Germans managed to launch some powerful offensives during the spring and again in the early summer of 1918; when these were checked the tide turned very suddenly. In August, Ludendorff himself came to the conclusion that hope of victory must be abandoned, and this was shortly followed by the fear of complete military collapse. If the fear was unfounded, or at least premature, the German leaders of 1918, in contrast with their successors of a later time, were at least rational men: if the struggle was futile, then it must be abandoned. The German government never questioned the verdict of the military from whom it meekly accepted the task of extricating the country from the war.[50]

[49] This situation made the Fourteen Points a highly useful tool of propaganda that could be, and was, used to undermine the enemy morale. But to write off the Fourteen Points as nothing but an instrument of propaganda, instead of an authentic declaration of intent, is a gross falsification of history. To the initial and most important statement of January 8 were added subsequent elaborations, in particular the Four Principles of July 4 and the Five Declarations of September 27.

[50] These events in September, 1918, in Germany are of extremely high importance. They betoken the overriding position of the military which endeavored

Having accepted the thankless task, the new Chancellor, Prince Max of Baden, through the intermediary of Switzerland, sent on October 4 a note to President Wilson declaring Germany ready to undertake negotiations for the restoration of peace on the basis of the American program and asking for the conclusion of an immediate armistice. The German note reached Washington on October 6.

There was indeed cause for concern and dispatch. It was at the end of September that a Balkan offensive had caused Bulgaria to withdraw from the war, opening the way to an invasion of Austria-Hungary from the south. The Bulgarian surrender made a considerable impression in Germany, unmistakable signal of the beginning of the end. Just a month later, on October 30, the armistice of Mudros likewise removed the Ottoman Empire from the war. This armistice was concluded by the British, essentially without consultation of their allies, a fact that presaged the renewal of rivalries among them now that victory was in sight.

This last aspect of things, differences among the victors, was likewise brought out by the German appeal to the United States. The end had come so suddenly that the Allies were unprepared with a concerted plan for action. The American program, the Fourteen Points and subsequent declarations, had received lip service from all—even the Germans had now discovered it—but this was very different from a formal commitment to this program as a basis for peace. On October 23, the American government informed its associates of its exchanges with the German and asked them whether they were prepared to make peace on the basis of the German request.

This gave rise to a vital discussion between the Allied leaders and the American representative, Colonel House, that lasted for several days at the end of October and the beginning of November. The debate was a close one, and at times became heated. The outcome of it was the acceptance of the American program by the Allies with but two minor reservations: the British did not feel that they could commit themselves in advance to any and all interpretations of the Freedom of the Seas (Point II) and wished to reserve their freedom in the matter; the French insisted on clarify-

---

to dissociate itself from the coming defeat. At this point the seeds were already being planted of the legends that Germany was never really defeated and that her surrender was due to a "stab in the back" at home, alternatively to Allied duplicity.

ing Point VIII, which spoke of "restoration" of damage, by speci-
fying that "restoration" was not subject to any prior limitations.
It may therefore be said that the Allies, of their free will—American insistence backed by the fact of American power assisting—
undertook a formal commitment to make peace on the basis of the
American program.[51]

To this a qualification must be made. The month of October
saw the internal collapse of Austria-Hungary. A last-minute manifesto of Emperor Charles, proclaiming a federal reorganization of
Austria, found no response among the subject nationalities. The
Fourteen Points, somewhat ambiguously, had spoken of "autonomy" for them; but the American reply, of October 21, to an inquiry from Vienna, in view of the changed circumstances,[52]
stated that the subject peoples must decide their own fate. In
Vienna, in Budapest, in Prague, and in Zagreb separate provisional
governments came into existence. The Austrian situation and an
Austrian request for an armistice were considered simultaneously
with the issue of acceptance of the Fourteen Points in the German
case. The Italians sought to safeguard their expected gains under
the Treaty of London of 1915 by entering a reservation to Point
IX in which "clearly recognizable lines of nationality" were mentioned. Here was an inconsistency obvious to all, one that could
not be blinked. Yet it was. For the moment, the compromise proposed by House was accepted: the issue was that of a reply to the
German request, which bore no relation to the Austro-Italian
question; that particular problem need not therefore be decided
at the moment.[53]

It was now possible for the American President to answer the
German request in the affirmative. But the armistice itself was a
military matter to be decided by the military leaders, with whom
the German command must therefore deal directly. At this point

[51] The argument of misunderstanding owing to insufficient clarity of definition of the Fourteen Points is invalidated by the record of the discussions that
took place at this time and by the detailed explanatory gloss on them prepared
for the occasion by Irving Cobb and Walter Lippmann.

[52] The American government had recognized the Czechoslovaks as belligerents
and declared itself in favor of Yugoslav independence. This is the basis for the
charge sometimes made that the Allies dismembered Austria-Hungary. The
chief disruptive force came from within, the simple fact of disparate nationalities, and
the contrast is revealing between the fate of Austria-Hungary and that of Germany which, apart from her eccentric losses, continued as a united solid block.

[53] The issue was thus postponed, but when it came up in the final peacemaking it was complicated by a controversy as to whether or not the Italians
were committed to the Fourteen Points. This episode is a perfect illustration
of the consequences of disposing of troublesome issues by dodging them.

the seeds of another ambiguity were planted. The fundamental reason for the German request was the conclusion reached by the German military leaders that Germany was not capable of continuing the struggle. The military terms of armistice presented by the Allied command therefore amounted to a demand for complete surrender, which Germany, having no real choice, accepted. The circumstances of the armistice were later to be used in Germany to sustain the legend that she was tricked into laying down her arms by Allied promises that were later not honored. To this there is one simple answer: why did Germany not discover the American program for peace until the power of her arms was broken?[54] The German military were alert to the possibility of extricating their own responsibility in the national disaster; their success in this endeavor was to have important future consequences and to cost heavily to all.[55] But this again clearly does not affect the validity of the Allies' commitment to the American program for the peace.

THE RUSSIAN SITUATION. While the war between the Allies and the Central Powers was being brought to an end during 1918, much confusion attended the Russian situation, which may be seen as a three-cornered contest involving the Bolshevik government, the Germans, and the Allies. The collapse of Russia had been formally registered in the peace of Brest-Litovsk of March, 1918. This arrangement left the Central Powers essentially in control of Poland, the Ukraine, and the Baltic lands. While the Ukraine was occupied militarily, in April a "national council" was set up in Riga, as a preliminary to the organization of the *Baltikum* as a region of German dependence and colonization; simultaneously, a German corps under General von der Goltz assisted the Finns in establishing themselves in independence within the frontiers they desired. The German defeat in the West thus found the Germans deeply established in former Russian territory.

In the eyes of the new Bolshevik government of Russia the issue was that of survival, the extent of territorial control being a

[54] It is the memory of this situation and the desire to avoid a possible repetition of it that were in considerable measure responsible for the demand for unconditional surrender at the end of the Second World War.

[55] This attempt to extricate the "honor" of the German army may seem a very crude one. Indeed it was. But it must be viewed in the context of the German military record during the war which was essentially one of victory until the very end, and of the fact that when the fighting ceased German armies were still deep in occupation of much enemy territory.

secondary matter for the moment. For Russia was involved in civil war, a number of anti-Bolshevik, or "white" armies operating in various sectors of the land. The Allies and the Central Powers held equally inimical views of the new Russian regime, but while the war between them was still in process the issue for both was how best to utilize what Russian power existed, or alternatively to neutralize its use against themselves. Conversely, on the Bolshevik side, the question was whether or not coöperation with either side in the still continuing war could be of use in insuring survival. Broadly speaking, it may be said that the fact and the circumstances of the Russian defection from the Allied side tended to orient the confused Russian situation along the line of coöperation between the Germans and the Bolsheviks on one side, between the Allies and the counterrevolutionary forces on the other, a situation that should be seen in the context of the record of past and future Russo-German relations.

On August 27 a secret agreement laid the bases of military coöperation between the Germans and the Bolshevik government. Meanwhile, as early as March, 1918, at the very time of the signature of Brest-Litovsk, a small Allied force had established itself in Murmansk. This expedition was too small to undertake important action, but the idea had already been considered of utilizing available Japanese forces for action in the Far East. The Allies, the United States especially, entertained considerable reservations on the score of the desirability of such action and discussions among them went on for a time, as well as between them and the Bolsheviks, in an attempt to decide whether such intervention would take place under the guise of friendly assistance or enmity. By July, the American consent was obtained to a plan that would coordinate Japanese action in Siberia with the activity of the Czech Legion in Russia.[56] In August, the Japanese began operations in Siberia where they constituted the bulk of the Allied forces, a token American contingent insuring the representation of non-Japanese interests. With the defeat of Germany in the West, two problems emerged: first procuring the relinquishment by her of the territories she had occupied in the East, then evolving a solution for the disposition of these same territories. This last was but

[56] This was a force recruited from elements who had deserted from the Austrian army to join the Allies. As a consequence of the revolution in Russia the Czech Legion aligned itself with the counterrevolutionary forces and operated mainly in Siberia.

one aspect of the larger issue of the fate of the revolution in Russia and of Russia's relations with the outside world. The Allies, especially the French, continued their support of the white armies and for some time Eastern Europe continued in a state of chaos and fluidity. The problem of peace with the defeated was dealt with in the meantime.

III. The Diplomacy of the Peace

PREPARATIONS FOR THE PEACE: THE PRECONFERENCE PERIOD

The task of restoring the peace in 1918 was comparable in its magnitude with that which had confronted the congress held in Vienna almost exactly one hundred years before; it was more complex than on the earlier occasion owing to the development of Europe during those hundred years and to the growth of the immeasurably more intricate relations of the economies of the belligerents. The circumstances of the war, the final and decisive importance of the western front, the French role, plus the convenience of location and of available facilities, made Paris the selection for the meeting of the coming peace congress.[57]

Then, as later, the popular fallacy held sway that the termination of active hostilities is synonymous with the restoration of peace, hence the great pressure to "bring the boys back home," especially among those peoples, the British and the Americans, to whom conscription was an alien practice, but in varying degree among all. The expectation was universal that even final peace would be promptly restored, though the leaders had a better understanding of the magnitude of the task and of the time that it would take to do it. Also, it was thought for a time that a formal peace could be established, leaving to later and calmer deliberations the settlement of the myriad specific problems that demanded solution.

In any case the fact that the victorious coalition was made up of democratic nations meant that heed must be taken of the state and the inclinations of popular opinion. The prevalent atmosphere was of high—and dangerous—expectation, for peoples had been fed with lavish promises that the colloquialism "pie in the sky" best expresses, and of which the American program was the clearest

---

[57] There was some criticism of this choice by those who felt that the French atmosphere was ill suited to dispassionate deliberations.

summation. The slogan of the war, "the war to end wars," commanded universal allegiance, followed as a close second by the belief in the merits of the democratic form of government. This put the United States in a unique position and cast President Wilson in the role of Messiah, bringer of the New Order to mankind, to a degree that caused concern to the rest of the Allied leaders.

Wilson himself embodied to an unfortunate degree the not uncommon American belief in moral superiority combined with suspicion of diplomacy in general, especially of that of Europe. Wilson's own background was academic and, despite his activity in American politics, his character was not devoid of doctrinaire content.[58] That Wilson was earnestly devoted to the realization of a high ideal may be granted; but no one other than himself would he entrust with the task of fighting for his ideal. As a consequence, he decided that he himself would head the American delegation to Paris, the wisdom of which decision was then and has since been much questioned, mainly on the ground that he was thereby bound to lose the asset of the Olympian arbitral position of prestige that was his. The phrase that he used when addressing the assembled American delegation during the passage on the *George Washington* aptly characterizes the man, "Tell me what's right, and I'll fight for it." The French Premier, Clemenceau, used more acid though perhaps no less appropriate language to describe the Wilsonian outlook; his phrase was "noble candor."

Wilson arrived in Europe in mid-December, but preparations for the peace congress were not yet quite complete. For one thing, its opening must wait upon the results of an election in Britain. His early contacts in Europe tended to confirm his belief that he was the more authentic representative of the hopes of the masses than their own elected representatives—a belief not devoid of a measure of truth, yet dangerous to a degree—while to his European peers the picture of cold aloofness was confirmed. To be

[58] In November, 1918, at the very time of the conclusion of the armistices, a mid-term election took place in the United States. In preparation for the coming peace negotiations Wilson reasoned that he needed strong endorsement at home, which he could best obtain through a sympathetic Congress. His appeal for the election of a Democratic majority laid him open to the charge of exploiting the foreign situation for party advantage; it backfired and the new Congress had a Republican majority, a situation that provided an interesting illustration of the operation and possible effects of the American constitutional system. Wilson made the further mistake, even after this outcome, of virtually ignoring, and thereby antagonizing, the Republican majority in his selection of the American peace delegation.

sure, the purpose of the peace ostensibly was justice, and justice is supposed to be blindfolded. But human beings have feelings; regrettable as it may have been, the passions that the war itself had aroused were realities no less solid than those of, say, economics. To ignore them was but to court disaster. Pascal's phrase comes to mind, *qui veut faire l'ange fait la bête.*[59] Finally, the consideration is apt, though not devoid of irony, that the Wilsonian personality and ideal would have been of little importance, hence would have warranted little attention, had it not been for the cruder fact of American power that Wilson represented.

Two more facts deserve mention. One was the failure, largely the result of American refusal, to accept any preliminary organized plan of procedure for the coming congress. The other was the decision to exclude the enemy from the deliberations of the peace congress. It was realized quite correctly that the reconciliation of the multitude of divergent interests among the victors would present sufficient difficulty without the intrusion of an enemy whose sole remaining weapon, in default of effective power, was the sowing and cultivating of dissension among others. The role of Talleyrand at Vienna had not been forgotten.

THE PEACE CONFERENCE OF PARIS

ORGANIZATION AND PROCEDURE OF THE CONFERENCE. Of preparations for the coming peace there had been considerable, especially on the part of the Americans, the British, and the French, but in default of an agreed plan of procedure, much was left to the accident of circumstances and improvisation. A good part of the world, some twenty-seven nations, was represented in Paris, but clearly, if for physical reasons of practicability alone, deliberations could not be conducted in parliamentary fashion in this areopagus of nations. Responsibility and power go together. Those who had done the work of achieving the victory and were possessed of real power would therefore take the leadership and assert the prerogative of ultimate decisions. Plenary sessions of the congress were few and far between and of no real significance. The directing agency of the war, the Supreme War Council, transformed itself into the directing agency of the peace, the Supreme Council. Japan alone was accepted as an equal, and thus the five victorious Great Powers, the United States, Great Britain, France,

[59] In free translation this may be rendered as: to pretend to ignore human nature can only lead to making a fool of oneself.

Italy, and Japan, represented by the heads of delegations accompanied by their foreign ministers became the Council of Ten.

But procedure was soon simplified even further. The Ten, attended by a bevy of experts and advisers, still made up a body in which discussion could be prolonged and not always wholly free. It soon became the practice for the heads of the four Western delegations—Japan was essentially unconcerned with any but Far Eastern questions—to hold informal meetings. The Council of Four became the central directing agency of the conference, the real seat of power wherein final decisions were made.[60]

But it was also evident that the Four lacked the necessary competence to make decisions on a host of matters that demanded technical knowledge. They therefore resorted to the device of appointing *ad hoc* commissions to report on such matters, reserving to themselves the power of ultimate decision in regard to the work of the various commissions, of which fifty-two were created. The initial phase of the conference lasted about one month; in mid-February, Wilson returned to the United States to attend to domestic matters. He was back in Paris a month later, by which time much of the work of the commissions or committees had been done. The Four were now in a position to make final decisions, on the basis of these reports of the committees, as well as on certain primarily political issues that they had reserved to themselves.

This they proceeded to do. Despite the difficulties they encountered—these will be discussed presently—they managed to have reached agreement in May on the text of the German treaty, by far the most important piece of business in the eyes of most of the Powers involved. The consequence of this in turn was that the initial conception of a quick preliminary peace was abandoned. There were grumblings at the delay in formally restoring peace, yet the final treaty with Germany was elaborated in an unexpectedly short time—too short some would say. At this point a German delegation was invited. Having come, it proceeded to register its

[60] The Four were accompanied by the two official interpreters, Sir Maurice Hankey and Paul Mantoux, French and English being the official languages of the conference. It so happened, however, that while Wilson and Lloyd George could not use French, Clemenceau had ready command of English; the consequence of this was that much of the discussion took place in the latter tongue, with the further effect of isolating Orlando, who had French but no English. Even apart from this accidental situation, the relative lack of Italian interest in German matters—those of greatest concern to the others—tended to make the Four into a Three, which the Supreme Council actually became when the Italians absented themselves in April. The Council of Four—or Three—held 145 meetings prior to the conclusion of the German treaty.

observations, in the form of numerous criticisms, on the text submitted to it.[61] These were essentially not entertained. Germany had no choice but to bow to the inevitable.[62] On June 28, 1919, the Treaty of Versailles was signed.

The occasion was a historic one, and appropriate ceremonial was devised to underscore its significance. To the day, this was the anniversary of Sarajevo. More important still, it was in the very same spot, the great Hall of Mirrors of the palace of the French kings at Versailles, where the birth of the German Empire had been proclaimed in 1871, that its death warrant was signed. There are few nicer instances of the continuity of history and of the weight of the past on the present; how fortunate and desirable such a condition is, is another matter again.

With the signature of the Treaty of Versailles, the Americans, the British, and the French felt that their main task had been finished; Germany had beyond a doubt been the chief enemy. Wilson returned at once to the United States. But much remained to be done, though many decisions had already been reached regarding Central Europe, the Balkans, and the Ottoman Empire. The peace conference continued its labors, though the Four were disbanded, their place falling to the heads of delegations that succeeded them. Treaties were eventually drafted for the remainder of the enemy states. On September 10, at St. Germain-en-Laye, a treaty of peace was signed with the new Austria. In November, the Treaty of Neuilly registered the terms of peace with Bulgaria.

There was some delay in the Hungarian case as the result of the episode of a Bolshevik revolution in that country in 1919. But once the regime of Bela Kun had been liquidated, negotiations were resumed, and the Treaty of Trianon, in June, 1920, made peace with Hungary as well. Last of all came the Ottoman Empire whose demise was registered in the Treaty of Sèvres of August 10, 1920.

The foregoing description of the process of reëstablishing the peace, as mentioned earlier, shows much that was improvised and unplanned. The process of peacemaking may be seen as the result of a response and adaptation to circumstances many of which were

[61] It is of interest that there were no verbal negotiations, but that instead the German observations had to be submitted in writing.

[62] This situation served to foster in Germany the view that the peace was a *diktat*. That the peace was essentially an imposed one is clear; whether or how far its provisions were sound or wise is, however, an entirely different issue, but the implications of unfairness in the word *diktat* had important consequences.

novel. We may now proceed to some consideration of the specific issues that were met and dealt with in the course of restoring the peace, and then examine its terms and the shape of the Europe that emerged from the First World War.

THE ISSUES OF THE PEACE.   The problems that faced the peace-makers were many, but priority among them properly goes to the most fundamental question of drawing the frontiers of Europe. This was bound to be so, so long as the world remains divided into the distinct political units that are states; frontiers have ever proved very difficult of alteration, and history can record few ex-amples, if any, of a change of frontiers save with the accompani-ment of war. It has proved much easier to make peaceful change in other arrangements, economic ones for example.

Ostensibly, a simple general principle, that of self-determina-tion, was to prevail in the drawing of frontiers. But this is not the easy thing that it appears on the surface to be. If lines of nationality tend to be fairly clear in the West, the case is otherwise in Central and Eastern Europe, where a variety of peoples had been under Austro-Hungarian and Russian rule for a long period of time; there are in that section of Europe substantial areas where popula-tions are mixed instead of being ethnically homogeneous. To apply crudely the criterion that all members of one nationality must be within one state could only result in the denial of the same test for others. Historic considerations would intrude at this point, but how far is it reasonable to attempt to undo history?[63] It may be pointed out in passing that no one suggested in 1919 the simple and crude device of making peoples fit frontiers; the much criticized peacemakers of that time never questioned the more humane ap-proach of making the frontiers fit the peoples, rather than the re-verse. In cases of doubt and in the face of contradictory claims, the wishes of the people themselves might be ascertained by hold-ing plebiscites. But a plebiscite is a deceivingly simple device: the area in which it is held may determine its outcome, no less than the decision of the qualifications for participating in it, to say nothing of conditions, economic and political, that may be momentarily prevailing. Plebiscites were resorted to in but a few instances.

[63] That there is no simple answer to the question is shown by the elimination after the First World War of the Greek colonies in Asia Minor established some 2500 years ago and by the setting up of the state of Israel after the Second World War. Europe is of more recent civilization than the Near East but no less affected by the shifting of peoples.

Moreover, a rigid adherence to the ethnic criterion alone, even assuming that it could be fairly tested, might in some cases lead to absurdities on other grounds. The economic viability of states, for instance, especially the new ones, must be assured; to deprive a country of her only outlet to the sea might be to put her at the mercy of an unfriendly neighbor. Nor could strategic considerations be altogether disregarded.

To all these arguments an easy answer could be given: the New Order that would insure everlasting peace and justice for all obviated the necessity of security measures as well as of economic independence. But such an answer was itself an absurdity tantamount to asking men to believe that the millennium had suddenly arrived. Peace and justice all wanted, but on how to insure peace and on what justice was, agreement was very limited.

The peacemakers must therefore face the task of effecting possible compromises. Much of the basis for the solutions that were eventually adopted was provided by the work of the *ad hoc* committees, but some issues were reserved for adjudication by the Supreme Council where they gave rise to debate, even crises, that must briefly be mentioned. The discussions themselves and the results to which they led considerably affected the future.

Of the details of European quarrels and their historic background Wilson had little knowledge. But one thing was close to his heart that he considered his own, and America's, peculiar contribution. The last of the Fourteen Points spoke of the organization of an association of nations to institute a rule of law among states, more narrowly to prevent the recurrence of war. In deference to Wilson's desire—and to the power that he represented—what came to be the League of Nations was the first important matter to be discussed at the summit level of the conference. The committee that was created, and of which appropriately Wilson himself held the chairmanship, proceeded to find some means of implementing this will-o'-the-wisp of mankind. At this point it will suffice to say that it immediately ran into what, in simplest terms, may be called the clash between the principles of sovereignty and of law. In different and more concrete form, what powers would the League have and whence would come the power to enforce its decisions?

Here also the outcome could not be other than compromise, but this meant that the League, even apart from being an untried instrument, was also one whose potentialities and precise powers were unknown. Such as it was, it meant a great innovation and a significant experiment. Whether the new creation would, as some hoped and claimed, change the future face of the world, whether it would become an instrument for the peaceful effectuation of change, or a tool for the preservation of the *status quo* unaltered, time alone could tell. Among Wilson's colleagues the reaction to the League ranged from hopeful sympathy to skeptical antagonism, but in general the specific terms to be written into the treaties of peace commanded the greater interest. It is for this very reason, and to make sure that the League could not be sidetracked, that the Covenant was incorporated into the various treaties of peace themselves.[64] The unexpected consequences of that decision will appear presently.

With the League safely attended to, the work of the committees making satisfactory progress, and Wilson back in Paris in mid-March, the Four were ready for the making of final decisions. The German problem was the largest issue, or perhaps it would be more accurate to say the current aspect of the Franco-German problem. The recovery of Alsace-Lorraine by France was never in question; this meant the frontier of 1870. But Clemenceau was fully alive to French weakness and to the inferiority, in the long term, of French power to German. France's own contribution to the common victory had been very large, but victory would not have been France's had she not had the good fortune of being part of a powerful coalition. This fortunate circumstance and its happy result must be exploited in order to insure the future safety of France. In concrete terms this meant two specific demands: the annexation of the Saar and the detachment from Germany of the left bank of the Rhine over which French military control would continue. But such arrangements would involve a violation of the principle of self-determination, since there was no question about the German character of the territories involved.

The issue became one between Wilson and Clemenceau, and the debate between them was prolonged and bitter, a major crisis in the peacemaking. The French desire for security had legitimate

---

[64] It is because of the precedent created by the incorporation of the Covenant into the post-First World War treaties of peace that the organization of the United Nations after the Second World War was carefully and deliberately divorced from the process of peacemaking.

enough foundation, but neither could Wilson's defense of self-determination be ignored. A way was found eventually out of the dilemma through a compromise. The Rhineland would not be detached from Germany but the French desire for security would be satisfied through the device of an Anglo-American guarantee to France against German aggression.[65] The regrettable consequences of this compromise, eminently sound in itself, will be discussed shortly; but for the moment this particular crisis of the peace had been surmounted.

No sooner was the French difficulty settled than there arose an even greater one from the Italian quarter. Where German matters were concerned the Italians had remained neutral, willing to accept the decisions of those more directly concerned with them. But they were anxious to procure a settlement of their own claims. The issue in this case was the clear one between the Treaty of London and the principle of nationality, as stated in Point IX in this instance; in concrete terms, it came to be a debate over two lines on the map: that of the Treaty of London and the so-called American, or Wilson, line, result of the recommendations of the American experts. The chickens now came home to roost that had been dodged during the armistice discussions of the preceding autumn.[66]

Realistically, Orlando, the Italian Premier, was prepared to compromise: the Treaty of London line, plus the city of Fiume,[67] in Istria, in exchange for yielding the northern half of Dalmatia promised to Italy in 1915. Unwisely, he began by staking out a claim for all that had been promised Italy, plus the city of Fiume, resting his case on a jumble of arguments: the sanctity of treaty obligations in one place, nationality in the other. The Yugoslavs, shrewdly from their point of view, capitalizing on the American

[65] The Rhineland was to remain under Allied occupation as a token of Germany's fulfillment of her obligations, but this was a temporary military measure. As to the Saar, it was detached from Germany and placed under the supervision of the League, pending the holding of a plebiscite in fifteen years. Ownership of the Saar mines went to France under the head of Reparation.

[66] See above, p. 357. Wilson had previously committed himself to acceptance of the Brenner frontier for Italy in the north. This was also a breach of self-determination, but had the contradictory effects of making him feel that the Italians ought to be all the more amenable when it came to their frontier with Yugoslavia, while it caused the Italians to question the solidity of his adherence to a principle which he had been willing to ignore in another instance. To Wilson, in turn, this took the guise of insult added to injury.

[67] The city of Fiume constituted an island of Italian population—it was about 50 percent Italian—almost contiguous, however, to the frontier drawn by the Treaty of London line which included the entire Istrian Peninsula.

prejudice in favor of small nations, let Wilson fight it out for them. The British and the French stood on the sidelines, acknowledging the validity of their 1915 signatures, but clearly impotent to coerce America. The result of it all was to turn an Italo-Yugoslav frontier dispute into an Italo-American quarrel. Wilson, whose temper was already frayed by this time as a result of other difficulties, saw it as a clear case of right versus wrong, good fighting evil. When on April 24th he elected to state his case in the French press, he thereby also shifted the ground of the debate. Taking the position that the authenticity of their mandate had been challenged by the American President, the heads of the Italian delegation went home to consult their Parliament, which in the circumstances gave them a resounding endorsement amid loud manifestations of outraged Italian national feeling at its worst.

If Italy could not be coerced beyond a certain point, clearly no one had the power to bend American will. The Italians came back to Paris empty-handed, but the Italian problem remained unsolved, so long at least as the American President insisted on exercising a power of veto in this particular question.[68] Since, however, this matter did not affect the German treaty, the latter could be proceeded with. The problem of the Japanese claims threatened for a moment a crisis as acute as the Italian. It has been pointed out that Japan had entered the war with a view to assuming the German position in the Far East and that the Allies had given their assent to her desire. Matters were complicated, however, by Far Eastern developments during the war. Taking advantage of the weakness of China and of the temporary absence of the Western Powers in the Far East, Japan had in 1915 forced upon China acceptance of her famous—or infamous—Twenty-One Demands that gave her far-reaching privileges in China. In 1917 China herself was induced to enter the war against Germany, and the Chinese representatives in Paris sought to recover for their country what her weakness had made it possible for either Germany or Japan to extract from her.

In the Sino-Japanese as in the Italo-Yugoslav dispute, America was not bound by the prior commitments of others, and, in addition, American interest, in the form of a traditionally pro-Chinese attitude, was far more sensitive to the Far East than to the Adri-

---

[68] It was resolved through direct Italo-Yugoslav negotiations in November, 1920, shortly after the Democratic defeat in the American election of that month.

atic.[69] The Japanese, shrewdly biding their time, chose the period of the climax of the Italian crisis to press their own demands; the skill of their diplomacy was rewarded and in the end they had their way, with the consequence that China was the only Power that refused to append its signature to the Treaty of Versailles.

There were many other sources of difference, the determination of the frontier between Poland and Germany, specifically the disposition of Danzig and of Silesia, conflicting claims among the heirs of the Austro-Hungarian state, the determination of the total of Reparation that should be asked of Germany, the disposition of the German colonies, and the fate of the Ottoman Empire, but none of these threatened to disrupt the peace congress as the French, the Italian, and the Japanese problems did. They were either definitely resolved at the time, or their solution was temporarily put off through a variety of devices (plebiscites, Reparation commission, etc.), so that it was possible to draft and to sign the treaties that have been enumerated with the five enemy Powers, Germany, Austria, Hungary, Bulgaria, and Turkey, during the period from June, 1919, to August, 1920.

THE SETTLEMENTS IN EASTERN EUROPE. But these treaties did not suffice to restore even a formal peace to all Europe. The thought was entertained for a time of having Russian representation in Paris, but in the end no satisfactory arrangements could be made for that purpose, with the consequence that the settlements in the borderlands of Russia were made quite independently of the peacemaking in Paris.

Russia was torn by civil war and some assistance went from the Allies to the counterrevolutionary armies. However, one by one these were defeated in the course of 1919 and 1920, until the Bolshevik regime was in control of the entire country. But in the West, Bolshevik Russia was confronted with the newly arisen states which the initial German victory had brought into existence.[70] The Allies abrogated the Treaty of Brest-Litovsk, but

[69] The Lansing-Ishii exchanges of November, 1917, reiterated the 1908 declarations, the United States recognizing that Japan's geographical position gave her special interests in China. In May, 1918, a Sino-Japanese treaty of alliance against Bolshevik Russia was concluded; it provided for the use in Siberia of Chinese troops under Japanese direction while concurrently Japanese loans for Manchurian development were arranged.

[70] In Siberia there was fighting that involved the Bolsheviks, the Czech Legion, and various White armies. There also the Bolsheviks gradually regained control which became complete after the Japanese evacuation of Vladivostok in October, 1922.

they experienced not a little difficulty in procuring the withdrawal of German forces from the *Baltikum*. A confused situation ensued in which these various states strove to maintain their independence against Russian efforts to regain control, first with German assistance, then, struggling to rid themselves of German influence, through their own power and some Allied aid. By 1919, the four Baltic states, Finland in the north and the three small units of Esthonia, Latvia, and Lithuania, had emerged, if only precariously.

Poland was a larger problem. In Warsaw, Pilsudski, liberated from German captivity, became head of the provisional government in November, 1918, and, though with some difficulty owing to divergent political orientation, managed to reach agreement with the Polish National Committee in Paris that the Allies had recognized. Poland had no frontiers, and if her border with Germany could be established in Paris, in the east, Poland found herself at war with Russia. The war ranged widely, from the depths of the Ukraine to the gates of Warsaw.[71] An equilibrium of forces was reached in 1920 that resulted in the conclusion of the Treaty of Riga in March, 1921. To the south of Poland the Rumanians, likewise taking advantage of Russian turmoil and impotence, had managed to establish themselves in Bessarabia, to the loss of which the Bolsheviks refused, however, to give formal sanction.[72]

IV. Europe and the World in 1920

THE NEW FRONTIERS

IN EUROPE. The combination of these developments and of the work of the peace gathering in Paris, had, by 1920, restored to Europe something like the semblance of peace. The various instruments, the treaties of peace, constituted the charter of the future and their detailed aspect warrants some close examination. Not for a century had Europe undergone such drastic rearrangements.

The western face of Europe, from the Atlantic to a line drawn

[71] In 1920 the hard-pressed Poles appealed to the Allies for assistance. From France they received credits and supplies and a military mission which enabled Pilsudski to retrieve the situation, driving the Russians back from Warsaw.
[72] A highly confused situation developed in the Caucasus where, in March–April, 1918, various states declared their independence. These were eventually reconquered by the Bolsheviks who concluded peace with Turkey in October, 1921, and in 1922 recombined these states into the Transcaucasian Socialist Soviet Republic, which became part of the larger U.S.S.R.

between Danzig and Fiume, was relatively little altered. France had recovered her lost provinces, but no more. The Saar was under care of the League for a time, and the left bank of the Rhine was under military occupation, but the sovereignty of it remained

German.[73] From Basle to Silesia the southern frontier of Germany was unchanged, but in the east Germany suffered appreciable losses; these were inevitable if Poland were to be reconstituted. In Silesia, a plebiscite was to be held, and Danzig, the sea

[73] Belgium acquired the small areas of Eupen, Malmédy, and Moresnet.

outlet of Poland, was likewise detached from Germany. This last was a clear case of a conflict between economic necessity and nationality: Danzig was a German city but was judged indispensable to Poland. The result was a compromise: like the Saar, Danzig was made the responsibility of the League, a free territory. Poland, however, held a strip of Baltic coast, the Polish Corridor, predominantly Polish in population, but East Prussia remained German land in recognition of the ethnic character of its people.[74] To complete the circuit of Germany's frontiers, a plebiscite in Schleswig, forgotten after the war of 1864, restored to Denmark part of that province. Despite these territorial losses, the bulk of Germany remained.[75]

Italy was also relatively little altered. She secured in the north the line of the Brenner frontier, and the Treaty of Rapallo in November, 1920, between herself and Yugoslavia, gave her essentially the frontier promised her in 1915 in Istria. Fiume was made a free city—the League was not involved in this case—but in the Eastern Adriatic Italy acquired only some islands adjacent to Istria and the city of Zara on the Dalmatian mainland.

There was to be a new Austria consisting of the purely German provinces of the former Habsburg Monarchy. Its southern frontier, with Yugoslavia, was established through a plebiscite held in the Klagenfurt area, and the fate of the Burgenland was likewise decided between herself and Hungary.[76] This last country also emerged as a new state peopled by Magyars, the old Hungarian state, the lands of the crown of St. Stephen, sustaining losses to all its neighbors.

In the north, the old Kingdom of Bohemia was restored within its historic boundaries, but to it were added the Slovaks to form the new state of Czechoslovakia that comprised also an extreme eastern fragment, Sub-Carpatho Ruthenia, with some 500,000 population. The case of Poland has been mentioned and the manner in which her frontiers were established. As the result of the Silesian plebiscite, held in March, 1921, the area was divided be-

[74] Owing to a dispute over a part of East Prussia a plebiscite took place in Allenstein and Marienwerder, as a result of which these districts remained German.

[75] Memel, a German city like Danzig, because of its importance to Lithuania, had been placed under Allied administration pending the adjudication of its fate. To forestall a solution similar to that adopted for Danzig, in January, 1923, the Lithuanians seized Memel and eventually made good their title to it.

[76] The Burgenland plebiscite did not take place until December, 1921.

tween Poland and Germany.[77] Over Teschen the Poles and the Czechs had rival claims, which the Conference of Ambassadors, successor body of the Supreme Council, adjudicated, dividing the territory between the two countries in July, 1920. In October, General Zeligowski, acting "independently," seized the city of Vilna from the Lithuanians. The Poles remained in possession, thereby creating a long-term issue between themselves and Lithuania.

The circumstances of the war provided Rumania with unexpected opportunities. In 1914 Rumanian irredentism was directed toward both Austria-Hungary and Russia. Rumania had thrown her lot with the Allies in 1916, only to find herself defeated, and the collapse of Russia had caused her to withdraw from the struggle. But the ultimate defeat of the Central Powers gave her an opportunity to reënter it while occupying Russian Bessarabia. Her claims were given recognition, with the result that a much enlarged Rumania emerged that included Transylvania as well as Bessarabia. The disputed Banat was divided between herself and the new Yugoslavia.

The South Slav problem had been the immediate occasion for the outbreak of the war. It may have been irresponsible on the part of hotheaded enthusiasts to risk the destruction of Europe for the sake of the satisfaction of their parochial wish; yet, in this case as in that of Poland, the destruction of the framework of 1914 was the necessary preliminary to the success of nationalistic aspirations. Preliminary arrangements made during the war led, upon its termination, to the proclamation of the union of the Serbs, Croats, and Slovenes under the Karageorgević dynasty of Serbia. The union was recognized by the Allies and its frontiers with Italy, Austria, Hungary, and Rumania were established in the manner that has been described. Despite some protests, Montenegro was absorbed into the Kingdom of the Serbs, Croats, and Slovenes.

Albania was barely born when the war had broken out and her continued existence seemed doubtful. The proposal for her partition between her two neighbors, Serbia and Greece, with Italy also having a share in the central portion around Valona, did not bear fruit. Of their own accord, the Italians relinquished their

[77] The plebiscite itself did not settle the issue, for a Polish attempt led by Korfanty, in May, 1922, to establish control of the Polish section led to a deadlock in the Supreme Council and to a final decision by the League in October that gave Poland the greater part of the mining resources of the district.

claim, retaining the island of Saseno alone, and the balance of surrounding interests led to the survival of pre-1914 Albania, the question of her southern frontier alone, that with Greece, remaining to be settled.

As in the Balkan Wars, Bulgaria emerged from the Great War in defeat. She suffered as a consequence some frontier rectification with Serbia and the loss of her access to the Aegean, Western Thrace passing under Greek sovereignty. This put Greece in territorial contact with Turkey. Amid the tortuousness of domestic politics, Venizelos, partisan of the Allied cause, emerged as the leader of his country in victory. Venizelos had grandiose plans, the *megala idea*, which may be described as making the entire Aegean a Greek lake through the incorporation of the Greek colonies, dating from classical times, whose descendants had survived on the western coast of the Anatolian mainland. Greece thus became a factor in the arrangements for the disposition of the Ottoman Empire.

IMPERIAL REARRANGEMENTS. These arrangements, made during the war, have been described. With some modifications, they were incorporated into the Treaty of Sèvres of August, 1920. The modifications were chiefly two: the elimination of Russia as a claimant, since the Bolsheviks denounced the secret treaties of tsarist Russia and renounced any imperial ambitions; and the intrusion of Greek claims. The Treaty of Sèvres sanctioned the death of the Ottoman Empire, from which the Arab part was severed. Arab nationalism was a young plant and the question was pertinent whether the Arab peoples had reached a stage in their political development that made the unqualified grant of independence to them a practicable matter. The combination of this fact, of the recognition given Arab nationalism, and of the imperial claims of European Powers resulted in an ingenious compromise, the Mandate system. Syria, Palestine, and Iraq were not to become unfettered British and French possessions respectively. Instead of this, title to these lands was vested in the League, which, in view of the conditions of these areas, assigned them as mandates to a politically more advanced Power. The theory was that the mandatory Power was to be responsible to the League for the administration of his mandate, and his role was to be that of educating the mandated area to the point where it would be prepared for independence. In the assigning of mandates, the interallied wartime arrangements were adopted. Thus, Syria became a French mandate, Iraq and Palestine British ones,[78] the main part of the Arabian peninsula, in which the British was to remain the most important external influence, remaining the independent battleground of rival chieftains.[79]

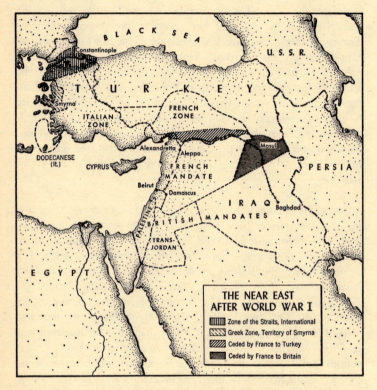

THE NEAR EAST
AFTER WORLD WAR I

|||||| Zone of the Straits, International
XXXX Greek Zone, Territory of Smyrna
//// Ceded by France to Turkey
████ Ceded by France to Britain

In the rest of the Ottoman Empire, a zone of the Straits, still nominally Turkish, was to be internationalized. The French ob-

[78] Direct Anglo-French negotiations resulted in a modification of the Sykes-Picot agreement, as a result of which the Mosul region became part of the British instead of the French mandate.

[79] The chief rivalry was between Sherif Hussein of Mecca, now King of the Hejaz, and Ibn Saud, a leader of the Wahabi sect. The British had dealt with both during the war and, in 1919, maintained an essentially neutral attitude in the struggle between them which resulted in the victory of Ibn Saud, though not until 1924. Meanwhile, two sons of Hussein had become established in Iraq and Transjordan, respectively, with the consequence that intra-Arab rivalries have continued ever since.

tained Cilicia, the section adjacent to their Syrian mandate, as a
sphere for their influence, and to the west of Cilicia, the region
of Adana likewise fell under Italian control. The Italians also obtained the Dodecanese Islands in full title, but the region around
Smyrna was turned over to Greece.[80] The impotent sultan signed
the Treaty of Sèvres, but in 1919 there were already rumblings of
Turkish discontent and objections to the just outlined partition of
Turkey, out of which Mustapha Kemal began to organize resistance in the Anatolian hinterland.[81] As a consequence, the Treaty
of Sèvres was to remain a dead letter as far as Turkey proper was
concerned; but that aspect of things is best left to subsequent treatment.

The Asiatic Near East may be regarded as a semicolonial area,
both because of its Mediterranean location and because of the degree of development of its peoples. It was otherwise in non-Medi-
terranean Africa. During the war, the British and the French had
planned a partition between themselves of the existing German
colonies in Africa. It would have been merely unrealistic to speak
of nationality or nationalism in Togoland or Tanganyika. Nevertheless, in Africa also the mandate principle prevailed, with an additional distinction. There were to be three categories of Mandates,
A, B, and C, corresponding to the degree of development of the
peoples who were placed under them. The Near Eastern mandates
were all in the first category, but those in Africa were either in
the second or third.

The outcome was a division of German Cameroon and Togoland, as B mandates, between Britain and France. German East
Africa became a B mandate to Britain, and German Southwest
Africa, sparsely peopled and highly undeveloped, was assigned as
a C mandate to the Union of South Africa. In addition, a section
of German East Africa, Ruanda-Urundi, was joined to the Congo
as a Belgian mandate. By way of compensation to Italy, France
ceded to her some territory that served to round out Libya in the
west, and the eastern frontier of that Italian colony was even-

[80] This was done in 1919 at the time of the Adriatic crisis; partly as a consequence of the irritation which developed with the Italians, Venizelos was asked
to send a Greek—ostensibly Allied—force to maintain order in Smyrna, an
opportunity that he seized with alacrity.
[81] In addition to the severance of the Arab lands from Turkey, the Treaty
of Sèvres also provided for an independent Armenia (whose boundaries remained
to be determined) and an autonomous Kurdistan. Both of these provisions were
destined to remain dead letters.

tually also readjusted on the Egyptian side. Jubaland was transferred from British East Africa to Italian Somaliland.[82]

Japan had fallen heir to Germany's position in the Far East. Germany's Pacific possessions, north of the Equator, were likewise assigned to Japan as a C mandate. Those south of the Equator and the former German section of New Guinea went to Australia, but Samoa was assigned to New Zealand and the island of Nauru to the British Empire as a whole.

Much has been written about the quality of these arrangements. The new map of Europe undoubtedly represented the nearest approximation ever achieved to ethnic boundaries. These were not perfect, nor could they ever be if populations were not to be displaced. The fact cannot be denied that the victors, and especially the new nations that emerged from the war on their side, profited from the asset of victory. In some cases at least, frontiers could have been drawn that would have left smaller minorities under alien rule. But that peoples were arbitrarily and callously bartered about is not true. If much was to be heard about the grievance of the Germans in Poland, the fact remains that the Corridor was predominantly Polish and that Danzig was not put under unqualified Polish rule. The largest minority in Poland was on her Russian border.

The question might be raised indeed whether such a thing as a Czechoslovak or a Yugoslav nationality existed or whether these were hybrid and synthetic creations. To such questions no clear and final answer could be supplied in 1920. Depending upon the course of the future, the possibility existed that such nationalities would become taken for granted as those of the Western peoples had become; the Western nationalities are the result not of ethnic factors alone, but of much history as well. Conversely, the possibility also existed that the final verdict of history might be that Serbs and Croats, for example, are distinct peoples. Continued peace and successful domestic operation, or the failure of the same conditions, over a fairly long period of time, alone could supply an answer to the questions. But these domestic conditions in the new states could also furnish some of the stuff of future international problems. One important innovation deserves mention. The new states in which substantial alien minorities existed were required to sign minorities treaties which gave these minorities protection through their right to appeal for redress to the League.

[82] A small area, the Kionga triangle, was added to Portuguese Mozambique.

Here was a clear intrusion into the domain of sovereignty, and, for that reason, it had all the more significance.

The same may be said in regard to mandates,[83] since the classical colonial relationship was modified by the intrusion of the League between the mandatory and the mandated region. The concept was new, and how the experiment would operate, again time alone could tell. The fact that the distribution of mandates followed essentially the wartime arrangements of the Allies naturally lent support to the contention that saw in the mandatory system a mere hypocritical cloak for the operation of traditional imperialism, adapting itself to the climate and the verbiage of the day. In actual fact, the record of mandates has varied.

THE LEAGUE OF NATIONS

But be it mandates or minorities treaties, the great innovation of the peace that followed the First World War was the League of Nations. The reception of this novelty ranged from snarly denigration to unrestrained optimism that hailed the League as the herald of the millennium; a more sober appraisal was that of a moderate mixture of skepticism and hopefulness. The League had no power distinct from that of its members, the French proposal of 1919 to create such power having been rejected. In its organization the League reproduced the structure of parliamentary democracy: an upper house, the Council, consisted of permanent members, the Great Powers, and of four elected nonpermanent members;[84] in the lower house, the Assembly, each member had one vote. Thus a compromise was achieved between the equality of sovereign states and the possession of effective power; in addition, the rule of unanimity applied.

The fundamental purpose of the League was the preservation of peace. Its success in this vital endeavor would also depend upon the course of the future, but some measures could be taken at once. Two things were widely accepted at the end of the war: the belief in the aggression of the Central Powers and the view that arms constitute in themselves a danger to the peace. They had the con-

[83] The concept of "mandate" as applied to the former German colonies and to some portions of the Ottoman Empire is to be credited in large part to the South African Marshal Smuts and to the American George Louis Beer.
[84] The composition of the Council varied in the course of time. At all times any Great Power member of the League had a permanent seat in the Council, but the tendency was to increase the number of nonpermanent members who, from 1922, constituted a majority.

sequence that the defeated enemy was disarmed, but this was intended as a mere preliminary step to general disarmament once order and security had been established on a reliable basis.

The Covenant of the League recognized "that the maintenance of peace requires the reduction of national armaments to the lowest point consistent with national safety and the enforcement by common action of international obligations" (Article 8), and the Council was to formulate plans for such a reduction. The members of the League guaranteed the territorial integrity and independence of all (Article 10), a provision that could be read as an attempt to freeze the *status quo*, but which was qualified by Article 19, which looked to the possible reconsideration of treaties that had become inapplicable.

As to the methods by which the peace should be preserved, there were no teeth in the League, which could, however, take any action that might seem advisable (Article 11); the members agreed to submit disputes among themselves either to arbitration or to inquiry by the Council, and not to resort to war until three months after the verdict or the report was rendered (Article 12). Any resort to war by a member in disregard of its League commitments would *ipso facto* be regarded as an act of war against all; the Covenant-breaking member would be subjected to financial and economic boycott, and the Council would recommend what armed contribution the members should make for the protection of the Covenant. This was as far as it was deemed possible to curb the sovereignty of a body of sovereign members. Since the League had no force of its own and no distinct existence apart from that of its members, clearly the door remained open to any action, to any degree of action, or even to no action at all, should the Council advise that it could recommend no action. The future fate of the experiment could, in 1920, obviously not be predicted; but this was the first time on record when states had committed themselves to do so much in a treaty bearing their signatures.

Also, the membership of the League consisted initially of those among the victors who were signatories of the treaties of peace, to whom were shortly added thirteen neutrals who adhered to the Covenant. The enemy was placed on probation, but would eventually be accepted into the company of the elect. For the League, quite appropriately, was universal in intent, open to all who accepted the obligations of the Covenant and whose admission would be sanctioned by a two-thirds vote in the Assembly.

APPRAISAL AND RECEPTION OF THE PEACE

This stress on the moral aspect of things instead of on the mere assertion of power must be seen as a reflection of the prevailing temper of the day, of which the emphasis on ideology during the war itself had been another facet.[85] It led to another and a very curious result. The vanquished enemy was not to be saddled with a classical indemnity of war; instead it was to make good the damage consequent upon the effects of its aggression. It thus came about that the Reparation section of the Treaty of Versailles opened with the famous so-called war guilt clause, the effects of which were to be very great and have in part already been indicated.[86] For the rest, it proved impossible to agree, during the peacemaking, either upon the extent of the damage or upon the enemy capacity for payment. Apart from demanding of Germany certain immediate payments and the delivery of certain goods, the treaty of peace merely provided for the creation of a Reparation Commission whose task it would be to assess the damage, then to organize arrangements for the discharge of the German liability. The other enemies, save Turkey, were also liable to Reparation, but the largest amount and the greatest problem by far was to be that of the German liability.

The charter of the future that the peace settlements constituted, especially those elaborated at Paris, and most of all the Treaty of Versailles, symbolic of all, has been the object of much debate and has given rise to a vast literature, much of it critical. This debate will not be entered into here, but some brief observations are relevant. First of all this, the settlements of 1919–1920, like other settlements of wars, embodied the results of past events and the registration of future expectations; but they were also the expression of existing relationships of power and of conditions at the time of their making. Treaties are not eternal; they are instruments that the future can use well or ill.

But this also is important that marked a departure from precedent. Here was an attempt to stress to a novel degree the moral aspects of the relations among states. This may be seen as progress, and certainly was intended as such by many at least of the peacemakers. Yet power had not been ignored, as indeed it could not

[85] The International Labor Organization, like the Covenant, incorporated into the treaties of peace, may be regarded as an expression of the temper of the time, a response to the demand and the pressure of the labor mass for recognition of its place in society.
[86] See above, Chap. V.

have been; the result was a curious mixture of power and morality, two elements that ever mix badly, or, in the specific case of Reparation, a compound of morality with economics—a novel experiment indeed. The outcome of the First World War, as we now know, was to be less than the final and lasting inauguration of the rule of law and of the reign of justice in the relations among states. Yet the hope had been there; the very frustration of it was to become a complicating factor for the future.

The peace, once it was made, elicited rather less than universal approval and rejoicing. That the defeated enemy should have found fault with its provisions was perhaps only to be expected; but beyond this, the German people were, with fair unanimity, appalled and bitterly resentful at what seemed to them gross injustice. But neither were the victors elated. Ostensibly, the British had rid themselves of the incubus of a German navy and had substantially enhanced their imperial position; yet the future appeared to them uncertain on the score of their economic position and of the general power balance in Europe. The French felt highly insecure, despite their victory, or rather just because the victory was theirs only in part; the treaty was presented to Parliament for ratification not as a great success, but with apologies as being the best that could be had in circumstances where France was only one in the victorious coalition.

The Italians felt frustrated and cheated, quite as much because of the manner in which their case had been handled as because of their failure to obtain all that they had hoped to get. Among the newly created states, especially in the case of the defeated, there subsisted a multitude of unresolved disputes. Everywhere it soon appeared that the peace had not automatically made the world "a place fit for heroes to live in." The necessity of reconverting from war to peace, in the economies of nations no less than in the private lives of individuals, was attended by much dissatisfaction; currencies had to find their own levels now that wartime controls and international agreements were abolished in the effort to reestablish free economies; labor unrest was widespread no less than political restlessness and psychological disturbance.

THE UNITED STATES AND THE PEACE. But in some respects the most interesting reaction was that of the United States. Without a doubt the United States had emerged from the war as far the greatest Power on earth, a fact which had found expression in the large voice of America in the shaping of the peace. This fact was clear to all, but meant relatively little to the American people who, the war finished, thought mainly in terms of a return to the temporarily interrupted course of their domestic concerns rather than in those of large participation in the affairs of the outside world. America was indeed unique, not least perhaps in her awareness of uniqueness, and the simple fact that power means inescapable responsibility was not part of the popular consciousness. Wilson himself had ever been aware of difference and had been given to suspicion of others, his "associates."

America, or Wilson, had not only bestowed the League upon the world, but had made certain that the world could not escape the League, whose Covenant was part of the treaties of peace drafted in Paris. As in other democratic countries, in the United States these treaties had to undergo the constitutional process of ratification, meaning in this case acceptance by a two-thirds majority of the American Senate. The Treaty of Versailles was duly considered after Wilson's return from Paris and a debate arose, the main issue of which was the Covenant of the League.[87] In simplest form, the fundamental question was that of the consistency, or lack thereof, between American sovereignty and the obligations that membership in the League entailed. The details of the debate do not belong in this story. There were extremists, Wilson demanding unqualified acceptance at one end, those advocating total rejection at the other. Between them, middle ground compromisers thought that sufficient votes might be obtained for qualified ratification in the form of certain reservations that would safeguard American rights. There were logical weaknesses in this last position, and the fact that politics is the art of the possible was uncongenial to Wilsonian rigidity. On the basis of an all-or-nothing position, unqualified ratification was not to be had.[88] Thus, the ironical result was achieved that, of the signatories of Versailles, the most important was the only one that failed to ratify that treaty.[89]

[87] This is worth stressing in view of the widespread popular misconception that the American refusal to ratify the treaty of peace with Germany was the result of dislike for its objectionable punitive features.

[88] The role of personalities in the episode was considerable. Senator Lodge, Republican Chairman of the Foreign Relations Committee, was a bitter hater of Wilson, who in turn fully reciprocated the feeling. It is in connection with the effort to secure ratification that Wilson embarked on a speaking tour of the country during the course of which he broke under the strain and suffered a stroke.

[89] Peace had to be established separately between the United States and Germany. This was done formally by the Treaty of Berlin in 1921 which may be described as the Treaty of Versailles minus the Covenant, thereby giving rise

To this situation there was a footnote, albeit one with important consequences. The tripartite Anglo-Franco-American treaty of guarantee to France was to have been considered at the same time as the Treaty of Versailles. In the heat of debate over the latter and its ultimate rejection, the former instrument never even reached the floor of the Senate. But that treaty constituted one side of a bargain, the other side of which had been written into the provisions accepted by France for the German treaty. The matter seemed remote and of little interest in America where it could be, and was, merely forgotten. The French view, quite understandably was other; out of it there grew a legitimate sense of grievance and a search for alternatives which became in itself an important feature of France's postwar policy. The consequences of this episode will appear in the following chapter.

In the United States the failure to ratify the Treaty of Versailles marked an important turning point, away from the involvement in world affairs and back toward the "normalcy" of the isolationist tradition. It was not long before the very intervention of the United States in the war came to be viewed as a mistake, a passing aberration, the consequences, if not the memory, of which were best forgotten and denied. The Republican victory in the election of 1920 may be regarded as the formal sanctioning by the American electorate of the turning away from the rest of the planet.[90]

Yet it is also true that the United States as a Great Power had come of age too suddenly. The slow and muddled operation of the democratic process demanded the passage of time before the implications of so sharply and suddenly altered conditions would penetrate sufficiently the consciousness of the nation. This fact itself was not the least of the problems of the postwar period, for Europe and for the world as a whole, but perhaps the sad consolation of understanding seems more appropriate a view of these things than the futile venom and bitterness of irrelevant recrimination.

---

to the quip that America chose to retain the questionable features of the peace while eliminating the more promising one.

[90] This is essentially correct despite the fact that, during the campaign, the Republicans paid at least lip service to the concept of the League.

XI

The False Recovery
and the
Era of Illusions, 1920-1930

It has been pointed out that one of the most important effects of the First World War was the emergence in the councils of nations of the United States to a position of ostensible significance commensurate with the reality of American power that circumstances alone had hitherto confined in isolation. Put in another form, the power structure of the world was radically, and irretrievably, altered by the war: instead of being, as until 1914, the powerhouse of the planet, Europe, enfeebled, was henceforth to be in what was an essentially defensive position, whether toward the dependent world over which it had been rapidly extending her sway, or *vis-à-vis* the preponderant power of America.

Yet this reality, in retrospect quite clear to all, was not to be acknowledged willingly by America until another world conflict had been fought. America's unwillingness to recognize the reality —and the consequent responsibility—of American power, understandable enough in the context of the historic American development, had not a little to do with the stresses and strains, ending in renewed collapse, of the long armistice. Whether she would or no, America could not help but have enormous influence on the course of world events; the effects of a policy of negation could be other, they could not be less significant and far-reaching, than those of active and deliberate participation. From the time of the First World War it is impossible to write a history confined to the limits of Europe.

To the distortion resulting from the American return to a policy of isolation, the refusal of existing power to assert itself, there was added what may be looked upon as an inverse distortion, in the form of too great a burden placed upon, or assumed by, an insufficient power. The injury that the war did to France has also been pointed out, together with the unexpected consequence of the war in the form of the collapse of the three European Empires of Russia, Germany, and Austria-Hungary; the result of this situation was to leave France the one effectively organized Power on the continent of Europe[1] and to enhance enormously, for the moment at least, the importance of French power. The ultimate insufficiency of French power was to be in the end no less significant a cause of ultimate collapse than the American attempt at withdrawal. In these fundamentals, rather than in the much debated merits and shortcomings of the specific terms of the peace settlements themselves, lay the roots of future developments.

To repeat again, the great problems of Europe after the formal restoration of peace, problems that far eclipsed in importance the myriad issues that strewed the map of Europe, were essentially three. They bore the names of the three great defeated Powers. Presumably, at some undetermined future time, Russia and Germany would recover internally and as a consequence seek to resume their place in the international community; the problem of Austria-Hungary was other: irretrievably destroyed by the successful force of nationalism, a vacuum of power now took the place of the former Habsburg domain. What place could be found in Europe for the fragments of power that had emerged in the Danubian area was a problem no less important and in some ways more complex than that of the reintegration of either Germany or Russia.

In the immediate sense, however, the problem of Danubia was not urgent, and Russia was in such chaos that she too could be forgotten, once it had become clear that the threat of world revolution would not materialize, an issue that the Russo-Polish War may be said to have settled. The case of Germany was different. That the defeat of Germany was ultimately thorough and her surrender unconditional may be granted; in 1920 Germany was completely powerless and disarmed. Yet Germany as an organized entity subsisted; her losses, if considerable, were not crippling, and

---

[1] It may be said that the same characterization held for Italy. But the destruction of the power balance of Europe that the defeat of Germany entailed robbed Italy of the chief asset of her foreign policy. She showed a remarkably limited range of interest in affairs other than those of immediate concern to herself and tended, for the rest, to assume an attitude of disgruntlement and a position of ineffectual criticism and of opposition to French policy.

her domestic revolution, if such it may be called, had not destroyed or even fundamentally altered the mechanism of an efficient state; moreover, Germany had only been defeated by the overwhelming weight of a world coalition and her wartime performance had placed her within reasonable distance of achieving hegemony over Europe. If such had been her deliberate purpose, the achievement of it did not seem a wholly utopian possibility.

France was victorious but bled white, further weakened by comparison with 1914 by the very war effort and the cost of victory; she was not unaware of the ultimate discrepancy between her power and the German. Self-appointed guardian of the peace, as much as thrust into that position by circumstances as France was, it was natural that the immediate postwar period should be dominated by the German problem, or better by the problem of the relations among herself, Germany, and the one other state that had emerged from the conflict with at least momentarily enhanced power, Great Britain.

I. The End of the Wartime Alliance or the Anglo-French Duel

Upon Britain and France, both in possession of effective power after the conclusion of the peace, lay the main burden and responsibility for the future organization of Europe. It makes for interesting speculation to contemplate what might have been the course of Europe and the world had these two countries contrived to agree upon and support a common policy. This they had every reason to do, being both "satisfied" Powers to whom the future, be it in the guise of a resurgent Germany clamoring anew for a place under the sun, a reconstructed Russia armed with the weapon of an aggressive ideology, or the overpowering growth of America, held common threats. Their failure to act in unison, on many scores their opposition, may be regarded as an illustration of the dead hand of the past, of incorrectly assimilated lessons of history, especially in the case of stronger Britain, less aware than weaker France of the necessity of union; at all events, the Franco-British duel vastly increased the fragility of the structure of peace that emerged from the war.

Yet the divergence was but the logical outcome of circumstances and tradition which the common democratic structure of the two countries made it all the more difficult to alter. Britain, too, had been injured and ultimately diminished by the war, though the evidence of her hurt was less concrete than France's: sunken ships and lost overseas markets make less impression on the eye than ruined fields and houses, though it might be more difficult to find a new place in the nation for the unemployed Lancashire mill hand than to rebuild a shattered house in Flanders or Champagne. The realities of warfare on her soil Britain had been spared, and the French feeling of insecurity and weakness she did not know. The result of this was that, on the one hand Britain's attention was focused on economic recovery, meaning trade, while on the other the defeat of Germany could be looked upon as just another episode in the tradition where the defeats of Spain, the Dutch, and Napoleon were precedents. On both scores Britain became rather sympathetic than otherwise to the recovery of Germany: a restored Germany could resume her place in Britain's trade while at the same time preventing the establishment of another hegemony—the French—in Europe. Aided by a distorted sense of fair play, the change in the mood of British opinion away from that of the somewhat hysterical khaki election of December, 1918, was surprisingly complete and rapid.

In the estimate of power for the long term lay Britain's capital error of judgment. Those in France who entertained Napoleonic visions belonged rather to the lunatic fringe than to the mass of the nation. This mass had had enough of war and if there was a feeling that commanded well-nigh universal adherence in France it was that of insecurity and fear; in more concrete and narrower terms, how could France guard herself against the recurrence of German aggression? But unanimity ceased when it came to the means that would insure this end. To destroy Germany, in the sense of undoing her unity, was not a realistic policy in the age of self-determination. America and Britain had been opposed to any such attempts, and even the limited effort at dismemberment that had encouraged a feeble Rhenish separatism had not received sustained support from Paris.[2] Basically, the Treaty of Versailles had sanctioned the survival of the united Reich.

The German Kaiser had fled, a German Republic been pro-

[2] In 1919 the French occupation authorities had already encouraged separatist tendencies in the Rhineland and General Mangin approved the proclamation of a "Rhenish Republic" in June, whereupon he was disavowed and removed by Clemenceau. For subsequent French support of German separatism, see below, p. 397.

claimed, and one might hope that defeat would have encouraged and magnified those forces in Germany unsympathetic to the military tradition. A genuinely peaceful Germany would solve France's problem, but it would have been at once more and less than human to expect France merely to gamble her security on such a possibility; French opinion would not have tolerated a policy of simple trust, especially in the overwrought atmosphere immediately after the war, and any government that advocated it could only be described as irresponsible. The "softest" policy imaginable that could be expected of France would not abandon guarantees. There were many indeed who favored thoroughgoing intransigence based on distrust nourished on past experience. Not surprisingly, the French election of 1919 had returned a Parliament, the *bleu horizon* Chamber, where the supporters of a "hard" policy were dominant.

Nevertheless the humanitarian tradition is strong in France and it was not long before the advocates of reconciliation and of at least a softer policy toward Germany made themselves heard. Thus, France was divided in her counsels, and in the contest between France and Britain, one half of France was at least half convinced that the British approach might be the more rewarding. This half may very roughly be equated with the Left, just as the traditional Right could claim a near monopoly of the opposite view. But, at first, the presence of Poincaré in the position of Prime Minister, and the Parliament of 1919, insured the pursuit of the more intransigeant course.

Germany, powerless, could but be relatively passive. That she would endeavor to recover her place and to mitigate the penalties visited upon her was inevitable, whatever her leadership, but in the pursuit of this general aim she, too, like France, might adopt the divergent tactics of conciliation or intransigence. Those elements in Germany that condemned the ways of the past, presumably the forces of the Left that stood for the Republic, like their French counterpart, were also fettered by an opinion which was well-nigh unanimous in deeming the peace settlement unjust and Versailles a *diktat* that superior force alone had imposed and that was not in keeping with the hopes engendered by Allied promises of fairness. Those who in Germany—and they existed—subscribed to the thesis of German war guilt were matched by those across the Rhine who thought French policy far from free of responsibility for the outbreak of war; in terms of national sentiment and opinion they were both insignificant minorities.[3]

FRANCE, BRITAIN, AND THE GERMAN PROBLEM

Such is the general background against which the actual operation of policy must be examined. France may have been disappointed at the failure to secure stronger guarantees for the future; she did nevertheless have in her hands a powerful instrument in the form of the treaty of peace. If the obsession of security dominated her outlook, clearly there was no immediate danger on that score. Her more immediate concern was with her own physical reconstruction, and for this too the peace had made provision in the section of it entitled Reparation. The peculiar innovation in a treaty of peace that was Article 231 has been mentioned, as well as the significance, political and psychological, of that innovation, reflection in the last analysis of the nature of the war itself. That aspect of the matter need not concern us further: be it regarded as the epitome of fairness or a brutal *diktat*, the validity of Versailles was not open to question; by it Germany stood liable to make good the damage of the war.

The issue of Reparation thus loomed overwhelmingly large in the immediate postwar years. Moreover, it has another aspect, mainly political, for the German obligation could be used as a device to maintain Germany in a position of subservience.

REPARATION: FROM THE TREATY OF VERSAILLES TO THE RUHR EPISODE. In the narrow sense, Reparation was an economic problem which could be reduced to two questions: what was the extent of the damage? how much of it and in what manner could Germany make it good? Even on the limited economic plane the problem was not simple, and the Treaty of Versailles had done little more than assert a principle; the task remained of assessing the damage and of determining the manner of discharge of the German obligation, a task entrusted to an *ad hoc* Reparation Commission. Meeting at Spa in July, 1920, the Allies had agreed upon their respective shares of compensation: France was entitled to receive 52 percent of the total, Britain 22 percent and Italy 10

---

[3] Historically, the role of the German critics of pre-1914 German policy was quite important, for they initiated the investigation of the issue of responsibility for the outbreak of the war and it is out of this activity that resulted the wholesale opening of pre-1914 archives, German and others.

percent;[4] the size of the French share was proper recognition of the French loss, France having furnished the chief and decisive battleground; it naturally gave France the greatest interest in insuring collection and a preponderant voice in future decisions.

By the beginning of 1921 the Reparation Commission had completed the task of assessment, set at 150 billion gold marks. A meeting with the Germans in London in March merely revealed an unbridgeable discrepancy between this estimate and the German offer, and this situation resulted in the taking of sanctions in the form of the occupation of the cities of Dusseldorf, Ruhrort, and Duisburg. A new meeting in April led to an ultimatum and to Germany's capitulation before the threat of an extension of the Allied occupation to the Ruhr.[5]

By May, 1921, the first fixed point had been reached. Britain had succeeded in somewhat reducing the total, but was not yet prepared to part company with her wartime allies, particularly France. Germany stood obligated for a total sum of 132 billion gold marks, to be discharged in the form of annual payments of 2 billion marks plus a 26 percent tax on her exports. Payments were begun on that basis and a further step was taken in October in the Wiesbaden agreement between France and Germany with a view to arranging for payments in kind. However, this Loucheur-Rathenau agreement was never ratified owing to the combined opposition to it of French industrial interests and of other claimants, mainly the British.

The whole story of Reparation may be summed up as a painful and costly lesson in economic realities. The approach, especially on the French side, was simple: Germany was saddled with a debt which, like other international financial obligations, it was her duty to discharge. International debts were no novelty, but, apart from rather exceptional voices of caution,[6] the understanding of

[4] The rest was allotted to Belgium (8 percent), to Greece, Rumania, and Yugoslavia (6.5 percent), to Japan (.75 percent), and to Portugal (.75 percent).

[5] This produced a ministerial crisis in Germany. The new Chancellor, Wirth, and his foreign minister, Rathenau, for the moment at least adopted the policy of fulfillment.

[6] The English economist, John Maynard Keynes, foresaw from the beginning the difficulties that would be encountered. He resigned from the British delegation during 1919 and laid the basis for his reputation with his sensational work, *The Economic Consequences of the Peace*. The book had very considerable influence, especially in Britain, but was marred by the flippancy of its tone which tended to defeat its purpose where criticism of the French position was concerned. It should be read in connection with the critique of it by Étienne Mantoux, *The Carthaginian Peace, or the Economic Consequences of Mr. Keynes*, Oxford University Press, 1946; Scribner, 1952.

their mechanism in many quarters may perhaps best be described as primitive. According to established custom, the German debt was specified in gold, but clearly there could be no question of Germany delivering precious metal in the quantities involved. What made possible the discharge of international financial obligations was the existence of a favorable balance of trade for the debtor; Britain's position as a large creditor of much of the rest of the world had been successfully maintained only because of the large unfavorable balance of her own trade. In the last analysis, therefore, Germany could accumulate the necessary credits for the discharge of her debt only through the building up of a large favorable balance of her foreign trade.[7] Even if one leaves aside the loss of German domestic territory and resources, of her merchant marine and colonies, for her to achieve the necessary position in foreign trade would have made her a far more successful rival and competitor of others than she had ever been before 1914. Therein lay an insoluble dilemma, a British dilemma especially,[8] though the opposition of French industry has been indicated as well. To sum it up briefly, the attempt to collect Reparation on the scale contemplated and under the conditions of a capitalist economy was an impossible one. To have said this in France would have been tantamount to treason, and politicians chose the easier and more popular course of merely repeating that "Germany will pay."

Difficulties were not long in appearing, during the second half of 1921, after Germany had met her first payment of 1 billion marks.[9] These difficulties might be no more than a reflection of German ill will, as many thought in France, but they might also

[7] Such considerations were not at all understood by popular opinion, particularly in France, where the problem was looked upon as a simple matter of the German state extracting the necessary funds from its people. It was indeed possible for Germany to tax herself, but the accumulation of German funds in Germany had nothing to do with the transfer problem which could only be solved through Germany's accumulation of foreign balances, that is, through a favorable balance of trade.

[8] Considerations of trade were of far greater importance to Britain than to France and explain the British inclination to leniency in the matter of Reparation. Allowing that the British position was a reflection of national interest, the fact remains that, in economic terms, the British early evinced a sounder understanding of the problem of the debts growing out of the war than either the French or the Americans. In August, 1922, Balfour proposed an all around cancellation of these obligations even though Britain was on balance a creditor.

[9] One manifestation of German difficulties was the course of the mark. Its value was cut in half between July and October and that last value again in half in November.

be the mere passing consequences of inevitable readjustment following the dislocation of war. A moratorium was granted to Germany in December, when it was also agreed that the British and French Prime Ministers would meet the following month.

Among the innumerable series of international conferences, characteristic of this period, the meeting of Lloyd George and Briand at Cannes from January 6 to 13, 1922, is of considerable importance. Looking beyond Reparation, Lloyd George was interested in an attempt to restore the economic health of Europe, Russia included. France, however, was not to be coerced, and Lloyd George thought to win concessions from her in the economic field with the political price of reviving the abandoned guarantee of the spring of 1919.[10] But France was not prepared at this time to make a choice between a weak and disorganized Germany that could not pay Reparation and a prosperous one that might at the same time be a danger; she wanted both security *and* Reparation. Briand's negotiations were viewed with suspicion in Paris whither he was summoned to furnish explanations; correctly assessing the temper of Parliament, Briand resigned without even seeking the test of its approval. His succession went to Poincaré from whom one could expect a staunch and intransigeant defense of French rights. Cannes was essentially a failure.

The meeting throws much light nevertheless on the essential Anglo-French divergence. Like most French statesmen, Poincaré set high store on the British alliance; he therefore continued the negotiation begun by Briand on the basis of Lloyd George's offer, but agreement proved impossible on two scores: rather than a British guarantee, implying a relationship of protection and subservience, Poincaré wanted a reciprocal insurance; in addition, the British guarantee, instead of being limited to the western frontier of France, should apply to the demilitarized zone of Germany and be extended further to the east of Europe. Such commitments Britain was not prepared to undertake at this time.

The rest of the year 1922 saw a further deterioration of the relations between France and both Britain and Germany. At Cannes it had been agreed that a meeting of all the Powers, including Russia, should be held to deal with economic questions. The substitution of Briand by Poincaré did not augur well, but the meeting took place nevertheless, in Genoa, in April and May.

[10] See above, p. 368. This was also the time of the Washington Naval Conference, a disappointment and a source of disgruntlement for France.

In Genoa much time was spent in futile haggling with the Russians who countered an attempt—predominantly French[11]—to secure recognition of the prerevolutionary debts repudiated by the Bolsheviks with a fanciful and much larger counterclaim for damages caused by Allied intervention. The tone of Anglo-Fench relations at this time may best be gauged by a headline blazoned in the London *Times*, surely no yellow sheet, on May 7: "Wrecking the Entente—Premier's [Lloyd George's] Threat to France." The Entente indeed *was* wrecked.

The Genoa meeting, however, provided a surprise. The Germans and the Russians chose the occasion for a separate negotiation of their own. On April 16, the foreign ministers, Rathenau and Chicherin, signed at Rapallo an agreement which made a clean slate of all past financial claims, restored diplomatic relations, and laid the bases of economic coöperation between their respective countries. The news came as a shock to all others. From the Russian point of view, the Treaty of Rapallo had the virtue of insuring against the inclusion of Germany in the ever-feared coalition of capitalistic states.[12] But for Germany this was clumsy diplomacy: to join her own impotence to the Russian could at the moment serve no useful purpose; it could instead quite effectively feed the French suspicion, rooted in much past history, of the potential and eventual dangers of a Russo-German alliance.[13] France for the moment had power and this was almost invitation to make use of it. Russia was far away, but not so Germany, whose will to resist might be broken.

REPARATION: THE RUHR EPISODE.   The occasion for a test of wills was at hand in the perennial of Reparation. The year 1922, despite the moratorium, saw no improvement in the German position, but rather a continued deterioration of it, which the accelerating fall of the currency reflected.[14] Poincaré was thoroughly unmoved by the spectacle of German distress—was it more than

[11] The Russian state debt amounted to some 12 billion gold francs, the major part of it in the hands of French holders.

[12] Just because Germany was at odds with France on account of Reparation, Russia feared that Germany might obtain mitigation on this score at the price of espousing France's policy toward Russia.

[13] Even at this stage Russia was not unwilling to play other cards than the German. A meeting took place at The Hague in June-July which, though barren of results, showed the Russians willing to trade recognition of the tsarist debts for diplomatic recognition and further loans.

[14] By November, 1922, the mark had fallen to 7,000 to the dollar; at the end of January, 1923, it had sunk to 50,000 to the dollar.

fair retribution?—which he regarded for that matter as the result of a deliberate German attempt at evasion. Germany must be convinced, through the application of France's superior force if necessary, that evasion could not succeed; and even realistic Britain would accept the inevitable instead of giving futile encouragement to German resistance once that resistance was proved hopeless. There was complete consistency of logic in the procedure adopted by Poincaré for all that the economic premises on which he based his reasoning might be fallacious.

Britain meantime underwent a change of administration when the withdrawal of Conservative support resulted in the fall of Lloyd George, an outcome not unrelated to the fact that Britain's half-hearted use of her power had had unsatisfactory results in Germany no less than in the Near East.[15] The change, however, resulted in greater British passivity, giving France a freer hand to try her more determined policy of force.

In December, 1922, the Reparation Commission had before it two resolutions submitted by its French chairman, Barthou.[16] The first, registering Germany's failure to make certain deliveries in kind, being a statement of fact, was unanimously approved; the second, stating that this failure constituted a German default, was adopted by a vote of three to one, the British delegate dissenting.[17] Ignoring British protests, that were no more than verbal, on January 11, 1923, French and Belgian troops began to move into the Ruhr.

The episode of the occupation of the Ruhr is of considerable importance in the story of the postwar period and has been much and variously commented upon. It was a manifestation of French policy, Britain remaining a passive and unsympathetic bystander; Belgium, though joining France in the operation, was anxious to evolve a compromise solution. As to Italy, she generally shared the British view of the unwisdom of the French action and was concerned about the extent of French power; taking a realistic view

[15] For the developments in the Near East at this time, see below, pp. 400 ff.
[16] A German request for a further moratorium in August had been blocked by France.
[17] France, Britain, Italy, and Belgium were represented on the Reparation Commission. The specific default was a trifling matter, the failure of deliveries of timber and telegraph poles, and the pettiness of France's legalistic position was much criticized. This is to miss the point, for the real issue was the far larger one of Germany's policy and of her relations with others, especially France; the technical German default was merely the pretext and occasion for the trial of a test of power and of wills.

of things, however, she thought it best to align herself with, instead of against, that power, though ever watchful for an opportunity to curb it. In America and among the neutrals French policy was highly unpopular and very severely criticized. The Ruhr episode may therefore be regarded as an isolated Franco-German conflict; Germany had no military weapons at her disposal, but in effect this was war, for which the later expression, "cold war," would have been apt description.

Ostensibly, France was applying the letter of the treaty of peace, enforcing sanctions for the German default. The sanctions were economic, the military force being for the sole purpose of protection of the M.I.C.U.M. (*Mission interalliée de contrôle des usines et des mines*) whose function it was to insure the collection of Reparation at its source, the heart of German industry; secondarily, but in the last analysis no less important, the awkwardness and inconvenience of the situation for Germany might induce her to accept the French view of what she ought to do in the matter of Reparation. In other words, the Ruhr occupation had the political purpose of procuring a new German surrender, in default of which France would be in a position to collect Reparation directly. Broadly speaking, it may be said that the economic operation, in the limited sense of direct and effective collection of Reparation, failed while the political purpose succeeded.

Germany was appalled and incensed and German feeling ran high. The German government protested and resorted to a policy of passive resistance, encouraging workers to strike and its officials to refuse coöperation with the occupying authority. This merely brought reprisals: the erection of a barrier between the Ruhr and the rest of Germany and widespread expulsions, while French and Belgian technicians were brought in to operate railways and mines. Of Reparation little was collected; the cost of occupation was little more than covered. But Poincaré was unmoved and prepared to sit it out, which Germany was not in a position to do. The policy of passive resistance was costly and, in the already straitened circumstances of Germany, proved the last straw leading to the complete unleashing of the printing presses, the great inflation, and the final and total collapse of the currency, with all the chaotic social consequences that such a condition implies.[18] Like

[18] The mark was worth 4,600,000 to the dollar in August, 1923, and 4,200,-000,000 in December. Inflation such as Germany knew does not greatly affect the wealth of the country as a whole, but it effects a chaotic redistribution of

it or no, as in 1918, Germany must once more acknowledge defeat, especially as there was fear that the political structure of the Reich stood in danger of disintegration.[19]

Poincaré would not enter into discussion save on the basis of a prior German surrender. A change of government in August brought Gustav Stresemann to the Chancellorship of Germany. Stresemann, of the *Deutsche Volkspartei,* a conservatively inclined group associated with large business, bowing before the inescapable necessity, began by withdrawing the legislation that had enacted passive resistance. This done, negotiations with France could be resumed.

A curious result ensued. Having won a clear victory, France in a sense surrendered it. Instead of securing political advantage or far-reaching economic arrangements between herself and Germany, by November Poincaré had allowed the intrusion of Anglo-American influence by agreeing to the constitution of two committees, one for the restoration of the German currency, the other, to be presided over by the American, General Dawes, to review the whole matter of Reparation. To a degree this may be seen as the result of Poincaré's own limited and legalistic outlook which failed to perceive and exploit the broader political implications of his own policy; but in a larger sense it was an expression of the limitations of French power.

One aspect of these limitations was the relative backwardness, in the economic and financial practice and thinking of France by comparison with Britain, America, and Germany. The overwhelming endorsement that the Chamber had given Poincaré when about to embark on the Ruhr expedition was misleading, based on the naïve view that "Germany will pay" if only sufficiently pressed. Germany had collapsed, but no payments had meantime been forthcoming, and the results were beginning to come home to roost of the careless management of French finances that had accumulated a huge debt for reconstruction on top of the wartime expenditure, all on the basis of the happy thought that Germany would reimburse it all. The franc, too, was beginning to show

---

property of which the middle class is the chief victim. Its social consequences are thus far greater than its economic; the youth of this bewildered and angered sector of society provided the best recruiting ground and much of the brains of the Nazi party.

[19] This period was the occasion for a revival of Rhenish separatism, but the movement could not long survive without the support of French bayonets and redounded to the discredit of French policy.

signs of weakness.[20] What appeared to the French elector was not large German payments but rather increased taxation; and the more liberally inclined segment of Parliament and the electorate, never too fond of Poincaré, was increasingly restive under the mounting criticism of French policy abroad. France's victory had, in the last analysis, been gained against an already defeated Germany. The outcome of this state of affairs was the defeat of Poincaré in the elections of the following May and the advent of a government, headed by Herriot, that represented the triumph of the *Cartel des Gauches*. France was resuming the more normal *sinistrisme* of her politics.[21]

REPARATION: THE DAWES PLAN. One of the issues of that election was that of acceptance of the so-called Dawes Plan which embodied the work of the experts who had been meeting in Paris from January to April, 1924. The scheme was finally adopted at a meeting in London in August. The restoration of German finances was to be assisted by an international loan, and for the next five years German Reparation payments would gradually rise from one billion to two and one-half billion marks, the transfer of which was to be in charge of an Agent General of Reparation in Berlin, under the supervision of a committee consisting of representatives of the United States, Britain, France, Italy, and Belgium. Nothing was said about the total of Reparation which presumably remained set by the London agreement of 1921.

The plan, based on a study of the German economy, represented a victory for those who had contended that Reparation was above all an economic issue; the principle of it was not questioned, but the discharge of the obligation was to be based on financial capacity. The "business" approach doubtless tended to remove much of the confusion resulting from the moral approach to an essentially financial question. No less significant, this was a victory for the Anglo-American view, the stamp of whose influence characterized the details of the scheme. These were in large degree of British inspiration, but the name of the American, Dawes, was given to the plan as a whole.

[20] From January to March the franc fell from 19.92 to 27.20 to the dollar. By May, with the impending acceptance of the Dawes Plan, it had risen again to 15.28 to the dollar.

[21] The word refers to what may be regarded as the "normal" tendency of the French electorate to favor the Left, a legacy of the revolutionary tradition and a measure of the respectability that attaches to the word "revolution" in France.

General Dawes had acted in this matter in the capacity of private citizen, for America still adhered officially to the position that she would have nothing to do with such European problems. Mention may appropriately be made at this point of the issue of the debts owed America by her wartime associates. These gave rise to not a little acrimony arising from two antithetic and irreconcilable views of the matter.

Owing to her unpreparedness and her late entrance into the war, America's military contribution had been relatively small. But, apart from the immeasurable factor of moral support, America had contributed large financial assistance; this had taken the form of loans to Britain, France, and others. If one took the view that the war was a joint enterprise for a common purpose, a strong case could be made for regarding the financial as America's contribution, that America should be glad to have made, hence cancellation of the Allied debts would seem no more than fair and reasonable. But if one took the view that America had no stake of her own in the outcome of the conflict, then what assistance she had given entitled her to gratitude, and repayment of it should be a point of honor. Apart from the fact that it is naturally easier for the debtor to perceive the validity of reasons for his exoneration, the dispute was involved in the then widespread view in America that she had been "bamboozled" into the war.[22] The British on the whole approached the entire question of war debts, whether due to America or owed by Germany, from the sensible standpoint of economic possibilities. In August, 1922, the Balfour note proposed all around cancellation of the financial obligations that grew out of the war.[23] But, in French eyes, for America to insist upon the collection of her debt while showing lenient inclination toward Germany's troubles easily took on the color of insult added to injury.

However that may be, the American view was best summed up in President Coolidge's terse comment, "Well, they hired the money," while any claim to a connection between the two sets of

[22] That issue is largely dead and it is both interesting and enlightening to note the manner in which America took to heart the lesson of the First World War debts. The useful fiction of Lend-Lease was the solution in the Second World War.

[23] In the refusal of the United States to entertain the suggestion, the British took the position that they would insist on collecting from their debtors only sufficient amounts to cover their own American obligation. Since they were creditors on balance, this policy may be regarded as dictated by intelligent understanding and enlightened generosity. The revival of international trade and the employment of her factory workers were more important to Britain than the collection of outstanding debts.

obligations was staunchly resisted. Nevertheless America did not press for immediate repayment and she was also willing to take into some account the difficulties of her debtors. In 1922 the Senate established the World War Debts Funding Commission and, between 1923 and 1926, arrangements were made with the various debtors.[24] With the conclusion of these agreements and the inauguration of the Dawes Plan the whole vexed issue of international financial obligations growing out of the First World War was removed from the domain of politics and feeling, and payment was duly made by all for a few years thereafter. Damage had been done nonetheless by the controversy and, in American eyes, France, using brute force in the Ruhr and last to come to terms on her own debts to America, was the greatest offender and obstacle to the restoration of genuine peace among the nations.

For, even under the more liberal dispensation of a government of the *Cartel des Gauches*, France was proceeding with caution *vis-à-vis* Germany. The inauguration of the Dawes Plan was to proceed alongside the evacuation of the Ruhr, which Herriot sought to make conditional upon the control of German disarmament. French suspicions on that score were not wholly devoid of foundation,[25] but somewhat lengthy and difficult negotiations finally led to an agreement: the Ruhr was evacuated by August, 1925, as well as the cities of Duisburg, Ruhrort, and Dusseldorf, occupied in 1921, and the evacuation of the British occupation zone of Cologne was likewise completed by the end of January, 1926. This last measure was tantamount to the assertion that Germany had lived up to the obligations of the treaty of peace and is connected with the name of Locarno, momentary symbol of a new era in the affairs of Europe. But before dealing with Locarno and the story of the large problem of security, it will be best to bring up to date developments in a different quarter.

THE NEAR EAST

The outstanding issue that dominated the international scene in 1922–1923 was undoubtedly that of Germany, be it in the

[24] Through a juggling of interest rates, adjusted to correspond to the varying financial capacities of the debtors, the debts were in effect substantially scaled down.

[25] Strictly speaking, Germany's violation of the disarmament provisions of the peace were not of great consequence (which made them also unwise and serving little purpose other than feeding suspicion), but General von Seeckt was doing excellent work in preserving the core of a future *Reichswehr* and especially a General Staff.

form of the possible consequences of domestic chaos in that country, of Reparation, or of Franco-German relations. But a close second to that issue arose from Near Eastern developments. In that quarter Germany was at this time a total stranger, her prewar interest in the Ottoman Empire having been completely destroyed. Yet, indirectly, the two issues were not unconnected, for just as Germany was a source of divergence between the two dominant Powers of the moment, Britain and France, so likewise Turkey was to be the scene of another aspect of the Anglo-French duel.

THE NEW TURKEY. The Treaty of Sèvres of August, 1920, had ostensibly written *finis* to the story of the Sick Man of Europe; its terms have been indicated.[26] Not only was the Ottoman Empire destroyed, but even in the Turkish homeland, the Straits, and the Anatolian peninsula, little independence was left; the feeble sultan had acquiesced in the intrusion of French, Italian, and Greek interests, plus independence or autonomy for Armenia and Kurdistan. But Turkey was destined to be the locale of a story that may well be described as both unique and romantic. As early as 1919, a young Turkish officer, Mustapha Kemal by name, associated with the Young Turk movement, had used the opportunity of a mission with which he had been entrusted to raise the standard of revolt in the interior of Anatolia, the remoteness of which put him beyond the reach of effective interference from the Powers or even from Constantinople. The sultan's writ of outlawry was a dead letter and, in January, 1920, Kemal had assembled a representative body of sorts which proclaimed in Ankara the Turkish Nationalist Pact, in effect a Turkish declaration of independence. The Straits were under international, mainly British, control, the French were in Cilicia, the Italians in Adalia, and the Greeks in Smyrna. The Greeks, relatively free of other distractions, could concentrate their attention and effort on the realization of the *megala idea*, a Greek-controlled Aegean empire. They were at war with Nationalist Turkey and their forces penetrated deeply into Anatolia during 1920. But the following year, after a period of military stabilization, saw a turning of the tide in the diplomatic no less than in the military field.

In March, 1921, Soviet Russia, friendly to all who were inimical

[26] See above, pp. 375–377.

to the dominant capitalist Powers, concluded a treaty with Nationalist Turkey. She relinquished the old Russian claim to Kars and Ardahan and furnished Kemal assistance in money and matériel. Shortly thereafter, in June, Italy, whose foreign policy was going through a phase of retrenchment, relinquished her claim to Adalia, and in October, France, following earlier military setbacks in Cilicia, adopted a similar course. The agreement negotiated by Franklin-Bouillon gave *de facto* recognition to the Kemalist government; the Sandjak of Alexandretta, adjacent to the Syrian mandate, was alone retained, and France supplied arms to Kemal. These agreements were resented by Britain who, quite correctly, saw in them a disintegration of the common front in the Near East. As between herself and France this was but another episode in the long tale of rivalry in that particular part of the world: France was maneuvering into a position of friendship with Turkey in opposition to which Britain was being isolated. Apart from her own small force at the Straits, Britain supported the Greeks, who constituted the bulk of active military opposition to the Turks. But, following a year of stability, the Greeks suffered a major defeat in September, 1921. Thereafter, the tide of battle moved on a steady course of uninterrupted Kemalist success, culminating in the Turkish entry into Smyrna in August, 1922. Literally and mercilessly, the Greeks were thrown into the sea amid much confusion. For Greece this was a major disaster and it had the domestic repercussions that might be expected.[27]

But larger international repercussions soon followed. The not unnaturally elated Turks moved toward the Straits where, in September, they faced the Allied occupying forces. Not only was Lloyd George unable to secure assistance from others, including the Dominions, but Poincaré ordered the withdrawal of the French contingent from Chanak on the Anatolian side of the Dardanelles.[28] It may be viewed as a measure of the statesmanship of Kemal that he declined to force the issue with Britain; on October 11, the armistice of Mudania between himself and the British and the Greeks ended hostilities, implying the final demise of the Treaty

[27] These events led to the abdication of King Constantine in September and to the trial and execution of some of his ministers. At the end of 1923 the Venizelists scored an overwhelming victory in the elections, the king left the country and Greece was proclaimed a republic in May, 1924.

[28] A discussion of unwonted violence ensued in a meeting between Poincaré and the British foreign secretary, Lord Curzon, who came out of it defeated and humiliated. This episode may be regarded as the low point in Anglo-French relations.

of Sèvres where Turkey proper was concerned. The Turkish Nationalists were allowed to administer Constantinople and proceeded to abolish the Sultanate in November. Kemal had made good the claim to independence and Turkey was launched on the path of modernization to which she has since essentially adhered. The Turkish revolution presents a fairly rare example in history, but the domestic record of her rejuvenation does not belong in these pages.

This may be pointed out, however. During October and November, 1922, France had surrendered her claims in Anatolia and accepted the prospect of a review of Reparation by an international body; these acts hardly constituted assertions of superior and successful power; at the same time, France had a stranglehold on Germany, who had just acknowledged defeat by giving up passive resistance, and with unusual harshness Poincaré had stood up to, not to say put in his place, the British foreign minister, Curzon. It is not difficult to understand that the more sensational manifestations of French power should be misread into a false estimate of the extent of that power.[29]

In any case, at the turn from 1922 to 1923, the German and the Turkish problems were the two issues that dominated the diplomacy of Europe. The first of these has been dealt with. During the first half of 1923 negotiations proceeded at Lausanne; they were lengthy and difficult at times but finally yielded the Treaty of Lausanne, signed on July 24, the international birth certificate of the new Turkey. Save that the Straits were to be demilitarized, Turkey was to be free of all servitudes (Capitulations were abolished); besides the Anatolian mainland, she retained Eastern Thrace in Europe.

The treaty also provided for what was essentially an innovation: the solution of a problem of nationalism through an exchange of populations. Save for those resident in Constantinople, the Greeks of Turkey were to go to Greece whence the Turks were to leave for Turkey. Inevitably, not a little hardship fell to the lot of individuals in the transfer of populations, yet the exchange was the result of a negotiated agreement and on balance proved an orderly procedure. That long-standing and seemingly unchange-

[29] If there was in Britain objection to and fear of the manifestations of French power, hence antagonism to it, the situation appeared in a different light to others who saw in it an indication of an Anglo-French *quid pro quo*, whereby France had given Britain a free hand in the Near East in exchange for British acquiescence in a free hand for France where Germany was concerned.

able component of eastern Mediterranean affairs, Greco-Turkish enmity, was thus dissolved, and before long coöperation and even a measure of friendship came to prevail between the two countries. It is an interesting reflection that our time was destined to see the closing of a story the beginning of which goes back two and a half millennia. The later rebirth of Israel to political independence is a comparable illustration of the continuity and persistence of historic development.

THE ARAB WORLD. The Turkey of Kemal was nationalistic, but thoughts of empire it did not entertain. The Arab world, formally severed from Turkey at Sèvres, was not affected by the Treaty of Lausanne save in the case of Iraq. The Turkish claim to the vilayet of Mosul, in which a substantial Kurdish element existed, proved impossible of resolution at Lausanne, where it was agreed instead to leave the matter to the League's decision. In October, 1924, the Council laid a provisional frontier, the so-called Brussels Line, which, after some further delay, became essentially the frontier between Iraq and Turkey, leaving to the former virtually the entire vilayet of Mosul.[30] Opposition to the British mandate also came from Mesopotamia itself; it was resolved by a treaty that Britain concluded with King Faisal, son of the King of Hejaz, whose election to the Iraqi throne the British had procured in August, 1921.

This election of Emir Faisal to the Iraqi throne was by way of compensation for his failure to secure the crown in Syria and Palestine. In the former territory the French had to resort to force to establish themselves in control of the mandate assigned to them, but General Weygand, the High Commissioner, succeeded in pacifying the land, for a time at least.

To the south of Syria, Palestine was another British mandate. The British interest in Palestine was primarily strategic, deriving from the proximity of the Suez Canal. But the situation was complicated by the intrusion of the Zionist claim to which the Balfour declaration of 1917 had given ambiguous support. The

[30] The matter was complicated by the presence of minorities: the Kurds, whom Turkey wanted to absorb and assimilate, and a group of Chaldean Christians. In addition, oil interests also intruded. The British rested their claim on a pre-1914 Turkish concession granted to the Turkish Petroleum Company, the German share in which (25 percent) was transferred to France. American interests also secured a share in Mosul.

British High Commissioner, Sir Herbert Samuel, endeavored with fair success, first to establish, then to maintain, the peace. By way of further appeasement of the Arabs, in 1923 the Palestinian mandate was divided into Palestine proper and Transjordan, which became autonomous under another son of the Sherif of Mecca, Abdullah, brother of King Faisal of Iraq.

These arrangements point to the lasting significance of dynastic relations and ambitions in the Arab world. In the remaining part of that world, the bulk of the Arabian peninsula, the rivalry between Sherif Hussein of Mecca and Ibn Saud, leader of the puritanical Wahabi sect, dominated the scene. The British dealt with both during the war. The fortunes of Hussein seemed to be rising, with himself in control of Hejaz and the Holy Places, and his two sons, Faisal and Abdullah, established in Iraq and Transjordan respectively.

But in the meantime Hussein's incautious ambitions and intransigeance lost him much support in Arab quarters; hostilities between himself and Ibn Saud proceeded sporadically, their course generally favorable to the latter. Hussein's assumption of the title of caliph in March, 1924, after the government of the new Turkey had declared the abolition of that office, proved the last straw. Resuming hostilities, Ibn Saud entered Mecca in October, 1924. Extending and consolidating his control, he created the state of Saudi Arabia. But the combination of religious differences—the Wahabis in control of the Holy Places—with dynastic rivalries— Ibn Saud in Arabia proper and the Hashemite dynasty in Iraq and Transjordan—was to provide a lasting source of division within the Arab world. Facilitated by the nomadic character of the desert people, raiding and counterraiding took place across frontiers that were not formally agreed upon until November, 1925, frontiers which, in addition, bore little relation to the facts of economic reality.

The nineteenth-century Egyptian ambition—Mohamed Ali's— to play a role of leadership among the Arabs was by no means abandoned. The war had made Egypt a British protectorate; the end of the conflict saw the emergence of the Wafd party, dedicated to the achievement of independence. Suppressed at first, subsequent negotiations between the British and the Wafd failed to produce agreement, but in February, 1922, Britain unilaterally announced the end of her protectorate, reserving certain rights pending the conclusion of a treaty with Egypt.[31] On March 15, Fuad I assumed the title of king.

II. The Search for Stability

A great revulsion against war was induced by the First World War; it had found expression in the introduction in the peace settlements of that innovation, the Covenant of the League, the first formal attempt at the international organization of peace. But there is many a slip between the cup and the lip. The debate which attended the drafting of the Covenant in 1919 has been mentioned; the fact that the Covenant emerged as an essentially Anglo-American document meant that the issue of what the real powers of the League were had been left unresolved. In simple fact, the League could be no more than the collection of its members, and its significance and fate would depend upon what these would make of it. The League was no supranational creation, standing above its component parts, but rather an experiment the future fate of which time alone could unfold.

THE FRENCH SYSTEM

The League, therefore, inevitably and to a large extent, depended upon the power of its larger members; since Germany and Russia were not among them and the United States had chosen to repudiate its own creation, this meant once more Britain and France.[32] The fundamental purpose of the League was to preserve the peace and to safeguard the security of all. In view of the overwhelming concern of France with security, the League might therefore be expected to be for her an attractive conception; it had indeed a strong and definite appeal, especially to those elements in France, primarily the Left in politics, responsive to the humanitarian, internationalistic outlook and tradition; but even these felt that the League should be endowed with concrete power. As to the more conservative and nationalistic elements in control of the government after the war, their attitude was rather of

---

[31] Such a treaty was not signed until 1936. The rights reserved by Britain in 1932 had to do with the security of imperial communications (the Suez), the defense of Egypt, the protection of foreign interests and of minorities, and the Anglo-Egyptian Sudan.

[32] Of the other Great Powers, Japan was essentially extraneous to European affairs and Italy was hampered by her weakness. Moreover, the advent of Fascism in 1922 brought into power a system unsympathetic to the League ideology.

reticence and suspicion; the League, in so far as it had any value, might serve to enlist others in defense of the *status quo*.

Correspondingly, among the defeated, Russia included and for that matter excluded at first, the tendency was to regard the League as a device designed to perpetuate the *status quo* of their own impotence and inferiority, a disguised coalition of the victors. In Britain the League ideal found genuine and sympathetic response but ran counter to the tradition that forbade the assumption of too far-reaching and too specific commitments in time of peace.

The League, therefore, began its life under at best uncertain auspices. Clearly, under the most favorable circumstances, it could not become at once a substitute for past conditions, and in no case could the role of power be ignored. This was made clear in 1920, the first year of the League's existence, and at the first meeting of the Assembly, which took place at the end of that year in Geneva, henceforth the seat of the organization.

The balance of power had been a long-honored principle of the community of states, mitigator of the anarchy implicit in the principle of sovereignty. It had led to the combination of shifting alliances, finally crystallized before 1914 into the two great rival blocs of European nations. Yet the balance of power had proved incapable of preserving the peace and, after the war, the pre-1914 system of alliances was widely regarded as responsible for the cataclysm that had engulfed the world. The very nature of the war had had considerable influence on the shape of the peace: defeated Germany was morally condemned and disarmed; there was no balance of power in Europe after 1919. Yet, curiously, the ostensible chief beneficiary of victory among the great continental Powers did not feel secure; this may have seemed a paradox after the war, yet, as events were to confirm, was based on an essentially sound view of the long-term deficiencies and limitations of French power.

France, therefore, had sought guarantees for the future. The best of them, the Anglo-American reinsurance, had ultimately been denied her; she thus felt impelled to organize security by other means, and out of this there grew what may be called the French system or the French organization (or at least attempted organization) of Europe in the form of a renewed system of alliances. As early as September, 1920, a Franco-Belgian alliance was concluded. After the German destruction of the guarantee of the neutrality of Belgium in 1914, the protection of French power seemed, from the Belgian point of view, a desirable substitute,[33] while for France, Belgium, though small, represented a valuable asset, whether in terms of strategy or resources.

Traditionally, French power had sought to counterbalance Central European, whether Habsburg or Hohenzollern, through eastern European connections; Turkey, Sweden, and Poland, and Russia more latterly, had had important places in the calculations of French diplomacy. In postwar Europe, Russia was not only in chaos but she was largely inimical, and France in fact became the prime exponent of the policy of Russian containment, then advocated under the name of *cordon sanitaire*. But a fairly large Poland had once more appeared on the map of Europe. Seen from Warsaw, the outside world held two great dangers that bore the names of her two large and normally powerful neighbors to the east and the west. France had assisted Poland in her war with Russia in 1920–1921. Circumstances were such that, be it toward Russia or Germany, the interests of France and Poland coincided to a large degree, a fact that found expression in the conclusion of a treaty of alliance between the two countries in February, 1921.

The Franco-Polish alliance also has interest as a reflection in its form of the changed circumstances of the post-war period. Professing their wish to protect the peace and their security "by the maintenance of the treaties which both have signed," and paying homage to the League, the treaty went to specify that

. . . if, notwithstanding the sincerely peaceful aims and intentions of the two contracting states, either or both of them should be attacked without giving provocation, the two governments shall take concerted measures for the defense of their territory and the protection of their legitimate interests, within the limits specified in the preamble.

The treaty was defensive in intent, and the way to preserve the peace was to maintain the *status quo*. A defensive Polish-Rumanian alliance in March may be regarded as a logical corollary of the Franco-Polish in that aspect of it which looked to maintaining stability in Eastern Europe.

It was in 1921 also that there came into existence the combi-

[33] Belgium would have preferred a tripartite arrangement that would have included Britain as well as France in her protection, but in face of the British reluctance to undertake such a commitment Belgium had to be content with the French alliance alone.

nation known as the Little Entente—so called from its being regarded as a smaller edition of the larger pre-1914 combination—as the result of the conclusion of three bilateral treaties that linked in pairs Czechoslovakia, Yugoslavia, and Rumania. These states, wholly or in large part emerged from the former Austro-Hungarian Empire, had in common the fear of a possible Habsburg restoration rather than of German aggression. The Little Entente was dedicated above all to the maintenance of the Treaty of Trianon, Hungarian revisionism being more intense than Austrian.[34] France had no quarrel with Hungary, having, in fact, to some extent been sympathetically inclined toward that country at the time of the peacemaking. But France had a large stake in the principle of opposition to revisionism and for that reason she was sympathetic to the aims of the Little Entente. Moreover, Czechoslovakia, though not possessed of former German territory, had an extended common frontier with Germany, along which resided the German-speaking Sudeten minority. Czechoslovakia thus became the connecting link between France and the Little Entente with the conclusion of a Franco-Czech alliance in January, 1924.[35]

Thus, by the middle twenties, a system for the organization of Europe had taken shape, which may well be called the French system. The three great problems of Europe—Germany, Russia and Danubia—were all provided for and for all the solution is best described by the phrase *quieta non movere*. The only gap in the network of alliances just described lay in the failure to effect a Polish-Czech connection, all efforts at making which foundered on the stumbling block of friction between the two countries, specifically on the issue of Teschen.

Save for this relatively minor flaw there was great strength in the French system, strength that derived from the totality of power that its participants commanded, no less than from the bond of common interest in preserving for all the fruits of vic-

[34] In March, 1921, ex-King Charles appeared in Hungary. Allied remonstrations and a Czech ultimatum caused him to withdraw. He returned once more in October, and although the Hungarian government successfully maintained itself, Czechoslovakia in particular insisted, even after his removal to Madeira, upon the enactment of legislation in Hungary that excluded the Habsburgs from the throne. As a consequence, Hungary retained nominally the monarchical form of government, but existed as a Kingdom without a king, pending whose arrival his place was held by a regent.

[35] The network of connections was completed with the conclusion of a Franco-Rumanian treaty in January, 1926, and a Franco-Yugoslav alliance in November, 1927.

tory. Nevertheless, there were flaws in the system, to the extent in fact that it may be said to have been built on false foundations. If the element of common interest was a solid binder, there were also the inevitable divergences that are part of any alliance. The common focus of the Little Entente was Hungary, but Rumania was even more concerned with Russia while Yugoslavia stood in fear of Italy.[36]

More serious was the fact that the political solution of the problem of Danubia, such as it was, contributed little to the solution of its no less important economic difficulties; though to speak, as often has been done, of the unwisdom of the destruction of Austria-Hungary, is essentially to put the cart before the horse, for that state succumbed to the force of nationalism with which it proved itself incapable of dealing. However, this did not alter the fact that the erection of a host of barriers in a large region where free trade had formerly prevailed made difficult the existence of an area in much of which the standard of life was none too high.

Czechoslovakia was a favored exception with an unusually well balanced internal economy, but most of Central-Eastern Europe was predominantly agricultural. France, largely self-sufficient, was not the logical complement of Danubia, which in the economic sense rather belongs with industrial Germany. French capital, though less available than before 1914, did to a point play a role comparable to that which it had played in tsarist Russia, but French loans usually had a large political content and tended to be used, in part at least, for armaments rather than for productive purposes.

Even more serious than the economic factor was the less ponderable one which may be put under the head of psychological or moral. If the totality of power gathered in the French system was considerable, France was in the combination much the most important single unit, without which the system would have little value. France was indeed attached to her security, but the mass of her people were at heart too deficient in aggressive will. An illustration may perhaps best explain a judgment that may seem to run counter to the widely accepted belief in French aggressiveness at the time. To the French people, the prospect of a number of Polish divisions attacking Germany in the event of German ag-

[36] The role of Russia and of Italy during this period will be examined later. See below, pp. 425 ff.

gression against France was indeed pleasing and attractive. But, naturally, the Polish interest in the alliance likewise derived from its value to the defense of Poland. Should Poland be attacked France would have to take the initiative of offensive action against Germany. No one in France raised at this time the later cry, "Why die for Danzig?" but French thinking and sentiment were too exclusively focused on France's *defense*, on holding the line of the Rhine. It was not many years before the flaws and weaknesses inherent in this outlook were to become apparent.

Had French power been greater than it was, provided one include under the heading of power that imponderable component, will, no less than natural resources, the French system might have been no less successful than Bismarck's. The system could exist and operate quite independently of the League and was in fact widely regarded as inimical to the spirit at least of the Genevan organization, owing to the implied distrust of the ability of the League to fulfill its peace-preserving function.[37] But there is another point of view, perhaps more realistic, that would simply take cognizance of the limitations of the League though not denying its validity or the desirability of its purpose: pending the day when all could depend on the League for their safety, any strengthening of security in a limited area would be a contribution to the larger ultimate purpose. The Franco-Polish treaty, for example, ostensibly professed the allegiance of its makers to the League; unlike pre-1914 alliances, its terms were public and duly registered in Geneva.

THE ISSUE OF SECURITY VERSUS DISARMAMENT

The war had had another, more limited, effect than that of inducing general and widespread revulsion against its recurrence. The old maxim, *si vis pacem para bellum*, honored before 1914

[37] The whole issue is implied here of whether regional combinations enhance or hinder the function of the wider world organization. That issue, much debated thirty years ago, has not been resolved. Both NATO and the Warsaw alliance of the present time purport to be defensive combinations, intended to make peace more secure, for all that they are in fact rival alliances.

The comparison between the two attempts to organize Europe in peace around one dominant Power is full of interest. The main differences are to be seen in the fact that Bismarck's Germany commanded greater relative power, that Bismarck did not run into the opposition of other Great Powers save one, and that his policies were not hampered by serious divisions in domestic opinion, to say nothing of the easier economic situation of his time. In the last analysis, the positive factor of excessive German power and the negative one of deficient French power were both major contributory causes in the outbreak of war in 1914 and in 1939 respectively.

as again in our day, was after the First World War considered a pernicious fallacy. Looking to the arms race before 1914, arms in themselves were regarded as one of the major causes of war. The partial truth of this view obscured a larger fallacy that amounted to a reversal of the order of causation: the accumulation of weapons is essentially the result and not the cause of a more fundamental condition, insecurity.[38] At any rate there was, after the war, widespread acceptance of the desirability of disarmament, or at least the reduction of armaments, and this became one of the chief concerns of Geneva.

The ten-year story of the efforts at agreement on the reduction of arms and of the attendant discussions, in Geneva and elsewhere, is one long sorry record of frustration. It may be summed up, in a nutshell, as an interminable and never resolved debate: Security versus Disarmament. To those that claimed that in the reduction of arms lay the path to greater security, the answer came forever: we shall disarm as soon as, or to the extent that, our security is guaranteed. The former position had the advantage of relative, and at least apparent, simplicity, while the latter tended to bog down discussion in the hopeless, yet inevitable, insistence on finding some concrete measure for security; for that reason it was open to the charge of disingenuousness on the part of its proponents. Yet it is clear that manpower is no less important than industrial potential, to say nothing of the less ponderable components of power.

The positions taken in the debate were the reflections of technical conditions and resulted in a broad division between land and naval Powers. The latter were more inclined to put reliance on trust; should their confidence prove mistaken, apart from the fact that important naval armaments would be difficult of surreptitious preparation, the natural protection that is provided by the oceans would make their error not irretrievable, and time would be granted them to organize their defense. Land Powers are in a different position, for it had become no less true that the British fleet could be of little use in the defense of Paris or Berlin. In the narrow confines of Europe, land Powers might quickly be

[38] To be sure, an armaments race tends to become a vicious circle and, undoubtedly, the mere existence of vast quantities of explosive material may enhance the likelihood of explosion. But we are now generally convinced that in strength lies the best guarantee of peace, though still endeavoring to deal with the outward manifestations rather than with the fundamental causes of insecurity.

overrun—what was the Schlieffen Plan? Land Powers therefore tended to be more insistent on prior carefully designed guarantees and elaborate schemes of inspection. The difference between the two positions was honest difference of opinion, not one between good and evil men: land Powers knew invasion, a concept possessed of little concrete reality in Britain and America. Given the circumstances of the time and the position of French power, it was but natural that the disarmament debate should in large measure be one between France and the English-speaking peoples. It did not add to the popularity of French policy with the latter.[39]

Nevertheless, from the beginning, the Assembly of the League had set up a Permanent Consultative Commission to look into the question of armaments, and in 1921 the Council appointed a Temporary Mixed Commission to examine the political, as well as the more limited military, aspects of the matter. In September, 1921, the Third Assembly of the League adopted the so-called Resolution XIV, a good expression of the thought of the time on the score of disarmament. The Resolution expressed the view that reduction of armaments should be general in order to be successful; that it should be a function for the various states, considering their peculiar positions, of the degree of their security; and that security could be provided by a general defensive agreement. This last point was qualified by the provision that "the obligation to render assistance to the country attacked shall be limited in principle to those countries situated in the same part of the globe." While indicating preference for a general treaty, the Resolution regarded regional arrangements (the French alliances) as permissible.

The atmosphere of 1922–1923 that saw the Franco-German issue reach its climax and that witnessed a low point in the climate of Anglo-French relations seemed hardly favorable to the enhancement of either disarmament or the general progress of the League. Nevertheless, a Draft Treaty of Mutual Assistance was elaborated

[39] It might be added that the defeated and disarmed Powers, Germany in particular, when she participated in the disarmament discussions, took the position that it was up to others to fulfill the promise of the Covenant by reducing their arms to the level of those that were disarmed. This was an effective debating position which turned into a claim for equality on whatever bases might be agreed by others. Russia, likewise, sought to make a virtue of necessity and favored reduction of armaments. The German and the Russian, however, were mere provisional positions, reflections of their weakness. What both countries were really interested in was, quite naturally, the recovery of their position of power.

and submitted by the League to members as well as to nonmembers at the end of 1923. The year 1924 saw a considerable change: the thorny Reparation issue was taken out of politics, Herriot replaced Poincaré after the French election, and Britain had her first Labour government under Ramsay MacDonald.[40] However, be it Labour, Conservative, or Liberal, the bulk of British opinion was not prepared at this time to undertake unspecified commitments beyond a narrow range that might at most include the Rhine; in addition, the Dominions, whose voice carried important weight in London, were even more provincial in their outlook: the Vistula seemed far away indeed in Ottawa or in Melbourne. This is how it came to pass that Britain, in a sense the most international of states, rejected the Draft Treaty in July, 1924, a rejection that signalized the death of this particular attempt.

Nevertheless, the team MacDonald-Herriot was symbolic of the altered mood of Europe in 1924; albeit somewhat in the abstract, it also held high the banner of international coöperation. Thanks to the work of able representatives of smaller powers, Beneš of Czechoslovakia and Politis of Greece in particular, what differences there were between the British and the French outlooks were reconciled in the Protocol for the Pacific Settlement of International Disputes, known for short as the Geneva Protocol. Taken up in the Assembly in October, the Protocol received unanimous endorsement.

The heart of the Geneva Protocol was expressed in the trinomial "arbitration, security, disarmament." States would agree henceforth that disputes between them, unless they fell under the jurisdiction of the Permanent Court of International Justice, would be amenable to arbitration. Aggression, a concept so recalcitrant to precise definition in law, would be the mere fact of refusal to accept arbitration, or the verdict of it. Should this occur, a majority of two-thirds of the Council would decide upon sanctions against the aggressor state, and this decision of the Council would become binding on all members.

Here was hopeful development indeed, all the more so that, as a genuine compromise, it represented substantial British concessions—the assumption of undetermined commitments—no less

[40] Actually a Labour-Liberal coalition since no party came out of the election of December, 1923, with an absolute majority. This situation naturally limited the freedom of operation of Labour over whose program the Liberals retained a power of veto.

than French concessions—putting trust in the untested League rather than in existing superiority of power. The small Powers were enthusiastic and a number of ratifications, the French among them, were soon forthcoming to Geneva.

But once again a stumbling block developed that was of British source. The unstable Labour-Liberal coalition having gone down in defeat, an election in November, 1924, yielded a clear Conservative majority that brought Stanley Baldwin to the Prime Ministership with Austen Chamberlain at the Foreign Office. If British Conservatives were perhaps less provincial than their Labour opponents, as a group they were also less responsive to the internationalist outlook; they were more accurate reflectors of the tradition that would encompass specific and limited commitments, if any. In March, 1925, Chamberlain, speaking in Geneva, announced his government's rejection of the Geneva Protocol, thereby spreading consternation in the ranks of the internationalist fraternity.

One may well speculate on what the subsequent course of events might have been had Britain shown on this occasion willingness to shoulder responsibilities that in the end she could not dodge, and wonder at the irony of the British decision at the very time when France showed willingness to abandon the path of intransigeance. Here, at any rate, was a prime illustration of the failure of the two chief Powers of Europe to work in harmony for the good of all no less than for their own. Yet all hope was not lost, for the British awareness of widespread criticism was an important factor in inducing Britain to be the sponsor of what came to be, shortly thereafter, the high point of international coöperation between the two World Wars, the Locarno agreements.

Before considering this development, however, brief mention should be made of armaments at sea. The difficulties surrounding the problem of reduction of armaments on land has been indicated. Matters were, or rather seemed to be for a time, more promising where naval armaments were concerned. Having retreated from Europe and her complexities, the United States had but a relatively secondary interest in land armaments, and the American military establishment had been largely dismantled after the war. But on the seas the United States emerged from the war as a Power second to none. Sharing, however, the widespread desire to reduce the burden of armaments as well as the belief in their causal function of conflict, it was appropriate that the United States should take the initiative in calling for a conference in Washington to deal with naval armaments.

The Washington Naval Conference met from November, 1921, to February, 1922, and achieved limited results. Its proceedings were simplified by the fact that five Powers only were involved: the United States and Britain were exclusively, or at least overwhelmingly, naval Powers; Japan put equal stress on naval and on land power; France and Italy were primarily concerned with the land, but were also possessed of substantial maritime interests and establishments. The United States enjoyed the asset of its overwhelming resources which, in the event of failure of agreement, would enable it far to outdistance all others in naval construction. Between itself and the British no substantial difficulty developed as a consequence of Britain's acceptance, with both good grace and wisdom, of the new American power: correctly postulating the unlikelihood of an Anglo-American conflict, Britain abandoned the claim to the two-power standard.

Faced with the discrepancy between America's and her own resources, Japan yielded to the American contention that the two-ocean situation warranted the existence of a larger American fleet. The French navy had been relatively neglected during the war and France was only partly successful in resisting the attempt to freeze naval power on the basis of existing levels. France was in fact more concerned with the Italian claim to parity with herself, which she opposed with an argument similar to that used by America *vis-à-vis* Japan: overall parity with Italy would mean inferiority for her in the Mediterranean; moreover, France had imperial commitments such as Italy did not have. It was a measure of France's power and of her isolation at Washington that in the end she yielded.

But the results of the Washington Conference were both limited and qualified. The fifteen-year treaty that was signed by the five Powers in February, 1922, established tonnage ratios of 5:5:3:1.67:1.67 for America, Britain, Japan, France, and Italy respectively; these ratios, however, only applied to the tonnage of capital ships (over 10,000 tons). Lighter ships and submarines, the poor man's weapon, despite American and British efforts, had to be excluded. The future was to show the limitations of the value of agreements obtained, partly at least, by coercion: Japan and France both felt that they had received rather less than due justice.

At Washington Britain had had to face another important decision. Unable to induce America to participate in her own alliance with Japan, she abandoned this alliance for the compromise of a Four-Power treaty, France being included in the arrangement, that guaranteed the *status quo* in the Pacific.[41] Of secondary importance for Europe, though highly significant in the Far East, was the Nine-Power treaty that sought to stabilize the international situation of China, at the time involved in domestic chaos. Powerless China had to rely for her defense mainly on the United States whose chief aim at this time was to prevent Japanese encroachment on the mainland of Asia.[42]

III. The Seeming Triumph of Collective Security

In Europe, the year 1924 had seemed a turning point in the story of the liquidation of the war. Germany was restored to domestic financial order and apparently wedded to the policy of fulfillment of her obligations. With the sympathetic support of Britain and others, and with a moderate government in France, she might, gradually and by peaceful means, regain her place in Europe. This was Stresemann's aim. Stresemann's character and his ultimate purpose have been the subject of much controversy. But there is little cause to debate the ultimate goal of his vision. Whether Germany would in the end become a peaceful member of the European community, satisfied with a proper place in the whole, or whether she would ultimately resume dreams of domination, she had in any case a long distance to travel before achieving mere equality. Toward this first goal Stresemann's efforts were directed; he was a patriotic German and a realist who understood that, in her position of weakness, a policy of conciliation and fulfillment would be the most rewarding.

THE LOCARNO AGREEMENTS

The idea of assuaging France's everlasting fears by giving her a freely consented guarantee of her eastern frontier appears in

[41] Britain's abandonment of the alliance rankled in Japan, who saw in the Four-Power treaty an implied Anglo-American alliance—not a wholly false interpretation—and an arrangement into which racial overtones could be read in addition.

[42] The Nine-Power treaty of February, 1922, asserted the sovereignty, independence, and the territorial and administrative integrity of China; it also reaffirmed the principle of the Open Door. Some concessions were made to China as in the promise, embodied in a separate convention, to abolish extraterritoriality when the domestic organization of China would have become such as to make such privileges unnecessary.

Germany as early as 1922.[43] It was premature at the time, but in the changed atmosphere of 1925, Stresemann, supported by the British ambassador in Berlin, Lord d'Abernon, thought the time ripe to revive the idea. Moreover, this was the time when the Geneva Protocol was becoming moribund and the question of the evacuation of the Ruhr had become entangled with the issue of Germany's fulfillment of her disarmament obligations; an Allied note in January, indicating German remissiveness, might hold for Germany the danger of a revived Anglo-Franco-Belgian coalition.

On February 9, 1925, a first German proposal, purposely loose and flexible, and which may be regarded as the opening step in formal negotiations, was submitted to the Allied governments. It evoked a guarded response at first in both Paris and London, but in March Austen Chamberlain mentioned his sympathy for the proposal. In France a favorable development occurred in the form of the overthrow of Herriot in April; Aristide Briand was foreign minister in the succeeding Cabinet. Like Stresemann, and even more than Stresemann, the figure of Briand dominates the second half of the twenties; his virtually uninterrupted tenure at the Quai d'Orsay, until his death in 1932, covers the brief span of years during which it was widely felt that the war had been truly and finally liquidated and that the League was taking on real significance. Of this atmosphere, Briand, as much as any other single European statesman, was both symbol and earnest promoter. Having securely tied his political fortunes to the star of Franco-German reconciliation, Briand was definitely sympathetic to the German proposal.

Negotiations proceeded during 1925, involving mainly Paris, Berlin, and London. By September 1, sufficient progress had been made for a committee of jurists to assemble in London in order to draft definite texts, on the basis of which the Powers gathered at Locarno in October to iron out final differences. The tone of the meeting and the relations among its participants are best described as a love fest; the "spirit of Locarno" of friendly compromise and accommodation has passed into the language as a phrase: on the evening of October 16, the collection of instruments that together constituted the Locarno Pact were signed.

[43] In December, 1922, the German ambassador to Washington approached the American Secretary of State, Hughes, with a suggestion that Germany and France pledge themselves to the United States not to resort to war for a generation. The awkwardly worded proposal was rejected by Poincaré as a "clumsy maneuver."

These consisted of the final protocol signed by all the participants, that is, Britain, France, Germany, Italy, Belgium, Czechoslovakia, and Poland, and of three categories of documents. These were:

1. Five annexes made up of

The main Rhineland Pact or Treaty of Mutual Guarantee between Germany, Belgium, France, Britain, and Italy;

Two identical Arbitration Conventions between Germany on one side and France and Belgium, respectively, on the other;

Two identical Arbitration Conventions between Germany and Poland and Czechoslovakia, respectively.

2. A collective note to Germany from the other Powers that gave an interpretation of Article 16 of the Covenant of the League.

3. Two identical treaties between France on one side and Poland and Czechoslovakia, respectively, on the other.

The first annex, the Rhineland Pact, often and mistakenly thought of as the entire Locarno arrangement, was undoubtedly the most important instrument. That which no French government during the whole period from 1871 to 1914 had ever been able or willing to do, a freely given acceptance of the Franco-German frontier, a German government was now prepared to underwrite: the frontier established by the Treaty of Versailles between Germany on one side, France and Belgium on the other, was guaranteed by the five signatories, as well as the provisions that established the demilitarized zone of Germany. Save in self-defense or in fulfillment of League obligations, France, Germany, and Belgium renounced the resort to war, and differences between them were to be settled by peaceful means in accordance with the procedures specified in the Arbitration Conventions.[44]

A breach of Article 2 of the Rhineland Pact or of Articles 42 or 43 of the Treaty of Versailles would entitle the aggrieved party to the immediate assistance of the other contracting parties. The Council would, in any event, be seized of the question, and all undertook to abide by its recommendations if concurred in by all save those engaged in the dispute.[45]

The German-Polish and German-Czech Arbitration Conven-

[44] Article 2 of the Rhineland Pact specified that a violation of Articles 42 and 43 of the Treaty of Versailles, those establishing the demilitarized zone of Germany, would constitute a case of self-defense for France, a provision that was to be of crucial significance in 1936.

[45] The Rhineland Pact also specified that the provisions of the Treaty of Versailles and those of the Dawes Plan remained unaffected by the new arrangements of Locarno. The final signature of these arrangements took place in London on December 1, after which ratifications were shortly forthcoming.

tions were identical with those between Germany and France and Belgium, but there was no equivalent of the Rhineland Pact for the frontiers of Germany with Czechoslovakia and Poland.

The Collective Note, taking into consideration the special conditions of Germany, specifically her disarmed state, explained that the obligations deriving from Article 16 of the Covenant were to be fulfilled to an extent compatible with the military situation and the geographical position of the members.

Finally, the treaties between France and Poland and between France and Czechoslovakia provided for immediate mutual assistance in the event of an unprovoked German attack. This was stated to be in fulfillment of Article 16 of the Covenant, with the further proviso that the commitment of mutual assistance would be operative, under Article 15, paragraph 7 of the same Covenant, even in the event of failure of unanimous decision in the Council.

Not many years passed before Mussolini was to observe that "the spirit of Locarno" had evaporated. Locarno represents nonetheless an important landmark in the story of the postwar era; the failure of the hopes that it embodied, and of the expectations that it in turn served to raise, does not detract from its significance. Locarno therefore warrants some closer analysis. The German contribution certainly was large, in the form of renunciation of any territorial claims in the West and of the acceptance of the disabilities embodied in Articles 42 and 43 of the Treaty of Versailles. But, unlike this last instrument, Locarno could not by any stretch of the imagination be called a *diktat*. Germany's signature was now freely given and the fact that she had negotiated as an equal represented a substantial gain for her. The guarantee of the western frontier as such may be seen as an unusually happy and skillful device, for it gave France the insurance that she craved without branding Germany with the stigma of unilateral suspicion. This was Britain's special contribution, as well as Italy's, though the latter country shared in the arrangement more from the feeling that it would have been awkward not to do so than from the positive motivation of genuine conviction. The French professed no aggressive intentions; but it must be remembered that, if their negative preoccupation with their own security was the authentic motivation of their policy, suspicion of their motives was also widespread in many quarters, as the phrase "French hegemony" in Europe bespeaks.

France was divided on the score of how to insure her security. Suspicion of Germany was widespread, but on the alternatives of coercion and conciliation sentiment varied. Poincaré and Briand were the authentic representatives of these contrasting views. In 1924, the *bleu horizon* Chamber, expression of war-induced emotion, gave way to one controlled by a coalition of the Left; Poincaré and his works were repudiated; Herriot, then Briand, took his place.[46] But if Briand was the apt representative of the current in France which held that Germans need not be regarded as irrevocably and congenitally aggressive, that the tendency of which German Social Democracy was the expression might become established in secure control, no responsible French statesman could be expected merely to throw away the solid and concrete assets that France possessed. These were of two kinds, the Treaty of Versailles and the alliances. Locarno therefore was a compromise: if Germany was to be admitted to the League, thereby implying that her moral probation was ended, the disarmament clauses of Versailles remained.

The matter of alliances was perhaps more delicate, and the solution in this case was also a compromise that was not devoid of some ambiguity. It took the form of asserting the compatibility of the French alliances with Czechoslovakia and Poland with the rest of the Locarno arrangements. But French assistance to these countries would be deprived of meaning if the possibility of French offensive action were ruled out. What effect would such a contingency have on the Rhineland Pact? Germany would not renounce the claim to frontier changes in the East, and there was no British, or other, guarantee of those frontiers. Clearly, a situation might occur where opinion in the Council would fail of unanimity. The answer was the provision mentioned before of the automatic and immediate operation of the French alliances.

Even so there were qualms, especially in Warsaw. The Poles were more realistic judges than the British, who persistently re-

[46] The Left, broadly speaking, inclined toward the internationalistic outlook and was sensitive to the charge of militarism often leveled against France, especially when that charge came from British quarters.

The Left coalition came to grief and split, as on other occasions, over fiscal issues. In 1925 the franc began to fall at a rate that the example of the great German inflation made all the more alarming. This led to the recall of Poincaré to the Prime Ministership. However, Poincaré's task remained strictly confined to financial restoration, which he successfully accomplished, the franc being stabilized in 1926 at one-fifth its prewar value, and the result was an interesting combination or compromise in the form of a team consisting of Poincaré and Briand, the latter remaining at the foreign office.

fused to acknowledge that Eastern European problems were of equal importance to Western, and in many respects far more delicate. If the French interest was primarily, as in fact it was, the defensive one of security, if France felt her security assured, might she not lose interest in the Polish alliance? The French hegemony of Europe, in so far as it was such, was for France merely one device for her protection. Locarno was looked at askance in Warsaw; it undoubtedly weakened, to a degree, the solidity of the French system to which it offered in effect a possible alternative.

As before 1914, the key to the future peace lay in Germany. Locarno was a step in the process of her rehabilitation; like all treaties, it registered conditions, material and moral, prevailing at the moment. If Locarno had any meaning for Germany, the process of German rehabilitation must continue; once it had been fully accomplished, the question would then inevitably arise: what were the aims of German policy? That question the future alone could answer, but the significant thing in 1925 was that an avenue seemed open for the preservation of peace by means other than the mere possession of superior force. The "spirit of Locarno" was a concrete reality, itself an important component of the stuff of European relations, and hopes ran high that the era was being entered into of the true liquidation of the legacy of the catastrophe of 1914.

THE FOREIGN POLICY OF GERMANY AND OF RUSSIA

That catastrophe, in broad terms, had been the result of pressures generated by the growth of Germany no less than by the rate of that growth. The German bid for dominance through the resort to arms had failed; Germany had had to acknowledge total defeat and had been made wholly impotent. That fact itself lent a measure of simplicity to the aims of German foreign policy after the peace; they reduced themselves to one purpose, the elimination of the disabilities that ensued from defeat and the recovery of a place of equality among the Powers. No German government, whatever its political color, could pursue any other aim. That aim achieved, and it could only be some distance away, one could then proceed to make choices.

The best, if not the only, tool of impotent power lies in the cultivation of differences among its opponents; for that reason the Germans had been kept away from the discussions that took place during the drafting of the peace. But differences existed, quite apart from any German encouragement of them, among the victors of 1918. Those between France and Britain have been mentioned. Generally speaking, it may be said that German hopes of exploiting these differences were deceived, mainly because of Britain's passivity; criticize and oppose France as she would, Britain did not have the means and the will to coerce French power determined to assert itself. The episode of the Ruhr was for Germany a source of disillusion; it showed to her conclusively that Britain could not be counted on to defend her effectively and that superior French power had to be acknowledged.[47]

But if that power could not be countered by frontal opposition, that might be all the more reason for considering the possibilities of the traditional alternative of German foreign policy, association with Russia, to which the re-creation of Poland and the Franco-Polish alliance might seem to give added point. France, as well as keeping Germany in subjection, was at the time the prime exponent of the policy of Russian containment. Matters at this point were somewhat complicated by the peculiar nature of the Russian regime and by domestic considerations in Germany. Revolution had occurred in Germany as well, but the main bulwark of the newly founded Republic, the Social Democrats, had firmly set their face against extremes; the bourgeois coalition of Weimar sternly suppressed from its beginnings any attempts to emulate the Russian model.[48]

What is more, the new regime in Germany showed little interest in radical modifications of the social structure of the country. The core of the old conservatism, traditional backbone of the armed forces, remained unaltered, its standing and prestige little affected, ready to reassert itself after the momentary unpopularity that had accompanied defeat. The first election in 1920 after the drafting of the constitution produced a loss of some one hundred

[47] If Britain, in any final test, would let France have her way, British opposition was not wholly futile, as the large role of British (and American) views showed in the formulation of the Dawes Plan. In a less tangible but important way, the influence of Britain's views on French opinion, as in the election of 1924, for instance, has been indicated. French financial difficulties were the most convenient wedge through which American and British influences could insinuate themselves.

[48] Communism can hardly be said to have constituted a danger. An attempted revolution in Berlin in January, and another in March, were ruthlessly put down by the army, and a short-lived Communist regime in Bavaria was likewise suppressed. One consequence of these episodes was to make the Social Democrats that were part of the government in a sense prisoners of reaction and to place added stress on the role of the armed forces.

seats for the Weimar coalition and a corresponding shift to the Right of the governing combination of parties. Within the limitations of the peace provisions, von Seekt proceeded to maintain the core and framework of the German army of the future; on the whole he accomplished his purpose with brilliance.

The Right in general, be it commercial interests or military ones, new version of the old alliance of steel and rye, rather than Liberals or Left, showed interest in a Russian connection; simple considerations of power can often override ideological differences. In April, 1922, the world was startled by the announcement of the conclusion of the Russo-German Treaty of Rapallo, at the time of the Genoa Conference. That move was at once premature and clumsy. The union of impotence to impotence could, however, be a warning of later possibilities; at the time it did no more than irritate and stiffen the determination and the fears of French intransigeance. Poincaré had no hesitation in using sharp language with Curzon and the Ruhr episode was not long in following.

The lesson was not lost on Germany and took the form of the emergence of Stresemann in 1923. Stresemann was of the Right, the German People's Party, in domestic politics; he stood for the policy of fulfillment, not because of any desire to atone for the German past, but because a realistic appraisal of the German present dictated this as the only feasible policy. German popular feeling about the *diktat* of Versailles and the iniquity of the Ruhr was well-nigh unanimous, but Stresemann secured from the Reichstag the abandonment of passive resistance, then the acceptance of the Dawes Plan. After that episode German economic recovery was rapid, aided to a degree by the influx of foreign capital, not least American.

In the context of the alternative orientations of German foreign policy, Stresemann may properly be called a Westerner. Locarno was his next achievement, the details and significance of which have been explained, and on his course he proceeded undisturbed. His task was aided by improved domestic conditions, which gave greater scope to those forces in Germany, the Left in general, which, like the Left in France, favored authentic reconciliation in the future and liquidation of the past legacy of strife.[49]

[49] The duality which existed in Germany, comparable to that which existed in France, found adequate expression in the Presidential election of 1925, precipitated by the death of the first President of the German Republic, Friedrich Ebert. Three candidates presented themselves, owing to the refusal of the Communists to join forces with the rest of the Left. The result was a failure of any

Much attention has been paid so far to the record of the Franco-German situation, and this is wholly warranted because that situation dominated at first the course of European affairs. But this condition itself represents a distortion, albeit an inevitable one, resulting from the self-imposed elimination of the factor of American power and from the reticence and inactivity of Britain. The absence of Russia was no less important, but it, too, was the result of circumstances and of the course of domestic Russian events. The war had exhausted Russia, and the first effect of the Revolution was further to impair what Russian power remained. The weariness induced by war in others alone permitted the survival of the Bolshevik regime. Rightly assessing the dearth of its own physical power, that regime at first staked its hopes on the occurrence of revolution elsewhere, and most of all in Germany, which in the eyes of its leaders constituted the key to all Europe. But, as mentioned before, Bolshevik hopes were destined to prove false in Germany.

As on later occasion, the Red bogey loomed large in the eyes of the governments of Europe; it may be said that for a time these governments and the Russian agreed upon one point and one alone, the impossibility of coexistence. The logic was sound on both sides that caused the Bolsheviks to encourage revolution everywhere and induced others to intervene in Russia. But this was to prove one instance where logic was belied by events. By 1921, with the conclusion of the Treaty of Riga and the stabilization of the Russo-Polish situation, both sides had been proved wrong. Coexistence might yet prove ultimately impossible, but the answer to this must wait upon a later day; the fact was that revolution outside Russia had failed, but on the other hand revolution in Russia survived. The first round in a continuing story had ended in a stalemate.

Yet Russia was more impotent than ever with the chaos of civil war heaped upon that of foreign; there was no choice for Russia but to endeavor to continue to survive while restoring some manner of order, nursing her wounds and rebuilding her life from a

---

one candidate to secure an absolute majority, and a second election in which Marshal von Hindenburg won by a narrow plurality. No more adequate personification of the old Germany could have been found than the old wartime leader and national hero, and his victory naturally raised doubts about the future of the German Republic. The parallel with France in the seventies is not far to seek. However, President von Hindenburg, during his first term of office, deceived expectations and fears alike by proving himself a loyal respecter of his oath of office.

level become incredibly low and primitive; there was no choice
for others but to seek to keep Russia at arm's length: the *cordon
sanitaire* was the answer, and in the fact that France was the chief
proponent of this policy may be seen the expression of an attempt
by France to supply an answer to the problem of the organization of Europe in this quarter as well. Here was another manifestation of the great fallacy of the postwar period; French power
was not for the long term adequate to maintain the organization
of Europe. In any case, Russia emerged again from war and revolution as a state among states, albeit in a unique position, for in
the arsenal of power her chief tool, for the moment at least, was
the imponderable one of ideology.

It was the very possession of this tool, or weapon, that largely
conditioned Russia's policy shaped by her great fear, a coalition of
others to encompass her destruction. It was wholly logical for
Russia to nurture discord among others, in the doing of which she
could, moreover, derive comfort from the thought that it was
written in her holy book that capitalist states are inevitably rivals
destined to recurring clash among themselves. Here was a point
of contact between herself and Germany, which also, from the
Russian point of view, should above all be kept from joining the
ring of her enemies; the Soviets enthusiastically endorsed German
grievances and were, logically again, particularly anti-French. In
this context Rapallo is quite understandable, though more in the
Russian than in the German context.

Despite the irritation of others at Rapallo, once coexistence had
become a fact and its cessation had become indefinitely postponed,
the tendency was strong to establish a *modus vivendi*. Obsessed
by her economic difficulties, Britain was particularly anxious to
resume with Russia a trade from which inordinately high expectations were held. This had indeed been Lloyd George's motivation in inviting the Russians to the Genoa Conference.[50] At Rapallo, the Soviets made not only commercial arrangements with
Germany but secured formal recognition from her. It was perhaps
symbolically appropriate that the first German ambassador to
Moscow should be the same Brockdorff-Rantzau whose lot it had
been to undergo the humiliation of putting Germany's signature

[50] Here again France was the chief opponent of Britain, being primarily concerned with her very large prewar Russian investment that the Bolsheviks had
repudiated. An Anglo-Soviet commercial treaty, involving *de facto* recognition
of the Russian regime, was concluded as early as March, 1921.

to the Treaty of Versailles. Gradually, from 1922 to 1924, Soviet Russia was granted *de jure* recognition by the majority of other states.[51] The process was aided by the fact that the Soviet regime, on the one hand definitely put world revolution on ice with the inauguration by Lenin of the New Economic Policy as early as 1921, while on the other hand the first Labour government took office in Britain in 1923 and the Left triumphed in France in 1924.

Relations between Soviet Russia and the outside world were sufficiently normalized for the former to participate in 1923 in the Lausanne Conference that regulated the status of the Straits. A stalemate of coexistence was thus achieved, but Russia's participation in international affairs continued relatively minor; she was definitely embarked on domestic reconstruction which absorbed all her energies. Lenin, the number one founding father, died in 1924; there ensued a bitter struggle for his succession in which Stalin was destined to win over the more brilliant and mercurial Trotsky, a fact which for the time at least served to insure continuance of the absorption in domestic problems.

In some respects the Russian Revolution was a denial of the Marxist gospel, since revolution such as had occurred was supposedly a stage in an inevitable course largely associated with industrial growth and maturity, while Russia was economically the most backward among important states. World revolution having failed, for the moment at least, Russia was saddled with a Marxist revolution without the supposedly necessary basis of it, a large industry and a correspondingly large and politically conscious industrial proletariat. Since industry had not produced the revolution, the inevitable course of history must be reversed and the revolution must proceed to create industry. This enormous task was to absorb for long the energies of Russia; the reversal of the "normal" course of historic evolution has not a little to do with the peculiarities of the domestic course of Russian events. With that aspect of things we are not concerned in this treatment, save that it must be borne in mind as an essential part of the background of Russian foreign policy. For some time, as a state among states, Russia was to remain relatively passive, leaving the initiative of leadership to the Western Powers.

[51] The first states to grant Russia *de jure* recognition, in 1920 and 1921, were her immediate neighbors, Esthonia, Lithuania, Latvia, and Finland, followed by Persia, Afghanistan, Poland, and Turkey. Among major states the one outstanding exception in granting Soviet Russia recognition was the United States, which did not resume diplomatic relations with her until 1933.

428   A DIPLOMATIC HISTORY OF EUROPE SINCE THE CONGRESS OF VIENNA

But this passivity did not mean indifference. Opportunities might arise that could be suitably exploited while the dread specter of a coalition must forever be watched and prevented from materializing if possible. In default of material power, the appeal of an ideology supported by propaganda of varying skill was an important tool of Soviet policy. The Communist International, organized as early as 1919, purported to resume the task of the Second International to which the war had been a vital blow; in effect, the revolution having been successful in Russia alone, the Comintern was an organ of the Soviet government, for all that the fiction was insisted upon that it was an international body in which the Russians were but one of the participants, a fiction which enabled the Soviet government to decline responsibility for the activities of the Comintern. In simple fact the directing personnel of the Soviet government, of the Communist party of Russia, and of the Comintern largely consisted of the same group of individuals.

The Russian Revolution had the effect of splitting Social Democracy in Europe, a split that was formalized in the immediate postwar period through the emergence of Communist parties, henceforth distinct from Socialist, in the various European countries; the enmity of rivals who both claimed legitimate descent from the Marxist origin was often bitter. The Socialists, becoming to all intents and purposes integrated into the democratic parliamentary tradition of the West, were branded traitors to the working-class movement by the Communists. The fear of the Red bogey soon subsided in the West where Communist parties did not emerge in threatening proportions; nevertheless, the existence in the body politics of European states of a group whose prime allegiance was to a foreign power served to introduce a new and complicating element in the conduct of international relations. To this condition no remedy exists and it occurs whenever powerful ideas capture the minds of men; it happened at the time of the French Revolution and in the days of the wars of religion: men are far easier suppressed than ideas. In actual practice, however, the effects of this situation were not to be substantial until the Russian state was to recover strength, thereby reminding one of Napoleon's dictum that a revolution is an idea that has found bayonets.

The German chaos of 1923, precipitated by the French occupation of the Ruhr, revived Russian hopes of revolution in Germany; but Karl Radek, the emissary of the Comintern, decided the time was not yet ripe. The surmounting of the German crisis served to discredit the encouragement of revolution, and the successful emergence of Stalin in control over his rival Trotsky went with the concentration of Russian effort on domestic reconstruction and the accompanying relative passivity of Russian policy previously mentioned.[52] Nevertheless, Locarno was disliked in Moscow where it revived the fear that the Western orientation of German policy that seemed to be Stresemann's might evolve into the dread anti-Russian coalition.

But if Stresemann's realism did in effect induce him to adopt a policy of appeasement toward France, he was not minded wholly to sever the wire to Moscow. From him, Chicherin, the Soviet foreign minister, obtained the conclusion of an economic agreement in October, 1925, that was followed in April, 1926, by the signature in Berlin of a treaty of friendship and neutrality: either party promised neutrality in the event of the other being the victim of aggression and undertook not to join others in financial or economic boycott. The assistance of German technique and technicians in the reconstruction of the Russian military establishment could continue; it provided for Germany a measure of evasion of the limitations that the peace had placed upon her own armed forces. Yet Germany went on to join the League in 1926, a move that disturbed Moscow, for whom the Genevan organization was but a capitalist coalition in disguise, dominated by Anglo-French influence that Germany might henceforth join and share.

MEDITERRANEAN DEVELOPMENTS

As it appeared at the time, Locarno was a turning point, the opening of a new chapter of genuine liquidation of the past, of an era of authentic coöperation among the Powers. For a few years this chapter seemed to unfold along a promising course. But before tracing the heyday of international coöperation and of collective security it will be useful to bring up to date developments elsewhere in Europe.

---

[52] With the political stabilization of Europe, Russian interest turned to the Far East where Russian advisers played an important role in the reorganization of the Chinese Kuomintang and in helping it secure control of the country under the leadership of General Chiang Kai-shek. But once successful, Chiang Kai-shek turned against his Communist supporters whom he ruthlessly suppressed after 1926. He was unable, however, to destroy a group that maintained itself under Mao Tse-tung to form the nucleus of the eventual Communist control of China twenty years later.

THE FOREIGN POLICY OF ITALIAN FASCISM. Little mention has been made so far in this story of the postwar role of Italy, and this is warranted by the fact that this role, like the Russian, was of relatively little importance for a time; European affairs as a whole were definitely dominated by the triumvirate of Britain, France, and Germany. But if Russia is possessed of vast numbers, space, and resources, which, once organized and developed, would supply Russia with enormous power that would entitle her to play a part of initiator and director of world policy, such cannot be the case of Italy, handicapped by exiguous means on which the pressure of numbers make for further weakness rather than added strength. Before and during the war Italian foreign policy had been conducted with both moderation and skill and, given Italian power, a good measure of success. The chief asset of Italy as a state among states was the balance of power, and the more delicate and unstable that balance the greater could her influence be and the higher the price that her exploitation of uncertainty could command.

The war and total victory, in which Italy shared, had the ironical effect of robbing Italy of her most valuable asset, for the destruction of Germany meant, for a time at least, that there was no balance in Europe. In this, as much as in the adventitious intervention of the United States and the specific faults of management of her affairs, lies the fundamental reason for the failure of Italy at the peace. In the dramatic clash of 1919 between the Italians and Wilson, the British and the French had stood on the side lines, not too displeased to let the Italians fight it out alone: they felt little love for what they regarded as the successful Italian exploitation of their plight written into the Treaty of London, nor did they see much need of courting Italian power at the time. What Italy failed to obtain from her share in the victory, and might or should in fairness have obtained, was, in terms of actual value, of relatively little consequence. But the phrase, "mutilated victory," best expressed the prevailing mood of Italy after the peace.

It was in September, 1919, that there occurred the episode of the seizure of Fiume by the poet-soldier d'Annunzio. The bombast and flamboyance that attended what may well be described as comic opera may seem of little importance, but the incident had symbolic significance and struck a responsive chord in the country. Of greater moment was the fact that the war had entailed a far greater effort than initially expected, with the result that a smaller absolute Italian contribution than the French or the British meant for Italy a proportionally greater strain. Here again the contrast is enlightening between the case of Russia which, left to her own resources, collapsed, and that of Italy to whom the avenues of assistance from her allies remained open.

The effect of these circumstances was to create in Italy after the war unusual stresses and strains for an economy that was weak and for a political regime that lacked solid roots. Weak governments ineffectively dallied with the situation, incapable of dealing with the financial problem and with labor unrest. In such conditions the extremes tend to flourish: unchecked illegality from the Left[53] began to be answered by corresponding direct action from the opposite pole. Mussolini, the former revolutionary Socialist of prewar days, turned interventionist in 1914, launched in 1919 the movement that came to be known as Fascism. What Fascism was, nobody, perhaps least of all Mussolini, could have explained with clarity. The early program of the movement had much in it that any socialist could espouse; it was a curious jumble of what had hitherto been strongly antagonistic tendencies, socialism and nationalism. It evoked very little response at first, but in the course of 1921 the movement became increasingly associated with the violent repression of labor, and the party, into which the movement transformed itself, obtained thirty-five parliamentary seats in the election of that year. The grand old man of Italian politics, the neutralist of 1915, Giolitti, was head of the government at the time; judging the situation in pre-1914 terms, he thought that a little violence from the Right might balance the same from the Left, and that time would cure a temporary fever. His fall in July, 1921, opened the door to a convincing demonstration of the ineffectiveness of Parliament in coping with conditions that were different from those of the prewar days.

In October, 1922, as a last resort, the king called upon Mussolini to form a government. The so-called March on Rome of the Fascist legions, an episode of not too great importance, is less significant than the fact that Mussolini's government received the endorsement of the same chamber in which his party held a mere thirty-five seats. The proceedings were wholly constitutional; they were tantamount to an abdication of Parliament, albeit most

[53] It was in 1920, as an episode in the widespread labor unrest, that there occurred the occupation of the factories by the workers, a novel form of action at the time and one that created considerable sensation and alarm.

of its members thought of it as a merely temporary surrender after which normality would soon resume its course and themselves control. Here was the first concrete instance of the suicide of a democracy, enacted in accordance with the laws of its own existence, a phenomenon whose recurrence was to be witnessed again in other places.

When Mussolini became Prime Minister of Italy no real revolution was thought to have occurred in that country. Fascism had no clear doctrine or program; it could mean all things to all men, and Fascist theory and practice in fact evolved relatively slowly and gradually, in large measure as a response and adaptation to circumstances. Despite the Acerbo law,[54] the election of 1923, in which the Italian people endorsed the new regime, was essentially free. This endorsement was little more than approval of the promise of the restoration of order; but some of the seeds contained in the original jumble of contradictory tendencies bore fruit. The intellectual content of Fascism was furnished by the Right, mainly by the small but able band of Nationalists with whom the Fascists were in early and close alliance. What came to prevail in Fascism was the assertion of the authoritarian principle—a response to the breakdown of constituted authority—and perhaps the most significant contribution of the movement, the implications of which reached far beyond Italian borders, is best expressed in the name of the German brand of the same product, National Socialism. This was an unexpected synthesis, yet a potent solvent of past conflicts: the claims of the rising masses, knocking at the door for their share of privilege, were asserted rather than denied, but these claims were to receive satisfaction through a revision of the Marxist doctrine of class struggle into a new version of struggle between rich and poor, haves and have nots, at the national level.

All this, little understood at first—and, for that matter, the theory only took shape with gradualness—did little to enhance the effective power of Italy. Nevertheless, when Mussolini came to power, a question mark was raised. Would Italy embark on some adventure, unwise though it might be? One of Mussolini's early contacts with his foreign peers was at Lausanne where the new

[54] This was a device for creating an effective and stable majority in Parliament. Whichever party received the largest popular vote—provided it was at least 25 percent of the total—would receive two-thirds of the seats in Parliament. A somewhat comparable scheme was attempted in the election of 1953.

treaty with Turkey was being negotiated; he indulged in some bombastic theatricals, but no more.

Perhaps because it was Italian, there was no mystical content in Fascism. To be sure, Mussolini forever exalted power, but he was also a realist who for a long time entertained a sound respect for and a correct appreciation of power, fitting in this respect into the classical tradition of Italian foreign policy. The acts of retrenchment of the preceding regime, the Treaty of Rapallo with Yugoslavia, the withdrawal from Asia Minor and from Albania, were not undone, for all that they were sometimes condemned as signs of pusillanimity. Yugoslav fears of Mussolini's Italy—they were the strongest—were set at rest with a clarification of the unsatisfactory situation in Fiume.[55]

Only the Corfu incident for a time rasied some doubts. The fate of Albania had been settled by the decision of the Conference of Ambassadors in November, 1921, that confirmed for that country the frontiers of 1913. But the task of delimitation remained; it was in the course of performing this task, in August, 1923, that the Italian General Tellini and some of his assistants were killed. The Italian reaction was reminiscent of that of Austria to the Sarajevo assassination, though far more prompt: an ultimatum to Greece was followed by the dispatch of a squadron to the island of Corfu, which was bombarded and occupied. But the quarrel was patched up with fair expedition through the mediation of the Powers, mainly Britain, more hesitantly of the League. Italy received the satisfaction of an indemnity for her show of force, but this minor flare-up was not followed by similar assertions of Italian power elsewhere.

The fundamentals of Italian policy remained, and Mussolini seemed to take reasoned account of them. French dominance of Europe was irksome to Italy *qua* Italy; it was natural that Italy should turn against that dominance and favor the restoration of some balance. This pointed to a continuance of the traditional Anglo-Italian identity of views and goes some distance toward explaining the tolerant British view of Italian Fascism. However, as already mentioned in the case of the Ruhr episode, Italy, sharing

[55] The life of the Free State of Fiume had been an uneasy one. In January, 1924, the Treaty of Rome, concluded between Mussolini and Pašić, sanctioned the annexation of the Free State to Italy. The further normalization of Italo-Yugoslav relations attempted by the Nettuno Convention of 1925 failed of ratification in the Yugoslav Parliament.

the British dislike of the French action, formally associated herself with that action. France would indeed welcome Italian support, but France could also dispense with that support at this time; Italy had no bargaining power and the French treatment of her was somewhat cavalier, which had in turn the effect of focusing more than ever Italian dissatisfaction with the peace into resentment against France.

Like Britain, Italy, misreading to a degree the extent and the intentions of French power, would therefore favor the recovery of German power—within limits, to be sure; despite the war, the tradition of Italo-German relations was one of friendship rather than the opposite and there had been no direct points of contact and difference between the two countries. However, Italy had obtained at the expense of Austria the Brenner frontier, placing within her borders some 250,000 German-speaking Tyrolese. In Austrian eyes the South Tyrol was an irredenta with connotations similar to those of Alsace for pre-1914 France. Little Austria was powerless, but her Germanic character, raising the possibility of *Anschluss* with Germany, made the Tyrolese irredenta potentially a German issue as well. Much as she would appreciate the restoration of a balance of power in Europe, Italy very soon came to take a determined stand on the independence of Austria. As a consequence, Italo-Austrian relations had an inevitable ambivalence in them, for Italy was at once the sharpest focus of Austrian irredentism and the most reliable defender of Austrian independence.

In Central Europe generally, in the former Habsburg domain, Italy might have expected to fall heir to at least some of the former German influence. But the new states of Central Europe, those that were beneficiaries of the war, leaned to the French association for two reasons: the greater French power and the greater reliability of France as an opponent of any alteration of the existing *status quo*. Thus it came to pass that, in default of German power, Central Europe became an arena of Franco-Italian rivalry, one in which Italy could not help but feel frustrated. This, in turn, caused Italy to veer ever more toward the espousal of revisionism and to associate herself with the other revisionist states, Hungary and Bulgaria.[56]

---

[56] In 1928 a shipment of arms, camouflaged as machinery, was intercepted by Austrian customs officials. An inquiry conducted by the League, at the instigation of the Little Entente, proved inconclusive, but it was widely believed that the arms had been surreptitiously sent from Italy to Hungary.

On economic grounds there was every reason for coöperation between Italy and Yugoslavia. Italy was indeed favorable to such coöperation, but, for political reasons, Yugoslav suspicion of Italy, and of Mussolini's Italy in particular, continued to exist; it was Yugoslavia who failed to ratify the Nettuno Convention of 1925. There was for that matter a Yugoslav irredenta, some three-quarters of a million Slovenes and Croats along Italy's eastern border, toward whom, as toward the Austrian Tyrolese, Fascism pursued a policy of enforced Italianization.[57]

Of her wartime claims to Dalmatia Italy had retained only some islands and Zara; the Italian minority in Dalmatia, legacy of the days of Venetian grandeur and concentrated in the urban centers, was a ready-made pretext for the possible assertion of spurious Italian Irredentist claims. But it was Albania that became the more active focus of Italo-Yugoslav rivalry and intrigue. In 1925 Ahmed Bey Zogu led a successful revolution that procured his election to the Presidency of Albania; he had been a refugee in Belgrade and his success appeared as one for Yugoslav influence, an impression confirmed by the prompt settlement, on terms favorable to Yugoslavia, of frontier claims against Albania. But this was a mere episode in a tale of Balkan intrigue. Once in power, Zogu became a willing recipient of Italian financial assistance.[58] In November, 1926, an Italo-Albanian Treaty of Mutual Assistance was signed. Like any alliance between vastly unequal Powers this one implied a relationship of dependence on the part of the weaker member; the arrangement was in the nature of a consolation prize for Italy in the face of the successes of French influence. It was itself a contributory cause to the conclusion in 1927 of the Franco-Yugoslav alliance, which completed the ring of connections between France and all three members of the Little Entente. Despite French reassurances and Mussolini's public acceptance of them, the Franco-Yugoslav alliance could not but have the color, in Italian eyes, of a guarantee against Italy of Yugoslavia by France.[59]

[57] Moreover, the new Yugoslavia was beset by the friction between Serbs and Croats, a situation suitable for exploitation by Italian intrigue.

[58] A National Bank for Albania was created in Rome in September, 1925, and in 1926 Italy granted Albania a loan of 5,000,000 gold francs. In 1928 a touch of Balkan comedy was introduced when President Zogu assumed the royal dignity, as King Zog I of Albania.

[59] The tone of Franco-Italian relations fluctuated somewhat. One source of friction was the problem of the *fuorusciti*, or Fascist exiles, whose number increased with the growing repressiveness of the Fascist regime after 1925, and whose main headquarters, for reasons of geographical proximity and of ideological congeniality, was in Paris.

With Greece, suspicion also persisted, that the Corfu incident had seemed to justify, and that Italian sympathy for Bulgaria, since Greco-Bulgarian relations were also unsatisfactory,[60] further confirmed; while from the Yugoslav point of view, Italian support of Bulgarian and Hungarian revisionist ambitions, combined with Albanian intrigue, could easily take on the appearance of a calculated policy of encirclement.

It was in 1928 that Mussolini openly espoused the cause of revisionism in the form of his reasserting the platitude that treaties are not everlasting; this was not devoid of some irony, being coupled with the reassertion of the sacredness of Italy's own frontiers. At all events Italian policy at this time cannot be called actively aggressive; the mere passage of time without the occurrence of active attempts to make good any of the Fascist claims in fact rather tended to confirm the impression that Fascist bombast was mainly for domestic consumption, while in effect Italian foreign policy was basically peaceful and reasonable. Such it was indeed at this time when Italy may be said to have been biding her time, waiting for opportunities that were not yet existent.

The Mediterranean has ever been the logical sphere of Italy's prime interest. In Libya, after the war, it proved necessary to undertake a task of reconquest and pacification, which lasted for a decade. The task was done and Libya was enlarged as the result of frontier rectifications on the Egyptian as well as on the Tunisian side. It is of interest, however, that whereas Italy took the position that the cessions made to her by Britain were adequate fulfillment of the colonial promises of the Treaty of London of 1915, she maintained that the French share of that bargain had not been satisfied, hence that the implementation of that instrument was still pending. This contention was to be of importance at a later date. Actually, Libya, save for possible reasons of strategy, was no asset to Italy but rather an expensive luxury,[61] and Mussolini's realistic appraisal was wholly sound that prompted him at one time to characterize Italy's imperial activity as an enterprise in the collection of deserts.

[60] Frontier incidents were frequent and in October, 1925, Greek troops crossed the border into Bulgaria. Following a Bulgarian appeal to the League, the Council was called to meet and hostilities were prevented when the Greeks consented to withdraw, thereby procuring a success for the League.

[61] A considerable effort was made to establish Italian settlers in Libya. The effort met with a measure of success, but in terms of its total accomplishment was of little significance for either Italy or Libya.

THE NEAR EAST. The Near East had more attractive possibilities and, in the context of imperial activity, the Italian attempt during the war to stake out a claim in Asia Minor had been sound. But in the face of postwar circumstances it had been equally sound to withdraw. In the Near East Italy pursued a policy of cultivating commercial and financial interests, in doing which she had fair success.

The most significant and striking development in the Near East was the rebirth of Turkey. Within the confines of Turkey proper, as she emerged from Lausanne, Kemal Ataturk set about a task of modernization and westernization reminiscent in some respects of that of Peter the Great in Russia. The trappings of parliamentary democracy were adopted, but Kemal ruled with a firm hand through his control of the single political party in existence; Kemal was an enlightened despot who did not abuse his power, and in one important respect Turkey differed from Russia: she had just given up an empire and showed no interest in intruding in the Arab world that had been her former domain. The secularization of the Turkish state, of which the abolition of the Caliphate was symbol, precluded the assertion of any claims to leadership in the Islamic world where religion still plays a central role that it has long forsaken in the West. Turkey, bent on domestic reconstruction and reform, was at peace with all.

In Syria the French had their difficulties, which remained confined to the internal level, but in neighboring Palestine seeds of conflict had been planted that were destined to have far-reaching implications. Palestine had been an Arab land for centuries; it held few Jews, who lived in it unmolested. But the ambiguous Balfour Declaration of 1917 opened the door to a stream of Zionist settlers. Would the "national homeland" seek to transform itself into a Jewish state? Incoming Jews could acquire land at high, even extortionate, prices; but they constituted the intrusion of an alien element, fundamentally Western in its techniques and methods, far in advance of those of the Arab world. In economic terms this situation could supply the foundation of fruitful coöperation from which the Arabs could profit handsomely.

But the Western virus of nationalism had penetrated into the Arab world, where its novelty caused it to operate in unusually virulent and irrational fashion. Therein lay the roots of insoluble conflict, and the fact that religion still holds a central place in the life of Islam, while the Zionist immigration contained an odd admixture of ancient Judaism with modern Western Marxism, held the possibility of giving a nationalistic conflict the ancient color of religious war. The Christian monks had quarreled, often in less than dignified fashion, over the Holy Places. Similar quarrels reappeared around the Wailing Wall, where in 1929 an open clash occurred between Arabs and Jews; petty as they may seem, they were symbolic of a clash of forces that, meeting in Jerusalem, meant Islam on one side, world Jewry on the other with all its Western connections.

Palestine was a British mandate, and the dilemma was Britain's —for the time at least. Britain had no solution and dallied with ineffective panaceas such as the regulation of Jewish immigration;[62] not surprisingly, she incurred the displeasure of both Arabs and Jews and even the charge that she was encouraging conflict in order to maintain her own position on the old theory of divide and rule. But the Palestinian situation was not out of control during the twenties; in the general picture of international relations it was no more than a small cloud on the horizon in a land in which, however, dragon's teeth were being sown.

Nationalism was rife throughout the Arab world. The British held Iraq with a lighter hand than the French used in Syria with the result that, generally speaking, the country made headway toward independence. By 1929 a formal promise of British support was given for the admission of Iraq to the League, implying termination of the mandate; it was followed in 1930 by a treaty of alliance that reserved certain vital military rights for Britain. A somewhat similar situation developed in Egypt. The grant of independence in 1922 was largely an illusion, since in connection with that grant Britain had reserved to herself the right to insure the security of imperial communications (the Suez Canal), that of the defense of Egypt, as well as the protection of foreign interests and of the status of the Sudan. The meaning of these restrictions was clear to Egyptian nationalists, the dominant Wafd party, and protracted negotiations broke down repeatedly. The situation had not been resolved by 1930.

The basic difficulty lay in the simple fact that, in the case of Egypt, as in that of other dependent lands seeking to emerge into

[62] During the administration of the first High Commissioner, Sir Herbert Samuel, the Jewish population of Palestine grew to some 120,000. Immigration was then virtually stopped and the prospect appeared of voluntary Arab-Jewish coöperation, which lasted until the incidents of 1929.

independence, the feeling was correct that Britain—or whatever imperial Power happened to be involved—was not willing to grant unfettered independence. On the side of imperial Powers there existed the feeling, likewise largely correct, that little reliance could be placed on mere promises to safeguard the interests in being. Agreement is difficult to produce out of mutual and warranted distrust, and, if produced, its meaning and value cannot but remain highly questionable. However, at this time, a decade after the termination of the war, none of these issues was yet out of hand; they seemed the manageable stuff of normal diplomatic activity. Another twenty years and a Second World War would be needed before they were to become issues of paramount importance for Europe and for the world as a whole.

THE HEYDAY OF COLLECTIVE SECURITY

Considering the small magnitude of conflicts and the low intensity of tensions, as well as the generally favorable economic situation, it is wholly understandable that for some years after Locarno the prevailing atmosphere of international relations should have been one of optimistic expectation that conflicts could be resolved and tensions further relaxed; in brief, that Europe and the world were entering an era in which the expectation of peace could be lasting.

The conjunction of two marked personalities, Briand in France and Stresemann in Germany, dominates the scene until the death of the latter in 1929. Though still disarmed and powerless, Germany remained in potential a great, if not the strongest, European Power. The issue of the rehabilitation of her power, hence that of Franco-German relations, naturally remained of crucial importance. Gifted in speech and endowed with keen sensitivity, careless of his personal appearance and none too precise in his thinking, Briand was genuinely devoted to the cause of peace in general and to that of Franco-German reconciliation in particular; the spectacle of war had induced in him a profound revulsion for that crude activity of mankind. Stresemann's political origins were the very opposite of Briand's, but, as pointed out before, he also acknowledged reality to the extent of adopting a policy of reconciliation.[63]

---

[63] The case of Stresemann and of his real and ultimate intentions has been the object of much controversy. At the very time of Locarno he wrote a letter to the ex-*Kronprinz* explaining the necessity of "*finassieren*," like Met-

Germany's acceptance of Locarno had been made subject by her to the evacuation of the Cologne zone of occupation. This having been agreed upon, the necessary legislation was enacted in Germany, though not without some difficulty and thanks to the support of Hindenburg, who had just become President. The next step was Germany's application for admission to the League. The German candidacy was warmly supported by Briand, but his government was overthrown in March, and Brazilian opposition prevented unanimity in the Council.[64] Despite the awkwardness of the resulting delay, the difficulty was overcome and Germany was admitted to membership in September, furnishing the occasion for a resounding and moving oration by Briand.

The time seemed auspicious for the initiation of a bold policy which Briand and Stresemann discussed in the convivial intimacy of a private meeting that they held in Thoiry. Briand was attracted to a large view of things; deliberately ignoring the bulky documentation of German breaches—mostly, no doubt, petty ones—of the disarmament clauses of the peace that the French war office had sent him, he was willing to consider the possibility of a complete evacuation of the Rhineland and even of a return of the Saar to Germany. Himself no financier, he thought that the French fiscal troubles of the moment—the still uncertain status of the franc—could be resolved through a "mobilization"[65] of the German debt that would make ready cash available to France. Stresemann proved a hard bargainer, and on the French side substantial opposition manifested itself to so far-reaching a relaxation of controls coupled with an insistence on the letter of the law of disarmament. When looked into more closely, financial possibilities appeared limited, and for that matter, Poincaré had succeeded in stabilizing the franc.[66] By December Briand had to acknowledge

ternich after 1809, in order to free Germany of the French stranglehold. The choice of the word, of French derivation (finasser), to which pejorative connotations can be attached, and even more the choice of the correspondent, give natural grounds for suspicion. The fact remains, however, that a different atmosphere was being created, favorable to the development of the forces of reconciliation, and the existence of which was a reality in both countries. In the immediate implementation of his policy Stresemann was charged with treason to the fatherland by the German nationalists and National Socialists.

[64] Brazil was not opposed to German membership as such but was intent upon securing permanency in the Council. In the end Brazil withdrew from the League.

[65] This meant the making of arrangements as a result of which the German debt could be used for the raising of immediately available funds.

[66] The franc was stabilized in fact in 1926, but legally not until 1928, when its value in terms of gold was redefined by legislation.

to Stresemann that the policy of Thoiry could not be implemented.

The time was premature, mainly on the French side, from which the larger concessions would have to come. Whether an opportunity was missed must remain speculation. It has been argued that a *grand geste* of generous forgiveness, a wiping of the slate clean by France, could have been the catalytic agent that would have insured the triumph of the forces of peace in Germany. The German *quid pro quo* was largely an imponderable, an authentic abandonment of aggressive intent. Partly at least because in her own right she lacked the confidence that strength alone can give, France did not have the boldness to make such a *grand geste;* much was still heard in France of the remissiveness of Germany and of the numerous German manifestations, in deed and word, of an impenitent intent. The passage of time might in itself gradually dissipate these suspicions, but there was also danger in that other effect that appeared at this time, the feeling in Germany that French concessions were ever reluctantly granted and that the obtaining of them was merely an argument for pressing for more that might be extracted from weakness, instead of constituting cause for gratitude; the counterpart in France was the feeling that there was total failure in Germany to appreciate concessions and any signs of generosity. If Germany were truly impenitent and aggressive, a policy of niggardly concessions had little to commend itself. The decision, in December, 1926, to abolish the military commission of control in the following month was, strictly speaking, based on a fiction, since it was tantamount to the assertion that Germany had fulfilled her disarmament obligations, whereas in fact that was not wholly true.[67] Clearly, there might be dangers in a policy of concessions to Germany; however, it was to take some years before these dangers began seriously to develop, in circumstances wholly different from those of the general economic well-being of the second half of the twenties.

Aided by this economic euphoria the hope of peace for the future continued to thrive for a time. Using the occasion of the tenth anniversary of the intervention of the United States in the war, Briand, in 1927, took up the suggestion of a Franco-American declaration renouncing war. This may have seemed innocuous enough, not to say a meaningless gesture. The reply of the American Secretary of State, Kellogg, was to propose a world-embrac-

[67] See above, p. 400, n. 25.

ing declaration. The outcome, after some months of negotiations, was the signature in Paris, on August 27, 1928, of the so-called Pact of Paris, or Kellogg-Briand Pact. This was an unusually brief statement that consisted essentially of two articles:

1. The High Contracting Parties solemnly declare in the name of their respective peoples that they condemn the resort to war for the settlement of international disputes and that they renounce the resort to war as an instrument of national policy in their mutual relations.
2. The High Contracting Parties recognize that the settlement of all disputes or conflicts, of whatever nature or origin they may be, that may arise between them, shall always be sought by peaceful means alone.

Fifteen nations signed the initial document, but very shortly virtually the whole world had adhered to the Pact of Paris, not excluding the Soviet Union.[68] That instrument was no more than a declaration of intent, wholly divorced from any enforcing agency or means; in retrospect it may appear quite futile, as in fact it was destined to be, and, under the best interpretation, the expression of naïveté that may seem difficult of understanding. To the enforcement and strengthening of peace the Kellogg-Briand Pact contributed not a whit, but it is a perfect expression and symbol of the widespread atmosphere of 1928. Briand characterized it as a date in the history of mankind, a view to which many at the time would have subscribed.

The liquidation of the past made further progress. It was on the occasion of the signature of the Pact of Paris that Stresemann raised the issue of the termination of the occupation. But Poincaré,[69] though not irrevocably opposed, insisted on linking that question with the issue of Reparation, the total of which he wished to see established, especially in view of the recently concluded agreement for the funding of the French debt to the United States.[70] Following the September meeting of the League in Ge-

[68] The only exceptions were Arabia, Argentina, Bolivia, Brazil, and Yemen.
[69] As pointed out before, the effect of the French election of 1928 was a compromise that took the form of leaving Briand at the Quai d'Orsay while Poincaré, in recognition of his fiscal accomplishment, continued in charge of finance. Thereafter, save on the score of Reparation, Poincaré did not play an important role in matters of foreign policy.
[70] Reparation payments were being duly made during this period in accordance with the arrangements of the Dawes Plan, which, however, had not dealt with the matter of the total of Reparation or the duration of payments. In 1926 a Franco-American agreement had fixed the payment of the French debt to the United States over a period of sixty-two years. The American contention that Reparation and interallied debts were unrelated problems was not accepted

THE FALSE RECOVERY AND THE ERA OF ILLUSIONS, 1920–1930

neva, a conference met at The Hague where, in August, 1929, it was agreed that the final evacuation of the Rhineland would begin in September, 1929, to be terminated the following June.

Meanwhile the problem of Reparation was taken under review during the first half of 1929 by a committee presided over by the American, Owen D. Young. The result was the new arrangement, known as the Young Plan, which fixed a terminal date in 1988 for the payment of German Reparation, thereby establishing a *de facto,* though not a formal, connection between the various financial obligations deriving from the war, whether enemy or inter-allied debts.[71] The evacuation of the Rhineland and the final settlement of Reparation were Stresemann's last accomplishments. He made a last appearance in Geneva, supporting Briand's project of European union, and died on October 3. Whatever appraisal may be made of the man and his motives, that he had served his country well is not open to question. What use Germany would make of her recovered position in Europe, an end toward the realization of which she still had some distance to travel, was left to other men and circumstances to decide. The flash of lightning in the economic sky that was to issue from across the Atlantic followed Stresemann's death by a few days.

THE PERENNIAL OF DISARMAMENT.   The conclusion of the Locarno agreements and the subsequent period of international euphoria were the heyday of the Genevan organization, when hopes rose high that peace would be lasting, the League become reality, and the reign of order come to prevail among nations as it had for long within those who called themselves civilized. Since the view still commanded wide acceptance that arms themselves are a major cause of wars, the time seemed an auspicious one for the discussion of disarmament, or more accurately, of the reduction of armaments. Much time and energy were spent on this discussion, which for that reason must be mentioned since it constituted an important segment of the international activity of the day. But in view of the sterility of the discussion, the record of

---

in France, and ratification of the Franco-American funding agreement was still pending in the French Parliament.

[71] The Young Plan provided for the payment of thirty-six annuities, part of which were nondeferrable, on a rising scale, payments thereafter to continue at the rate then reached. The Reparation Commission was abolished, but a Bank of International Settlements was created in its place; the bank had no political powers, Germany thus recovering her financial independence.

which is that of a dreary tale of impotence, it can also be summed up with brevity.

It was in 1925 that a Preparatory Commission, intended, as its name indicates, to pave the way for a Disarmament Conference, presumably before too much time had elapsed, was appointed by the Council of the League. After some delay, the Preparatory Commission held its first meeting in May, 1926; participation in its work was not confined to League members, the United States being represented, and eventually the Soviet Union as well. The debate was again in large measure Anglo-French, and the chief difficulties arose from French objections. The French ever insisted that security must precede disarmament and raised a host of issues, all relevant indeed, but also hardly possible of resolution at the purely technical level. They may best be summed up under two heads: the estimation of potential, and the necessity of methods of supervision and control as prerequisites to the enactment of reduction of armaments.[72] Interminably and wearily, the debate droned on, producing only deadlock. A momentary compromise, reached by direct Anglo-French discussion, merely aroused opposition from others,[73] and matters were not helped by the genial proposal of the Soviet representative, Litvinov, at the end of 1927, for the complete abolition of all armed forces, in which others saw nothing but a device, never sincerely meant, but merely calculated to procure their common embarrassment.

In these debates Germany held a special position since she was already disarmed, or at least largely so. For debating purposes her stand was effective which amounted to saying that others should follow her example, or alternatively on insisting not so much on

---

[72] Additional reduction would be more accurate, for the French military establishment had been considerably reduced. What mattered, however, was not the absolute degree of armament but rather the institution of measures equally applicable to all.

To the American reader it is enlightening to observe the shift in the American position in these matters from one of general opposition to French views during the twenties, to one, after the Second World War, very reminiscent of the French position after the First World War. Just as, after that war, French power was the single concrete reality that could insure the preservation of peace, so likewise after the second war American power found itself in a somewhat comparable situation and it was reluctant to face the risks that the absence of adequate controls might entail.

[73] This compromise involved the British acceptance of the French view in the matter of trained reserves in exchange for the French acceptance of the British view in certain naval matters. With the assistance of premature press revelations it was misconstrued as British espousal of French supremacy in Europe and proved equally unpopular in America, in Italy, and in Germany.

any one scheme or method of disarmament as on the recognition of the right of equality for herself. The German demand for *Gleich-berechtigung* naturally evoked a popular response at home, and some uneasiness on the part of others was created by the meeting of Count Bernstorff and Litvinov in Berlin in 1928. The Preparatory Commission could report no progress in 1928, three years after its creation. In that same year a Committee on Security produced, under the leadership of Beneš of Czechoslovakia, a so-called General Act for the Pacific Settlement of International Disputes. The Act purported to create machinery for the implementation of the Pact of Paris. By 1930 it had gained some acceptances, but not a single one from a major Power.

On a more limited scale, efforts were made to follow up the accomplishments of the Washington Naval Conference of 1921–1922. An American invitation to a new naval conference in June, 1927, met with a French and an Italian refusal to participate; those two countries could not accept the view that arms in a special category (on the sea) could be dealt with in separation from others, while America had little interest at the time either in land armaments or in the contention that security must precede arms reduction. The American aim was to extend the mathematical ratios of 1922 to smaller categories of ships, but the divergent needs of Britain and America had not been previously explored; the lack of adequate diplomatic preparation was in part responsible for the breakdown in August of the three-Power naval conference.[74]

Better preparations preceded the meeting in London in 1930 of another naval conference in which both France and Italy participated. Anglo-American agreement was further facilitated by the existence of a Labour government in Britain; the British Prime Minister, MacDonald, found pacifistic views congenial; he thought, as he put it, that "the risk of war was practically nil" and Britain's "absolute" requirements were set at an unusually low level, while it proved also possible to adjust American-Japanese differences. The result was a tripartite agreement, the London Naval Treaty of April, 1930, which resulted in the scrapping of some capital ships and a new allocation of tonnage by categories. France and Italy accepted only the part of the agreement dealing

---

[74] It was in connection with this conference that the above-mentioned Anglo-French compromise was evolved, which only led to recriminations. The whole episode is a good illustration of very poor diplomacy. The almost simultaneous signature of the Kellogg-Brian Pact served, however, to relieve the atmosphere of tension.

with capital ships and the regulation of submarine warfare. Here were useful, but certainly small, results.[75]

Small as they were, they served to create a measure of optimism and, by the end of 1930, the Preparatory Commission had succeeded in producing a Draft Disarmament Convention. The next step was the actual meeting of a disarmament conference; the Council of the League set the time for this meeting in February, 1932. But events were beginning to move at an accelerated pace; the climate of 1932, as will be presently explained, was wholly different from that of Stresemann's day, or even of 1930, to the extent that the discussion of disarmament in 1932 no longer bore significant relation to existing reality.

The French had finally quit the German Rhine in June, 1930. That step was the occasion for considerable soul searching in France where gloomy forebodings were voiced. France still held in her hands some valuable assets for her security: the Rhineland was still demilitarized and the disarmament clauses of Versailles were still valid. But the trend was clear: one by one the fetters that the peace had imposed upon Germany were being broken. The decision to construct powerful fortifications along the German frontier, the so-called Maginot Line, may be interpreted as an indication on the French side of an attitude of pessimistic realism, an implied admission of lack of faith that security could be insured much longer through mere enforcement of the letter of the law of German disarmament.

Consequently, much importance attached to ultimate German intentions. That the evacuation of the Rhineland should be cause for rejoicing in Germany needs no explanation. But an election took place in Germany in September, the results of which were good cause for anxiety. The followers of Adolf Hitler had hitherto played the role of a lunatic fringe in German politics; there were twelve of them in the existing Reichstag. The rantings of *Mein Kampf* could be dismissed as preposterous aberration, just as the abortive Munich *Putsch* of 1923 could be regarded as a performance the chief aspect of which was the ridiculous.[76] But the

[75] Subsequent developments make even the "useful" questionable in the case of Britain. The agreement was much disliked in Japan where the Naval Minister received upon his return the present of a dagger, a suitable instrument for suicide, which a member of the Naval General Staff actually committed.

[76] On November 9, 1923, General Ludendorff and Adolf Hitler attempted an abortive coup in Munich. Hitler was arrested and sentenced to a prison term in Landsberg fortress; the time he put to use in writing *Mein Kampf*.

election of September, 1930, returned 107 Nazi representatives to the Reichstag; here was a strange manifestation of gratefulness for the concession of premature evacuation of the Rhineland. The seeming liquidation of the war, characteristic of the past five years, the harmonious duet of the Briand-Stresemann conjunction, economic good times—all this was but illusion, a passing dream prelude to a rude awakening. The return to a harsher reality, the legacy of issues which the war had itself partly created, but to some of which the war had merely given sharper point and added momentum, and the fumbling attempts to deal with the new problems we must now proceed to examine.

XII

The Return to Reality, 1930-1936

I. The Political Importance of Economics

THE NEW CLIMATE OF THE 1930'S

Ten years after the conclusion of the treaties of peace the signs of the year 1930 pointed toward the future in uncertain direction. The Young Plan, supposedly final settlement of the problem of German Reparation, became effective in May; some, though small, progress was made in disarmament with the conclusion of the naval Treaty of London and the continuing labors of the Preparatory Commission. But it could be pointed out that both these last developments left many issues unresolved, that Germany was straining for the removal of still remaining disabilities, and that the Nazis had achieved a marked and unexpected success.

It was within some days of the death of Gustav Stresemann that the New York stock market was the scene of a sensational collapse in security prices. The sudden American crash can hardly be held accountable for the subsequent ills of the world, but it was a symbolic occurrence, a date from which conveniently to mark a turn in the story of the postwar years. An economic and financial turn primarily, but the fact remains undeniable of the important interaction between economic and political events. The general economic well-being of the second half of the twenties had not a little to do with the relaxation of political tensions, which relaxation in turn was favorable to the promotion of political agreement. The cycle of boom and depression was a familiar one to the free capitalist economy; under its supposedly self-regulating operation Europe and the world had prospered during the nineteenth century and risen to an unprecedented level of material comfort. The whole world was about to embark on a depression of unparalleled magnitude and duration which was to have the effect of invalidating much of the classical approach to economic problems.

It is outside the scope of this treatment to dwell in detailed fashion and at length upon matters primarily economic; but these questions assume such overwhelming and all-prevading importance that brief mention at least must be made of them. One word, maldistribution, as much as any single one sums up the central difficulty; it applies to the supply of gold in the world as well as to the operation of the processes that establish a balance between the production and the consumption of raw materials and of industrial goods.

Overproduction is a term of relative content; it may be used, however, to describe the failure of production to be consumed, whatever be the reasons for the maladjustment. There was evidence in 1929 of an oversupply of raw materials, such basic ones as wheat and cotton. The effects of this situation were therefore naturally felt at first among the producers of these primary products, within the various countries, and, among countries, in those mainly engaged in the production of these commodities. The fall of raw material prices in turn impairs the purchasing capacity of raw material producers with corresponding repercussions on the sellers of manufactured goods. Such developments cannot but have an important political impact within nations; agricultural interests will clamor for subsidies and tariffs, which last appeal especially to industrial interests, while industrial workers will equally resist a diminution of their wages and, if wholly deprived of employment, will turn to the state for assistance. These are powerful pressures, and the tendency was thereby highly accelerated that urged the modern state to assume vast responsibilities for its members, most of all for the industrial workers, generally deprived of capital reserves and wholly dependent for their very existence upon the income of regular employment. The right to vote may, in such circumstances, take on the guise of an ironic luxury by comparison with the right to work; at most, the former makes it inevitable to take into account the latter. Much was to be heard about "economic democracy" as distinct from "political," and the first was often regarded as the more fundamental of the two. The crisis generally spread in Europe from east to west, from the agricultural toward the industrial states, while it created much political unrest in all.

In these developments the United States occupied a unique position. During the middle and late twenties American prosperity was such, outside the relatively depressed agricultural sector of the country, as to lead to much talk of the new economic era that an uninterruptedly ascending curve characterized. But there were maladjustments in America as well, of which overexpansion of credit and reckless speculation were rather symptoms and effects than causes. Hence the stock market crash of 1929 that ushered in the deepest depression ever known in the history of the United States and resulted in the repudiation in 1932 of the ruling administration.

American economic developments affected the rest of the world in two ways. The war had had the effect of brusquely changing the United States from a debtor to a creditor country while at the same time boosting the productive capacity of the nation. This called for readjustment that was not understood by the ruling political powers of the period. America endeavored to be at the same time the universal creditor and to build up a large favorable balance of trade. In 1928, for instance, the foreign balance due America amounted to about $1,600,000,000, divided almost equally between balance of trade on the one hand, debts and the return on foreign investments on the other. The balance was reëstablished[1] through the simple device of exporting American capital in the form of additional loans.

This device had been used for some time; it had in large measure made possible the successful operation of the Dawes Plan; Germany had duly paid Reparation, while payments on the American war debts by the Allies had been likewise forthcoming. But such a method was no more than a temporary palliative, which, for the long term, merely postponed a reckoning that the passage of time would tend to make all the more difficult of liquidation. In addition, much of the world's gold had found its way to America. In these phenomena, to a large degree unperceived when not willfully unrecognized, lay the key to much of the successful operation of the European economy during the twenties. It was a fallacy about to be revealed, for the effect of domestic difficulty in the United States was to dry up at its source the golden stream of American capital export; as if to compound a bad situation, the understandable American reaction was to concentrate on the domestic aspects of the problem, to emphasize isolation, political

---

[1] Roughly half of this amount was balanced by so-called invisible payments, American tourist expenditures and immigrant remittances abroad.

no less than economic; specifically, to raise the level of the existing American tariff.

THE GERMAN SITUATION.   Among the major European states, economic difficulty was especially marked in Germany. To a degree, Germany, like America, had indulged in overexpansion and she was unusually dependent on the influx of foreign capital;[2] she was first to feel the repercussions of financial difficulty in the agricultural European East. Germany, it must be remembered, had been severely shaken in the aftermath of the war; her prosperity had been too short-lived to erase memories of the chaos of the great inflation, while the political system of Weimar was also young and little tried, hence less capable than that of older established democracies to withstand unusual strains.

The death of Stresemann had brought into the Cabinet a far less able substitute, Dr. Curtius, no other change occurring in the government of Chancellor Müller. The impact of economic crisis brought divisions in the government and the Reichstag over the issue of sound finance—balanced budgets versus the claims of social legislation, specifically the unemployed. The accession to the Chancellorship of Dr. Brüning marks the beginning of the end of the Weimar experiment in Germany. Able, respected, and uncommonly aloof, Brüning was also deficient in the more congenial attributes of the politician's craft; the Republic he would preserve, but with the support of the Social Democrats, its most reliable defenders, he would willingly dispense. Defeated in the Reichstag in July, his response was to dissolve that body. The ensuing election belied his expectations: while the Catholic Center and the Social Democrats held their own, the Nazis, as mentioned before, emerged with a sixfold increase of the popular vote and a Reichstag membership that rose from 12 to 107.

Brüning could only remain in office with the support of the Social Democrats, grudgingly given him as the lesser evil from their point of view. From 1930 on it was difficult to organize in Germany a government that had either stability or authority; the Republic could only be maintained through the resort to the emergency provision of its own constitution, increasingly putting power into presidential hands. Von Hindenburg made no attempt to abuse these powers, but the emergency was never overcome

[2] It is calculated that, during 1927–1928, Germany borrowed abroad an amount equal to five times the total of her Reparation payments.

within the framework of Weimar. The years from 1930 to 1932 witnessed the agony of the Weimar Republic. The great democratic wave had begun to recede from the heart of Europe, a state of affairs highly inimical to hopes that, until 1929, had found expression mainly in Geneva.

The fate of the scheme of European union is symbolic of the altered atmosphere. In a variety of forms the desirability of some sort of union of Europe had been advocated by a variety of individuals and organizations. The concept has an old history that inserts itself into the memory of universal Rome and universal Christendom. But the rise of the national state had been inimical to it, and all attempts at unification by force had been successfully defeated by the differences among European states, encouraged and sustained by the traditional policy of Britain. Under the dispensation of Geneva the prospect was now raised of union by consent.

Briand himself, among statesmen in a position of importance and responsibility, came to espouse the idea, the advocacy of which, albeit in vague and guarded terms, he made the subject of one of his great orations, in September, 1929, on the occasion of the tenth Assembly of the League. Stresemann gave him warm support—it was almost the last act of his life—and Briand was entrusted by the delegates of the European Powers in Geneva with the task of drawing up a more concrete proposal. This was forthcoming in May, 1930, and was sent to the Powers. The gist of it lay in an effort to create security in Europe through an extension of the Locarno type of arrangement and to approach the task of integration at the political rather than at the economic level.

The response was discouraging, for when it came to facing the concrete possibility, individual differences and objections asserted themselves. To say nothing of the smaller Powers, among the major ones, Germany, as at Locarno, was reluctant to abandon her revisionist hopes in the East; Italian Fascism had little sympathy with the internationalist outlook; in Britain, too, despite the existence of a Labour government, the national tradition prevailed: Britain's imperial position, the voice of the Dominions, was a reason, or a convient pretext, for minimizing the possible extent of integration to vague and loose "collaboration," which Henderson defended against Briand's insistence on the necessity of federal and political links. In September, 1930, the eleventh Assembly of the

League created a "study commission" to examine the project. For all that he assumed the presidency of the commission, Briand did not misunderstand the significance of this classical form of polite burial.

THE AUSTRO-GERMAN CUSTOMS UNION PROPOSAL. These same years, 1930–1931, witnessed an interesting manifestation of the interaction among matters political, economic, and financial. The new Austria that had emerged from the disintegration of the Habsburg monarchy had, from the first, had a troubled existence, in large measure owing to the problem of readjustment to her newly restricted territory and circumstances; the Germanic character of Austria gave rise in her case to the special issue of possible *Anschluss* with larger Germany. But the initial crisis of the post war years was surmounted[3] and little Austria achieved a measure of stability in which some saw the possibility of a successful new Switzerland. In 1930, the meeting held at The Hague for the purpose of making final arrangements for the enactment of the Young Plan had exonerated Austria from the payment of further Reparation.

But Austria felt the impact of economic crisis, especially in the form of repercussions from the financial difficulties of the neighboring agricultural countries of Eastern Europe. Out of these circumstances, and on the rather specious plea that Germany and Austria could relieve each other's distress, came the agreement in March, 1931, of what was tantamount to the economic union of the two countries, signed by the respective foreign ministers, Curtius and Schober.[4]

To Briand this announcement was a source of irritation and embarrassment, especially as he had just voiced in France the opinion that any danger of *Anschluss* was past. To be sure, the proposal was limited to customs "coördination," but it could easily revive memories of the nineteenth-century *Zollverein*, prelude to political union; the French reaction to the ill-timed proposal was

[3] In 1922, in response to the appeal of the Austrian Chancellor, Monsignor Seipel, the League appointed a commissioner to supervise the task of restoration of Austrian finances. The success of the operation resulted in the termination of League supervision in 1926. In connection with the League intervention of 1922 Austria's obligation to maintain her independence—meaning renunciation of the *Anschluss*—was reaffirmed.

[4] This project was in part a response to the attempt of the Little Entente and Poland to organize an agricultural bloc.

one of unusual violence.[5] In May, the French Chamber as well as the Little Entente expressed their opposition to the scheme; when it came up for consideration before the Council of the League, opposition was likewise expressed by the French, British, and Italian delegates, and the outcome was a unanimous agreement to submit the matter to the Permanent Court of International Justice at The Hague. The question was whether or not the Austro-German scheme was compatible with the treaties of peace of Versailles and St. Germain and with the obligations undertaken by Austria in connection with the assistance that she had received in 1922.

Pending the Court's advisory opinion, the Austrian government agreed to take no further action. But this was just the time when the impact of economic crisis took a more concrete financial shape. The failure of the largest Austrian bank, the Viennese *Creditanstalt*, was declared on May 12, resulting in a governmental crisis. By July, Germany was also in the throes of a banking crisis that resulted in the suspension of payments. In August, Austria once more appealed to the League for financial assistance.

The impact of the financial crisis was felt unequally among countries. The German crisis especially had marked repercussions in England, to the extent that, in August, in response to domestic emergency, the Labour government yielded place to one of National Union over which MacDonald continued to preside.[6] Britain was in no condition to offer immediate assistance which, at the same time, could only come from France, seemingly still immune to the crisis and where gold was in ample supply. But France was little minded to assist Austria in the circumstances, and one may see in this occasion an illustration of the use of French financial power for political ends reminiscent of pre-1914 years. The Court's

[5] This should be seen, from the French point of view, in the context of the succession of events that were the anticipated evacuation of the Rhineland in June, 1930, the German election of September, and finally the economic *Anschluss* proposal of March, 1931. This last, which also had the value of an attempted diversion from domestic political difficulties in both Austria and Germany, was, on Germany's part, less than skillful diplomacy.

[6] The specific issue over which the political crisis arose was that of the budget, to balance which unemployment benefits must be curtailed. The Labour government was split and most of the party refused to follow that portion of its leadership which gave priority to financial soundness. Consequently, Labour suffered a disastrous setback in the election of October, 1931, and the coalition continued to govern under the Union label and the presidency of MacDonald, while in effect the bulk of its support became Conservative. As a result of the continued drain on her gold reserves, Britain abandoned the gold standard in September.

decision was to be delivered on September 5; on the 3rd, Austria and Germany announced their voluntary abandonment of the economic *Anschluss*. The Court's opinion, when rendered, sustained the French contention, though the eight to seven· division of the judges suggested as much political as legal content in the verdict, and the whole episode left behind it a train of suspicion.

This was also the time that saw the final liquidation of German Reparation. Between the cessation of the flow of American capital abroad and the impact of the Eastern European crisis, Germany found herself unable, in 1931, to meet her Young Plan obligation. It is appropriate expression of the true reality of the mechanism under which the international financial obligations growing out of the war had been met that an appeal for relief should issue from the President of Germany, the universal debtor, to that of the United States, the universal creditor. The result was President Hoover's proposal of a year's moratorium on all such international payments, to begin on July 1, 1931. The proposal was accepted, but the French resented the cavalier treatment of their interest: instead of being previously consulted in a matter where they had to forego a large credit balance, they had been placed in a position where their refusal would have isolated them in opposition to a measure desirable for the recovery of all. Matters were hardly helped when, on the occasion of his visit to Washington in October, the French Prime Minister, Laval, encountered the usual American refusal to acknowledge a formal connection between Reparation and war debts, despite the *de facto* link that the American President had himself just established.

That contention was still maintained when the year's moratorium came to an end. At the conference that met at Lausanne in July, 1932, the impossibility for Germany to resume Reparation payments was acknowledged by her European creditors; the payment of a final lump sum of 3 billion marks—even that payment was never forthcoming—would wipe completely clean the slate of Reparation. The resumption of payments to the United States— the next payment fell due in December—gave rise to heated debate, most of all in the French Parliament. America's creditors were fundamentally agreed in their view of the matter, but the French alone in the end elected to incur the moral onus of willful default. The eloquent appeal of Herriot, the French Prime Minister, to honor the country's signature regardless of the rights and wrongs of the case, could not overcome the resentment to which American obduracy gave rise in France. Herriot fell and France defaulted, a fact that, needless to say, in turn created considerable resentment in America.[7]

Over these last developments Briand did not preside in France. His long tenure at the Quai d'Orsay came to an end in January, 1932, to be followed within two months by his death. His passing, like Stresemann's, was symbolic; a shadow of himself toward the end of his period of office, he died a disillusioned man, fully aware that failure had attended his efforts, the focus of which had been the maintenance of future peace. It was also appropriately symbolic of the changing times that, in 1931, rather than devote his attention to the furtherance of European union and Franco-German reconciliation, Briand should preside over matters that had to deal with the first serious and fundamental challenge to the Genevan institution. That challenge arose not in Europe, but in the remote Far East. It will be dealt with briefly for that reason, but in view of the far-reaching implications that it held for Europe as well, mention of it must be made.

THE LEAGUE AND THE MANCHURIAN EPISODE

The background of the Manchurian crisis of 1931 lay in two things: Chinese nationalism and Japanese imperialism, a clash between which need be little cause for surprise.

Out of the long-standing chaos of China the possibility of reconstruction had seemed for a moment to emerge. During the 1920's the Kuomintang, or Nationalist party, effected a reconquest of the whole country. Nationalist China was antiforeign and, logically, had received advice and assistance from the Soviet Union. However, the reconquest once effected, the leader of Nationalist China, Chiang Kai-shek, turned against his Communist allies whom he ruthlessly suppressed in China. By 1931 it appeared that the control of all China was rather less than either complete or final: apart from the recurrent scourges of famine and flood, some areas were still under Communist rule, such as Fukien and Kiangsi, seces-

[7] The French contention may be regarded as basically sound, though the manner of implementing it was unfortunate. In face of the persistent American obstinacy, after a short time all the debtors, save "honest" Finland, came to default, a position in which, technically, they have remained ever since. Eventually, America, too, acknowledged economic reality and the skillful device of Lend-Lease used in the Second World War was in large part intended to avoid the recurrence of the situation and the recriminations that followed the first war, accepting as it did the contention of the Allies of the first war that the war was a joint enterprise for a common purpose of equal importance to all.

sion reappeared in Canton, banditry was rife, and rebellion occurred in the north as well. The Nationalist government was beset
by more urgent cares than the effort to rid China of the "unequal
treaties," the most irksome manifestation of which was in the
existence of foreign concessions and of extraterritoriality.

On the Japanese side the astonishing record of the development
of Japanese industry and power is familiar. But this Japanese
growth had the effect of creating a colossal pressure of population
—increasing at the rate of close to 1,000,000 a year—on exiguous
native resources, and hence made foreign trade a matter of vital
importance for Japan. Much of Japanese trade flowed to the United
States and to China. But Chinese chaos interfered with this commerce no less than did nationalistic boycotts, and the American
depression dealt a severe blow to the silk trade of Japan. In 1931
economic stress was severe in Japan.

More narrowly, Manchuria had become the special focus of
Japanese interest which, by 1930, was dominant in the southern
part of that province. Manchuria was mainly Chinese in population,
but effective control was in the hands of a local chieftain, or war
lord, Chang Hsueh-liang, who, in alliance with rather than under
the obedience of Nanking, was striving to consolidate his power.
This in itself was cause for alarm to the Japanese who had invested
considerable capital in the development of Manchuria, its mineral
resources and soybean cultivation. Moreover, the Japanese enjoyed
certain rights in Manchuria, particularly that to administer and
garrison the so-called railway zone of the South Manchurian railway, for which purpose they maintained a force of some 25,000
men.

To these privileges Chinese nationalism understandably took
exception, and the successes of this nationalism, in coöperation
with Chang Hsueh-liang, were correspondingly a cause of Japanese suspicion, no less than the steady influx of Chinese settlers
in Manchuria. Moreover, on the Japanese side, the impact of economic stress had the political effect of promoting the influence
of the military element; ruthless and aggressive, the Japanese military were not reluctant to use assassination to cow their opponents
at home, a device not condemned by much of Japanese opinion.
Some at least of the military leaders nurtured grandiose visions of
the outright conquest of Manchuria as a first step toward the creation of a vast empire on the mainland of Asia, of which Mongolia
and North China, and possibly all China, would be part. Reminis-

cent in some respects of pre-Weimar Germany, the military held a position of privilege in the Japanese state.

This background, briefly sketched, explains why, in 1931, conditions in Manchuria were ripe for the occurrence of a clash. Incidents were customary fare, and one of these served to initiate a larger development. Following the murder of a Japanese captain, in August, on September 18 the Japanese seized control of Mukden after promptly cowing the Chinese garrison in that city.[8] The Mukden incident, small enough in itself, was the starting point of a long train of events. Of the local aspects of the matter it will suffice to say that, disregarding the more moderate tendency in their own government, the Japanese military proceeded with their own plans, which the advent to the war office of General Araki, a domestic victory for them, made it easier to pursue. While hostilities took place for a time in Shanghai, this was essentially a diversion from the main center of activity in Manchuria where the superior military machine of Japan easily accomplished its purpose. By February, 1932, a puppet self-appointed Manchurian convention approved the declaration of Manchurian independence, over which the dethroned emperor of China, Pu-yi, was to preside as K'ang Tê, Emperor of Manchuria. The state of Manchukuo was born, which Japan recognized and with which a convention was made in September that recognized Japan's right to insure domestic security and external defense. Call it protectorate or colony, Manchuria was in effect a Japanese preserve.[9]

Such episodes had not in the past been infrequent. But what gave this affair an unwonted significance was the fact that China, in her distress and impotence, immediately appealed to the League for assistance against Japan's aggression, thereby presenting that body with the first major test since its original formation. The

[8] The Japanese claimed to have taken this action as a result of the blowing up of a section of the South Manchurian Railway and of Chinese attacks against them. The effectiveness of their action, which took the Mukden garrison by surprise, pointed to careful prior planning and the Japanese charges were widely disbelieved. That aspect of the matter is, however, relatively secondary; incidents were frequent occurrences and once the Japanese determination to seize Manchuria is acknowledged, the finding of pretexts for initiating action becomes a minor issue.

[9] Not content with their accomplishment in Manchuria, the Japanese extended their operations into Jehol and into China proper, crossing the Great Wall and threatening Peking. The Chinese government of Chiang Kai-shek yielded at this point, in May, 1933, concluding an armistice with Japan in which, however, it did not surrender its political claims

rights and wrongs of the case might be argued, for all that Japanese intent was clear, since under existing treaties Japan did have legitimate grievances; but in essence the issue was whether the dispute could be resolved by peaceful means, and therefore whether or not the writ of Geneva was valid. From the point of view of the League the circumstances of the case were particularly awkward. In the last resort, the power that the League could use, should it come to the use of power to enforce decisions, was in the main British naval power. The problem therefore was to a special degree also a British problem.

Such a problem it was in two senses. Britain had her own extensive Far Eastern interests. The generally antiforeign attitude of the Chinese Nationalists—much anti-Britishness had accompanied their rise to power in China—might point to the desirability of the older British tendency to act in the Far East in combination and agreement with Japan, even though the formal alliance had fallen victim to the British desire to conciliate American feeling. Here was a situation where Britain stood to bear the chief burden as peace-enforcing agent for much of the rest of the world. To be sure, this was a crucial test; if the League could prove effective in this instance, its prestige would be enormously enhanced and it could command much respect from other would-be aggressors. Much would depend, therefore, on the view that Britain took of things, but it must be remembered that the traditional British approach to foreign policy is inimical to the assumption of generalized commitments with a view to meeting theoretical future possibilities.

Further difficulties arose from the special conditions that surrounded the Far Eastern clash. Apart from the principals in the dispute, three major Powers had significant interests in the area, Britain, the Soviet Union, and the United States. But the last two were not members of the League at the time. The Soviet state was still relatively weak; disillusioned with the anti-Communist turn of Chiang Kai-shek, but highly inimical to Japanese expansion in Asia, the Soviet role appeared uncertain and might reduce itself to extracting what advantage might accrue from the course of events. The United States, broadly speaking, was sympathetic to China and correspondingly antagonistic to Japan, but the United States was not anxious to commit itself very far in underwriting League action; more concretely, the question was raised of the

American attitude in the event of Far Eastern naval complications. Might it possibly insist on the rights of neutrals at sea in wartime?[10]

These general considerations affected in considerable measure the response of the League to the problem; it is best summarized in two words, evasion and inaction. In September, and again in October, the Council summoned Japan to withdraw her forces. Aware of the lack of power to enforce these demands, Japan refused to comply; in December the Council appointed the Lytton Commission to conduct a local investigation and to report on the facts. By the time the Lytton report was forthcoming, in September, 1932, the Japanese invasion had made considerable progress. The report was a judicious document which, while not exonerating China, recognized Japan as the aggressor.

In the end no action was taken. The value of purely verbal condemnation instead of simple silence may be questioned. Japan withdrew from the League in March, 1933. Had it not been for the existence of the League, the Japanese conquest of Manchuria could have been viewed as one chapter in the book of imperial activity, the effects of which are by no means all detrimental. But the conditions of 1931 put the Manchurian affair in a wholly altered context. Apart from having breached her obligations under the Nine-Power Treaty of 1922, no less than under the Kellogg-Briand Pact, Japan had with success defied the unanimous verdict of Geneva. The severity of the blow to the hopes of collective security can hardly be overstated and this is the main significance of the Manchurian episode in the present story. Some comfort could be derived, however, from the consideration of the special circumstances of the case—the absence of the United States and of the Soviet Union from the League, and the fact that the League was essentially a European organization that might yet prove capable of dealing with primarily European issues. No more than two years were to pass before the validity of that hope would be tested.

To consider the perennial of disarmament at such a time and in such circumstances may be viewed as an exercise in futile beating of the air. It was precisely that, and the matter need not detain

[10] There was no prospect at any time that the United States would join in naval action in the Far East. The American contribution remained largely confined to the enunciation by Secretary of State Stimson, in January, 1932, of the doctrine of nonrecognition of the results of aggression, an empty gesture in the circumstances.

us, save briefly for the sake of completeness. The London Naval Conference of 1930 had produced results essentially confined to the consent of the three chief naval Powers, the United States, Great Britain, and Japan, while France and Italy remained in disagreement. Franco-Italian discussions continued for a time; of them it may suffice to say that they furnished the occasion for some bombastic, if vague, threats by Mussolini; in the end, failing of agreement, they left a legacy of recrimination. But the general disarmament conference did meet, as planned, in February, 1932, at the very height of the Far Eastern crisis. Discussion more than ever was futile though it went on around schemes of varying degrees of ingenuity. Perhaps the most significant development, harbinger of more important things soon to come, was the notification by the German government, on September 16, of its decision to withdraw from the conference since it perceived no signs of progress toward the accomplishment of its particular desire, equality of rights. This new turn of events was met with ingenuity; a meeting of five Powers (the United States, Britain, France, Italy, and Germany) produced a formal declaration that recognized the German claim "in a system which would provide security for all nations." Even the French could underwrite this meaningless collection of words. It had the effect of bringing the Germans back into the disarmament conference, but a limit had been reached in that particular aspect of the diplomatic art which consists in the use, or abuse, of language for purposes of concealing reality. Even that aspect of the art is at times not devoid of value, but it cannot serve indefinitely as a substitute for the solution of differences.

The League successfully defied, disarmament attempts hopelessly deadlocked, the world wrapped in deepest economic crisis, in turn creator of domestic stress and of international tensions, the stalemate was about to be broken through a return to the crude reassertion of the brute rights of power.

II. Europe and Nazi Germany

NAZISM AND ITS ADVENT TO POWER

There are at all times large quantities of matter printed to which sane and serious-minded men will devote no attention. But on occasion, out of the literary trash, something emerges the importance of which is no less, but rather more, for its having defied the ordinary canons of common sense and good taste. *Mein Kampf* by Adolf Hitler is an important book.

The abortive Munich *putsch* of 1923 had earned one of its leaders, Hitler, a prison term in Landsberg fortress. The enforced leisure he used to write *Mein Kampf*. Be it on the score of literary merit or at the level of the content of ideas, the product could only be rated very low, the rantings of a disappointed man, envenomed and frustrated, of which little heed need be taken. Yet the book contained a program and the outline of methods for achieving this program that were destined to be put into action. Fanaticism and aberration well describe much of it; the wonder is that such rantings could capture the imagination and for a time control the destinies of what for long had called itself—a claim granted by others—a great civilized nation.

In simplest terms and for our purposes, of Nazism some things alone need be retained. The name itself is significant, derived from that of the party, *National Sozialistische Deutsche Arbeiter Partei*, or National Socialist German Workers party. Like Fascism, of which this was a more virulent and, in the test, effective version, the combination of the first two words represents a new view of by this time classical conflicts. The workers, the people, the mass are indeed the fundamental and important core of the nation; their stake, however, and the hope of satisfaction and their needs, lies not in the divisive and costly struggle of classes, but in union for purposes of strengthening the nation, whose energies should be directed toward the securing of its proper place among other nations. For Germany, in contrast with Italy, that place must be not only a high one, but indeed the first, the right to it deriving from the simple fact of superiority to all others. The racial theories of Nazism were not novel; the French Gobineau and the English Houston Stewart Chamberlain had long ago expounded them, but now for the first time these theories were to be in control of a state that was to use its power to carry out their implications to the extremes of logical conclusion. Leaving aside the colored peoples, wholly beyond the pale, between the poles of Germanic Nordic and Jew, intermediaries ranged in weird gradation: the master race had the right to rule others, to insure if necessary the physical elimination of their polluting influence.

In order to procure the enactment of the consequences of German superiority, the German nation needed unity, enforced by coercion if necessary. Hence the stress on conformity, the intolerance of opposition, the coördination (*Gleichschaltung*) of all aspects of activity, the totalitarian state, the assertion of authority, and over all the principle of blind allegiance to leadership. It is not altogether fortuitous, but rather a form of adaptation to the circumstances of our time, that so much common ground should have existed between the systems and practices that prevailed for a time in Germany and Italy and still obtain in Russia. The fact that the last rests in the last analysis on a serious philosophy and has a large rational content, while the other two were compounded of much emotion and irrationality, may account for their demise while the Russian still prospers. In lighter vein, and with reference to Nazi racial views, the quip used to be current that the perfect Nordic must be blond like Hitler, slim like Göring, tall and well-shaped like Goebbels, and bear a typical German name like Rosenberg; yet this strange collection of men managed to extract from Germany and organize to most telling effect power of unsuspected dimensions.

After the election of September, 1930, when the Nazis scored their first notable success, their progress in the troubled conditions of Germany was rapid. The period from 1930 to 1932 witnessed the breakdown of parliamentary government in Germany; repeated consultations of the electorate furnished no clearer answer in the form of producing workable majorities. Like it or no, Catholic Center and Social Democrats must at least tolerate each other to the extent of making possible emergency government by decree and the use of the presidential prerogative. In 1932 Hindenburg's term came to an end. The result was not devoid of irony, for he was induced to be a candidate for his own succession by the defenders of the Republic, his opponents of 1925, who now saw in his name, his prestige, and his record the best hope of stemming the rising Nazi tide. Hindenburg was reëlected, though as in 1925 again, only on a second ballot, the Communists once more refusing to make common cause with the republican forces. Nazis and Communists were bitter enemies who would with enthusiasm resort to violence against each other; yet to a point they worked to the same end, both being dedicated to the destruction of the Weimar regime, from which destruction each group thought of itself as the ultimate beneficiary.

Hindenburg was eighty-five years of age. The grand old man commanded universal respect, but the malicious or humorous tales that circulated about him were not inaccurate expression of the impaired condition of his faculties, and he fell increasingly under the influence of men of his own social ilk, the old military class of Germany. He dismissed Brüning, who had indeed become unpopular in all quarters, and, to the general surprise, availing himself of Article 48 of the Weimar constitution, constituted a "government of barons" under the presidency of an irresponsible intriguer, von Papen, perhaps most aptly described as a combination of the fox and the snake.[11] It is a measure of the weakness of the liberal forces of Germany that the Prussian government of Otto Braun meekly allowed itself to be ousted in July, von Papen appropriating the post of High Commissioner for Prussia. Here was a preview of *Gleichschaltung*.

An election, also in July, returned 230 Nazis backed by a popular vote of nearly 14,000,000. They were nearing the point of absolute majority in the Reichstag, but Hindenburg would not yet yield to Hitler's demand for full powers. Yet the Reichstag showed its nearly unanimous distrust of von Papen to whom it gave an adverse vote of 513 to 32. Another dissolution, followed by another election, marked a setback for the Nazis; their loss of some 2,000,000 votes gave rise to the hope in some quarters that the tide had passed its full crest and might begin to ebb. Despite his personal liking of von Papen, Hindenburg now called to the Chancellorship the minister of the *Reichswehr*, General von Schleicher. The activity of von Schleicher is proper cause for some interesting considerations on the attribute of honorability and forthrightness that the leaders of the German military class have been fond of claiming for themselves. His oversubtle and unscrupulous intrigues and calculations had the effect, within two months, of inducing the weary Hindenburg to call Hitler to the Chancellorship of the Reich, on January 30, 1933.

Allowing for some important differences, here was a repetition of what had happened in Italy just ten years earlier. But the molding of the Third or Nazi Reich proceeded far more rapidly than that of the Fascist state. For all that opposition to the Versailles *diktat* and rantings about Germany's rights and greatness were

---

[11] Von Papen had first come to public notice when, as military attaché to the Washington Embassy during the First World War, his recall had been demanded by the American government owing to his improper activities. It is a measure of the man, and a credit to his eel-like abilities, that, having served all the successive German regimes, he emerged in exoneration from the post-Second World World trials.

useful tools in the Nazi armory, the chief concerns of the German people were domestic. To insure their recovery Hitler must be free of the dead weight of an impotent and stalemated Parliament. An election in March, the last free one in Germany before the war, gave him a broad mandate.[12] With other groups he dealt in simple fashion: briefly, the opposition was eliminated and outlawed; more congenial groups, the Nationalists for instance, could be absorbed. The Enabling Act gave him the full powers he asked and made him complete master of Germany; Hindenburg was reduced to an impotent shadow, and when he died in 1934 was not even replaced. The Führer's power was absolute and dictatorial.

This domestic background is of the greatest importance, which is the reason why it has been briefly sketched, and we may now return to the larger European scene. What importance attached to Nazi xenophobia and *Mein Kampf* was uncertain in 1933; clearly, in any case, effective German power could not become a reality for some time. Nevertheless a large question mark was posed to deal with which the optimistic ideology of Geneva, the spirit of Locarno, seemed hardly adequate.

THE FOUR-POWER PACT

It might have been expected in the circumstances that the strongest and most definite reaction to these events would have come from France, the Power on whom more than any other the structure of Europe depended for its unaltered preservation. Yet this was not the case. The year 1932 was an election year in France; it was also the time during which the seeming French immunity to the impact of world crisis was shown to be illusion. The economic crisis did not reach highly severe proportions in France where the financial position was still very strong;[13] it did nevertheless induce a degree of malaise that found political ex-

[12] Out of a poll of nearly 40,000,000 the Nazis obtained more than 17,000,000 votes which, with 3,000,000 Nationalist votes, constituted a majority of the popular vote. The Catholic Center, the Social Democrats, and the Communists roughly held their own with 5,500,000, 7,000,000, and 4,800,000 votes respectively, and this outcome, despite a measure of coercion, warrants speaking of the election as free.

[13] The importance of Britain in world trade caused a number of countries to follow suit when Britain abandoned the gold standard in 1931. These constituted the sterling bloc, in contrast to the gold bloc, of which the United States and France were the most important members. When the United States in turn abandoned the gold standard in 1933, France continued to adhere to it along with some other European countries.

pression. The result was not alarming and did not threaten the regime as in Germany; ostensibly, the French election of May, 1932, represented no more than a return to the normal *sinistrisme* of French politics, expressed in the form of a victory at the polls of the *Cartel des Gauches*. However, the legislature of 1932 was the one during whose life the postwar structure of Europe was destined to collapse. In view of the role and position of France as cornerstone of that structure, the domestic condition of France during the subsequent four years assumes no less international importance than that of Germany, out of which the Nazi state was born.

The continued discussion of disarmament in the circumstances of 1933 may seem like mere unrealistic aberration, which in fact it was. It is enlightening to recall some dates: On January 30 Hitler became Reichschancellor, on February 2 the disarmament conference resumed its sessions, on February 24 Japan gave notice of her intention to withdraw from the League. But the British Prime Minister, MacDonald, would not allow his optimism to be damped and appeared in Geneva in March with a new draft convention, the details of which need not detain us beyond noting that it proposed tentatively concrete numbers of effectives for the various Powers, including Germany.

Mussolini had other ideas. Priding himself on realism, Geneva and all that it stood for had never held much attraction for him; the institution of peace was a utopia that some age yet to come might realize, but the present day was still one of struggle among the competing forces that were nations. The advent of Hitler in Germany was not displeasing to Mussolini who felt flattered instead by what he took to be the compliment of imitation; German power, restored to a degree, would in addition revive the possibilities of the traditional Italian position in exploiting the balance of power. From Geneva the British ministers were called to Rome, whither they went and were presented with a first draft of the proposal that came to be known as the Four-Power Pact.

The essence of the concept was simple. There were in Europe four Great Powers, Britain, France, Italy, and Germany. On the basis of equality among themselves they should shoulder the responsibility for the organization of Europe and the preservation of peace. Here was, in other words, a formalization of the old concept of the Concert of Europe. This would imply, of course, a recognition of the German claim to equality and the lifting of

German disabilities—not at once, but over a period of time—and Mussolini's proposal consistently laid stress on the need for the revision of treaties, adding also mention of readjustment in the colonial field.

The devotion of the British ministers to the League was evidently not such as to prevent their favorable reaction to the Mussolinian proposal. On their way home they took it up in Paris where, more surprisingly perhaps, the opposition that might have been expected was not found. But if the French did not or pretended not to see the full implications of the scheme, there were others who did. The Little Entente ministers[14] raised a loud cry of alarm, fully warranted by the suggestion that "others" might be induced to accept whatever decisions the Big Four might reach among themselves. The Poles and the Belgians were likewise alarmed and the fears of France's allies had repercussions in Paris.

France dealt with the situation with diplomatic skill. Rather than reject out of hand the Italian proposal, negotiations went on and counterproposals were submitted which became the bases of the Four-Power Pact that was eventually signed in Rome on June 7. By that time Mussolini had largely lost interest in the scheme, and rightly so, for the final result bore no resemblance to the original conception. Where the need of treaty revision had been stressed, the possibility was now acknowledged of such revision *only* under agreed procedures—a meaningless reassertion of Article 19 of the Covenant—through the agency of the League rather than that of the Four-Power directorate, and not without consultation of those concerned.

The alarm of the small states was fully justified, just as was their support of collective security and the League. Nevertheless, it may be pointed out that if the League was destined to be impotent, a return to the older concept of the Concert of Europe was not wholly devoid of merit. For Germany it would have meant a very substantial gain, another great step forward on the path to full liberation and equality. Neither Britain nor Italy were, in the last analysis, desirous of encouraging a German dominance of Europe though neither would be loath to diminish the role of "French hegemony"; but a case could be made for believing that Germany could be more effectively controlled if she were a member of the inner directing circle of Europe, since any at-

[14] In February, 1933, the Little Entente countries strengthened their association by creating a Permanent Council of their foreign ministers.

tempt on her part unduly to enhance her position would automatically have tended to create against her a coalition of her three associates.

Perhaps the most significant aspect of the Mussolinian proposal was the challenge that it contained to the existing order of Europe. Under this scheme the position of France would be considerably diminished and France was faced with the dilemma of choosing between her allies and accepting a position of equality as one among four. The possibility also existed that agreement among the four and the peace of Europe might be preserved, as had happened on earlier occasions, through their agreement at the expense of the smaller Powers; what else could in fact be the meaning of the stress on revision and on inducing others to accept the verdict of the Four? For the moment French diplomacy saved the day and, having emasculated the original proposal, went on to reassure France's allies, among whom the episode left none the less some lingering suspicion.

The negotiations attending the Four-Power Pact served to prolong for a time the discussion of disarmament. Hitlerian diplomacy was already embarking on the practice of skillfully mixing and alternating conciliation and threats. On May 17 Hitler delivered himself of an unexpectedly moderate speech, following which Germany adopted an attitude of coöperation that made agreement possible on the basis of the MacDonald plan. The relaxation of tensions thereby procured was short-lived. When the disarmament conference reconvened in the autumn it was faced with German demands for a substantial degree of rearmament. Having given no prior warning of its intentions, on October 14 the German government brusquely gave notice of its withdrawal from the conference, a notice soon followed by the declaration of its intention to withdraw from the League altogether. In December Hitler stated that he would resume negotiations only on his own terms.[15]

FRANCE AND THE GERMAN PROBLEM

The efforts to achieve agreement on the score of the degree of armament were in effect dead; Mussolini's judgment was sound

[15] These were a conscript army of 300,000 endowed with all the weapons that the conference had declared "defensive"; the para-military organizations, the S.A. and the S.S., were to be excluded from the count of armed forces, and the immediate return of the Saar was also demanded. Hitler's position at home had meanwhile been fortified by the endorsement of the plebiscite held on November 12.

when he stated in December that, in the failure of revision through the Four-Power Pact, the voice would belong henceforth to his majesty the cannon. Some futile negotiations nevertheless went on, based on a direct German memorandum to France, and on a British effort to reconcile the two extreme positions. The French condition of a prior German return to Geneva having been rejected, some further negotiations were followed by a French declaration of April 17, 1934, that virtually closed the door to discussion. Stating that she refused to give the sanction of legality to the rearmament of Germany, France would henceforth insure her security by her own means.[16] These were brave words; there was much to be said for not wasting further time and effort on the illusion of the worth of agreements concluded with Hitler's Germany. But what did the words mean unless France was prepared in the event to avail herself of the rights that legally were still hers? The likelihood that France would adopt the logical suggestion of nipping in the bud the threat of German rearmament by preventive war stood little chance of acceptance;[17] meanwhile, in British eyes, France bore the onus for the final break in negotiations.

That doubts existed on the score of French intentions was revealed by the action of France's most important ally. Poland had two great enemies, the two great Powers to the east and west of herself, but the greatest danger of all for her lay in the possibility of agreement between these two, agreement most easily procured at her expense. The combination of the highly nationalistic content of Nazism with the long-standing German grievance over the "bleeding frontier" of the east might seem proper cause of alarm for Poland. But the ideological dislike of Soviet Russia, that Nazi Germany professed to share, also provided common ground. Nevertheless, the announcement on January 26 of the conclusion of a ten-year agreement between Germany and Poland was cause for general surprise. This did not mean that Germany renounced her eastern claims or that Poland had suddenly become blindly enamored of Germany; it was a temporizing move in the increasingly fluid situation of Europe: the two countries merely agreed

[16] The French government was divided on the issue, some arguing the value of an agreement that would bind Germany, even if they were not sanguine over the value of Hitlerian promises. The totally uncompromising position taken by France seems to have been motivated in part by the belief in the fragility of the Nazi regime.

[17] It was thrown out in May in Mussolini's paper, *Popolo d'Italia.*

that for ten years they would renounce the use of force in the settlement of their differences. Promises cost Hitler little, and for that matter it would take some years before Germany, even if unimpeded by outside interference, could recreate a military force of consequence. Poland did not renounce the French alliance, but clearly the Nazi-Polish Pact was a severe blow to that alliance and had the significance of a pointed warning to France.

Doubts about the solidity of French purpose were further warranted by the conditions of the domestic French scene. The impact of economic crisis in France, combined with the example of her eastern neighbors, created some response in France to the appeal of totalitarian methods, but mainly it produced confusion and unfocused unrest. Leagues of varying nomenclature—an old tradition in France—of which the *Croix de Feu* came to be the best known, appeared upon the scene. It was on February 6, 1934, that rioting in Paris resulted in a few casualties. The event in itself was small and its occurrence largely accidental;[18] but it created a profound impression in the country no less than outside. The main significance of it lay in calling attention to the degree to which the postwar democratic wave had receded,[19] when at the very center and heart of the democratic tradition on the continent of Europe the authority of Parliament could be challenged by that of the street and the mob. But of greatest importance in the present context was the fact that the display of divisions so violent in the state hitherto most responsible for the maintenance of the structure of Europe, especially in the face of the German challenge, could but give heart to those who wished to alter that structure, while correspondingly instilling doubts and dismay in the opposite camp.

FRANCE, ITALY AND CENTRAL EUROPE.   Almost simultaneously with the Parisian flurry, far more serious disturbances were taking place in Vienna. From her beginnings little Austria had suffered from the handicap of the imbalance between the large capital,

[18] The French political scene was further confused at this time by the occurrence of scandals reminiscent of the Panama affair. The most notorious of these centered around the activities of one Stavisky, a financial adventurer of Eastern European provenance, whose manipulations were made possible by his political connections, thereby providing ammunition to the enemies of the régime and to the critics of the parliamentary institution.

[19] To say nothing of the Italian and the German cases, in 1926 Poland had become a semidictatorship under Pilsudski, and in 1929 King Alexander had suspended the Yugoslav constitution. In Central and Eastern Europe Czechoslovakia was the only authentic democracy still extant.

Vienna, long center of a great empire and stronghold of the Left in politics, the "Red" city, and the "Black" countryside dominated by the clerical influence. Once the euphoria, economic and political, of the second half of the postwar decade had given place to the recurrence of crisis, the issue of Austria's viability was raised once more. The attempted economic *Anschluss* of 1931 and its failure have been mentioned. The success of Nazism in Germany could not but have deep repercussions in the neighboring Germanic state. The preservation of Austria required, internally, the coöperation of her clerical and democratic forces. But their traditional rivalry proved insuperable; in February Austria was in the throes of virtual civil war. The outcome of it was the thoroughgoing defeat and suppression of the Socialists by the government of the day, and Chancellor Dollfuss proceeded to reorganize his government increasingly along the lines of the Italian model.

This outcome was not wholly displeasing to Italy which, at this time, was firmly wedded to the preservation of Austrian independence. In order to achieve this aim, the Italian position toward Austria was becoming increasingly that of protector, a relationship that Dollfuss was willing to accept. Since the preservation of the independence of Austria was equally an aim of French policy, this might have furnished ground for Franco-Italian coöperation. It was in fact on February 17 that a joint Anglo-Franco-Italian declaration reiterated the common view of "the necessity of maintaining Austria's independence and integrity in accordance with the relevant treaties."

Austria's economic difficulties, and those of the smaller states of Central Europe as well, might have been alleviated through the adoption of common policies based on coöperation. That was in fact the aim of the Danubian scheme sponsored by France in 1932; but the traditional suspicions of the Little Entente, combined with the opposition of Italy, prevented any fruit from being borne of the French proposal.[20] Italy preferred to pursue the extension of her influence into Central Europe through a more lim-

[20] A French scheme was proposed for economic collaboration among the five Danubian states. Although acceptable to the Little Entente, it was opposed by Austria because of its failure to include Germany and Italy, a condition that France in turn would not entertain. Nothing came of the proposal save a further manifestation of divergence between France and the Little Entente on the one hand, Austria, Germany, and Italy on the other, the last two countries regarding the scheme as a device to confirm and enhance French influence in Central Europe.

ited association with Austria and with Hungary. In March the
Rome Protocols were signed, which emphasized the association of
the three countries, Italian assistance to Austria and to Hungary
tightening the relationship of dependence of the last two countries on the former. Italy was still adhering to the policy of leading a league of the malcontents.

The Central European situation was becoming complicated by
the reintrusion of German influence, which created at once the
possibility of Franco-Italian union against that influence and the
temptation for Italy to enhance her own position by exploiting
the factor of Franco-German difference. Germany at this stage
was still militarily impotent and her chief tool remained agitation and propaganda, for which Austria provided the most fertile
ground. On July 25 an internal Nazi coup was attempted in Vienna. The attempt was a failure, despite the brutal murder of Dollfuss, and though there was little doubt of German implication
and connivance, the German attitude remained ostensibly "correct," denying interest and concern in the purely domestic affairs
of Austria. But Mussolini did not need to let himself be entangled
in the niceties of legalistic delays and discussions; he could answer
Hitlerian methods in kind, which he did in the form of mobilizing
Italian forces on the Brenner frontier.

On the score of Austrian independence, France and Italy saw
eye to eye on the basis of an authentic common concern. It is of
interest that the attempted Nazi *putsch* in Vienna provoked a
clear and unmistakable Italian reaction while France was still content with verbal condemnation. The events of February in France
had led to the formation of a union ministry of sorts in which,
under the paternal guidance of the elder statesman Doumergue,
such diverse personalities as Herriot and Tardieu could both serve.
But the supposed political truce had no solid foundation and was
consequently short-lived. While some signs of economic improvement were beginning to appear in various countries, the French
situation itself continued to deteriorate; an attempted policy of
deflation, contrary to the general practice elsewhere, further restricted the scope of French economic activity; budgetary problems reappeared and there were few who dared advocate the device of devaluation in France, where instead the defense of the
franc was a popular slogan accompanied by a stubborn adherence
to gold. It was in these difficult circumstances that an attempt was
made to pursue a stronger foreign policy.

FRANCE, THE SOVIET UNION, AND EASTERN EUROPE. This was largely the work of Barthou, also an elder statesman, called to the Quai d'Orsay by Doumergue. Barthou belonged to the generation and the school of thought of Poincaré. Intelligent, full of determination and energy, Barthou set about the task of reinstilling life into the French system. This he would do in two ways: by breathing life again into the existing alliances and by extending the scope of alliances. To accomplish these purposes he visited Warsaw in April, and again in June he undertook a tour of the capitals of France's eastern allies. The reception he met, especially in Warsaw, was a personal tribute that accomplished, however, little of his larger purpose; he could not overcome the skepticism of the dying Pilsudski or the more definite unfriendliness of the foreign minister, Colonel Beck.

Barthou's ideas took the form of a proposal, often referred to as an Eastern Locarno, a defensive alliance that provided for immediate military assistance in the event of aggression and would include Germany, the Soviet Union, the four Baltic states, Poland, and Czechoslovakia; it would be open to other states such as France. In addition, Barthou envisaged a Franco-Soviet treaty of mutual assistance. The Eastern Pact proposal was submitted to Germany but rejected by her in September on the plea that she could not envisage the possibility of having to go to the assistance of her ideological archenemy, the Soviet Union. Poland followed the German lead, arguing her reluctance to contemplate the possibility of Russian troops on her territory. The failure of the scheme, to which Czechoslovakia and the Soviet Union alone responded favorably, could only further strain Franco-Polish relations.

The Soviet Union had begun to have second thoughts on the score of a policy that had professed to watch with equanimity the Nazi success in Germany. Communists in that country had been dealt with in thoroughly ruthless fashion and, after the events of June, 1934, the power of Hitler seemed to be firmly established at home.[21] The German claim to *Lebensraum* could best find satisfaction in the east which had the twin advantages, from the Nazi point of view, of providing unlimited space and being occupied

---

[21] This was the result of a clash between contending tendencies within the Nazi movement. Without hesitation, Hitler, standing as the sole and self-appointed judge of the German nation, instituted a ruthless and thoroughgoing purge that effectively crushed any opposition to himself within the movement.

by inferior Slavs. For that matter, the Soviets had begun to hedge even before the advent to power of Hitler; in 1931 and 1932 nonaggression treaties were concluded with all the bordering states in the west, save Lithuania and Rumania, as well as with France.[22]

Simultaneously, the Soviet tune began to change from the classical one of attacks on the iniquitous treaties of peace to one of opposition to revisionism, a position that accorded well with the abandonment of the stress on world revolution in favor of a policy best expressed by the slogan of socialism in one country.[23] This evolution led Russia to discover the merits of collective security; with the corresponding change in France in the face of the potential German danger, the outcome was the invitation to the Soviet Union, issued by the League in September, to join that body. Thus it happened that the Soviet Union became a member of the institution that it had so often reviled as the hypocritical cloak for an effective coalition of the victors; it suited the Soviet book for the moment to join the ranks of the forces of conservation. It was a logical next step to return to the pre-1914 Franco-Russian alliance, a connection of which Germany was the *raison d'être;* but before that step was taken, a few months later, other events took place that must now be recounted.

France's obsessive fear of insecurity could never find enough assuagement in collecting the promise of assistance from others; Barthou's efforts have been mentioned to put new life into the existing alliances. France, as well as Russia, would gladly enlist Italy. The difficulty of bringing both Russia and Poland under one roof manifested itself in the failure of the Eastern Locarno proposal. A parallel to this difficulty may be seen in the attempt to deal in similar fashion with Yugoslavia and Italy. But in the latter case things took a somewhat different turn.

While in Belgrade, Barthou had arranged for a visit of King Alexander to France. Accordingly, the king landed in Marseilles on October 9. It was while crossing the city from the harbor to the railway station that King Alexander was shot while Barthou, who accompanied him, likewise fell victim to the assassins' bullets. The deed was the work of Croatian terrorists, reminiscent in

[22] This hedging policy was motivated by the uncertainties arising from the successful Japanese aggression in the Far East at the same time that the Nazi star began to rise in Germany.

[23] This reorientation of Russian foreign policy was the counterpart of the definitive triumph of Stalin over Trotzky and of the consequent concentration on domestic development after 1928.

some respects of 1914 Sarajevo. For the problem of Yugoslavia was, to a point, comparable to that of the old Habsburg monarchy; Croatian grievances against the dominant Serbs had led to serious friction that threatened the existence of the state to the extent that, in 1929, King Alexander had suspended the constitution, setting himself up in a dictatorial position instead. This only exacerbated Croatian resentment and, as in the case of pre-1914 Austria, Croatian terrorists, the Ustashi, had found shelter and assistance in neighboring states, particularly Hungary and Italy.[24] Hungary entertained irredentist grievances toward Yugoslavia, while Italy was not loath to contemplate a disruption of that state; the Croatian portion might offer an easier field for the extension of her influence.

THE LAVAL-MUSSOLINI AGREEMENTS. But the assassination of King Alexander and Barthou did not lead to serious international complications. Tension was for a time severe, especially between Yugoslavia and Hungary, but the restraining and pacifying influence of others, not least of France, served to tide over a difficult passage. The fact that Barthou's succession in France went to Laval was in large part the reason for a minimum of difficulty where Italy was concerned. Laval had views of his own on how best to protect the position of France in Europe; he agreed with Barthou's policy of alliances, but the emphasis that he placed upon it had a different bent. While Russia evoked from him a minimum of enthusiasm, he set considerable store by the Italian connection.

In pursuit of this aim, within less than three months Laval went to Rome where, on January 7, 1935, the news was announced to the world that all Franco-Italian differences had been liquidated. In actual content these differences were small. The colonial claims of Italy, stemming from the unfulfilled provisions of the 1915 Treaty of London, were satisfied through the French cession of some desert (the Fezzan) that enlarged Libya to the south, a minute strip of French Somaliland with the small strategic island of Doumeirah, and some shares in the Djibouti-Addis Ababa railway. This was small coin, and even for so little, Italy paid a price in the eventual surrender of her Tunisian rights.

[24] There was this important difference with 1914—the Croatian malcontents did not wish to rejoin free brethren, but rather wanted separation from Serbia or at least a wide autonomy in the Yugoslav state. In this respect, therefore, Hungarian and Italian complicity in 1934 had quite a different motivation from that of 1914 Serbia.

That France and Italy should reiterate their support of the continued independence of Austria needs no explaining since this was a genuinely common interest of the two countries. But it would have been surprising that Italy should join the French camp without obtaining a substantial price in the process. In fact, if Mussolini was willing to join in the containment of Germany, the time had not yet come when Germany was an actual threat, and he did exact a price from Laval. There was more to the Rome agreements than met the eye; it was the French acquiescence to an Italian "free hand" in Abyssinia. The term "free hand" is elastic and the Laval-Mussolini understanding soon proved to have been a misunderstanding and a source of mutual recriminations. Laval subsequently claimed to have spoken of French *désintéressement* and only of economic *désintéressement*, while Mussolini put a broader interpretation on the French acquiescence. The debate may never be fully resolved, but in any event the effects of Franco-Italian agreement and misunderstanding were not to appear for some time. For the moment at least, France could turn her undivided attention to the German problem, which was indeed the major question mark of Europe.

What precisely German intentions were was not wholly clear at this time and was, outside Germany, the source of divergent interpretations: these intentions might range all the way from a minimum that could be described as the redress of legitimate grievances, the lifting of what disabilities still remained, the achieving of complete control of her own house and full equality with others, to a maximum that would entail the realization of *Mein Kampf*'s wilder visions, in broad terms the control of Europe by Germany. That Germany was in process of rearming herself was no secret; she was therefore passing through a delicate and dangerous period in which it behooved her to proceed with caution lest she induce actions by others that might cut short the recovery of her power, a result that at this time could still have been procured with ease.

It is a credit to the skill of Hitlerian diplomacy that it achieved results that can be called astounding through the judicious intermingling of force and threats, with cajoling and promises based on a shrewd appraisal of the psychology of the German people no less than of others. Psychological understanding has ever been useful in diplomacy, but the modern art of exploitation of the mass was brought by Hitler to a point of perfection that commands no less admiration for its having been diabolical in intent, unprincipled in method, and catastrophic in its final outcome. For good or ill, mostly for ill so far, it may be said that a new dimension was introduced in diplomatic practice.

THE SAAR PLEBISCITE. A concrete test was at hand for the practice of the Hitlerian technique. The fifteen-year period of trial provided in the treaty of peace for the territory of the Saar was coming to an end in 1935; a plebiscite was to be held in which the people of the Saar would decide their future allegiance. The German character of the Saar had not changed during those fifteen years, but the advent of Nazism in Germany and its persecution of Socialists as well as Catholics gave some basis for the belief that the people of the Saar, among whom both Socialists and Catholics were numerous, might hesitate to rejoin Hitler's Reich. The result was that they were to be offered the third choice of a continuation of the existing status instead of the alternatives of Germany or France. On the German side there was determination to turn the plebiscite into a resounding nationalistic success, and to that end all available means of pressure, from propaganda to dark threats, were freely used. On the French side the advent of Laval made matters easier, his attitude seeming to have been that of the Saar he knew little and cared less; certainly a case could be made for taking the position that, if the outcome was foregone in any event, there was little merit in a policy of pinpricks and futile opposition.

Franco-German negotiations during 1934 led to a financial agreement for the repurchase by Germany of the French state property (mines and railways) and to the French acceptance of noninterference with German propaganda in the Saar. Under the supervision of a League Committee of three, presided over by the Italian Aloisi, the plebiscite took place in orderly conditions on January 13, 1935. It showed that 90 percent of the vote favored outright return to Germany, a return which took place on March 1 amid much rejoicing. Hitler used the occasion to declare that Germany was now satisfied and entertained no further claims against France with whom he wished to live on amicable terms. Had this been a true statement, the relatively smooth return of the Saar to Germany might have been but the manifestation of simple realism and good sense and an authentic contribution to the normalization of Europe. But in the opposite event it could be a token of weakness on the part of France and a corresponding encouragement for Germany to proceed with the redressing of other grievances, real or imagined.

Time was in fact pressing for Hitler, who could derive further encouragement from the failure of any meaningful reaction to the illegal rearmament of Germany. In this matter also, a case could be made for the adoption of a policy of realism that would not forever insist on discrimination; such an approach had considerable appeal in Britain where the feeling of "guilty conscience" toward Germany, deriving from the "iniquities" of the peace, was widespread. Even the French had wearied of their reliance on the law of Versailles, by now already substantially modified. From their discussions with the British a proposal emerged, known as an "air Locarno"—a mutual undertaking to give immediate air force assistance to the victim of an aggression—coupled with suggestions for involving Germany in regional agreements of mutual assistance in both the West and the East. The German response was not an outright refusal of these suggestions, but while negotiations were under way Hitler judged the time ripe for his next coup.

THE REARMAMENT OF GERMANY AND THE STRESA FRONT.   In March, a British White Book was published that justified increased military expenditures in Britain on the plea of German rearmament. In March also the French government submitted to Parliament a law for the extension from one to two years of the term of military service in order to compensate for the manpower deficiency produced by the lean births of the war years. Using these as pretexts, on March 16 the German government issued a decree that reintroduced conscription in the Reich.[25]

The sensation was great, partly because of the size of the proposed German army, but quite as much because this was the first formal repudiation of a clause of the treaty of peace. But Hitler's intuition was again proved correct. The British, the French, and the Italian governments issued solemn protests while the French brought the matter to the attention of the League. Following a preparatory meeting of these three Powers at Stresa—of which

[25] A week earlier Germany had already given official notice of the existence of an air force. The announcement divulged no secret and failed to provoke strong reaction in any quarters, a fact which encouraged Germany to proceed with the next step, conscription.

more presently—the Council met in extraordinary session in April, an occasion on which the mountain gave birth to a mouse. To be sure, it was found that Germany was guilty of a breach of her obligations, to which finding was added a hint that naughty Germany must henceforth behave better else the next time others might act. Moral lecturing unaccompanied by sanctions is highly questionable practice; it could irritate Germany who was, in effect, allowed to reap the benefits of her action. Hitler's prestige, needless to say, did not suffer, either at home or abroad, from his successful operation. To a degree matters had indeed been clarified and the situation had shifted from the ground of irksome legalistic disputation to the more realistic one of the relationships of power.

The impotence of the League, registered through its meaningless action, was thus demonstrated to all. That impotence in turn derived from the fact that the League was but the collectivity of its members. Among those who could have taken action, the most concerned of all, France, lacked the necessary will. It may be pointed out that, even had she been minded to act at this time, France would have found no support, but rather opposition, in Britain; Italy had matters of greater interest in mind and Mussolini had in fact issued preliminary warnings in Italy that no high expectations should be held of the Stresa meeting. The Stresa conference accordingly did no more than register a condemnation of the German method and a reaffirmation of loyalty to Locarno and of devotion to the continued independence of Austria; these innocuous expressions of sentiment were reflected in the subsequent Genevan sermon. The Stresa meeting had nevertheless significance for it contained the possibility of the revival of a common Anglo-Franco-Italian front, which might effectively bar the realization of further German ambitions. French opinion, and British even less, could not be aroused to action by what many regarded as the negative German act of removing a disability; this, to be sure, might be but a preliminary step toward future aggression, but Hitler was correct in judging that the pacifically inclined public opinion of the Western countries would refuse to equate with aggression the mere restoration of German armed power.

In view of subsequent events especial interest attaches to the decision at Stresa, repeated at Geneva, that such action as Germany had just taken should call for appropriate measures "in the event of its having relation to undertakings concerning the security of peoples and the maintenance of peace in Europe." Why the qualification *in Europe?* Certainly one could read in it the implication, as was later contended in Italy, that the intention was to exclude from the applicability of the declaration issues outside of Europe.[26]

THE FRANCO-SOVIET AND SOVIET-CZECH ALLIANCES.   But Stresa and the so-called Stresa front were not the only consequences of the rearmament of Germany. Mention has already been made of the gradual reorientation of Soviet policy coincident with the rise of the Nazis in Germany and the corollary of that reorientation in the form of a Franco-Soviet rapprochement. The nonaggression pact of 1932 contained the reciprocal engagement not to join a coalition directed against the other party. The pact was ratified in the French Chamber in May, 1933, by a vote of 520 to 0, an interesting and rare manifestation of national unanimity: for purely military reasons on the Right, for combined military and ideological reasons on the Left, the pact commanded support in all quarters in France.

The course of German events from the beginning of 1933 could only strengthen the bonds that drew France and Russia together and we have seen Barthou's unavailing attempts to bring the Soviet Union into the circle of Eastern European security. After Barthou, Laval pressed the rapprochement with less eagerness, but negotiations continued nonetheless, at the military level for one, and led to the signature in Geneva of a Laval-Litvinov protocol, prelude to an exchange of verbal amenities in both countries. The events of March, 1935, precipitated matters, registering among other things the definitive failure of any multilateral arrangements *à la Locarno* for Eastern Europe.

The final negotiations were concluded between Laval and Litvinov in Geneva in April, and on May 2 a Franco-Soviet Pact was signed in Paris. On May 16 a similar agreement was signed in Prague between Czechoslovakia and the Soviet Union. The Franco-Soviet Pact provided that in the event of threatened aggression by a European state against either party, the two contractants would consult with a view to accelerating and strengthening the operation of Article 10 of the Covenant. If the League

[26] It may be argued that the Stresa meeting and declaration were clearly intended to deal with the German situation alone. On the other hand, it is worth noting that Litvinov's attempt in Geneva to remove the restriction *in Europe* failed, and it is strange, to say the least, that in view of the current warlike preparations of Italy in East Africa no discussion of the Abyssinian problem should have occurred at Stresa.

decided on sanctions against a European state, either party would lend assistance to the other; but in case of an unprovoked attack against either partner the other would lend immediate assistance, even in the event of failure of the Council to achieve unanimity. The intent of the pact was clear and its German focus unmistakable; the pact was exclusively European, Far Eastern matters remaining outside its purview. But some uncertainty persisted around the meaning of "immediate" assistance. How much time would the Council be given for its deliberations? Also, in deference to French wishes, the pact was subordinated to the Locarno agreement by a protocol that provided that, in the event of German aggression, it would become operative only if that aggression were recognized as such by the guarantors of Locarno, Britain and Italy.

It should also be mentioned that the Soviet-Czech Pact had a special provision that made it operative only in the event that France lent assistance to the attacked party, a provision whose subsequent effect was to be considerable. As before 1914, the German danger had brought together France and Russia. There were differences nonetheless. Evidently some reticence persisted on the French side which would indeed welcome the asset of Russian power but, rightly on the whole, gave priority of importance to the role of France's neighbors in the West; the reticence had its counterpart on the Russian side and was registered in the special provision just mentioned of the Soviet-Czech treaty. Finally, it should be pointed out that Poland did not participate in these arrangements. Poland would under no conditions consider the possibility, even for purposes of assistance to herself, of Russian forces on her soil; and this in turn meant that Russia had no direct land contact with either Czechoslovakia or Germany.

If the Franco-Soviet Pact was generally popular in France, ideological considerations also made for reticence. To a point, the circumstances of forty years earlier were now reversed, for in the eyes of all, France included, it was now Russia who held the former French place as the radical state of Europe; the tendency existed in France to look with interest, and even some sympathy, to the domestic German and Italian models, especially the latter, a sympathy that could easily overflow into a wish to explore the possibility of understanding with those Powers. This made for confusion in France and for a crossing of the normal tendencies of political alignment. It was the Left that was anti-Nazi, hence would tend to be anti-German, while what sympathy there was for the Reich and the experiment of Nazism was to be found in the traditionally nationalistic Right. These differences were of degree, but their confusing effect was to appear before long. More immediately, the spectacle of the French Communists espousing with enthusiasm the cause of French military power, the virtues of which had been discovered by the Soviet Union was not devoid of humor;[27] whatever expediency might dictate, for the long term France was still, after all, a doomed capitalist state.

The Franco-Soviet connection was not welcome in Italy, while in Britain it elicited what may best be described as a lifting of eyebrows. There was little, if any, ideological sympathy for Nazism in Britain, though to many the strongly anti-Communist aspect of Nazism was not displeasing. For Germany as such and the redressing of her grievances understanding was considerable; eyes would often be shut to the cruder manifestations of the Nazi regime and these would be dismissed, as in the United States, with knowing reference to the earlier tales of Germany's wartime atrocities. These were the days of much pacifism in Britain, of the Oxford oath,[28] and consolation could be found in the consideration that it was French intransigeance that had driven Germany to the unilateral repudiation of her obligations. Had not Hitler repeatedly proclaimed that he had no ambition beyond the restoration of Germany to the rank of self-respecting equal among nations? Those who had taken the proper measure of Hitler's Germany and insisted at least on strong precautionary measures of rearmament—there were some in Britain—were dismissed as alarmists and reduced to the status of voices crying in the wilderness. The official leadership was supine, making some feeble gestures toward rearmament, but preferring the easier course of drifting on the current of prevalent opinion, loath to look unpleasant facts in the face.

In Germany the press could expatiate on the spread of the Communist danger, and Hitler, in a speech that he delivered on

[27] Since the war the Soviet Union had been a consistent and harsh critic of French "hegemony" in Europe, regarding France—quite correctly—as the chief barrier against change. The novel circumstances of the time had brought Russia around to the view that, for the moment at least, in opposition to change lay her best interest.

[28] On February 9, 1933, by a vote of 275 to 133, the Oxford Union passed the resolution that "this House will in no circumstances fight for its King and Country." While no overwhelming importance should be given to this particular manifestation of pacifistic aberration, it was nonetheless significant; it created a considerable sensation and received very widespread notice, in England no less than outside.

May 21, pointed out that the new alliances had introduced into the Locarno arrangements an element of legal insecurity that he would like to see clarified. The point was not ill taken, for the initial ambiguity of Locarno had indeed been compounded by that of the Franco-Soviet Pact. But, for the rest, Hitler's speech made a generally favorable impression, since he reaffirmed Germany's loyalty to Locarno[29] and chose the occasion to deny once more German interest in the domestic affairs of Austria, let alone any thoughts of annexation or *Anschluss*. Hitler well understood and skillfully exploited the wishful thinking of the West and the almost pathological wish of most peoples for peace.

From Britain there emerged at this time an interesting manifestation of combined realism and wishful thinking. Britain is naturally most sensitive to naval matters. Within the limits of her disarmament obligations, even before the advent of Hitler, Germany had already launched a "pocket" battleship in 1930; Hitler was now building forbidden submarines, for all that he had stated that the desirability of British friendship, while he pursued his other ends (destruction of French hegemony and eastward expansion) meant renouncing a German navy. It was thought practical politics in Britain to seek to control Germany's naval rearmament by giving open consent to it.

Hitler had nothing to lose and Anglo-German negotiations promptly led to an agreement that was disclosed on June 18: Germany undertook to keep her navy to the ratio of 35 percent of the British; within that limitation of tonnage she could build submarines to the total tonnage of the whole Commonwealth. That Hitlerian promises were not worth the paper they were written on was not, in 1935, proved beyond possible question and the not unreasonable British argument was that in freely given consent lay the best hope of keeping German ambition within reasonable bounds. Nevertheless, the manner of achieving this purpose was both unfortunate and clumsy. Britain's unilateral sanction of a modification of the treaty of peace created, in France especially, a most unfavorable impression and reaction. To say the least, the Anglo-German naval treaty showed on the British side either unawareness or unconcern, or both, over the fact of the basic similarity in the British and French positions *vis-à-vis* the outside world. It was certainly calculated to impede Anglo-French

[29] In retrospect, considerable importance attaches to the reservation, "so long as the other partners on their side are ready to stand by that pact," as evidence of the development of a clearly thought out policy.

coöperation at a moment when a larger issue made that coöperation more than ever desirable.

III. The End of the Versailles System

The picture of European relationships in mid-1935 must be seen in the light of these developments: the unopposed German rearmament, the Stresa Front, the Franco-Soviet and Soviet-Czech treaties, and the Anglo-German naval agreement. Which of these were solid realities and which were paper structures the future was soon to test and to reveal.

When the Stresa meeting took place in April, Italy was as much, and rather more, concerned with matters African as European. As early as 1927, Mussolini had delivered himself of the opinion that "We shall be in a position then—tomorrow—when, between 1935 and 1940, we shall find ourselves at a point which I shall call a crucial point in European history—we shall be in a position to make our will felt, and to see our rights recognized." This was to prove a remarkably accurate and prescient forecast, but it was made in the days when Fascism gave little concrete evidence of aggressiveness, and, for all the disparaging statements about democracy and the League, Italy was rather coöperating with Geneva than the opposite. Mussolini's statement was no cause for alarm at the time. However, the first half of the 1930's witnessed the gradual return of Germany to the councils of European power. But it would take some years before Germany would again be an effective military factor, and this transitional period Italy might exploit to secure some advantage for herself, after which she would be in a position to make her influence—possibly an enhanced influence—felt again in the councils of Europe. Such a calculation was not devoid of shrewdness; in the circumstances of the day, the implementation of it called for skill and the willingness to take certain risks, in neither of which attributes Mussolini was deficient. The story of the Abyssinian imbroglio is a tangled tale, a combined tragedy and comedy of errors, but its initial outcome may be said to have justified Italian calculations.

THE LEAGUE AND THE ITALIAN CONQUEST OF ABYSSINIA

Italy's East African dreams were of long standing, and the failure of them under Crispian mismanagement has been told.[30]

[30] See above, Ch. VI.

Italian imperial activity thereafter had been, in Mussolini's scorn-
ful but accurate phrase, an enterprise in the collection of deserts.
In the classical context of imperialism, the creation of an East
African empire seemed for Italy wholly reasonable; it may be
granted that such an empire could have developed into an economic asset for Italy and even that, on balance, it would have
been of benefit to Abyssinia. To this consideration two qualifications must be adduced. In the days when the greatest existing
colonial empires, the British and the French, had already begun
to recede under the pressure of the combined impact of their own
inner weakness[31] and of native nationalisms, was Italy, with the
more limited resources of her power, capable of going against the
dominant current? Secondly, in the world of 1935 there existed
an institution, the League, of which it happened that Abyssinia
was a member.[32] Such is the background of the development that
we must now consider; it will be told briefly, without recourse to
the detailed and intricate complexities of its legal and legalistic
aspects, but mainly with an eye to its effect on European relations.

Italian plans for the conquest of Abyssinia can be traced to
1933, if not earlier. The opening gun for action was provided by
the incident of Walwal in December, 1934.[33] Acting under the
provisions of the Italo-Abyssinian treaty of 1928, the Abyssinian
government proposed arbitration that Italy refused, thereby inducing an Abyssinian appeal to the League. This last move coincided with the visit of Laval to Rome, and the understanding, or
misunderstanding, that took place between him and Mussolini
is an important part of the episode. From the French point of
view, Laval's especially, trouble in Abyssinia was an awkwardness
to be avoided at all costs, and Mussolini was therefore in a strong

[31] At this point the Italian—and German—contention must be borne in mind
that the democracies were decadent Powers to which the new rising Powers
were destined to fall heirs, a contention that, in the limited sense of a decline
of the aggressive will on the part of the peoples of Britain and France, may
indeed be granted.

[32] The point might be legitimately debated whether or not Abyssinia, in view
of the degree of her political development, should have been a member of the
League. Her membership was undoubtedly based on the acceptance of certain
fictions, but the fact remains that she *was* a member at this time. Not a little irony
attaches to the circumstances of her admission to the League in 1923, an admission
which took place with Italian and French support but in the face of British
skepticism.

[33] A military encounter with some casualties that took place in territory on
the border between Abyssinia and Italian Somaliland, which had been under
Italian occupation since 1930.

bargaining position, especially in dealing with the unprincipled Laval. The first result, however, was an Italian acceptance of arbitration, but on the terms of it agreement proved impossible. There followed an appeal by Abyssinia to the League under the terms of Article 15 of the Covenant. It will be noted that the date of this appeal, March 17, almost coincided with that of the announcement of German rearmament and preceded by three weeks the Stresa meeting. On this last occasion, strange as it may seem in the circumstances, Abyssinian affairs were not under discussion.

The Abyssinian matter was an awkward one for Britain and for France, who found themselves at the same time engaged in negotiating the formation of a united anti-German front with Italy and confronted with a situation in Geneva where Italy was being charged with aggressive intent. They could react in two divergent ways. On the one hand, a strong stand against aggression could strengthen the League and rally to it those who might on a future occasion be called upon to resist a German aggression; the price of this would be the estrangement of Italy. Or else they might let Italy have her way in order to retain her support in Europe; this would entail a delicate and awkward operation that would once more underline the impotence of the League. To be sure, it might be argued that the League had already proved powerless in Manchuria; but then what was the League, if not in large measure Britain and France? The issue in simplest form was this: how did Britain and France intend to preserve the peace, an end on the desirability of which they agreed, through their support of the League, or, forgetting the League, through direct combinations of power?

What complicated matters further was the fact that, beyond their general peaceful intent, Britain and France disagreed on methods. The direct interest of Britain in East Africa far exceeded the French; this last was limited, while the possibility of a large Italian establishment in that region had considerable significance for the British route to the East, no less than for the water supply of the Nile, hence Egypt and the Anglo-Egyptian Sudan. On the basis of her own imperial interests, therefore, Britain was more anxious to prevent the success of Italian aggression than was France, who could accept the price of it to herself for the sake of Italian support in Europe.

The effect of these national differences was a curious reversal of the usual French and British positions at Geneva: France, who had always insisted on the desirability of giving power to the League and making it effective, was the more reluctant to let the issue come to a head; while Britain, ever averse to extending her commitments under the League, now began to discover the virtues of a League endowed with power. France was driven into assuming an inconsistent position, while the sudden British devotion to the League she found both irritating and suspect. This must be said for the French position that, while it was both inconsistent and inglorious, it appeared in the nature of a *reductio ad absurdum* to let matters come to the possible point of a Franco-Italian clash when Germany was France's prime concern and when no assurance could be gained from Britain that the Abyssinian precedent would be eventually of use in the German case. The Abyssinian affair was to be the source of much antagonism and resentment between Britain and France.

The immediate effect of this state of affairs was, not surprisingly, tergiversation. On May 25 the Council declined to take action other than leaving the dispute to the parties involved for two months. Time was thus gained, not least for Italy, whose military preparations, in the form of accumulating matériel and troops in East Africa, went on apace. Negotiations meanwhile were proceeding between the three European countries most interested, the British seeking to effect some compromise that Italy rejected;[34] Anglo-French divergence was playing into Mussolini's hands and Italian conviction was growing that Britain would not dare to act, a conviction that was reinforced by domestic events in Britain where the results of the "Peace Ballot" were announced in June.[35]

In the failure of either compromise or direct Italo-Abyssinian agreement, the Council went into extraordinary session on July 31. There was some humor in the activity at this stage of the Commission of Inquiry into the initial Walwal incident; it resulted, in September, in the exoneration of both parties by the Council,

[34] In June Foreign Secretary Eden went to Rome with a proposal for an Abyssinian cession of territory to Italy in exchange for the British cession of Zeila to Abyssinia, thus giving her access to the sea.

[35] This was a poll of public opinion (not a sampling, since some 11,500,000 answers were received) organized in 1934. The sense of this poll has been adequately summarized thus: "Go as far as you can, in combination with other members, to secure and observe loyalty to the Covenant, and to resist aggression; do all you can to keep out of war, even in company with other member-States; and we give no support at all to military measures which will fall exclusively or preponderantly on British shoulders." G. M. Gathorne-Hardy, *A Short History of International Affairs*, Oxford University Press, 1950.

which had meantime entrusted negotiations to an Anglo-Franco-Italian conference whose efforts proved sterile. The curious Anglo-French proposal of a tripartite mandate over Abyssinia was rejected by Mussolini despite the preponderant role offered to Italy. Mussolini had by now decided to burn his bridges; even the British naval demonstration in the form of a large concentration of the fleet in the Mediterranean left him unmoved. That gesture served little purpose other than to exacerbate Anglo-French relations, irritate Italy, and prove the danger of bluff in diplomacy. On October 3, 1935, the Italian forces began active operations in Abyssinia.

The fact of open hostilities of itself created a new situation, for there is a limit beyond which the denial of reality becomes impossible. Accordingly, on October 7, the Council unanimously found Italy guilty of aggression, a view in which the Assembly concurred.[36] The next step was the imposition of sanctions, of which it may suffice to say that they were purposely designed to insure their ineffectiveness. The summation of Laval in the French Chamber in December was accurate that "We [himself and Sir Samuel Hoare] found ourselves instantaneously in agreement upon ruling out military sanctions, not adopting any measure of naval blockade, never contemplating the closure of the Suez Canal—in a word ruling out everything that might lead to war." The simple fact was indeed that Britain and France would have peace for themselves at any price.

The aggression of Italy was not open to question nor her disregard of the League; hence she obviously bears the prime and full responsibility for the affair and its consequences.[37] Italy had in effect succeeded in destroying the League. But this in turn hardly exonerates the bungling diplomacy of Britain and of France. These countries no doubt wanted peace, but to secure the peace there were two roads. One was determined support of the League from the beginning; the risk of war with Italy was fairly small, and such a war, had it occurred, might well have prevented a

[36] Switzerland made a reservation in respect to participation in the imposition of sanctions, and Austria, Hungary, and Albania, owing to their relation to Italy, dissented.

[37] It is of interest that, to this day, this view commands little response in Italy. At the time the Italian feeling was that the League was a convenient tool of which Britain and France were availing themselves to prevent Italy from doing that which they had themselves done many times in the past. The episode produced in Italy well-nigh unanimous support for the regime for which it probably marked the highest point of popularity.

greater. The other would have been to make with Italy an old-fashioned colonial bargain; to be sure, this would have been difficult to contrive, especially in view of the existing temper of British opinion.

But the fact remains that the course adopted, if understandable, was the worst possible of all: the League was wrecked in the end, and France and Britain emerged from the episode discredited, enabling Mussolini to indulge in empty bombast about the Italian defiance of fifty nations. Unprincipled Laval had overreached himself and there was poetic justice in the outcome of Italian recriminations against France. French irritation and annoyance turned in large measure against Britain, on the score of whose hypocritical moralizing harsh and unreasonable things were said. Britain replied in kind with moral indignation, at the popular level especially, directed toward both Italy and France.

The course of war is ever unpredictable and, like its termination, often bears little relation to the plans that govern its outbreak. There were many who thought, with memories of Adowa, that Italy had undertaken an operation that she would find it difficult to bring to a successful conclusion; even the limited economic sanctions imposed upon her might have effect. These expectations were belied. After some initial fumbling, once the ineffective de Bono had been superseded by the more competent Badoglio, matters proceeded rapidly. The modern tools of war that Italy possessed found little difficulty in disposing of Abyssinian weapons of Adowa vintage; even apart from military action Abyssinia was difficult country, the penetration of which redounded to the credit of Italian engineering skill, of the never lost talent for road building. By May, 1936, native resistance had been broken, the Emperor had taken flight, and the annexation of the country was proclaimed by Italy whose king assumed the imperial title of Abyssinia.

The clear Italian success was measure of the discomfiture of the League. Sanctions had miserably failed and obviously no one would undertake at this point the task of ousting the Italians from their newly won possession. The League acknowledged its defeat with the lifting of sanctions in July, and one by one over a period of time the states came to recognize the validity of the Italian title. Meantime the period of the war itself was accompanied by important developments on the European scene.

To the British and French the episode was full of awkwardness.

Broadly speaking, France may be said to have been willing to write off Abyssinia; even among the most ardent supporters of the League in France there was little desire to let the issue degenerate into a Franco-Italian dispute, and Laval's annoyance at Mussolini's intransigeance and ungratefulness while he was loyally endeavoring to block and nullify League action is understandable. The British position was rendered particularly delicate by the trend of opinion, of which the results of the Peace Ballot were indication. The government chose this time, November, 1935, for the holding of a general election; ostensibly, it was still a coalition or Union government, now under the presidency of Conservative Stanley Baldwin; but in actual fact it was a Conservative government. It was thought expedient, for electoral purposes, to lay stress on the government's devotion to Geneva, a somewhat newly found devotion in the intensity of its professions and perhaps not wholly above suspicion, but the device served its electoral purpose.

The government's realistic approach may be described as a desire to cut its losses and to effect a compromise acceptable to Italy that would restore the peace. The outcome was the notorious Hoare-Laval plan which would have given Italy some two-thirds of Abyssinia and a virtual protectorate over the rest. Had the arrangement proved acceptable to Mussolini it may still be questioned whether the task of "selling" it to Parliament and opinion would not have taxed even the dialectical abilities of Sir Samuel Hoare, the British foreign minister. But the test was never made, for premature revelations in the press resulted in such an outburst of indignation as to force the resignation of Hoare whose succession went to Anthony Eden on December 22.[38] This episode furnished fresh fuel for Anglo-French recriminations and the legend was popular, if inaccurate, for a time in Britain of the unprincipled and crafty French minister having "bamboozled" his innocent and upright British opposite number. In France, Laval, though with little glory, survived another month.

Germany was not directly involved in any of these matters. No longer in the League, she did not have to participate in the application of sanctions, but rather derived out of them some prof-

---

[38] The disclosure of the terms of the Hoare-Laval plan occurred first in the French press and has been credited to the activity of some French journalists in London, who used this means to bring about the failure of the scheme.

itable trade with Italy. It was widely believed in Germany that Italy had involved herself in a long and difficult operation for which she found little sympathy in German opinion; but the most significant aspect of the matter from the German point of view was the disruption of the Stresa combination and the neutralization of Italy in Europe. The three-way falling out between the members of the Stresa front was highly welcome and provided an unexpected opportunity for another demonstration of Hitlerian tactics.

THE REMILITARIZATION OF THE RHINELAND

Since March, 1935, German rearmament was an open matter and was being carried out with both vigor and speed. The reaction to it has been mentioned, but one important part of that reaction, the Stresa front, had already been nullified. There remained the Franco-Soviet connection, signed on May 2, 1935. The German view of that instrument has also been indicated, and in June an exchange took place in the form of a German note to France, wherein the inconsistency was argued between the Franco-Soviet and the Locarno pacts; this was countered by a French rejoinder that reiterated French adherence to Locarno. There matters rested for a time while the Abyssinian affair unfolded.

The Franco-Soviet treaty still wanted ratification in France and indications were forthcoming from the French ambassador in Berlin that the ratification might induce German action in the still demilitarized Rhineland. From this the conclusion was drawn of the desirability of a clear line of action in either one of two forms: France might negotiate some arrangement along the pattern of the Anglo-German naval agreement, thereby obtaining the freely given promise of some German restraint, or alternatively, France might give unmistakable warning that a breach of the demilitarization provisions would be resisted by force. Hitler, meantime, made the most of the significance of the Franco-Soviet pact as a success of Communism in France, directing the argument to French as well as to world opinion.

Neither policy was adopted by France, but the successors of Laval, Prime Minister Sarraut and foreign minister Flandin, brought up the Franco-Soviet treaty for ratification in Parliament, arguing its consistency with Locarno and even offering, as earnest of their good intentions, to submit the question to the Interna-

tional Court at The Hague. At the end of February and the beginning of March the treaty was ratified in both French houses.[39]

German plans for the remilitarization of the Rhineland go back
to the middle of 1935. They gave rise to considerable discussion
in the inner circles of the government and much opposition was
voiced by the military in view of the existing state of German
military forces and of the possibility of French action. Disregarding these, Hitler preferred to follow the promptings of his intuition which, on this occasion again, proved to be based on sound
psychological judgment. On March 7 the German foreign minister, von Neurath, called the ambassadors of the Locarno Powers
to whom he handed a note denouncing the Rhineland Pact and in-
forming them that, at the very moment, "symbolic detachments"
of the German forces were entering the demilitarized zone. Simultaneously, Hitler was addressing the Reichstag where he conveyed the same information. The German action was justified on
the ground of the alleged prior violation of the Locarno Pact by
France through the conclusion of the Franco-Soviet Pact. However, dedicated as he was to the preservation of peace no less than
to the restoration of German rights, Hitler also offered to France
and Belgium the conclusion of a twenty-five year nonaggression
pact as well as of an air pact, like Locarno, under British and Italian guarantee; in addition, he also proposed the conclusion of
agreements similar to the Nazi-Polish Pact with Germany's other
eastern neighbors.

This, it must be emphasized, was taking place in March, 1936,
when Italy was making rapid progress in Abyssinia and her relations with France and Britain were rather less than cordial, while
Anglo-French relations were also not at their warmest. To expect
in these circumstances that the Anglo-Italian guarantee of France,
envisaged at Locarno, could come into effect may seem visionary.
It was therefore up to France to decide whether, with or without
assistance, she would act. Whatever might be said of the German
contention about the Franco-Soviet Pact, that Germany had violated the Treaty of Locarno, no less than that of Versailles, was

[39] The vote for the pact was 353 to 164. This was the occasion for an
incident which, however, caused a minor sensation at the time. Hitler had granted
a very friendly interview to a French journalist, Bertrand de Jouvenel. The purpose of it had been to influence opinion in France, and the delay in publication
of the interview until after the vote in the Chamber was taken by Hitler as a
deliberate maneuver on the part of the French government.

clear beyond cavil; the French case for action was therefore
equally clear.[40]

THE ABDICATION OF FRANCE.   Understandably, the news caused
a profound sensation in France and the government met to deliberate. But Sarraut's spirited declaration about not tolerating the
threat of German guns over Strasbourg was no more than words.
Unable to come to a decision, the governors of France seemed
more concerned to avoid the taking of responsibilities, military and
civilians each seeking to put the burden of decision on the other.
From the outside, especially from Britain, counsels of moderation were forthcoming, Eden condemning the German action,
but proceeding to add that, fortunately, it did not contain the
threat of hostilities. France doing nothing, Hitler's intuition was
proved right, and the outcome was correspondingly an enormous
success, for him personally no less than for Germany.

What followed was meaningless shadowboxing. Meeting in
London, the Locarno Powers decided to submit the matter to the
Council which, also meeting in London on the 14th, went through
the motions of solemnly declaring that Germany was guilty of a
breach of her obligations. The Locarno Powers went on to take
up the earlier French proposal of consulting The Hague tribunal,
meekly asking the Germans to proceed with moderation pending
a new agreement; they also issued mutual guarantees of their territories against German aggression. This was tantamount to tacit
acquiescence in the latest German coup and Hitler declined to accept "humiliating conditions." Further strengthened by the verdict
of a domestic plebiscite, held on March 29, that endorsed him by a
99 percent vote, on April 1 Hitler went on to pose as advocate of
peace, proposing a vast plan based on his initial memorandum of
March 7. Despite the French refusal to negotiate unless German
forces first withdrew from the Rhineland, French counterproposals were forthcoming that Germany rejected in turn. None of
these moves need detain our attention for they had little bearing
on reality and led to no results.

That reality was the simple one that Germany was proceeding
on an unvarying course and had achieved one more success on

[40] We may recall the provision of the Rhineland Pact of 1925, which had
specifically mentioned such action as Germany was now taking as constituting
a breach of the Locarno Pact. See above, p. 419.

the path that was taking her from impotence, through restored equality, to superior force designed for aggression. This occasion may be seen as the last instance in which it lay within the power of France to stem the changing tide of power; that is the reason why so much importance attaches to the failure of French action. It is true that Britain showed reluctance to act, even sought to restrain possible French action, for the feeling at this time was still very strong in Britain that Germany was seeking no more than her own; hence the fond hope that Hitler's peaceful declarations might still be taken at face value. Even among responsible quarters in Britain comfort could be derived from the consideration that the removal of Germany's last grievance, if awkwardly contrived, was essentially a contribution to the restoration of confidence through the reëstablishment of a basically desirable German equality.[41]

But this does not exonerate the French inaction, makes it in some respects all the more serious, for in France there were fewer illusions. The inaction of France is explainable in the domestic context of the country. Since 1934 especially, France had been increasingly torn by internecine quarrels and the sharper division between Right and Left. The response to the events of that year, the supposed threat to the regime that the semi-Fascist leagues represented, had been the formation of the coalition that came to be known as the Popular Front. Following the reorientation of Soviet policy, for the first time the Communists adopted a policy of coöperation with other forces of the Left, instead of clinging to the doctrinaire view that any setback to any capitalist regime—for instance, to Weimar Germany—would ultimately redound to their advantage. The Communists became the most enthusiastic supporters of the Popular Front, in France the coalition of themselves, the Socialists, and the more reticent Radical Socialists. The French political context was particularly suitable to this Communist *volte face*, for the Jacobin tradition of France made easy the adoption of the patriotic slogans of the Great Revolution without at the same time renouncing the revolutionary tradition itself.

When Hitler sent his formations into the demilitarized Rhine-

---

[41] A significant and revealing gauge of British opinion is to be found in the leading article of the London *Times* of March 9 that dealt with the Rhineland situation. While reproving German methods, the *Times*, judging "the old structure of European peace, one-sided and unbalanced" saw in the recent happenings a hopeful opportunity for rebuilding on a sounder basis. One is hard put to find a neater illustration of false realism.

land the government of France was almost in the nature of a care-taker government, holding office until the impending elections, due to take place on April 26 and May 2, would give a new clear mandate of the French people. That people, in their mass, was not sympathetic to the German and Italian experiments in government and they were generally fearful of the rising German power; but also in their mass they were largely wrapped up in the more im-mediate and more clearly discernible effects of the economic crisis, whose impact upon France was not alleviated by the passage of time. The legislature of 1932, now reaching the end of its life, had started under the domination of the *Cartel des Gauches;* economic and financial stress had once more the effect, as on other occasions in France, of disrupting the Left coalition and of shifting the ful-crum of control nearer the center. This period has aptly been de-scribed as that of the *années tournantes,* critical years of indecisive search for an evanescent stability, and for solutions which in the foreign field led to renunciation and inaction. As the time for elec-tion approached, anti-Fascism combined with social reform made a fine slogan for the Popular Front.

The Popular Front won the election handsomely, at least at the parliamentary level,[42] and the result led to the formation of a gov-ernment under the Socialist leader Léon Blum. But France was bit-terly divided, the fear of the Reds competing with the fear of Germany, a fact that found expression in the violence of talk about the two hundred families to which the slogan "rather Hitler than Blum" was the answer. Blum was a cultivated gentleman, some-what starry-eyed, doctrinaire and idealistic, but not a strong per-sonality. As leader of the Popular Front government his first cares were two: the institution of a far-reaching, and in France long overdue, program of social reforms, and the avoidance, so far as possible, of the exacerbation of the divisions of the country. The fact that France is a democracy goes a long way toward explain-ing her weak foreign policy at this time. The German danger was real and mounting, but still remote in concrete terms of possible

---

[42] The three chief component parties of the Popular Front were returned with 330 deputies, to which may be added 56 of other Left groups, leaving 222 members in the Right opposition. By comparison with 1932, however, the Left gained less than half a million votes and the Right lost less than 200,000 in a total poll of nearly 10,000,000. Within the Left, however, there was a marked shift toward the extreme, the Communists nearly doubling their popular vote to a total of 1,500,000.

496 A DIPLOMATIC HISTORY OF EUROPE SINCE THE CONGRESS OF VIENNA

aggression; to nip it in the bud would have required aggressive will
that France did not possess as a nation. Social and economic problems were the stuff of current existence, hence they must receive
first attention.[43]

[43] This fundamental aspect of the French milieu must be borne in mind
when one considers the subsequent actions and role of France and the not infrequent berating of her. Given her resources, it was difficult for France, unlike
America for instance, to manage both guns *and* butter. But unlike Germany,
France would not make a choice that could only have been implemented at the
cost of emulating German methods of coercion. This is indeed credit to the
strength of the French democratic tradition, but went to the inevitable accompaniment of a divided nation.

XIII

Preparations for War, 1936-1939

I. The Realignment of Power

The 7th of March, 1936, is as significant a date as any in the story of the relations of the states of Europe during the entire period of the long armistice: the consequence of the success of the Hitlerian gamble was the collapse of the structure of Europe that had existed since the restoration of peace. As pointed out before, French power was the cornerstone of that structure. It mattered little at this point whether the condition that had existed was the result of French ambition or of the failure of others willingly to assume their proper share of responsibility; the relevant consideration for the future was that the bases of European relationships had been altered.

Germany was not yet fully armed, for all that her rearmament had been proceeding actively for some time; however, even at this stage, it was only reasonable to assume that German power would soon be fully restored and that full weight must be given henceforth to the voice of Germany in the councils of Europe. A situation had therefore arisen which was in some respects not dissimilar from that which had existed before the First World War: for Europe as a whole the paramount question was, what were the aims of German power? An important corollary of this question was the estimate that others would make of these aims, for it would be their reading of the situation—right or wrong—that would determine their positions and their actions. In any case, after 1936, Germany lies at the center of the story of Europe which she dominates by her own positive initiatives no less than in the reactions of others to these.

The French system had suffered a blow from which recovery was well-nigh impossible. The League having already proved its inadequacy there was no clear focus of power, nor center of direction in Europe, but instead a highly fluid condition, a free-for-all in which each single unit must reappraise the total situation and seek to insure its own advantage or safety as best it could. Confused and hesitant groping is thus characteristic for a while of the picture of European relations until clearer alignments emerged.

In this confusion Germany may be said to have enjoyed a definite advantage from the singleness of her direction and purpose; power may be disliked, but power that asserts itself successfully commands respect and tends to attract other power. Germany's success had consisted in breaking the circle that the French system of alliances had forged around Germany and there was every reason for her to pursue the rewarding tactics of divisiveness and to insist on dealing with issues and with states in isolation, instead of accepting the collective approach for the treatment of European problems or the organization of international relations.

If the French system had been effectively destroyed, France's own power had not; reduced to what some would regard as adequate dimensions, it was still considerable and an important factor in Europe. But power means little without the willingness to assert itself, and the most significant aspect of the March crisis had been the unwillingness of French power to do precisely that; no amount of *ex post facto* explanation could alter the profound impression that the abdication of France had created. In France herself and in the English-speaking countries this abdication might appear as the manifestation of reasonableness and of one of the "nicer" aspects of peace-loving democracy; that interpretation carried little conviction elsewhere, where the stress was on the aspect of weakness. Even in France many had qualms. The Popular Front coalition that took over the government in June had little cause to cherish sympathy or to entertain illusions where Nazi Germany was concerned. But it felt hampered by the need to give priority to the domestic situation as well as by the fear of exacerbating the bitterness of internal divisions. Confronted with an outburst of social unrest, most awkward since it came from its own supporters, the government of Léon Blum was fully occupied in creating a French version of the American New Deal. Whether desirable or not, social legislation makes demands upon the exchequer. The economic and fiscal policies of France had not been producive of recovery. To assume the new burdens that social policy entailed, in addition to those of an enlarged military establishment, might be too great a load, for France is not possessed, like the United States, of resources that make it possible to have both guns *and* butter. But neither did France have the German system that made it possible to impose a choice between the two commodities, if both could not be had at once. The French people would have butter and were reluctant to face the implications of trying to have guns as well. In September it had already been decided that the franc must at last be devalued,[1] a move that was but a stage in a continuing record of financial difficulties. Though not necessarily fatal, these difficulties could only further detract from the strength of the French position.

It was sound in such circumstances for France to draw the conclusion that the connection with Britain took on greater importance than ever. That, *vis-à-vis* the rest of the world, Britain and France had fundamentally the same position of satisfied, declining Powers, whose interest was primarily defensive may seem to constitute the most solid foundation for a common policy. Indeed it was, but apart from the fact that the mismanagement of the Abyssinian imbroglio had left a train of mutual recriminations, in public opinion especially, there was in Britain, at all levels, a profound misreading of the international situation, the manifestations of which have already been mentioned. At most, and by way of insurance, Britain would see to some strengthening of her neglected armaments. For the moment, Britain favored negotiations with Germany; in response to the German offer of the end of March, a British questionnaire was sent to Germany on May 6. The tone of it may be described as clumsy and the German reaction was one of at least pretended annoyance: a Great Power would not submit to the indignity of being catechized by another as to whether or not it was in a position to undertake "genuine" commitments. More to the point, having met mere verbal opposition to the coup of March, Germany saw little cause to negotiate. There is in fact no reason to dwell on any further consideration of discussions related to the Rhineland episode. Germany's repudiation of Versailles was an accomplished fact and future calculations must be based on that solid reality.

The Soviet Union viewed the recovery of German power with natural alarm and suspicion; its new policy, in the form of the alli-

[1] The extent of the devaluation, 30 percent, was designed to bring the franc in line with the British pound. The belated operation failed to have the hoped-for effect of reviving the French economy. At the same time France was undertaking a substantial rearmament program, a source of added deficit.

ance with France, had in fact been the German pretext for the remilitarization of the Rhineland. However, the Soviet Union was a party to neither Versailles nor Locarno, and in the failure of France to respond to the German action had no cause to take action on its own. A policy of watchful waiting, tempered by general suspicion of all, seemed best indicated in the circumstances.

These same circumstances gave unusual importance to the Italian role. Italy's action in Abyssinia had had very considerable repercussions in Europe; wrecking the League and straining to the breaking point the possibility of common action with Britain and France, it had opened for Germany the opportunity that she had so effectively used. Italy was not averse to the restoration of a balance in Europe and her Four-Power proposal of 1933 expressed that view, but Italy could have no interest in abetting a German dominance of Europe. There had been no organized Italo-German coöperation during the Abyssinian episode; but out of its unfolding *de facto* coöperation developed. If Italian activity had been most useful to Germany, so likewise the German action of 1935 had been a useful deterrent to Anglo-French, and more particularly French, action against Italy.[2] It is significant that, despite the state of her relations with Britain and France, Italy joined in the London meeting of the Locarno Powers called in response to the Rhineland coup. If the Western democracies would accept the legitimacy of the Italian conquest, Italy might yet act on the basis of Mussolini's declaration that she was now a satisfied Power and join the forces of conservation in preserving the new existing order.

But this must also be said. The unexpected success of the Abyssinian affair, both locally and in defiance of the Western Powers, combined with the effective interplay of Italian and German action, constituted for Italy a temptation. Success can be a heady draft that clouds the judgment: boldness might secure further gains, in the pursuit of which the German card might be of further use;[3] this would involve an element of gambling to which Fascism was not necessarily averse. There was between Germany

---

[2] Germany, no longer in the League, was not involved in the application of sanctions. She did some profitable trade with Italy as a result, and Italy was grateful for the benefits of German trade—even at a high price.

[3] Mention may be made again of the frequent Fascist reference to decadent democracy. The actual performance of the democracies was indeed calculated to foster the belief that these assertions might be more than rhetoric, thereby giving encouragement to further aggression.

and Italy one major possible source of dissension, the continued independence of Austria, on the score of which Italian policy had hitherto been both consistent and firm. But it was on June 11 that a bilateral Austro-German agreement was concluded. The declaration issued on that date, simultaneously in Berlin and in Vienna, was not devoid of ambiguity, for while it stated that Germany recognized the full sovereignty of Austria, it also contained the commitment that Austrian policy would be based "on principles which correspond to the fact that Austria has acknowledged herself to be a German state."

This may be said to have sanctioned ambiguity rather than clarified Austria's status. But the stamp of Mussolini's approval of the declaration was indication that, at the very least, Germany had agreed to put the Austrian problem "on ice," thereby paving the way for easier relations with Italy.[4]

THE SPANISH CIVIL WAR

The opportunities for coöperation were soon to be greatly enhanced by an unexpected turn of events in a wholly different quarter. The role of Spain in the affairs of Europe has generally been such as not to warrant mention of the country. Spain's Moroccan difficulties[5] during the preceding decade had resulted in some coöperation with France in putting down the Riff rebellion; at home a dictatorship of sorts had been instituted under General Primo de Rivera that had lasted until 1930. A reaction followed the next year that ousted the king and proclaimed a Republic; but the course of the Republic was troubled, oscillating between wide swings of opposite extremes. The most recent development on the Spanish political scene had been an election in February, 1936, that showed the country very evenly divided but gave a clear majority in the *Cortes* to the *Frente Popular*, a combination broadly similar to that which was to triumph under the same rubric in the French elections of April–May.

Despite initial moderation of the new regime, Spain was torn by increasing strife and violence that the government seemed unable to bring under control. The murder of one of the leaders of

---

[4] Hungary likewise signified her approval of this declaration.

[5] In 1921 Spain had suffered a military disaster at Anual in Morocco where some 12,000 out of a body of 20,000 troops had been killed. The mismanagement of military operations in Morocco and the king's role in these matters led to the suppression of the results of the investigation by a committee of the Cortes and to the subsequent one of the constitution.

the Right, Calvo Sotelo, was seized upon as the occasion for the launching of a revolt that had been planned for some time; on July 17 the army rose, in the Moroccan zone first, then in most garrison cities in Spain. Such an event was hardly novel in Spain and might have merely been a passing episode without significance beyond the borders of the country had it been either quickly successful or promptly suppressed. But neither happened, and within a short time a situation developed that found the country split into two halves, under the control respectively of the rebellious army and of the existing government, rebels or nationalists on one hand, loyalists on the other, as they came to be commonly known. In the uncertain situation of the Europe of 1936 the Spanish Civil war was not allowed to unfold as a purely Spanish affair and Spain became instead the battleground of contending ideologies and interests.

THE POWERS AND THE CIVIL WAR: NONINTERVENTION. It was to take the better part of three years before the drama of the Spanish Civil War was played out; the war itself was accompanied by much brutality and slaughter in Spain and by considerable diplomatic activity on the part of the Powers, the record of which constitutes a lengthy and generally dreary tale; the episode in its domestic and international aspects is still source of much controversy, and the high points of it alone will be considered.

Precisely what preparations the revolting Spanish army leaders had made for assistance cannot be said with final certainty. But some Italian assistance was forthcoming very early.[6] A change of government in Spain from the existing one to one more favorably disposed toward the Fascist outlook would obviously be pleasing to Italy; at small cost, through a coup rapidly executed, Italy could gain the asset of a sympathetic regime which would have the further advantage of acting as a potential pressure on France.

The very same considerations, in turn, might be expected to induce an opposite reaction in France, especially as the factor of ideological sympathy linked the new government of that country with the existing one of Spain. This lends all the more interest to the behavior of France at this time. Never a forceful or a belliger-

[6] That Italy was implicated in the preparation of the Spanish army coup was confirmed by the incident of Italian airplanes on their way to Spain mistakenly landing in French Morocco at the end of July.

ent man, Premier Blum was in addition confronted with a delicate situation at home;[7] it was a French initiative on August 1, addressed at first to Italy and Britain, that proposed that the Powers undertake to refrain from intervening in Spain 'and come to an agreement among themselves to that end. In addition to the evident purpose of minimizing the possibility of complications, the French suggestion was designed to secure solidarity with Britain. For Britain, which became in fact the most authentic advocate of, as well as adherent to, the practice of nonintervention in Spain, was truly desirous of avoiding an extension of the Spanish disturbance and not especially concerned over the prospect of a change in the rule of that country. It was quite consistent for France, after the abdication of March, to align her own policy with the British.

The British response to the French proposal was therefore wholly favorable,[8] and further exchanges with other Powers led to the formal acceptance of it and to the setting up, appropriately in London, of a so-called Nonintervention Committee.[9] The deliberations of that body were destined to be both laborious and, from the standpoint of its ostensible purpose, quite futile; into them we shall not enter and it will suffice to say that the most, if not the only, useful aspect of the Nonintervention Committee was that it served to conceal behind diplomatic verbiage the reality of intervention. To that extent it may also be seen as a safety valve. For it became apparent very early that some Powers had no intention of refraining from intervention in Spain. The most flagrant offender by far was Italy, who sent to Spain substantial quantities of matériel and increasingly large regular army formations, dubbed at first "volunteers." The Italian position may be summed up in simplest form as follows: Italy, perhaps having made an initial miscalculation, found herself committed to the ultimate triumph of the forces of General Franco in Spain; from this position

[7] The advent of the Popular Front government was the signal for a great outburst of social unrest that created a delicate situation for the government, which hastened to enact its program of social reforms while seeking to put an end to the numerous strikes. There was no danger of revolution but tension was nevertheless considerable and opinion bitterly divided.

[8] The Italian reply, an acceptance in principle, was in effect essentially a quibble that foreshadowed the future Italian behavior in the matter of nonintervention.

[9] By implication, the ban on assistance to either side in the civil war tended to place the rebels on the same plane as the legitimate government which, for that reason, objected to its being denied the possibility of purchasing war matériel abroad.

she would not retreat, whatever the consequences, and the Spanish disturbance could only be contained in Spain if Italy could have her way.

But if the Italian intervention was the most substantial, Nazi Germany likewise sent valuable assistance, mainly in the form of matériel and technicians, and this was also the case with the Soviet Union, which contributed political commissars in addition.[10] From the German point of view the Spanish affair, like the Abyssinian, was another wholly satisfactory occurrence. If the testing of new war matériel was technically useful, far more important were the political aspects of the matter. The increasing Italian involvement had the combined effects of hampering the effectiveness of the Italian role in Central Europe as well as minimizing the likelihood of Italy regaining the Western camp. However, Germany did not seek to take advantage of the situation at the expense of Italy at once, abiding by the terms of the freshly-made Austro-German declaration of June. The outcome therefore was Italo-German coöperation where Spain was concerned, be it in the form of material assistance to the Franco forces, or in that of preventing agreement and effective action in the interminable discussions of the Nonintervention Committee. For Italy a major decision was involved, the long-term consequences of which, for herself no less than for Europe, could be of enormous import. Committed as she was in Spain, she elected to strengthen her *de facto* collaboration with Germany and to formalize it into an open agreement.

THE ROME-BERLIN AXIS

Thus the Rome-Berlin Axis was born. On the German side there had been some hesitation, but it too was overcome.[11] The replacement at the Italian foreign office of Suvich by Mussolini's own son-in-law, Count Ciano, in June,[12] the formal German rec-

[10] There was also a measure of more or less surreptitious assistance from France. In addition, volunteers who were authentic anti-Fascists went individually to the assistance of the government, which organized them into an International Brigade. The number of such volunteers was always small by comparison with the numbers sent by Italy.
[11] Some share in doing this goes to a British memorandum on "the German danger," drawn up by Anthony Eden, of which the Italians were able to secure possession and which they transmitted to the Germans. This helped counter the effect of contacts that Hitler had had with some British leaders, such as the aging Lloyd George, who had a friendly meeting with him at Berchtesgaden and made himself in Britain the advocate of a pro-German orientation.
[12] Ciano had been in charge of the propaganda ministry where his place was taken by Alfieri, an advocate of the closer connection with Germany. Ciano

ognition of the Italian title to Abyssinia, and an increasing frequency of official visits were the preliminaries to the agreement that was made on October 24, on the occasion of Ciano's visit to Germany. It was the Spanish War that had brought out in full the merits of a common policy, and on that subject the two governments saw eye to eye; they decided in fact to grant recognition to the government of General Franco. For the rest, their possible differences in Central Europe were for the time amicably adjusted —or concealed. Germany did not seek to challenge the Italian position, but in turn Italy was willing to accept the German position in Europe, especially in Central Europe, while her own would be paramount in the Mediterranean.

The Axis was aptly named. Mussolini, who coined the expression in a speech of November 1, meant to assert the claim to leadership of the new vigorous regimes that held sway in Rome and Berlin, by contrast with the decadent Western democratic systems on one side and with the Eastern threat of Bolshevism on the other. The theme of anti-Bolshevik crusade, of the defense of civilized Europe against barbaric Marxism, one of which Hitler was even fonder than Mussolini, was often to be reasserted. In the eyes of its sponsors it was more than meaningless verbiage and fraudulent propaganda; but it was also a very useful propaganda tool of which they made effective use in confusing opinion and therefore weakening the resolution of the Western democratic Powers. It was also in 1936, in November, that a German-Japanese agreement, usually known as the Anti-Comintern Pact, added point to the crusading aspect of Axis policy.

This lack of resolution and weakness of the West, so patently brought out in the manifestations of French policy, gave point to the assertion that the Rome-Berlin Axis was henceforth to be the combination around which Europe would revolve, and the prevailing uncertainty found reflection in the gropings of the smaller Powers which, in default of strength, were particularly sensitive to shifts in the relationships of power.

Belgium had been the first, in 1920, to enter the circle of the French system. But the events of 1936, especially the remilitarization of the Rhineland, were cause for second thoughts in Belgium. Even before that event Belgium had manifested the desire

---

was only thirty-three years of age. Not devoid of intelligence and charm, he was also possessed of not a little irresponsibility and was anxious to make a mark for himself.

to renounce the French alliance and to confine her obligations to those of the Locarno agreement. But even that had lost its meaning after the coup of March and the subsequent failure of the Locarno Powers to come to any meaningful understanding. Belgium took the decision to resume an "independent" policy and attend to her own defense, accepting no obligations beyond those that derived from her membership in the League, another superseded instrument. The true significance of this was the obvious attempt of Belgium to disengage her policy from the French,[13] public notice of loss of faith in the validity of the French system. The Belgian wish was given recognition in the subsequent Anglo-French declaration of April 24, 1937, while in January Hitler declared in the Reichstag his willingness to acknowledge the inviolability of both Belgium and Holland.[14] To a degree, therefore, Belgium may be said to have returned, or at least attempted to return, to the status of pre-1914.

Unlike Belgium, Poland did not seek to withdraw from her formal commitments, but she had already embarked upon a hedging policy with the conclusion of the agreement with Germany at the beginning of 1934. Subsequent relations between the two countries were hardly marked by an increasing cordiality, though Poland could not fail to take notice of the growing German strength accompanied by French inaction. If France could derive comfort from the contemplation of her eastern fortifications, the Maginot Line would be of little use to Poland, especially when the German undertaking of fortifications in the west, the Siegfried Line, could contribute to the immobilization of France. The Franco-Polish visits that were exchanged in 1936—General Gamelin to Poland; General Smigly-Rydz, Pilsudski's heir, to France—were cordial enough, but could not alter the fact that Poland was adhering to a watchful attitude; General Göring, too, had been entertained in Poland. Poland had little liking for the Franco-Soviet connection, which the accompaniment of a Czech-Soviet pact did little to endear to her. In brief, the Franco-Polish alliance still had formal existence, but little more than that.

Like Poland, the Little Entente was part of the French system, though its chief motivation and focus had been Hungarian revi-

---

[13] A movement of general Fascist tendency, that went by the name of Rexist, had made its appearance in Belgium. Under the leadership of Léon Degrelle, the Rexists secured twenty-one seats in the election of 1936.

[14] This was reasserted in a German declaration of October 3, 1937.

sionism and the fear of Habsburg restoration. The resurgence of Germany and the growing Italo-German collaboration were the outstanding facts in Central Europe, corresponding to the weakening of the French influence. So long as Italy and Germany saw eye to eye, both Austria and Hungary could benefit from their joint protection.[15] The danger of Habsburg restoration was small, for it suited neither the German nor the Italian book, but it might be otherwise with Hungarian revisionism that the spectacle of Germany's unopposed success could not but encourage. The same applied in the case of Bulgaria which Italy especially was sponsoring.

Czechoslovakia had little choice and continued to adhere to the older connection with France and the newly made one with Russia. But the internal ties of the Little Entente were loosened by the changing picture of the distribution of power. Yugoslavia, like Poland, continued to adhere to the French alliance, but the conclusion of a Yugoslav-Bulgarian Pact of Friendship on January 24, 1937, shortly followed by an Italo-Yugoslav nonaggression pact on March 25, were clear indications of the drift of Yugoslav policy. The tour of Eastern European capitals that the French foreign minister, Delbos, had made in December, 1936, was barren of concrete results.[16] The smaller states of Central and Eastern Europe had little cause to welcome or encourage German resurgence, but must adapt themselves as best they could to changing circumstances; in so far as they could benefit from a condition of equilibrium among the greater Powers, it was the possibility of balance between German and Italian influence that was of interest to them; at this stage that aspect of the matter was not a realistic calculation. As to the Soviet Union, with the exception of Czechoslovakia, these states were all characterized by their strong dislike of the Bolshevik state.

MEDITERRANEAN READJUSTMENTS

Meanwhile, the most concrete issue that occupied the foreign offices of the Powers was that presented by the Spanish Civil War. In view of the special involvement of Italy, the entire Mediter-

[15] In November, 1936, Ciano and the Austrian and Hungarian foreign ministers met in Vienna where a secret protocol was signed that envisaged the neutrality of its participants should one of them find itself at war.

[16] Rumania, too, was veering away from the French connection. In August the pro-French and pro-Little Entente foreign minister, Titulescu, was forced to resign.

ranean equilibrium was affected and that sea was the scene of re-adjustments comparable to those just indicated in the Central European world. The most concrete aspects of them took place, however, at the eastern end of that sea where they affected most notably Turkey and Egypt.

For some time Turkey had shown dissatisfaction with the status of the Straits, demilitarized at Lausanne in 1923. The failure of the disarmament discussions and the consequent rearmament of Germany, together with shifting Balkan alignments, caused Turkey as well to consider a new program of armament. The Abyssinian war had also had the effect of creating tension and uncertainty at the eastern end of the Mediterranean, while the success of the German coup was an obvious inducement to others to take matters into their own hands.

It is significant that while Turkey's reiterated wishes for a change in the status of the Straits had hitherto gone unanswered, the Turkish note of April 10, 1936, led to prompt action.[17] The result was the conference that met at Montreux in June–July, 1936. Over mainly British opposition Turkey gained her ends: she was allowed to remilitarize the zone of the Straits, and the guardianship of the somewhat altered conditions of passage through them was put in Turkish hands instead of those of an international commission. Although the terms of the Montreux Convention entailed some advantage for Russia, their main significance lay in the restoration of Turkish control.

A comparable situation occurred in the case of Egypt. Anglo-Egyptian negotiations had been deadlocked since their breakdown in 1930.[18] The Abyssinian war seemed a good occasion for reopening them, especially on the Egyptian side. The effects of that war pointed in opposite directions: Egyptian sympathy was, understandably, with Abyssinia, and British power might be a desirable protection for Egypt; on the other hand, Egypt might become the battleground of an Anglo-Italian conflict; the Italian success, resulting in the Italian control of the sources of the Blue Nile, was

[17] The Turkish case for revision rested mainly on the changed circumstances and on the undependability of the guarantees undertaken in 1923. In the face of various breaches of international agreements it was thought desirable to avoid one more such, especially in view of the hint that Turkey might take matters into her own hands in the event of failure to achieve her wishes by recourse to legal methods.

[18] In 1935 the chief Egyptian parties joined in a National Front which secured from King Fuad the restoration of the suspended constitution of 1923. Following this Egypt sought the resumption of discussions with Britain.

naturally of much concern to Egypt. There was difficulty in reaching an understanding, owing to some British reluctance and to Egyptian suspicion of British tergiversation, but agreement was eventually achieved, which was written into the Anglo-Egyptian treaty of August 26, 1936.

This was an important landmark in the story that had begun fifty-four years earlier. The status of Egypt, beclouded since the termination of the British protectorate, was now made clear: a fully sovereign and independent state, Egypt entered with Britain into a relationship of alliance, as the result of which Britain retained the right to maintain certain forces in Egypt and received additional facilities in the event of war or emergency. The status of the Sudan was restored to that of condominium.[19]

Somewhat comparable developments took place in the Syrian mandate of France. An attempt to alter the French position in Syria along the lines of the Anglo-Iraqi arrangement of 1932[20] had proved unsuccessful. But the advent of the new government in France in June revived a seemingly unpromising negotiation that led to the signature in September of a Franco-Syrian treaty, followed by a similar one with Lebanon in November.[21]

To the Syrian situation there was a footnote. The Sanjak of Alexandretta has a majority of Turkish, or at least Turkish-speaking, population; it had enjoyed a special status since 1921, and the conclusion of the Franco-Syrian treaty was occasion for Turkey to raise the issue of its new position. Through the League, in 1937, a Franco-Turkish agreement was reached that further loosened the connection of the Sanjak with Syria, a step along the road of its absorption by Turkey.[22]

The story of the Palestinian mandate had been troubled from its beginning as a consequence of the ambiguity of Britain's wartime arrangements. Britain did not feel able to relinquish her man-

[19] The treaty was well received at the time, both in Britain and in Egypt, but as subsequent events were to show, it proved but a stage in a continuing story rather than the closing of it.
[20] In 1933 an agreement had been sketched which, however, remained a dead letter owing to opposition in Syria and to the reinstitution of repressive measures by France in 1934.
[21] These treaties, too, remained dead letters owing to the failure of their ratification by the French Parliament, a fact that naturally fed discontent in Syria and Lebanon.
[22] The Sanjak was to remain in customs and monetary union with Syria. Elections that were to take place in 1938 were postponed owing to local disturbances, and a new agreement was made that was superseded in 1939 with the outright incorporation of the Sanjak into Turkey.

date, as in the case of Iraq, owing to her Zionist pledges, and a trickle of Jewish immigration continued to flow into the land. The racial policies of the Third Reich gave a great impetus to this movement after 1932; in 1935, over 60,000 Jews entered Palestine legally.[23] The Palestinian Arabs began to have visions of becoming a minority and losing control of their own land, while the British failure to produce a compromise acceptable to Arabs and Zionists alike resulted in an outbreak of Arab violence in April, 1936, reflection also of the diminished standing of Britain that the Abyssinian affair had produced. Peace momentarily restored, the British evolved a solution for the partition of the small country into a Jewish and an Arab state. Unsatisfactory to both Arabs and Jews, the proposal was not put into effect and Britain continued in charge of the mandate under conditions that were essentially impossible and led to increasing deterioration: there was no reconciling the inconsistent aims of the two groups, while for Britain the problem was to maintain her own position in a vitally strategic region and to avoid losing the friendship of those Arab states—Arabia, Iraq, and Transjordan—whose rulers were still favorably inclined toward her.[24]

THE THREE POWER CONSTELLATIONS OF EUROPE

These Near Eastern developments reflected the diminished standing of the Western states, of which the outcome of the Abyssinian episode was one clear outward manifestation, and the French renunciation of March the latest confirmation. With the destruction of the League and the abdication of France, nothing was left of any structure that had held Europe together since the First World War. In the new contest for power three groups or units were taking shape toward the end of 1936. The Western states, Britain and France, had in common their dedication to the democratic ideal; more concretely and immediately, they were subjected to a threat of universal dimensions. Holders of hitherto preponderant strength, they were possessed of large empires that could be menaced no less by the ambitions of European rivals, claiming to have been so far deprived of their rightful place under

[23] Illegal entries reached a large figure during this same period; in 1932 the figure of entries was about five thousand.

[24] The Palestinian situation was to become increasingly difficult and the final solution of the creation of the state of Israel in 1947 has merely altered the terms of the conflict that remains to this day unresolved. See below, pp. 607–608.

the sun, than by the rising tide of the desire for freedom of the dependent peoples in these same empires.[25]

At the opposite end of Europe, the Soviet state had come to the conclusion that peace was for the time its best interest, but the revolutionary urge had been temporarily restrained rather than permanently denied. Between the two, athwart Central Europe, Nazi Germany and Fascist Italy, Hitler and Mussolini, represented the most active forces of change, urged on besides by the desire for quick returns. The smaller Powers, anxiously watching the fluid situation, were concerned above all to maintain their own independence, though some of them inevitably saw their best hope in conservation while others thought they could best profit by change.

Given the three-cornered situation just mentioned among the greater Powers, the possibility existed of the combination of any two of the groups should the proper basis for an accommodation be found. Russia in fact had formal links with the West in the form of the French alliance, and the nature of the French regime might be thought suitable to solid collaboration. But Russia, like others, had cause for second thoughts on the solidity of French purpose, while on the French side, the very fact of the Soviet alliance was a divisive element. The Popular Front government of France must not in any case, it felt, part company with Britain; but Britain's enthusiasm for the Franco-Soviet connection was, to say the least, moderate.

In this connection reference must be made to the domestic course of events in the Soviet Union. After the definite triumph of Stalin over his rival Trotzky and the secure establishment of the former in control, stress had been put on the internal growth of the country. Broadly speaking, the succession of Five Year plans had two aims: the building up of heavy industry and the collectivization of agriculture, but the pursuit of them did not go without severe internal stresses, the manifestations of which, in the Soviet milieu of secrecy, were at times bewildering to outsiders. The attempts at rapidly enforced collectivization had led to opposition that had been brutally and ruthlessly suppressed, though generally with success. But the assassination of Kirov in 1934 was the

[25] In North Africa France had to contend with local nationalist agitation, the most serious manifestation of which was the revolt of Abd-el-Krim in Morocco, which it took several years to repacify. She faced similar difficulties in Indochina, while in India Gandhi was conducting his persistent campaign for emancipation from British rule.

opening signal for a series of political purges. This is no place to go into the details of these Byzantine performances, of which we need only retain the shocking extent. That the flower of the "old Bolshevik" leadership, close associates of Lenin, should suddenly appear in the guise of saboteurs and traitors, and most astonishing of all undergo the public humiliation of abject recantations, was calculated to tax the will to believe. Many were executed, and even the army leadership seemed to be unreliable and was extensively purged.[26] Much of Soviet leadership seemed to be fated to destruction.

That such a state of affairs should cast doubts on the reliability of Russia's policy and, more concretely, on the dependability of her strength, is the least that could be expected, even apart from the element of revulsion that such barbarity induced among many, especially in the Western states long accustomed to the rule of law and to the practice of open and fair trial. The importance of this factor of doubt where Russia was concerned is difficult of measurement, but the significance of it is worth bearing in mind when one comes to consider the possibility of a solid connection between the Soviet Union and the Western states. Nevertheless, the likelihood of an opposite association between the former and the Central European totalitarians seemed an even less probable prospect in view of their mutual and loudly proclaimed hatred: the "Fascist beasts" were fully dedicated to the destruction of the common enemy of mankind.

This might point to the possibility of association between the democracies and the Fascist states, a prospect never absent in Russian calculations. From the point of view of the Fascist states the most important consideration was to prevent a combination of others against themselves and to weaken whatever connection existed. The League they had successfully destroyed, and collective security, after 1936, was but a hollow phrase, though still mouthed in Geneva. The German coup of March had weakened the French position in general and the Franco-Soviet connection in particular; it had in some degree drawn France and Britain closer, and the French attitude in the Spanish War might augur well for the pur-

[26] In June, 1937, Marshal Tukhachevsky and some other high-ranking generals were executed after a secret trial in which they were accused of plotting the overthrow of the regime with foreign Powers (Germany and Japan). Whether the charges were justified or not, such happenings could not but make a considerable impression on the outside world and raise doubts about the solidity of the Soviet regime.

suit of further common policy. But Britain did not share France's fears; most of all she wanted peace and for the preservation of it she would pay a high price. There was in Britain considerable willingness to recognize the legitimacy of German demands in particular, and this was tantamount to a major decision based on an estimate of the aims of German policy.

Another possibility may be mentioned in the unfolding of the three-cornered power competition. If a showdown in the form of an open clash was fated to occur, each of the three contenders would find it advantageous to see it occur between the other two, letting the warring rivals wear each other out while reserving the use of its own power to procure the outcome most satisfactory to itself. This may be said to have been Britain's traditional policy toward the Continent though by no means a British monopoly of outlook. The consideration is relevant that such a policy, which some would describe as Machiavellian, would be more difficult of implementation in the democratic milieus of the West, with free and open discussion in Parliament and press, than in the rigidly controlled totalitarian states. These broad considerations are the fundamental background of the European scene as the year 1936 was drawing to a close, the background against which the record of the steady progress toward ultimate catastrophe must be seen.

THE WESTERN POLICY OF APPEASEMENT. That German aims knew no limit and that what seemed the lunatic ravings of *Mein Kampf* was a program for action meant in earnest we now know, both from the events that occurred and from the available record of Nazi documentation. But Hitler was a shrewd appraiser of human psychology, and just because his program seemed fantastic and his lies were very big, the tendency was widespread to discount much of them as propaganda meant for domestic consumption, the stock in trade of demagoguery, and to seize upon the sweeter seeming reasonableness of other pronouncements that he was also capable of making.[27]

The wish, father to the thought, was strong in Britain to believe in the fundamental moderation of German aims. However, the close association of the Fascist states was potentially dangerous;

---

[27] Hitler exploited with skill the technique of explaining, after each coup, that it was his last and that he had henceforth no additional claims. After the Rhineland coup of 1936 he proposed the conclusion of a twenty-five-year nonaggression pact with France and Belgium, presumably a more reliable commitment because freely consented to by himself.

at the very least it enhanced their bargaining power. To break that association was therefore a desirable end, the question being how best this could be done: would it be easier to give satisfaction to Germany or to Italy? In either case some price would have to be paid in order to appease the hunger of the claimant. Out of this view was born the policy that goes under the name of appeasement. The word has fallen into disrepute and is now often used to damn a person or a policy. It may not be amiss to recall its original meaning devoid of unfavorable connotations; appeasing the appeasable is a most reasonable endeavor, but whetting the appetite of the insatiable is mere suicidal folly. It is not therefore the policy of appeasement as such that merits condemnation, but the correct or faulty judgment on the score of appeasability that warrants praise or blame.

One more consideration may be added before proceeding to the examination of the specific record of events. Britain was the prime pursuer of appeasement, but France showed herself willing to follow in that path. Having allowed the structure of Versailles to collapse, the eminently wise decision of France not to be separated from Britain seems to have been unaccompanied by a determination to insist on the fact that the Anglo-French association was rooted in the fundamental community of interests between two equal partners, each of equal importance and need to the other—the French army, a powerful instrument, was also the only tool that the partnership possessed for immediate use on the Continent. France instead meekly surrendered to the British leadership, no doubt an easy way to maintain concordance, but an additional manifestation of the abdication of France. This is all the more remarkable that there was generally in France, among the directors of policy, a rather clearer understanding of the whole European situation than was to be found at the same level in Britain.

The Spanish Civil War was the most concrete and potentially dangerous issue that confronted Europe at this time. The Nonintervention Committee, established in London, served the function of safety valve rather than fulfilling its ostensible purpose. The record of its lengthy, tedious, unrealistic, in some ways humorous, deliberations will not be detailed; the basic position of the various Powers in connection with the war has been mentioned. In the circumstances, the Nonintervention Committee served nevertheless the useful purpose of making it possible to keep alive the fiction that the Powers were striving to find some common ground among themselves. But since there was no common ground in fact, the Spanish episode may fairly be summed up by saying that Britain and France had reconciled themselves to letting the Axis, Italy in particular, have its way in Spain, and largely shut their eyes to the sending of sufficient assistance to insure the victory of General Franco.[28] In view of the fact that, albeit on a small scale, there was assistance to the Loyalist side as well, the role of diplomatic activity was in effect to prolong the agony of Spain. Some of the manifestations of policy in connection with the Spanish War deserve mention, however, as revealing indications of the evolving relations of the Powers.

After the dropping of sanctions against Italy in July, 1936, Britain, seeking to cut her losses, endeavored to revive a measure of understanding with Italy. During the latter part of the year negotiations were undertaken in Rome which led to the conclusion, on January 2, 1937, of a so-called "gentleman's agreement" in which both countries disclaimed any desire to entertain alterations in the status of the Mediterranean.[29] But the agreement failed to modify Italian policy in Spain where Italian assistance continued on an ever-increasing scale, until Mussolini, throwing away the pretense of "volunteers," took to acknowledging and even boasting of the presence of regular army formations in Spain. It was during the summer of 1937 that occurred the episode of "piratical" submarines, an occasion that caused a more vigorous and successful British reaction,[30] but no improvement of Anglo-Italian relations.

If appeasement was unrewarding in the Italian case, it might be tried at the northern end of the Axis. The new British ambassador, Sir Neville Henderson, appointed to Berlin in May, was a firm believer in Anglo-German understanding, to which end he labored

[28] In 1937 there was instituted a naval patrol of the Spanish coasts with the participation of Britain, France, Germany, and Italy. The effect of this arrangement was not very substantial and it led to some serious incidents between the Spanish government and the Axis Powers.

[29] The Italians had for some time been in effective control of the Balearic Islands, a matter of especial concern to France, who welcomed the conclusion of the gentleman's agreement.

[30] Attacks on ships directed to loyalist Spain by "unknown" submarines occurred, even in the Eastern Mediterranean, and the suspicion was widespread that the submarines were Italian. The British Admiralty issued orders to counterattack any attempt on British ships, and a French proposal resulted in a meeting at Nyon where, despite Italian absence, arrangements were made for Anglo-French patrolling of the Mediterranean. A subsequent agreement with Italy entrusted her with the patrolling of central Mediterranean and Dodecanese waters. Piratical submarines promptly ceased to appear.

assiduously, while in November Lord Halifax paid a visit to Hitler. Though no concrete results were procured, there was apparent relaxation of tension that likewise affected Franco-German relations. Germany needed time to proceed with her rearmament and stood to reap no advantage from irritating Britain and France, but she strove simultaneously to strengthen the loose bonds of the Axis. Exchanges of visits between the two countries culminated in a royal reception given to Mussolini at the end of September,[31] and this was followed by the formal adherence of Italy, on November 6, 1937, to the Anti-Comintern Pact of the preceding year. The Rome-Berlin Axis was thus enlarged into the Rome-Berlin-Tokyo triangle.[32]

II. The Year 1938. Germany Begins to Move

It had become a custom in Nazi Germany to hold celebrations on the 30th of January, anniversary of the appointment of Hitler to the Chancellorship. An important pronouncement of the Führer before the claque of a docile Reichstag was a common accompaniment of the festivities. It was that date in 1937 that he had chosen to proclaim, not without humor perhaps, the end of the "policy of surprises"; the relaxation of tension during the rest of the year has been noted. Special interest therefore attached to the announcement that the meeting of the Reichstag had been postponed to February 20. There was reason indeed for this interest: Germany had been putting to good use the passage of time in reconstructing her armed forces and was about to launch into the next phase of her program.

On November 5, 1937, an important meeting had already been called by Hitler with some of his most important advisers, in the course of which he had disclosed to them his future plans. The first step was the integration under a single rule of the German community in Europe; this meant the incorporation into the Reich of both Austria and the Sudetenland. Although Britain and France

[31] He made a speech in German before a huge assemblage in Berlin in which he stressed the solidity of Fascist friendship.

[32] In the Far East Japan was proceeding with her aggression initiated by the Manchurian episode. In 1937 she resumed active hostilities against China, though never formally declaring war. By the end of the year Shanghai and Peking were in Japanese hands and the Japanese went on to occupy Canton and Hankow in 1938. All the while an uneasy peace was maintained between Japan and the Soviet Union, the latter being anxious not to become embroiled in Far Eastern hostilities owing to the uncertain situation in Europe.

had, according to Hitler, probably written off Czechoslovakia, they would tend to oppose the extension of German power in Europe as well as overseas.[33] The contemplated operation therefore involved certain risks of war, but the moment for taking these was favorable in view of the head start in German rearmament in contrast with the lag of British and French preparations; the passage of time would, on the other hand, enable those Powers to make up their lag and restore an equilibrium detrimental to Germany.

In the pursuit of the aims of German policy, opinion in the directing group was divided between what may be called the moderate and the radical tendencies, the former being represented by the foreign office and the *Wehrmacht*. It was significant that on February 4, 1938, the foreign minister, von Neurath, was replaced by the incompetent and irresponsible von Ribbentrop, hitherto Germany's representative in London. Simultaneously was created an *Oberkommando der Wehrmacht*, at the head of which was placed the subservient General Keitel, while the war minister, von Blomberg, and the Commander-in-Chief, von Fritsch, old line military leaders, were ousted.[34] Hitler was definitely taking into his own hands the direction of foreign policy as well as that of the armed forces.

THE ANSCHLUSS AND ITS CONSEQUENCES

Italy's adherence to the Anti-Comintern Pact was the occasion for discussion of the Austrian problem, the outcome of this discussion being that Mussolini came to accept that, in view of Italy's increased Mediterranean interest and of the state of Italo-German relations, the Austrian question had lost much of its importance. Subject to "no surprises" Mussolini thus removed his veto on the *Anschluss*. Free of this obstacle, and anticipating correctly that the Western Powers would offer no effective opposition, Hitler felt able to move against an Austria deprived of any external support. Austrian Nazis had not been inactive in the internal affairs of

[33] According to Hitler's plan colonial questions should be postponed to a more suitable time, when Britain would encounter difficulties in her own possessions; meanwhile the possibilities of Anglo-Italian and Anglo-Japanese difference should be fostered. On Eden's resignation and its significance, see below, p. 521.

[34] The "socially unsuitable" (by old German army standards) marriage of the War Minister, von Blomberg, was occasion for the demand for his resignation by the Commander-in-Chief, von Fritsch. Hitler resolved the dilemma with which this situation confronted him through a decree that placed him in command of the armed forces and through a reshuffle of the army command.

Austria, and the regime of Chancellor Schuschnigg lacked a sufficient basis of positive support in the country as well as a forceful personality in its leader.[35] On February 12, 1938, Schuschnigg accepted a summons to Berchtesgaden where he met scant courtesy, a severe lecture from the Führer, and a virtual ultimatum; as a consequence, the Austrian Nazi leader, Seyss-Inquart, became minister of the interior. The writing on the wall was clear and Schuschnigg's belated attempt at resistance merely precipitated the outcome. A new German ultimatum[36] placed Seyss-Inquart in the Chancellorship; pretexting the need of assistance for the preservation of order, the first gesture of the new Chancellor was to call in German forces. These entered unopposed and marched to Vienna. On March 13 Austria joined the German Reich, of which it became a new province, the Ostmark. A plebiscite in Greater Germany, on April 10, endorsed the result with a 99 percent vote.

Hitler had judged correctly; no one reacted. The event was nonetheless a shock and the significance of it was considerable. This was a strange commentary on the recent Hitlerian promise of "no more surprises," for the formal pretext used in the operation was too flimsy to deceive anyone; the question was raised anew of the extent of German aims. Quite apart from the nature of any particular regime in Germany, a case could be made for the *Anschluss* on the simple basis of the German nationality of Austria, where feeling for union with Germany had always existed since the war in substantial, though varying, strength. The *Anschluss* might therefore be regarded as a not unreasonable German desire and not necessarily indicative of aggressive intent. This was the view that prevailed in the British government of the day and even in France the policy of appeasement had not a little support.

France was involved at this time in domestic difficulties, mainly financial; these were reflected in a rapid succession of Cabinets, the orientation of which was toward a Center combination, away from the Popular Front coalition. The Prime Minister, Chautemps, and the foreign minister, Georges Bonnet, both Radical Socialists, like Chamberlain in Britain, were partisans of cutting losses and

[35] Chancellor Schuschnigg attempted to be at the same time anti-Nazi and anti-Socialist. In addition, his personal leanings were monarchical. The combination was well calculated to assure the opposition of all his neighbors and of much of the Austrian people.
[36] On March 9 Schuschnigg announced the holding of a plebiscite on the 13th on the issue of independence. This move caught the Germans by surprise, but, determined to prevent the testing of Austrian opinion, they reacted promptly, demanding the resignation of Schuschnigg, who yielded on March 11.

definitely favored a Franco-German understanding, the corollary of which was the inevitable acceptance of certain German claims, perhaps even the recognition of German primacy in Central Europe.[37] Such a policy could indeed be defended as one of reasonableness, especially if two assumptions were made: that German aims were limited, that Germany was the strongest bulwark against the Communist danger. It was a policy that was welcome in Britain where French intransigeance had been so often criticized in the past. The least that can be said of the interpretation of the Western Powers is that it entailed a substantial renunciation of position, and the successful *Anschluss* appeared to all as the outstanding German victory that in reality it was.

A different interpretation was possible, the correct one as we now know, based on a different view of German intentions. There was a substantial German minority in Czechoslovakia, and the *Anschluss* had the effect of vastly diminishing the defensive possibilities of that country, as a mere glance at the map will conclusively show. The judgment was old that, in military terms, whoever controls Bohemia controls Central Europe. Needless to say, Czechoslovakia was alarmed, but Hitler had no difficulty in issuing profuse reassurances. The issue of the fate of Czechoslovakia could not escape the West, but the impact of that consideration may be summed up by saying that it had little effect in Britain, where the tendency was strong to give Germany the benefit of the doubt, while in France it served to accentuate the cleavage of opinion.

The case of Italy is of especial interest. To Italian opinion the *Anschluss* generally appeared as the unmitigated disaster that it was. But opinion in Italy carried little weight and Mussolini professed to be entirely satisfied, for taking which position Hitler expressed to him undying gratitude.[38] The reality was fairly simple: Hitler had taken advantage of Italy's involvement in Spain, of the

[37] This period was characterized by unusual governmental instability in France, owing to domestic circumstances, mainly economic and financial. Bonnet became foreign minister in April, 1938. In December, 1937, Delbos, foreign minister at the time, had undertaken a tour of Eastern European capitals, reminiscent of Barthou's in 1934, the results of which were even more disappointing than on the earlier occasion, owing to the considerable deterioration of the French position during the intervening years. In December, 1937, also, both Chautemps and Bonnet, in the course of conversations with von Papen, had given Germany reason to believe that France might be willing to accept German dominance in Eastern Europe.

[38] In retrospect, there is not a little irony in Hitler's assurance that Italy's frontier in the north was henceforth as safe as France's.

drain that this meant on her resources, coming as it did immediately after the Abyssinian adventure, and of her estrangement from the Western states; in the circumstances Mussolini felt he had no choice but to *faire bonne figure au mauvais jeu.* But in effect the *Anschluss* meant a shifting in the Axis relationship, in which Italy was passing from the position of equal partner to that of prisoner.[39] Her influence in Central Europe suffered a severe setback, a condition of which the smaller states of that region showed awareness.[40]

Yet Italy still had some freedom to maneuver, and though the passing of time rendered the operation increasingly difficult, she still might have rejoined the Western Powers. For all that this was the heyday of appeasement in both Britain and France, certain elementary precautions must be taken. Both countries had begun to rearm, though still at a moderate pace by comparison with the German program, and Britain especially was seeking some accommodation with Italy. The disappointing result of the gentleman's agreement of January, 1937, had not discouraged Chamberlain. Anglo-Italian negotiations were resumed in earnest at the beginning of 1938; Austria, Spain, and Abyssinia were the subjects of discussion. On the last of these Italy was adamant in demanding formal recognition of her title, a request that Chamberlain was willing to grant; there was indeed little virtue in a futile refusal to acknowledge the *fait accompli* if no prospect of altering it existed. In Spain Italy was committed to a Franco victory, an outcome also acceptable to Britain; Austria was written off during the negotiations. Agreement could thus be reached that was signed on April 16. It dealt mainly with various aspects of British and Italian interest in the region of the Red Sea, extent of armed forces, bases, exchange of information, the headwaters of the Blue Nile; Britain would give others the example of recognition of the Italian conquest of Abyssinia and Italy disclaimed the desire to secure any position of privilege in Spain or her possessions. The liquidation of the Spanish War remained in fact a prerequisite to the coming of the agreement into effect, but this result was expected to materialize in the very near future.

[39] One manifestation of Italy's dependence was the institution of racial legislation along the lines of the German, an action for which Germany had been pressing. In the Italian context this policy was at once abject and absurd.

[40] In March Lithuania yielded to a Polish ultimatum that demanded the restoration of normal relations between the two countries, at odds since the Polish seizure of Vilna in 1923.

It is worth mentioning that, in Britain, Foreign Secretary Eden represented the tendency of distrust of either partner of the Axis and of opposition to the policy of appeasement to which the Prime Minister was so firmly wedded. It is in connection with the Italian negotiation that the breach between the two became irretrievable, resulting in the resignation of Eden, a fact that in itself could not but influence the attitude of confidence of the Axis powers.[41] Italy gave little heed to the spirit of the agreement where Spanish affairs were concerned, though in July she went so far, together with Germany, as to agree to the British proposal, already a year in the discussing, for the evacuation of foreign "volunteers" from Spain. General Franco declined to accept the arrangement, and the Spanish War went on for another nine months. It may fairly be said that complications were avoided by the British unwillingness to react effectively to almost any degree of Italian intervention.

THE DESTRUCTION OF CZECHOSLOVAKIA

While the Spanish War was dragging to its appointed conclusion, inevitable in the circumstances, the attention of Europe was drawn away from Spain by an acute crisis that held for a while a major threat to her peace. Mention has been made before of the program outlined by Hitler to his own advisers in November, 1937. Austria had been his first victim, but it was not long after the events of March before the Czech problem was brought up in acute form.

THE CZECH PROBLEM.   The facts of the Czechoslovak situation may be recalled briefly. As the result of the decisions of 1919 a Czechoslovak state had emerged that contained slightly less than ten million Czechs and Slovaks and nearly half that number of other nationalities. Among the latter, far the largest was the German, some three million, two hundred thousand Sudeten Germans, spread along the rim of the frontier of Czechoslovakia with Germany and Austria, who had never been part of the German Reich.

[41] It came to a meeting between Chamberlain, Eden, and the Italian ambassador, Grandi, in the course of which Chamberlain took the unusual position of taking sides against his own foreign minister. The report of such happenings in Rome and the subsequent resignation of Eden gave Mussolini cause to feel that he had brought about this resignation. This outcome was just the sort of thing calculated to foster belief in the validity of Fascist talk about decadent democracies, when Britain bowed to Italy, an unprecedented occurrence.

Some grievances they had, but in comparative terms at least, they could hardly be described as an oppressed minority, and the relatively benign rule of Czech democracy might have led to their willing absorption into the composite state.

The advent of Nazism in Germany changed all this. By 1935 there had emerged a *Sudeten Deutsche Partei*, under the leadership of Konrad Henlein, which commanded the allegiance of some 70 percent of the Sudeten Germans—according to the 1935 election—and was in close contact with the German Nazis. The *Sudeten Deutsche Partei* did not demand at first more than the redress of specific grievances within the framework of the Czechoslovak state, but the *Anschluss* emboldened it to formulate more far-reaching demands. The eight points of the Carlsbad program of April, 1938, were tantamount to a demand for autonomy; simultaneously, a plan was being made ready in Germany for an attack on Czechoslovakia, while the German press began to take a new interest in the "oppressed" Sudeten German brothers. The Carlsbad program was intended to lead to negotiations, out of which a crisis would develop that would be the pretext for armed intervention. This, briefly, is the background and essence of the Czech crisis, the unfolding of which adhered fairly closely to the German plan of action.

There was no possibility in Czechoslovakia of using the technique of the Austrian coup; a German response, even to a Sudeten appeal, could not be made to appear as other than outside interference, unwanted by the legal government; the attitude of other Powers was consequently of great importance, especially as, weakened though it was, the French alliance was still in existence. On the French alliance hinged the operation of the Russian, but the French attitude would be greatly influenced by the British in view of the faithful adherence of France to the British connection. In the new French government that had been formed in April, Daladier was Prime Minister, while Bonnet held the foreign office; in the failure to obtain a firm British commitment to a common line of policy for Czechoslovakia, the result was joint advice to the Czechs to make concessions to the demands of Henlein.

A preview of later happenings took place in May. Suspecting, incorrectly on this occasion, the possibility of German action in connection with the municipal elections, the Czechs mobilized some forces. Britain made strong representations in both Berlin and Prague while cautioning the French that she would only intervene in the event of direct aggression against them: this was expression of the British view of how best to contribute to the preservation of peace. However, since the German timetable did not call for action until the autumn, the crisis proved to be a mere false alarm. France in the meantime still reasserted the validity of the Czech alliance.

But, clearly, the issue had not been resolved and a new crisis could be expected momentarily. French diplomacy busied itself exploring the implementation of the Soviet alliance; Russia was willing to intervene, but could do so only by crossing Polish or Rumanian territory: Poland, the more suitable route, opposed a flat refusal, while Rumania would tolerate the passage of aircraft.[42] These were unpromising results which had the effect of placing France in the dilemma of taking the initiative of action or following in the wake of British decisions.

Britain wanted to preserve peace above all, if not at any price, at almost any price. Central and Eastern European complications were things to be eschewed, and the phrase subsequently used by Chamberlain that referred to Czechoslovakia as "a far away country about which we know little"—odd words from the lips of a British Prime Minister—was apt rendering of the British outlook at this time. It was in July, while the British sovereigns were on a state visit to France, that the British foreign minister, Lord Halifax, announced that Lord Runciman would go to Prague as unofficial mediator. The purpose of the Runciman mission was to produce agreement on the Sudeten claims within the Czech milieu. The Czechoslovak government was loath to grant the full extent of these demands, tantamount to a federal reorganization of the state, but these negotiations do not warrant excessive attention, save perhaps as an illustration of the techniques of Nazi diplomacy. Henlein was fully supported by Hitler, as the latter publicly acknowledged on September 1. Under the mounting pressure of German threats and of British urging of concessions, the Czech government finally acceded to nearly the whole of the Carlsbad program. Much more than this could hardly be expected unless the Czech state were to consent to its own demise. The issue therefore was no longer the domestic one of the Sudeten

---

[42] France also sought to improve relations with Italy, following in the wake of the Anglo-Italian agreement of April. But Mussolini publicly drew a sharp distinction between Italo-British and Italo-French relations. To seek to draw a wedge between Britain and France was a logical part of Axis policy.

problem, but rather of the use that Germany wanted to make of that question for purposes of larger policy.[43]

THE SEPTEMBER CRISIS. Germany's open intervention, which made the Sudeten question a European issue and precipitated a major European crisis, occurred on September 12. On that date Hitler delivered himself of a violent and ranting speech, for which occasion he chose the annual gathering of the party congress in Nuremberg. The gist of it was simple: the Sudeten Germans were being subjected to unendurable oppression by the Czech government and Germany would see to their protection. This barely veiled threat of war induced Chamberlain to take an unusual step: he offered to meet Hitler in person, which he proceeded to do on the 15th.[44] The spectacle of a British Prime Minister, the representative of the power and pride that were Britain's, a man of seventy, for the first time in his life resorting to airplane transportation, in order to plead with the Austrian upstart, was in itself a sensation of the first magnitude; it was a measure of the acuteness of the crisis, of Britain's devotion to the preservation of peace, and of the power commanded by Germany; perhaps one should add of the degree of recklessness and irresponsibility of that power.

The meeting between Hitler and Chamberlain took place in the former's mountain retreat of Berchtesgaden. On the limited and specific issue of the Sudetenland Hitler was adamant and intransigeant; he would not be content with less than outright annexation, once again the last remaining German claim. This Chamberlain was willing to accept, though he must consult his own government and the French, for which purpose he returned to England. He would then come once more to Germany to meet Hitler again.

Despite some differences the British Cabinet accepted the principle of annexation of the Sudetenland. The French government was sharply divided on the issue, in the Cabinet no less than

[43] The reply of the *Sudeten Deutsche Partei* to the Czech offer was an outbreak of violence, but relative quiet was momentarily restored while negotiations were supposed to continue—actually waiting for the German decision.

[44] This was also the date on which Henlein, having broken off negotiations with the Czech government, for the first time demanded the annexation of the Sudetenland to Germany. These developments rendered futile the efforts of Lord Runciman, and Chamberlain's precipitate decision was caused by the fear that the situation might become locally uncontrollable.

among the military advisers.[45] Anglo-French discussions in London won the day for the British thesis and, as a consequence, joint Anglo-French proposals were submitted to the Czech government on the 19th. This last, it will be noted, had hitherto not been a party to the discussion and waited upon the outcome of it among the greater Powers with understandable anxiety. Confronted with a demand of territorial cession, it pointed out the significance of so radical a measure and appealed to the German-Czech Treaty of Arbitration of 1925. But this response was not entertained by the British and the French who instead notified the Czechs that unless they yielded they would be left to face Germany unassisted. France was in effect denouncing her alliance, and feeling ran high in Prague; but there was little choice in the circumstances, and the Czech government yielded on the 22nd. Chamberlain could now bring back a favorable answer to Hitler whom he went to meet in Godesberg the next day.

THE MUNICH SETTLEMENT AND ITS AFTERMATH. But the crisis was not so easily resolved, for the British offer was no longer acceptable to Hitler who now brought forth additional demands.[46] Unable to accede to these new requests of German unreasonableness, Chamberlain went home empty-handed. Following another violent speech of the Führer on the 26th, preparations were begun for mobilization in Germany, France, and Britain, Czechoslovakia having already resorted to this measure. On September 28, a final effort was made by Chamberlain, who proposed a meeting of the heads of the British, French, German, Italian, and Czech governments. It was left for Mussolini, who had so far not been involved in the negotiations, to seize the proposal and Hitler yielded to his urgings.[47]

[45] In the Cabinet Paul Reynaud was in favor of resistance while foreign minister Bonnet was the chief advocate of yielding. Among the military, the chief of staff, General Gamelin, advocated resistance but much was made of the weakness of the French air force, currently in process of reorganization, partly as a result of which airplane production had fallen to an extremely low level.

[46] The date of October 1 as a deadline for the satisfaction of German demands, conditions for the holding of plebiscites in certain areas, and the satisfaction of Hungarian and Polish claims, in Slovakia and in Teschen respectively.

[47] During the later stages of the crisis Mussolini had made a series of bellicose speeches supporting the German demands. In actual fact he was not desirous of war for which Italy was not prepared. His eleventh-hour intervention enabled him to pose as the savior of peace, a role that gained him much popularity at home.

Thus came about the famous conference of Munich that met on the 29th of September and, after some close but relatively brief discussions, reached agreement in the early hours of the 30th, the Czechs having been excluded from the meeting. This agreement was essentially achieved on the basis of Hitler's demands at Godesberg, modified in minor respects only—an extension to October 10 of the Czech evacuation, the supervision of an international commission to settle the details of the new frontier line, and a six-month option granted to the Czechs in the surrendered territory. Confronted with agreement among the four Powers, the Czechs, cavalierly excluded from the discussion of their fate, had little choice but to yield.

Thus peace was saved at Munich, an outcome for which the peoples of Europe were generally grateful. But it was only saved for a brief time, and the subsequent course of events made clear the full significance of Munich, the climax of appeasement. The ostensible justification of the arrangement just contrived at the time was the avoidance of war. Czechoslovakia had been treated with unnecessary brutality, but that fact might be overlooked for the sake of the larger achievement. If the validity of the principle of nationality be granted without qualification, a case could indeed be made for the surrender of the Sudetenland to Germany, and this was largely the argument that made the arrangement palatable in Britain, where Hitlerian declarations of peaceful intent were widely accepted. After the Munich agreement Hitler and Chamberlain signed an Anglo-German declaration professing mutual good will and stating their common intention to use the method of negotiation in the solution of any differences. This accomplishment, "peace in our time," as Chamberlain described it, was highly welcome in Britain as was the author of it, whose reception at home was triumphal. Clearly, the validity of this view entirely depended upon that of the Hitlerian declaration of future peaceful intent.

But even if such a patent fraud were taken at face value, very great significance attached to the manner in which the Czech crisis had been resolved. Peace had been saved by the agreement of four Great Powers, an agreement the cost of which was to be borne by a fifth smaller one whom the four had "induced" to acquiesce in the necessary consequences; Munich was the precise implementation of the Four-Power proposal that Mussolini had made in 1933. The directorate of Europe had come into effective existence and others must take notice of its collective power and will; it had indeed the power to preserve the peace so long as it continued to function. Here was confirmation, if any were still needed, of the demise of the French system and of the Versailles arrangements.

There were in France fewer illusions than in Britain, but France had followed the initiative of the latter country; it was indeed the French excuse, Bonnet's for example, that France could not afford to run the risk of war alone in the definite refusal of Britain to assist her unless she were directly attacked. Yet it remains that it was France who had a formal alliance with Czechoslovakia that she never regarded as a little known faraway country. The joint Anglo-French guarantee given the new reduced Czechoslovakia, a guarantee in which Germany and Italy were eventually supposed to participate, was a thin consolation prize in the eyes of the smaller Powers. If already in 1936 there had been cause to doubt the solidity of French intent, the acid test had now come that France had failed to meet; the French role at Munich was certainly inglorious.[48]

If, on the other hand, Germany's declarations of future peaceful intent were mere sham—as indeed they were—then Munich takes on a different significance. The Czech position, in military terms, had been rendered precarious by the *Anschluss;* nevertheless Czechoslovakia still had a significant army and powerful frontier fortifications. These had to be surrendered along with the Sudetenland—Germany was insistent that they should remain undisturbed—and the country now became thoroughly undefendable, demonstration that the strategic considerations of 1919 had had some solid *raison d'être*. In military terms, no less than in moral and psychological ones, the German victory at Munich was great.

In the circumstances, what justification there may have been for the Munich surrender lies in the argument that, in view of the state of preparedness, or rather unpreparedness, of the British and French they traded space for time in which to remedy their deficiency. A balance should therefore be struck between the gains and losses that Munich entailed. The loss was clear and has

[48] It has become the fashion to criticize France for her behavior in 1936 as well as in 1938. The criticism is warranted, but it is well to recall that in the eyes of the critics of earlier French intransigeance—and they were numerous—the French acceptance of Munich was evidence, like that of the reoccupation of the Rhineland, of a novel and welcome reasonableness.

been mentioned: in concrete terms the asset of Czech force, in moral terms the distrust sown among other Powers. But there was a much larger issue involved, for the Soviet Union had not been present at Munich. This in itself added to the extent of the German victory, for the Franco-Russian connection was thus in practical effect largely severed. This point has been and will be the source of much dispute, hardly capable of final resolution, for it implies judgment on two points: the reliability of Soviet intentions and the military capabilities of the Soviet Union. On both scores, the spectacle of the existing Russian scene, whether correctly assessed or not, gave ground for legitimate doubts. But in any event, Russia, like others, could not but take notice of her exclusion from Munich and entertain in turn serious doubts about the true nature of the Western Powers' intentions. Munich might be but a prelude either to a European coalition against the Soviet Union or to the granting to Germany of *carte blanche* in the East. More than ever the possibilities were fluid of alignment between the three great power centers of Europe, the Western democracies, the Axis and the Soviet Union.

III. The End of the "Long Armistice"

FROM MUNICH TO PRAGUE

There were footnotes to Munich proper, but they deserve no more than passing mention, for they affected little the basic distribution of power in Europe. The partition of Czechoslovakia followed its ruthless course. Where the German claims were concerned, the operation of the international commission may fairly be described as a farce, comparable to the Nonintervention Committee of the Spanish War; even the pretense of real plebiscites was shortly abandoned, German claims being acknowledged instead in nearly all instances. With little grace, but with German support against French and Russian objections, Poland made good her claim to Teschen. In the failure of direct agreement between Czechoslovakia and Hungary, the former country accepted the arbitration of the Axis: in Vienna, on November 2, Ribbentrop and Ciano decided the extent of the cession to be made to Hungary. It was quite logical in the circumstances for Czechoslovakia to have renounced the Soviet alliance in October; she had become a thoroughgoing satellite of the Axis, a fact that found appropriate expression in the personality of her new foreign minister.[49] These events were propitious to the assertion of internal centrifugal forces; in November the Czechoslovak Parliament gave its sanction to the autonomy of Slovakia and of Subcarpatho Ruthenia, proclaimed in the preceding month.

The Munich crisis overcome, there was again momentary relaxation of tensions. The Anglo-German "peace in our time" agreement that Chamberlain seems to have taken at face value was followed by a Franco-German nonaggression Pact signed on December 6 in Paris: no further claims existed and consultation would be used in the event of future differences. Paper and ink are inexpensive commodities.

The effort to extend this relaxation to the southern end of the Axis was also pursued at this time. The Anglo-Italian gentleman's agreement went into effect in November without waiting for the prior conclusion of a similar Franco-Italian understanding. Mussolini had declined to make such an arrangement in May, and the appointment of a new French ambassador to Rome[50] did little to improve relations between the two countries. It was during a speech by Ciano in the new Italian Chamber of Fasci and Corporations that a "spontaneous" manifestation raised the cry of "Jibuti, Tunis, and Corsica!" which the press promptly amplified to include Nice and Savoy.[51] The representations of the French ambassador were met by the formal Italian denunciation of the Laval-Mussolini agreement of 1935 in December, and France in turn countered with a firm reassertion that she would yield no land under her flag. The path of the Four-Power directorate of Europe was clearly less than smooth; rather than finding common ground among themselves, the association of the Axis was tightening, while Britain, if with some hesitancy and reluctance, tended to associate herself more closely with France.

Chamberlain's optimism was a sturdy growth that German action alone could in the end destroy. This action was forthcoming in March when an internal quarrel with Slovakia resulted in an

---

[49] Following upon the Munich agreement the government of Hodza resigned, to be succeeded by a new one, organized by General Sirovy, in which Chvalkovsky, of Germanophile orientation, held the foreign portfolio.

[50] Italy refused to receive a French ambassador unless he were accredited to "the King of Italy and Emperor of Ethiopia," in other words unless France gave *de jure* recognition to the Italian conquest of Abyssinia.

[51] Ciano had for some time been making preparations to put forward claims under the heads of Jibuti, Tunis, and Suez.

appeal to Hitler by Monsignor Tiso, the Slovak Prime Minister. The Czech President, Hacha, was summoned to Berlin where, during the course of a night of which lurid accounts have been given, and under the threat of an immediate German air destruction of Prague, he put his signature to the German Protectorate of Bohemia and Moravia—henceforth Czechia. Prague was under German occupation by 9 o'clock the next morning, Slovakia achieved full independence, and a Hungarian occupation of Subcarpatho Ruthenia established direct territorial contact between Poland and Hungary.[52]

While these readjustments were taking place in Central and Eastern Europe, at the opposite end of the Continent the Spanish War was drawing to a close. After the fall of Barcelona at the end of January, 1939, there seemed little point in either denying or delaying the accomplishment of the inevitable end. At the end of February both France and Britain recognized the government of General Franco to whom Madrid surrendered a month later. Appropriately enough, Franco joined the anti-Comintern. The Spanish disturbance was ended and it had proved possible to prevent its extension beyond the borders of Spain, no doubt a substantial achievement; but that result had been contrived only because, in the last analysis, the Western Powers had been willing to accept the Axis success that the triumph of Franco entailed.

Italy, pleased at the outcome and boasting of her share in it, maintained nevertheless that she had no direct ambitions in Spain from which she would withdraw her forces. This in effect she did, but the new Spanish regime was both in debt to the Italian and by its nature sympathetic to it. In the unstable and fast-changing European scene, should open conflict break out, the possibility could not be overlooked that France, the land bulwark of the Western democracies, was in effect encircled, a fact calculated to induce in her second thoughts and suitable to the extraction of further concessions from her. If the policy of appeasement had hitherto succeeded in preserving the peace, it had also had the effect of introducing in the eyes of all an element of dangerous uncertainty: what price would the appeasers pay; what precisely was the limit of the demands that could be made of them; or was there possibly no limit?

[52] This time was also used by Germany to redress another minor grievance. Following the receipt of an ultimatum, Lithuania retroceded the territory of Memel that she had seized and incorporated in 1923.

THE REACTION TO THE GERMAN SEIZURE OF PRAGUE. But in March, 1939, the sudden presence of the Germans in Prague was the greater sensation. Considering that the Western states had in the preceding October acquiesced, in fact themselves assisted, in the destruction of Czechoslovakia, the presence of the Germans in Prague altered the fundamentals of the situation but little; from the Nazi point of view there was deficiency in logic in balking at the logical consequences of an earlier decision. But there was balking, and very violent balking, especially in Britain, which is what makes the occupation of Prague so important an episode.

This must be emphasized, for it provided a very good illustration of the fact that new forces had entered into the conduct of the relations among states. Hitler had not, in terms of concrete and material reality, greatly altered the situation in March, 1939; the real change had been accomplished at Munich. But Hitler had accomplished a great change by tearing off the veil of British illusions. Some humor may be seen in the degree of British indignation at the fact that Hitler had broken his word. But Prague could not be called German, unlike Austria and the Sudetenland; here, therefore, was an act of naked aggression, a gross violation of democratic rights, of which the *Anschluss* and Munich could be presented as being fundamentally implementations. For Germany to talk *Lebensraum* could only bring home the realization that in German designs there might indeed be a threat to British interest.

All this may seem naïveté, and to a point indeed it was; what is perhaps more surprising but equally important is that the British Prime Minister should himself have shared the popular reaction. The outcome was an interesting one, for though the former critics of the policy of appeasement so determinedly pursued by Chamberlain were now proved right, they were not called upon to take the leadership in his place; in March, 1939, no less than in October, 1938, Chamberlain was the authentic representative of the feeling of the British people. Here may be seen a perfect manifestation of the democratic process, but equally significant was the cohesion of British opinion about to embark on what amounted to a revolution in British policy for Europe. The British scene has been stressed, for Britain had for some time been the leader of the Western coalition in which France had become the willing attendant. Britain would continue to lead, but in a new direction, rather the one that France might have been expected to pursue in the days when this would have earned her criticism in Britain. All that had happened had to happen before the extent to which British and French interests were identical was at last brought out in full light.

FROM PRAGUE TO DANZIG

THE POLISH PROBLEM.   Whatever British feelings may have been at this point, there could be little question of giving effect to the five-month-old guarantee of Czech integrity. For the moment verbal protests again must suffice. But if Germany's intent was aggressive, the case for seizing Prague might equally apply elsewhere; Poland, despite a fair degree of collaboration with Germany, would be the logical next German objective. Until March 15, the outward manifestations of German-Polish relations were cordial—it was a fundamental and sound tenet of Nazi foreign policy to isolate its objectives and deal with them one at a time— though the question of Danzig had been mentioned to Colonel Beck, possibly in connection with a joint scheme of aggression directed toward the Ukraine. Poland failed to respond to these feelers. But the month of March was not out before Poland was asked to join formally the anti-Comintern combination while the matter of Danzig was raised in more insistent fashion.[53]

The Polish situation was the occasion for the first outward manifestation of the new orientation of British policy. The form of it was unusual, for it came in the shape of a unilateral British guarantee to Poland issued on March 31;[54] France joined in this two weeks later, reaffirming the still formally existing alliance. Poland, it might be pointed out to Chamberlain, was hardly nearer or better known in Britain than deceased Czechoslovakia; the significance of the British gesture was therefore that of a clear warning to Germany that she must put a halt to her expansion and her methods. It was in keeping with the new orientation and mood that, on April 13, Britain and France should give similar guarantees to Rumania and Greece; a month later an Anglo-

[53] Parallel with the Nazi successes in Germany, the local Nazi organization in Danzig had become increasingly obstreperous, gaining control of the local administration, and making it difficult for the League Commissioner to fulfill his duties. In a speech of April 28 Hitler publicly declared that the Danzig problem must be solved.

[54] This procedure was due to the urgency of the situation; Anglo-Polish relations were to be placed on a more customary basis through the negotiation of an alliance.

Turkish agreement was concluded for mutual assistance and co-operation in the event of hostilities in the Mediterranean, and here again France followed suit.[55]

The shadow of impending conflict was growing darker and the eventual alignment was being clarified. Hitler used the occasion of a speech that he delivered on April 28 to denounce both the Polish agreement of 1934 and the naval agreement with Britain of 1935; almost simultaneously, Poland had been notified of a formal German claim to Danzig and to extraterritorial rights of communication across the Corridor. It was at the beginning of April that Hitler had ordered the *Wehrmacht* to be ready for an attack on Poland on September 1—a fact, needless to say, not revealed until after the Second World War. The British decision, on April 28, to introduce peacetime conscription was, in the light of Britain's historic tradition, another token of the seriousness of the situation.[56]

How convincing were to others these somewhat frantic exertions of British and French diplomacy remains questionable. In view of the by now long record of appeasement, doubts might subsist. There was also the question of the actual state and quality of British and French armaments; both countries had for some time undertaken programs of rearmament which were, however, proceeding in relatively leisurely fashion, especially by contrast with the feverish German pace. Given some years, as Hitler had judged in 1937, the German advantage might indeed disappear. With consistency, Germany was organizing her economy for war; bearing in mind the blockade of the First World War, she had embarked on a program of self-sufficiency, or autarchy, of which her attempted economic dominance of southeastern Europe was another corollary aspect. The simple fact is that Hitler, caught in his own nebulous dreams of primitive heroics, relished the prospect of war for its own sake; he was resentful of the Munich compromise that had robbed him of the opportunity to put force in action.

[55] Franco-Turkish negotiations were somewhat complicated and agreement was delayed by the Turkish claim to Alexandretta, which France ceded in June. The legality of this transfer was open to question in view of the fact that title to the original Syrian mandate rested with the League rather than with France.

[56] Following an address to the Board of the Pan-American Union on April 14, President Roosevelt sent a personal message to Hitler and to Mussolini asking them to commit themselves for ten years to refrain from aggression against a number of specified countries. The proposal merely elicited abuse and derision in the German and Italian presses.

THE PACT OF STEEL.   Heroic talk and exaltation of the martial virtues occurred in Italy as well, where, however, they fell on less responsive ears. Nevertheless, the directors of Italian policy, Mussolini and Ciano, had cause to be elated by the success of their bluster, a fact which may have robbed the Duce of the clarity of judgment that had been his in the past. After Abyssinia and Spain there was every reason for Italy to digest her large gains while attending to the deficient state of her military forces and her economy. But instead of aligning herself with the satisfied Western Powers, whether fearful of their eventual revenge or hopeful that more bluster might at small cost secure for her yet more gains, she chose to tighten the bonds of the German connection.

Ciano was the prime exponent of the German orientation and Italy's newly proclaimed demands against France have been mentioned.[57] Italo-German cordiality was not devoid of reticence and the possibility was ever feared by either partner of the Axis that the other might desert him and come to terms with the Western Powers: Hitler had not been pleased with Mussolini's role of mediator at Munich and the latter had seen with a jaundiced eye the conclusion of the Franco-German nonaggression agreement in December. The latest German coup in Prague, of which Italy had had no premonition, was cause of both irritation and humiliation, which Mussolini endeavored to compensate for by acting in similar fashion in Albania.[58] Having rejected in October Ribbentrop's advances, made with a view to the outbreak of war in the autumn of 1939, and disturbed by the prospect of impending Polish complications, Mussolini came to the decision to enter into a formal alliance with Germany. The alliance might help give his voice greater weight in Axis planning, for if Mussolini had by this time accepted the prospect of war, he did not wish it to happen until 1943, when Italy would have had time to complete her military preparations and have held, in 1942, the projected universal exposition in Rome.

Ciano explained these things to Ribbentrop when they met in Milan in May, but with the levity characteristic of his methods

[57] Immediately after the termination of the Spanish War, Italy sought to open negotiations with France on the subjects of Jibuti, Tunisia, and Suez, but was confronted with an adamant *non possumus*.

[58] On April 7 Italian troops were landed in Albania. The seizure of Albania was effected smoothly, King Zog taking flight, and the Albanian crown was added to those of Italy and Ethiopia on the 8th.

he yielded to the German view. On May 28 the so-called Pact of
Steel was signed in Berlin. It was an offensive alliance which
committed either participant to join the other should he be involved in hostilities with one or more Powers. Although no date
was set for war, in view of the nature of German activity, the
pact had the effect of solidly tying Italy to the German chariot,
making her little more than a satellite.[59]

THE SOVIET UNION TERTIUS GAUDENS. With this consolidation
of the Axis, intending to embark on a program of military adventure, and with the growing affinity between Britain and France,
the position of the Soviet Union assumed ever greater importance.
Between the Soviets and the Axis relations were ostensibly marked
by a cordial reciprocity of hatred to which their propaganda gave
unrestrained expression. But recent events had aroused Russian
suspicion of the West, and the rash Anglo-French guarantees after
Prague were perhaps less convincing to Russia than the concrete
performance of Munich from which Russia had been excluded.
Might not the Western Powers contrive to get the Soviet Union
embroiled with the Axis while retaining for themselves the role
of *tertius gaudens?*[60] Such designs could hardly be avowed openly,
but in the naked and ruthless contest of power currently under
way they seemed entirely plausible, nor was the West devoid of
advocates of so sensible an outcome. Since there was little likelihood that the initiative of aggression would come at this time
either from the truly pacific Western democracies or from the
Soviet Union, for whom peace was at the moment the more
desirable condition, the question perhaps reduced itself to one of
deflecting the coming Axis aggression away from oneself.

But the probable Axis initiative in aggression also created
bonds between the West and the Soviets; following the German
seizure of Prague, negotiations for an agreement were undertaken
in April. The Anglo-French desire to have Russia share in their
guarantee of Poland and Rumania was countered by the Soviet
Union's proposal that such guarantees be extended to all its western

[59] Following this an agreement was made in July for the settlement of the
issue of the South Tyrol. The German-speaking population was to be given an
option between Italian nationality and emigration to the Reich. A consultation
took place in December but the scheme was only partly implemented; by 1943
fewer than 80,000 persons out of 185,000 who had opted for emigration had
actually left.

[60] Such a view was expressed by Manuilsky in a speech to the Congress of
the Russian Communist party on March 11.

neighbors, the Black Sea as well as the Baltic states. This suggestion ran into the difficulty that the states in question, Poland most of all, but Rumania and the Baltic states as well, did not seem very anxious to have a Russian guarantee. Perhaps unwisely, yet understandably in the light of their historic experience and of their knowledge of their eastern neighbor and its ways, these states were reluctant to enter into too close an association with the Soviet state, feeling that this might increase the likelihood of making them the objects of Nazi anger. Also, it should be mentioned that in terms of ideology the governments of these states had greater affinity to the German than to the Bolshevik, a fact which in turn went to feed Russian suspicion. This suspicion could only be increased by the seeming Anglo-French reluctance to assume too rigid a commitment, the very thing Russia desired. As a consequence, negotiations made but slow and painful progress till the end of May when an impasse seemed to have been reached over the British refusal to guarantee the Baltic states against their own desire.[61]

Discussions were renewed in June and, thanks to Anglo-French concessions to the Soviet point of view, they seemed to have made sufficient progress by the end of July to warrant the consideration of the conclusion of a military convention. The British and the French appeared to proceed in surprisingly leisurely fashion, for their delegates did not reach Moscow until August; they found a corresponding Russian leisureliness and concrete Russian difficulties, the most important of which was the requirement of formal Polish consent to the passage of the Red army. This Poland would not give, despite much French pressure, and in the failure of it Russia would not bind herself, as Voroshilov informed the French delegate on August 21.

THE NAZI-SOVIET PACT AND THE OUTBREAK OF WAR.   The last phase of the negotiation was largely futile in any event, for Russia had been simultaneously conducting similar discussions with none other than Nazi Germany; she was in the desirable position of being courted by two opposite sides, hence able to raise her bid, bide her time, and choose the higher offer. Actually, the initiative

---

[61] The abrupt replacement of Litvinov, the advocate of collective security and of a prowestern orientation, by Molotov at the Commissariat of Foreign Affairs in May was indication of a shift taking place in Russian policy and widely interpreted as such.

of the Nazi-Soviet rapprochement seems to have come from the Soviet side. Using the occasion of relatively minor economic discussions, Soviet representatives in Germany began very tentative approaches in April. The Nazi regime found itself confronted with a major decision, but by the end of May it opted to explore the possiblity in earnest.[62] There was much ground to travel considering the widely advertised ideological difference, and exchanges were cautious for a time. By the end of July a point had been reached where the Russians acknowledged the advantages of a rapprochement, while the Germans put stress on the common ideological opposition to the democratic states and to the greater advantages that Germany could offer by comparison with Britain.

From this point progress was very rapid; Germany could not wait if her projected attack on Poland were to take place as scheduled on the 1st of September. While Molotov was haggling with the British and the French, the Russians suggested that a high-ranking German personality come to Moscow. The date of August 26–27 was agreed upon, then advanced to the 23rd, Stalin having acquiesced to a personal request of Hitler to hasten the proceedings.

Ribbentrop reached the Soviet capital on that date, provided with plenipotentiary powers, and negotiations had already made such progress that the Nazi-Soviet agreement was signed during the very night after his arrival. The world was thus confronted with the announcement of the conclusion of a Nazi-Soviet non-aggression pact. The significant public part of the treaty was the commitment by each participant not to join a third Power at war with the other. No less, in fact rather more, important was the simultaneous secret protocol which defined the spheres of influence of the two states: the Baltic states, save Lithuania,[63] were to be Russia's, and Poland was divided along the Narew-Vistula line; the Russian interest in Bessarabia was likewise acknowledged by Germany.

The startling news, sprung out of deepest secrecy upon an unsuspecting world, created a profound sensation. The spectacle

[62] Von Schulenburg, the German ambassador in Moscow, was an adherent of the Bismarckian view of the desirability of Russo-German association and despite the nature of the regimes strove to effect a rapprochement between them.

[63] Lithuania, to which Vilna was to be added, fell in the German sphere. The question of whether to maintain an independent Polish state, and within what boundaries, was left to later decision, on the basis of amicable understanding and of subsequent developments.

of Stalin drinking the health of the Führer was indeed cause to make one wonder about the nature of reality; confusion was widespread, not least among Communists outside the Soviet Union. Actually, this reality was fairly simple and the Nazi-Soviet Pact a revealing indication of the methods and possibilities of totalitarian diplomacy. To barter away, in secrecy and in advance, the existence of other states was more than a parliamentary democracy could accomplish in conditions of peace;[64] but the systems of Germany and Russia labored under no comparable limitations from opinions and parliaments which must, in a democracy, at least be educated and prepared for major shifts of policy. In the open contest between the three power constellations of Europe, the totalitarians enjoyed the telling assets of greater freedom of action and rapidity of decision.

That Germany was set on her course in any event may be granted, but clearly the Russian pact was an open invitation to proceed with war. In the immediate sense and from the point of view of Soviet interest, the pact was a master stroke: the tables had been turned and it was up to the Western Powers whether or not they would resist German aggression in Poland; should they live up to their declarations, the result would be a conflict that Russia could contemplate with equanimity in the prospect that all her enemies would greatly weaken, if not wholly destroy, each other; biding her time, Russia could derive whatever further profit might seem eventually available. For the moment, she was assured of a considerable extension of her influence and of the corresponding asset to her defense that the enlarging of her borders would constitute. Whether such calculations were sound, or perhaps overclever, the future alone could decide.

In any case, the Nazi-Soviet Pact may be regarded as Russia's endorsement of Germany's immediate plans. For some time the world had been treated to the spectacle of a mounting tempo of German complaints against Poland, by now familiar prelude to

[64] The importance of the difference between democratic and totalitarian systems must be stressed in this connection. In the Nazi book, and purely in terms of power, the Anglo-French consent to the annexation of the Sudetenland could well imply their acceptance of the Prague coup, since the former event had effectively destroyed the significance of Czechoslovakia. But, especially in British eyes, there was all the difference between Munich (an implementation of self-determination) and Prague (the denial of it). There could be no justification for the bartering of the independence of the Baltic states other than crude considerations of power. Relevant as these might be, they would have aroused a storm of moral indignation in Britain. Thus, fundamentally divergent ideologies lead to authentic misunderstanding and consequent recriminations.

some Nazi action. Having obtained at Munich redress of her "last" grievance, Germany now rediscovered the bleeding eastern frontier: justice must be obtained for the persecuted Germans in Poland and in Danzig; "incidents" began to occur in increasing numbers and it was not even thought necessary to go through the sham of negotiations with Poland, against whom demands were merely asserted.[65]

In these circumstances, British and French efforts to save the peace through a German-Polish agreement were doomed to futility; Hitler wanted to have his war. Not even a repetition of the Munich performance would satisfy the Führer this time, and the only possibility of averting a generalized conflict was to abandon Poland altogether. This possibility was thought by some to exist and was the cause of momentary delay; but Chamberlain announced in Commons on the 24th that Britain would honor her commitments and an Anglo-Polish alliance was signed on the 25th. Britain did not wish to open herself to the 1914 accusation that her failure to clarify her position had encouraged Germany to embark upon war.

The Polish answer to the public disclosure of German demands was general mobilization on August 30. At dawn on September 1 German armed forces crossed the frontier into Poland while the annexation of Danzig was proclaimed; it was not thought necessary to observe the formality of a declaration of war.

At Munich a year earlier Mussolini claimed much credit for having saved the peace. On August 31 he proposed the meeting of a conference, a suggestion that France was willing to entertain, but on condition that Poland be one of the participants. The German invasion on September 1 caused Poland to refuse the proposal. In view of the outbreak of actual hostilities, with hesitation and reluctance Mussolini passed on his suggestion to Hitler on September 2. But Britain and France would only consider a conference subject to the prior withdrawal of German troops from Poland. This caused the conference proposal to be withdrawn and instead of it a British ultimatum was delivered to Germany on the 3d: unless the German government had consented to withdraw from Poland by 11 A.M. the next day, Britain would declare

---

[65] One can hardly describe as negotiations the mere formulation of demands and the virtual ultimatum that embodied the German claims. On the pretext that the Polish ambassador was not entrusted with plenipotentiary powers, Ribbentrop refused to negotiate with him and the German demands were merely made public on August 30.

war, which, in the German refusal, she did. France acted likewise.[66] By September 4, 1939, three major European Powers and
Poland were at war; the Second World War had begun. The issue
of responsibility for its immediate outbreak has given rise to no
debate corresponding to that which surrounded the circumstances
of 1914. Only the degree of the effect of the Russian role in concluding the pact with Germany has been variously estimated.

[66] It is of interest, and symbolic of the degree to which France continued to
follow in the wake of British initiative, as she had since 1936, that the French
ultimatum and declaration of war followed the British by some hours. Doubts
were entertained in some quarters, German and Polish among them, as to whether
France, where Bonnet was still foreign minister, would not seek to repeat the
performance of Munich.

XIV

The Second World War and Its Immediate Aftermath, 1939–1947

I. The European War

THE "PHONEY" WAR

For the moment at least diplomacy must yield once more to the language of guns, but as in any war there was soon cause for much diplomatic activity, be it between belligerents and neutrals or among the members of a coalition. In addition, the peculiar course of the war gave rise to some special forms of activity. It is with those aspects of things that we are here concerned though, clearly, military developments, decisive in the last analysis, cannot be ignored.

The attitude of peoples everywhere was very different from that of 1914; even in Nazi Germany, for all the popularity of Hitler and the widespread desire to redress alleged wrongs, active martial enthusiasm was limited. The Western peoples accepted war as a grim necessity forced upon them in self-defense, which indeed it had been, though there were some, especially in France, who doubted the wisdom of it or the appropriateness, as it was put, of dying for Danzig. The German war machine had been brought to a high pitch of efficiency; the recent resumption of the German rearmament was itself an advantage, for it meant up-to-date weapons as well as novel thinking. By contrast, the Polish forces had neither; left to themselves, the only question was how long they could withstand the German. In the West there was the French army; despite its deficiencies, especially in the air arm, it was a powerful instrument generally held in considerable esteem; the British could supply some forces, well equipped and of high quality, but relatively small in size. The first question was whether France would launch an offensive in Germany in order to relieve the pressure on Poland.

As in 1914 France was free to concentrate the bulk of her forces in the North owing to the Italian declaration of neutrality. Mussolini, as pointed out before, had no objection to war, but he needed more time for his preparations. His Axis partner had been extremely cavalier, taking little trouble to inform him of the negotiations with Russia;[1] not until August 25 did Hitler write to Mussolini to explain his recent dealings with Russia and his intentions toward Poland. This treatment was naturally resented in Italy whence came the reply that, in view of her unpreparedness, Italy would have to abstain from immediate participation in the war unless Germany could make good her deficiencies. The list of Italian demands, when presented, was impressive and wholly outside Germany's capacity to meet; Hitler declared that he understood the necessity of Italy's abstention. As in 1914, therefore, Italy regained her freedom of action and the problem was again for her the same, how best to profit from the conflict. But, whereas in 1914 there had been in Italy a strong current of sympathy for the Western Powers, Italy had for some time been closely associated in the Axis; the issue now, by contrast with 1914, was between neutrality and intervention on the German side. The course of military events would in all probability have much influence on the ultimate decision.[2]

THE DESTRUCTION OF POLAND AND REARRANGEMENTS IN EASTERN EUROPE. France did not attempt an offensive against Germany, but remained content instead to keep her forces in readiness in the shelter of the Maginot Line; consequently Germany could proceed unimpeded with the eastern operations. The war in Poland was a demonstration of the effectiveness of new techniques: for all their bravery the Poles could not withstand the onslaught of German mechanized forces working in close co-

[1] Not until August 11–12 did Ribbentrop, in the course of a meeting at Salzburg, give Ciano an idea of the impending conclusion of an agreement with Russia, showing at the same time no disposition to discuss Germany's plans for immediate war.

[2] As in 1914, however, Italy was in the position of being courted by both sides, the West being anxious to keep her in a state of neutrality that she in turn found profitable. In October Hitler reasserted that the Mediterranean was Italy's preserve.

ordination with the *Luftwaffe*. Less than three weeks sufficed to destroy the organized armed forces of Poland, a result that brought into operation the arrangements of the Nazi-Soviet Pact.

Using the pretext of chaos in Poland and that of the alleged persecution of the non-Polish minority in the East, Soviet forces penetrated into Poland as early as September 17. A line of Russo-German demarcation, fixed on the 22d, was modified on the 28th when a new Nazi-Soviet treaty was signed in Moscow: in exchange for a larger German share of Poland, Lithuania would fall into the Russian sphere.[3] The fourth partition of Poland had been accomplished.

The rapid march of events raised anew the question of the purpose and prospects of the war. If German aggression must be curbed and the wrong done to Poland undone, the Western Powers must envisage a long and costly war, one moreover in which they would find the Soviet Union bound to Germany by her complicity in the sharing of spoils. Might not some accommodation be found now that the destruction of Poland was a *fait accompli?* Such a view was not without supporters and it was expounded by Hitler in a speech before the Reichstag on October 6: if Britain and France would only recognize the Eastern situation, now guaranteed by two powerful states, apart from some colonial claims, Germany asked for nothing of either Power. But the roster was long by this time of meaningless Hitlerian promises; Britain and France would adhere to their fundamental purpose as was declared by their Prime Ministers, Chamberlain and Daladier, in their public replies to the Führer's invitation.[4]

However, this was not the prelude to active hostilities in the West and there followed instead for some months a twilight period of inactive war that came to be known as the "phoney" war. Two things took place during this interval: a consolidation of positions and the so-called war of nerves. The Soviet Union ostensibly behaved as a loyal ally of the Nazis and nowhere was this better exemplified than in the tone and content of Russian propaganda. This was especially significant in France where the large Communist party had been outlawed; driven underground, French Communists, once they had absorbed the shock of the

[3] A secret protocol provided for the reciprocal freedom of emigration of nationals of either country who found themselves in the other's sphere.

[4] Suspicious of German designs, in November Belgium and Holland offered their good offices to Germany, Britain, and France. Their mediation was rejected by Hitler, and the British and the French did likewise.

Nazi-Soviet Pact, accepted the Soviet interpretation of the war as an adventure of their own imperialist governments; they did their best to weaken the morale of their country, even resorting to occasional sabotage, while Nazi propaganda on its side untiringly dinned the theme of the useless war. Thus propaganda came into its own, making full use of the modern techniques of communication as a tool of warfare and diplomacy.

But the Nazi-Soviet connection, if highly profitable to both its makers at the moment, was at best a *mariage de convenance;* little love or trust was squandered by either partner on the other. Impressed by the performance of German arms in Poland, Russia sought to extract the maximum advantage from the continuing war. Toward the end of September and the beginning of October, representatives of the three small Baltic states, Esthonia, Latvia and Lithuania, went on forced pilgrimages to Moscow where they signed nonaggression treaties with the Soviet Union; they were forced in addition to cede naval bases and to maintain Soviet troops in their territories. They were thus receiving with a vengeance the benefit of the Russian guarantee that they had previously declined, perhaps not unaware of the likely nature of Soviet protection.

Not content with these gains, Russia put forth similar demands toward Finland whose refusal to entertain concessions resulted in a Russian attack on November 30. This pleased no one and gave rise to some interesting, though futile, gestures. In response to Finland's appeal the League formally expelled the Soviet Union from its membership on December 14. The occasion was thought by some to provide a new possibility of settlement among the belligerents[5] while among the Western Allies, where opinion was strongly sympathetic to the Finns, what in retrospect must seem a fantastic notion was entertained of sending military assistance to Finland, the most likely way to bring Russia actively into the war on the German side. Britain and France were prevented from implementing this quixotic scheme by the firm adherence to neutrality of the Scandinavian countries, which declined to grant facilities for the transit of armed forces.

Mention should be made in this connection of the use of ideology as an instrument in international affairs: having penetrated

[5] Mussolini seems to have favored such a compromise but Hitler remained deaf to his suggestion.

a small portion of Finland, the Russians on December 1 proclaimed a Finnish People's Republic, a potentially useful tool in subsequent Russo-Finnish relations. Of the Finnish war little need be said. It did not merge into the larger war and much of the world contemplated with admiration and satisfaction the unexpected difficulties that the Russians encountered. But the final outcome could be one thing alone: on March 12, 1940, peace was restored with the cession by Finland of the Karelian Isthmus with Viborg and a thirty-year lease for the establishment of a Soviet naval base on the Hangoe Peninsula. Considering the circumstances, these were surprisingly lenient terms.

PRELIMINARIES IN THE WEST: SCANDINAVIA AND THE LOW COUNTRIES. The "phoney" war could hardly drag on indefinitely and must either end in a negotiated compromise or give way to authentic hostilities. In France a new government, organized under the leadership of Paul Reynaud on March 22, might be expected to assert a more vigorous policy.[6] Taking the pretext of the declared intention of the Western Powers to mine Norwegian territorial waters,[7] on April 9 the Germans put into execution a plan well prepared in advance: Denmark was overrun and Norway invaded. There was no Danish resistance and that of Norway was broken by the end of the month; the government fled to England while the puppet, Quisling, organized a government in Norway under Nazi protection.[8] An Anglo-French force sent to the assistance of Norway had to be evacuated in June from its last foothold in the extreme north at Narvik.

These Scandinavian operations were only the prelude to greater activity in the West where Germany unleashed a major offensive on May 10. The German plan of 1940 was broadly similar to that of 1914, with the variant that both Holland and Belgium, instead of the latter alone, were attacked.[9] Holland, treated to a

[6] But it is significant that Reynaud was endorsed by a vote of 268 against 156 with 111 abstentions, that is, by a majority of a single voice.

[7] In February a British destroyer had seized in those waters the German ship *Altmark* carrying British prisoners of war. This incident led to representations with Norway by both the British and the Germans.

[8] The seizure of Denmark resulted in the separation of Iceland which was subsequently occupied by the British.

[9] On this occasion, by contrast with 1914, Germany did not plead the higher law of necessity but pretexted the safeguarding of the neutrality of the two countries.

demonstration of the efficiency of Nazi frightfulness in the air bombardment of Rotterdam, was quickly overrun; she gave up the struggle on May 15, her government, like the Norwegian, taking refuge in England. Meanwhile German mechanized forces had opened a breach in the French line in the Ardennes; putting to good effect the new technique of the *blitzkrieg*, they reached the Channel a week later, cutting off the Anglo-French forces in Belgium from the remaining bulk of the French army. It proved impossible to close the gap, and the decision was to evacuate at Dunkirk what could be saved of the surrounded force. The operation was accomplished in masterful fashion, but the extent of the German success could not be denied: virtually all that existed of British matériel for land war, as well as a substantial part of the French, had been either destroyed or captured.

THE COLLAPSE OF FRANCE

THE WAR IN FRANCE. These momentous events were accompanied by important political repercussions. King Leopold of Belgium ordered his armies to lay down their weapons on May 28;[10] unlike the Dutch Queen, he chose to remain among his own people, but the disagreement of his ministers, who made their way to London, served to create a controversial and confused status for Belgium. The French government of Reynaud was reshuffled while General Weygand of First World War fame was put in charge of military operations in replacement of the more scholarly than martial Gamelin. In Britain, likewise, discontent had been mounting against Chamberlain of appeasing fame; the failure in Norway brought it to a head and it was on the same May 10 that his place was taken by Winston Churchill at the head of a coalition government. Britain at last had found an authentic war leader.

France was now left essentially alone to meet the German onslaught. On June 6–7 the French line on the Somme was broken and thereafter the total defeat of France was but a matter of time. It was swift, Paris being entered on the 13th, while the French armies in a state of disorganization could oppose little more than sporadic and local resistance to a virtually unimpeded German advance. The military aspect of the matter is not part

---

[10] For this action he was sharply reproved at the time by Reynaud. This and his subsequent behavior during the war were to be the source of much controversy and troubled the Belgian political scene until his abdication in 1951.

of this story,[11] but the effects of it, needless to say, were far-reaching. Consultations between the British and the French leaders during May and June were frequent; the desperate French calls for help Britain was unable to meet, and even in the air, once the course of the battle had become clear, Britain decided that her limited forces must be husbanded for the defense of the homeland. Regardless of events in France, Britain was determined to carry on the struggle, a resolution to which Churchill gave magnificent expression in his famous speech of June 4. On May 31 he had given Reynaud assurance that, even if France fell, Britain would not abandon her.

In France facts had to be faced and the question was how to deal with them. Since, beyond question, the chief military tool of the allies had been broken, the debate was between those who felt that the war had been lost, that Britain would soon herself be likewise defeated or else seek an accommodation with Germany, and those who took the contrary view that a major battle was lost but that the war could yet be won: in concrete terms, the French government should move to North Africa where, behind the shelter of the British and its own naval power, it could wait in the hope of a better day.

The discussion went on for some days to the accompaniment of intense Anglo-French negotiations. Britain would not oppose the conclusion of an armistice, but before releasing France from the obligation not to make separate peace she wanted to be informed of the eventual German demands and to make sure that the French fleet above all would not fall into German hands. It is at this juncture that, with the support of some British and French leaders, Churchill made the proposal of a complete union of the two countries. Whether wholly seriously meant or not it was both unprecedented and highly imaginative, and one cannot help speculate on what the effects might have been for the future of such an example given to the world by two of its Great Powers. However that may be, the proposal fell on relatively deaf and certainly exhausted French ears.

The 16th of June was the crucial date when the French de-

[11] The French defeat of 1940 has been the subject of a great deal of discussion. There is no little irony in the fact that the German technique of mechanized warfare had been initially advocated in France and that France was possessed of substantial armor. The use of it, however, and in general the methods of the French command, were antiquated, a fact symbolically reflected in the personalities and ages of the French military leaders.

cision was made in favor of ending hostilities.[12] The triumph of the more pessimistic view was reflected in the displacement of Reynaud by Marshal Pétain on that date. Pétain was a respected military leader of the First World War, now well into his eighties, not so much a political figure as a symbol. Old-fashioned in his military thinking, sea, air, and armored forces meant relatively little to the man; the war was lost; he would use his prestige and his person to seek honorable terms from the enemy.

CONSEQUENCES OF THE COLLAPSE OF FRANCE. France, though defeated at home, was not wholly deprived of bargaining assets in the armistice negotiations: she still had a vast empire and an important fleet. If pressed too hard she might throw these assets to Britain or herself continue in the war; the desire was equal on the part of the British and the Germans that the French fleet should not fall to the adversary. Agreement was thus reached in the end and was written into the armistice that came into force on June 25.[13] Apart from the inevitable military terms of surrender, France was divided into two zones, some three-fifths of the country to be under German occupation, made up of the northern part of the country and of the entire Atlantic seaboard to the Spanish frontier. The fleet was not to be surrendered, but, apart from the portion of it needed for imperial defense, the rest was to return to its home ports where it would be disarmed under German (or Italian) supervision. The German government solemnly undertook not to make use of the French fleet, but in view of the well proved value of the word of Hitler, this arrangement could hardly be reassuring to Britain.

The rapidity of the unfolding of events in France during May and June had created a major issue for Italy. Feeling that it would be injurious to Italian interest to let the war be won by Germany alone, now that no risks seemed to be left, Mussolini on June 10 declared war on both Britain and France. If not devoid of logic, the gesture was equally vacant of glory and calculated to con-

[12] Reynaud had succeeded in putting off decision on the armistice pending the reply to a message to President Roosevelt. The answer to a request for "clouds" of (nonexistent) American planes could be one thing only, words of sympathy and reference to Congressional prerogatives. Roosevelt was anxious nevertheless that France continue the struggle in North Africa.

[13] Some delay was caused by the discussion of the armistice with Italy. For the signature of the German armistice Hitler insisted on the literal reënacting of the 1918 ceremony, in the identical location and in the very same railway car used in 1918.

THE SECOND WORLD WAR AND ITS IMMEDIATE AFTERMATH

firm the not uncommon epithet of "jackal" used to characterize Italian policy. The Italian share in military operations was equally inglorious, some small advances in the Alps, but naturally Italy shared in the German victory and an Italian armistice had to be concluded before the German came into effect. A 50-kilometer zone along the Franco-Italian frontier was demilitarized as well as the French naval bases in the Mediterranean.

The consequences of the French collapse were very great indeed. It came as a universal shock and brought out in full clarity the place that French power had filled in maintaining the organization of Europe. Unless Europe were to be organized under complete German domination, others must henceforth supply the force and carry out the task that the French army was to have done for all. There were only three Powers in the world possessed of sufficient resources for such an undertaking: Britain at war, the uneasy German ally that was the Soviet Union, and the United States, where opinion was still in the throes of the debate the fundamental gist of which was whether or not the country was part of this planet.

But more immediately the relations of power were radically altered. The nature of the French defeat made it appear as if French power had been a nonexistent fiction; from the exaggerated picture that was prevalent until 1940, the opposite and equally erroneous and extreme estimate now tended to be made, a fact that was to bedevil subsequent attempts at recreating equilibrium. For the moment, however, French power had beyond a doubt been annihilated, thereby creating an enormous vacuum in Europe. But French resources still existed that, in combination with the fleet and the empire, could play an important role for the belligerents. Up to a point, at least, France still had it in her power to withhold these or to throw them on either side of the balance.

EUROPE UNDER GERMAN DOMINATION

The German gain was commensurate with the French loss. Germany was mistress of Europe outside the Soviet Union, and for her the immediate problem was to make use of the resources of the Continent in the prosecution of the war against Britain. Britain still dominated the sea and her resources were immense, though, for the moment at least and for a long time at best, she could not hope to meet Germany in land war. The Napoleonic situation had once more developed of a dominant sea power facing a state all-powerful on land, with the corollary that a compromise must be found or else either power must develop means with which effectively to destroy the weapons of the other. Should it come to accommodation, each held important bargaining assets; the future place of France, for example, might well be subject to discussion.

The events of June, 1940, had raised for all, belligerents and neutrals alike, the paramount question, would the war continue or not? The answer to it lay in Britain's hands and it was soon forthcoming as an unmistakable positive. The British people were thoroughly aroused at last and they had the good fortune of having found in Churchill a leader who was himself possessed of dogged determination, while he had also the ability to give voice to the common resolve in memorable language. This last aspect of the matter was not without considerable value, for at the moment Britain had little more than words with which to meet German power.

If Britain, then, was determined to eschew compromise, the further question was raised of the likely course of the conflict. That German victory over Britain was possible in the age of air power can hardly be called an unreasonable expectation, one bolstered besides by the impressive impact of the Nazi performance in France. Pending clarification, it would be unwise to antagonize German power, just as it would be unwise for Germany to press others beyond a certain point. Thus there was a brief lull during the summer and early autumn while Germany prepared, then launched, the Battle of Britain. It was an episode of high drama and heroic dimensions, which may be summed up by saying that the *Luftwaffe* failed; there was to be no invasion of Britain,[14] and the Battle of Britain had an effect comparable to that of the Marne in 1914: Germany was deprived of the possibility of a short and successful war. This changed the situation altogether; if the war must be one of indefinite duration both sides would, among other things, endeavor to secure the assistance of neutrals and the war would in all probability extend its theater. There was ample room for diplomatic activity in this state of affairs.

On the Continent there was little prospect that anyone would court the suicide that joining Britain in active hostilities would certainly have meant at the moment, since German arms on land

[14] This time again, and perhaps for the last time, it may be said that the Channel proved the salvation of England.

were all-powerful. British efforts would therefore be directed toward minimizing the extent to which others would coöperate with Germany, while correspondingly Germany would seek to obtain the maximum of such coöperation. In the pursuit of these antagonistic aims a distinction must be made between the smaller Powers of Central and Eastern Europe and others.

In regard to the smaller states, German policy was generally directed to the avoidance of political or military disturbances, the ultimate effects of which may always be difficult to control, preferring to have the use of their resources on the basis of economic agreements, one-sided, draconian, and imposed if necessary. But both the Soviet Union and Italy held different views in the matter; like everyone, the former had been impressed, though not comforted, by the collapse of France, which nullified calculations based on the existence of a military equilibrium in the West that would result in a costly war of attrition. The Soviet tendency was thus to consolidate and increase the extent of the gains already obtained in connection with the destruction of Poland.

While the French armistice was still being negotiated, on June 15–16, the three small Baltic states received Russian ultimatums. The operation was conducted in conformity with the technique that the world has seen repeated since on numerous occasions and in a large variety of states. The installation of puppet governments —not wholly Communist at first, but under barely disguised Soviet control—was the initial step, prelude to elections which produce invariably satisfactory results. The new parliaments of Esthonia, Latvia, and Lithuania petitioned for incorporation into the Soviet Union whither they were admitted at a special session of the Supreme Soviet at the beginning of August.

In June again the Soviet Union informed Germany of its desire to recover Bessarabia and to acquire Bucovina, this last never before a Russian possession. German objections to the latter could at most reduce the extent of the Russian demands while Rumania was confronted with an ultimatum asking for the surrender of Bessarabia and Northern Bucovina. This led to an operation reminiscent of that of which Czechoslovakia had been victim after Munich. The Rumanian appeal to Germany and Italy found no response at first and there was no choice but to yield. On August 2 a Moldavian Soviet Republic was formed that proceeded to join the Soviet Union. The ideological factor was a useful tool of Soviet diplomacy, which it provided with flexibility in performing such operations. In simple fact and in older and more classical terms, Russia had, since 1939, annexed vast territories that contained some 23,000,000 people and which brought her back nearly to the 1914 frontiers. Germany had no choice, though she found little cause for satisfaction in this Russian progress.

Within the sphere of dominant German and Russian power, both ruthlessly used, the individual wishes of the smaller states, in terms of their own national grievances, found some occasion to assert themselves. The Soviet annexation was shortly followed by Bulgarian and Hungarian demands against Rumania. The former received satisfaction in the agreement of August 22 that yielded the Southern Dobrudja to Bulgaria; but the Hungarian claims were not adjusted until an Italo-German arbitration was imposed. Meeting again in Vienna at the end of August, Ciano and Ribbentrop decreed a partition of Transylvania.[15] Shortly thereafter, in October, on the pretext of protecting the Rumanian oil wells from allied sabotage, the remainder of Rumania was placed under German occupation. The bases had been laid of growing Nazi-Soviet difference and it is in fact from this time that operation Barbarossa, the Nazi plan for the attack of Russia, was taken under study.[16] Consistently, the bonds of the Rome-Berlin-Tokyo triangle were strengthened with the signature in Berlin, on September 27, of a new and more far-reaching tripartite pact.

MEDITERRANEAN STRATEGY AND DIPLOMACY: ITALY AND SPAIN. Hitler had recognized the prior claim of Italy to dominance in the Mediterranean. However that might be in future, it was clear for the present that Italy was being excluded from the Eastern European sector. Italy was disappointed with the outcome of the defeat of France, from which she had reaped meager concrete rewards; she was anxious to obtain some immediate advantage, at least in the Adriatic, and by September had succeeded in overcoming German opposition to action on her part in that quarter. Without warning to Hitler, and incidentally to pay him back with some of his own coin of surprise while restoring some equilibrium of power and prestige, on October 28 Italy launched an attack against Greece from the Albanian border. Technically, the operation had

[15] Following this King Carol abdicated in favor of his son, Michael. On September 12 a new Council of the Danube, from which Britain and France were excluded, was created to replace the International Commission established in 1921.

[16] It was a logical result of these alterations that both Hungary and Rumania should, in November, join the tripartite alliance of Rome, Berlin, and Tokyo.

been so ill prepared that the Italians suffered setbacks at the hands of the Greeks and became hopelessly bogged down in the wild mountains during the winter months. Rather than gaining prestige, here was a further humiliation; there was laughter abroad and Italy sank ever deeper into the position of German satellite.

From the German point of view it might be debated whether Italy was more asset than liability. The stalemate with Britain had the effect of enhancing the importance of the Mediterranean, and this meant that belligerent Italy, defeated France, and neutral Spain were all deeply involved. Italy was established in Libya and might be expected to move against Egypt, taking advantage of Britain's preoccupation with her home defense and the exiguity of her resources. Italy, however, did not move with alacrity for all Mussolini's bombast about his coming march into Cairo. When the Italian forces moved into Egypt in September their progress was sluggish and limited; the British had meantime concentrated in Egypt a substantial part of what was left of their armor. With it they were able to launch an attack in December that penetrated deep into Libya; by February Tobruk and Bengasi had fallen, yielding much booty and a large number of prisoners. Almost simultaneously British and Imperial contingents began to move into the various Italian East African possessions.[17] Even in her own Mediterranean and African preserve, Italy must call upon Germany for assistance; this was forthcoming, and General Rommel, heading the *Afrika Korps*, took over the direction of the war in Libya, thereby demoting Italy one further notch.

For purposes of Mediterranean strategy, the role of Spain could be of great importance. Negotiations between her and the Axis were protracted and arduous and destined to be barren of results; they can be summed up briefly. As might be expected in view of his indebtedness to the Axis, Franco was profuse of sympathetic declarations; he was not averse to entering the war, but owing to the deplorable condition of Spain just emerged from the civil war, he wanted the assurance of substantial economic aid; he demanded in addition a high price for his services: Gibraltar, French Morocco, Western Algeria, and other African territories farther south. Finally, he wanted the outcome to be conclusively assured by a prior successful German invasion of England. After this last had failed negotiations continued, characterized by growing Span-

---

[17] The East African possessions were shortly overrun, Addis Ababa capitulating in April, 1941, thereby sealing the fate of the short-lived Italian dream of empire.

ish reticence and prudence; the mission to Berlin and Rome of the Spanish foreign minister, Serrano Suñer, was unproductive, and when Hitler and Mussolini met at the Brenner in October they found difficulty in reconciling overlapping Spanish, Italian, and German claims in Africa. The Italian setback in Libya could only increase Spanish prudence; the initial opportunity having passed, the role of Spain in the war consisted in putting off the Axis with fair but vague and inexpensive words, ever urging the deficiencies of Spain as a pretext for putting forward impossible requirements. It was skillful diplomacy, in sharp contrast with the Italian; Spanish neutrality was destined to return handsome dividends.

VICHY FRANCE AND "FREE" FRANCE.   The Spanish claims in Africa were all at the expense of France, and that fact in itself was an obstacle for the reason that to punish France beyond a certain point might have the effect of causing her to throw the fleet and the empire into the hands of the enemy of the Axis. For that reason primarily France was therefore possessed of a measure of power to the significance of which German diplomacy, far more than Italian or Spanish, was sensitive. As mentioned previously, from the point of view of the belligerents, chiefly Britain and Germany, the problem of France was the negative one of preventing the use of her remaining resources from passing into the adversary's hands. France therefore must be treated with deftness. But there was also the French side of the equation. France, any France, could hardly do other than seek to minimize the consequences of her defeat. How this was to be done implied judgments and decisions that might, if incorrect, prove costly; there was of necessity a premium on hedging and tergiversation. Dealing from a position of weakness, French diplomacy may be said to have conducted a delicate operation with fair skill.

But what precisely was France? The government had taken the decision not to leave metropolitan France; it had concluded an armistice, but not formal peace, thus still remaining technically at war though not engaged in hostilities. More than half of the country was under enemy occupation, over which the French government had limited control. In the chaotic aftermath of military disaster the seat of government was transferred to Vichy in the unoccupied zone. There, on the 10th of July, the regularly constituted organs of the French state, the French Parliament, surrendered their power to Marshal Pétain, henceforth the Head of the French State, entrusted with full power to govern and to draft a new constitution. The tale of the mean and pitiful attempt to rejuvenate France by putting back the clock to the heyday of the *ancien régime*, in modern terms by creating some sort of authoritarian system presiding over some modified version of the Italian corporative state, under the leadership of the initially respected figure of an aged and increasingly senile military man, never well versed in politics, does not belong in these pages. Inevitably, Pétain would fall under the influence of his advisors whom, however, he could choose and dismiss at will.

Among these Pierre Laval was prominent. This unattractive personality will long remain controversial. Unprincipled but not unintelligent, Laval's policy may be described as one based on the assumption of German victory; from this it followed quite logically that French interest could best be served by recognizing the inevitable and accepting its consequences; by willing coöperation with the New Order France might prove more useful to Germany than either Italy or Spain for instance. It was, in this context, consistent to advocate a complete breach with Britain.[18] Britain had justified cause for suspicion, especially on the score of the fate of the French fleet. Feeling in her peril that the risk was too great, on July 3, following the rejection of an ultimatum, the British fleet attacked the French at Mers-el-Kebir[19] where various ships were sunk or disabled. French feeling ran high, especially in naval and military circles, but Pétain refused to retaliate despite the urgings of Laval and Admiral Darlan. However, diplomatic relations were severed between Vichy and London.

To complicate even further these delicate Anglo-French relations, a Free French movement had raised its banner in London. On July 17 General de Gaulle, holder of a minor ministerial post and early advocate of the technique of warfare so successfully appropriated by Germany, had flown to London from Bordeaux. De Gaulle was an advocate of continued resistance; after the

---

[18] Laval felt little love for Britain, especially since the Abyssinian affair, while conversely he had no rooted antagonism for totalitarian systems. Whatever role these predilections may have played, the more important consideration was his judgment of the existing situation and its probable unfolding; though the judgment eventually proved erroneous, it was, as mentioned earlier, widely shared in many quarters in and outside of France.

[19] The ultimatum demanded that the French fleet join the British or else sail to the West Indies or to the United States. At the same time French naval units in Britain were seized and a local agreement resulted in the disarmament of the French units in Alexandria.

French surrender he remained in England where he proceeded to organize the just mentioned Free French movement, maintaining that a battle but not the war had been lost and that France should continue to be represented as an active belligerent. At the end of July de Gaulle organized in London a Council of Overseas France which obtained the adherence of a number of French colonies, most importantly in Central Africa. This development could be of value to Britain, who understandably encouraged it; with a view to extending the range of its control, an expedition to Dakar, hoping to secure the allegiance of French West Africa, was agreed upon by Churchill and de Gaulle. The attempt, in late September, was a failure with the result of lessening in British eyes the importance of the Free French movement.

The legality of the Vichy government was hardly open to question, and despite the uncertainties of the French position it might be best not to antagonize it to the point of open enmity. After the fiasco at Dakar a fragile *modus vivendi* was established as the result of some contacts between British and French representatives in Madrid: both sides tacitly recognized the existing divided status of the French empire and agreed to refrain from aggressive attempts to alter it.

The reliability of such understandings must obviously remain forever uncertain. In October Laval contrived at Montoire an interview between Pétain and Hitler where the former acknowledged the desirability of collaboration with Germany. The simultaneous advent of Laval to the foreign office served to renew British suspicion; Laval was indeed willing to declare war against Britain, though not before conditions would be suitable, and Hitler had to reassure Mussolini, chagrined at the prospect of having been supplanted. Nothing came of all this and the dismissal of Laval in December was reassuring to both Britain and Italy while raising corresponding doubts in Germany. French feeling and opinion were still largely inert, stunned by the impact of defeat and willing in the main to put trust in the Marshal, while on the German side the policy of inducing willing acceptance of the new order of Europe was still being pursued: it would be of considerable value to Germany if she could use with others the example of voluntary French acceptance; France must not be pressed too hard, while the "correct" behavior of the occupying forces must give a favorable picture of Germans. But doubts inevitably persisted on the German side on the score of France as they likewise persisted on the British, doubts that the French policy of trimming could only cultivate.[20] Laval's perhaps apocryphal comment seems a fair summary: unless Britain is defeated shortly we shall be criminals.

NAZI-SOVIET RELATIONS AND THE SPREAD OF THE WAR IN EU-
ROPE. But, however much diplomatic ingenuity might be spent on the delicate relations at the center of which lay defeated France, the solution to the greater issue of the war must come from other and more powerful quarters. As in the First World War, and even more than in that conflict, there was no possibility of compromise and reconciliation between limited interests; instead of this, contending and violently divergent ideologies must fight it to a finish through the instrumentality of total war. Hitler must be taken quite literally when he spoke of a thousand-year Reich or alternatively of bringing down in chaos the whole house of Europe.

Mention has been made of readjustments in Central Europe where German, Russian, and Italian influences met. The last was the least difficult to deal with owing to the weakness of Italy; but it was otherwise with the others. In October–November, 1940, an important Russo-German negotiation took place, the essence of which was an attempt at definition of the respective spheres of influence on a world-wide basis. In reply to an advance by Ribbentrop, Molotov visited Berlin on November 12–14; he proved as ever a close bargainer and no agreement was reached on that occasion. The Russian counterproposals, submitted on November 25, were equally unacceptable to Germany. They were not answered, Hitler proceeding instead with the preparation of operation Barbarossa. The failure to agree had come over the Balkan perennial; Russia wanted complete control of the Black Sea and the Baltic, for which purpose German forces must withdraw from Finland and, more important, Bulgaria fell in the Russian security zone. Under those conditions Russia was willing to join the tripartite Rome-Berlin-Tokyo Pact.

Germany's grand strategy had two foci, Central Europe and the Mediterranean. In the latter sector Spain was again brought into the picture but steadfastly continued to resist German and

[20] There were further Anglo-French contacts toward the end of 1940, of which it is difficult to form a clear picture, owing to the great British reticence on this subject. The state of Anglo-French relations may be described as having continued for some time on the basis of reciprocal caution and suspicion. Cf. J.-B. Duroselle, *Histoire diplomatique de 1919 à nos jours*, Paris, 1953, pp. 325–330.

Italian pressure at the turn from 1940 to 1941.[21] An Axis offensive in Libya in the spring of 1941 cleared the country, save Tobruk, of British forces.[22] One reason for this North African success was the weakening of these British forces, depleted as a result of Balkan developments. For the other aspect of German preparations was an effort to consolidate the control of Central Europe and the Balkans. Hungary and Rumania had become Axis satellites and Italy was at war with Greece. This left Bulgaria and Yugoslavia. Bulgaria was the scene of the sharpest Russo-German diplomatic contest. Having refused the offer of a Russian guarantee, or the alternative of a pact of mutual assistance in November, 1940, in March, 1941, Bulgaria adhered to the tripartite pact and, despite Soviet protests, allowed German forces to enter the country.

Simultaneous negotiations had been taking place with Yugoslavia which adhered to the tripartite pact on March 25. But at this point an unexpected turn of events took place. The regent, Prince Paul, was ousted and under the leadership of King Peter II, declared of age though minor, a new government was constituted. Nazi power would not allow such independence and responded with yet another manifestation of frightfulness. Yugoslavia was attacked on April 6 and once more the outcome was the only possible one in the circumstances. The country was promptly overrun and, as a consequence and to the further discomfiture of Mussolini, the Greek war was also terminated with the German occupation of the country.[23]

Both the Greek and Yugoslav governments went into exile, the latter having previously entered into a pact of nonaggression and friendship with the Soviet Union. But while in Athens the Germans set up a puppet regime, the Yugoslav state was completely destroyed.[24] Signs were multiplying of German preparations

[21] In December Admiral Canaris went to Madrid in an effort to obtain the passage of German troops for an attack on Gibraltar. In February, 1941, a meeting between Mussolini and Franco at Bordighera was equally barren of results.

[22] Under German and Italian prodding a coup took place in Iraq in April under the leadership of Rashid Ali. When the anti-British orientation of the new Iraqi regime became clear, in May, prompt military action on the part of the British forestalled the arrival of adequate German assistance. Rashid Ali took flight and the situation was restored for Britain.

[23] It was for the purpose of assistance to Greece that British troops had been withdrawn from North Africa. They were unable to stem the German tide and even had to yield the island of Crete in May.

[24] Slovenia was partitioned between Germany and Italy and Croatia became an independent state, the crown of which was to be borne by an Italian prince who, however, never actually assumed the post. Montenegro was likewise to be independent under the Italian crown. Both Hungary and Bulgaria regained ter-

against Russia, the attack being delayed some weeks by the unexpected Yugoslav resistance. Russia was much concerned, but the gestures of appeasement that she made were futile, for the Führer's mind was made up. Since the invasion of Britain had had to be abandoned Germany would turn east, acquire there vital space, and commandeer the resources of that region for a protracted war. On June 22, 1941, the Nazi war machine moved across the uneasy line of demarcation between the zones of German and Soviet control.[25]

Hitler was quite correct when he described this move in a letter to Mussolini of June 21, as "the most important decision of my life," for the consequences of it were to be great. For Britain, which had for just a year been holding the fort singlehanded, and whose prospects of victory were at best nebulous and remote, this was a heaven-sent opportunity to which Churchill responded by declaring at once that Britain would give all possible aid to Russia, a commitment that was formalized in the agreement of July 13. Apart from the immediate extension of the theater of hostilities, the effect of the Nazi action was to bring Russia back into European affairs in a way that she had not been since the revolution, with consequences that will be long in the unfolding. Needless to say, Communists everywhere could now return to the earlier pre-Nazi-Soviet Pact allegiance; they docilely made a new about face and, from having generally done their best to aid the German purpose, turned to the opposite end. Their contribution at first could not be very significant, but they played an increasingly important role in the resistance movements throughout the Continent, a fact the consequences of which were to be of the highest import for the future.

The purely military aspects of the war in Russia will not be dwelt upon. The Nazi war machine demonstrated once more its capacities, penetrating deep into Russia. By the end of the year Leningrad and Moscow were invested, the Ukraine overrun, and even Sebastopol besieged; Russian losses were very large, but the significant thing is that Russia's military power was not broken. There was more room in Russia than in France; the Russian spaces and the Russian winter proved again valuable assets and the Rus-

---

ritory lost after the First World War and Bulgaria annexed the bulk of Macedonia, as well as of Thrace taken from Greece, which retained Salonika. Albania was also somewhat enlarged, and a small, supposedly independent Serbia, was left, corresponding to the pre-1914 state.

[25] A Soviet-Japanese nonaggression pact was signed on April 13, 1941.

sians were even able to mount an offensive that regained some ground for them. For the moment the German purpose had been foiled. Nor did Germany obtain the benefits that she might have expected from the large territory that she held; there were appreciable defections from Soviet rule, but the stupidly consistent application of the Nazi racial outlook was to the occupied populations a more convincing argument for resistance than the shortcomings of the Soviet regime were for coöperation with the Germans. As the year 1941 was drawing to a close German control of the Continent was firmly established; but the war, if its range had been vastly extended, was still a stalemate. Moreover, the closing of the year had witnessed another development whose effects were to be ultimately decisive in the outcome of the struggle.

II. The War Becomes Worldwide

JAPANESE PLANS IN THE FAR EAST

The war having engulfed the virtual totality of Europe, two world Powers were still, nominally, at peace, the United States and Japan. Both had been participants in the earlier world conflict and both were destined to share in the second. Both, however, were extra-European and had a point of contact in Far Eastern affairs. There has been occasion to mention Nazi-Japanese contacts, the basis of which was the potentially common Soviet enemy; Japan had signed the Anti-Comintern Pact as early as November, 1936, but the Nazi-Soviet Pact of August, 1939, had naturally put an at least temporary quietus on the possibilities of continued collaboration directed against the Soviet Union. The German attack of June, 1941, might reëstablish the prospect, but the Japanese foreign minister, Matsuoka, having visited both Moscow and Berlin, the result was the Soviet-Japanese nonaggression pact of April. For the time being Japanese nonparticipation in the European conflict was insured.

Japanese interests were exclusively Far Eastern and the main significance for Japan of European complications was an enhanced opportunity to proceed with her plans of which the main focus was China. After the successful aggression of 1931 and the setting up of the puppet state of Manchukuo matters were quiescent for a time while Japan proceeded to digest and organize her conquests. From that time on the European Powers, involved in a succession of crises nearer home, were not in a position to take effective action in the Far East, either individually or through the agency of a moribund League of Nations. Japan was consequently relatively free to proceed with her designs in China and this led to the resumption of active hostilities in July, 1937.[26] It was war in effect, though neither side issued a formal declaration of it, and Japan seemed bent upon obtaining the establishment of an amenable and subservient government in China rather than upon the acquisition of specific territorial gains. But in spite of their military successes that brought increasing sections of China under their control, the Japanese did not contrive to overthrow the regime of Chiang Kai-shek which, having moved to Chungking, continued the struggle from there.[27]

THE UNITED STATES AND THE WAR

The United States was inimical to these Japanese activities but found itself handicapped by its inner entanglements in its efforts to oppose them. This was in the United States the heyday of isolationism. The American people, having convinced themselves that their involvement in the First World War had been a mistake, had come to the simple, logical, and erroneous conclusion that the best hope of peace for themselves lay in avoiding entanglements in the affairs of the outer world. The fast deteriorating European situation after the advent of the Nazis in Germany, and especially after 1935, caused the American Congress to give expression to the American desire for peace in the form of the curious legislation embodied in the Neutrality Acts. Lest America find herself implicated through the machinations of even her own wicked merchants of death[28] or bankers, as early as August, 1935, the Congress passed the first Neutrality Act, which decreed an embargo on arms shipments to any belligerent. This was in force when the Abyssinian conflict broke out and was renewed upon expiry the following February. The new act allowed the President to decide upon the existence of a state of war, a provision that proved useful in making possible assistance to China in the undeclared Sino-Japanese War.

The Spanish Civil War was an awkward dilemma owing to

[26] The Soviet Union was naturally concerned over Japanese aggression in China, but, despite some military encounters with the Japanese, adhered to an attitude of caution and avoided a formal breach with Japan.

[27] A puppet regime was set up in Nanking at the beginning of 1940.

[28] The Nye investigation in 1935 was an expression of this temper which its report helped in turn to strengthen.

its domestic nature; quite consistently the United States refused to be involved in the activities of the nonintervention committee set up during that war. That such self-imposed restrictions might have the undesirable effect of working to the benefit of an aggressor (as in the Italo-Ethiopian conflict for instance) was regarded as less important than the risk of involvement, and the new law of May, 1937, a permanent piece of legislation, strengthened its expired predecessor by introducing the "cash and carry" provision: American ships might not carry goods destined to the belligerents, who in addition must pay cash for their purchases. What all this meant in effect was that the United States was deciding severely to hamstring the possibilities of an effective foreign policy.[29] Little wonder that Roosevelt's peace efforts in the form of pleas addressed to Hitler and Mussolini in the spring of 1939 fell on deaf ears. Nevertheless American feeling was increasingly antagonized by the behavior of the Axis Powers, a fact which tended to create for it a dilemma of sorts.

These were the conditions of the American scene when war broke out in Europe in September, 1939. The very real sympathy that existed for the victims of aggression did not to any large extent translate itself into the belief that America had any stake in the war. Neutrality was declared on September 5 and, by way of further insulation of the entire American Continent from the conflict, the Pan American Conference decreed on October 2 the existence of a 300-mile zone along the Atlantic coast in which hostilities were barred.[30] The debate was meanwhile raging with increasing vigor, but few signs of its resolution appeared, between the advocates of neutrality *à outrance* and those who pointed to the undesirable effects of abstention, especially in the Far East. Tentatively, in November, the Congress lifted the embargo on arms.

During the period of the "phoney" war some repetitions occurred of the pre-1917 situation: the Allies' control of and activity on the seas gave rise to a degree of friction, especially with

[29] The somewhat pathological American reaction to the very word war is well illustrated by the episode of the Ludlow resolution (a popular referendum required to make a declaration of war effective, save in the event of invasion) and by the unfavorable reception of President Roosevelt's so-called Quarantine speech in 1937.

[30] In December, 1940, the German pocket battleship *Graf Spee*, cornered by three British cruisers, sought refuge in Montevideo harbor; when forced to leave it was scuttled by its crew. These activities gave rise to protests addressed to the belligerents by President Roosevelt speaking for the American governments.

Britain. But of greater significance was the beginning of the strengthening of the American military establishment. If Premier Reynaud's appeal at the time of the French disaster for "clouds of planes" from the United States was wholly chimerical, it was at this very time that an expansion of the army and the navy was decreed while an ambitious scheme was launched for an airplane production of 50,000 units—clouds of planes indeed. In September the unprecedented step was taken of enacting a selective service measure in peacetime.

The collapse of France made a substantial dent on American complacency and gave added point to the question of whether or not America had a stake in the outcome of the conflict in Europe. Feeling was generally sympathetic to the Allied cause but remained strong against direct involvement; while there were those who favored intervention, others preferred the concept of fortress America. That greater strength was desirable seemed accepted, and on June 17 the declaration was made that no transfer of territory in the Western Hemisphere from one European Power to another would be recognized, thus in effect neutralizing French and Dutch holdings in the Americas.

The outcome of these divergent American tendencies may be described as a policy of compromise that constituted a step on the road to involvement. In August a joint United States–Canadian Board of Defense was set up; of greater consequence was the so-called destroyers-bases deal in September. As early as May, one of the first acts of Churchill after his assumption of the Prime Ministership had been a request to President Roosevelt for the loan of forty to fifty overage destroyers; negotiations followed a renewal of the request in July and led to the acquisition by Britain of fifty such ships; in exchange for them the United States obtained ninety-nine-year leases for naval and air bases in a number of British possessions.[31] The destroyers were, in the circumstances, of vital importance to Britain and the bases were clearly advantageous for the defense of the Americas. The arrangement undoubtedly constituted a measure of American involvement; it may fairly be described in Churchill's words as marking the transition from neutrality to nonbelligerency and was a major setback for the isola-

[31] These bases were to be located in Newfoundland, Bermuda, the Bahamas, Jamaica, St. Lucia, Trinidad, Antigua, and British Guiana. In keeping with earlier Pan-American agreements, the use of them was also made available to other American states.

tionist tendency. It is of interest that the arrangement was made on the eve of the American election in which President Roosevelt decided to break the two-term presidential tradition.

The substantial victory that he gained—nearly a 5,000,000 majority of the popular vote—gave him increased freedom to pursue the policy to which he was firmly wedded of giving Britain all assistance short of war. Britain could indeed make use of all possible aid and she had by this time already made very substantial purchases in the United States which, in accordance with the existing American law, had had to be made on the cash-and-carry basis. As in the First World War the question was beginning to appear of the continued financing of such purchases, a matter that Churchill brought to Roosevelt's attention in December. The Johnson Act excluded the possibility of American loans, but the difficulty was eventually circumvented through the skillful device that went under the name of Lend-Lease, an Act passed by Congress that became law on March 11.

The Act gave the American President very extensive powers that could be used in highly flexible fashion, for under it "any country whose defense the President decrees vital to the defense of the United States" was made the eligible recipient of American aid in almost any form in exchange for whatever compensation or advantage the President was to judge adequate. What this actually meant was that Britain could be assured of unlimited aid. The terms of the arrangement also constituted a tacit acceptance by the United States of what had been the debtors' view in the controversy over the first war's debts, that the war was an enterprise in which America's stake was no less than that of others. By a stroke of the pen the possibility of the renewal of the unrealistic controversy that had grown out of the First World War in the matter of financial arrangements was thus eliminated.[32] When Germany launched her attack against Russia, three months after the passage of the Lend-Lease Act, the Soviet Union became one of the countries whose defense was found vital to the defense of the United States. Following the visit to Britain and to Russia of Roosevelt's personal trusted representative, Harry Hopkins, the arrangements were shortly formalized for American and British aid to Russia.

[32] The closeness of the personal relationship that grew up between Roosevelt and Churchill was a factor of the first order of importance in the Second World War.

The Grand Alliance was fast taking shape and the growing American acceptance of responsibility for the shape of the world that would emerge from the conflict was further evidenced by the meeting between Roosevelt and Churchill that took place off Newfoundland on August 9–11. From it emerged the joint declaration of peace aims known as the Atlantic Charter: both countries renounced any desire for territorial aggrandizement and underwrote the right of peoples freely to choose their governments, as well as that of the access of all to raw materials; states should collaborate to promote social and economic progress; the seas should be free; the future peace must insure international security and lay the bases for the general reduction of armaments. This is reminiscent of the Fourteen Points, but, unlike that earlier American charter of the future, it was not the result of careful preparation and study; consequently and deliberately it was made far less precise. Bearing in mind the fate of the League, no concrete reference was made to a future international organization.

Despite the deepening American involvement in the conflict,[33] the American debate was raging on in vigorous and inconclusive fashion between interventionists and isolationists; even among those who saw the defeat of the Axis as necessary for the security of America the hope was strong that aid short of war might obviate the necessity of direct participation. The debate might have remained unresolved but for developments in the Far East that led to its abrupt conclusion.

THE UNITED STATES ENTERS THE WAR

Japan's activity in China has been mentioned as well as the American dislike of Japanese encroachment.[34] But the operation of American policy was fettered in the Far East no less than elsewhere by its unresolved contradictions; antagonistic to Japan and sympathetic to China as it was, the United States, ever fearful of involvement, hesitated to coöperate with other states, Britain and the U.S.S.R. in particular, whose anti-Japanese interest was broadly similar to its own. The war in Europe had the inevitable effect of lessening the effectiveness of British and Russian opposition to

[33] Since January military consultations had been going on in Washington between American, British, and Dominion staffs. In April, an agreement with Denmark allowed the United States to assume the defense of Greenland, and in July American forces landed in Iceland.

[34] See above, pp. 459, 561. As a manifestation of American displeasure the 1911 commercial treaty was allowed to lapse in January, 1940.

Japanese designs and correspondingly emphasized the American quandary.

The Nazi-Soviet Pact had not been welcome in Japan; while Soviet-Japanese relations remained in a state of mutually suspicious watchfulness, the course of the European war during 1940 further enhanced for Japan the alternative possibility of southern expansion. Before the German occupation of Holland Japan had already been pressing for economic concessions in the Dutch East Indies.[35] The French collapse opened still larger opportunities; Japan demanded the right to place forces in French Indochina and obtained from Britain the closing of the Burma Road, one of the last remaining avenues for supplying aid to China. Despite American warnings the Japanese, having extracted through an ultimatum concessions from the Vichy government, clearly impotent to act in the Far East, proceeded to occupy Indochina in September.[36]

The American retort in the form of cutting off supplies of scrap iron and steel was characterized by Japan as an unfriendly act and it was at this time that Japan acceded to the tripartite pact with the Axis. By way of counterpart to the New Order in Europe Japan had begun to speak of a New Order for Asia, which the awkward sounding phrase, Greater East Asia Coprosperity Sphere, was used to describe. There was no counterpart, however, to the tension that soon began to develop between Germany and the Soviet Union, whose relations with Japan remained on the same basis of watchful waiting; there was, if anything, some relaxation of tension as witnessed by the conclusion of the above-mentioned Soviet-Japanese nonaggression pact in April, 1941. But the German attack against Russia in June had the effect of liberating Japan from doubts of possible action from the Soviet quarter; Japan in turn did not elect to use the opportunity for action in the north but concentrated instead on her southern designs.

The year 1941 saw an intensification of Anglo-American cooperation on a world-wide basis. It was out of the secret staff discussions that began in January and of the Atlantic Charter meeting that understandings took shape with a view to a distribution

[35] There was not yet at this time any Japanese intention of occupying the Dutch possessions, but the United States issued a warning in April that it would oppose any attempt to alter the status of the Dutch East Indies by nonpeaceful means. In June the local government agreed to place no restrictions on exports to Japan.

[36] Shortly thereafter the hostilities that had broken out between Thailand and French Indochina were terminated as a result of Japanese intercession.

of forces and of labor in the event of American participation in the war and of its extension to the Far East. From the spring of 1941 also dates the Japanese decision to proceed with the plans for expansion that made war virtually unavoidable; with the definite establishment in control of the army point of view[37] little hope was left of possible accommodation. Nevertheless Japanese-American negotiations continued during the summer and autumn. The details of these will not be dwelt upon in this story from the point of view of which their main significance and interest lies in the impact of American and Japanese intervention in the more general conflict.

Positions on both the American and the Japanese sides were assuming increasing rigidity: Roosevelt had declared that further Japanese expansion by force would compel the United States to take all measures necessary for the safeguarding of its interests, while Churchill had announced that in the event of failure of conciliation, Britain would be unhesitatingly at the side of the United States; in Japan the decision was taken at the beginning of September that, if within a month Japanese demands seemed impossible of acceptance, war against the United States, Britain, and Holland would be considered. These demands were in fact much too far-reaching for the United States to entertain[38] and the last negotiation in Washington, conducted by the Japanese Ambassador Nomura assisted by a special envoy, were wholly futile. The final American rejection in the form of counterproposals, equally unacceptable to Japan, came on November 26. On the 22d a Japanese fleet was already prepared to sail in the direction of the Hawaiian Islands. The formal Japanese decision for war dates from December 1, and negotiations on the Japanese side were only continued thereafter with the intent to deceive and to provide the advantage of surprise. Despite warnings by its ambassador in Tokyo in November of the possibility of an unannounced attack, and despite much knowledge of Japanese doings derived from possession of

[37] There were divisions and hesitations in Japan, largely on the score of tactics, the Navy being more reluctant than the Army to face the prospect of war with the United States. These differences were finally resolved with the reorganization of the Cabinet in July, as a consequence of which the Army point of view, represented by the war minister, General Tojo, prevailed. A new reorganization in October put Tojo in the Premiership and was the prelude to action.

[38] The minimum Japanese demands aimed at securing uninhibited access to economic resources in the Far East and the lifting of American trade restrictions. But the United States insisted on the evacuation of Japanese forces from China and Indochina *prior to* the negotiation of a trade treaty with Japan.

the Japanese code, the attack on the base of Pearl Harbor on December 7 found the United States totally unprepared and consequently succeeded in inflicting very substantial damage.[39]

The action at Pearl Harbor naturally elicited in the United States a reaction made up in equal parts of shock, indignation, and anger. More importantly, it resolved at one stroke the unending debate between intervention and neutrality; like it or no, in rudest fashion the United States was catapulted into the war. That the major European war should proceed parallel and unconnected with another major war in the Pacific was hardly to be expected. The initiative of making the connection between the two conflicts came from the Axis; on December 11 Germany and Italy observed the formality of a declaration of war on the United States. The war indeed was world-wide.

THE COURSE OF MILITARY OPERATIONS

The war had now been going on for just over two years and had taken a shape that would have been difficult of prediction at the time of its outbreak. Ranged on one side stood the Rome-Berlin-Tokyo triangle, already well on its way to a formal alliance in September, 1939. But on the other side things had vastly changed; France, the initial mainstay of the Western alliance, had been eliminated as an active contestant, and for a year beleaguered Britain had held the fort alone, able to do little more than survive. The aggressive dynamic of the triangle had, in the course of six months, totally changed the face of the war; unwilling Russia and reluctant America, forced to defend themselves, were now joined to Britain. The prospects of the Grand Alliance, for the long term at least, were bright, though some time was to pass before these prospects began to show signs of realization. Not until the vast potential of unprepared America had been sufficiently transformed into actual weapons did the tide turn and begin to unroll to its appointed end.

The war in its military aspects is not the primary concern of this treatment, but the course and shape that it took could not but have important repercussions and must therefore ever be borne in mind when considering the relations of states, whether belligerent or neutral. For the sake of simplicity of presentation it will

---

[39] The events of Pearl Harbor have been the source of much controversy, not least in the United States, where even the Axis version that they were contrived by President Roosevelt as a device to bring the United States into the war has found some supporters.

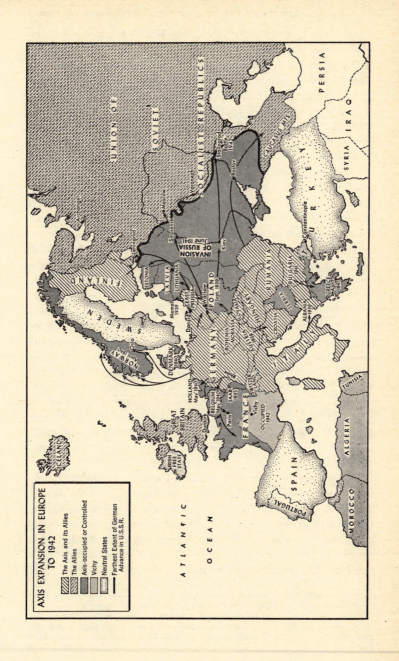

AXIS EXPANSION IN EUROPE
TO 1942

The Axis and Its Allies
The Allies
Axis-occupied or Controlled
Vichy
Neutral States
Farthest Extent of German
Advance in U.S.S.R.

therefore be convenient to recall very briefly the chief developments of the conflict itself.

American participation gave an enormous boost to British and Russian prospects and morale, yet the year following Pearl Harbor marked the low point of allied fortunes and correspondingly the high tide of Axis and Japanese success. At Pearl Harbor the Japanese had inflicted crippling damage on the American fleet; it was America's good fortune that she enjoyed the asset of the protection of two oceans: unhurt at home and beyond the reach of invasion, she could proceed undisturbed to mobilize her people and her industry. The Japanese meantime pressed their advantage hard. As the year 1942 opened they had captured Guam and Wake Islands, as well as British Hongkong, and overrun the Philippines; from French Indochina they forced Thailand into the war on their side and descended into British Malaya, seizing the base of Singapore in February. A month earlier they had begun to move into the Dutch East Indies; by March they were invading Burma and threatening Australia, the invasion of which was frustrated in the Battle of the Coral Sea in May. They met failure again at Midway the next month and the second half of the year witnessed a halt in their progress, prelude to the great offensive that gradually, during the next two years, evicted them from their conquests. It was in mid-1944 that the war was brought to the home islands in the air while the Philippines were invaded in October; by 1945 the Japanese were being forced to retreat in Southeast Asia and were being mercilessly pounded from the air in Japan proper. It was only a matter of time before Japan herself would be invaded. The war in the Pacific was, on the allied side, largely an American operation.[40]

But despite the great effort that the Pacific war entailed, Roosevelt had agreed with Churchill, even before America was involved in hostilities, that priority must go to operations against the Axis. The Axis, or more precisely Germany, was master of the Continent where it was organizing the New Order while mobilizing resources for the prosecution of further operations. Of this New Order little need be said, for it was soon to be wiped

---

[40] Operations in Southeast Asia had been put under the command of Lord Mountbatten in 1943. Japanese activity on the mainland of Asia was no less imperialistic than that of European Powers; nevertheless the defeats inflicted by an Asiatic Power on Western Powers had a profound and lasting effect on the peoples of Asia, supplying a great stimulus to their desire for emancipation from European control.

out; traces of it and complications were nonetheless its future legacy. Some governments were operating at home while others had gone into exile, leaving the Axis to set up puppets in their place. In varying but increasing degrees German exactions aroused everywhere opposition, and underground resistance movements sprang up throughout the Continent; to these movements the attack on the Soviet Union gave a great boost for it threw in their ranks the well disciplined Communist parties, while American participation naturally raised the hopes of all opponents of the Axis. But the resistance by its very nature was also bound to put a premium on illegality; it thus brought into the life of the European nations an element of lawlessness and a cleavage of opinion that were to play a large role in the aftermath.

The Germans and their satellites—Italian, Hungarian, and Rumanian—had penetrated deep into the Russian land. After a halt, and even some retreat during the first winter, they launched a new offensive in the summer of 1942 that brought them to Stalingrad and to the Caucasus. The whole direction of the war, even in the Italian theater, was essentially in German hands. In North Africa the war was one of wide movement. A new British offensive in December, 1941, did not stop until El Agheila was reached, but a counterdrive in May cleared again all of Libya and the next month reached into Egypt to within 70 miles of Alexandria. The Middle East thus became the focus of Germany's grand strategy; poised at the Caucasus and El Alamein a huge pincers might overrun the whole intervening area. If successful, a still more grandiose plan could be envisaged that would effect a junction with a Japanese drive toward India.

But this was the zenith of Axis fortunes. Instead of taking Stalingrad, the Germans had to face a Russian offensive in November, and the stubbornness of their leadership had merely the effect of allowing an army to be surrounded that finally surrendered to the Russians in February; thereafter the Russian drive gained in intensity and the German retreat began that did not end until Berlin was reached.[41] Almost simultaneously with the Russian drive at Stalingrad a British offensive was launched at El Alamein at the end of October; it met with success and three months later Tripoli was entered by the British. Thus the tables

[41] This outcome, prolonging the war long beyond the point of certain defeat, may be credited to the combination of the steadfastness and fighting qualities of the German army with the insanity of Nazi leadership.

were turned and instead of the pincers on the Middle East it was the turn of the Axis to be trapped in North Africa. For on November 8 a large allied armada had brought forces to French North Africa where landings were effected in Morocco and Algeria. The end in Africa was to take place in Tunisia where the remainder of the Axis forces were trapped and captured in May, 1943.

The invasion of North Africa had caused the Germans to occupy all of France,[42] but Spain continued neutral. As to Italy, where discouragement and disgruntlement were rife, she was already under virtual German control where military matters were concerned. The clearing of North Africa was followed in July by an attack on Sicily, the overrunning of which was completed in August, while a *coup de théâtre* in Italy brought the fall of Mussolini on July 25. Both the Italian and the French situations thus became highly confused and complex.[43] Within six weeks the new Italian government of Marshal Badoglio sued for an armistice and surrendered, while the Allies moved on to the Italian mainland. The country thus became a battleground instead of extricating itself from the war as it had hoped, for the German forces that took over the bulk of Italy had to be painstakingly driven virtually the entire length of the Peninsula during the next two years. Rome was not entered until June, 1944.

When the Allies entered the Holy City the event was overshadowed by the landing of an Anglo-American force on the Normandy beaches two days later. The success of this operation made the handwriting on the wall quite plain; *Festung Europa* was clearly not impregnable, but the nature of the Nazi leadership also prevented a repetition of the 1918 situation when Germany surrendered once her military leaders had come to the conclusion that the war was effectively lost. True to his own mad genius, Hitler must literally bring down the house of Europe if he could not make it his own. Paris was liberated in August while the Allies were proceeding north and east toward the Rhine. Into Germany

---

[42] An attempt to seize the French fleet at Toulon was foiled by the scuttling of it by its crews.

[43] On the Italian situation, see below, pp. 575, 582–583. In North Africa the Anglo-Americans were at a loss with whom to deal; for a time they recognized the authority of Admiral Darlan, Pétain's heir apparent, who seized the opportunity to attempt to maintain his own position by dealing with the Anglo-Americans. This situation had a confusing and complicating effect on the various French factions.

the war had to be brought while the country was reduced to rubble from the air. In April the Elbe was reached by the Western Allies and the Russians arrived in Berlin where, in the setting of a true *Götterdämmerung*, the Nazi regime collapsed while Hitler put an end to his days. The junction of the allied forces was effected on April 25 on the Elbe; following the surrender of a group of German armies to the Western Allies, May 8 was proclaimed V-E Day, the end of the war in Europe.[44]

While the Axis was being destroyed in Europe the fate of Japan had been sealed for some time. The steady retreat toward the home islands continued to proceed through the years from 1943 to 1945; like Germany, Japan was subjected to increasing air bombardment and preparations were in progress for the launching of an invasion of Japan herself. At this point an unexpected development took place, the effects of which were destined to be profound, not only on the limited matter of the Japanese war, but on the wider aspect of the future conduct of international relations. No clearer and more significant illustration of the effects of technical developments in the military field can be found than the production of the atomic bomb. For some years physicists, mainly in America, had been addressing themselves to the problem of nuclear fission;[45] one result of their successful endeavors was the manufacture of the atomic bomb, a weapon whose destructive power was incomparably greater than that of any hitherto in existence. On August 6 such a missile was dropped on Hiroshima; a single bomb destroyed half the city where it caused casualties in the order of 100,000, as well as a shudder of horror to run through the whole world. More immediately, this meant an incalculable magnification of American power; it also meant that in face of the literal possibility of physical obliteration Japan hastened to acknowledge her defeat, inevitable in any event. The final surrender took place on board the American battleship *Missouri*

[44] The end in Italy occurred at the same time, but not without having given rise to recriminations from the Russians who suspected the Western Allies of attempting to exclude them from that quarter.

[45] The problem did not date from the war, but the military possibilities of the release of atomic energy caused the American government to support a large program of research in the field. For practical reasons American and British resources were pooled and the actual work was done mainly in the United States. It is one of the unexpected, but not the least significant, consequences of Axis ideology that it resulted in much scientific talent being made available to its enemies. The leadership in the field of nuclear fission was to a considerable extent in the hands of exiles from Central Europe.

on September 2. Against all their enemies the Allies had achieved total victory; the fate of the world lay in their hands.[46]

III. The Diplomacy of the War

SHIFTING POSITIONS OF POWER

But who, precisely, were the Allies? As in the case of any war, some correlation inevitably exists between the contribution made to its prosecution and the weight carried in decisions of the wartime as well as of the peacemaking. One fact stands out quite clearly, namely that the burden of the war had been carried by three states, the United States, the Soviet Union, and Great Britain. Among these three Powers, however, substantial differences existed: the United States emerged from the war uninjured, in fact a beneficiary in the sense that the very war effort had acted as a stimulant to the rate of its economic growth and thus increased its potential; also the United States had sole possession of the atomic bomb. By contrast Britain had suffered great injury. Among the victors no injury could compare with that sustained by the Soviet Union, be it in terms of ravaged lands or of enormous casualties; in this respect the role of the Soviet Union in the war is also comparable to that of France in the earlier conflict, but by contrast with France after 1919, the recuperative capacity of the Soviet state, enhanced by the nature of its political system, was very great. For the longer term, partly because of their sheer dimensions and numbers, it appeared that two Powers, the United States and the Soviet Union, had emerged in a position that placed them in a category by themselves, outside the range of any others.

The United States is not a European Power and whether the Soviet Union is or is not has been argued; it is in any case on the fringes of Europe. Britain, too, is European with marked qualifications, not least in her own eyes. Though Britain was undoubtedly, during the war and at its end, a member in full standing of the Big Three, whether or not Britain would remain in the category of her two companions was an open question. The effect of all this, where Europe was concerned, was thus unique and unprecedented, for Europe was essentially at the mercy of forces

---

[46] The surrender of the Japanese forces in China was arranged on September 9 in Nanking with Generalissimo Chiang Kai-shek. Also, on August 8, the Soviet Union declared war on Japan and proceeded to invade Manchuria, thus acquiring a voice in the surrender arrangements.

that were largely extraneous to her. France had been in the war from the first, but the events of 1940 had had the effect of removing her from significant military participation in it. Nevertheless, by way of redressing the unbalanced situation of European representation, France was also admitted to the inner councils of the victors. Similarly, on the opposite side of the planet, Chiang Kai-shek's China, an active belligerent throughout, albeit not a very effective contributor to the final outcome, was, like France, admitted in the same group. Thus there emerged the Big Five, but the concept was partly fiction, possibly useful, of any sort of real equality within this inner group. If the British standing was not devoid of ambiguity, clearly both France and China held their formal positions by the courtesy of others.

This was not all. Apart from the factor of pure power, the French situation contained troublesome ambiguities that derived from the initial defeat, the events of 1942, the nature of the Vichy regime, the emergence of the Free French, and the confused process of the liberation. Italy likewise presented a complex situation; after the fall of Fascism in 1943 the new government had joined the Allies, under the ambiguous status of cobelligerent, while an Italian Social Republic, under German-liberated Mussolini, continued in the war on the German side. Similar complexities were present in the whole region of Central and Eastern Europe, from the Baltic to the Aegean. These circumstances largely derived from the course of the war itself, which is the reason why a brief account of it was given in the preceding pages. The various arrangements that were made among the Big Three, whether for purposes of adjusting their mutual direct relations, or with a view to planning for the future of others and of the world as a whole, were the background of the effort—mortgages on it if one will—to establish some sort of international order. To these, therefore, we must, if only briefly, turn back.

It has been indicated that, even before Pearl Harbor, the United States was becoming increasingly entangled with the belligerents: all aid to Britain short of war, Lend-Lease, the Atlantic Charter, the eligibility of the Soviet Union to Lend-Lease assistance, were the chief manifestations of this involvement. After Pearl Harbor there was no longer need for subterfuge, but every reason instead for the three Powers to organize and coördinate their efforts without reticence. As ever in a coalition, the solidity of it is in direct relation to the strength of the binder that the common threat constitutes; as the danger recedes the emphasis on mutual differences tends to reappear. There were differences between the United States and Great Britain, but these were relatively minor and never too difficult of adjustment; to a very large extent the two countries, endowed with common institutions, spoke in a real sense the same language. It was otherwise with the Soviet Union, operating under a political system far more akin to that of its totalitarian enemies, long confined to relative isolation, and dedicated to an ideology that forecast the demise of the systems under which its Allies operated. From the Soviet point of view the war was but an episode in the long record of inevitable conflict among imperialistic states; skillfully, at first it had allowed, even aided, others to clash among themselves, but had unwittingly found itself brutally removed from the enviable position of *tertius gaudens*. The Soviet Union, struggling for its very existence, could indeed for a time gladly welcome all aid, the British declaration of June, 1941, and the American $1 billion lend-lease credit of November. But long-standing distrust could not so easily be eradicated by a stroke of the pen; there was, therefore, throughout the conflict an element of reticence and mutual suspicion between the Soviet Union and the Western Powers, more particularly the fear on either side that the other might find accommodation with the enemy at its expense. This fundamental background must ever be borne in mind when considering the relations of the three chief participants in the coalition against the Axis and Japan.

Within two weeks of Pearl Harbor Churchill arrived in Washington where he remained three weeks, being joined by the Soviet Ambassador, Litvinov, in some of the discussions. From these consultations emerged, on January 1, 1942, the so-called Declaration of the United Nations, twenty-six states joined in war against the Axis. The Declaration was a broad statement of principle, similar to the Atlantic Charter;[47] more concretely, the United Nations undertook to use all their resources in the struggle and not to make separate peace. The purely military aspects of the war were examined and the world divided into zones of operation under distinct, but in each case unique, commands; it was also agreed that the main enemy was Germany but that the Western Allies were not in a position to launch a major attack against her. Of necessity, the main burden of the war had to be borne

[47] Freedom of religion was added.

for the time being by Russia. Her foreign minister, Molotov, visited London and Washington in May; while in the former city he signed a twenty-year treaty of alliance with Britain, looking to coöperation during the war and after and containing the provision that neither state would join a coalition directed against the other. In Washington he obtained some reassurance on the score of his most urgent plea, the opening of a second front in Europe in 1942.

But Western resources were not yet equal to such an undertaking. Churchill was decidedly opposed to it, as well as some of the American leaders, and after his visit to Washington in June preparations began in earnest for Operation Torch, the invasion of North Africa. Not surprisingly, this decision served to revive Russian suspicions, only partly allayed during Churchill's visit to Moscow in August, followed by that of Hopkins in September. Stalin complained and, conversely, doubts were entertained in the West over the possibility of Japanese mediation bringing about a Russo-German compromise. The success of the North African invasion softened Russian dissatisfaction for a time.

There had been repeated suggestions of a meeting between Stalin and Roosevelt, but, pretexting the urgency of operations in course on the Russian front, Stalin declined to join in the meeting of Roosevelt and Churchill at Casablanca at the beginning of January, 1943. The favorable course of the North African campaign, both in the West and in the East, and the turn of the tide on the Russian front opened up definitely brighter prospects for the Allies, and though victory and peace were still distant this had the effect of intensifying political and diplomatic activity, which was very intense during the year 1943. The purposes of the Casablanca meeting were mainly three: the future of Mediterranean operations, the French situation, and relations with the Soviet Union. The first of these was easily disposed of and led to the subsequent invasion of Italy mentioned before. The French situation, however, was a delicate and troublesome matter about which something may appropriately be said at this point.

THE PROBLEM OF FRANCE

The position of France after the defeat of 1940 may fairly be described as a passage through limbo. From the French point of view, and quite apart from ideological predilection, the issue was how best to defend French interest; this implied a judgment on the probable outcome of the war. If, as seemed not unreasonable in June, 1940, German arms were to be victorious, it would be expedient not to persist in a futile resistance that would merely invite additional reprisals; willing collaboration would be the more rewarding course. Laval was the exponent of this policy to which he became irrevocably committed; something might yet be saved from the wreckage, especially where Italian and Spanish ambitions were concerned, that Hitler alone was capable of arbitrating and minimizing. The best that could be said of such a policy was that it might be called realistic. Pétain was more cautious; after the meeting at Montoire and fair words about collaboration with Germany he dismissed Laval in December and adhered to what may be described as hedging.

From the point of view of the belligerents the problem was, as indicated before, how to annex as much of French resources as possible to their own purpose, or alternatively how to minimize the exploitation of them by the opponent. German policy toward France was unresolved and ambiguous, unable to come to a clear decision between the respective advantages of coercion and wooing. A similar dilemma faced Britain, sympathetic to the French plight, yet of necessity conditioned by the overriding fact of the war; the result was Mers-el-Kebir and Dakar, and an uneasy *modus vivendi*.[48] The Free French might be useful, yet were also a complication; their support at home was scanty and the French military in particular, though not enamored of Germany, maintained their allegiance to Pétain and his government. There was in addition some divergence between the United States and Britain on the score of how best to deal with the French situation. While diplomatic relations were broken between Vichy and London, there had been no occasion for a similar development between Vichy and Washington. America continued to be represented at Vichy and to deal with it on the basis of what has aptly been described as "our Vichy gamble." The German failure in the Battle of Britain, the attack on Russia, and the entrance of the United States in the war were all calculated to induce in France greater caution in associating herself with Germany whose prospects of victory were becoming ever more beclouded and tenuous; resistance at home began to develop and the prospects of the Free French to improve. German policy reacted to these developments with an assertion of greater harshness and

48 See above, pp. 556–557.

more rigid control; in April 1942 Pétain was induced to bring Laval again into his inner council.

The Anglo-American decision to proceed with Operation Torch gave renewed emphasis to the problem of France. The American view prevailed that the Free French should not be associated in it or even informed of its preparation; this decision was the result of the American estimate of the weakness of the Free French movement,[49] as the result of which opinion an attempt was made to enlist the support of General Weygand as leader of a revolt against Vichy.[50] The outcome was not a little confusion; when the Anglo-American forces arrived in North Africa on November 8 they met some armed resistance that was, however, neither intense nor prolonged. Admiral Darlan in Algiers ordered a cease fire and, propounding the theory that Pétain was no longer a free agent, entered into an agreement with the American command.

This move had important repercussions. Convinced of French treachery, Hitler decided upon the occupation of all France while Laval, summoned to Munich, refused to enter into a formal alliance with the Axis to which, however, he granted the use of Tunisian bases. Pétain was truly no longer a free agent; his protests against allied and German actions were futile gestures that had no influence on the course of events[51] and the Vichy regime virtually ceased to count in the story of the position of France toward the outside world.

But this, if it simplified, did not solve the French problem, which was therefore one of the main issues at the Casablanca meeting, for there were now two groups of French engaged in the struggle against the Axis—the initial Free French, or Gaullists, understandably incensed at having been kept out of the African operation, and a new group consisting of much of the empire that followed the leadership of Darlan. This ambiguous personage having been eliminated in December by the bullets of

[49] In December, 1941, some Free French naval units went to St. Pierre and Miquelon, whose allegiance to their cause they secured. The Vichy government naturally protested, and the episode produced considerable annoyance to the American government. Secretary Hull's derogatory reference to the "so-called Free French," needless to say, did little to improve relations with them.

[50] Weygand had been in command in North Africa until November, 1941, when he had to be recalled as the result of German distrust of his activity. An American representative met him in Nice in January, 1942, but failed to shake his obedience to Pétain.

[51] Formally, the Vichy regime continued to exist but in August, 1944, Pétain was forcibly taken to Germany.

a young Free French enthusiast, Roosevelt and Churchill contrived—or perhaps better compelled—a meeting of Generals de Gaulle and Giraud in Morocco.[52] Not until May, however, after protracted negotiations that tried the patience and the temper of all concerned, was a French Committee of National Liberation established in Algiers. Though a long internecine struggle continued within the Committee, some sort of French unity had been contrived that, nominally at least, may be said to have put France back into the war against the Axis.[53]

DIPLOMACY BY CONFERENCE

Russia's dissatisfaction was the other chief issue dealt with at Casablanca and an effort was made to allay her suspicion by subscribing to the total destruction of German and Japanese military power. The simple formula of unconditional surrender expressed this decision.[54] But Russian recriminations continued, chiefly over the delay in establishing a second front, and they led to some lively exchanges while nourishing the Western fear of possible Russian defection. One difficulty arose from Churchill's preference for action in the Balkans, for the British Prime Minister, for all his loyalty to the alliance, had fewer illusions than his American allies about Russian aims and behavior; as a consequence he was more alive to the importance of who would be in physical possession of what when the end came. A meeting of the foreign ministers in Moscow in October–November succeeded in allaying Russian fears through the definite setting of the following spring as the time when a second front would be established in France. It was also agreed that a European Consultative Commission would meet in London to elaborate a specific solution of the German problem, and it was finally decided that the three

[52] American distrust of the Free French was largely responsible for the attempt to find an alternate French leader in the person of General Giraud who, in the event, proved to have little following of any consequence.

[53] Eventually de Gaulle emerged in full control, the politically inexperienced Giraud being gradually evicted. In June, 1944, the Committee became the Provisional Government of the French Republic. Although relations with Vichy had meantime been severed, partly because of the difficult relations between Roosevelt and de Gaulle, the Provisional Government did not obtain formal recognition until October, 1944. At the Quebec Conference, in August, 1943, the Algiers Committee had been recognized as the administrative government of the French overseas territories that owed allegiance to it.

[54] The decision was also influenced by the memory of the situation which had developed after the First World War when much was made in Germany of the alleged breach of the Fourteen Points to which the Allies had committed themselves during the armistice negotiations.

heads of government, Roosevelt, Churchill, and Stalin, would at last meet together. At the request of Stalin the meeting would take place in Teheran.

One cause of Russian suspicion was the ease and closeness of relations between the English-speaking Powers. These did in fact have important discussions out of which emerged a large measure of agreement in regard to the shape of the future. This was the chief purport of the two-weeks visit that foreign minister Eden paid to Washington in March; the Western Allies would accept the incorporation into the Soviet Union of the three small Baltic states, of the portion of Poland east of the Curzon Line of 1920 fame, and of Bessarabia. It would indeed have been difficult to prevent the occupation of these territories by Russia or to dislodge the Russians from them thereafter. There was awkwardness, to be sure, in the fact that Britain had initially gone to war as a result of her guarantee of Poland's integrity; some compensation, however, could be offered Poland in the acquisition of East Prussia;[55] here was a good illustration of the effect of the necessities of war in prejudging the shape of its settlement. The principle of the dismemberment of Germany was likewise accepted in the course of these discussions, which also dealt with the Far East. The islands under Japanese mandate would pass to the United States in some form, but the Americans and British held divergent views on the future prospects of China as a Power, as well as on the more immediate issue of which French government to recognize.

The meeting two months later, in Washington again, attended by Churchill, dealt primarily with military matters though it was also agreed on this occasion that extraterritorial rights in China would be surrendered.[56] It was in June that Stalin made the interesting, but not too significant, gesture of dissolving the Comintern; for this made little difference in the relationship between the various Communist parties and the Muscovite center of control of them. Once more, in August at Quebec, the Western Powers met, attended this time by a Chinese representative. In

[55] Some indication of the state of Russo-Polish relations was given by Moscow's severance of relations with the Polish government-in-exile in London on April 27. This was followed within a few days by Stalin's somewhat ambiguous expression of the hope of friendly relations with a "strong, independent Poland." The meaning of "independent" in the Soviet vocabulary was to be clarified by subsequent events.

[56] As a result of this meeting negotiations were undertaken by Britain with Portugal that resulted in the grant of allied bases in the Azores.

addition to further military decisions—the creation of a South-east Asia command under Lord Louis Mountbatten—a declaration was drafted in regard to a future international organization that would continue, or supersede, the League of Nations.[57]

THE PROBLEM OF ITALY. This was the time when the political aspects of the Italian situation demanded attention. Mention has already been made of it[58] but something should be added. The poor Italian showing in the war has also been mentioned; by contrast with the Abyssinian episode, Italy's participation in the current conflict commanded a minimum of enthusiasm at home and led to a vicious circle of deficient morale and defeats, in a mutual and cumulative relationship of cause and effect. In these circumstances Italy became a complete dependent of Germany, even in the direction of military operations. Mussolini, who had taken over the direction of foreign affairs from Ciano in February, 1943, was in the unenviable position of having to beg for ever more assistance from his ally; ill and despondent he yet would not accept the view, increasingly held even in Fascist ranks, that a separate peace was Italy's only salvation. The evacuation of North Africa,[59] followed by the overrunning of Sicily now brought things to a head.

A long session of the Grand Council of Fascism on July 24— it had not met since December, 1939—found Mussolini opposed by nineteen of its twenty-eight members. In pursuance of prior arrangements, when Mussolini went to see the king the next day, he was informed of his dismissal and, upon leaving the meeting, was arrested. The earlier preservation of the monarchical institution served the purpose of effecting a momentarily smooth passage out of the Fascist episode, for hardly a finger was lifted in the country in support of the discredited system when Badoglio proclaimed three days later the dissolution of the Fascist party. There was instead an outburst of pent-up rejoicing over what was taken to mean the termination of the war. This failed to take into account the realities of the conflict. The new government wanted indeed to extricate the country from the struggle,

---

[57] The recall of the Russian ambassadors in Washington and London gave point to rumors of a rift, but the Moscow meeting of foreign ministers in October redressed the situation. It was during his American sojourn that Churchill, in a speech at Harvard University, made the suggestion of common Anglo-American citizenship, a proposal that met much the same response and fate as his earlier one of Anglo-French union.

[58] See above, pp. 572, 575.

[59] For the fate of the other Italian possession, see above, p. 553.

but the operation was a delicate one that could not help but be awkward and confused. Simultaneously, Badoglio publicly declared that Italy remained in the war while secretly he made approaches to the Allies, seeking to explain the necessity for the moment of playing a double game. It was a double game indeed and the bare-faced lying of the new foreign minister, Guariglia, proved not altogether convincing to the Germans, who nevertheless hesitated on what course to adopt. The Allies felt similar uncertainties and finally decided to insist on unconditional surrender; terms could be subsequently softened if Italy assisted in the war against Germany. Surrender terms were signed on September 3, not to be made public until the 8th in order to make possible the arrival of allied air-borne troops in Rome. The scheme miscarried for the Germans' suspicions had been sufficiently aroused to cause them to seize control of the capital, whence the king and the government managed to escape to Brindisi while the conclusion of the armistice was made public by General Eisenhower.

Great confusion ensued. What was left of the Italian military power had been effectively destroyed; the Germans took over the country, disarming Italian formations, and moved south from Rome to meet the advancing Allies. They also rescued Mussolini whom they set up as a puppet in the Italian Social Republic he established in the north.[60] The Germans used the occasion of Italy's collapse to bring the South Tyrol, Istria, and Trieste under their direct rule. An earnest of future complications could be seen in the growing activity of Yugoslav partisans operating with Russian support.[61] The issue of Italy's eastern frontier was to prove extremely difficult of resolution after the war.

THE TEHERAN CONFERENCE

Needless to say, the Italian collapse made an equally profound impression on both sides of the belligerent lines. The hopes of ultimate success to which it gave rise among the Allies were added

[60] They exacted revenge from the opposition in the Grand Council. The nineteen members who had voted against Mussolini were tried in Verona; five of them who were present, including Ciano, were executed. Mussolini himself came to an ignominious and gruesome end when he was captured by partisans while trying to escape to Switzerland at the time of the final collapse, on April 28, 1945.

[61] With the passing of time Yugoslav resistance came to be dominated by the Communists under the leadership of Tito (Josip Broz), with the consequence that a three-cornered struggle ensued involving the Axis and the two rival resistance movements. The legacy of this situation was a bitter intra-Yugoslav feud resolved by the eventual triumph of Tito after the war was ended.

reason for their effecting an understanding among themselves in regard to the shape of the peace. There was much business to transact when Roosevelt, Churchill, and Stalin met in Teheran on November 28. The fact of war, where Russia was concerned, had tended to reëmphasize the national over the ideological component and Russia was pursuing the traditional aims of Russian foreign policy, meaning protection from external attack and expansion toward warm and open waters. The contest between these Russian aims, ultimately translated into the desire for extension of territory, or at least of spheres of influence, and the contrary effort to limit the extent of this Russian wish for expansion was beginning to take concrete shape.

The role of personality must be borne in mind at this point for the power residing in the hands of three men, allowing for the varying extent of limitations imposed by the diverse nature of their respective milieus, was in any event enormous. It is not unfair to say that the Britisher and the Georgian had a more realistic and hard-headed approach to the fact of power, particularly in its international aspects, than the more dilettante American President. Roosevelt, not without justification, set high store by his ability to deal with people in general, relying on his personal charm, which could be considerable. Geniality was not beyond the ken of the Russian dictator, who made a not unfavorable impression on Roosevelt and who was judged by him accessible and not beyond the reach of reasonableness. Relations between Churchill and Roosevelt were generally easy and cordial, based on reciprocal liking and esteem; certainly the possibility never occurred to either that the other might find or even seek direct and one-sided accommodation with the enemy. But Britain was too dependent on American assistance and must, in the last analysis, defer to American power. Especially in the face of Russo-American agreement, Churchill must acquiesce.

Thus his favorite project of Balkan operations by the Western Powers was thwarted by determined Russian opposition, which America supported. The second front would be launched on the Atlantic shores alone. For the rest, no final decisions were made at Teheran in regard to Europe, but schemes were discussed for the destruction of German power, admitted by all to be the greatest danger, through the breakup of the German state into a number of fragments; these proposals were to be referred to a Consultative Commission for Europe. The Ruhr, the Saar, and the

THE SECOND WORLD WAR AND ITS IMMEDIATE AFTERMATH

Kiel Canal were all to be placed under international control. Also, Stalin indicated that the frontiers of Poland should extend in the west to the Oder. There was also discussion of the future organization of the United Nations, the central core of which was to consist, in Roosevelt's estimation, of the Big Four, the three at Teheran plus China.

THE MIDDLE EAST AND THE FAR EAST. Churchill's desire for operations in the Balkans did not stem from disagreement on the score of giving priority to the German danger, but rather from a sound realization, fully shared by Stalin, of the importance of the large but fragmented area of Central and Southeastern Europe. Churchill was well aware of the significance of the whole Mediterranean region, and beyond the Mediterranean of the entire Middle East, which this is a convenient occasion to bring up to date. During the whole duration of the war the Moslem world, from Egypt to Iran, was kept under allied control with relative ease; what issues arose there it proved possible to deal with without great difficulty, but all the while much ferment was seething under the surface that would later emerge into crises.

Until the landings in French North Africa in November, 1942, Egypt had been the only base of North African operations. The government of that country was in many respects more favorably inclined toward the Axis than toward its opponents, and the threat of penetration of the country by the Axis forces brought matters to a head at the beginning of that year. A British military demonstration in Cairo in February forced upon King Farouk a new ministry under Nahas Pasha, leader of the Wafd party. Nahas was hardly pro-British and kept demanding revision of the treaty of 1936 as well as evacuation of the Canal zone and incorporation of the Sudan. With his advent, however, and the military successes that began at El Alamein later in the year, an end was put effectively to the prospects of Axis intrigues in Egypt.

In Syria and Lebanon an awkward situation grew out of the French defeat. The French forces in the mandate remained loyal to the Vichy regime, but the permission granted by Vichy for the use of landing fields by German planes caused intervention in June, 1941, by combined British and Free French forces.[62] After some fighting Syria and Lebanon joined the Free French cause, but, later in the year, were given a promise of independence,

[62] On this episode, see above, p. 558 and note 22.

underwritten by General de Gaulle. The ambiguous position of the Free French made for dilatory implementation of promises; not until 1943 were elections held that resulted in a nationalist success. The reaction of the French authorities in the form of attempted suppression led to local disturbances and to strong Anglo-American pressure on the Free French Committee of National Liberation. In December the full transfer of power to Syrian and Lebanese governments was granted by the Free French, thereby in effect putting an end to the French mandate.[63]

In neighboring Palestine the British had been faced before the war with the makings of a seemingly insoluble dilemma made up of the irreconcilable wishes of Arabs and Jews. But like the Irish poser of 1914, the Palestinian one was put on ice for the duration; the Zionist opposition would not embarrass the British engaged in war against Nazi Germany. The Grand Mufti of Jerusalem, unhampered by any such considerations, would willingly collaborate with the Axis but had to flee, first to Iran, later to Germany.

His departure from Iran was caused by foreign intervention in that country where German influence had made substantial inroads during the thirties.[64] The ruler, Shah Riza Pahlevi, was not averse to this encroachment as a counter to the traditional dominance of British and Russian influence. Iran was one possible avenue through which assistance could be conveyed to Russia. In August, 1941, Iran was occupied by Russian and British forces who compelled the expulsion of German agents and the grant of facilities for transportation; simultaneously, the Shah was forced into retirement, to be replaced by his more amenable son. In January, 1942, Iran was in formal alliance with Britain and Russia and the following year joined in the war against Germany. By this time America, large supplier of Russian needs, was also involved in Iran. It was in the Iranian capital of Teheran that the Big Three chose to meet; to Iranian affairs they devoted little attention, save that they issued on December 1 a declaration asserting their intention to respect the country's territorial integrity and independence as well as that of continuing to give it economic

[63] A virtual British guarantee had been announced in November. This episode inserts itself in the long story of Anglo-French rivalry on the Near East; especially in the circumstances of French weakness at the time, it served to feed anti-British suspicion in France.

[64] By 1940–1941 Germany accounted for nearly half of Iran's foreign trade, her share of it having risen from less than 10 percent when Hitler came to power.

assistance. But, simultaneously, the old Anglo-Russian rivalry had reasserted itself; in the North the Russians seemed to be doing rather more than insuring the safety of lines of communication, dealing highhandedly with native no less than with supposedly allied authorities, while they also gave support to the Iranian pro-Communist Tudeh party. Competition became increasingly acute between the Russians and the Anglo-Americans[65] over the grant of oil concessions. The tension was kept under control by the necessities of the common war, but the bases were laid for complications after its termination.

As guardian of the Straits and because of her own military establishment, Turkey was the most important single unit in the Middle East. Turkey was neutral; her arrangements of 1939 with Britain and France had been largely nullified by the collapse of the latter country, while toward Russia she had long since returned to her traditional distrust. The British in particular would have liked to secure Turkish participation in the war with an eye on the perennial of Balkan operations. But the meeting in Cairo on their return from Teheran of Roosevelt and Churchill with the Turkish President, Inönü, and his foreign minister at the beginning of December could not overcome Turkish objections.[66] Turkey therefore never entered the war.

It thus appears from the brief foregoing sketch that the Allies, during the war, were able to control and use the Middle East for their purposes. The successes of their arms from 1942 helped to maintain stability and order, but it was also true that much of the area was a seething cauldron of unresolved issues and tensions. Their story belongs to the postwar period.

One more issue was dealt with in connection with the meeting at Teheran. On their way to that meeting Churchill and Roosevelt met Chiang Kai-shek in Cairo. There ensued the Declaration of Cairo of December 1 that proclaimed the common intention to reduce Japan to surrender; as punishment for her aggression Japan would have to restore all conquests, not only since the aggression of 1931, but also the acquisitions from the First World War and even the island of Formosa and Korea, this last to become an independent state. Russia, a nonbelligerent in the Far

---

[65] To a lesser degree the competition was also between American and British interests.

[66] Churchill had paid a visit to Turkey at the beginning of the year and Eden had met his Turkish counterpart shortly before Teheran.

East, did not participate in these arrangements, but was no less interested in Chinese and Japanese affairs. In China the war against Japan was complicated by the division of the country between the Nationalist government of Chiang Kai-shek and the Communists, who controlled substantial parts of the interior. An uneasy truce prevailed between the two factions which negotiations in 1943 and 1944 and even American efforts at mediation failed to resolve into unity. The Russian attitude may be described as one of cautious watchfulness; bound by her treaty of nonaggression with Japan of 1941, Russia's assistance to China was reduced to a minimum. The fact that in 1943 the Soviet press assumed a critical attitude toward Chiang Kai-shek was, in this quarter also, a prelude to later complications.[67]

THE LAST PHASE, 1944-1945

RUSSIA AND EASTERN EUROPE. The meeting at Teheran had taken place in a generally friendly atmosphere, and the great question of the future, the attitude of the Soviet Union toward others, seemed possible of resolution on the basis of reasonable coöperation, though optimism on that score was greater in American than in British quarters. It was only a question of time before Germany and Japan would have to surrender; the retreat of the Germans and of whatever satellites they had been able to involve with them against Russia was on the whole a steady one. Once it had been decided that the Western Allies would refrain from operations in the Balkans, the corollary followed that the occupation, or liberation, of Eastern and Central Europe would be a Russian task—or prerogative. This took place during 1944, and the manner in which Russia proceeded is of the highest significance. The Russian fear of aggression, of German aggression in particular, was both legitimate and understandable; from it derived the wish of reinsurance in the form of Russia's determination not to tolerate unfriendly governments along her borders. But the word "friendly" is capable of elastic interpretation, to say nothing of the possibility that a conflict might arise between friendship and independence. The governments of these bordering states had for the most part been highly suspicious of Russia, be it on national or on ideological grounds.

[67] In 1942 Chinese authority had been reasserted over Sinkiang which had, prior to that time, been subjected to considerable Russian penetration and influence, both economic and political.

Moreover, the status of these states in the war varied. Rumania, Hungary, and Finland were German satellites at war with Russia; Poland and Czechoslovakia had governments-in-exile and were, nominally at least, in the allied camp; so were Yugoslavia and Greece, while Bulgaria, at war with the Western Powers, was still at peace with Russia. Also, internal resistance movements were active in varying degrees in a number of these countries, but the degree to which these movements did or did not owe allegiance to the governments-in-exile was, in a number of instances, and again in varying degrees, a source of division and of potential future complications. Everywhere the Communists took a leading part, and often a highly effective one, in the resistance. The formal dissolution of the Comintern had had no effect on the degree of control that Moscow exercised over the various national Communist parties.

An indication of possible Russian intentions was already contained in Moscow's withdrawal of recognition from the Polish government-in-exile in April, 1943. It was in June, 1944, that the Russians in their steady advance reached the gates of Warsaw where they paused for some months.[68] In July they gave recognition to the Polish Committee of National Liberation, an authentically Polish resistance organization, but also an amenable Communist puppet established in Lublin. Czechoslovakia enjoyed the distinction of having been the first non-German victim of Nazi aggression; she was also the one Central European state whose relations with the Soviet Union had been amicable before the war. Ex-President Beneš, leader of the Czechs in exile, was highly favorable toward Russia, rather feeling that he had been betrayed by the West in 1938. He went to Moscow at the end of 1943 where he signed a new treaty of alliance, having received the assurance that Russia favored the reconstruction of his state within its pre-Munich frontiers.[69]

Finland, Rumania, and Hungary were in the clear category of enemies. The first of these, having reëntered the war with Ger-

[68] The approach of the Russians gave rise to the tragic episode of the rising in Warsaw which, left unassisted, was crushed by the Germans. The failure of the Russians to help Warsaw was the source of much subsequent controversy and recrimination. Likewise, the massacre of some 10,000 Polish officers in Katyn forest, claimed by the Russians to have been a Nazi deed, was believed by many Poles to have been a Russian operation.

[69] Beneš's willingness to believe the best of Russia made all the more disappointing to him the Russian-fostered separatist activity in Subcarpatho Ukraine in 1944.

man assistance, was compelled in September to sign a second armistice that confirmed the cession to Russia of the territories lost in the first war; she was also saddled with a $300,000,000 war indemnity. A similar punishment was inflicted on Rumania[70] when she, too, signed an armistice shortly after the entrance of the Russians in Bucharest at the beginning of the month; from her Russia recovered the acquisitions made in 1940, Bessarabia and Northern Bucovina. But there was compensation for Rumania, for the annulment of the second award of Vienna of August, 1940, enabled her to recover Transylvania from Hungary against whom the war was still in progress at this time. A Hungarian armistice was signed in January, 1945.

For some time Bulgaria had been seeking to extricate herself from the war, having sent for that purpose representatives to Cairo. Russia declared war upon her on September 6, a war that was a pure formality and lasted but some hours, but entitled Russia to be a party to the Bulgarian armistice finally signed in October. Like Poland, Yugoslavia had never joined the enemy; the resistance in Yugoslavia was vigorous, but, as mentioned before, was divided between the adherents of the government-in-exile and those, increasingly powerful and sponsored by Russia, led by the Communist Josip Broz, better known as Tito. The rival factions, instead of coöperating, fell out among themselves, making at times the country the scene of a three-cornered struggle. As Tito's effectiveness and stock rose, so correspondingly did the fortunes of the rival Mihailovitch decline, and the Western Allies, especially the British, tended to throw their support to the former. What this meant in effect was that Yugoslavia was the object of a contest, largely Anglo-Russian, for the purpose of delimiting the reach of the respective spheres of their influences. The United States at this time still showed relatively little sensitivity to the extension of the sphere of Russian control. In October Russian forces and partisans in combination liberated Belgrade. It was only a week earlier that the British had liberated Athens; in Greece they found themselves confronted with a situation comparable to the Yugoslav, virtual civil war within the larger war. By January they had managed to secure control, but the effect of all these developments was to lay the bases for future interallied differences; except for Greece, the smaller states of Eastern Europe were fall-

---

[70] Rumania and Finland had earlier broken relations with Germany. Theoretically, these armistices were concluded with the United Nations.

ing one by one under Russian domination as a consequence of the fact that their "liberation" was essentially the work of Soviet armies.

WESTERN EUROPE. Correspondingly, in the West, the presence of Anglo-American armies gave Britain and America a similar advantage, despite the pressure of powerful Communist elements in the resistance. While Italy was being slowly and painstakingly reconquered, virtually all of France was liberated in 1944. The case of France was in some ways a special one. Inevitably, the extent of French material assistance in the war had been small, not in a category with the contribution of either the United States, Britain, or Russia, for all that the French empire had been a valuable asset. The events of 1940 naturally caused the prospects of French power to be held in low esteem, but the political consideration was important of the future place of France in Europe. The three main architects of allied victory were all in varying degrees non-European; was not France, after all, likely to be the most useful cornerstone on which to base the reconstruction of Europe? To this consideration the British were the most sensitive and responsive, stressing the desirability of a strong and powerful France. But the United States and Russia were less disposed to give France a large voice. Not until October, 1944, was *de jure* recognition granted to the provisional government[71] established in Paris, and not until November was France associated as a member of the Consultative Commission for Europe. In large measure these results were accomplished as a consequence of British urgings.

On the French side it was only natural that every effort should be made to reassert the position and role of the country. Shorn of effective power as he was, General de Gaulle had deliberately and consistently let no occasion pass to assert and insist upon the rights of France, a position that often made him a trying and cantankerous partner, especially where the American President was concerned.[72] With the grant of formal recognition the pos-

---

[71] This was the result of the merger, in September, of representatives from the Algiers Committee and the internal resistance. General de Gaulle was leader of this Provisional Government, in which Georges Bidault, president of the National Council of Resistance, held the foreign ministry. De Gaulle hastened to state that elections for a National Assembly would be held with the shortest possible delay.

[72] Apart from the rigidity of a primarily military personality, this attitude was consciously adopted by de Gaulle as the best calculated to assert France's presence. With Churchill he had numerous difficulties but found a general ap-

sibility of a more independent policy was enhanced. Clearly France could not expect to regain in her own right a place of power commensurate with the American or Russian, but the very existence of these superpowers might enhance the possibility of assuming a role of leadership for the rest of Europe. More narrowly and immediately, might not France play a balancing role of mediation between the Western Allies and the Soviet Union?

With such ideas in mind de Gaulle and Bidault journeyed to Moscow in December, 1944. The result of their visit was the conclusion of a twenty-year alliance, comparable to the Anglo-Soviet treaty of 1942; reminiscent of the pre–First World War connection, the focus of the 1944 alliance was the German danger. But also, by contrast with 1892, the stress was now on disparity between French and Russian power. For all the stress on ideology, the Russian leaders were sensitive to little more than crude power, the number of divisions in being; they were not long in showing their lack of regard for French power and wishes, an attitude for the manifestation of which the Yalta conference soon provided occasion.

THE YALTA CONFERENCE AND THE END OF THE WAR IN EUROPE. This meeting, which took place in the Crimea from February 4 to 11, 1945, was made desirable by two things: the imminence of the end of hostilities and interallied divergences that it would be preferable to reconcile before that point was reached. Some differences there were between America and Britain, whether on the score of France or Italy[73] or elsewhere, but perhaps more importantly on how to deal with the underlying forces struggling for control, another aspect of which difference was the issue of Russian intentions. Though Roosevelt was more inclined than Churchill to put reliance in Stalin and his promises, concrete Russian actions, as in Poland, for instance, were inescapable cause for concern.

The German problem was foremost at Yalta, but no concrete arrangements were made on the score of either the dismember-

---

preciation of the soundness of his tactics; from Roosevelt he elicited mainly misunderstanding and irritation. De Gaulle remained immovable, as shown by his refusal to travel to Algiers in February, 1944, in order to meet Roosevelt on his way home from Yalta.

[73] Broadly speaking, Britain, or Churchill, tended to support the more conservative forces, in contrast with the American tendency to favor the elements of the Left. In the particular case of Italy, Secretary of State Stettinius supported Count Sforza, distrust of whom was publicly voiced by Churchill.

ment of the country or the extent of reparation, both principles being, however, accepted. Owing mainly to British urgings it was agreed to give France an equal voice in future German arrangements and she was also to share in the occupation of Germany, but the French Zone was to be carved out of what was to have been the American and the British shares. For Poland, Russia insisted on the Curzon Line as the Russo-Polish frontier; Poland could then be compensated from German territory in the West. On the troublesome issue of the rival governments of Poland, the most that could be done was the appointment of an Anglo-Russo-American commission that would see to the enlargement of the Lublin government through the adjunction of some representatives of the Polish government-in-exile in London.[74] Making use of the word "democratic" in widely different senses, without attempt to clarify the irreconcilable nature of these divergences, it was possible to agree, for Poland and for others, on the wording of a Declaration which pledged assistance to the liberated countries and support for the establishment in them of democratic governments issued from free elections. Support was pledged likewise for an international organization dedicated to the preservation of peace.[75]

At Yalta also Russia's intervention was sought in the Far Eastern war, the American expectation being at this time that the defeat of Japan, if ultimately foregone, would prove both lengthy and high in human cost. Russia agreed to declare war on Japan within three months of the German surrender, but exacted for this the pledge that she would recover the positions that she had lost as a consequence of her defeat by Japan in 1905. Taking Russian commitments at face value, President Roosevelt seems to have been satisfied with the results of the Yalta meeting, feeling that misunderstandings had been cleared up and harmony restored among the chief Allies.[76] He had been continuously in office for twelve years and had guided his country and much of

[74] Matters were not helped by the highhanded behavior of the Russians in Poland, either directly or through the amenable agency of the Lublin government. But all protests of the London Poles were unavailing to put an end to these arbitrary acts, trials, and deportations of Poles suspected of opposition to Russia.
[75] For this purpose a United Nations conference was to meet in San Francisco in April.
[76] The aftermath of the Yalta Conference has led in the United States to a heated controversy reminiscent of that associated with the events of Pearl Harbor.

the world through a time of unwonted stress; the sight of him at Yalta bespoke the strain that he had undergone. Within two months of his return, on April 12, 1945, he met sudden death from a cerebral hemorrhage, thereby leaving in his vacated post the American Vice-President, Harry S. Truman.

The change in American leadership could by this time have no effect on the military course of the war. The Rhine had been crossed in March, and from both East and West the Allies were moving to a junction which they effected on the Elbe on April 26. Berlin fell to the Russians, where their fury vented itself, and the Nazi state literally dissolved. With the signature of unconditional surrender at Rheims on May 8, confirmed the next day with Russian participation in Berlin, the German phase of the war was at an end; the entire country was under occupation, in accordance with previously agreed lines of respective demarcation and wholly at the mercy of its conquerors.

But peace was far from restored. In the most favorable of circumstances, and even if a common purpose and good will had moved all the great Allies, it would have taken time to unscramble the effects of nearly six years of war. Instead of this the task was vastly complicated by the appearance of wide divergences, mainly between the Anglo-American combination and the Russians. The latter were not slow in giving indications of their interpretation of the Yalta agreements. As early as February, Vishinsky went to Bucharest where the king had to submit to a brutal ultimatum that forced upon him a Communist-dominated Cabinet; this was a peculiar interpretation of free and friendly government, but American objections were of no avail.

Poland, original occasion of the whole war, constituted a particularly significant test of Soviet intentions and behavior. It proved extremely difficult to implement the decisions of Yalta in regard to her government in the face of Molotov's recalcitrance that direct appeals from Roosevelt and Churchill to Stalin could not overcome. In April the *de facto* provisional government signed a twenty-year treaty with Russia, but its representatives failed to gain recognition at the San Francisco conference where the United Nations was being organized.[77]

This last-mentioned meeting was the result of much prior prep-

[77] Not until June 23 was a Polish national government organized through the adjunction of five members of the London group to the Moscow-sponsored Lublin government.

aration and of the desire to avoid a repetition of the situation that had grown out of the First World War, when the incorporation of the Covenant of the League into the treaty of peace with Germany had resulted in the rejection of that instrument by the American Senate. The treaties of peace and the Charter of the new international organization would be wholly separate undertakings. From the meetings at Dumbarton Oaks and the Yalta Conference[78] the shape of the United Nations had emerged, very similar to that of the defunct League, but some issues were still unresolved when the San Francisco Conference met on April 25 to deliberate for two months. The somewhat preposterous Soviet claim that the sixteen Soviet Republics should be admitted as distinct entities had been resolved through the compromise reached at Yalta that would admit only three members of the Soviet Union, Russia proper, the Ukraine, and Byelorussia. Although the Big Three agreed on the veto for the permanent matters, full agreement on voting procedures was left to the meeting that it was decided to call in San Francisco of all states signatories of the United Nations Charter and of all those having declared war on Germany before March 1, 1945. The San Francisco meeting, while ending in agreement, did not pass without some additional friction between the United States and the Soviet Union.[79]

The war in Italy ended simultaneously with the German but through the separate surrender to the British Commander, a fact which aroused sharp Russian protests. Moreover, the Yugoslav forces of Tito succeeded in overrunning the whole region of Julian Venetia before the Western Allies were able to occupy all northern Italy within her 1939 frontiers. There ensued a delicate and tense situation, finally resolved by a compromise between Marshal Alexander and Tito: the Yugoslavs relinquished Trieste but remained in control of the bulk of the province. Here was another point of physical contact between the victors from the East and the West where their influences stood in rival and precarious balance.

---

[78] In September–October, 1944, at Dumbarton Oaks, an agreement was reached on the principal features of the future United Nations Organization in the course of meetings between the Americans and the British, first with the Russian, then with Chinese representatives.

[79] The admission of Argentina, which the United States supported and eventually secured, for reasons of its Latin-American policy, was the subject of heated controversy owing to the nature of the Argentine regime.

This deterioration of relations between the members of the victorious coalition led to the American effort at elucidation in the form of the mission of Harry Hopkins to Moscow in May–June, 1945. To the American grievances he found there corresponded Russian; Stalin was irritated by the admission of Argentina to the United Nations at San Francisco, he resented the abrupt American decision to terminate Lend-Lease deliveries, he objected to the presence of France on the Reparation Commission, and he suspected Western designs to reëstablish anti-Russian influence in Poland. Russia, according to him, was willing to enter the Far Eastern war in accordance with the Yalta agreement, that is, by August 8, but he required the prior Chinese acceptance of this same agreement in regard to Manchuria. These matters were to be considered at another meeting of the top leaders that would take place at Potsdam.

THE POTSDAM CONFERENCE AND THE END OF THE WAR WITH JAPAN. The Potsdam conference met on July 17 and concerned itself primarily with matters European. The mutual recriminations, Anglo-American complaints about the highhanded Russian behavior in Rumania and Bulgaria, where their own interests and representatives were being wholly disregarded, countered by Russian criticism of the Greek situation under British control, were left unresolved.[80] For the broader purpose of reëstablishing peace, here again the 1919 procedure was inverted; the relatively simpler problem of peace with the five satellites of Germany (Italy, Rumania, Bulgaria, Hungary, and Finland) would be dealt with first, leaving the more important and difficult case of Germany for later settlement. The drafting of the satellite treaties would be directed by a Council of Foreign Ministers, consisting of the Big Five, but in each case only those representatives of Powers signatories of the surrender would be participants; this had the effect of excluding France from a voice in Eastern European affairs, but the provision was made that in the matter of the Italian treaty she would be counted a signatory.

For Germany some general principles were stated that were to apply to her treatment in the initial stages of interallied control. Germany was to be wholly disarmed and demilitarized as well as

[80] The palliative was merely resorted to of setting up Anglo-Russian and Russo-American commissions of experts.

de-Nazified,[81] and in an effort to promote decentralization there was to be no central German government. Elaborate provisions were devised for the control of German industry and for enabling Russia to receive at once some share of reparation, from her own zone and to some degree from the others as well. No final decisions were made in regard to frontiers, but mortgages were issued in the form of an Anglo-American commitment to support the transfer of a part of East Prussia with Königsberg to Russia, while the territories east of the Oder-Neisse line were to be temporarily under Polish administration. A Russian effort to secure access to the Mediterranean through control of the Straits and the claim to Libyan trusteeship was not successfully advanced.[82] According to Secretary of State Byrnes, newly appointed to the post, the conference was a success; if so it was short-lived.

There remained to liquidate the war with Japan, the outcome of which was foregone, but the conclusion of which might be drawn out if Japanese resistance persisted. Unlike Hitler, the leaders of Japan were not bent on either total victory or destruction. A joint ultimatum demanding unconditional surrender, issued by the United States, Britain, and China on July 26, was rejected, but the atomic bomb dropped on Hiroshima on August 6, followed by another on Nagasaki on the 9th induced Japan to accept the ultimatum. Between these two events there came another, the Russian declaration of war against Japan on the 8th.[83] The only qualification granted Japan to unconditional surrender was the tacit acceptance of the Mikado's own position.

IV. Between War and Peace

THE WORLD IN 1945

There now remained the enormously complicated task of restoration of a world torn by six years of strife on a scale far more widespread than that of the First World War. The recurrence

[81] The undertaking to de-Nazify Germany led to the enactment of regulations for the abolition of Nazi legislation and the removal of individuals, to the supervision of education, and to the famous Nuremberg trials of war criminals.

[82] On July 25 the conference adjourned to await the outcome of the British election. The overwhelming victory of Labour resulted in the new Prime Minister, Attlee, and his foreign minister, Bevin, taking the place of Churchill and Eden for the rest of the Potsdam discussions. At Churchill's invitation Attlee had attended the first part of the conference as well.

[83] The treaty of neutrality of 1941 had been denounced by Russia in April and Russian forces had been gathering in the Far East.

of conflict within less than a quarter century, clear evidence of the failure to establish lasting peace in 1919, served to create in 1945 a climate wholly different from that of 1918. If victory was pleasant to the victors, its achievement was attended by a minimum of elation; unlike the 11th of November, V-E Day and V-J Day have not become dates for commemoration. It would have been difficult in 1945 to contend that the war was an unfortunate, avoidable accident and that the world could go back to the interrupted course of normality; few thought of 1939 as a time fondly remembered and the conditions of which they would like to restore. The climate of 1945 was far more realistic than that of 1918, but the problems now to be faced were no less. Also, they were vastly different.

The First World War had seen the collapse of four empires, the Russian, the German, the Austrian, and the Ottoman. Of these the last two were gone beyond hope of resurrection and to that extent the conflict had registered lasting results. But the main differences between the two postwar periods were two: the distribution of power and the relations among the victors. Twice in a generation German power had brought down the house of Europe and the issue of responsibility was far clearer in 1945 than on the earlier occasion. The responsible Nazi leadership—and the Japanese likewise—were branded war criminals to be tried for their crimes; in fact they were, but that aspect of things will not detain us here.[84] The distrust of Germany was deep and widespread and was to be rather more lasting than after the first war.

The peace of 1919 had been the work of the victorious coalition, mainly three Powers, the United States, Great Britain, and France, and of the three the weakest, France, had emerged as the chief upholder of the European structure. The effects of this unbalanced situation of power have been examined and their role explained as one of the chief causes of the failure of the earlier peace. The power situation in 1945 was closer to the long-term reality. The role of Britain in the second war is to a point comparable to that of France in the first; her contribution had been great, but as with France earlier, the cost of victory had been too great and the achievement of it had done Britain drastic injury. In terms of power, Britain, for all that she was counted one of

---

[84] While the magnitude of Nazi crimes is not debatable, an important precedent and a highly controversial issue were created by the retroactive action and by the fact that the victors set themselves up as judges of their defeated enemies.

the Big Three, was sharply demoted. By contrast with the First World War Russia had survived the conflict; injured indeed she had been, but the prospects for her, because of her very extent and physical nature, were of recovery in a way that Britain could not contemplate. By contrast again with the earlier conflict, the United States had found it necessary this time to carry much of the burden of actual military operations. But American power emerged in all respects enhanced rather than injured; American losses were relatively small, certainly compared to the Russian, and there had been in America no physical destruction but rather an acceleration and a vast expansion of economic capabilities, to the extent that many feared difficulty and depression in the return to peacetime operation; America had shown that she could have guns and butter at once.

In terms of power, therefore, the Second World War may be said to have had a clarifying effect: the United States and the Soviet Union emerged from it as superpowers in a category by themselves that far outdistanced all others. But here another factor intervened. The victors of 1919 had had a common ideology; they were all democratic states. Differences among them on the score of rival national interests indeed existed and led to serious clashes; nevertheless they shared in large degree a common outlook and spoke the same language. In 1945 the ideological conflict was deep among the victors; the fact that the necessities of war had induced Russia to a measure of coöperation and that the Russian military performance commanded much admiration and respect among the other Allies could not conceal for long the fundamental clash, evidences of which in the late stages of the war have been mentioned.

A further complication ensued. The nature of the Soviet system left control firmly in the hands of its directing group, especially of Stalin. But in America and Britain popular opinion and feelings could not, beyond a certain point, be disregarded. Churchill was ousted in 1945 in the midst of the Potsdam conference. To say nothing of the fifth columns that were in effect the Communist parties everywhere, there was in the West a favorable climate of opinion where Russia was concerned. One aspect of this response to popular feeling was the rapid dismantling of the American war machine: the war had been fought by America with a minimum of flag waving and elation; the thankless task accomplished, foolishly equating the termination of active fighting with the restoration of peace, the pressure to "bring the boys back home," a pressure that came from the boys themselves, their mothers, their sisters, and their Congressmen, could not be resisted.

But America was possessed and had for the moment the monopoly of that terrifying weapon, the atomic bomb, twice demonstrated in Japan. Thus a curious and unprecedented equilibrium was established between American atomic power and the huge armies that were the form of Russian power. In limited terms of interest that may be called national, Russia wanted security that she achieved through the effective control of large territories in Eastern Europe in which her armies were in actual occupation. But the Marxist book contained the assurance that all Europe, not to say the whole world, must eventually fall under the sway of its allegiance. The chaos of war and the misery of its immediate aftermath were highly suitable conditions for the propagation of political unrest; Communist parties were strong and were represented in the governments of both France and Italy. What if either or both of those countries could by ostensibly peaceful and legal means come to the point where they should elect to become Soviet Republics? This is the background against which the relations of the immediate postwar period must be seen. Matters were fluid and the outcome uncertain for some two years, when the hoped-for One World began to crystallize into Two. Before examining the manner in which this occurred, it will be convenient to consider briefly two other concrete developments: the United Nations organization and the treaties of peace with Germany's satellites.

INSTRUMENTS OF PEACE

THE UNITED NATIONS ORGANIZATION. Of the United Nations something has already been said.[85] The new international organization finally emerged at San Francisco in June, 1945, and came into formal existence in October when the Charter was ratified by twenty-nine states; when the first session met in London in January, 1946, fifty-one member states were present. The United Nations formally became heir to the League of Nations when the last Assembly of the latter, meeting in Geneva in April, endorsed the transfer of its assets and powers. The structure of the United Nations was very similar to that of the League, consisting of a General Assembly, a Security Council, and a Secretariat; there

[85] See above, p. 595.

was in addition an Economic and Social Council from which stemmed and depended a number of specialized agencies, such as the International Monetary Fund, the World Health Organization, the International Labor Organization, the Food and Agriculture Organization, the International Refugee Organization, the Educational, Scientific and Cultural Organization (UNESCO), and a number of others.

A Trusteeship Council perpetuated the concept of mandate, taking over still existing League mandates as well as new ones, such as the former Italian colonies. An International Court completed the roster of the five chief organs of the United Nations.

Like the former League Assembly, the General Assembly of the United Nations, consisting of all members, was essentially a deliberative and consultative body deprived of powers of decision. It fell to it, however, to elect the nonpermanent members of the Security Council as well as the membership of the Economic and Social Council, the Trusteeship Council, and the International Court. It would also decide upon the admission of new members and upon the exclusion of delinquent ones, upon recommendation of the Security Council.

This last body was the true repository of power, for out of its eleven members the five permanent ones enjoyed the right of the veto. If this was realistic recognition of the role of power, it was also admission of the fact that, beyond a certain point, power could not be made subject to the rule of law. A conflict involving a major Power or Powers could in the last analysis only be resolved through the time-honored methods of compromise and conciliation, or in the failure of these open conflict. Such a situation occurred at the very beginning over the issue of the nomination of the Secretary General, the choice falling eventually to the Norwegian Trygve Lie, a compromise candidate.[86]

Almost immediately the limitations of the United Nations became apparent, the chief obstacle to its successful operation stemming from the above-mentioned clash between irreconcilable ideologies. The charter members had been those who had declared war against Germany, but others could join the organization if accepted. Spain was a Fascist state that had only escaped involvement in the collapse of the Axis through a judicious adherence to

[86] The "working languages" of the United Nations were to be English and French, but there were five official languages, Russian, Spanish, and Chinese, in addition to the other two.

neutrality; but there was little love for Franco among the United Nations membership, some of which was even bent upon contriving the downfall of his regime; Franco survived, but Spain was placed beyond the pale of admission. There were other candidates in 1946, but only three, Afghanistan, Iceland, and Sweden, achieved membership, the others, Eire, Portugal, and Transjordan, being blackballed by Russia. During 1947 the Soviet Union and the United States blocked a number of each other's candidates. Thus, Germany's ex-satellites, even after the conclusion of peace with them, found themselves for a time excluded.

THE SATELLITE TREATIES OF PEACE.   At Potsdam the Council of Foreign Ministers had been charged with the task of proceeding with the drafting of treaties of peace with the five secondary enemies in Europe, Italy, Bulgaria, Rumania, Hungary, and Finland.[87] The negotiation of these treaties was laborious and extended from September, 1945, to the end of 1946, through a series of meetings in London, Paris, Moscow, and New York, in which at various times the foreign ministers, their delegates, and the Big Three themselves took part. At the long-drawn-out Peace Conference of Paris from July to October, 1946, where the defeated countries were allowed representation, the treaties were finally drafted, leaving the finishing touches to be put by the Four meeting in New York in connection with a session of the United Nations. The five treaties were signed in Paris on February 10, 1947; the effects of their provisions may be examined briefly.

The application of the principle of self-determination was supposed to be, as in 1919, the foremost consideration in the drawing of frontiers. To a considerable degree it was applied, with the consequence that the new map of Europe bore substantial resemblance to that of 1937. There were nevertheless notable alterations, mainly along the Soviet frontiers, but these last changes were, to a point at least, sustained by the facts of nationality. No appreciable changes occurred in the West where the 1939 frontier was reestablished between France and Germany;[88] from Italy France

---

[87] It was also decided at Potsdam to demand the evacuation of Tangier by Spain, who had taken over the International Zone in January, 1940. A special conference on Tangier met in Paris in August–September without the participation of Spain. Spain complied with the demand for evacuation, and a provisional regime was set up in Tangier, in which America and Russia both participated.

[88] Alsace had been incorporated into the Reich during the war. On the Saar, see below, pp. 618, 621, 634, 635, 643, 662.

EFFECTS OF WORLD WAR II
IN CENTRAL AND
EASTERN EUROPE

NORWAY

SWEDEN

FINLAND

KARELO
FINNISH
(S.S.R.)

DENMARK

Acquired
from
Germany

ESTONIAN
(S.S.R.)

LATVIAN
(S.S.R.)

LITHUANIAN
(S.S.R.)

EAST PRUSSIA

Danzig

EAST
GERMANY

WEST
GERMANY

POLAND

U. S. S. R.

WHITE
RUSSIAN
(S.S.R.)

CZECHOSLOVAKIA

UKRAINE
(S.S.R.)

BUKOVINA

SWITZER-
LAND

AUSTRIA

HUNGARY

SUB CARPATHIAN RUTHENIA

MOLDAVIAN
(S.S.R.)
(BESSARABIA)

Trieste

RUMANIA

ITALY

YUGOSLAVIA

BLACK
SEA

BULGARIA

ALBANIA

TURKEY

GREECE

To Yugoslavia and Bulgaria
Soviet Acquisitions
German losses
Sphere of Russian control
Frontiers of 1938
Frontiers of 1947

acquired some minute parcels of land, minor rectifications of the Alpine frontier. The Austrian claim to the South Tyrol was not entertained and the Austro-Italian frontier remained unchanged along the Brenner line, but the issue of Italy's eastern frontier proved extremely difficult of resolution for, behind the rival claims of Italy and Yugoslavia, stood the powerful influences of East and West. Eventually, a compromise was found, based on a French proposal, as the result of which Italy relinquished most of her post–First World War gains in the East; for Trieste, special bone of contention, the solution was adopted of creating a Free Territory, consisting of the city and a small surrounding area. Even then, it was impossible to agree on the choice of a governor and Trieste continued under Western allied occupation.[89] Albania, loosened from the Italian connection, regained full independence.

Hungary and Bulgaria were reduced to their pre-1938 frontiers, save that Bulgaria retained the Southern Dobruja. But if Rumania recovered Transylvania, the loss of Bessarabia and northern Bucovina to the Soviet Union, as first arranged in 1940, was confirmed. In the far north Finland had to yield to Russia the losses she had sustained during her first war and some additional territory that gave the Soviet Union a common frontier with Norway. Although peace was not established with Germany, the temporary arrangements that were made were treated as essentially final by her Eastern neighbors. Thus East Prussia was partitioned between Poland and the Soviet Union, which received the northern half of it with Königsberg, henceforth Kaliningrad; Poland established control of territory up to the Oder-Neisse line, including the port of Stettin, depriving Germany of the Silesian industrial complex with its capital, Breslau, renamed Wroclaw. This was compensation to Poland for the lands east of the Curzon Line retained by the Soviet Union, in which the small Baltic states also remained incorporated. Even supposedly friendly Czechoslovakia had to yield (in June, 1945) Subcarpatho Ruthenia to the Soviet Union. But for the rest Czechoslovakia was reconstituted within her pre-Munich frontiers. Austria, too, would be restored as before the *Anschluss*, but for the time, like Germany, she remained under the temporary regime of quadripartite occupation.

The post–First World War settlements had often been criticized

---

[89] This provisional situation lasted until the settlement of 1954 which did away with the Free Territory.

for their failure to adhere to the proclaimed canon of self-determination; it is true that, after 1919, substantial minorities subsisted,
especially among the new states of Central Europe. To a degree
this had been unavoidable, and at all events the peacemakers of
1919 had adhered to the humane principle that the land belongs
to the people and that frontiers therefore must be adapted to
their existing distribution. Things were now otherwise and the
ethnic map of Europe was brought into much closer agreement
with its political divisions through the simple, if crude and in-
humane, device of making the peoples fit the frontiers. In considerable measure this was retribution for the ruthless application
of Germany's racial vagaries. Germany in future would no longer
have an opportunity to set forth claims to lands because German
communities existed in them. Thus German nuclei scattered
throughout Central Europe were expelled, in particular those in
the Sudetenland. Going beyond this, much German population
was evicted from the ethnically German lands brought under
Polish rule, where their place was taken by Poles from the eastern
regions ceded to Russia. The merits of this superficially simple
solution of frontier problems may be tested in future.

There were also political clauses in the satellite treaties; following the 1919 pattern, these provided mainly for the limitation
of the armed forces of these states and for the payment of reparations. In the latter case, however, the lesson of the post–First
World War experiment was taken to heart and the obligations
imposed, if onerous, were of relatively brief duration and of manageable dimensions. For the successor states of the old Dual Monarchy the status of the Danube is of prime importance. The war
had resulted in the abolition of the international bodies that had
regulated the Danube which had, in effect, come under German
control. The situation was now reversed, Russia taking the place
of Germany. The conference that met in Belgrade in June, 1948,
in fulfillment of the decision of the Council of Foreign Ministers
of December, 1946, resulted in the *de facto* exclusion, despite
their protests, of Britain, France, and the United States from Danubian affairs. From Austria to its mouth the Danube was effectively under the exclusive control of Russia and what were by
that time her own satellites.

The arrangements that prevailed in the Far East will be no
more than mentioned in this treatment. Japan and China became
the concern and to a point the battleground of American and

Soviet influences; for the rest the bases were laid for the eventual liquidation of the French and Dutch positions in Asia. The British relinquishment of Burma and the new status granted India in the Commonwealth were likewise manifestations of the world-wide retreat of Europe's imperial position. In Africa, Italy's dream of empire came to an end beyond the hope of resurrection; while Abyssinia was restored to complete independence, following the precedent of the disposition of the German colonies after the First World War, the fate of the older Italian possessions of Eritrea, Somaliland, and Libya was to be dealt with by the United Nations.

TWO WORLDS INSTEAD OF ONE

THE PROBLEMS OF THE MIDDLE EAST.   Libya was Arab land and constituted for that reason one aspect of the larger problem of the Arab world as a whole, of which, owing to its proximity and close relation to Europe, brief mention at least must be made, especially as it was destined to become one of the sharper foci of antagonism between the East and the West. The problem of the Arab world has two aspects, the internal and that of its role as an object of contending external forces.

It was the First World War, with its consequent destruction of the Ottoman Empire, that had given the Arabs their opportunity. Thereafter the Arab world continued to struggle, in its separate units, for the achievement of total independence and made along that road substantial progress, the manifestations of which have been mentioned. The Arab world is vast, reaching from the Atlantic to the Persian Gulf; it is, in varying degrees, in a state of considerable political and economic backwardness, and what unity it possesses is largely of a cultural nature, the shared legacy of Islam. One step toward the achievement of unity, or at least of coördinated action, was the formal organization of the Arab League, whose charter was signed in Cairo in March, 1945, by the Prime Ministers and foreign ministers of six independent Arab lands.[90] The purpose of the League was the preservation of intra-Arab peace and the promotion of contacts and of common action *vis-à-vis* the outside world to the end, among others, of aiding the

[90] Yemen signed the Charter in May. The beginnings of the Arab League may be traced to 1936 with the conclusion of a treaty between Iraq and Saudi Arabia. Thereafter contacts and exchanges among the Arab states continued and multiplied, leading to the preparatory conference in Alexandria in 1944 where the bases were laid of the charter of the future League.

independence of those parts of the Arab world still deprived of it. It asserted that Palestine was Arab land.[91]

The Arab world, free or independent, is possessed of little power. Some of it is endowed with valuable resources, of which by far the most important consists of the largest known oil deposits in the world. Its geographical location, at the meeting point of three continents and athwart the communications between Europe and farther Asia, gives it in addition strategic significance. The British dream that seemed for a brief moment to have materialized in 1920 proved to have been an illusion, but British influence remained nevertheless the single most powerful external element in the Middle East, a fact which had been of the utmost usefulness during the Second World War. Britain was desirous of maintaining a preponderant position in the Arab world and, in 1941, Eden had expressed himself as favorable to Arab unity. The United States at the end of the war had no particular political interest in the Near East, but the Soviet state had inherited the tsarist policy in the area, especially at the Straits.

The war was the occasion for the final liquidation of France's political interest in the Levant, and this may also be regarded as a first success for the Arab League. In 1944 trouble had already broken out in Syria and Lebanon, whose suspicion of French promises of independence persisted; a virtual English ultimatum to de Gaulle put a stop to the fighting and was the prelude to British intervention. France had to promise to evacuate her forces, which she did in 1946, in face of the local insistence supported by American, British, and Russian pressure.

This French retreat was not a British gain, for Britain was having serious difficulties of her own in Egypt and in Palestine. The former country insisted on a revision of the treaty of 1936, demanding the complete evacuation of the British forces and the union of the Sudan with itself. Futile negotiations in 1946, broken off the next year, left both sides standing on their respective positions, the treaty of 1936 for Britain, for Egypt the denial of it.

In Palestine the inner contradictions of British policy were becoming ever more apparent, with the influx of Jews on the one hand and the general courting of the Arabs on the other. An

[91] The Arab states asserted the claim to Palestine as Arab land. While sympathizing with the plight of European Jews, the Arab countries stated that "nothing would be more arbitrary and unjust than to wish to settle the problem of European Jews through another injustice of which the Palestinian Arabs would be victim."

Anglo-American investigation in 1946, which resulted in the recommendation of the continuance of the British mandate and increased Jewish immigration, aroused Arab discontent. It was set
aside and another British plan proposed the division of the land
into four segments, but an attempt to bring together the various
interested parties in London was stillborn owing to the Jewish
refusal to attend the sessions of the conference. In desperation
Britain turned the problem over to the United Nations. After
investigation and report, followed by prolonged debate, the outcome was the adoption of a partition plan by a vote of 33 against
13 and 10 abstentions on November 27, 1947. The state of Israel
had thus received its charter; this was undoubtedly a great success
for the Zionist cause, but as much as a final solution of the thorny
problem it was a planting of dragon's teeth, owing to the steadfast
Arab refusal to recognize Israel.

A treaty with Iraq in 1948, similar to the 1930 agreement
which it superseded, was rejected by the latter country, leaving
Anglo-Iraqi relations in a condition of suspense. The artificial
creation that was Transjordan—a kingdom from 1946—alone
seemed to remain loyal to the British connection. Altogether,
British influence in the Middle East was fighting a retreating
action.

The Russian interest in the Middle East was most intense along
the Soviet borders, in Turkey and Iran, and also in Greece, about
which more presently. The various allied forces in Iran were
scheduled to evacuate the country within six months of the end
of the war. The Iranian request that the evacuation be anticipated
met a favorable British response, but Russia gave every indication
of having no intention of abiding by her commitment. Instead of
this, following a technique by this time familiar, the pro-Communist Tudeh party organized a revolt in Azerbaijan in August, 1945,
while Russian forces prevented the central government's police
from acting. After an election of the appropriate nature in such
circumstances, an autonomous Azerbaijani Republic was proclaimed in December. Russia having rejected an Anglo-American
proposal of evacuation by January 1, 1946, Iran appealed to the
United Nations whose impotence was reflected in the recommendation of direct Soviet-Iranian negotiations.

The passage of the terminal date for evacuation, March 2,
found the Russians still in Iran and evoked strong American, British, and Iranian protests. But unexpectedly, on March 26, the

Soviet Union declared its intention to withdraw. This in fact it did, and the year 1946 witnessed the complete restoration of the control of the central government over all Iran, including reincorporated Azerbaijan, and a corresponding setback for Communist influence in the country,[92] as well as for Soviet prestige in general.

It was as early as 1945, with the European war still unfinished, that Russia launched a strong diplomatic attack against Turkey. Her demands were two: territorial cession of the Armenian vilayets of Kars and Ardahan, and a revised status of the Straits that would place them under joint Russo-Turkish control. American proposals for a revision of the Convention of Montreux of 1936 in regard to the status of the Straits having proved unsatisfactory to Russia, the Turkish *status quo* was maintained in all respects, but Turkey was subjected to the strongest pressure, which the assurance of Anglo-American support helped her withstand.

The British were primarily responsible for the liberation of Greece and for the restoration of order in that country, a badly needed requirement owing to its bitter divisions; the local resistance movement, E.A.M., was under Communist control and operated as an arm of Russian influence, already established in neighboring Bulgaria. Greece and Greek politics thus became the battleground of rival Russian and Western—meaning at this point British—influences. A Communist regime in Greece would serve to outflank Turkey, on the eastern side of which the Azerbaijanian situation has been mentioned. Greece, Turkey, and Azerbaijan were thus in 1945–1946 three aspects of the same Russian policy aiming at southern expansion.

In Greece as in Iran the British acted with determination and vigor. In 1944, shortly after their arrival in Athens, they had already effectively put down an E.A.M.-organized revolt. Despite the failure to procure agreement among the various factions, elections were held in March, 1946, that resulted in a Monarchist victory, confirmed by a plebiscite in September. But this merely served as a signal for a recrudescence of civil war; the Communist forces in Greece were receiving from Yugoslavia and Bulgaria assistance that amounted to barely veiled intervention. A Greek

[92] As condition for their withdrawal the Russians demanded the dropping of the issue in the United Nations and the conclusion of a Russo-Iranian oil agreement, to obtain which they encouraged direct Iranian-Azerbaijani negotiations. The year 1946 continued as a troubled one in Iran, the British reacting strongly to a strike with political overtones against the Anglo-Iranian Oil Company.

appeal to the United Nations had the inconclusive effect of divergent reports turned in respectively by the pro- and anti-Communist members of the investigating commission that had been appointed. Greece in effect was largely prevented from falling under Communist control by the presence of British forces.

THE YEAR 1947: AMERICA ASSUMES THE LEADERSHIP OF THE WEST.   Greece was but one of the commitments with which Britain was saddled, and the totality of them amounted to a burden of such magnitude that the question had to be faced in London whether the means existed to sustain the load, and in the opposite event, which of them ought to be relinquished. It is a measure of the strain on Britain that, despite the importance of the Near East to her, she felt compelled to announce, in February, 1947, that she could no longer shoulder the responsibility of the defense of Greece. A Communist regime in Greece had great potential implications of which the United States had become conscious by this time; the outcome of the British renunciation was the taking over of the British responsibility in that quarter by the United States.

With little preparation or warning, on March 12 President Truman, addressing a joint session of Congress, requested from it an appropriation of $400,000,000 for immediate assistance to both Greece and Turkey for the purpose of preventing a repetition of what had happened to various states in Eastern Europe, brought under Russian control through the device of Communist or Communist-dominated governments. The request was granted the next month, thereby initiating a clearly defined new orientation of American policy. The Truman Doctrine was unmistakable notice to the world at large, and to the Soviet state in particular, that the United States would use its endeavors to contain further Russian expansion.

American-Soviet divergence and antagonism were becoming more sharply defined, and the problem of Germany, if less immediately urgent than that of Greece, provided much occasion for irreconcilable difference.[93] Differences on the score of Germany were mainly of two kinds, political and economic, and the conference of the foreign ministers that met in Moscow in March–

[93] From the beginning of the year the American and British Zones of occupation had been united into a single Bizone, to which the French Zone was added, but not until the end of the following year.

April was largely barren of concrete results. Anglo-American, Russian, and French views disagreed on the nature of the future political structure of Germany; where economic matters were concerned, America was aiding substantially the recovery of the shattered country, while Russia was primarily interested in extracting from it the maximum of value, seeking to obtain a voice in the control of the Ruhr, in which endeavor she failed. Like difficulties were encountered in Austria[94] and no effective progress could be made toward the conclusion of either a German or an Austrian treaty; the consequence was that both countries had to continue in the limbo of the provisional status of occupation.

There was little merit, from the American point of view, in subsidizing an unfriendly Russia through the indirect device of promoting German recovery. Yet this recovery was deemed essential lest material distress prove fertile ground for the prosperity of social and political unrest. Not Germany alone, but the other countries of Europe were going through a difficult period of reconstruction. In both France and Italy the Communists participated in the government while they commanded in elections between a quarter and a third of the popular vote. In both countries it appeared that the prospect was not wholly utopian that, even without resort to violence, they might succeed in obtaining control; the governments conducted, with skill and success on the whole, the delicate operation of preventing the securing of crucial Cabinet positions by Communist ministers. It was in May, 1947, that in France and in Italy the Communists were ousted from the government altogether, thus throwing a powerful party into unrestrained opposition.

This made it all the more important to bolster the economic recovery of Europe[95] and again an American response was forthcoming. In concrete terms, Europe was in need of financial assistance to enable her to fill the gap of a large adverse balance of trade while her own productive equipment was emerging from the ruins of war. Using the occasion of a speech at Harvard

[94] The Russians wanted the cession of Carinthia to Yugoslavia, which the Western Powers opposed, but the chief bone of contention was the definition of German assets, which had been assigned to Russia at Potsdam under the head of reparations.

[95] There were no difficulties in Britain from the existence of a large Communist party, but economic readjustment was proving very troublesome. The loan of $3,750,000,000 granted by the United States in December, 1945, and supplemented by a Canadian credit of $1,250,000,000, became exhausted within two years, much sooner than had been envisaged.

University in June, 1947, Secretary Marshall[96] launched the proposal out of which eventually grew the plan that bears his name:
a coördinated and long-range program of massive assistance that
would consider Europe as a whole in place of the series of more
or less effective *ad hoc* arrangements that had hitherto prevailed.
This was leadership calculated to capture the imagination. Some
preliminary negotiations led to the gathering in Paris in July of
sixteen countries and to the eventual formulation of the Marshall
Plan, which was to be one of the most successful financial operations of all time. The fact that the proposal may fairly be described as an unusually perceptive manifestation of enlightened
self-interest detracts not a whit from the generosity of the American initiative.

So important a scheme could not be devoid of political implications, and in the end it served to accentuate the cleavage between
the United States and the Soviet Union, more broadly between
East and West. The proposal was initially open to all, and the
Soviet response, if hedged with suspicion, was not at first unfavorable. But the requirements that Russia insisted upon caused her
shortly to exclude herself from the discussions, after which she
took the position that the scheme was merely a manifestation of
American imperialism in Europe and was of fundamentally anti-
Soviet intent.[97] To a degree, and in large part as the result of
Russia's own action, the scheme did have the effect of tying the
free countries of Europe to the United States and of emphasizing
the containment of Russia. The formal Russian answer was the
Cominform, organized in September, revived and revised version
of the Comintern that had been formally abolished in 1943. The
Soviet Union proclaimed the cleavage of the world into two
camps, the imperialist-capitalist under American guidance, the
other anti both, led by the Soviet Union. Leaving aside the adjectives, this was a correct description of fact: out of the war had
come two worlds, not one.

[96] His appointment in February, 1947, foreshadowed the initiation of a more
vigorous American policy. To the State Department General Marshall brought
the highly desirable attributes of competence, clarity of vision, and determination.
[97] Finland, with regret, and for "political and geographical reasons," declined
the invitation issued by Britain and France to all European countries to meet in
Paris on July 12 in order to discuss the American proposal. Czechoslovakia accepted the invitation, but, after the visit of her Communist Prime Minister to
Moscow, changed her mind. Other Communist governments took positions similar
to the Russian.

For the four foreign ministers to meet under such auspices may have seemed wholly futile. It was so indeed, but meet they did nevertheless in London in November–December, 1947. No understanding of any sort was possible and the conference turned into a test of the patience of the Western representatives and of the dogged persistence of the Russian delegate, Molotov, in the ability to keep on saying no. This London meeting may be seen as adequate registration of the developments of the year 1947. But if there were two worlds, highly antagonistic, the test of arms and the holocaust of war had been too recent an experience for all; the term "cold war," a twilight zone that was not war, nor yet peace, aptly describes the state of relations thereafter.

XV The Search for a New Equilibrium

That the Second World War conclusively sealed the demotion of Europe and her irrevocable displacement as a prime mover in world affairs may be regarded as an outcome both permanent and final; from that standpoint the conflict closed a chapter of which the First World War had been the introduction. But beyond this result—to be sure, of overwhelming significance—the record of the postwar period is too close upon us and we cannot discern in reliable fashion those lines in it that a more distant future, possessed of the advantage of perspective, will regard as its shaping directions. Events, crises, disputes, which at the time of their occurrence fill the horizon of significance, will in due course appear to have had relatively little importance, while conversely, in little-noticed happenings the seeds will be discovered of far more telling developments. But which is which we may not tell and time alone will reveal the true shape of the present. Our world is fast evolving, and the relationships of its component parts are numerous and tangled; the single trees obscure for us the woods. For these reasons, and allowing that the difference is of degree rather than kind, we may not hope to treat the recent past in the same fashion as we have the events of the long armistice, let alone those of the Napoleonic aftermath.

A mere chronological story of the last quarter of a century could be made very full and cluttered with the record of much activity. This mass of raw material would have little shape, and this concluding epilogue will be an attempt to disentangle—in avowedly tentative and provisional fashion—what at this writing seem to be developments and trends that may have lasting meaning. Because of its provisional nature this treatment will therefore be brief, attempting no more than to organize in some order and shape a mass of information that is at once incomplete and overwhelming.

Some things would seem established with reasonable clarity.

The just mentioned demotion of Europe is one; the corresponding emergence of the two superpowers, the United States and the Soviet Union, to a position far above that of any others and whose rivalry dominates the world scene, Europe included, is another facet of the same phenomenon. It might indeed be questioned whether it is still possible, or meaningful, to write of Europe alone. Nevertheless, the place of Europe has been such for so long, and Europe still contains such resources of numbers, industry, and skills, that at the very least it must be a prime coveted prize for others. In a more optimistic vein there have been those, in and outside of Europe, who have envisioned the possibility of the component parts of Europe, or some of them at least, in combination, organizing a new center of power, a Third Force, that could at least act as a balancing or mediating factor between the other two.[1] In any case Europe will continue to be the focus of the present treatment.

Equally clear is the contrast between the dominant climates of the two postwar periods of our time. If in 1919 it was possible to look upon the war just finished as an unfortunate accident, mere interruption in the course of nineteenth-century progress that could therefore simply be resumed, there were few in 1945 who thought in terms of merely restoring the *status quo ante bellum*. Put in other words, the fact of change is more generally faced and accepted; whether or not to an appointed end and purpose, the world does move; moreover it does so at an accelerating tempo, the very rate of which raises some unexpected questions.

By 1947, with the taking by the United States of firm positions, of which the Truman Doctrine and the Marshall Plan may be regarded as the outstanding manifestations, a measure of clarification had occurred and some short-lived illusions of the immediate postwar era were definitely shattered. The next five years may be seen as a period during which the initiative of decisions was in large measure in American hands. Provisionally, therefore, we may regard the postwar period as falling into three parts: first, a consolidation and a hardening of positions; then, a groping search for a *modus vivendi* based on the existing power balance. More recently, the two main blocs centered around the two superpowers have felt

[1] The possibility of Europe's emergence as a third major center of power illustrates the point that the importance of current happenings is difficult to appraise. China, too, has been knocking at the gates of recognition, but she has a considerable distance to travel before she reaches the American and the Russian levels.

the impact of centrifugal forces and the world has been engaged in the attempt to find a new equilibrium, the shape of which is currently in the making.

I. The Cold War

Fear is the counselor of much of human action; whether or not it is justified matters less than the fact of its existence. Between the United States and the Soviet Union it does not seem unfair to say that mutual fear and suspicion have been at the root of relations. Who is to blame for this may make an interesting subject of debate, one which, however, from our point of view is largely irrelevant and sterile; it may suffice to say that a vicious circle had been entered upon of action and counteraction, needless to say attended by much recrimination and vituperation, in keeping with the custom of our day. This last aspect of things also will not concern us here.

THE STRUGGLE OVER GERMANY

Whatever may be thought of the vagaries of the Nazi aberration, the German military performance in the Second World War had been unquestionably impressive. In 1945, far more than in 1919, there was agreement about the desirability of keeping German power destroyed. The role of the French fear of German power after the First World War has been examined in detail in earlier chapters; the former French view had gained wider support. But the context was now wholly different. For, if Russia shared the French fear, Bolshevik Russia had also always thought of the control of Germany as the key to that of all Europe. From the Russian point of view, therefore, the ideological weapon might be used to annex Germany; but, failing or pending this outcome, German power must not be restored. The initial arrangements for Germany had placed the entire country under the firm control of the victors. The classical approach of German foreign policy of enhancing its role by exploiting the differences between East and West could hardly be at first a relevant consideration since Germany had not even a government of her own, let alone the direction of her own policy. Germany could at most be a pawn whose assets might be of use to others.

Russia was in direct control, through occupation, of a substantial portion of Germany; indirectly, she may also be said to have

had a dominant voice in that portion of Germany, east of the
Oder-Neisse line, where Polish rule held sway. Russia was also interested in collecting reparation from Germany, her right to which
had been acknowledged by others. There had been much talk of
internationalizing the Ruhr, Germany's arsenal and the heart of her
industrial power.[2] But, after the events of 1947, it became increasingly difficult to operate the quadripartite arrangements for the
control of Germany, while the prospects of agreement on the terms
of a treaty of peace became ever more distant. Disagreement was
confirmed by the meeting of the Western Powers held in London
in February, 1948, to discuss the future of Germany. What hope—
or pretense—there still was that Russia might join in common arrangements was conclusively shattered with the breakdown of the
four-Power control in Berlin.[3] The London sessions were resumed
and the first bases were laid for the organization of a German government in the three Western Zones.

The institution in them of a new currency, the *Deutsche Mark*,
was cause for Russian protests, and by July 1 the breakdown in
Berlin was complete with the closing of the *Kommandantura*. The
next Russian move was an attempt, through the institution of arbitrary regulations, to isolate Berlin from contact with the West.
But the Berlin blockade provoked a bold and imaginative answer
for which America was mainly responsible; rejecting the idea of
breaking through the blockade by force, the experiment was undertaken of supplying West Berlin by air. The airlift was costly,
but its purpose was successfully achieved and the Russians on their
side, somewhat taken aback, recoiled from a cruder test of force.

It took a year to resolve the impasse.[4] Meanwhile, in April,
1949, agreement was reached in Washington by the three Western
Powers on the organization of their portion of Germany, despite
some opposition mainly of French source; this last was eventually

[2] There was also much discussion of the desirability of de-Nazifying and
democratizing Germany. Some individuals were tried and punished as war criminals, and the Nuremberg trials have created an interesting precedent, some of
the eventual consequences of which may prove unforeseen and surprising. The
attempt to teach the Germans democracy must be viewed as a well-meant enterprise, but one of questionable value. Such changes, if they are to have any substance, must come from within.

[3] After the March 20 meeting of the Interallied Control Council in Berlin,
abruptly ended by its chairman, Marshal Sokolovsky, all the quadripartite organs
in Berlin, save the *Kommandantura*, ceased to function.

[4] The issue of the Berlin blockade was taken up by the Security Council
of the United Nations in October, but the United Nations, in face of the Soviet
veto, had to abandon its mediating role.

overcome for, in contrast with the period of the early twenties, the French voice now carried little weight by comparison with the American and British.[5] In these circumstances a meeting of the Council of Foreign Ministers that took place in Paris in May–June, 1949, was essentially futile, though it was possible, as a result of direct Russo-American contacts before and after this meeting, to establish a new *modus vivendi* for Berlin that eventually reopened access to it from the West.

The airlift had been successful in defeating the Russian blockade. But the movement initiated by the Western Powers was not abandoned. The ultimate effect of the Washington agreements of April was the emergence of a German state, a federation of eleven *Länder* who approved the federal constitution, or fundamental law. Elections took place in August, and in September the first government of this new German state, the German Federal Republic, came into existence; Konrad Adenauer was its Chancellor, a position in which he remained until 1963.

The Russian reaction to these Western initiatives may be described as imitation; in their own zone, in October, a German People's Republic was proclaimed whose government was ostensibly endowed with extensive powers, even in the field of foreign relations. In appearance at least the Western Powers retained greater control over the Federal Republic through the Allied High Commission, but in effect the new western German state soon asserted itself; in November, the Petersberg agreements virually put an end to reparations and terminated the policy of dismantling the German industrial plant; any thoughts of internationalization of the Ruhr had by this time been abandoned.

From the German point of view these developments were two-edged. They were on the one hand a step toward the reintegration of Germany in the community of Europe, but it was rather two Germanies than one, for the events of 1949 had the effect of crystallizing the division of the country into two segments fated to exist under widely divergent rules and influences. Such a division of Germany would not be displeasing to either Russia or France, both fearful of a reunited, independent Germany, despite the universally professed devotion of all to the ideal of a reunited Ger-

---

[5] One difficulty was the problem of the Saar, which France was desirous of detaching from Germany and possibly incorporating. The issue of the Saar, until its final disposition ten years later, perpetually recurred and will be mentioned on various occasions. See below, *passim.*

many. The German people were not blind to this state of affairs; completely stunned at first by their defeat, they would begin to recover and reassert themselves. Given the circumstances, each German state was bound to profess the desire for reunion, but the fact that each would only entertain it on its own terms, considering the divergence of the German regimes, would in effect tend to accentuate the cleavage. The proposal by Bonn of all-German elections in 1950 was taken as a propaganda move rather than as a token of serious intent.

That many, especially in Europe, should remain suspicious of Germany was inevitable after the Nazi experience, and for the long term the thoughts and temper of the German people therefore remained of paramount importance. Had the experience of two wars and two defeats, the last complete and catastrophic beyond precedent, changed this temper? Had they genuinely espoused democracy and the desire for peace? These must remain unknowns that the future alone can elucidate, but one fact seemed to be of considerable significance, the German fear of becoming the battleground for others as Germany had been during the Thirty Years' War; if others would resort to violence, let it be *ohne mich*. This last factor was to become relevant when, in the continuing stalemate and hardening of positions, the effort took increasingly clearer shape to draw Germany into the Western alliance. Here was at once for Germany danger and opportunity. For Europe as a whole a new twist was given to the course of her development and to that aspect of things we may now turn.

THE INTEGRATION OF EUROPE

The fear of being the battleground for others was not confined to Germany alone. The various members of the European community, or some of them at least, in combination, might gather sufficient power to avoid being reduced to the mere role of pawns at the mercy of decisions that would be made by others; they might successfully defend themselves against attack, or alternatively have an important voice in the making of those decisions. The prime motivation of the older concept of European unity had been that of finding solutions for intra-European quarrels. When it came to creating a united Europe, the war thrust upon others by Nazi Germany naturally created an obstacle to her acceptance into an integrated whole; understandably, the alliances of the wartime and those concluded shortly after its termination, the Anglo-French

Treaty of Dunkirk of May, 1947, for instance, had had an anti-German focus.

The growing dissension between the two great rivals of the postwar period gave a new turn to the search for security. An Anglo-French proposal at the beginning of 1948 led, in May of that year, to the conclusion of the Treaty of Brussels, a fifty-year alliance in which the Benelux states joined Britain and France, and the main purpose of which was the provision of automatic assistance in the event of aggression against one of the participants in Europe. The treaty also envisaged the creation of a permanent Consultative Council.

Such a development was welcome from the American point of view and correspondingly objectionable to the Soviet Union. The movement for European integration or union had thus two aspects: one that may be regarded as primarily internal or European; the other, in considerable part of American inspiration, stressed the factor of European force to resist Russian encroachment. The two are distinct but inevitably overlap.

THE EUROPEAN MOVEMENT.   What is known as the European Movement, coördinating the various groups and associations long at work, may be said to have been formally launched with the meeting at The Hague in May, 1948, of a congress that gathered over eight hundred delegates from various European countries, simultaneously be it noted with the conclusion of the Brussels Pact, whose signers may be seen as constituting a kernel around which a larger Europe could unite in some form.

Much discussion at the governmental level went on after the Hague congress, in the course of which reappeared the usual British reluctance to assume too far-reaching commitments toward the Continent, for all that Churchill himself had been an enthusiastic sponsor of European union. However, in January, 1949, the Consultative Council of the Brussels Treaty Powers was able to produce a compromise solution between French and British proposals. In May the Statute of the Council of Europe was signed by these Powers, to which were joined the Scandinavian countries, Italy, and the Irish Republic. The Council was to consist of two organs: a committee of the foreign ministers, and a Consultative Assembly with purely deliberative functions.[6]

[6] There were to be in the Assembly eighteen members each for Britain, France, and Italy; six each for Belgium, the Netherlands, and Sweden; four each for Denmark, Eire, and Norway, and three for Luxembourg.

The Council of Europe held its first session in Strasbourg in August–September, 1949. Perhaps the most important issue that it debated was that of the admission of Germany, which was put off for the time being.[7] The Belgian foreign minister, Henri Spaak, elected President of the Council, was wholly right in stressing the need for patience and further study. As things turned out, whatever hopes centered around the Council of Europe were destined to be frustrated; it may by now be seen as one more milestone on the road to a distant goal, the desirability of whose achievement is on a par with the difficulties that attend its realization. Even among the advocates of a united Europe there were differences on how to proceed, some feeling that to attempt too much was to court failure and that more limited and gradual ambitions, at the purely economic level for instance, stood better prospects of success. One aspect of the difficulty was the by now traditional French fear of Germany, and this in turn took the form of a French desire for British participation lest otherwise Germany assume too large a place and influence in a united Europe. To the extent therefore that Britain was reluctant to join Europe, France tended correspondingly to be cautious and hesitant. Following, however, the conclusion in January, 1950, of an agreement between France and the Saar,[8] the next year Germany was admitted to the Council of Europe. But when this happened the significance of it was much reduced owing to the meagerness of the accomplishments of the movement for European union. Nevertheless this may also be seen as another step in the process of the recovery by Germany of her position in Europe. The control of the Western Powers over the Federal Republic was being steadily relaxed; in September, 1950, the Federal Republic had been allowed to reëstablish its own foreign office, a position that Chancellor Adenauer himself filled, and to resume diplomatic relations with all states.

Germany, any Germany, could clearly do no other than to seek to recover her place, and on the whole it may be said that the policy of Chancellor Adenauer—like that of Stresemann after the First World War—was based on achieving this aim by methods of conciliation that would allay the fears of others. France did not

[7] The issue of the Saar intruded at this point, France insisting that it have separate representation, a move clearly designed to stress its separation from Germany.

[8] France negotiated at this point a direct agreement with the Saar which aroused German feeling. The United States and Britain endeavored to mediate between France and Germany by supporting the former's policy of economic integration of the Saar, while taking the position that its ultimate disposition must wait the conclusion of a treaty of peace with Germany.

now possess the controlling power that she had held thirty years earlier, yet she too could not be coerced beyond a certain point. Dealing like Germany from a position of weakness, she might fare better through amenability—or dilatoriness—than by attempting a frontal opposition to the desires of American policy, for instance. She might also attempt to capitalize on her technical position as a victor in order to crystallize what advantages she might secure on that score.

THE SCHUMAN PLAN.   One way of doing this was by taking the initiative of certain actions. The so-called Schuman Plan may be seen as such an attempt, though this does not detract from its merit as a proposal genuinely intended to foster the integration of Europe in general and the solution of her age-old quarrels. It could also be seen as an alternative, more hopeful because more modest, to the perhaps overambitious Council of Europe.

The proposal[9] was launched in May, 1950, that looked to the integration of the French and German production of the two basic commodities, coal and steel. Out of it was to grow the European Coal and Steel Community which came into existence with the signature of the treaty of April 18, 1951. It joined six European states—France, Germany, Italy, and the Benelux group—and consisted of four organs: the High Authority, empowered to make decisions and recommendations; the Council of Ministers, made up of delegates of the governments; the Assembly, in which the members were represented on a proportional basis, and which controls the High Authority; and a Court of Justice.

The European Coal and Steel Community must still be regarded as an experiment; highly involved and technical, it may be said, however, to have been of greater significance than the Council of Europe. It holds in addition the possibility of serving as a model for other similar organizations of a concrete and limited nature. The Schuman Plan, though primarily an economic device, could not be devoid of important political implications; the "scrambling" of the production of such basic commodities as coal and steel could serve to impede the resort to their use for warlike purposes by the individual members of the community. Also, to a degree, the powers of the High Authority entailed a *de facto* surrender of a measure of sovereignty.

---

[9] Much of the credit for the orgnization of the Coal and Steel Community goes to Jean Monnet who became first president of the High Authority.

The Schuman scheme was highly welcomed by the United States where any step in the direction of European integration was encouraged. Britain, under a Labour government at the time, could not see her way to abandoning any of her sovereignty and refused to participate in the Paris meeting of June, 1950, where the first discussion of the Schuman Plan took place. Not surprisingly, the scheme was regarded as inimical by the Soviet Union.

THE ATLANTIC ALLIANCE. The Schuman Plan was only one of various developments that provoked an unfriendly Russian reaction. The economic and political integration of Europe could be expected to be a long-term development of relatively small immediate effect; it might be otherwise with the revival of her military power. In the immediate aftermath of the war there could be no question that priority must go to economic reconstruction. Europe went through a difficult passage, especially from 1945 to 1947, but, American aid assisting, made on the whole a remarkable economic recovery. The Marshall Plan has been mentioned and the refusal to participate in it by Russia and by the states where Russian influence was dominant. The Marshall Plan itself thus became a contributor to the widening rift between East and West, more concretely between the United States and the Soviet Union. With the ousting of the Communists from the government in both France and Italy in 1947 and the episode of the Berlin blockade in 1948 tension was high in that year. America still enjoyed the monopoly of atomic weapons, but that privileged position would in all likelihood not be of very long duration.[10] The reconstruction of armed power in that part of Europe free of Russian control was, from the American point of view, desirable; with the signature of the Brussels Treaty the path was open to the coördination of European arrangements with American. Discussion of this possibility had in fact preceded the conclusion of the Brussels Pact and it continued during the rest of the year.[11] It led to the signature in Washington in April

[10] The first Russian atomic explosion took place in September, 1949, rather sooner than had been expected. The significance of it was very considerable, for the disappearance of the American advantage in the monopoly of atomic weapons altered the balance of power and the calculations that were based upon it. It was one reason for placing stress again on ground forces and conventional arms, of which Russia was well provided.

[11] In view of the traditional tendency of American foreign policy, considerable importance attaches to the adoption by the Senate of the Vandenberg Resolution, in June, 1948, which authorized the conclusion of alliances outside the American continent in peacetime.

624 A DIPLOMATIC HISTORY OF EUROPE SINCE THE CONGRESS OF VIENNA

of the Atlantic Pact. The North Atlantic Treaty Organization is somewhat loosely labeled for, in addition to the initial kernel of the Brussels Powers, plus the United States and Canada, it joined in the common alliance wholly Mediterranean Italy as well as the Atlantic states of Norway, Denmark, Iceland, and Portugal, these having accepted the invitation to join extended to them in March.

The Atlantic Pact was a military alliance of the classical type for the common defense of its members who professed their peaceful intent. Like the French alliances of the 1920's its avowed purpose was the strengthening of peace; however, the declared intention of using force in the event of aggression, if it could be presented as conforming with the intent of the United Nations, also betokened doubt of the ability of the larger organization to act with adequate effectiveness or promptitude. The similarity with the role of the League is obvious; the issue has not been resolved whether regional alliances tend to enhance or detract from the function of the world organization. Allowing the authenticity of the defensive intent, that the Atlantic Pact was an instrument designed for Russian containment is clear. That it should have provoked Russian objections was no less than could be expected; these were in fact forthcoming in the form of a Soviet memorandum—the text of the treaty had been made public even before its signature—at the end of March. These objections had no effect though the Russian contention was cogent that raised the issue of the consistency of the new alliance with the existing ones in which Russia was a participant.

In the circumstances the American role in the alliance was bound to be overwhelming. The signature of the treaty was in fact immediately followed by a request for American military aid by the Brussels Treaty Powers. This was approved in October by the American Congress, spurred on by the announcement of the first Soviet atomic explosion the preceding month.[12] Gradually, the mechanism of the alliance took shape, beginning with the decision, taken in London in May, 1950, at a meeting of the twelve countries involved: committees of finance ministers and of defense ministers —these last assisted by a committee of chiefs-of-staff—were set up

[12] The Atlantic Pact was but one aspect of the American policy of containment of Russian expansion, the possibilities of which in Asia were of no less concern to the United States. The new program of military assistance also raised the issue for the United States of the respective allocations for that purpose and for the continued support of the economic recovery of Europe.

under the direction of the permanent Council of Foreign Ministers. For military purposes a Standing Group, consisting of the United States, Britain, and France, would sit in Washington, and the theater of operations was divided into five zones: United States–Canada, North Atlantic, Northern Europe, Western Europe, Southern Europe and Western Mediterranean.

Another meeting in December in Brussels designated General Eisenhower, of World War II fame, as supreme commander of the organization whose military headquarters came to be established at Rocquencourt in France. The details of the further evolution of the North Atlantic Treaty Organization, the twelve and the three "wise men," set up in 1951, need not be dwelt upon at length, but some aspects and implications of NATO must be considered.

In broad terms it may be said that there was some difference between the European and the American views of the arrangement. In the eyes of the former the guarantee of American power was indeed welcome, but there was also fear lest the increasing rigidity of alignments magnify the danger of conflict, and there were even those who looked askance at the too close integration of Europe with the United States; the desire not to become a battleground was understandably strong among Europeans who found little cause for cheer in the prospect of eventual liberation that would liberate little more than a cemetery. In some cases this went the length of espousing a wholly neutralist position. Even among those who realistically felt that Europe lacked the power to pursue an effective policy of neutrality the tendency was to make use of the strength of the newly created alliance for the purpose of reaching some *modus vivendi* with the Soviet Union. This was indeed ostensibly the American position as well, to contain Russia first by convincing her that she might not with impunity attempt further expansion, then to approach her from a position of strength in order to achieve equilibrium. But, understandably also, there was, in some American quarters at least, less reluctance to envisage the possibility of open conflict and a tendency to look upon the European allies as mere additions to American strength and upon European lands as useful advance bases of defense or, if need be, attack. Thus there was in Europe fear that America might be unduly rash, intransigeant, or impatient, and the feeling therefore that she, too, must be at times restrained; more concretely, the tendency was for the Europeans to "drag their feet" in the matter of implementing the re-creation of their armed forces to which they stood committed,[13] while America persistently urged the pursuit of European rearmament. Thus, for all the general agreement on broad purpose, there were stresses and strains within NATO and some underlying mutual suspicions among its members.

If the building of armed strength was essential to the containment of Russia, the more such strength existed the better. Thus two questions were raised. One was the enlargement of the alliance by extending it to include Greece and Turkey, to the assistance of which and to the preservation of whose independence America had for some time been committed. Though such a step would be straining the usually accepted geographic definition of the Atlantic Ocean, there was logic in it. After the meetings in Rome and in Lisbon of the Atlantic Council at the beginning of 1952 both countries were invited to join the North Atlantic Treaty Organization.

The other matter was more delicate; it stemmed from the desire to enlarge the available military force of Europe. In the search for possible additional divisions the thought must inevitably occur that a German contingent might be added to others, a consideration that could further be strengthened by the argument that Germans could be expected to contribute to their own defense, instead of leaving it entirely in the hands of others, American, British, and French. Logically, the proposal was of American origin, but that the prospect of a rearmed Germany should disturb many Europeans, on whichever side of the Iron Curtain they might happen to be, needs no explaining. Among the NATO Powers it might be expected that France would be the one to voice the strongest reservations. The discussions that centered around the organization of the European Defense Community were to be protracted; they occupied much of the diplomatic activity of the following years. For reasons of chronology it will be best to deal with them subsequently and to bring up to date first some other aspects of our story.

THE RUSSIAN REACTION

That story up to this point has largely been centered on the actions of the Western states. But Russia was not idle during the

[13] There was also, in European eyes, the important consideration that too great a stress on rearmament might jeopardize the still incomplete recovery of European economies; alternatively, how much rearmament could the European economies support? Needless to say, the Communist parties in the West were strenuously opposed to the Atlantic alliance and to rearmament.

years from 1947 to 1952 and something must be said of her activity. In general terms it may be said that the initiative of action in this period belonged to the West and that Russian moves were in the nature of reactions to these Western initiatives. But it is equally true that in large measure, especially where America was concerned, this situation was itself a reaction to the manner in which the Soviet Union had acted immediately after the war. As indicated earlier, the formulation of the Truman Doctrine may be regarded as the turning point in the orientation of Western, more specifically American, policy.

The episode of the Berlin blockade has been mentioned as well as the highland manner in which the Soviet Union interpreted "independence" for the section of Europe that her forces occupied.[14] Technically, these occupations were justified by the fact that, pending the conclusion of treaties of peace with Germany and Austria, the Russian army must maintain lines of communication with its forces of occupation in these two states. But this condition was in turn an inducement to delay the conclusion of those treaties, a situation particularly clear in the Austrian case where the remaining points of difference were of little substance.

Among the smaller states of Central Eastern Europe two had a special place and role. Owing to her long, and in that region unique, record of friendship with the Soviet Union, Czechoslovakia might, and in fact did, hope to serve as linking bridge between East and West. The Russians had used a relatively light hand in Czechoslovakia, which enjoyed the distinction of having the largest authentic (meaning freely given) Communist vote of any country —some 38 percent in the election of 1946. The initial Czech acceptance, then refusal, to participate in the Marshall Plan negotiations seems to have been a turning point. In February, 1948, the aged, ailing, and disillusioned President Beneš yielded to Communist pressure in a manner reminiscent of that in which Hacha had yielded to the Nazis in 1939, and a nearly all-Communist government was constituted. The reality was clear, for all that, ostensibly, this was a purely internal development, which made discussion of

[14] Allowance must be made for the misunderstanding that grew out of divergent interpretations of independence and free elections. Given the nature of the Soviet milieu and the manner of its operation, there was logic from the Russian point of view in misreading these terms into Western acquiescence to an unqualified free hand. To what extent America particularly was authentically deceived, or deceived herself, in underwriting these arrangements remains a debatable question.

the matter in the Security Council futile. Czechoslovakia was being "integrated" (*gleichgeschaltet* used to be the word) into the Soviet orbit, and the connecting link is strong that runs through the Prague coup, the Berlin blockade, and the opening negotiations of the Atlantic alliance.

THE CASE OF YUGOSLAVIA. The Czech coup was but a move in the larger policy of closer integration of the whole East Central European domain into the Soviet orbit, the aspects of which integration were economic no less than political.[15] Soviet behavior may be described as heavy-handed and showing undue lack of sensitivity in its dealings with peoples with traditions of distinct national consciousness and in some ways more advanced than the Russians themselves. The presence of Russian forces was therefore an essential factor in maintaining allegiance to the Soviet Union of states where native communism was often weak.

Yugoslavia, after a bitter internecine struggle, had emerged under Communist control, but this control was native, led by the energetic Tito. Save for Albania, Yugoslavia was the only country with a Communist regime but no Soviet forces in occupation. Tito had been on friendly terms with Russia, but some friction began to develop in the spring of 1948 owing to the extent, manner, and clumsiness of the attempted control by Moscow. The outcome was an open break, the first manifestation of which was the condemnation of Yugoslav deviation at the meeting of the Cominform which the Yugoslavs did not attend. This was in June, 1948.

Yugoslavia is a small country, but the nature of the Communist ideology and the insistence in the Communist world on discipline and unquestioning obedience to the writ of the Kremlin gave this affair significance far greater than the mere power of Yugoslavia would have ordinarily warranted. It may be best understood in terms of the significance of heresies in the Church. Muscovite fulminations had no effect in shaking the hold of Tito over his domestic following, while they tended, on national grounds, to rally behind him the support of elements in the country that communism would normally alienate. For the rest, agreements with the Western countries enabled Yugoslavia to surmount economic

[15] In September, 1947, the Cominform was organized, partly by way of counter to the Marshall Plan. It was essentially a revived Comintern, ostensibly designed to insure coördination among the Communist states. In 1949 a Council for Mutual Economic Aid, reminiscent of the Marshall Plan, was also organized among these same countries.

difficulties that might otherwise have proved fatal. Despite all means of pressure short of war by the members of the Cominform, and the accompaniment of lusty mutual vituperation, the Yugoslav heresy survived to challenge successfully the Muscovite claim to the sole and exclusive possession of the Marxist orthodoxy. Yugoslavia, however, showed no signs of renouncing that gospel or of aligning herself with the West;[16] the possibility that she might join the Atlantic alliance was not pursued very far. This episode, a result of Tito's determination and skill, as well as of the suppleness of the West in exploiting an unexpected opportunity with moderation, was a serious setback for the Soviet Union.

It was all the more reason for tightening Soviet control over the rest of Eastern Europe. Religious persecution was one aspect of this endeavor, of which the arrest, followed by the trial and sentence to life imprisonment, of Cardinal Mindszenty in Hungary at the beginning of 1949 was the most sensational single manifestation. Beyond the elimination of opposition, the tightening of party and Russian control led to the repetition in the satellite countries of the phenomenon that had appeared in Russia herself on earlier occasions. Bulgaria, Hungary, Poland, Rumania, even Albania, saw their existing leaderships accused of a variety of treasonable crimes, commonly charged to Western or Titoist collusion, and the displacement of them by other, presumably more amenable, puppets. Whether this betokened greater Soviet strength or weakness was not clear at the time, but this tightening of controls by Moscow was accompanied by growing tension between East and West.

Nevertheless, and to repeat, it may be said that this period was one that registered success for the policy of Russian containment. This did not mean the abandonment by the Soviet Union of her ultimate aims or beliefs, but, more immediately, as on past occasions when Russia had met successful resistance in one direction, she focused her attention on another quarter. Far Eastern developments were suitable to this change of emphasis; they will be treated here primarily with an eye to their effects on the European scene.

THE KOREAN WAR

Of the course of Chinese events it will suffice to say that steady and continued disintegration was the lot of the Kuomintang forces

---

[16] In the United Nations, for instance, the Yugoslav vote was usually cast with those of the Communist bloc. It was in June, 1948, that the Danube Conference met in Belgrade; see above, p. 605.

of Chiang Kai-shek, accompanied by corresponding success of the Communists led by Mao Tse-tung. The former finally took refuge on the island of Formosa, and by the end of 1949 the entire mainland was under Communist control, the new regime, the People's Republic of China, being recognized by the Soviet Union, its satellites, and some other states.[17]

Meanwhile, in adjacent Korea, a situation had developed that was in some respects reminiscent of the German stalemate. After the failure of the Russo-American commission to arrange country-wide elections, there emerged in 1948 two separate units: a Republic of Korea south of the 38th parallel, and a People's Republic of Korea north of that line; both states were denied admission to the United Nations owing to the exercise of respective American and Russian vetoes. In the summer of 1949, following upon the termination of military government, American occupation forces were withdrawn from South Korea.

Despite warnings of local origin during the first half of 1950, there was surprise in America and the West when the news came on June 25 of the crossing of the 38th parallel by North Korean forces. However, the American reaction was swift; asking for an immediate convocation of the Security Council, the American government obtained in it the passage of a resolution condemning North Korean aggression.[18] Of equal, or greater, importance was the immediate decision by President Truman to furnish armed assistance to the Republic of Korea, while the action of the Security Council maintained the international character of the operation. In actual fact, while a number of states participated in it in at least token fashion, the overwhelming burden of military operations was carried by American forces. What precisely may have been the Russian role in precipitating the Korean War has been much debated; naturally, Russia and her satellites voiced violent protest

[17] If there was little prospect that Chiang Kai-shek could reconquer the mainland, the question was raised of the representation of China in the United Nations, a matter of special importance owing to the possession of the veto by China. Following a policy similar to that pursued after the Bolshevik revolution of 1917, the United States refused to recognize Communist China, and Nationalist China continued, largely as a result of the American attitude, to represent China in the United Nations. This patent fiction has even been a source of difference between the United States and some of its allies.

[18] The fact that the Russian delegate was currently boycotting the sessions of the Security Council eliminated the possibility of a Russian veto on this occasion.

against the illegality of the alleged American-led "aggression." This was of no avail, and the Russians could do no more than impede the effectiveness of the proceedings of the Security Council once they resumed attendance at its sessions.[19]

Thereafter the role of the United Nations in the Korean War was relatively secondary. From the beachhead of Pusan to which they had been reduced, the American and South Korean forces launched an offensive in September that carried them back to the 38th parallel. The issue appeared at this point of whether or not to cross that line, a move to which there was much opposition, even among supporters of the United States. Following an unanswered ultimatum to the North Koreans General MacArthur, the American commander of the United Nations forces, ordered the crossing of the line. But the success of the advance toward the Yalu had the effect that some had feared and predicted of bringing about the intervention of Chinese Communist forces, ostensibly "volunteers," but in effect well-organized formations.

On this occasion again, if the action of the Peking government is not open to doubt, the same is not the case of possible Russian collusion. In any case the prospect had arisen of a vast enlargement of the conflict, and the possibility that America might resort to the use of atomic weapons against Communist China—a precipitate retreat in Korea had followed the Chinese intervention—was cause for widespread alarm. In December, 1950, British Prime Minister Attlee made a hurried visit to Washington to urge upon the American government the desirability of caution.[20] The Korean War thus went on with alternating fortunes, essentially resolving itself into a stalemate in the vicinity of the 38th parallel. Despite the general reluctance in all quarters to enlarge the war, it proved extremely difficult to translate this *de facto* stabilization into a formal armistice or peace; negotiations to that end, initiated in July, 1951, were protracted and did not reach success until July, 1953. Their result, broadly speaking, was to create in Korea a situation similar to that

[19] One consequence of this obstructionism was the adoption by the Assembly on November 3 of a resolution labeled "United Action for Peace," which made it possible for the Assembly to take action in the event of a stalemate in the Security Council.

[20] The tendency of General MacArthur to take independent action in disregard of instructions led to his recall by President Truman in April, 1951. This action, somewhat of a sensation in the United States, was generally welcomed abroad, where the fear was considerable lest the scope of the war become extended.

which had developed in Germany, crystallizing the division of the country into two segments the prospects of whose reunion was indefinitely adjourned.

THE JAPANESE TREATY OF PEACE.   It may be mentioned at this point that this Far Eastern situation also had repercussions in Japan. Here again, as in Germany, America took the leadership in integrating Japan into the anti-Communist bloc. The Japanese case was simpler and easier to deal with than the German owing to the absence of Russian forces in Japan. Following the publication of a draft treaty of peace with Japan in July 1951, a conference was called by the United States to meet in San Francisco where peace with Japan was signed on September 8 by all save the Soviet Union, Poland, and Czechoslovakia.[21] Japan was reduced to the home islands, her sovereignty restored, and occupation forces were to be withdrawn unless special agreements were made for their continued presence. This is what happened, for Japan, like the Bonn Republic, was desirous of the protection that this continued presence of American forces insured.

EUROPE AND THE KOREAN WAR

These Far Eastern arrangements, especially the integration of Japan into the American system of defense against Communist aggression, may be seen as giving further shape to the American policy of containment—encirclement from the Russian and Chinese points of view—of the Communist world. They were the counterpart of the efforts to re-create effective force in Europe as well as to coördinate and integrate that force into a more effective tool than separate national entities could provide. These efforts, in the form of the Atlantic alliance, have been mentioned. The outbreak of hostilities in Korea gave them an added impulse and, in general, that conflict had important repercussions in Europe. These must be indicated.

Not least among these repurcussions perhaps was the rise in commodity prices that ensued and which presented a threat to the hitherto quite successful economic recovery of Europe, to

[21] India, Burma, and Yugoslavia did not accept the invitation to the San Francisco Conference. At the same time, to allay the fears of Australia, New Zealand, and the Philippines of a revival of Japanese militarism, the United States concluded separate treaties with those countries.

which an added threat was contained in the prospect of diverting increasing resources to rearmament. The European states wished to give first priority to the economic aspect of their life, while the American tendency was to place relatively greater stress on arms; the difference was of degree in relative allocations, but it served to create some divergence, and American aid to Europe took the form of increasing military appropriations while diminishing those for economic recovery; the revival of Europe did in fact make economic assistance less urgent than in the years immediately following the war. The European peoples were in addition divided between their wish for security, hence for American protection and coöperation with America in military arrangements, and the fear lest too aggressive an American policy render more likely a conflict that they wished above all to avoid. Hence on their part the tendency to some suspicion of American policy and intentions and to remain alert to possibilities of negotiation. Even the widespread and genuine enthusiasm which had greeted the initial American reaction to the outbreak of hostilities in Korea had largely evaporated and given place in many cases to criticism of too vigorous, or rash, American action in that theater.

THE REARMAMENT OF GERMANY AND THE EUROPEAN DEFENSE COMMUNITY. In more limited and immediate fashion, the idea of adding twelve German divisions to the existing force did not appear in many European quarters to be the obviously desirable and simple thing that it seemed to be in Washington. Opposition to it was especially strong in France, as might be expected, but there was much of it in Germany herself as well; Britain, too, was divided on the score of German rearmament, which evoked enthusiasm from Churchill but doubts and reservations from the Labour government of the day.

The impulse that the outbreak of Korean hostilities gave to the rearmament of Europe found a first expression in the adoption by the Consultative Assembly of the Council of Europe, meeting in Strasbourg in August, 1950, of a resolution of Churchillian sponsorship that aimed at "the immediate creation of a unified European army under the authority of a European minister of defense, subject to proper European democratic control, and acting in full coöperation with the United States and Canada." This was an interesting concept that called for clarification; in view of the difficulty of the political integration of Europe, to propose the creation of a European army—the army is the clearest and most sensitive organ of sovereignty—was, to say the least, a bold gesture.

The idea was further discussed at a meeting in New York in September of the American, British, and French foreign ministers, Acheson, Bevin, and Schuman. In 1950 France lacked the power totally to prevent the rearmament of Germany by merely opposing it. She adopted subtler tactics in the form of the Pleven Plan, sponsored by and named after her defense minister, which the United States promptly endorsed. Thus was initiated a three-year-long discussion, barren of results in the outcome, but which during that time absorbed much of the attention of foreign offices. The heart of the Pleven Plan was the "scrambling" of small units into European divisions. German forces could thus be used, but no German national army or German General Staff would come into existence. The practicability of the scheme seemed very doubtful to many and the question had also to be explored of its acceptance by the Bonn government; it was, however, as much as could obtain at this time the reluctant consent of France.

The discussion were lengthy and made little progress during 1951;[22] the details of them need not be examined. Quite naturally, from the German point of view, apart from the widespread opposition in the country to any form of rearmament, here was an opportunity to take an important step in the rehabilitation of Germany to a position of equality among others. Quite naturally, also, the prospect of German rearmament was highly displeasing to the Russians who, besides customary vituperation, sought to contrive a four-Power meeting on the German question. The prospect of a neutralized Germany might prove an attractive bait in Europe but it alarmed the Bonn government, which obtained on that score reassurances from the United States. The spring of 1951 saw protracted negotiations between the Western and the Russian representatives in an attempt to formulate a mutually acceptable agenda for a later meeting of the foreign ministers. These discussions once more turned into a test of patience and a maneuvering for position which served no other purpose than to establish that there was no suitable ground for compromise between the West and the Soviet Union.

[22] The Saar issue appeared again at this juncture as a source of Franco-German difference and was the cause of some delay until a temporary accommodation was found.

This failure was added inducement for the West to proceed with its defense arrangements, negotiations for which went on during the rest of the year. These were complicated again by the consideration of the impact of a substantial rearmament program on the still fragile economies of Europe, hence discussion of the proper allocation of respective military contributions and costs, and by the deep-rooted French reluctance to accept any German rearmament; on the German side, Chancellor Adenauer now firmly espoused the position that German rearmament was desirable, even from the point of view of achieving German reunification. In January, 1952, the French Parliament, though hedging it with conditions and reservations where Germany was concerned, unenthusiastically approved the plan of a European army. Debates in Bonn reflected corresponding hesitations in acquiescing to what many regarded as unwarranted discriminations—the Saar perennial intruding here again—but finally on May 27 the treaty creating the European Defense Community was signed by the foreign ministers of Little Europe: France, Germany, Italy, and the Benelux countries.[23] This occurrence, taken in combination with the almost simultaneous completion of the process of ratification of the treaty that established the European Coal and Steel Community,[24] seemed to justify the hopes of those who had been working for the unity of Europe, even though it was so far a fraction of the whole, albeit a highly important fraction. Not enough weight was being given, as events were to show, to the fact that French acceptance had been reluctantly given, to a degree extracted from French weakness, and did not represent true consent and conviction. There can be many a slip between the cup and the lip, as the process of ratification of EDC was to show.

Thus, as the year 1952 was drawing to a close the future could only appear very cloudy. The most significant development was the hardening and crystallization that had taken place in the rival American and Soviet camps. The United Nations was obviously an unsatisfactory solvent of tensions, and even its spectacular success in the initial phase of the Korean episode had largely been the result of accident, the momentary Russian absence. Europe had not emerged as a third balancing force, but had rather been drawn into

[23] Simultaneously an agreement was signed that redefined the relations between the Bonn Republic and the occupying Powers, which may be regarded as a further step in the rehabilitation of Germany.

[24] The last ratification, by Italy, took place on June 16.

the respective orbits of the rival camps. The writ of the Kremlin was ruthless law among its satellites; that part of Europe that was authentically free had nonetheless, even if in slower and more laborious fashion, been integrated into the American camp. In many ways the German problem remained, as well as many others, which, since they concern in large part the dependent or formerly dependent world, will best be dealt with separately.[25] As stated before, the five years just elapsed may be regarded as representing a success of American leadership and initiative; America herself avowed it as her purpose to build positions of strength from which to conduct negotiations since Russia understood and respected nothing but existing force.

The atmosphere was therefore laden with much distrust and fear that was authentic in all quarters, and the vicious circle had been entered of competition in armaments, expression of the fears of insecurity, which in their turn they feed and compound. It is not surprising therefore that, in the circumstances, the discussion of disarmament should have been largely a repetition of the dreary record of that which followed the First World War. For that reason no attempt will be made to analyze the details of an essentially sterile debate. The French position of the 1920's, so often criticized at the time, had now been wholly espoused by America: we shall disarm, and gladly so, as soon as and to the extent that we feel secure.

The debate unfolded, however, in the novel context of technical developments in the field of arms for which no precedent had validity. The Russian success in producing atomic weapons, restoring a temporarily broken equilibrium, was a spur to the further search for destructive advantage. The far more powerful hydrogen bomb was successfully produced almost simultaneously in the United States and in the Soviet Union in 1953. In addition, the rate of progress—if progress this can be called—in this line of endeavor is such as to give new and unprecedented importance to the factor of obsolescence. This makes for a high degree of instability and affects the technique of conducting international relations as well: the time-honored devices of ultimatums and formal declarations of war, the possibility of consultation in the event of crisis, take on quite a different meaning in a situation where effectiveness of the priority of decision to take action may hingle on a matter of hours

25 See beow, pp. 646 ff.

at most. Some have sought comfort in the hope that, in the face of such colossal responsibility as the decision to act now entails, safety may yet turn out to be the child of terror.

II. The Tentative Relaxation of Uneasy Coexistence

THE EQUILIBRIUM OF BALANCED FORCES

CHANGES IN WASHINGTON AND IN MOSCOW. The fears in 1952 that major conflict might break out were belied. The large place that the United States filled in the world gave the Presidential election of November, 1952, importance far beyond the confines of the country. Presidents Roosevelt and Truman had on the whole succeeded in pursuing a policy that may be called bipartisan, avoiding in that respect the mistakes of their last Democratic predecessor; too much was now at stake and there seemed to be a large measure of agreement that politics must stop at the edge of the ocean.

But the world had now been at peace, however uneasily, for some years and the attacks on the existing administration, followed by the election of the Republican candidate, General Eisenhower, especially in view of the long absence of the Republican party from office, was cause of doubts and qualms abroad lest the direction of American policy alter. For all the criticism of the vigorousness or intransigeance of American policy, the last thing that free Europe wanted was to see the American guarantee of protection, more concretely American assistance and American forces in Europe, in any way diminished.

Domestic American quarrels do not belong in this treatment. Of them it may suffice to say that the violence of their unfettered expression was misleading[26] General Eisenhower, ex-head of NATO, would give little comfort to any isolationist tendencies in his party, and of the foreign policy of the new administration it may be said in general that it was merely a continuation and extension of that of its predecessor. Whether, as some have felt, with the successful achievement of containment, the time was ripe for an alternative approach, and what fruits such a new approach might have borne, are questions difficult of assessment. It seems

[26] The chief accusations, in part justified, in part wholly unwarranted, against the Democratic administration, had to do with the Yalta arrangements and with the responsibility for the loss of China to Communism. They were in any case meant for domestic consumption.

not unfair to say, however, always speaking in broad terms, that the initiative now shifted in considerable measure to the Communist camp, while Western policy tended to be one of reaction to these initiatives, thus reversing, to a degree at least, the condition that had prevailed during the preceding five years. However that may be, the emergence of new leaders in Washington might serve to facilitate a change of climate and direction.

Far more sensational and of greater consequence for all than the appearance of a new President in Washington was the demise of the autocrat of all the Russias. On March 5, 1953, the world was apprised of the death of Stalin, in circumstances that led some to suspect that the operation of the forces of nature had been assisted in the final stages by the works of man. At all events Stalin was no more; the enormous power that had been concentrated in his hands and the nature of the Soviet system raised the question of the future course of Russia, more specifically of on whom, if anyone, Stalin's mantle would fall. A struggle might ensue among individuals, the consequences of which would be hard to predict. The arrest, followed in December by the execution, of Beria, one of the possible contenders, lent credence to tales of dark intrigue. The answer to the question is not yet forthcoming, if ever it will be, and the Byzantine methods of the Kremlin allow little more than speculation on the nature of the relationships of its tenants. Malenkov for a time seemed to emerge to a position of primacy, then went into eclipse to make way for Khrushchev, but unlike luckless Beria, Malenkov was not liquidated; the army, too, seems to have played a significant role. What we may retain of all this is a marked change, for a time at least, in Russian tactics if not ultimate aims.

THE RESUMPTION OF NEGOTIATIONS BETWEEN EAST AND WEST. The passing of Stalin was a suitable opportunity for modifying a rigidity of posture which had been in large measure responsible for the developments that have been outlined in this chapter. Softer words began to issue from Moscow, not only about the customarily asserted one-sided devotion to peace, but about the possibility of achieving at least a *modus vivendi*. There were many abroad only too ready to explore any possibility of relaxing the tension that had been mounting for some years, and the term "coexistence" began to take the place of "containment." All this was encouraged by domestic Russian developments where stress seemed to be placed on the granting of a larger share to amenities—consumer goods—

instead of dinning the need for continued austerity that the persisting demands of armed vigilance entailed. A situation might develop, reminiscent of that of a quarter of a century earlier, when Russia had begun to emphasize her domestic development and the possibility of socialism in one country; given time and continued peace, Russia and the other Communist states might evolve into manageable members of the world community. Had not the French Revolution been tamed during the nineteenth century?

Gradually it seemed as if a thaw might be occurring in the frozen rigidity of irreconcilable antagonisms. Following negotiations during the first half of the year and a meeting in Washington in July of the foreign ministers of the United States, Britain, and France, these countries sent similar notes to Moscow with a view to exploring the possibilities of German reunification and of concluding final peace with Austria.[27] The conclusion of an armistice in Korea in July, after what had seemed hopelessly protracted and stalemated negotiations, although ostensibly Russia had no connection with that matter, further aided the process of relaxing tensions. Negotiations between the Western Powers and Russia went on for the rest of the year; they made slow progress, partly because the West kept on saying "Germany" and the Russians insisted on replying "China," but eventually they led to the meeting of the four foreign ministers in Berlin in January–February, 1954.

Whatever fears existed in Germany that the Four might come to terms among themselves in some respects at her expense were at least premature. Behind the impossibility of agreeing on a criterion for free elections lay the more solid fact that Russia was not prepared to relinquish the asset of her control of an important segment of Germany, to say nothing of the fact that a treaty of peace with a reunited Germany would have had as a logical consequence the withdrawal of Russian forces from the satellite countries—while conversely the Western states would not consent to any arrangement that might involve the risk of extending the area of Communist control to the Rhine. The Berlin conference was thus barren of results in Europe. But British and French insistence extracted the reluctant consent of the American Secretary of State, John Foster Dulles, to the holding of a meeting in Geneva for pur-

---

[27] Save for the issue of the so-called German assets in Austria, agreement had essentially been reached on the terms of peace with that country. In addition, by contrast with Germany, Austria had continued to exist as a single political unit.

poses of discussing Far Eastern matters.[28] While in Europe Russia was adhering to the defensive position of holding her own, the focus of her more active policy was being turned to the East and in general to the ferment of the dependent world. To this we shall turn presently, but one aspect of Eastern problems, of crucial importance for Europe, more specifically for France, may be mentioned at this point.

THE INDOCHINESE AFFAIR.   Two issues were of prime importance at the meeting that opened in Geneva on April 26. On Korea, the same situation prevailed as in Germany, inability of the two sides to agree on the meaning and implementation of so-called free elections. But in April, 1954, far more important and dramatic than the Korean situation was that fast approaching a climax in Indochina.

Of Indochina it will suffice to say that, following the events of the war period, the French had returned to that land in a much weakened position. In addition, when faced with local demands they dealt with these with less than skill and suppleness, missing in 1947 an opportunity to come to terms with Ho Chi Minh, leader of the movement for a measure at least of autonomy. The consequence had been hostilities, conducted amid the welter and confusion of French no less than of Indochinese politics, a tale highly involved and not a little sordid. This distant war had been a severe drain on France, absorbing roughly the equivalent of American aid to her, presumably for reconstruction in Europe. The total Communist conquest of China, establishing direct contact between Indochina and Communist-controlled territory from which assistance could easily be sent, served to intensify the struggle, and the war had been going ill for the French, despite increasing American involvement through various forms of assistance short of military intervention. An ill-considered French military operation resulted in the besieging of a French garrison in Dien Bien Phu in the interior. The fate of it seemed sealed, and the Chinese delegate in Geneva, Chou En-lai, could await the outcome with complacency. The possibility of more direct American intervention seems to have been considered at this juncture, on the plea, in a sense quite correct, that French in Indochina was fighting the extension of the area of Communist control no less than the United States has done

[28] One important source of American objection lay in the participation of Communist China in the Geneva discussions.

in Korea. But the decision was eventually against interference and Dien Bien Phu finally fell.

This was but an episode in a much larger contest, albeit one that was dramatic and sensational. It had a great impact in France, where it brought to the public consciousness realization of the seriousness and significance of a distant adventure.[29] A month later the Laniel government fell, to be succeeded by one under the Premiership of Mendès-France. Though a Radical Socialist, Mendès-France was in the nature of a maverick in French politics; a clear-headed and severe critic of successive governments, he had been out of office since his resignation in 1945 as the result of differences over economic policies. The crisis gave him his opportunity. Realistically, he understood the deficiencies of French power and the folly of a policy that failed to take proper account of the relationship between ends and means. He also understood the value of shock tactics and created the proper sensation when, on assuming office, he undertook to put an end to the Indochinese imbroglio within one month.

This he succeeded in doing. Dealing from a position of weakness, but perhaps skillfully playing on the prospect of American intervention in the event of too great Communist intransigeance, following discussion with Chou En-lai in Switzerland, he contrived on July 21 an agreement comparable to the one that had been made in Korea. Indochina was divided into four parts: Laos and Cambodia became separate entities, while the rest and the most important part, Vietnam, was cut in two by an armistice line along the 17th parallel.[30] Considering the circumstances, this outcome may be seen as rather more favorable than might have been expected; it was promptly ratified in France where relief at the escape from what had become a hopeless impasse was the dominant note. It was less pleasing to the American Secretary of State who gave vent to his dissatisfaction at this manifestation of French independence, but granted in the end his grudging and reluctant consent.

With the situation stabilized in Indochina, for the time at least,

[29] The Indochinese war had, in some respects, been highly unpopular in France, to the extent that the government did not dare make use of the conscript army. The war, however, proved a severe drain on the supply of officers and thus indirectly interfered with the reorganization of French armed force in Europe.

[30] The provisions for elections and unification have had the same fate as the similar ones for Korea; in Vietnam, as in Korea, the armistice line has crystallized the emergence of two distinct states.

American policy endeavored to erect in Southeast Asia a barrier comparable to that which the Atlantic alliance constituted in Europe. On September 8, 1954, in Manila, two instruments were signed: a Pacific Charter professing devotion to self-determination and the promotion of self-government in East Asia; a Southeast Asia Collective Defense Treaty that provided for a Southeast Asia Treaty Organization (SEATO), a consultative pact rather than a military alliance like NATO. The participants in these agreements were the United States, Britain, France, Australia, New Zealand, the Philippines, Thailand, and Pakistan. India and Indonesia preferred to maintain a more neutral position.

THE END OF EDC AND THE PARIS AGREEMENTS.   The Indochinese armistice, disliked in America, was not, however, the only or last disillusion that French had in store for American policy. The EDC treaty stood still unratified by the French Parliament, one reason for this being the reluctance of successive French governments to face a test of uncertain outcome. France's prospective associates in EDC were growing impatient, no less than America, at French tergiversation; yet France could hardly be coerced, and held a *de facto* power of veto from the simple fact that there could be no EDC without France. The dynamic Mendès-France decided to put an end at least to the uncertainty. Himself unenthusiastic, though not formally committed to any position, but feeling that the treaty was unlikely of ratification in Paris, he sought in August at Brussels to gain additional concessions from the other members of EDC. Meeting impatience, annoyance, and refusal, he submitted the treaty to the French Parliament in its existing form, the government adhering to a neutral position. On August 30, by a vote of 319 to 264, EDC went down in defeat.

Rightly or wrongly, France was not prepared to associate herself with Germany in the manner that had been contemplated. Outside of France there was dismay, and even anger,[31] but recriminations were futile; Mendès-France did not seek to deny the Atlantic alliance and the inescapable issue of German rearmament must in any event be faced. The day was saved by a British initiative, the call to London of a meeting of the EDC powers, Britain, the United States, and Canada. The agreements provisionally reached

---

[31] Despite the fact that the other governments had ratified EDC, the existence of substantial opposition to it and the reluctant acceptance of it outside France must be borne in mind.

in London were soon implemented with the signature of the so-called Paris Accords later in the month.[32] These accords provided as follows: an agreement between the occupying Powers and the Bonn Republic for the liquidation of the occupation regime;[33] the nine above-mentioned Powers agreed to enlarge the Brussels Treaty into a Western European Union that would include the Federal Republic and Italy; the former would create an army of twelve divisions, an air force of 75,000 men and a navy of 25,000 for coastal use; West Germany would join NATO under whose supreme commander her forces would be placed; a Franco-German agreement provided for the "Europeanization" of the Saar, which would have political independence while retaining her economic connection with France. The Saar would also have representation in the Western European Union, the Council of Europe, and the Coal and Steel Community, and the arrangements to that end were to be submitted to a local vote.

The success of these arrangements depended upon French and German acceptance of them. In both countries they met with substantial opposition, but ratification was forthcoming in the French Parliament on December 30—albeit by the close vote of 287 to 260 —and Bonn followed suit in February. France could wreck EDC; but in the larger context of the competition between East and West she did not, in the last analysis, possess the power to prevent the adjunction of German power to the Western forces. These circumstances had thus made possible another significant step in the rehabilitation of German power. What the ultimate consequences of this will be time alone can tell. It is of interest that three years after the endorsement of German rearmament the bare effective beginnings of it were taking place in Germany. However, the process once launched would be unlikely to be reversed.

The rearmament of Western Germany may be seen as an additional step in the process of builing up strength of anti-Communist intention. This it undoubtedly was, and strong condemnation of it issued from Russia. Moscow's efforts to procure a four-Power meeting on the subject of German reunification were unavailing; a meeting with the satellites in Moscow issued fulminations but also showed that Russia wished to keep open the avenue of further

[32] A last-minute obstacle in the form of the problem of the Saar was overcome when an agreement was reached between Mendès-France and Adenauer.
[33] This did not mean a withdrawal of the occupation forces, but, as in the case of Japan, a redefinition of their status.

negotiations.[34] In fact, despite these moves by the East and the West, a measure of relaxation was taking place. In the side of the West the tendency in France and Britain was likewise, despite American ill humor, to favor negotiations with the Russians now that a position of greater strength had been established. The thaw was accentuated by a shift in the Russian position to willingness to discuss Austria separately from Germany. Following a visit to Moscow of the Austrian Chancellor and his foreign minister, an Austrian treaty of peace was signed in May by the four Powers. Austria was restored to full independence within the boundaries of January 1, 1938; she was, however, forbidden to unite with Germany and to enter into military alliances. The neutralization of Austria naturally suggested the possibility of creating a large buffer zone in mid-Europe by eventually extending to Germany a similar arrangement.

THE SUMMIT CONFERENCE OF 1955 AND ITS AFTERMATH.   It was now the turn of the West to issue a call for a four-Power meeting. In June Russia accepted the proposal made the preceding month in notes from Washington, London, and Paris for a meeting in Geneva of the four heads of government. The meeting on July 18, 1955, in the Palace of Nations in Geneva of President Eisenhower and Premier Bulganin, Prime Minister Eden, and Premier Faure attracted worldwide attention. The somewhat sensational proposal made by President Eisenhower that the United States and Russia exchange information on their respective military establishments and grant each other facilities for aerial inspection had perhaps in it more drama than substance. Actually, nothing concrete was achieved at this summit conference, but the tone of the meeting nevertheless raised hopes of possible later accomplishments, and the talk of the "spirit of Geneva" was reminiscent of that of the "spirit of Locarno" of thirty years earlier.

But it took much less time for the spirit of Geneva to evaporate than for that of Locarno. If the West had succeeded at Geneva in convincing the Kremlin that its devotion to peace was authentic this may have served to foster the conclusion in Russia that there was little risk in intransigeance. When Chancellor Adenauer and his foreign minister went to Moscow in September, essentially to explore the price of Russian consent to German reunification, they

[34] In 1955 the Warsaw Pact and the Warsaw Treaty Organization provided for the integration of the armed forces of the Soviet Union and its satellites in a manner comparable with NATO.

came back empty-handed, for all that diplomatic relations were reëstablished between Moscow and Bonn. In addition, Russia insisted on treating Bonn on a par with its puppet German Democratic Republic and gave its position added point by signing a treaty with that state on September 20. The meeting in Geneva at the end of October of the four foreign ministers took place in an atmosphere wholly different from that of the summit conference of the preceding July.

It does not seem unreasonable to speculate—though in the dearth of adequate information speculation this must remain—that the course of Russian behavior was motivated by authentic fear of aggressive intent on the part of the West, more particularly of America,[35] or alternatively by the success of the American policy of containment, but that this fear was to a point allayed by such events as the summit conference. The consequences of this were to induce the new leadership that followed that of Stalin to seek some authentic but cautious relaxation of tensions. Account should also be taken of the stresses and strains that existed inside the Soviet milieu and in the satellites. Little more can be said than that such tensions existed. The rising of the workers in East Berlin and the subsequent events of Poznan[36] undoubtedly were serious food for thought in the Kremlin. It was startling, to say the least, to see Khrushchev go humbly to Canossa, in the form of traveling to Belgrade, there to apologize in abject fashion for past Russian mistakes *vis-à-vis* Yugoslavia. Tito's stock was naturally enhanced by this, and the dismissal of Molotov from the foreign office in 1956 was widely interpreted as a gesture of appeasement toward Yugoslavia.

More surprising still was the speech by the same Khrushchev in February, 1956, an attack of seemingly unnecessary violence on the misdeeds of the Stalin regime. The precise meaning and intent of such a performance is difficult to estimate; that there was an increase of free discussion and criticism in the Soviet milieu was clear,

[35] Allowing that the intent of American policy has been authentically defensive, it is enlightening nevertheless to glance at a map that shows the ring of bases that have been established on the periphery of the Communist world. In 1951 the American magazine *Collier's Weekly* devoted a special issue to a fictitious reporting of 1960 of a successful atomic war and its subsequent "liberation" of Russia. As publicity this was eminently successful, but it was understandably taken by many, and not in Russia alone, as an indication of the trend of American thinking.

[36] In June, 1953, there were strikes and riots in East Berlin that were severely put down. A comparable situation occurred in Poznan in October 1955, but there was no Russian intervention on this occasion.

but whether the permission of it was the result of a sufficient accumulation of pent-up and widespread discontent or a calculated move of the leadership as a safety valve, whether it was the prelude to real change or a diversionary sop, this too must remain speculation, especially in view of the subsequent reassertion by the Muscovite leaders that they were all Stalinists. On balance, many if not more questions were raised than were answered by the seeming gyrations of Soviet leadership, whom some suspected of instability and of uncertain direction, or alternatively of Machiavellian calculations designed to confuse and deceive.

At any rate there was undoubtedly, for some time at least, some relaxation in the tension between East and West, especially in the European arena of conflict. This coincided with a greater concentration of Soviet attention on issues elsewhere in the world. Of these some mention must be made for, given the imperial involvements of Europe, they had important repercussions on Europe as well.

THE REVOLT AND EMERGENCE OF THE DEPENDENT WORLD

The view is of long standing that it is the fate of imperial activity ultimately to lead colonial possessions to independence. The great imperial accomplishments of Europe during the latter part of the nineteenth century have been discussed in the second part of this volume; their magnitude and their success served for a time to eclipse what may be called the defeatist view of imperialism. But the First World War brought about a sharp reversal in the rising tide of imperial expansion, despite seeming, but misleading, further successes as were registered in such an instrument as the Treaty of Sèvres of 1920. During the long armistice imperial Powers had to contend with the ripening seeds of a nationalism all too successfully planted in the dependent world. The Second World War had the effect of giving a tremendous impulse to the movement for emancipation of the dependent peoples of the world. The defeat of France and the setbacks suffered for a time by Western Powers at the hands of the Japanese naturally redounded to the discredit of those Powers in the eyes of their subject peoples. The Second World War had also the effect of destroying the Japanese and Italian Empires, just as the first had liquidated the German, thereby further reducing the number of imperial Powers.

The struggle for emancipation was, in addition, also compli-

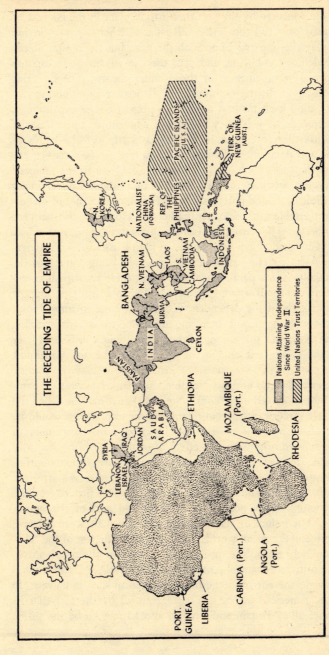

THE RECEDING TIDE OF EMPIRE

Legend:
- Nations Attaining Independence Since World War II
- United Nations Trust Territories

Map labels:
N. KOREA, S., NATIONALIST CHINA (FORMOSA), REP. OF THE PHILIPPINES, PACIFIC ISLANDS (U.S.A.), TERR. OF NEW GUINEA (AUST.), BANGLADESH, LAOS, N. VIETNAM, S. VIETNAM, CAMBODIA, BURMA, INDONESIA, INDIA, CEYLON, PAKISTAN, ETHIOPIA, SYRIA, LEBANON, ISRAEL, IRAQ, JORDAN, SAUDI ARABIA, MOZAMBIQUE (Port.), RHODESIA, ANGOLA (Port.), CABINDA (Port.), LIBERIA, PORT. GUINEA

In the western hemisphere European control still extends to French and Dutch Guyana, British Honduras, and some Caribbean islands (British, French, and Dutch). British Guyana and the rest of the Caribbean islands formerly under British, French, or Dutch control have achieved independence. Rhodesia declared independence unilaterally in 1965 (UDI) but her independence has not been acknowledged by the United Kingdom or in the United Nations.

cated and confused by the fact that it took place in the context of the Russo-American competition. Russia, whether tsarist or Soviet, could play the imperial game with the best, but the nature of the Soviet ideology could be, and was, used to advantage to espouse the cause of emancipation of those under the sway of capitalist imperialism, while the contiguity of Russian acquisitions to the Soviet Union itself made it possible to present Soviet expansion as a consequence of voluntary accession. The simple line of Soviet policy has therefore been to espouse and support the cause of Asiatic and African nationalisms. Here a qualification may be entered in the case of China. The addition of China to the ranks of Communist states has created a situation of a unique nature, owing to the dimensions and potentialities of China, of an order of magnitude comparable to those of Russia herself. However, the incipient rivalry between the two great Communist states did not materialize at first. China stood in a better position than Russia to assert leadership in Asia, her chief rival in that endeavor being India, but the two initially took a parallel position. Thus, there was broad agreement between the Russian, Chinese, and Indian attitudes in support of the struggle of the dependent peoples for emancipation. However, power being power, behaving according to its own laws, the agreement did not prove long lasting. Something will be said later on of the falling out among the three would-be anti-imperialist states.

American views and policies in these matters have been hampered by unresolved inner contradictions. What may be called the instinctive American reaction to the fact of imperialism would be characterized by some as *simpliste*. The legacy of the memory of America's own origins has the effect of evoking *a priori* sympathy for the desire for freedom anywhere, another form or extension of the enthusiastic American espousal of self-determination after the First World War. The application of this principle proved troublesome enough in the politically most evolved part of the world, Europe. The failure to acknowledge differences between Europe, the Arab and the Asian worlds, not to mention the rest of the African, is merely unrealistic, just as the notion that the simple introduction of the mechanical trappings of democratic government will be a magic solvent of domestic political problems is naïveté. In addition, American policy has been troubled by the fact that its two chief allies, Britain and France, also happen to be the prime imperial Powers, chief targets as a consequence of the rising of the dependent peoples. The efforts—squirmings sometimes—of American policy to effect some reconciliation between the contending desires to favor independence everywhere and to support allies is not one of the least interesting aspects of American foreign policy, which is in addition plagued by the dilemma created by a competitive courting with Russia for gratitude and influence among peoples in process of achieving emancipation. Economic assistance, Point Four programs, alliances sometimes, have been some of the tentative responses. They have been welcomed and at the same time regarded with a measure of suspicion by some of their objects, lest they be skillful adaptations of the old imperialism to novel conditions, and the Soviets have endeavored, not wholly without success, to tar America in the eyes of others with the brush of imperialistic intent.

Thus the dependent world has not only been struggling to emancipiate itself from its masters, but has found itself caught in the meshes of the larger struggle between East and West, a situation that it has understandably sought to exploit to its own best advantage. To examine the detailed record of this struggle would take us too far afield, and its accomplishments and consequences to date alone will be examined.

THE DUTCH AND INDONESIA. The Dutch had created in Indonesia a regime that was neither unprogressive nor inefficient, though its paternalistic tendency allowed a minimum of scope for self-rule. When the Dutch returned to Indonesia after the Japanese defeat they found a native government in existence that resisted their control. By 1947 they recognized three states that were to be linked with Holland in a Netherlands-Indonesian Union under the Dutch crown. But a recrudescence of hostilities led two years later to another agreement that recognized the sovereignty of the Republic of the United States of Indonesia, still in union with Holland. This was but a step toward the complete severance of all links by the Republic of Indonesia, established in 1950. This development was abetted by other Asiatic peoples and by the Communist states, but it also had the blessing of the United States. To American pressure the Dutch were especially sensitive, while feeling resentment of it, stemming as it did in their eyes from misunderstanding. Holland lacked the power to maintain by force her position in Indonesia in the face of the combination of pressures to which she found herself subjected. What the Republic of Indonesia would evolve into remained an open question.[37]

BRITISH RETREAT AND ADAPTATION.   Winston Churchill had declared during the war that he had not become His Majesty's Prime Minister in order to preside over the liquidation of the British Empire; dominion status for India was the extent of concession that he would contemplate for that subcontinent. But the advent of a more amenable Labour government in 1945, combined with the inability of Hindu and Moslem to agree on a constitution, resulted in the emergence in 1947 of two states, Hindu India and Moslem Pakistan, who eventually agreed—save in Kashmir—on their frontiers.[38] Both states have, through a somewhat nebulous link, remained in the Commonwealth, as did Ceylon, which emerged as another separate unit. Burma, however, elected to sever all connections with Britain and peaceably achieved full independence in 1948.

The emergence of India and Pakistan to their new status must be seen as a highly significant development in the evolution of the British imperial record. India especially, because of her dimensions and numbers, though possessed of little effective power, has aspired to a role of leadership in world affairs. Her natural sympathy for and support of other peoples seeking to achieve independence like herself, together with the continuing British connection, and the fact that she was led by Nehru, a man whose political outlook came closest to that of British Socialism, placed her in a favorable position to act as neutral and possible mediator between East and West. The future long-term course of India remains a question mark, but the impact upon much of the rest of the non-Western world of her success or failure in establishing an authentic and native democratic regime in an Asian milieu will be considerable. In her endeavor to show the way to others, her great rival, as mentioned before, is China. India has played on the whole a moderating and skillful role on the world stage—even if at times one trying to her Western friends and admirers. Her dispute with Pakistan over Kashmir has caused some to feel that when it comes to issues of national interest

---

[37] By contrast with the Dutch, the Belgians had for a time no serious difficulty in their possession of the Congo, a less advanced region than Indonesia, where their policy may be described as one of firm paternalism.

[38] The settlement of the frontiers between India and Pakistan resulted in a large migration of Hindus and Moslems that was attended by not a little hardship and even in some instances by outbreaks of violence and massacres.

and power India may not be very different from other states. In any case, however, the evaporation of any legacy of bitterness toward the former rulers of India and the retention of a Commonwealth link were developments of a unique and hopeful nature. One may point out that the West rather takes pride in, instead of bemoaning, the legacy of the imperial days of Rome.

In farther Malaya, a Federation of Malaya was established in 1948, which moved toward possible dominion status. Thus the British Commonwealth continued to evolve. The state of Ghana (former Gold Coast) emerged into existence in March, 1957, the first Negro African unit to achieve emancipation, and a Caribbean Dominion was adumbrated. Whether such developments were steps in the disintegration of empire or promising manifestations of a changing but possibly continuing relationship between widely diverse peoples was a question that time alone could answer.

FRANCE AND THE FRENCH UNION. The French conception of empire differs from the British, rather resembling in some respects the Roman, and the statement often made that the French have had easier relations with dependent peoples than the British is on the whole correct. However, it has ceased to be true in our time. This is probably a result of the very success that the French have had in turning into Frenchmen leaders of their dependent peoples; once the virus of nationalism becomes injected into the situation the French emphasis upon the Rights of Man easily turns into an all the more effective tool of opposition to French control; in addition, the highly centralized rigidity of French administration, by contrast with the greater flexibility of the British, makes alteration more difficult in the French imperial structure. Finally, the simple fact may be mentioned that French weakness during and after the war was a natural invitation to take advantage of it. The unfortunate Indochinese record has been mentioned.[39]

In an attempt to cope with the rising tide of nationalism in the dependent world the French reorganized their imperial domain into a French Union, the outlines of which were sketched in the constitution of the Fourth Republic. The Union was to consist of four categories of territories: metropolitan France and the overseas departments, the overseas territories, the associated states, and the

[39] See above, pp. 640-641. It was the same Mendès-France, who had negotiated the Indochinese armistice, who also acceded to the Indian demand that France relinquish her remaining outposts in India.

associated territories. The first two categories had direct representation in the French Parliament, a fact that did not serve to simplify the operation of French politics into which it introduced a body of representation whose primary concerns were not those of the metropolitan French. It may suffice to say that the French Union did not prove a successful experiment and France was beset by mounting difficulties, especially in her North African domain.[40] These centered at first in the Tunisian and Moroccan protectorates. It was again Mendès-France who, in 1954, took the initiative of breaking the Tunisian deadlock. The convention signed in June 1955 that granted internal autonomy to Tunisia was the first step toward the achievement of complete independence. Morocco, after many difficulties, some bloodshed, and lengthy negotiations, likewise achieved sovereign status, and both states were admitted to membership in the United Nations in 1956.

These struggles for independence had the support of the Communist world, as well as that of the dependent or ex-dependent peoples; America was generally sympathetic to them and welcomed French concessions, though she was often restrained and embarrassed by the necessities of the French alliance.[41] In the process, the French, like the Dutch and the British, have often felt that there was little understanding of their problems in America. What hopes for the future may be contained in the independence of Tunisia and Morocco are still impossible to discern with clarity. From the end of 1955 France was involved in Algeria in guerrilla warfare that eventually drew to North Africa the greater part of her armed forces. The Algerian problem was rendered particularly recalcitrant to solution by the presence in Algeria of over a million Europeans, some 12 percent of the population, a state of affairs that resembled that existing in the Union of South Africa.[42]

THE TROUBLED MIDDLE EAST. The attempt to evict France from North Africa had the support, moral and in some measure material,

[40] In March, 1947, rioting in Madagascar was countered by ruthless repression which effectively pacified the island.

[41] Algeria, constitutionally a part of France, was as a consequence included in NATO, while in neighboring Morocco the United States had a number of bases, as a result of agreements negotiated with France, the protecting state.

[42] In the Union of South Africa, the European minority, or at least the Afrikaans-speaking part of it, has been seeking to carry out a policy of *apartheid*, or segregation, designed to insure the permanence of white supremacy, with the consequence of building up explosive tensions. On the final outcome of the Algerian situation, see below, p. 679.

of the Arab League. The Arab world of the Middle East has been an area of high instability. In that region the war had the effect of terminating any French control, leaving Britain alone to face the problem of how to maintain some influence in the Middle East. The Egyptian insistence on complete British withdrawal, even from the remaining base of Suez, supported by the Arab League and by sympathy from America, led to the accomplishment of that end in 1956. Even the British treaty connection with Jordan was liquidated at the request of that country, from which all British forces were withdrawn.

In Cyprus, too, the British were faced with the demand for *enosis*, union with Greece, which resulted in outbreaks of violence and a situation somewhat comparable to that of French North Africa.[43] The Cypriot situation has had the further effect of introducing an unsettling element in the relations between Greece and Turkey.

But the most troublesome fact of the Middle East has been the intrusion of Israel, whose success in war against the Arab states in 1948 resulted in an uneasy truce and a highly explosive situation, most embarrassing to the West. From the Arab point of view Israel is essentially a new version of Western imperialism, a view difficult of understanding in America, who finds herself caught in the dilemma—a dilemma in part of her own creation— of simultaneous sympathy for the establishment of Israel and for the Arab struggle against British and French control. To support Israel while keeping Arab goodwill is a feat that has so far exceeded the capabilities of American diplomacy, a diplomacy which, moreover, has been characterized in this matter by rather less than deftness and skill.

But such a state of affairs has been eminently satisfactory to Moscow which, after its initial vote in favor of the establishment of Israel, has increasingly turned to courting Arab favor, partly by providing military assistance, especially to Egypt.[44] The intrusion of Soviet influence in the Middle East has tended to divide it into rival camps and to increase uncertainty and tension. Turkey has

[43] As a result of the Turkish conquest and of the long period of Turkish rule, the population of Cyprus, amounting to some 500,000, is divided in the proportion of four to one between Greeks and Turks, with the consequence that the Turkish minority, supported in this by Turkey, was opposed to the relinquishment of British rule. The significance of Cyprus derived from its being the last remaining British base in the Eastern Mediterranean.
[44] The arms sent to Egypt were at first of Czech rather than of Russian provenance but in such matters it is not unreasonable to think of the Communist world as a unit. Syria, too, received Russian arms.

been a steady bulwark against Russian expansion and, in February, 1955, concluded with Iraq an agreement for consultation in the defense of the Middle East. The pact was later in the year extended to include Iran, Pakistan, and Britain, the United States giving the arrangement—the Baghdad Pact—its blessing but declining formal participation in it lest it jeopardize its influence in other Arab states.[45] Hurdling this barrier of the Baghdad Pact states, Russia has endeavored to establish her influence, especially in Syria and in Egypt.

Mention may also be made at this point of the attempt of the states newly emerged to independence to coördinate their action and their influence. The most characteristic manifestation of this tendency was the conference that met at Bandung in Indonesia in April, 1955, and at which twenty-nine Asiatic and African countries were represented. Needless to say, imperialism was condemned at Bandung, but the meeting did not turn into a mere attack against the West for there were some to point out the imperialistic nature of Soviet policy. Also, the Bandung Powers were much concerned over the friction between the United States and Communist China, but the latter showed after the Bandung meeting some signs of relenting in her attitude.

THE CRISES OF 1956

THE EGYPTIAN IMBROGLIO.   That the conditions of the Middle East should lead to an explosion can hardly be a cause for surprise. The occasion for it was the decision of Colonel Nasser, on July 26, to nationalize the Suez Canal, anticipating by twelve years the termination of the initial ninety-nine-year contract, a decision that seems to have been precipitated in turn by the abrupt American about-face in negotiations for a loan for the building of a dam on the Nile at Aswan. The Egyptian initiative, followed by some inconclusive negotiations, had the effect of a catalytic agent that united several components: the Israeli fear of aggressive Egyptian intent; the British feeling that their evacuation of Suez had been

[45] In conjunction with the Baghdad Pact, the setting up of a Middle East Treaty Organization (METO) could be regarded as forging a link between NATO and SEATO, through the Greco-Turkish connection in the West and the Pakistani in the East, that, save for the gap of India, completed the encirclement of the Communist world. With the withdrawal of Iraq from the Baghdad Pact, following a revolution in 1948, that organization became the Central Treaty Organization (CENTO). The United States only participated as an observer rather than a full member in the Baghdad Pact and in CENTO.

read as a sign of weakness and a prelude to further liquidation of their position in the Middle East; a similar French feeling, exacerbated by resentment at Egyptian support of the North African rebellion.[46] Thus Israel, Britain, and France, apparently convinced in addition that American policy was one of tergiversation and of

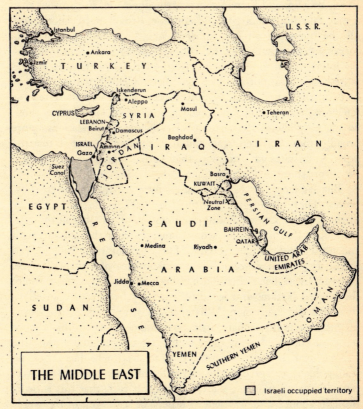

THE MIDDLE EAST

☐ Israeli occupied territory

evasion of pressing and vital issues, came to focus simultaneously on what they regarded as an Egyptian threat. On October 29 the Israeli army launched an attack in the Sinai Peninsula, the bulk of which it overran in four days. Two days later Britain and France attacked Egypt from the air and followed this by landings at Port Said on November 5.

[46] Mention may be made in addition of the dependence of Europe upon Middle Eastern oil. However, as subsequent events were to show, this dependence may not be as crucial as had been thought to be the case.

The United Nations immediately took cognizance of these hostilities, and the General Assembly called for a cease-fire. This would be an opportune occasion to digress on the proper definition and meaning of aggression, but most of the world, including the United States, took the position that the initiation of hostilities by Israel, Briitain, and France constituted aggression. For reasons that it may take long to clarify and appraise, Britain and France called off the operation on November 6 and the withdrawal of their forces was eventually effected through the agency of an intervening international force collected by the United Nations. Israel was more recalcitrant but she, too, eventually yielded, withdrawing in favor of the same United Nations forces. There matters rested for ten years, leaving still unresolved a number of local issues: those having to do with the status of Israeli-Egyptian relations; more broadly, those between Israel and all her neighbors, for all that the other Arab states gave no more than verbal support to Egypt; and the future status of the Suez Canal.

But far larger issues were raised by the Middle Eastern hostilities. They obviously constituted a challenge to the authority of the United Nations, raising the question of whether in the final reckoning that institution would emerge from the episode with enhanced or diminished credit. The incident may have served to clarify certain matters. The common plea of Britain, France, and Israel was that a situation had been allowed to develop where the United Nations and legalistic casuistry had become an effective cloak for aggression. Whatever one may think of the merits of this contention in that particular instance, it is one that cannot be simply disposed of by mere denial; from attempted evasion the League died. In the last resort, the fact has to be faced that no state is likely to agree to the surrender of what it views as interests vital to its existence merely because it feels that this is being brought about by the consent of others, be it the rest of the whole world. A case indeed may be made from the point of view of the rest of the world even for the desirability of the demise of certain states; the old Concert of Europe did at times enforce its decisions with success at the expense of weaker states. But there is no instance on record of a major state thus being peaceably coerced.

The extent to which the formal equality of sovereign states is a fiction, the usefulness of which is being strained increasingly by the steadily growing membership of the United Nations, has also been brought out by recent events, and the same is true of the correlation between the fact and the responsibility of power. This last consideration seems particularly relevant in the operation of American policy. The initial American reaction to the outbreak of hositilities in the Middle East was one of strong condemnation of the ostensible aggressors and of support of the United Nations. But the result cut athwart other desiderata of American policy and there was cause for second thoughts when the United States found itself joined to the Communist states in condemnation of its principle allies, who were in turn bewildered and resentful.

Without a doubt the Middle Eastern crisis dealt a severe blow to the Atlantic alliance, efforts to restore which were subsequently made. In a more limited terms, the outcome served to expose British and French weakness, and both these states emerged with much diminished standing. The parallel with 1936 is not far to seek; not so much in the sense that Nasser was another incipient Hitler, as some contended, as because in 1936 France abdicated by declining to make use of the power that was hers. Twenty years later France and Britain together did the same thing again, though it seems that Britain was this time the prime mover in the policy of abdication. If in this outcome one chooses to see one of the more desirable aspects of democracy, the sensitivity to opinion, both domestic and foreign, it also raised in acute form the question, mentioned on other occasions in this treatment, of the operation of foreign policy in a democratic milieu. Pending the day, seemingly distant, when the whole planet will be a democracy, the factor of power seems to have lost little of its importance in the conduct of the relations among states. There will be occasion to return to this point.

THE HUNGARIAN EPISODE. That the Soviet Union should condemn the aggression against Egypt was only natural. It even went the length of issuing dark threats of its own intervention, threats that some thought safely callable bluff. However that may be—the issue was not tested—the cessation of hostilities in Egypt removed for the time being the danger of a spread of the conflict.

But it also happened that at the very time when hostilities broke out in Egypt the Soviet Union found itself confronted with an awkward development in its own domain. The policy of (relative at least) liberalization that the Soviets had adopted for some time both at home and in their satellites, more particularly since the astonishing speech of Khrushchev in February, 1956, proved in some ways the opening of a Pandora's box. There was restiveness in the satellites, of which the most ostensible signs were for a time in Poland. The rioting workers of Poznan were not ruthlessly suppressed as their counterparts had been in East Berlin in 1953; the trial that ensued was open and fair, resulted in mild reprobation and sentences, and provided an opportunity for an uncommonly free airing of grievances. There were changes in the leadership of Poland, where the once condemned and imprisoned Gomulka reëmerged in control.

Whatever the Kremlin's view of these happenings, the new leadership of Poland, still Communist to be sure, maneuvering with skill on the tightrope between continued subservience and impossible opposition, contrived to assert a surprising measure of independence.

But things went otherwise in Hungary where a similar ferment was at work that led, partly by accident it would seem, to open and uncontrolled violence. The flimsiness of the hold of Communism in Hungary was exposed, and, following a period of intense confusion, ruthless Russian intervention restored the *status quo ante*. Ostensibly, the Russians had merely responded to a call of the Hungarian government to assist it in restoring order and in suppressing a revolt that went officially in the Communist book as counterrevolution of Fascist and foreign-imperialist inspiration.

These matters, too, came before the United Nations whose thorough impotence they served to expose in this case. If indeed the official Communist version of purely domestic trouble and friendly Russian assistance be accepted, what call could there be for outside intervention? But this, as in the case of Egypt, raised once more the question of how much fraud, pretense, and legalistic obfuscation of reality can be of use to the successful operation of the United Nations. It should be mentioned that there was far less unanimity in the United Nations in the Hungarian than in the Egyptian case. This resulted from the fact that, apart from the ostensibly greater ambiguity of the Hungarian situation, Russian troops shooting Hungarian workers (Europeans fighting Europeans) and British and French forces killing Egyptians (Europeans fighting Africans) appeared like wholly different matters, especially among non-Europeans. Even supposedly impartial Nehru responded to this emotional legacy of European imperialism among Asiatics and Africans. Such a response is quite understandable in human terms; it leaves unanswered, however, some rather vital questions and has naturally given rise to the charge that two weights and two measures were being used in the United Nations.

All this may have seemed highly damaging to the world organization. In a way it was, though it was possible to hold the optimistic view that even so much pretense and the use of two measures might in the long term serve the useful purpose of making possible a difficult passage in peace. But it was also possible to take another view of these developments. If power was still the great and most important regulator of the relations among states, might not the simultaneous weakening of the American-led coalition and the internal difficulties of the Communist bloc serve to relax the tensions arising from their opposition? Were this to happen, might not greater scope be found for the influence of many who would not be loath to take the position "a plague on both your houses," Third Forces, neutralists, or what have you? This might in turn enhance the prospects of negotiations and of finding a *modus vivendi* of coexistence.

III. The Erosion of the Blocs

It is within the framework of the possibilities just suggested that we shall proceed to a brief survey of the past fifteen years. In contrast with the twenty-year period of the long armistice, the post–Second World War does not have so clear a shape and marked divisions, a condition emphasized by the fact of proximity; it appears so far on the whole as a time of groping transition toward a future the shape of which remains unclear, containing a variety of possible outcomes. Where Europe is concerned, the most important development may be seen as the launching of the European Economic Community,[47] the kernel of the little Europe of the Six, with inherent possibilities of further integration and expansion. This may be in process of realization, but the shape, fate, and role of Europe remain open questions, though some things of significance have happened that will be discussed presently. However, even a united Europe, under the most favorable of suppositions, can only be at most one of the main repositories

[47] The Treaty of Rome, which came into force on January 1, 1958, launched the European Economic Community. This included France, West Germany, Italy, and the Benelux countries and constituted a further step on the path of integration initiated by the European Coal and Steel Community.

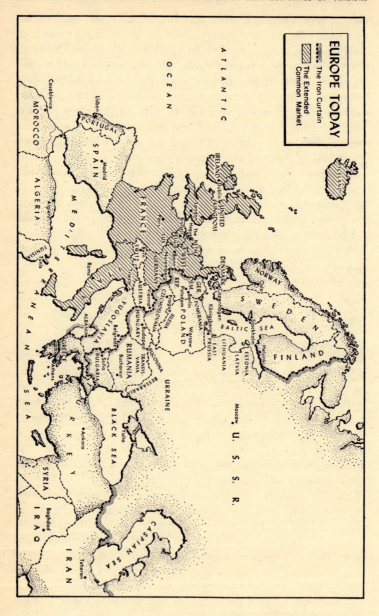

of world power. The larger world meantime has been evolving
and it will therefore be convenient to proceed first to a survey
of its course, after which we shall turn to an examination of the
more narrowly European developments seen in the context of the
larger framework.

The World Framework

In what has become "One World," if not in Wendell
Willkie's sense, at least in the sense that no one segment of the
whole remains unaffected by what happens in others, the most
significant change has been the trend toward the loosening of
blocs, with the consequent tendency away from bipolarity. Something therefore must be said about the manifestations of this
loosening, the evolution that has taken place within each of the
two rival camps, and the impact of that evolution upon their
mutual relations.

THE ARMS RACE

The ancient maxim *si vis pacem para bellum* has been honored
throughout most of history; it is only during brief aberrant
periods, such as the decade following the First World War, that
the idea that peace can be the result of disarmament has achieved
any degree of popularity; even then little that was concrete was
accomplished. The Cold War that followed the Second World
War has been discussed; in more than one aspect it continues,
and so does the armament race. The reasons for Cold War rather
than active hostilities have been two. One is the normal sequel
of exhaustion and weariness in the train of a major conflict, when
first priority goes to recovery; the other is more narrowly technical and in large measure new, the current state of weaponry,
truly without precedent.

Once the United States had made the decision not to exploit its
monopoly of the possession of the atomic weapon—be that decision
judged wise and humane or the opposite—the inevitable consequence was the acceptance of some sort of armed equilibrium. The
Russians proceeded to produce their own nuclear arsenal, and
Sputnik in 1957 was a severe jolt to American complacency. The
somewhat panicky reaction that followed was but a passing phase,
and the recovery of confidence was best expressed in President

Kennedy's commitment to put a man on the moon by 1970, a deed performed in July, 1969. The military implications of the performance need no elaboration any more than do other accomplishments, such as the appearance of earth satellites, of great use in peaceful communications as well as for military purposes. Leaving aside a lengthy and intricate tale of technical progress, warning systems, silos, nuclear submarines, ABMs, MIRVs, and others, the result may roughly be summed up as the achievement of parity between the United States and the Soviet Union. Each had acquired the capacity to destroy many times over the other; hence the balance of terror, the current form of equilibrium, a fragile reed on which to rest the confidence in the durability of peace.

For the balance is not static and the possibility ever exists of a technical breakthrough that may tip the scales on one side or the other. Another consideration intrudes at this point, the fantastic cost of modern weapons, hence the importance of economic resources. Since those of the Soviet Union are in the order of half the American, the strain of keeping up the race is far greater for the former; its political system, however, makes possible the necessary diversion of resources to that end. But even in the American case, especially in the context of the totality of American commitments, the strain has been considerable, reflected in the difficulties into which the American economy ran, the rate of inflation being one of its manifestations.

Thus, economic considerations create the common ground of a similar interest in at least moderating the competition. So far the control of nuclear weapons has been in responsible hands, another fragile reed but also another common condition. This emphasizes the desirability of avoiding the proliferation of such weapons, all the more as the roster of nations capable of producing them inevitably grows. At this point, in addition to the two superpowers, there are three other members in the nuclear club—Britain, France and China—interestingly those possessed of the veto power in the Security Council of the United Nations; quite a number of others possess the necessary techniques and resources but have so far refrained. The problem, therefore, has had two aspects: on the one hand, how sufficiently to overcome the mutual suspicion between the United States and the Soviet Union in order to reach some meaningful and applicable understanding for the limitation of armaments; on the other, how to induce others to consent to a permanent status of inferiority.

Discussions have been protracted, tangled in highly complex technicalities, and in some ways reminiscent of the dreary Genevan debate on a comparable issue during the interwar period. The high points alone will be mentioned. In August, 1963, a treaty was signed in Moscow barring nuclear tests in the atmosphere, but not underground.[48] This was followed in January, 1967, by an agreement on the demilitarization of space and in July, 1968, by a nonproliferation treaty. This last was adhered to by a large number of states, though neither France nor China were among them; the West German and the Japanese consents were reluctant. In November, 1969, the SALT (Strategic Arms Limitation Talks) discussions were initiated in Helsinki. They have continued since, in that city and in Vienna, to the accompaniment of shifting positions on the part of the participants. At this writing here is discussion of a European Security Conference that would further stabilize the equilibrium of forces in Europe.[49]

Needless to say, the approach taken by the United States and the Soviet Union, apart from the solid ground of common interest just indicated, has been influenced by other developments, in particular by those within their respective blocs, both of which have been subjected to centrifugal forces. Each will be considered, following which some attention will be given to their contacts and relations.

THE COMMUNIST BLOC

The speech delivered by Nikita Khrushchev at the Twentieth Party Congress in 1956 had truly opened a Pandora's box. It was in keeping with the colorful and mercurial personality of the Soviet leader, who for some years thereafter maintained his position of primacy in the Soviet state. But there were inner contradictions in his methods, and some of his initiatives proved to be rather less than successful. His blustering revival of the Berlin

[48] Prior to this, in March, 1958, the Soviet Union suspended tests but resumed them in August, 1961, following which American testing was also resumed.

[49] As early as 1956, the Rapacki Plan, so named from the Polish foreign minister who suggested the idea, proposed a denuclearization of a section of central Europe. Though not implemented, the proposal inserts itself into the subsequent interest of the United States and the Soviet Union, as well as of the European states in both blocs, in relaxing tensions between them.

problem at the end of 1958 was followed by a tacit retreat; most of all the ill-considered adventurousness that resulted in the Cuban missile crisis in 1962[50] did not redound to his or to Soviet prestige. In October, 1964, he was ousted from power and, though not otherwise punished, was confined to quiet retreat.[51] Again there was a return to a form of collective leadership, with the figures of Leonid Brezhnev and Alexei Kosygin emerging, the former drawing ahead as the years passed. The new Soviet leadership may fairly be described as consisting of intelligent, cautious, and unimaginative bureaucrats; it had to deal with problems that anteceded its emergence.

A fundamental one, essentially domestic, must at least be mentioned because of its impact on the general Soviet stance and possibilities. It grew out of the desire of the Soviet people for a greater share of the goods of this earth, the issue of guns versus butter, the allotment of resources between heavy industry and consumer goods in one of its aspects. After two generations that had undergone heavy hardships and sacrifices, the younger people especially have shown signs of impatience. That impatience has also manifested itself in the more restricted but highly important sector of the intelligentsia, chafing at the restrictions on its freedom. Ever since the demise of Stalin, having renounced the clarity of his ruthlessness, his successors have dealt with this opposition in irresolute and inconsistent fashion, alternating between permissiveness and repression in a manner reminiscent of pre-revolutionary days. While scientists in some domains, physics for example, have escaped persecution and have been allowed manifestations of courageous and sharp criticism, others have fared less well; the tribulations of the Nobel-Prize-winning writer Solzhenitzyn are sufficiently known, to cite but one among a long list of examples.

THE RUSSO-CHINESE RIFT. This hesitancy in dealing with a domestic problem has had its counterpart in the foreign domain. In this the most important occurrence, pregnant of long-term future consequences, has been the change in the Russo-Chinese relationship. The successful Communist take-over of China under the leadership of Mao Tse-tung in 1949 was at first at least

[50] On Berlin and Cuba, see pp. 672–673.
[51] Khrushchev essentially disappeared from the public scene until his death in 1971.

officially welcomed, even though Stalin's enthusiasm for communism in China had always been highly qualified.

Here was undoubtedly a great extension of the area controlled by the Marxist ideology, but it took little prescience to foresee that, because of her dimensions and numbers, China could not remain in the same subservient position as the small European satellites of the Soviet Union; Peking was a potential rival of Moscow. There is also the highly significant difference that, for all its worship of Marx and Lenin, the Chinese leadership, in this respect more realistic and wiser than the Russian, acknowledged from the first that it was dealing with a society of peasants and hence has not attempted to base itself on a largely nonexistent industrial proletariat or to force the pace of industrial growth.

For a time the two great Communist regimes behaved as brothers in Marx, and the Russians gave aid and advice to the Chinese. But by 1960 a breach manifested itself, which the passage of time has only made wider. In April of that year criticism was voiced in Peking of Moscow's revisionist policy—meaning Khrushchev's deviation from the Stalinist line—and Moscow responded by withdrawing its technical personnel from China. Interestingly, Chinese influence gained a foothold in Europe, in little Albania of all places, which until 1971, in the United Nations for example, took pride in being the spokesman for 800,000,000 people.[52] In December, 1961, Albania achieved the distinction of Muscovite excommunication, which it was able to survive. Sour exchanges between Moscow and Peking continued despite some attempts, mainly on the Soviet side, to patch up the quarrel; in 1964 China refused to participate in a world conference of Communist parties, an attempt to restore the Russian position of leadership in the whole Communist world.

Russia's initial support of Chinese communism fitted the anti-imperialist stance. But to insist upon the validity of the unequal treaties that Russia at one time, like other imperialist Powers, had imposed upon China, can only be regarded as an example of inner contradiction. When the issue was raised by the Chinese, the Soviet reaction, as expressed in Pravda in 1964, was very sharp. It is particularly significant that, despite the withdrawal of Russian

[52] The Albanian position must be understood in the context of differences with Yugoslavia, hence in turn in the context of the relations between that country and the Soviet Union. The climate of these has fluctuated, but on the whole both sides have hesitantly striven for rapprochement.

technical assistance, in November, 1964, China succeeded in exploding her first atomic device; it was in fact a source of general surprise, in view of the backwardness of the Chinese economy, that progress in the nuclear domain should be so rapid as to enable China to set off an H Bomb in 1967.[53]

In this atmosphere of growing tension border clashes occurred in 1969, reminiscent of those that had taken place between the Japanese and the Russians in the late thirties. Open conflict did not occur, though the expectation of it was widespread in 1970. It is also natural in the circumstances that the thought of preventive war, especially with a view to destroying in the bud the Chinese nuclear development, should have been seriously entertained in Moscow; but for the time being the doves, to use modern parlance, prevailed. The Chinese experience with Russian encroachment is a matter of past record; the Russian fear of the huge Chinese mass is authentic and for the long term certainly not devoid of foundation. Here also the Marxist ideology has failed to overcome the national factor, and one is sometimes tempted to recall the Kaiser's Yellow Peril or, more recently, General de Gaulle's views about the future prospects of Russia in Asia.[54]

THE SOVIET UNION'S EUROPEAN SATELLITES. The importance of Yugoslavia's emancipation from subservience to Soviet control in 1948 has been indicated; the significance of this success of heresy cannot be overemphasized, for the condition was irretrievable and the example infectious. The Chinese case and its Albanian footnote have just been mentioned. The case of Hungary in 1956 must be seen as an attempt to stop the possible spread of the disease. If Moscow effectively reasserted its power on that occasion, it was at high cost to its standing; the fiction of capitalist intrigue as a pretext for intervention was wearing thin. The Bulgarian purge of pro-Chinese and pro-Stalinist elements in November, 1962, indi-

[53] The Chinese to be sure have had their own internal problems. The Great Leap Forward in 1958, a misguided attempt at industrial development, turned into costly economic setback, and the Cultural Revolution after 1966 has also had profound—if not too well understood by the outside world—and unsettling effects. But these domestic occurrences do not seem to have affected the general Chinese position *vis-à-vis* the outside, a fact reflected in the durability of Chou En-lai in the direction of foreign policy.

[54] Kaiser William II brandished the Yellow Peril as an argument for unity—under German guidance—of the European peoples. General de Gaulle on various occasions voiced his opinion that much of Russia's Asiatic domain is destined to escape from Russian control.

cated an adaptation in that country to the dominant tendency in the Soviet Union at the time of its occurrence. But the erection of the Berlin Wall in August, 1961, was also an indication that elements of discontent persisted among the Soviet satellites in Europe.

One source of difficulty was the fact that the Soviet Union itself was less advanced and developed, in economic terms for one thing, than some at least of the states it dominated—and to a point exploited. A measure of flexibility was introduced in their relations, as witness for example the altered direction in the German Democratic Republic, whose economic development began to assume impressive proportions.

But a dose of liberalization, in the political domain especially, is a dangerous thing. The year 1968 witnessed in Czechoslovakia what is usually described as the dawn of the Prague spring, not indeed a rejection of the Communist ideology, but an opening of hitherto closed windows to the drafts of freer thought and reform. The change was observed with attentive anxiety in Moscow until it was decided that things had gone too far and that the danger of imititave spreading of the tendency could not be longer endured.

The implementation of the decision was dramatic. After some awkward negotiations, in August, 1968, the forces of the members of the Warsaw Pact except the Rumanian invaded Czechoslovakia, where they met no active resistance but a very cold reception indeed. The pretext was again that of subversive capitalist intrigue and the danger of attack from West Germany, which made possible the fiction that Czechoslovakia was not being attacked but merely assisted by brotherly regimes following the (nonexistent) call for such assistance from within the country. From the standpoint of reasserting Russian control the operation was successful, the Czech leader Dubcek and his government being gradually replaced by a set of suitably subservient puppets, and the country *gleichgeschaltet*. Thus the so-called Brezhnev Doctrine was asserted, the claim to rightful intervention in the affairs of a socialist state that showed deviationist tendencies. It was a doctrine of far-reaching implications and it had a divisive effect among other Communist parties, such as the French and the Italian, an aftermath that seems to have been the source of second thoughts and hesitancy in Moscow.

When the Polish workers of Gdansk and other Polish cities

at the end of 1970 rose again in protest, not against the Communist ideology but more prosaically against certin economic decisions, the response was not an invasion of Poland but the displacement of Gomulka and the grant of concessions to the Polish workers.

It had been pointed out that Rumanian forces had not participated in the invasion of Czechoslovakia. For her increasingly independent attitude Rumania was not punished, maneuvering with skill and suppleness under the leadership of Ceausescu. President de Gaulle in May, 1968, and President Nixon in 1970 both visited Rumania, and the Rumanians have declined to endorse condemnation of China, with which they have maintained friendly relations.

To speak of a Rumanian-Yugoslav-Albanian combination representing Chinese opposition in Russia's European domain would be a premature exaggeration, and to contemplate within any foreseeable future the return of real independence to the Soviet Union's European satellites would be visionary. But there is no denying that the competition between the two great rival claimants of orthodoxy enhances the possibilities of independence on the part of the smaller adherents to the faith, among whom a variety of heresies may prosper. "National" communism, even if it is still communism, has become a solid reality.[55] The legacy of Marxism, as happened to the earlier one of the French Revolution, is in the process of being absorbed into the preexisting state systems.

THE WESTERN OR FREE WORLD

AMERICAN UNCERTAINTIES.   These internal problems and centrifugal tendencies in the Communist world have had their counterpart in the Western, or free. The liquidation of the Korean War, one of the early accomplishments of the Eisenhower administration, had initiated a relative pause in the driving urge of American policy. It was not a return to isolationism by any means, and indeed the Cold War continued—relentlessly conducted by the American Secretary of State, John Foster Dulles, who died in May, 1959. Nevertheless, it was on balance a comparatively inward-looking period on the part of the American people after their strenuous endeavors in the war and its immediate aftermath.

The election of John F. Kennedy to the Presidency in 1960,

[55] The admission of Communist China to the United Nations has had the effect of bringing out into the open more sharply and clearly the Sino-Soviet controversy. Western imperialists could hardly have found harsher language than that used by the Chinese delegate in the Security Council in December, 1971, in excoriating Soviet imperialism for its position in the Indian-Pakistani clash.

by the narrowest of margins over his rival, Richard M. Nixon, introduced a new and more colorful style of leadership. The figure of the youthful American President captured many an imagination, no less abroad than at home; in many eyes, especially among the young, he took on the guise of a knight in shining armor. Leaving aside the domestic scene, where the accent was placed on reform, in the foreign domain he was confronted with two especially important issues—they will be discussed later—in addition to what may be described as the normal, long-standing one of relations with the Soviet Union, the face of the Cold War. His approach to foreign affairs was well expressed in the words he used in his inaugural address: "Let every nation know, whether it wishes us well or ill, that we shall pay any price, bear any burden, meet any hardship, support any friend, oppose any foe to assure the survival and the success of liberty," an assertion of the willingness to assume once more responsibilities of world-encompassing dimensions.

In the proximate island of Cuba a native revolutionary movement finally achieved success when its leader, Fidel Castro, marched into Havana in January, 1959. The American reaction to the Cuban change was not initially and *a priori* hostile, but the possibility of friendly relations, owing to mishandling on both sides, soon evaporated. After two years the breach seemed irrevocable. It was a few months later, in April, 1961, that occurred the episode of the Bay of Pigs. Cuban dissenters, with American assistance, attempted a landing on the island. But the assistance was halfhearted and inadequate, resulting in failure to the accompaniment of embarrassment and discredit to the United States. While it proved possible to carry along the Latin American rest of the continent in quarantining Cuba, the newly proclaimed policy of the Alliance for Progress—an attempt by the United States to show greater concern for the Latin American countries—proved on the whole barren of results.

It has been possible for Cuba to survive American displeasure, to which its response has been of two kinds. One has been to seek to foment discontent south of the American border. In this endeavor success has been very limited;[56] but discontent and instability have been rife in the Latin American world, where the year 1970 saw the advent in Chile of an avowedly Marxist regime.

[56] The quixotic attempt of Che Guevara to foment revolution in Bolivia, where he was captured and met his death, may be cited as an illustration.

It is an awkward dilemma for the United States, torn between the desire for political stability and the protection of its economic interests on the one hand—a desire that has in places and at times led to the endorsement of reactionary, authoritarian regimes—and the realization of the need for reform, yet qualified by the fear lest revolution open a Pandora's box of uncertain possibilities on the other. In the world of today the claim to the legitimacy of the revolutionary mantle has been successfully appropriated by others. But the Latin American situation exceeds the bounds of this treatment and it is only mentioned because of its impact on the United States, the leader of the Western bloc.

The other Cuban reaction was to turn elsewhere for support, in doing which it found a ready Soviet response. Russian aid to Cuba was at first economic, and costly—the purchase of much of its sugar crop; but it extended beyond this to the military domain. The Cuban missile crisis of 1962 will be dealt with presently, after another troublesome American problem and its consequences have been discussed.

THE VIETNAM WAR. The Genevan accords of 1954, which liquidated the French position in Indochina, had divided Vietnam into two parts along the 17th parallel. The North was under solid Communist control, and the prospected elections did not take place in the South. Instead there was local rebellion, with the consequence that the United States, on the plea of unholding the South's independence—one form of the containment of Communist expansion—embarked, on a small scale at first, on a degree of involvement. It was Kennedy's decision at the end of 1961 to increase to 15,000 the number of American "advisers" in South Vietnam. Seizing the bear by the tail is an apt simile, for the American involvement became increasingly deep and substantial. Here also the American dilemma was that between the reluctance to assume direct control and the fiction of assistance to a friendly, independent regime.

When President Kennedy was assassinated in November, 1963, his successor, Lyndon B. Johnson, inherited a situation not of his making. He elected to continue on the same path of involvement, which grew by leaps and bounds, until more than 500,000 American troops were in Vietnam. Never officially declared, it was war nonetheless, a stalemate in effect, reminiscent of the French operation in Algeria. The enormous American war machine, placing too much reliance on air power, yet in a sense never fully unleashed, proved incapable of insuring full, let alone swift, victory, even though a much greater weight of bombs was dropped on the small country, as well as on Cambodia and Laos, than had been used in the entire Second World War. Once more the limitations of conventional warfare in dealing with guerrilla tactics were demonstrated in Vietnam as they had been in other places.

The consequences of this state of affairs have been very great, and some of them are relevant to our discussion. The experience of stalemated conflict is unfamiliar to the American people, whose reaction was increasingly one of revulsion; one is reminded of Chamberlain's "far away country about which we know little." Great as American resources are, the cost of the Vietnam War, added to that of other commitments, had an appreciable impact on the economy; inflation and balance of payment problems were some of the manifestations.

But far more serious was the moral impact, the divisiveness that pervaded the American body politic. A measure of it may be seen in the implied admission of failure that was President Johnson's announcement in March, 1968, that he would not seek reelection.[57] His successor, Richard M. Nixon, proceeded to deescalate and to "Vietnamize" the war, reversing the trend of increasing the size of the American forces in Vietnam. Meanwhile, in June, 1968, peace negotiations were opened up in Paris between Washington and Hanoi; they have so far been barren of results.

Of greatest significance from the standpoint of the present treatment has been the impact of the Vietnam War on America's world position. Where the United States itself is concerned the realization has been brought home that its resources, hence its power, are not without limits. The consequence of this has been a rethinking, a reappraisal of priorities. If the extreme isolationist tendency made no appreciable headway—the time for it is irretrievably past—it was otherwise with the more sober understanding of the necessity of choices.

As to the outside world, America's Vietnam War reminds one of Britain's Boer War at the turn of the century, meaning well-nigh universal condemnation. Such a stance on the part of the Communist, or even the neutralist, world could be expected, but it extended to America's allies, whose position ranged from

[57] The clumsy, secretive, and disingenuous handling of policy, and the subsequent disclosures and controversy, further undermined American morale.

embarrassed reticence to sharply expressed disapproval.[58] Apart from moral judgments, which were abounding, the question for the Europeans was whether the Far Eastern involvement did not imply a diversion of American interest—and capabilities—away from the Atlantic and from Europe. Thus a vicious circle developed: European doubts about the validity of the American commitment in Europe suggested the possible desirability of a more independent policy while, conversely, doubts were fed in America about the dependability of her European allies; each might undercut the other in seeking accommodation with the Soviet Union.

The greatest independence and the most severe criticism were voiced by the French president, General de Gaulle, at times in language that seemed deliberately designed to cause irritation. The effect was a loosening of the Western bloc comparable in some respects to that which has been indicated in the Communist milieu, a condition rife with uncertain possibilities, not all necessarily undesirable, containing among them that of a new, more flexible equilibrium. Before closing these considerations with a somewhat more detailed analysis of more strictly European affairs, something will be said of the relations between the two blocs, especially of those between the United States and the Soviet Union. They are still an important part of the framework within which the rest of the world operates.

RELATIONS BETWEEN THE EASTERN AND WESTERN BLOCS

BERLIN AND CUBA. It was in November, 1958, that the Russians decided to test once more the Berlin situation. This took the form of a long note addressed to the Western Powers that carried overtones of an ultimatum. Contending that existing arrangements were obsolete, it was proposed to make Berlin into a totally independent entity, access to which would have to be negotiated with the German Democratic Republic, to whom the Soviet Union would transfer its functions. Failure to reach agreement among the four occupying Powers within six months would result in separate arrangements between the Soviet Union and the German Democratic Republic; meanwhile indications were given in speeches that the former would support the latter against any attack.

---

[58] The first has been characteristic of the British position, the second of the French, especially during the period of General de Gaulle's tenure. His speech in Phnom Penh in August, 1966, may be cited as an illustration.

The episode may be summed up by saying that the Soviet attempt to test the solidarity of the West resulted in a confirmation of that solidarity. In the face of this situation the six-month deadline was forgotten in Moscow and things continued in Berlin as they had been before. In fact it was in May, 1960, that a summit meeting was to take place in Paris. But by this time Khrushchev seems to have changed his mind about the utility of the meeting. Using the windfall of an American spy plane shot down over the Soviet Union, he made demands with which President Eisenhower refused to comply and nothing came of the meeting.[59] The meeting in Vienna in June, 1961, between the new American President, Kennedy, and Khrushchev unfolded in a somber atmosphere, and the Berlin wall was erected in August, an effective device for staunching the steady flow of escapees from the German Democratic Republic to the West.

The Cuban situation has been mentioned. In August, 1962, evidence was forthcoming that Soviet assistance to Cuba was taking the form of installing nuclear missiles and launching ramps on the island. After much thought and consultation, on October 23, 1962, Kennedy announced his decision to institute a blockade of Cuba. There followed a tense passage, until the Soviet leader decided to back down before what was essentially an American ultimatum. The confrontation had been sharp and from it the United States emerged with enhanced credit and prestige, having successfully met the test of power.

The significance of the episode is considerable. America had taken the decision alone, a fact that strengthened the doubts of Europeans about their place in American councils. When told of it, de Gaulle heartily endorsed the decision but asked pointedly whether he was being "informed or consulted." Yet between the United States and the Soviet Union the incident also had a clarifying effect and introduced a stage of better understanding and relations—the test ban treaty dates from 1963—though it did not enhance Khrushchev's domestic standing. The Cuban situation remained static thereafter, even if Castro too had to draw the conclusion that when it came to vital issues between the two superpowers his own wishes could be bypassed, a lesson others could take in as well.

[59] The American U-2 plane was shot down on May 1, two weeks before the planned summit meeting. The incident was thus no more than a convenient pretext for sabotaging the meeting.

The Vietnamese situation was naturally another source of divergence between the United States and the Soviet Union, though it never became acute. For material assistance Hanoi was largely dependent on the Russians. The Chinese could see eye-to-eye with both Hanoi and Moscow on the score of America's imperialistic behavior in Southeast Asia, but that did not prevent differences and rivalry between them and the Russians over assistance to the Vietnamese.

THE MIDDLE EAST.   Russo-American rivalry thrived in another quarter as well. Following the proclamation of the so-called Eisenhower Doctrine[60] in January, 1957, the middle of 1958 saw intervention by American forces in Lebanon and British forces in Jordan. Both were withdrawn and the incident had no morrow, but the Soviet involvement in Egypt continued and increased. The situation in that country, the 1956 war and its aftermath, was favorable to the extension of Soviet influence in the eastern Mediterranean, where it asserted itself by bypassing the barrier of a suspicious Turkey.[61]

The accumulation of arms and the reiteration of Arab threats, more concretely the closing of the Strait of Tiran and the Egyptian demand for the withdrawal of the U.N. forces, promptly complied with, finally led Israel to the conviction that a confrontation was imminent. It decided to meet the danger by preventive action. In May, 1967, virtually the whole of the Egyptian air force was destroyed on the ground in a matter of hours, and the Israeli forces started an advance across the Sinai Peninsula that brought them to the Suez Canal in a matter of days. They fared equally well on the west bank of the Jordan and against the Syrians on the Golan Heights. The Six Day War was a masterful performance that could only command respect for its technical competence. But it settled little.

The newly occupied territories gave Israel the asset of better

[60] This somewhat nebulous statement, asserting the right of intervention if locally requested, constituted a further step in the process of increasing American involvement in the Middle East.

[61] The island of Cyprus, following the relinquishment of British control, was torn by the clash between the Greek majority and the 20 percent Turkish minority. An uneasy peace has been maintained on the island by the presence of a United Nations force. But when a clash between Greece and Turkey, both members of NATO, seemed imminent in 1964, the sharp intervention of President Johnson, in the form of a letter to the Turkish government, created strong resentment in that country.

frontiers, and the United Nations resolution of November, 1967, demanding their evacuation has been ignored by her. Her distrust of Great Power guarantees is wholly understandable and warranted, but the problem remains of peace in the Middle East, which became an area of increasingly sharp Russo-American confrontation.

This was emphasized by the fact that in the Six Day War French-manufactured aircraft had been the backbone of the Israeli air force. But, on the plea that Israel was guilty of aggression, the French position underwent a sharp about-face, cutting off the supply of military assistance to Israel. This shift was related to the fact that, following the liquidation of the Algerian War, France set about reëstablishing her position in the Arab world; eventually she even agreed to supply aircraft to Libya. The success of this French endeavor remains problematic, all the more so as the Arab world, despite its reiterated assertions of unity, continues to be torn by dissensions. These stem from two main sources: the internal stresses of societies seeking to insert themselves into the modern stream of economic and social change; and rivalries between various centers of power. Cairo has aspired to a position of leadership among the Arabs, but has been challenged by others, Algeria for example. The United Arab Republic, an Egyptian-Syrian union proclaimed in January, 1958, was dissolved three years later; a later comparable attempt involving Egypt, Libya, and the Sudan remains a question mark.[62] The one uniting factor shared by the Arab world seems to be the negative one of hatred of Israel.

The Soviet reaction to the Arab defeats of 1967 was to intensify the scope of its assistance, in the form of both arms and advisers. The counterpart of it was a correspondingly increased American involvement in maintaining a balance of forces through assistance to Israel, a condition that reflects the current version of rival imperial competition. In this contest such an element as the French behavior becomes a complicating factor: it can be read as an alternative to a too-exclusive Soviet monopoly of influence among the Arabs, and as such welcomed by them, but it also raises the question of whether it assists or hinders the American effort to accomplish the same purpose.

In any case the American interest in the Mediterranean, the

---

[62] The discovery of oil in Libya has provided that territorially large but mostly desert state—its population is about 2,000,000—with very great financial resources, a fact that has had the effect of distorting its position of power.

eastern part of it especially, has been emphasized by the presence of the Sixth Fleet. In the naval domain as in the nuclear, the Soviet Union has striven to achieve parity, so far with impressive results. Russian craft in the Mediterranean have appeared in increasing numbers, and while both Powers have recoiled from open confrontation, neither will yield to the other and they have been indulging in a game that so far remains a delicate and dangerous bluff. It contains the contrary possibilities of clash, either by accident or owing to the uncontrollable initiative of their respective dependents, but also of accommodation. The prospect of agreement between the United States and the Soviet Union, with its possible consequence of an attempt at an imposed solution, is suspected and feared by their local Mediterranean clients, even though in the Egyptian case it could have the contrary advantage of furnishing a face-saving alibi. The model and the accomplishments of the nineteenth-century Concert of Europe are neither wholly irrelevant nor totally forgotten. The Middle East remains a highly sensitive point of East–West confrontation.

The Continued Devolution of Empire

But this particular situation, the evolution of the Arab world and its repercussions, must be seen as but one local aspect of a larger condition: the continuing struggle of the formerly dependent world to solve its own problems and to find its place in the larger context of the whole world and of the rivalries of the Great Powers. What may be called the first wave of decolonization has been dealt with; considerable remained to be done at the close of the decade of the fifties, and that tale will be briefly summarized at this point.

By way of introduction two general observations are useful. One is the fact that the attempt to adopt the model of Western institutions has met with but mediocre success. Democracy and representative institutions have had enough difficulty in securing their purpose in their original native milieus, where they had at least the advantage of being the outcome of a long evolutionary process. Abstract ideals, noble as they may be *in abstracto*, can also in practice be tantamount to a denial of reality. It is not therefore very surprising that the democratic practice should have fared ill among societies where it lacks roots. We shall not attempt to rehearse the roster of coups and the succession of regimes that have been characteristic, amounting to a normal pattern rather than the exception, of the course of a large number of states newly risen to independence. The Soviet or the Chinese pattern, for all their ultimate dedication to the achievement of egalitarian democracy, may well in their present coercive stage be a better-suited model for emerging states. To this must be added the all-important fact of economic conditions. To industrialize is all very well, but how do it, where to find the necessary capital resources, is an altogether different question. We shall not enter into a discussion of the problem of foreign aid beyond saying that it has been generally diminishing and that, even so far as it has been forthcoming, it has not brought the boons expected of it; the gap between the rich and the poor, at the level of states, has if anything been widening.

The second consideration is the fact that a crude application of the democratic idea in combination with the fetish of sovereignty has resulted in a proliferation of states, some of them of highly questionable viability. This condition has been reflected in the operation of the United Nations, where the clearest result has been a devaluation of the pronouncements of the General Assembly.[63] This has been touched upon and will not be repeated. Some salient events alone, because of their wider implications, will be indicated.

In the British milieu the retreat of empire continued, essentially in orderly fashion. Thus in March 1957, the former Gold Coast, renamed Ghana, achieved independence; its leader, Nkrumah, until his downfall in 1966 sought to establish a position of leadership among the emerging African states. After a while little was left in Africa of British control. The federative tendency encouraged by the British, in East Africa and the Caribbean for example, sensible as it may have been, on the whole has not met with success. The civil war that tore Nigeria from 1966 to 1969, though it did not achieve separateness for Biafra, is an illustration.

The Rhodesian federation broke up and a special problem arose in Southern Rhodesia, where the controlling white element,

[63] In connection with the Korean War American influence was able to secure the adoption of the "Uniting for Peace" resolution, a device enabling the General Assembly to intervene in the event of a stalemated situation in the Security Council. The long-term effect of this *ad hoc* measure has to a large extent been a devaluation of United Nations resolutions and a disregard of Article 19 of the Charter, as witness the cases of the Congo and the six-day Arab-Israeli war in 1967. See below, p. 680, n. 67.

although a mere 5 percent of the population, issued a Unilateral Declaration of Independence in 1965 rather than yield its privileged position. Britain had neither the means nor the desire to use force to suppress what was unquestionably rebellion, and the sanctions decreed by the United Nations proved on balance ineffectual.[64]

The racial issue has bedeviled the Commonwealth. The Union of South Africa refused to heed Macmillan's hint in a speech he delivered in February, 1961, suggesting that the "winds of change" called for greater flexibility in the domain of race relations. South Africa has adhered to the frank policy of race discrimination that is *apartheid;* she has also refused to divest herself of the mandate for Southwest Africa, again despite United Nations demands. Eventually she quit the Commonwealth in 1961, thereby giving point to the question of the meaning and content of that institution.

Other members of the Commonwealth have also had difficulties, of which the persisting difference between India and Pakistan over Kashmir is an example. It flared up into brief hostilities in the summer of 1965, the matter being provisionally settled owing to the intromission of Soviet good offices. Considerable significance attaches to the fact that India and Pakistan, both of them members of the Commonwealth, should have met in Tashkent rather than in London,[65] an episode that marked a step in the extension of Soviet influence in the Indian subcontinent.

There have been differences between India and China as well. Despite their repeated assertion of community of views, on the score of their opposition to imperialism above all, their incipient rivalry for leadership among the newly free flared up into open conflict when the Chinese, after they had reëstablished control over Tibet, asserted border claims in the Himalayas. Though militarily successful, the Chinese did not push their advantage in 1962, essentially content with the humiliation of India. A later consequence of this state of affairs has been to bring India closer to the Soviet Union, while China has cultivated the friendship of Pakistan. Power rivalries are by no means the exclusive appanage

[64] Subsequent negotiations between Britain and Rhodesia led, at the end of 1971, to an agreement that would give Rhodesian independence the stamp of legality. But this has only been achieved at the cost of putting off the possibility of majority rule to a very distant and problematic future.

[65] On the further British retreat from Asia and the Indian Ocean, see below, p. 681.

of the great European Powers, and Europe counts for little in the Indian subcontinent, save insofar as one considers Russia European.

Indonesia, too, having shaken off the influence of Europe, Dutch in her case, under the leadership of Sukarno, showed signs of aspiring to a role of leadership in the Third World. She secured possession of the last remnant of Dutch control in Western New Guinea, West Irian, but eventually Sukarno was displaced by an internal coup in 1965. Concurrently, the substantial Communist influence in Indonesia was destroyed in the crude form of a blood bath.

Imperial devolution has followed a less smooth course in the French case than in the British, as already indicated before. The eviction of the French from Indochina has been dealt with, and the Fourth Republic's attempted solution of a French Union was essentially barren of results. During the second half of the fifties France became involved in Algeria in a situation reminiscent of the Indochinese. Proximity, a population that was 10 percent of European derivation, and the fact that Algeria was constitutionally part of France added to the difficulty of the problem.

The situation had serious repercussions in metropolitan France, where it led to the downfall of the Fourth Republic. General de Gaulle, called back from retirement as the savior once more, having become convinced that French control could no longer be maintained in Algeria, maneuvered with patience and skill until the Evian accords in May, 1962 granted the Algerians their wish—to join the ranks of independent states. At the same time he dealt in drastic fashion with the rest of the empire. The result was that in 1960 fifteen new states, largely former French administrative divisions, gained admission to the United Nations.

With the exception of Guinea most of these states have retained some connection with France, economic and cultural in the main. On a proportionate basis, France has made the largest contribution of any country to assistance to the underdeveloped world. But that assistance, which has been diminishing, has been directed exclusively to her former possessions. The outcome of that policy, whether continued influence and fruitful association or a passing phase, remains to be tested. Algeria, the keystone, has given indications of restlessness and has shown a marked interest in responding to Soviet advances, especially since the advent of Colonel Boumedienne to power in 1965.

The French model of abrupt imperial devolution was followed

in the case of the Belgian Congo. On July 1, 1960, it achieved full independence, a condition for which the large country was poorly prepared, almost totally lacking native administrative cadres. The result was chaos and a mutinous army; the issue of national integrity was at stake for a time amid the competition of diverse ethnic groups and of rival leaders. The United Nations, to which the Congo had gained admission, concerned itself with the problem and intervened in the form of material assistance and of sending military contingents from various small Powers. Behind this intervention lurked the rival influences of greater Powers, especially the United States and the Soviet Union.

Eventually, the integrity of the Congo, recently renamed Zaire, was preserved and a measure of order restored.[66] Much of the assistance, other than troops, had been provided by the United States, and it is of interest that the Soviet Union and France, though not making use of the veto power, have refused to pay their share of the assessment for the operation.[67]

At all events the decade of the sixties witnessed the total emancipation of Africa, in formal terms at least, from European control, save for the Portuguese possessions; Portugal, the first European colonizer, has so far refused to follow the example of others. The rapidity of the transformation has raised as many questions as it has answered, largely because of the unpreparedness of the liberated. It might well have been better for all concerned, colonizers and colonized alike, had the process been more gradual. But this is a hypothetical question by now beside the point. The collectively suicidal policy of the European states has produced this result. Yet, as also pointed out, the need for capital and technical assistance has the effect of prolonging the role of outside influence. A number of African states retain membership in the British Commonwealth, and most of the francophone ones are associated with the Common Market. Inevitably, American interest has developed in Africa and so has Russian; this last, however, save in the Arab section, has achieved but meager results. The Chinese, too, have given indica-

[66] It is in connection with the United Nations operation in the Congo that Dag Hammarskjöld, the Secretary General of the organization, met his death in an airplane accident in the Congo.

[67] This has raised an awkward issue for the the United Nations. Under the provisions of Article 19 of the Charter, the Soviet Union and France should have been deprived of their voting rights. Rather than face the problem, the breach of Article 19 has been overlooked. The Russians and the French have contended that the Security Council alone was possessed of the power to make appropriations for the Congo operation.

tions of interest, in Tanzania for example, but only on a rather modest scale so far.

The retreat of Europe's imperial position continued elsewhere as well. The British have quit Singapore and have given notice of their intention to withdraw from east of Suez. Their position in the Persian Gulf and on the periphery of the Arabian Peninsula has reached the last stages of renunciation.

But the result of imperial devolution has not been the emergence of a coherent and effective Third Force. The unforeseen—at the time of its birth—proliferation of membership in the United Nations is an accomplishment of questionable value; by the time Malta and the Seychelles have each one vote in the General Assembly, to mention but two among a large and growing number of ministates, there is validity in questioning the usefulness of what is tantamount to a *reductio ad absurdum* of the principle of sovereignty and to a patent denial of the facts of power. One concrete result so far, as already indicated, has been the devaluation of General Assembly resolutions, ignored with impunity by large and small states alike.

Europe in the World Today

THE STATE OF EUROPEAN INTEGRATION

Speaking of Third Forces, the candidacy of Europe, or at least of that part of it which is free to exercise that role, has often been discussed. Certainly the potential exists. We shall therefore turn in these closing pages to more strictly European developments; these must be considered while always bearing in mind the larger framework of the whole world, which is the reason why an outline of it has been sketched.

That the former Great Powers of Europe have no possibility of recovering their earlier position may be regarded as established fact; individually they lack the dimensions, numbers, and resources of the superpowers. The issue therefore becomes that of whether they can effect some sort of union, for which accomplishment an obvious prerequisite is the abandonment of the insistence on the prerogative of national sovereignty. That the peoples of Europe are no longer infected, to the degree at least that they once were, by the nationalistic virus would be difficult to deny. But the weight of historic tradition persists, and the well-entrenched apparatus of state power resists a diminution of its role.

THE NORTH SEA TRIANGLE.   More narrowly, what matters above all are the relationships and the positions of three states, what may be called the North Sea Triangle—Great Britain, France, and Germany. If these three can come to terms, they constitute a sufficiently powerful core that would easily attract the rest of the free and might even contemplate, in an unspecified future, extending that attraction to the domain of the Soviet satellites. Open conflict among the three Powers just mentioned is usually considered, probably correctly, to have receded outside the domain of the possible; but that does not mean that competition among them for at least priority of place has completely ceased, or even that the possibility of some combination of two has wholly disappeared. In a novel context and in attenuated fashion the traditional relationships of European Powers have not totally lost their meaning.

The European Coal and Steel Community was in part an attempt to solve the Franco-German problem. The British refusal to join it was an expression of the British feeling of uniqueness and distinctness. In British eyes union with Europe was but a third, reluctantly considered possibility, to which two others were preferred. The first of these, the imperial or Commonwealth solution, has had to be put down as a failure; enough has been said in the preceding pages to establish that point. The second, close association with the United States, the special relationship, has fared little better. The last-named country prefers to deal with equals, or alternatively to encourage the unity of Europe. Here lies the essence of the British dilemma, and facing it has been a slow process. Something more will be said presently of the latest developments in that domain.

The German case presents a very special situation. It makes for interesting reflection to observe that, one hundred years after unification, the German people are in a sense back to first base; though in a manner geographically different from that existing before 1871, Germany is again divided. The intervening period has been at once a great success story and a dismal failure. In some respects the success story continues, as witness the economic performance of the Federal Republic; the German Democratic Republic, since the reversal of the Soviet attitude in its regard, has also been the scene of an impressive economic revival. Fear of German power persists in Europe, and the peculiar nature of the Nazi interlude, in combination with Germany's impressive wartime military record, makes probable the continuation of German disabilities for some time longer, though not for an indefinite time. The characterization of Germany, West Germany especially, as an economic giant and a political dwarf has had validity, but that condition has been changing.

In these circumstances the policy of the Federal Republic has been conducted with moderation and skill, reminiscent of that of the Stresemann period. German politics have also operated in orderly fashion. The transition has been effected with smoothness from the period of Christian Democratic dominance, first under the strong and able leadership of Konrad Adenauer until his retirement in 1963, through the less deft chancellorship of Ludwig Erhard, through the grand Christian-Social Democratic coalition led by the team of Kiesinger and Brandt, and finally to the purely Social Democratic administration led by the latter. As the prospect of reunification has receded into an indefinite future, the more pressing question has been that of managing relations with the rest of the Western alliance while unfreezing a rigid stance toward the East, of which the Hallstein Doctrine[68] was the best expression. The importance of the Franco-German relationship has been mentioned before.

THE FIFTH FRENCH REPUBLIC. France, too, has undergone some unexpected developments. Under the Fourth Republic she made an excellent economic recovery and the reversal of the demographic situation—France now numbers 50,000,000—is also significant. But the politics of the Fourth Republic were confused, uninspiring, and not suited to the day. It was the inability of that regime to deal with the imperial problem, more specifically the Algerian War, that brought the threat of civil war to France. General de Gaulle returned to power, initially as Prime Minister and on his own terms, in May, 1958. His tasks were two: the preservation of internal order and some solution of the imperial impasse. On the score of the first, it will suffice to say that a new constitution was enacted with overwhelming popular endorsement. Thus the Fifth Republic was born, of which the chief characteristic was the enhanced power of the executive, a solution to which France has returned again and again and has equally repeatedly rejected. At any rate, under the presidency of de Gaulle, and even since his retirement in 1969, France has known governmental stability.

Whatever the final judgment of history may be on this odd

[68] The Hallstein Doctrine asserted the refusal of the Federal Republic to have relations with any state, other than the Soviet Union itself, that granted recognition to the German Democratic Republic.

and larger-than-usual star in the political firmament, his interest in and understanding of the facts of power and his skill in manipulating them, are difficult to deny; he belongs in the Richelieu tradition. His approach to the imperial problem could be deduced from his appraisal of the Syrian situation shortly after the First World War: "My impression is that we hardly penetrate this region, and that the people remain as alien to us—and conversely—as they have always been. . . . We must either achieve this penetration, or leave." It was consistent that he should let Algeria and the rest of the empire go in the manner that has been described.

But his did not mean renouncing a belief in the role and greatness of his country, though not the entertainment of obviously outdated Napoleonic ambitions. This approach shaped the main lines of his policy, which may be put under three heads: adherence to the Western alliance, but with a diminution of dependence on the United States; a diminution also of the British position, achieving a rought parity with it for the French; exploitation of the disabilities with which Germany was saddled.

The first two of these aims found expression in the memorandum he sent to President Eisenhower very shortly after his return to office, as early as September, 1958. It was essentially a demand for the creation of an Anglo-Franco-American world directorate. This was clearly pretense, for if a case could be made for Anglo-French parity, the dimensions of American power were obviously in a different category. Whatever merit there may have been in the proposal, it did not meet with a favorable response.

This raises another question. De Gaulle believed in Europe, in a united Europe of some sort, but not in a merger in which the component parts would lose their identities; a "Europe of states" was his phrase. Innocent of aggressive intent, he saw in the arrangement a possibility of French leadership, a *primus inter pares* position for France; the appanage of sovereignty would not be surrendered.

It is of interest that nothing was done by France to interfere with the implementation of the Treaty of Rome, which had come into effect on January 1, 1958.[69] But it is also undeniable that the movement for European integration suffered a setback. De Gaulle's pronouncements were not altogether convincing to others, among

[69] The Treaty of Rome, signed in 1957, created the European Economic Community, consisting of France, West Germany, Italy, and the Benelux countries. A 20 percent devaluation of the franc gave France a useful commercial advantage during the years immediately following the inauguration of the Common Market.

whom they revived fears of hegemonic French intent reminiscent of the period following the First World War.

BRITAIN AND EUROPE.   By this time the British government of Harold Macmillan had come to the conclusion—the aftermath of Suez is important in this connection—that the imperial and American options seemed unrewarding and that Britain should therefore apply for admission to the Common Market, which seemed to be a thriving concern. One is tempted to speak of a tragicomedy of errors at this juncture. It is well to bear in mind that on the prerogative of sovereignty the British and the French attitudes are close to each other, much more inflexible than those of other Europeans; this very similarity makes agreement all the more difficult.

In any case, Macmillan's visit to de Gaulle in December, 1962, was immediately followed by a meeting between the former and Kennedy in Nassau.[70] That meeting was ill prepared and ill contrived, with the consequence that de Gaulle felt he had been double-crossed and disregarded. He chose the occasion of one of his press conferences the following month to announce in his wonted lordly manner, of which brutality could be a calculated part, a French veto on Britain's admission to the small Europe of the Six. His contention that the British were not truly European may be accepted as valid; the conclusion that they must be excluded instead of being converted through participation is another matter again. The real issue was the fact that de Gaulle was suspicious of what he mistakenly regarded as a too intimate Anglo-American connection—in more homely language, Britain as the Trojan horse of American influence in Europe.

THE FRANCO-GERMAN RELATIONSHIP AND ITS IMPACT.   But other possibilities might be open. The French veto on Britain's admission to the Common Market was generally a cause of dismay to the other members of the organization. But in Germany, Chancellor Adenauer was a sincere believer in Franco-German reconciliation. When he had met de Gaulle the two aging statesmen had found each other highly congenial, and just because the latter's patriotism was above suspicion he was in a better position than anyone else in

[70] A revision of the military arrangements between the two countries was made necessary by the American decision to abandon the production of *Skybolt*. The subsequent invitation to France to participate in the new arrangement conveyed to de Gaulle the impression of a slighting afterthought.

France to extend the hand of reconciliation to Germany, a gesture that was highly appreciated across the Rhine. Almost simultaneously with the blackballing of Britain took place the conclusion of a Franco-German treaty of amity, harbinger of possible future close cooperation between the two countries.

Although the treaty was welcome in Germany, it also gave rise to some questions for it made sharp the dilemma in which the Federal Republic was placed by its close association with France. Adenauer was willing, to a point at least, to accept a backseat position and to follow French leadership. The difficulty lay in the fact that one of the aims of French policy was the diminution of American influence, a condition that in turn points to the common dilemma of all free Europe: natural restlessness over dependence on American power and lingering doubts about the solidity of American purpose are combined with the consciousness of Europe's own deficiencies, in the matter of defense in particular. Thus Europeans, and not the French alone, have criticized and berated American actions and policies while some of them, especially the Germans, have raised worried outcries whenever any suggestion has been made of a reduction of American forces in Europe.

On these matters de Gaulle had the advantage of self-confidence and clarity of thought. Should it come to the ultimate test, for reasons of self-interest if no others, America would come to the defense of Europe; the Atlantic alliance therefore retained its validity. But that test was unlikely to occur because of lessened Russian aggressiveness, consequence among other things of the mounting difficulties in the Communist milieu. It was consequently safe to take what to many appeared as a strong anti-American stance, and France increasingly withdrew from cooperation with NATO, until the headquarters of it had to be moved to Belgium.[71]

A double and contradictory effect was involved for American policy. Insofar as the French, or the Europeans more generally, pursued a policy of greater accommodation toward the Soviet Union, they were adopting a position similar to the American one of seeking relaxation of tensions with that country, while at the same time they were weakening the American bargaining position. And it should be borne in mind all the while that the inconclusive Vietnam War pointed to a diversion of American attention and in-

[71] Beginning with the withdrawal of the French fleet from the NATO command, the French tendency of disassociation from that organization culminated in the withdrawal of France from it in 1969.

terest away from Europe toward the Pacific and the Far East. It all added up to a loosening of the blocs and somewhat greater freedom of action for the Europeans, to whichever bloc they belonged, a condition expressed by increasing contacts and exchanges across the Iron Curtain.

As to Germany, the last thing she wanted was to be faced with a clear choice between Washington and Paris, and her leaders strained every effort to retain the connection with both. Therein lay the weakness of the French position, for clearly French power could not offer itself as a substitute for American. As a consequence, the Franco-German treaty proved largely barren of results. There was a measure of agreement among Europeans with the fundamental aspects of French policy *vis-à-vis* America,[72] even if no one else would couch criticism in the peculiar shape of Gaullist rhetoric; the net result therefore was a degree of French isolation and certainly a setback for the movement of European integration.[73]

The American reaction to these circumstances was, at the governmental level at least, the intelligent one of not attaching exaggerated importance to French criticism and pinpricks; de Gaulle received near-royal treatment when he attended Kennedy's funeral. The simple fact is that French power does not carry sufficient weight to balance the American. Nevertheless some important and valid issues had been raised that may be summed up in the question of whether the rigid attitude of the Cold War did not call for readjustment. Important changes took place at the turn from the sixties to the seventies; close as they are to us, hence unsuited to dependable appraisal, they yet contain numerous possibilities of changed orientation.

THE EVENTS OF 1968 AND THEIR SEQUEL

De Gaulle's services to his country have been considerable, and they may be summed under the two heads of restoration of self-

[72] There has been considerable discussion centering around the American economic penetration of Europe. It has given rise to the divergent reactions of opposition and of the desirability of imitation of American methods and ways. This second view has been expressed in Jean-Jacques Servan-Schreiber's book, *The American Challenge* (New York, Atheneum, 1968).

[73] The Common Market countries have experienced considerable difficulty in the attempt to agree on agricultural policy. France, because of the possibilities of her own agriculture, has proved the most recalcitrant negotiator and has on occasion resorted to high-handed pressure in an effort to make her views prevail.

respect and position and of having opened the possibility of a more adequate constitutional practice. As to the substance and reality of French power, the situation remains best summed up in his own phrase, *les choses sont ce qu'elles sont* (things are what they are). France is one of the chief components of Europe outside the Soviet Union, no less but no more.

The revolt of the young is one of the interesting phenomena of our time, consequence of the continuing rise of the mass in the affluent society, in which that revolt has chiefly manifested itself. It is of interest to note how widespread it is, from Berkeley to Tokyo by way of Paris and Rome, but discussion of it exceeds the bounds of this treatment. It may be observed, however, that the tendency is highly fragmented; hence it would seem to contain little promise of the possibility of effectiveness associated with hard-thinking, coördinated, revolutionary movements.

However that may be, the normally governmentish French were becoming increasingly weary of the monarchical authoritarian aloof, though not unduly repressive, behavior of their president. A minor squabble in the University of Paris in May, 1968, soon escalated into what reminded one of the atmosphere of February, 1848. Before long the country was paralyzed by well-high universal strikes. It was a situation not devoid of irony, for while the students were spouting revolution, the Communist leadership of the workers, supposedly the proprietor of that tendency but in effect a conservative force of order, was desperately trying to maintain itself in the leadership of its own troops from the rear. In the end nothing of political substance was accomplished, and the French people rallied to their existing leadership once enough of them had been sufficiently frightened.

Yet the regime had been seriously shaken, and the following year, undergoing defeat in a referendum that he proposed to the country,[74] de Gaulle quit power.[75] He was eventually succeeded in the presidency by Georges Pompidou. The fundamentals of French policy have not been seriously modified and there is little prospect that France will rejoin NATO, even if her manner has become more accommodating and softer. Certainly the flamboyant style of Gaullist policy has disappeared, but the issue of the fate of Euro-

---

[74] The referendum awkwardly combined two unrelated proposals, a reform of the Senate and a regional reorganization of the country. It has even been suggested that it was purposely so designed in order to insure its defeat.

[75] General de Gaulle went into retirement and died in 1971 while occupied in writing his memoirs.

pean integration and of the solidity, or lack of solidity, of the blocs remains.

It was shortly after the abortive French events of May–June, 1968, that, as indicated before, an end was put to the Prague spring. But the Brezhnev Doctrine, if it meant a reassertion of Soviet control, hence a consolidation of the Soviet bloc, could not conceal the rising ferment in that bloc. The Rumanians have skillfully walked a tightrope, asserting greater independence, and the Polish events of 1970 have also been mentioned; but the Yugoslavs are concerned about the possibility of Russian action in connection with the succession of Tito. The Russians did not see their way to interfering in either Poland or Rumania, and the disruptive impact of multiplying assertions of independence has continued to assert itself.

The Western reaction to the invasion of Czechoslovakia was one of indignation and of sympathy for the victims of Russian heavy-handediess, but it did not go beyond verbal expression. The Russians in a sense were right, for if the pretext of plotting and of danger from Western attack was too flimsy to merit serious consideration, their problem was the very real one of the degree of deviation that they could afford to allow among their satellites; it could well become a dangerous infection. Thus, in a curious way, their action in Czechoslovakia, like their Cuban attempt in 1962 and their subjection of Hungary in 1956, eventually served to enhance stability between the opposing blocs—neither would interfere in the domain of the other—though it was also at least a momentary setback to the tendency toward détente and possible rapprochement between them. The solidity of the blocs was thus reaffirmed, but it was at the same time made clear that within both a disruptive ferment was at work.

The removal of General de Gaulle from the political scene, if it did not alter the fundamentals of French policy, nevertheless introduced greater flexibility into it. The events of 1968 in France had clearly shown the limitations of French power, in the economic domain among others.[76] In Britain the Labour government of Harold Wilson was having little success in dealing with the economic situation—the pound was devalued in 1967—and, despite

---

[76] Concurrently there was a French attempt, in the form of an attack on the dollar, to force a revision of currency arrangements, especially of the role of reserve currencies, the dollar and the British pound. The attempt failed at the time, but the issue recurred in 1971. See p. 691, n. 78.

another French veto in 1966, decided to persist in the attempt to join the Common Market. A mis-timed general election in June, 1970, unexpectedly brought the Conservatives back to power. Edward Heath, the new Prime Minister, had always been a staunch advocate of Britain's membership in Europe. Negotiations were pursued in earnest and came to a successful conclusion in Brussels; in October, 1971, the British Parliament endorsed this result. Though little enthusiasm for it existed at the popular level, but rather an attitude of resignation before the inevitable, the change on both sides of the Channel may be taken as recognition of the facts of life—to put it another way, acknowledgment, as in 1904, that Britain and France are in the same boat.

There is, however, a great difference between 1971 and 1904; yet, even though no threat of armed conflict seems to exist, the fact of German power is again a factor. As the Franco-German association proved meager of results, as time passes and the memory of the German record becomes attenuated, and as Germany—even West Germany alone—has emerged as the strongest economic unit of the Continent, a greater German assertiveness has become manifest. By the slenderest of margins the Social Democrats secured control of the government in that country after the election of 1969. The new Chancellor, Willy Brandt, just because of the unimpeachability of his record, was in a better position than anyone else to initiate the new *Ostpolitik*, a tentative attempt to find a new basis for relations with the Soviet bloc, including he German Democratic Republic and the Soviet Union itself. Having discarded the Hallstein Doctrine, the new West German policy implied in addition the acceptance of the Oder-Neisse frontier and at least the tacit or implicit acknowledgment of the present division of Germany.

These endeavors found a willing response in Moscow and an even readier one among its satellites, the German Democratic Republic being the most hesitant.[77] The Russians, concerned with the Far East, have been anxious to secure stability on their western border.

All this of course must be seen in the larger context of world-wide developments. Napoleon is credited with the phrase, *impos-*

---

[77] Following the resignation—or ouster—of Walter Ulbricht, the policy of the German Democratic Republic became somewhat more accommodating, until, even though not without considerable difficulty, it proved possible to conclude a direct agreement between it and the Federal Republic.

sible n'est pas français (nothing is impossible to the French). It looked for a time as if the United States had made the slogan its own, but America, too, has come like Napoleon to acknowledge that there may be limitations to her power. The problems of America are many, not least that of an economy beset at once by inflation and unemployment. But the single most important source of unrest and dissatisfaction in the American body politic has been the stalemated Vietnam War. The election of 1968 brought Richard M. Nixon to the Presidency. His policy of deescalation of the war and the stalemated negotiations with Hanoi in Paris have been mentioned. The outcome of it all remains uncertain.

THE LATEST REORIENTATION. The past two years are too close to us for dependable appraisal of their import. Nevertheless, certain developments took place during their course that, while they may turn out to have little lasting significance, also contain the possibility of a changed orientation. For that reason, brief mention of them is warranted by way of conclusion to our discussion.

The unresolved problems of the United States—mainly the state of the economy and the war—resulted in President Nixon taking a bold initiative in the summer of 1971, an apparently abrupt reversal of his previous course, variously interpreted as unprincipled behavior or intelligent flexibility. Within a short interval two startling decisions were announced: the introduction of economic controls[78] and a visit by Henry Kissinger, the President's chief adviser on foreign policy, to Peking, in preparation for a visit by the President himself to China. Both announcements were generally welcomed by the American people, weary of a too onerous and ambitious world role.

One consequence of the second announcement was the admission of Communist China to the United Nations in November, 1971.[79] Acknowledgement of the existence of by far the largest among the world's nations had been unduly delayed by ideological considerations and by the extent of American influence; the acceptance of reality is undoubtedly a gain, but the facts of power

[78] Simultaneously, the dollar was detached from gold and a 10 percent surcharge imposed on imports. These measures, designed to redress the American balance of payments, which was running into a very large deficit, led to a small devaluation of the dollar and a general realignment of currencies.

[79] A fine point of law was raised in this connection on the issue of whether Nationalist China, which had nominally held the Chinese seat, was being evicted from the United Nations or whether China continued to be represented in the world organization, but by Peking instead of Taiwan.

have not altered. In general development the Soviet Union remains a considerable distance behind the United States, and China a greater distance behind both; yet in terms of potential the equation of the three is warranted. The problem of their relations and possible alignments—there were also three main centers of power before 1939—will constitute the most important single issue of the international politics of the near future.

Almost immediately upon the admission of Communist China to the United Nations that body was confronted with the issue of open hostilities between India and Pakistan. From the standpoint of the present treatment the most significant aspect of the matter has been the added proof of the total incapacity of the Security Council to take any action, hamstrung as it is by the veto.[80] Interestingly, the vetoes have been Russian and Chinese, the two having in addition indulged toward each other in vituperation hitherto reserved for the capitalist, imperialist West and confined between them to the level of party disputes. Also, the Soviet Union supported India and China supported Pakistan. The facts of power and the game of power politics continues, but does so in this case in a region and over issues in which the role of the West, certainly of Europe, has been reduced to minimal proportions.

Coming back to Europe, especially in view of what has just been said, only in union could it constitute an entity of dimensions comparable with the other three centers of world power. Hence the importance of the admission of Britain to the Common Market,[81] which reopens the possibility of a fresh start in the movement for European integration. It has been indicated that the British and the French remain the most jealous adherents to the prerogative of sovereignty, an appanage that they cannot fully retain if Europe as a whole is to have a place in the world commensurate with its potential. At best it will take time for the transformation to be effected, and the outcome will be molded by the issue of the

[80] The handling of the Indo-Pakistani dispute has had implications for other situations, that of the Middle East for example. Israel's conviction of the worthlessness of international action and guarantees was confirmed, and the Arab-Israeli conflict was at least momentarily displaced from its position of priority among international concerns.

[81] On January 1, 1973, Britain, together with Denmark and the Republic of Ireland, joined the European Economic Community. The opposition of the leader of the Labour Party, who reversed his former stand on the issue, and the lack of enthusiasm of the British people failed to prevent this outcome.

Britain has also been troubled by a recurrence of the problem of Ulster, where a resumption of violence has created for some time an awkwardly deteriorating situation.

relationships among the three main European centers of power, Britain, France, and Germany.

But in the most favorable hypothesis, that of success of the endeavor, Europe will be but one of four world Powers. To achieve that full status it would, in addition, have to attend to its own defense unaided, no longer relying on the umbrella of American protection, which inevitably creates a condition of inferiority and dependence. The capability of developing nuclear weapons has long existed in Europe; the British and the French each have their own small nuclear arsenal. There have been suggestions that the two could be merged, but the obvious question appears at this point of how long Germany can be expected to accept a disability imposed upon her as a consequence of a war terminated more than twenty-five years ago. The elimination of nuclear weapons by all would of course be an answer.

The relationships between the actual or would-be members of the Big Three have continued to evolve along the course on which they have been set of late. The visit of President Nixon to Peking in the spring of 1972 went off well. Not surprisingly, it gave rise to Russian suspicions, which it was the purpose of a subsequent visit by the American President to Moscow to alleviate.

It is reasonable speculation to believe that the thaw in the Sino-American relationship lay at the root of a breakthrough in the seemingly unending and stalemated discussions between Washington and Hanoi in Paris. An agreement between the two was somewhat prematurely announced in October 1972,[82] but the chief significance of it lay perhaps not so much in the conclusion of an unrewarding and inconclusive clash as in its meaning for the world at large.

Where America is concerned the prospect of disengagement from Southeast Asia has been highly welcome to the American people. It will have been an educative episode, the main result of which may be the acknowledgment of the limitations of American power. Taking a large and long term view of the course of events since Sarajevo, it would appear that the intrusion of ideologies, as happened with the French Revolution, for a time complicated and

[82] The announcement was made on the eve of the American Presidential election, but not implemented before that event took place. The reelection of President Nixon by a large majority of those who voted (55 percent of the electorate), while it promises continuity of policy in the foreign domain, was also a reflection of weariness among the American poeple, yearning for an elusive stability in that domain no less than in the domestic.

distorted the "normal" or "classical" operation of power. The Marxist ideology has failed to conquer the world and has instead been absorbed into the framework of the world structure of states; "national" communism is an existing reality. The United States has likewise failed to make the world in its own, democratic image. The tacit recognition of common failure provides common ground, and the confirmation in office of the American President in the election of November, 1972 bodes continuity of policy on the American side.

All are subject to, or victims of, the impact of a fast evolving and increasingly complex technology, not least its military aspects. Under the circumstances all are perhaps returning, *faute de mieux*, to an acceptance of power equilibrium. It is a game of which the chief rules have in the past been two: the acceptance by all of the right of all to exist and the legitimacy of competition within the bounds of the first rule. It is a risky game as 1914 showed; whether the new technology, because of the present state of weaponry, will now make peace more durable is a question for the future to answer.

Where the smaller powers are concerned, the peace based on the equilibrium maintained by the big powers offers prospects of a mixed nature. They naturally fear agreement at their expense; the Concert of Europe at times imposed its will on the Balkans, even when they flared up in war among themselves. The unresolved Mideastern situation comes to mind. The suspicion exists even among the former great, currently demoted to second rank. Japan, startled and shocked by the abrupt American reorientation, reacted by adopting a more independent policy. The same applies in Europe. Europe, free Europe that is, is still in transition. The Norwegian refusal to join the Common Market has reduced the prospective expansion of that grouping from ten to nine. It is expansion none the less, and the accession of Britain especially could give renewed impact to Euorpean integration, even if the economic house of Britain needs putting in order before the full impact of British influence can be felt.

There has been in addition a tendency toward relaxation and rapprochement among the European dependents of the Big Two. Chancellor Brandt's *Ostpolitik*, the abandondent of the Hallstein Doctrine in favor of a more realistic acceptance of the facts of political life, including the existence of the German Democratic Republic, have been the clearest manifestations of that trend.

There has been talk, perhaps not devoid of some irony,[83] of two German states in one German nation and of two Germanys in the United Nations. There has also been discussion of a European Security Conference in which the United States would participate. Bilateral discussions on the subject of arms control and reduction have been going on all the while between this last and the Soviet Union. That particular issue is regarded by some as the most crucial single issue for the future.

The point was made at one time that the historic course of empire, beginning with the days of Rome, has been in a westward direction. One may be tempted to wonder whether the circle is not being closed. The Atlantic superseded the Mediterranean, and while it still remains the most heavily traveled avenue of commercial exchanges, the larger political issues of the day seem to be gravitating toward the Pacific.

Allowing that we live in an age of unprecedentedly rapid transition, hence instability, but recognizing also that the fundamental stuff of history, humankind, has changed but little in historic times, one can only speculate whether the world, Europe included, is moving toward unprecedented chaos, toward the dawn of universal peace and well-being hitherto unknown to mankind—or, more prosaically, continuing to meet from day to day, in fumbling fashion and within little-changing human limitations, essentially old issues clad in novel garb. The only safe prediction is that the problem of power persists. The continuing story of it, if it lasts and so long as it lasts, promises to remain full of undiminished interest.

---

[83] The irony lies in the fact that, one-hundred years after Bismarck's masterful accomplishment of German unity and a subsequently impressive performance in a variety of domains, Germany finds herself again divided, as she was before 1871, albeit along different lines.

Bibliography

In this bibliography no attempt is made to give an exhaustive list of primary sources and secondary works. In regard to the former the reader is referred to certain books which contain such bibliographical information, often critically annotated, and are readily accessible. Biographies of statesmen and diplomats and their memoirs are, likewise, generally not included in the following references. Save in a few instances, no attempt has been made to list works which deal with related aspects of diplomatic activity, economic, military, etc.

The present bibliography will therefore confine itself in the main to secondary works which will be of use to the reader desirous of pursuing further the study of some particular problem or issue. It was also felt that to give bibliographies for each chapter would entail an undue amount of repetition and duplication. The scheme has been adopted, therefore, of dividing this bibliography into three sections —in addition to a general and introductory one—that correspond to the three main divisions of the book. Within each section references are grouped either topically or chronologically according to the arrangement that seemed most suitable. This seems a preferable organization to the grouping by countries for a subject that deals with the relations among countries.

To repeat, the present bibliography makes no pretense at completeness. It is no more than a guide to further reading, an adequate one in the author's estimation, though doubtless a different list could have been compiled.

I. INTRODUCTORY AND GENERAL

For a description and discussion of primary sources, documentary collections for example, the following are useful guides:

The seven volumes of the Langer Series, "The Rise of Modern Europe," that cover parts of the period.

Artz, Frederick B., *Reaction and Revolution: 1814–1832* (New York, 1934).

Langer, William L., *Political and Social Upheaval: 1832–1852* (New York, 1968).

Binckley, Robert C., *Realism and Nationalism: 1852–1871* (New York, 1935).

Hale, Oron J., *The Great Illusion: 1900–1914* (New York, 1971).

Hayes, Carleton J. H., *A Generation of Materialism: 1871–1900* (New York, 1941).

Sontag, Raymond J., *A Broken World: 1919–1939* (New York, 1971).

Wright, Gordon, *The Ordeal of Total War: 1939–1945* (New York, 1968).

The two volumes of the collection "Clio," *L'Époque contemporaine* (*1815–1919*) that deal with the nineteenth century.

Vol. I: Droz, Jacques, Lucien Genet, et Jean Vidalenc, *Restaurations et révolutions* (*1815–1871*) (Paris, 1953).

Vol. II: Renouvin, Pierre, Edmond Préclin, et Georges Hardy, *La Paix armée et la grande guerre* (*1871–1919*) (Paris, 1947).

The volumes of the collection "Peuples et Civilisations" published under the editorship of Louis Halphen and Philippe Sagnac.

Weill, Georges, *L'Éveil des nationalités et le mouvement libéral* (*1815–1848*) (Paris, 1930).

Pouthas, Charles-H., *Démocraties et capitalisme* (*1848–1860*) (Paris, 1948).

Hauser, Henri, Jean Maurain, et Pierre Benaerts, *Du libéralisme à l'impérialisme* (*1860–1878*) (Paris, 1939).

Baumont, Maurice, *L'Essor industriel et l'impérialisme colonial* (*1878–1904*) (Paris, 1949).

Renouvin, Pierre, *La Crise européenne et la première guerre mondiale* (Paris, 1948).

Baumont, Maurice, *La Faillite de la Paix* (*1918–1939*), 2 vols. (Paris, 1951).

Also,

The Cambridge History of British Foreign Policy (*1783–1919*), edited by A. Ward and G. P. Gooch, 3 vols. (Cambridge, 1922–1923).

Droz, Jacques, *Histoire diplomatique de 1648 à 1919* (Paris, 1952).

Holborn, Hajo, *The Political Collapse of Europe* (New York, 1951).

Potemkine, Vladimir P., *Histoire de la diplomatie*, 3 vols. (Paris, 1946–1947). This is a translation of the Russian collective work, published under the editorship of Potemkin, of which the second half of the first volume and the second and third volumes deal with the period covered in this book.

Ragatz, Lowell J., *The Literature of European Imperialism, 1815–1939* (Washington, 1944).

The four volumes of the series "Histoire des relations internationales" by Pierre Renouvin.

Vol. V: *Le XIXe. Siècle. I. De 1815 à 1871* (Paris, 1954).

Vol. VI: *Le XIXe. Siècle. II. De 1871 à 1914* (Paris, 1955).

Vol. VII: *Les Crises du XXe. Siècle. I. De 1914 à 1929* (Paris, 1957).

Vol. VIII: *Les Crises du XXe. Siècle. II. De 1929 à 1945* (Paris, 1958).

Seton-Watson, Robert W., *Britain in Europe, 1789–1914* (Cambridge, 1955).

Taylor, A. J. P., *The Struggle for Mastery in Europe 1848–1918* (Oxford, 1954).

Covering a more limited period, that after 1871 or parts of it, the following contain good bibliographies.

Albertini, Luigi, *Le origini della guerra del 1914*, 3 vols. (Milan, 1942–1943). Bibliography in Vol. I.

An English translation of this work is available under the title, *The Origins of the War of 1914* (Oxford, 1953–1957).

Fay, Sidney B., *The Origins of the World War*, 2 vols. in 1 (New York, 1932).

Langer, William L., *European Alliances and Alignments, 1871–1890* (New York, 1939).

Langer, William L., *The Diplomacy of Imperialism, 1890–1902*, 2 vols. (2d. ed., New York, 1951).

Duroselle, J.-B., *Histoire diplomatique de 1919 à nos jours* (Paris, 1953).

In addition to the preceding, the following works of a general nature may appropriately be listed here.

Albin, Pierre, *Les grands traités politiques. Recueil des principaux textes diplomatiques depuis 1815* (Paris, 1923).

Albrecht-Carrié, René, *The Concert of Europe* (New York, 1968).

Albrecht-Carrié, René, *Britain and France: Adaptations to a Changing Context of Power* (New York, 1970).

Allen, Henry C., *Great Britain and the United States; a History of Anglo-American Relations, 1783–1952* (London, 1954).

Ancel, Jacques, *Manuel géographique de politique étrangère*, 2 vols. in 3 (Paris, 1936).

Bailey, Thomas, *A Diplomatic History of the American People* (New York, 8th ed., 1969).

Bemis, Samuel F., *A Diplomatic History of the United States* (New York, 5th ed., 1965).

Gitermann, Valentin, *Gechichte Russlands*, 3 vols. (Zurich, 1944–1949).

Hartmann, Frederick, H., *Basic Documents of International Relations from the Treaty of Chaumont to the North Atlantic Pact* (New York, 1951).

Headlam-Morley, James W., *Studies in Diplomatic History* (London, 1930).

Hertslet, Edward, *The Map of Europe by Treaty*, 4 vols. (London, 1875–1891).

Joll, James, *Britain and Europe, 1793–1940* (London, 1940).

Mowat, Robert B., *History of European Diplomacy 1815–1914* (London, 1927).

Oakes, Augustus and Robert B. Mowat, *Great European Treaties of the Nineteenth Century* (Oxford, 1918).

Petrie, Charles, *Diplomatic History 1713–1933* (London, 1948).

Seaman, L. C. B., *From Vienna to Versailles* (New York, 1956).

Temperley, Harold and Lillian M. Penson, *A Century of Diplomatic Blue Books, 1814–1914* (Cambridge, 1938).

Temperley, Harold W. V. and Lillian M. Penson, *Foundations of British Foreign Policy, 1782–1902* (London, 1966).

Vernadsky, George, *Political and Diplomatic History of Russia* (Boston, 1936).

Vietsch, Eberhard von, *Das europäische Gleichgewicht* (Leipzig, 1942).

Vietsch, Eberhard von, *Das europäische Gleichgewicht* (Leipzig, gart, 1950).

Windelband, Wolfgang, *Die auswärtige Politik der Grossmächte in der Neuzeit von 1494 bis zur Gegenwart* (Essen, 1936).

Finally, by way of general introduction to the subject of diplomacy and in order to obtain some background for the study of its operation, the following are recommended.

Cambon, Jules, *The Diplomatist* (London, 1931).

Laue, Theodore H. von, *Leopold von Ranke: The Formative Years* (Princeton, 1950). This is a translation of Ranke's essay of 1833, "Die grossen Mächte."

Mowat, Robert B., *The European State System* (New York, 1931).

Mowat, Robert B., *International Relations* (London, 1933).

Mowat, Robert B., *Diplomacy and Peace* (London, 1935).

Nicolson, Harold, *The Evolution of Diplomatic Method* (London, 1954).

Nicolson, Harold, *Diplomacy* (London, 1955).

Also, the collective work published under the editorship of Duroselle, *La politique étrangère et ses fondements* (Paris, 1954).

II. THE PERIOD 1815–1870

In addition to the preceding references the following, insofar as they deal with this period, may be mentioned under the rubric of general treatments.

Bell, Herbert C., *Lord Palmerston*, 2 vols. (London, 1936).

Bibl, Viktor, *Metternich in neuer Beleuchtung* (Vienna, 1928).

Bourgeois, Émile, *Manuel historique de politique étrangère*, 4 vols., of which the second and third cover the period 1789–1878. (Paris, 1922–1927.)

Debidour, Antonin, *Histoire diplomatique de l'Europe, 1814–1878*, 2 vols. (Paris, 1891).

Guizot, François, *Mémoires pour servir à l'histoire de mon temps*, 8 vols. (Paris, 1858–1867).

Grünwald, Constantin de, *Trois siècles de diplomatie russe* (Paris, 1945).

Jenks, Leland H., *The Migrations of British Capital to 1875* (New York, 1938).

Rain, Pierre, *Histoire diplomatique de 1815 à 1870* (Paris, 1949).

Srbik, Heinrich von, *Metternich, der Staatsmann und der Mensch*, 2 vols. (Munich, 1925).

Stern, Alfred, *Geschichte Europas seit den Verträgen von 1815 bis zum Frankfurter Frieden von 1871*, 10 vols. (Berlin, 1894–1924).

The following cover specifically the Congress of Vienna and the period immediately following.

Kissinger, Henry A., *A World Restored; Metternich, Castlereagh and the Problem of Peace, 1812–1822* (Boston, 1957).

Nicolson, Harold, *The Congress of Vienna. A study in Allied Unity, 1815–1822* (New York, 1946).

Webster, Charles K., *The Congress of Vienna* (London, 1945).

The following cover the period of the Restoration.

Bourquin, Maurice, *Histoire de la Sainte Alliance* (Geneva, 1954).

Buckland, C. S. B., *Metternich and the British Government* (London, 1932).

Näf, Werner, *Zur Geschichte der Heiligen Allianz* (Bern, 1928).

Perkins, Dexter, *A History of the Monroe Doctrine* (Boston, 1955).

Phillips, Walter A., *The Confederation of Europe* (London, 1914).

Pirenne, Jacques H., *La Sainte Alliance (1815–1848)*, 2 vols. (Neuchâtel, 1946–1949).

Schenck, H. G., *The Aftermath of the Napoleonic Wars. The Concert of Europe, an Experiment* (London, 1947).

Sweet, Paul R., *Friedrich von Gentz, Defender of the Old Order* (Madison, 1941).

Temperley, Harold W. V., *The Foreign Policy of Canning, 1822–1827* (London, 1925).

Webster, Charles K., *The Foreign Policy of Castlereagh, 1815–1822* (London, 1925).

Webster, Charles K., *Britain and the Independence of Latin America, 1812–1830*, 2 vols. (London, 1938).

These works cover the events of 1830 and their aftermath.

Franqué, Wolfgang von, *Luxemburg und die belgische Revolution* (Bonn, 1932).

Guichen Eugène de, *La révolution de 1830 et l'Europe* (Paris, 1916).

Lannoy, Fleury de, *Histoire diplomatique de l'indépendance belge* (Brussels, 1930).

Perelman-Liwer, F., *La Belgique et la révolution polonaise de 1830* (Brussels, 1948).

Steinmetz, Rudolf, *Englands Anteil an der Trennung die Niederlande, 1830* (The Hague, 1930).

The Eastern Question is a hardy perennial which, in changing shape, appears throughout the nineteenth and the twentieth centuries. Some general treatments of it may be indicated here.

Ancel, Jacques, *Manuel historique de la question d'Orient (1792–1925)* (Paris, 1926).

Anchieri, Ettore, *Costantinopoli e gli Stretti nella politica russa* (Milan, 1948).

Driault, Édouard, *La question d'Orient depuis ses origines jusqu'à la paix de Sèvres* (Paris, 1921).

Goriainov, Sergei Mikhailovich, *Le Bosphore et les Dardanelles* (Paris, 1910).

Hurewitz, Jacob C., *Diplomacy in the Near and Middle East*, 2 vols. (Princeton, 1956).

Marriott, J. A. R., *The Eastern Question; an historical Study in European Diplomacy* (Oxford, 1940).

Miller, William, *The Ottoman Empire and its Successors, 1801–1927* (rev. ed., Cambridge, 1934).

Silva, Pietro, *Il Mediterraneo dall'unità di Roma all'impero italiano* (Milan, 1941).

The following deal more specifically with the problem during the period covered in Chapter II.

Cattaui, René, *Le règne de Mohammed-Ali d'après les archives russes en Égypte*, 3 vols. in 2 (Cairo, 1931–1935).

Charles-Roux, François, *Thiers et Méhémet-Ali* (Paris, 1951).

Crawley, C. W., *The Question of Greek Independence. A Study of British Policy in the Near East, 1821–1823* (Cambridge, 1930).

Driault, Édouard et Michel Lhéritier, *Histoire diplomatique de la Grèce de 1821 à nos jours*, 5 vols. (Paris, 1925–1926). Vol. I deals with this period.

Guichen, Eugène de, *La crise d'Orient de 1839 à 1841 et l'Europe* (Paris, 1921).

Mosely, Philip E., *Russian Diplomacy and the Opening of the Eastern Question in 1838 and 1839* (Cambridge, Mass., 1934).

Politis, Athanase G., *Le conflit turco-égyptien de 1838–1841* (Cairo, 1931).

Puryear, Vernon J., *International Economics and Diplomacy in the Near East. A Study of British commercial Policy in the Levant 1834–1853* (Berkeley, 1935).

Rodkey, Frederick S., *The Turco-Egyptian Question in the Relations of England, France, and Russia, 1832–1841* (Urbana, 1924).

Swain, James, E., *The Struggle for the Control of the Mediterranean prior to 1848, a Study of Anglo-French Relations* (Philadelphia, 1933).

Webster, Charles K., *The Foreign Policy of Palmerston, 1830–1841* (London, 1951).

Grouped together follow some references to a number of specific European issues and to matters outside of Europe.

Costin, William C., *Great Britain and China, 1833–1860* (Oxford, 1937).

Grosjean, Georges, *La politique extérieure de la Restauration et l'Allemagne* (Paris, 1930).

Guyot, Raymond, *La première entente cordiale* (Paris, 1926).

Hoffmann, Kurt M., *Preussen und die Julimonarchie, 1830–1834* (Berlin, 1936).

Näf, Werner, *Die Schweiz in Metternichs Europa* (Bern, 1940).

Parry, E. J., *The Spanish Marriages* (London, 1936).

Price, A. H., *The Evolution of the Zollverein, 1815–1833* (Ann Arbor, 1949).

Renouvin, Pierre, *La question d'Extrême-Orient* (Paris, 1946).

Rieben, Hans, *Prinzipiengrundlage und Diplomatie in Metternichs Europapolitik 1815–1848* (Aarau, 1942).

Robertson, R. S., *France and Latin-American Independence* (Baltimore, 1939).

Schefer, Christian, *La politique coloniale de la monarchie de Juillet* (Paris, 1928).

On the mid-century disturbance of 1848 and its immediate aftermath, see the following.

Greer, Donald M., *La France, l'Angleterre et la révolution de 1848* (Paris, 1925).

Guichen, Eugène de, *Les grandes questions européennes et la diplomatie des puissances sous la seconde République*, 2 vols. (Paris, 1925–1929).

Meier, E., *Die aussenpolitischen Ideen der Achtundvierziger* (Berlin, 1938).

Meinecke, Friedrich, *Radowitz und die deutsche Revolution* (Berlin, 1913).

Moscati, R., *La diplomazia europea e il problema italiano nel 1848* (Florence, 1947).

Scharff, Alexander, *Die europäische Grossmächte und die deutsche Revolution. Deutsche Einheit und Europäische Ordnung 1848–1851* (Leipzig, 1942).

Schwarzenberg, Adolph, *Prinz Felix zu Schwarzenberg, Prime Minister of Austria, 1848–1852* (New York, 1946).

Taylor, A. J. P., *The Italian Problem in European Diplomacy 1847–1849* (Manchester, 1934).

The following deal with the Italian question and the unification of Italy.

Bourgeois, Émile et E. Clermont, *Rome et Napoléon III (1849–1870)* (Paris, 1907).

Bourgin, Georges, *La formation de l'unité italienne* (Paris, 1929).

Matter, Paul, *Cavour et l'unité italienne*, 3 vols. (Paris, 1922–1927).

Mazziotti, Matteo, *Napoleone III e l'Italia* (Milan, 1925).

Mollat, Guillaume, *La question romaine de Pie VI à Pie XI* (Paris, 1932).

Omodeo, Adolfo, *L'opera politica del Conte di Cavour* (Florence, 1945).

Salata, Francesco, *Per la storia diplomatica della questione romana. Da Cavour alla Triplice Alleanza* (Milan, 1929).

Valsecchi, Francesco, *L'unificazione italiana e la politica europea, 1854–1859* (Milan, 1940).

Valsecchi, Francesco, *Il Risorgimento e l'Europa. L'alleanza di Crimea* (Milan, 1948).

Wagner, F., *Cavour und der Aufstieg Italiens in dem Krimkrieg* (Stuttgart, 1940).

On the Eastern Question during the period of the Second Empire, see these works.

Bapst, Edmond, *Les origines de la guerre de Crimée* (Paris, 1912).

Borries, Kurt, *Preussen im Krimkrieg* (Stuttgart, 1930).

Douin, Georges, *Histoire du règne du khédive Ismaïl Pacha*, 3 vols. in 4 (Cairo, 1937).

Edgar-Bonnet, G., *Ferdinand de Lesseps. Le diplomate, le créateur de Suez* (Paris, 1951).

Friedjung, Heinrich, *Der Krimkrieg und die oesterreichische Politik* (Stuttgart, 1911).

Guichen, Eugène de, *La guerre de Crimée (1854–1856) et l'attitude des puissances européennes* (Paris, 1936).

Hallberg, Charles W., *The Suez Canal. Its History and Diplomatic Importance* (New York, 1931).

Henderson, G. B., *Crimean War Diplomacy* (Glasgow, 1947).

Morand, E., *Le canal de Suez et l'histoire extérieure du Second Empire* (Paris, 1936).

Puryear, Vernon J., *England, Russia and the Straits Question 1844–1856* (Berkeley, 1931).

Rheindorf, Kurt, *Die Schwarze-Meer Frage vom Pariser Frieden von 1856 bis zum Abschluss der Londoner Konferenz 1871* (Berlin, 1925).

Riker, Thad W., *The Making of Roumania, a Study of an International Problem, 1856–1866* (London, 1931).

Seton-Watson, Robert W., *The Rise of Nationality in the Balkans* (London, 1917).

Tarlé, Eugene, *The Crimean War* (in Russian), 2 vols. (Moscow, 1944–1945).

Temperley, Harold W. V., *England and the Near East: the Crimea* (London, 1936).

Wilson, Arnold T., *The Suez Canal* (London, 1939).

Zaionchkovski, Andrei M., *The Eastern War of 1853–1856 in Connection with the Contemporary Political Situation* (in Russian), 2 vols. (St. Petersburg, 1908–1912).

On the German Question and the unification of Germany, together with related aspects of that issue, see the following.

Bardoux, Jacques, *Les origines du malheur européen. L'aide franco-anglaise à la domination prussienne* (Paris, 1948).

Brandenburg, Erich, *Die Reichsgründung* (Leipzig, 1922).

Brüns, Gerhard, *England und der deutschen Krieg 1866* (Berlin, 1933).

Clark, Chester W., *Franz-Joseph and Bismarck. The Diplomacy of Austria before the War of 1866* (Cambridge, Mass., 1934).

Dorn, Arno, *Robert Heinrich Graf von der Goltz* (Mainz, 1929).

Ebel, W., *Bismarck und Russland vom Prager Frieden bis zum Ausbruch des Krieges von 1870* (Frankfort, 1936).

Eckhart, Franz, *Die deutsche Frage und der Krimkrieg* (Berlin, 1931).

Engel-Jánosi, Friedrich, *Graf Rechberg. Vier Kapitel zu seiner und Oesterreichs Geschichte* (Munich, 1927).

Friedjung, Heinrich, *Der Kampf um die Vorherrschaft in Deutschland 1859 bis 1866*, 2 vols. (Stuttgart, 1916–1917).

Friese, Christian, *Russland und Preussen vom Krimkrieg bis zum polnischen Aufstand* (Berlin, 1931).

Goldschmidt, Hans, *Bismarck und die Friedensunterhändler 1871* (Berlin, 1929).

Grenu, R., *La question belge dans la politique française de 1866 à 1870* (Paris, 1931).

Grob, Ernest, *Beusts Kampf gegen Bismarck* (Zurich, 1930).

Henderson, W. O., *The Zollverein* (London, 1930).

Lord, Robert H., *The Origins of the War of 1870. New Documents of the German Archives* (Cambridge, Mass., 1924).

Michael, Horst, *Bismarck, England und Europa* (Munich, 1930).

Oncken, Hermann, *Die Rheinpolitik des Kaisers Napoleon III 1863–1870 und der Ursprung des Kriges vom 1870–1871*, 3 vols. (Stuttgart, 1926).

Redlich, Josef, *Das Oesterreichische Staats- und Reichsproblem*, 2 vols. (Leipzig, 1920–1926).

Rheindorf, Kurt, *England und der deutsch-französische Krieg 1870–1871* (Bonn, 1923).

Salomon, Henry, *L'incident Hohenzollern* (Paris, 1924).

Scheidt, H., *Konvention Alvensleben und Interventionspolitik der Mächte in der polnischen Frage, 1863* (Munich, 1937).

Sempell, Charlotte, *England und Preussen in der Schleswigholsteinischen Frage* (Berlin, 1932).

Sorel, Albert, *Histoire diplomatique de la guerre franco-allemande*, 2 vols. (Paris, 1875).

Srbik, Heinrich von, *Deutsche Einheit*, 4 vols. (Munich, 1935–1940).

Stadelmann, R., *Das Jahr 1865 und das Problem von Bismarcks deutscher Politik* (Munich, 1933).

Steefel, Lawrence D., *The Schleswig-Holstein Question* (Cambridge, Mass., 1932).

Stolberg-Wernigerode, O., Graf von, *R. H. Graf von der Goltz, Botschafter in Paris 1863–1869* (Berlin, 1941).

Sybel, Heinrich von, *Die Begründung des deutschen Reiches durch Wilhelm I*, 7 vols. (Munich, 1901).

Taube, Alexander von, *Fürst Bismarck zwischen England und Russland* (Stuttgart, 1923).

Valentin, Veit, *Bismarcks Reichsbegründung im Urteil englischer Diplomaten* (Amsterdam, 1937).

These works are mainly on extra-European issues and on some aspects of the policy of the Second Empire.

Barié, Ottavio, *Idee e dottrine imperialistiche nell'Inghilterra vittoriana* (Bari, 1953).

Bienstock, Gregory, *The Struggle for the Pacific* (New York, 1937).

Bratianu, Georges, *Napoléon III et le problème des nationalités* (Paris, 1930).

Case, Lynn M., *French Opinion on the United States and Mexico, 1860–1867* (New York, 1936).

Charles-Roux, François, *Alexandre II, Gortchakoff et Napoléon III* (Paris, 1913).

Grünwald, Constantin de, *Le duc de Gramont, gentilhomme et diplomate* (Paris, 1950).

Hail, William J., *Tseng Kuo-Fan and the Taiping Rebellion* (New Haven, 1927).

Hallberg, Charles W., *Franz Joseph and Napoleon III, 1852–1864* (New York, 1955).

Kaiser Karl, *Napoleon III und der polnische Aufstand von 1863* (Berlin, 1932).

La Gorce, Pierre de, *Napoléon III et sa politique* (Paris, 1934).

Recke, Walther, *Die polnische Frage als Problem der europäischen Politik* (Berlin, 1927).

Sansom, George B., *The Western World and Japan* (New York, 1950).

Schefer, Christian, *La grande pensée de Napoléon III. Les origines de l'expédition du Mexique, 1858–1862* (Paris, 1939).

Schüle, Ernst, *Russland und Frankreich vom Ausgang des Krimkrieges bis zum italienischen Krieg* (Berlin, 1935).

III. THE PERIOD 1871–1914

The circumstances which make our knowledge of the diplomacy of this period unusually full have been explained in Chapter V. A description and discussion of the great documentary collections, some of them, like the French and the Italian, still in course of publication, will be found in the bibliographical guides mentioned in the first part of this bibliography.

The best general discussions of the diplomacy of the period are to be found in the above-mentioned works of Albertini (Vol. I), Fay (Vol. I), Renouvin (Vol. VI), and Taylor. Also, the two works by Langer, each covering sections of the period, are fundamental. In addition to these references, some general discussions of the whole period or of parts of it may be added here.

Brandenburg, Erich, *From Bismarck to the World War* (London, 1927).

Hauser, Henri, *Manuel de politique européenne. Histoire diplomatique de l'Europe 1871–1914*, 2 vols. (Paris, 1929).

Salis, J. von, *Weltgeschichte der neueuren Zeit*, Vol. I (Zurich, 1951).

Sontag, Raymond J., *European Diplomatic History, 1871–1932* (New York, 1933).

The following works, either of a general nature, or dealing with certain aspects or related aspects of the subject, will be found useful.

Barthélemy, Joseph, *Démocratie et politique étrangère* (Paris, 1931).

Carroll, Eber M., *French Public Opinion and Foreign Affairs, 1870–1914* (New York, 1931).

Carroll, Eber M., *Germany and the Great Powers, 1866–1914. A Study of Public Opinion and Foreign Policy* (New York, 1938).

Feis, Herbert, *Europe, the World's Banker, 1870–1914* (New York, 1936).

Gooch, G. P., *Franco-German Relations, 1871–1914* (London, 1923).

Gooch, G. P., *Before the War. Studies in Diplomacy*, 2 vols. (London, 1936–1938).

Gooch, G. P., *Recent Revelations in European Diplomacy* (London, 1940).

Gosser, F., *The Management of British Foreign Policy, 1880–1914* (Leiden, 1948).

Knaplund, Paul, *Gladstone's Foreign Policy* (London, 1970).

Kohn, Hans, *Panslavism: its History and Ideology* (New York, 1960).

Pribram, Alfred F., *England and the International Policy of the Great European Powers, 1871–1914* (Oxford, 1931).

Robbins, Lionel C., *The Economic Causes of War* (London, 1939).

Schreiner, A., *Zur Geschichte der deutschen Aussenpolitik, 1871–1945*, Vol. I, *1871–1918* (Berlin, 1952).

Schuman, Frederick L., *War and Diplomacy in the French Republic* (New York, 1931).

Valentin, Veit, *Deutschlands Aussenpolitik von Bismarcks Abgang bis zum Ende des Weltkrieges* (Berlin, 1921).

Wittkowski, G., *Die deutsch-russischen Handelsbeziehungen in den letzten 150 Jahre* (Berlin, 1947).

During the two decades that followed the Franco-Prussian War the direction of European diplomacy was dominated by Germany, more specifically by Bismarck, undoubtedly one of the outstanding statesmen of all time, yet a highly controversial figure whose role and influence have been much debated and are currently undergoing reevaluation. On Bismarck the following may be cited.

Bismarck, Otto von, *Bismarck, the Man and the Statesman* (translation of Bismarck's memoirs) (New York, 1966).

Darmstaedter, Friedrich, *Bismarck and the Creation of the Second Reich* (London, 1948).

Eyck, Erich, *Bismarck*, 3 vols. (Zurich, 1941–1944). An English condensed version of this work has appeared under the title *Bismarck and the German Empire* (London, 1955).

Meyer, Arnold O., *Bismarck, der Mensch und der Staatsmann* Stuttgart, 1949).

Robertson, Charles G., *Bismarck* (London, 1919).

Taylor, A. J. P., *Bismarck, the Man and the Statesman* (London, 1955).

Zechlin, Egmont, *Bismarck und die Grundlegung der deutschen Grossmacht* (Stuttgart, 1930).

For various aspects of the diplomacy of the Bismarckian period, centering mainly around Germany, see the following.

Aydelotte, William O., *Bismarck and British Colonial Policy: the Problem of South West Africa, 1883–1885* (Philadelphia, 1937).

Becker, Otto, *Bismarcks Bündnispolitik* (Berlin, 1923).

Becker, Otto, *Bismarck und die Einkreisung Deutschlands*, 2 vols. (Berlin, 1925).

Coolidge, Archibald C., *Origins of the Triple Alliance* (New York, 1919).

Fuller, Joseph V., *Bismarcks Diplomacy at its Zenith* (Cambridge, Mass., 1922).

Hagen, Maximilian von, *Bismarck und England* (Stuttgart, 1941).

Heller, Eduard, *Das deutsch-oesterreichische ungarische Bündnis in Bismarcks Aussenpolitik* (Berlin, 1925).

Holborn, Hajo, *Bismarcks europäische Politik zu Beginn der siebziger Jahre und die Mission Radowitz* (Berlin, 1925).

Jantzen, Günther, *Ostafrika in der deutsch-englischen Politik, 1884–1890* (Hamburg, 1934).

Japiske, N., *Europa und Bismarcks Friedenspolitik, 1871–1890* (Berlin, 1927).

Krausnick, H., *Holsteins Geheimpolitik und die Aera Bismarcks, 1866–1890* (Hamburg, 1942).

Rachfahl, Felix, *Deutschland und die Weltpolitik. Die Bismarcksche Aera* (Stuttgart, 1923).

Rothfels, Hans, *Bismarcks englische Bündnispolitik* (Berlin, 1933).

Wienefeld, Robert H., *Franco-German Relations, 1878–1885* (Baltimore, 1929).

Windelband, K., *Bismarck und die europäische Mächte, 1879–1885* (Essen, 1942).

The following deal particularly with the Eastern Question, but also cover some other phases of Mediterranean activity.

Charles-Roux, J., *L'isthme et le canal de Suez*, 2 vols. (Paris, 1901).

Chiala, Luigi, *Tunisi* (Turin, 1895).

Corti, Egon C., *Alexander von Battenberg; sein Kampf mit den Zaren und Bismarck* (Vienna, 1920).

Goriainov, Sergei M., *La question d'Orient à la veille du traité de Berlin, 1870–1876* (Paris, 1948).

Grüning, Irene, *Die russische öffentliche Meinung und ihre Stellung zu den Grossmächte, 1878–1984* (Berlin, 1929).

Harris, David, *A Diplomatic History of the Balkan Crisis, 1875–1878: The First Year* (Stanford, 1936).

Medlicott, William N., *The Congress of Berlin and After: A Diplomatic History of the Near East Settlement, 1878–1880* (London, 1938).

Sabry, Mohammed, *L'empire égyptien sous Ismaïl et l'ingérence franco-anglaise, 1863–1879* (Paris, 1933).

Schinner, Walter, *Der oesterreichisch-italienische Gegensatz auf dem Balkan, 1875–1896* (Stuttgart, 1936).

Seton-Watson, Robert W., *Gladstone, Disraeli and the Eastern Question* (London, 1936).

Sumner, Benedict H., *Russia and the Balkans, 1870–1880* (Oxford, 1937).

Woodward, Ernest L., *The Congress of Berlin* (London, 1920).

Also, on other aspects of European relations, consult the following.

Bloch, Charles, *Les relations entre la France et la Grande Bretagne (1871–1878)* (Paris, 1955).

Chabod, Federico, *Storia della politica estera italiana dal 1870 al 1896*, Vol. I, *Le premesse* (Bari, 1951).

Crispi, Francesco, *Questioni internazionali* (Milan, 1913).

Knaplund, Paul, *Gladstone's Foreign Policy* (London, 1970).

Medlicott, William N., *Bismarck, Gladstone, and the Concert of Europe* (London, 1956).

Salvemini, Gaetano, *La politica estera di Francesco Crispi* (Rome, 1939).

Wertheimer, Eduard von, *Graf Julius Andrássy. Sein Leben und seine Zeit*, 3 vols. (Stuttgart, 1910–1913).

The fall of Bismarck was the beginning of the transitional period that finally resulted in the division of Europe into two rival camps. The first step in that process was the formation of the Franco-Russian alliance. On that subject, see these works.

Langer, William L., *The Franco-Russian Alliance* (Chicago, 1930).

Michon, Georges, *L'alliance franco-russe, 1891–1917* (Paris, 1927).

Nolde, Boris, *L'alliance franco-russe* (Paris, 1936).

Wiederkehr, Ernst, *Les origines de l'alliance franco-russe: les années 1878–1881* (Fribourg, 1942).

The recrudescence of imperial activity during the period of readjustment played a very important role in the relations of the European Powers. The following focus on imperialism in general, more particularly on African developments, and especially on the impact of these on Anglo-French relations.

Andrew, Christopher, *Théophile Delcassé and the Making of the Entente Cordiale* (New York, 1968).

Berger, E., *Die grosse Politik Delcassés* (Berlin, 1941).

Ciasca, Raffaele, *Storia coloniale dell'Italia contemporanea* (Milan, 1938).

Darmstädter, Paul, *Geschichte der Aufteilung und Kolonisation Afrikas,* 2 vols., Vol. II, *1870–1919* (Berlin, 1913–1920).

Friedjung, Heinrich, *Das Zeitalter des Imperialismus 1884 bis 1914,* 3 vols. (Berlin, 1919–1922).

Garvin, James L., *The Life of Joseph Chamberlain,* 4 vols. (Vol. IV by Julian Amery) (London, 1932–1935, 1951).

Giffen, Morrison B., *Fashoda, the Incident and its Diplomatic Setting* (Chicago, 1930).

Hallgarten, Wolfgang, *Imperialismus vor 1914* (Munich, 1951).

Hardy, Georges, *La politique coloniale et le partage de la terre aux XIXe. et XXe. siècles* (Paris, 1937).

Lovell, Reginald I., *The Struggle for South Africa, 1875–1899. A Study in Economic Imperialism* (New York, 1934).

Mandelstam, N., *La politique russe d'accès à Méditerranée au XXe. siècle* (Paris, 1935).

Moon, Parker T., *Imperialism and World Politics* (New York, 1934).

Neton, A., *Delcassé* (Paris, 1953).

Pigli, Mario, *L'Etiopia moderna nelle sue relazioni internazionali, 1859–1931* (Padua, 1933).

Pyrah, G. B., *Imperial Policy and South Africa, 1902–1910* (London, 1955).

Sommaruga, Rodolfo, *Le potenze europee in Africa, 1878–1919* (Milan, 1938).

Vialatte, A., *L'impérialisme économique et les relations internationales pendant le dernier demi-siècle* (Paris, 1923).

Yerusalimski, A. S., *Vneshnaia politika i diplomatika germanskogo imperialisma v Kontze XIX v.* (2d. ed., Moscow, 1951).

These books cover imperialism in Asia, particularly in the Far East.

Becker, Otto, *Der Ferne Osten und das Schicksal Europas, 1907–1918* (Leipzig, 1940).

Chang, Fu-Chang, *The Anglo-Japanese Alliance* (Baltimore, 1931).

Galperin, A., *Anglo-iaponskii soiuz* (Moscow, 1947).

Hudson, Geoffrey, *The Far East in World Politics* (Oxford, 1937).

Joseph, Philip, *Foreign Diplomacy in China, 1894–1900* (London, 1928).

Krupinski, Kurt, *Russland und Japan. Ihre Beziehungen bis zum Frieden von Portsmouth* (Berlin, 1940).

Lobanov-Rostovski, Andrei, *Russia and Asia* (Ann Arbor, 1951).

McCordock, Robert S., *British Far Eastern Policy, 1894–1900* (New York, 1931).

Minrath, Paul, *Das englisch-japanische Bündnis von 1902* (Stuttgart, 1933).

Reid, John G., *The Manchu Abdication and the Powers, 1908–1912* (Berkeley, 1936).

Romanov, Boris A., *Russia in Manchuria 1892–1906* (Ann Arbor, 1952).

Willoughby, Westel W., *Foreign Rights and Interests in China* (2d ed., Balitmore, 1927).

Zabriskie, Edward H., *American-Russian Rivalry in the Far East, 1895–1914* (Philadelphia, 1946).

The question of Anglo-German relations took on particular importance during the transitional period of realignment. On that issue and, more generally, on German policy, the following may be mentioned.

Anderson, Pauline, *The Background of anti-English feeling in Germany, 1890–1902* (Washington, 1939).

Banze, Angelika, *Die deutsch-englische Wirtschaftsrivalität* (Berlin, 1935).

Becker, Willy, *Fürst Bülow und England 1897–1909* (Greifswald, 1929).

Bülow, Bernhard von, *Memoirs of Prince von Bülow*, 4 vols. (Boston, 1931–1932).

Fischer, Eugen, *Holsteins grosses Nein* (Berlin, 1925).

Hamman, Otto, *The World Policy of Germany, 1890–1902* (New York, 1927).

Hoffman, Ross J. S., *Great Britain and the German Trade Rivalry, 1875–1914* (Philadelphia, 1933).

Huene-Hoeningen, Heinrich von, *Untersuchungen zur Geschichte der deutsch-englischen Beziehungen 1898–1901* (Breslau, 1934).

Kanner, Heinrich, *Kaiserliche Katastrophenpolitik* (Vienna, 1922).

Klein, W., *Der Vertrag von Björkö* (Berlin, 1931).

Lichnowsky, Karl M., *Heading for the Abyss* (London, 1928).

Marder, Arthur J., *The Anatomy of the British Sea Power; a History of British Naval Policy in the pre-Dreadnought Era, 1880–1905* (London, 1940).

Meinecke, Friedrich, *Geschichte des deutsch-englischen Bündnisproblem* (Munich, 1927).

Nowak, Karl F., *Kaiser and Chancellor; the Opening Years of the Reign of Kaiser Wilhelm II* (New York, 1930).

Nowak, Karl F., *Germany's Road to Ruin; the Middle Years of the Reign of Emperor William II* (London, 1932).

Oncken, Friedrich, *Das deutsche Reich und die Vorgeschichte des Weltkrieges*, 2 vols. (Leipzig, 1932).

Penson, Lillian M., *Foreign Affairs under the Third Marquis of Salisbury* (London, 1962).

Schmitt, Bernadotte E., *England and Germany, 1740–1914* (Princeton, 1918).

Sontag, Raymond J., *Germany and England, Background of Conflict, 1848–1918* (New York, 1938).

Tirpitz, Alfred von, *Politische Dokumente*, 2 vols. (Berlin, 1924, 1926).

Willis, Edward F., *Prince Lichnowsky, Ambassador of Peace; A Study of the Pre-War Diplomacy, 1912–1914* (Berkeley, 1942).

Wolff, Theodor, *The Eve of 1914* (New York, 1936).

Woodward, Ernest L., *England and the German Navy* (Oxford, 1935).

Ziekursch, Johannes, *Politische Geschichte des neuen deutschen Kaiserreiches*, 3 vols. (Frankfurt, 1927–1932).

These deal with the role of Italy.

Billot, A., *La France et l'Italie. Histoire des années troubles, 1881–1899*, 2 vols. (Paris, 1905).

Cataluccio, Francesco, *Antonio di San Giuliano e la politica estera italiana dal 1900 al 1914* (Florence, 1935).

Chabod, Federico, *Storia della politica estera italiana dal 1870 al 1896*, Vol. I, *Le Premesse* (Bari, 2d. ed., 1962).

Gallavresi, Giuseppe, *Itàlia e Austria, 1859–1914* (Milan, 1922).

Glanville, James L., *Italy's Relations with England, 1896–1905* (Baltimore, 1934).

Hoernigkh, R., *Italien zwischen Frankreich und dem Dreibund* (Berlin, 1931).

Italicus (*pseud.* Ernst E. Berger), *Italiens Dreibund politik 1870–1896* (Munich, 1928).

Salvatorelli, Luigi, *La triplice alleanza, 1877–1922* (Milan, 1939).

Sandonà, Augusto, *L'irredentismo nelle lotte politiche e nelle contese diplomatiche italo-austriache*, 3 vols. (Bologna, 1932).

Serra, E., *Camille Barrère e l'intesa italo-francese* (Milan, 1950).

Silva, Pietro, *L'Italia fra le grandi potenze (1882–1914)* (Rome, 1931).

Tommasini, Francesco, *L'Italia alla vigilia della guerra. La politica estera di Tommaso Tittoni*, 5 vols. (Bologna, 1934–1941).

Volpe, Gioacchino, *L'Italia nella triplice alleanza, 1882–1915* (Milan, 1939).

Wollemborg, Leo, *Politica estera italiana, 1882–1917* (Rome, 1933).

More particularly on the Eastern Empires of Russia and Austria-Hungary see the following.

Conrad von Hoetzendorff, Franz Graf, *Aus meiner Dienstzeit 1906–1918*, 5 vols. (Vienna, 1922–1925).

Frantz, Gunther, *Russland auf dem Weg zur Katastrophe* (Berlin, 1926).

Hoyos, Alexander Graf, *Der deutsch-englische Gegensatz und sein Einfluss auf die Balkanpolitik Österreich-Ungarns* (Berlin, 1922).

Korff, Sergei A., *Russia's Foreign Relations During the Last Half Century* (New York, 1922).

Molden, B., *Alois Graf Aehrenthal. Sechs Jahre äussere Politik Oesterreich-Ungarns* (Berlin, 1917).

Musulin, Alexander von, *Das Haus am Ballplatz* (Munich, 1924).

Pribram, Alfred F., *The Secret Treaties of Austria-Hungary*, 2 vols. (Cambridge, Mass., 1920, 1921).

Pribram, Alfred F., *Austrian Foreign Policy 1908–1918* (London, 1923).

Sazonov, Serge, *Fateful Years, 1909–1916* (London, 1928).

Seton-Watson, Hugh, *The Decline of Imperial Russia, 1855–1914* (London, 1953).

Stieve, Friedrich, *Izvolsky and World War* (London, 1926).

Szilassy, Julius, *Der Untergang der Donaumonarchie. Diplomatische Errinerungen* (Berlin, 1921).

Taube, Mikhail, *La politique russe d'avant-guerre et la fin de l'empire des Tsars (1904–1917)* (Paris, 1928).

Wedel, Oswald H., *Austro-German Diplomatic Relations, 1908–1914* (Stanford, 1932).

The decade preceding the outbreak of war in 1914 was marked by an accelerating tempo of crises. The two such crises that grew out of the Moroccan question are dealt with in these works.

Anderson, Eugene N., *The First Moroccan Crisis, 1904–1906* (Chicago, 1930).

Barlow, P., *The Agadir Crisis* (Chapel Hill, 1940).

Caillaux, Joseph, *Agadir. Ma politique extérieure* (Paris, 1921).

Hallmann, Hans, *Spanien und die französisch-englische Mittelmeer-rivalität, 1898–1907* (Stuttgart, 1937).

Nava, Santi, *La spartizione del Marocco* (Florence, 1940).

Saint René Taillandier, Georges, *Les origines du Maroc français* (Paris, 1930).

Tardieu, André, *Le mystère d'Agadir* (Paris, 1912).

For the Tripolitan war, see the following.

Askew, William C., *Europe and Italy's Annexation of Libya 1911–1912* (Durham, N.C., 1942).

These cover Balkan developments.

Bickel, Otto, *Russland und die Entstehung des Balkanbundes, 1912* (Königsberg, 1933).

Calgren, W. M., *Iswolsky und Aehrenthal vor der Bosnischen Annexionskrise* (Uppsala, 1955).

Drosos, D., *La fondation de l'alliance balkanique* (Athens, 1929).

Helmreich, Ernst C., *The Diplomacy of the Balkan Wars* (Cambridge, Mass., 1938).

Nintchitch, Momtchilo, *La crise bosniaque (1908–1909) et les puissances européennes*, 2 vols. (Paris, 1937).

Schmitt, Bernadotte E., *The Annexation of Bosnia* (Cambridge, Mass., 1937).

Seton-Watson, Robert W., *The Role of Bosnia in International Politics, 1875–1915* (London, 1932).

Vucinich, Wayne S., *Serbia Between East and West: the Events of 1903–1908* (Stanford, 1954).

Other aspects of the Near Eastern Question are covered by the following.

Earle, Edward M., *Turkey, the Great Powers and the Baghdad Railway* (New York, 1923).

Giesl, Wladimir von, *Zwei Jahrzehnte im Nahen Orient* (Berlin, 1927).

Howard, Harry N., *The Partition of Turkey; a Diplomatic History, 1913–1923* (Norman, Okla., 1931).

Iorga, Nicolae, *Comment la Roumanie s'est détachée de la Triplice* (Bucharest, 1933).

Krainikowski, Asen I., *La question de Macédoine et la diplomatie européenne* (Paris, 1938).

Wolff, John B., *The Diplomatic History of the Bagdad Railroad* (Columbia, Mo., 1936).

The following may also be mentioned.

Gelber, Lionel M., *The Rise of Anglo-American Friendship, A Study in World Politics, 1898–1906* (London, 1938).

Heindel, Richard H., *The American Impact on Britain, 1898–1914* (Philadelphia, 1940).

Manger, J. O., *Die Triple Entente* (Utrecht, 1934).

Nicolson, Harold, *Sir Arthur Nicolson, Bart., First Lord Carnock—A Study in the Old Diplomacy* (London, 1930).

Paléologue, Maurice, *Un grand tournant de la politique mondiale, 1904–1906* (Paris, 1931).

Poincaré, Raymond, *Au Service de la France*, 10 vols. (Paris, 1926–1933).

Rachfahl, Felix, *Deutschland und die Weltpolitik, 1871–1914*, Vol. I, *Die Bismarksche Aera* (Stuttgart, 1923).

Schmitt, Bernadotte E., *Triple Entente and Triple Alliance* (New York, 1954).

Siebert, B. de, *Entente Diplomacy and the World (1909–1914)* (London, 1921).

Stieve, Freidrich, *Izwolsky and the World War* (London, 1926).

Wright, Gordon, *Raymond Poincaré and the French Presidency* (Stanford, 1942).

Wullus-Rüdiger, J. (*pseud.* Armand Willus), *La Belgique et l'équilibre européen* (Paris, 1935).

IV. THE PERIOD SINCE 1914

The events of the five weeks that elapsed between the Sarajevo assassination and the general outbreak of hostilities have given rise to an immense literature. This is adequate expression of the fact that 1914 marks one of the great turning points in the history of Europe, and reflects as well the different nature of the present century, be it in the shape of the rising of the mass or in that of the nature of the warfare of our time, two developments intimately related. Likewise related to these facets of novel conditions is the great controversy that has raged around the issue of responsibility for the outbreak of war in 1914. Of this enormous literature a few samples only can be cited among the most important and durable, in addition to the first volumes of the works of Albertini and Fay previously cited.

Anrich, Ernst, *Die englische Politik im Juli 1914* (Stuttgart, 1934).

Barnes, Harry E., *The Genesis of the World War. An Introduction to the Problem of War Guilt* (New York, 1927).

Bourgeois, Émile, *Les origines et les responsabilités de la guerre* (Paris, 1922).

Dedijer, Vladimir, *The Road to Sarajevo* (New York, 1966).

Fischer, Eugen, *Die kritischen 39 Tage von Sarajevo bis zum Weltbrand* (Berlin, 1928).

Isaac, Jules, *Un débat historique. 1914, le problème des origines de la guerre* (Paris, 1933).

Lutz, Hermann, *Die europäische Politik in der Julikrise 1914* (Berlin, 1930).

Magrini, Luigi, *Il dramma di Sarajevo. Origini e responsabilità della guerra europea* (Milan, 1929).

Montgelas, Max, *The Case for the Central Powers* (London, 1925).

Pourtalès, Friedrich, *Am Scheideweg zwischen Krieg und Frieden. Meine letzten Verhandlungen in Petersburg, Ende Juli 1914* (Charlottenburg, 1919).

Renouvin, Pierre, *Les origines immédiates de la guerre, 28 juin–4 août 1914* (2d. ed., Paris, 1927). English translation, *The Immediate Origins of the War* (New Haven, 1928).

Schmitt, Bernadotte E., *The Coming of the War*, 2 vols. (New York, 1930).

Seton-Watson, Robert W., *Sarajevo. A Study in the Origins of the War* (London, 1936).

Stanojević, Stanoje, *Die Ermordung des Erzherzog Franz Ferdinand* (Frankfurt, 1923).

Wegerer, Alfred von, *A Refutation of the Versailles War Guilt Thesis* (New York, 1930).

Wegerer, Alfred von, *Der Ausbruch des Weltkrieges*, 2 vols. (Hamburg, 1939).

On the diplomatic activity of the war period and on the armistice negotiations, see the following.

Antonius, George, *The Arab Awakening: The Story of the Arab National Movement* (Philadelphia, 1939).

Bethmann-Hollweg, Theobald von, *Betrachtungen zum Weltkriege*, 2 vols. (Berlin, 1919–1922).

Churchill, Winston S., *The World Crisis*, 4 vols. in 5 (London, 1923–1929).

Czernin, Ottokar, *In the World War* (London, 1919).

Dahlin, Ebba, *French and German Public Opinion on Declared War Aims* (London, 1933).

Danilov, I. N., *La Russie dans la guerre mondiale, 1914–1917* (Paris, 1927).

Fainsod, Merle, *International Socialism and the World War* (Cambridge, Mass., 1935).

Fester, Richard, *Die Politik Kaiser Karls und der Wendepunkt des Weltkrieges* (Munich, 1925).

BIBLIOGRAPHY

715

Frangulis, A. F., *La Grèce et la crise mondiale*, 2 vols. (Paris, 1926–1927).

Gatzke, Hans W., *Germany's Drive to the West* (Baltimore, 1950).

Glaise von Horstenau, Edmond, *The Collapse of the Austro-Hungarian Empire* (London, 1930).

Gottlieb, Wolfram W., *Studies in Secret Diplomacy During the First World War* (London, 1957).

Johnson, Humphrey, *Vatican Diplomacy in the World War* (Oxford, 1933).

Kammerer, Albert, *La vérité sur l'armistice* (Paris, 1944).

Kedourie, Elie, *England and the Middle East. The Destruction of the Ottoman Empire, 1914–1921* (London, 1956).

Kennan, George F., *Russia Leaves the War* (Princeton, 1956).

Maurice, Frederick B., *The Armistices of 1918* (London, 1943).

Mayer, Arno, *Political Origins of the New Diplomacy, 1917–1918* (New Haven, 1959).

Mermeix (*pseud.* Gabriel Terrail), *Les négociations secrètes et les quatre armistices* (Paris, 1919).

Pingaud, Albert, *Histoire diplomatique de la France pendant la grande guerre*, 3 vols. (Paris, 1938–1940).

Rudin, Harry R., *Armistice 1918* (New Haven, 1944).

Salandra, Antonio, *La neutralità italiana* (Milan, 1928).

Salandra, Antonio, *L'intervento* (Milan, 1931). This and the preceding work are translated together in English as *Italy in the Great War* (London, 1932).

Schramm von Thadden, Ehrengard, *Griechenland und die Grossmächte 1913–1923* (Göttingen, 1953).

Seymour, Charles, *American Diplomacy During the World War* (Baltimore, 1934).

Smith, C. Jay, Jr., *The Russian Struggle for Power, 1914–1917* (New York, 1956).

Toscano, Mario, *Il patto di Londra* (Bologna, 1934).

Toscano, Mario, *Gli accordi San Giovanni di Moriana* (Milan, 1936).

Toscano, Mario, *Guerra diplomatica in estremo oriente*, 2 vols. (Turin, 1950).

Volkwart, J., *Brest-Litowsk* (Stuttgart, 1937).

Wheeler-Bennett, John W., *Brest-Litovsk, The Forgotten Peace, March 1918* (New York, 1939).

These works cover the peace settlements that were the result of the war and the manner in which they were contrived.

Albrecht-Carrié, René, *Italy at the Paris Peace Conference* (New York, 1938).

Aldrovandi-Marescotti, Luigi, *Guerra diplomatica, ricordi e frammenti di diario* (Milan, 1937).

Almond, Nina and Ralph Lutz, *An Introduction to a Bibliography of the Paris Peace Conference* (Stanford, 1935).

Baker, Ray S., *Woodrow Wilson and the World Settlement*, 3 vols. (New York, 1922).

Birdsall, Paul, *Versailles, Twenty Years After* (New York, 1940).

Crispi, Silvio, *Alla difesa d'Italia in guerra e a Versailles* (Milan, 1937).

Deák, Francis, *Hungary at the Paris Peace Conference. The Diplomatic History of the Treaty of Trianon* (New York, 1942).

Haskins, Charles H. and Robert H. Lord, *Some Problems of the Peace Conference* (Cambridge, Mass., 1920).

Holfeld, A., *Versailles und die russische Frage* (Hamburg, 1940).

Jaszi, Oscar, *The Dissolution of the Habsburg Monarchy* (Chicago, 1929).

Keynes, John M., *The Economic Consequences of the Peace* (New York, 1920).

Luckau, Alma, *The German Delegation at the Paris Peace Conference* (New York, 1941).

Mantoux, Paul, *Les délibérations du Conseil des Quatre (24 mars–28 Juin 1919): Notes de l'interprète*, 2 vols. (Paris, 1955).

Marston, Frank S., *The Peace Conference of 1919* (New York, 1944).

Mayer, Arno, *Politics and Diplomacy of Peacemaking. Containment and Counter-Revolution at Versailles, 1918–1919* (New York, 1968).

Mermeix (*pseud.* Gaston Terrail), *Le combat des Trois* (Paris, 1922).

Miller, D. Hunter, *The Drafting of the Covenant*, 2 vols. (New York, 1928).

Nicolson, Harold, *Peacemaking 1919* (London, 1933).

Noble, George, *Policies and Opinions at Paris, 1919* (New York, 1935).

Nowak, Karl F., *Versailles* (New York, 1929).

Scott, James B. and James T. Shotwell, eds., *The Paris Peace Conference. History and Documents. I. The Origins of the International Labor Organnization*, 2 vols. (New York, 1934).

Stein, Boris, *Die russische Frage auf der Pariser Friedens-Konferenz, 1919–1920* (translated from the Russian) (Leipzig, 1953).

Tardieu, André, *The Truth about the Treaty* (Indianapolis, 1921).

Temperley, Harold W. V., ed., *A History of the Peace Conference of Paris*, 6 vols. (London, 1920–1924).

Torre, Augusto, *Versailles, Storia della conferenza della pace* (Milan, 1940).

Vedovato, Giuseppe, *Il trattato di pace con l'Italia* (Rome, 1947).

Zeigler, Wilhelm, *Versailles. Die Geschichte eines missglückten Friedens* (Hamburg, 1933).

The period since the First World War has seen an enormous growth of the sources of information. Much of the business of states is now conducted *coram populo*. This has a distorting effect, for while it makes it possible to treat of contemporary developments on the basis of substantial information, there is still much that remains unrevealed.

Also, the practice of publicity varies with states. In the democratic countries the tendency has been to be very free in making state papers public, and private individuals have been very ready, not to say at times anxious and premature, in giving their versions of important negotiations in which they have participated; this tendency has been especially marked in the American milieu. By contract, the Russians, for all that they were the initiators in the opening of archives, have maintained a great measure of reticence, and the same applies to totalitarian regimes in general. The fact remains that, in varying degrees, the disclosure of state papers is often made with an eye to the effects of publicity on opinion, both domestic and foreign, rather than for the purpose of aiding the historian. The diplomatic history of our time will be long in the writing, but it is also true that our knowledge of contemporary events is extensive.

In addition, the Second World War resulted in the German archives falling into the hands of the Allies. This documentation, and the Nuremberg trials that followed the war, have been the bases of voluminous publications which clearly constitute invaluable sources of information, especially, of course, on German policy, but also on Russian policy on the score of which native documentation is difficult to obtain.

The publication of the British Royal Institute of International Affairs, *Survey of International Affairs*, begun in 1925 as a yearly publication, initially under the editorship of Professor Toynbee, despite the factor of immediacy has achieved a high level of reliability and objectivity. Interrupted by the war, but since resumed, this series constitutes the best single source of information on current developments. The same high standards apply in general to the topical publications of the R.I.I.A. The American quarterly *Foreign Affairs*, published by the Council on Foreign Relations, gives useful briefly annotated bibliographies of current publications; these bibliographies have been conviently collected in the four volumes, *Foreign Affairs Bibliography*, for 1919–1932, 1932–1942, 1942–1952, and 1952–1962, respectively. Journals dealing with current international affairs are numerous; guides to them and to further bibliographies will be found in some of the general works listed at the beginning of the present bibliography. Note in particular, Vol. VIII of Renouvin, pp. 3–6.

For the period between the two world wars as a whole the following works may be indicated.

Carr, Edward H., *Britain. A Study of Foreign Policy from the Treaty of Versailles to the Outbreak of War* (London, 1939).

Carr, Edward H., *International Relations Since the Peace Treaties* (rev. ed., London, 1941).

Carr, Edward H., *The Twenty Years' Crisis, 1919–1939* (2d. ed., London, 1948).

Céré, Roger and Charles Rousseau, *Chronologie du conflit mondial (1935–1945)* (Paris, 1945).

Chastenet, Jacques, *Vingt ans d'histoire diplomatique* (Geneva, 1946).

Foerster, F. W., *Europe and the German Question* (New York, 1940).

Francois-Poncet, André, *De Versailles à Potsdam* (Paris, 1948).

Gathorne-Hardy, Geoffrey M., *A Short History of International Affairs* (4th. ed., New York, 1950).

Jouvenel, Bertrand de, *D'une guerre à l'autre*, 2 vols. (Paris, 1940–1941).

Laroche, Jules, *Au Quai d'Orsay avec Briand et Poincaré*, 1913–1926 (Paris, 1957).

Macmillan, Harold, *Winds of Change*, 1914–1939 (London, 1966).

Medlicott, William M., *British Foreign Policy Since Versailles, 1919–1939* (London, 1940).

Miller, Jane K., *Belgian Foreign Policy Between two Wars, 1919–1940* (New York, 1951).

Mowat, Charles L., *Britain Between the Wars, 1918–1940* (Chicago, 1955).

Petrie, Charles, *The Life and Letters of the Rt. Hon. Sir Austen Chamberlain*, 2 vols. (London, 1939–1940).

Rain, Pierre, *L'Europe de Versailles (1919–1939)* (Paris, 1945).

Schmidt, Paul, *Statist auf diplomatischer Bühne, 1923–1945* (Bonn, 1950).

Toynbee, Arnold J., *The Conduct of British Empire Foreign Relations Since the Peace Settlement* (London, 1928).

Van Zuylen, Pierre, *Les mains libres. Politique extérieure de la Belgique, 1914–1940* (Paris, 1950).

Wambaugh, Sarah, *Plebiscites Since the World War, With a Collection of Official Documents*, 2 vols. (Washington, 1933).

Wiskemann, Elizabeth, *Europe and the Dictators, 1919—1945* (London, 1966).

Wolfers, Arnold, *Britain and France Between Two Wars: Conflicting Strategies of Peace Since Versailles* (New York, 1940).

In varying forms the German problem remained central during the entire period between the two world wars. The first half of that period, roughly the decade of the twenties, was dominated by the relations among France, Britain, and Germany. On these, and particularly on the issue of Reparation which played such an important role, see the following.

Benoist-Méchin, Jacques, *History of the German Army Since the Armistice* (Zurich, 1939).

Bergmann, Carl, *The History of Reparations* (New York, 1927).

Carr, Edward H., *German-Soviet Relations Between the Two World Wars, 1919–1939* (New York, 1966).

Chamberlain, Austen, *Down the Years* (London, 1935).

Chastenet, Jacques, *Raymond Poincaré* (Paris, 1949).

Cowan, L. Gray, *France and the Saar, 1680–1948* (New York, 1948).

Craig, Gordon A., *The Politics of the German Army* (New York, 1945).

d'Abernon, Edgar V., *The Diary of an Ambassador*, 3 vols. (Garden City, 1929–1931).

Gatzke, Hans W., *Stresemann and the Rearmament of Germany* (Baltimore, 1954).

Herriot, Édouard, *Jadis*, Vol. II, *D'une guerre à l'autre 1914–1936* (Paris, 1952).

Jordan, W. M., *Great Britain, France, and the German Problem 1918–1939* (London, 1943).

Kochan, Lionel, *Russia and the Weimar Republic* (New York 1954).

Nicolson, Harold, *Curzon; The Last Phase 1919–1925* (New York, 1934).

Paul-Boncour, Joseph, *Entre deux guerres; souvenirs sur la troisième République*, 3 vols. (Paris, 1945–1946).

Stresemann, Gustav, *Gustav Stresemann: His Diaries, Letters and Papers*, 3 vols. (London, 1935–1940).

Suarez, Georges, *Briand, sa vie, son oeuvre*, 6 vols. (Paris, 1938–1941, 1952).

Tirard, Paul, *La France sur le Rhin. Douze années d'occupation rhénane* (Paris, 1930).

Toynbee, Arnold J., *The World After the Peace Conference* (London, 1925).

Wambaugh, Sarah, *The Saar Plebiscite* (Cambridge, Mass., 1940).

Weill-Raynal, Étienne, *Les réparations allemandes et la France*, 3 vols. (Paris, 1948).

Wentzke, Paul, *Ruhrkampf, Einbruch und Abwehr im rheinisch-westphalischen Industriegebiet*, 2 vols. (Berlin, 1930).

Wheeler-Bennett, John W., *The Wreck of Reparations, being the Political Background of the Lausanne Agreement, 1932* (New York, 1933).

The League of Nations was a novel experiment the main purpose of which was the preservation of peace. On it and on the related issues of disarmament and security, see the following.

Brugière, Pierre F., *La sécurité collective, 1919–1945* (Paris, 1946).

Carter, G. M., *The British Commonwealth and International Security* (Toronto, 1947).

Jessup, Philip C., *Elihu Root*, 2 vols., Vol. II (New York, 1938).

Lapradelle, Albert G. de, *La paix moderne (1899–1945). De La Haye à San Francisco* (Paris, 1947).

Morley, Flex, *The Society of Nations* (Washington, 1932).

Rappard, William E., *The Geneva Experiment* (London, 1931).

Rappard, William E., *The Quest for Peace* (Cambridge, Mass., 1940).

Walters, F. P., *A History of the League of Nations*, (New York, 1965).

Webster, Charles K., *The League of Nations in Theory and Practice* (London, 1933).

Wheeler-Bennett, John W., *Disarmament and Security Since Locarno* (New York, 1932).

Wheeler-Bennett, John W., *The Pipe Dream of Peace* (London, 1934).

Zimmern, Alfred, *The League of Nations and the Rule of Law* (New York, 1936).

On the economic difficulties that arose at the end of the twenties and their political impact, see the following.

Basch, Antonin, *The Danube Basin and the German Economic Sphere* (New York, 1943).

Hodson, Henry V., *Slump and Recovery, 1929–1937* (London, 1938).

Moulton, Harold G. and Leo Pasvolsky, *War Debts and World Prosperity* (Washington, 1932).

Robbins, Lionel C., *The Great Depression* (London, 1934).

Ronde, Hans, *Von Versailles bis Lausanne* (Stuttgart, 1950).

Truchy, Henri and Maurice Byé, *Les relations économiques internationales* (Paris, 1948).

Varga, Eugen, *The Great Crisis and its Political Consequences* (New York, 1935).

On the role of Italy and of Fascism, see the following.

Alatri, Paolo, *Nitti, d'Annunzio e la questione adriatica* (Milan, 1959).

Albrecht-Carrié, René, *Italy from Napoleon to Mussolini* (New York, 1951).

Christopoulos, Georges C., *La politique extérieure de l'Italie fasciste* (Paris, 1936).

Currey, Muriel I., *Italy's Foreign Policy, 1918–1932* (London, 1932).

Kirkpatrick, Ivone, *Mussolini: A Study in Power* (New York, 1964).

Macartney, Maxwell H. H. and Paul Cremona, *Italy's Foreign and Colonial Policy, 1914–1937* (London, 1938).

Moodie, A. E., *The Italo-Yugoslav Boundary* (London, 1945).

Perticone, Giacomo, *La politica italiana nell-ultimo trentennio*, 3 vols. (Rome, 1945–1947).

Zoli, Corrado, *Expansione coloniale italiana 1922–1937* (Rome, 1949).

The Soviet Union and Communism are covered by the following.

Beloff, Max, *The Foreign Policy of Soviet Russia, 1929–1941*, 2 vols. (London, 1947–1949).

Borkenau, Franz, *The Communist International* (London, 1938).

Carr, Edward H., *German-Soviet Relations Between the Two World Wars, 1919–1939* (New York, 1966).

Coates, William P., *A History of Anglo-Soviet Relations*, 2 vols. (London, 1945, 1958).

Dallin, David J., *Soviet Russia's Foreign Policy, 1939–1942* (New Haven, 1943).

Dallin, David J., *Soviet Policy and the Far East* (New Haven, 1948).

Deutscher, Issac, *Stalin: A Political Biography* (New York, 1949).

Fischer, John, *The Soviet in World Affairs*, 2 vols. (2d. ed., Princeton, 1951).

Gurian, Waldemar, *Bolshevism. An Introduction to World Communism* (Notre Dame, Ind., 1952).

Laserson, Max M., *Russia and the Western World* (New York, 1945).

Moore, Harriet L., *Soviet Far Eastern Policy, 1931–1945* (Princeton, 1945).

Taracouzio, Timothy A., *War and Peace in Soviet Diplomacy* (Cambridge, Mass., 1940).

Warth, Robert D., *The Allies and the Russian Revolution* (Durham, N. C., 1954).

On the unresolved problems of Central and Eastern Europe and on Balkan affairs, see the following.

Ball, Margaret M., *Post-War German-Austrian Relations, 1918–1936* (Stanford, 1937).

Braunthal, Julius, *The Tragedy of Austria* (London, 1948).

Crane, John O., *The Little Entente* (New York, 1931).

Eichstadt, Ulrich, *Von Dollfuss zu Hitler* (Berlin, 1957).

Gulick, Charles A., *Austria From Habsburg to Hitler*, 2 vols. (Berkeley, 1948).

Hanč, Joseph, *Tornado Across Eastern Europe* (New York, 1942).

Kerner, Robert J. and Harry N. Howard, *The Balkan Conferences and the Balkan Entente, 1930–1935* (Berkeley, 1936).

Krofta, Kamil, *Germany and Czechoslovakia*, 2 vols. (Prague, 1937).

Macartney, Carlile A., *Hungary and her Successors: The Treaty of Trianon and its Consequences, 1919–1937* (London, 1937).

Mackray, Robert, *The Struggle for the Danube and the Little Entente, 1929–1938* (London, 1938).

Morrow, Ian F. and C. M. Sieveking, *The Peace Settlement in the German-Polish Borderlands* (London, 1936).

Roucek, Joseph S., *Balkan Politics; International Relations in No-man's Land* (Stanford, 1948).

Seton-Watson, Hugh, *Eastern Europe Between the Wars, 1918–1941* (2d. ed., Cambridge, 1946).

Shotwell, James T. and Max M. Laserson, *Poland and Russia, 1919–1945* (New York, 1945).

Szembek, Jan, *Journal 1933–1939* (Paris, 1952).

Vondracek, Felix J., *The Foreign Policy of Czechoslovakia, 1918–1935* (New York, 1937).

Wiskemann, Elizabeth, *Czechs and Germans. A Study of the Strug-*

gle in the Historic Provinces of Bohemia and Moravia (London, 1938).

The League met its fate as the result of happenings the locale of which was outside Europe. On such problems, see the following.

Boveri, Marget, *Mediterranean Cross-Currents* (New York, 1938).

Buss, Claude A., *War and Diplomacy in Eastern Asia* (New York, 1941).

Cumming, Henry H., *Franco-British Rivalry in the Post-War Near East* (London, 1938).

Driault, Edouard, *La Question d'Orient, 1918–1937* (Paris, 1938).

Hall, Duncan, *Mandates, Dependencies and Trusteeships* (Washington, 1948).

Hyamson, Albert M., *Palestine under the Mandate, 1920–1948* (London, 1950).

Lapradelle, Albert G. de, *Le Conflit italo-éthiopien* (Paris, 1936).

Logan, Rayford W., *The African Mandates in World Politics* (Washington, 1948).

Mandelstam, André N., *The conflit italo-éthiopien devant la Société des Nations* (Paris, 1937).

Monroe, Elizabeth, *The Mediterranean in Politics* (London, 1938).

Pavlovsky, Michael, *Chinese-Russian Relations* (New York, 1949).

Pollard, Robert T., *China's Foreign Relations (1917–1931)* (New York, 1933).

Quigley, Harold S., *Far Eastern War, 1937–1941* (Boston, 1941).

Royal Institute of International Affairs, *Great Britain and Palestine, 1915–1945* (London, 1946).

Seton-Williams, M. V., *Britain and the Arab States: A Survey of Anglo-Arab Relations, 1920–1948* (London, 1948).

Silva, Pietro, *Italia, Francia, Inghilterra nel Mediterrano* (Milan, 1939).

Stimson, Henry L., *The Far Eastern Crisis* (New York, 1936).

Toynbee, Arnold T., *The Islamic World Since the Peace Settlement* (London, 1929).

Willoughby, Westel W., *The Sino-Japanese Controversy and the League of Nations* (Baltimore, 1935).

With the rearmament of Germany and the assumption by that country, under the Nazi regime, of a role of leadership, the European community reverted to a state of anarchy. See the following for what may be called the prelude or the background of the Second World War.

Bonnet, Georges, *Défense de la paix*, 2 vols. (Paris, 1946–1948).

Ciano, Galeazzo, *Diario 1938–1943* (Milan, 1946).

Ciano, Galeazzo, *Ciano's Diplomatic Papers* (London, 1948).

Ciano, Galeazzo, *Diary 1937–1938* (London, 1952).

Coulondre, Robert, *De Staline à Hitler* (Paris, 1950).

Feiling, Keith, *The Life of Neville Chamberlain* (London, 1947).

François-Poncet, André, *Souvenirs d'une ambassade à Berlin* (Paris, 1946).

Gafencu, Grigore, *The Last Days of Europe* (New Haven, 1948).

Gibson, Hugh, ed., *The Ciano Diaries* (Garden City, 1946). This edition is unsatisfactory; the French one, published in Neuchâtel, Switzerland, is preferable.

Gilbert, Martin, *The Roots of Appeasement* (New York, 1966).

Hadley, William W., *Munich, Before and After* (London, 1944).

Haines, C. Grove and Ross J. S. Hoffman, *The Origins and Background of the Second World War* (2d. ed., New York, 1947).

Henderson, Nevile, *Failure of a Mission* (New York, 1940).

Hitler, Adolf, *Mein Kampf* (Reynal and Hitchcock edition, New York, 1940).

Hofer, Walther, *Die Entfesselung des zweiten Weltkrieges* (Frankfurt-am-Main, 1964).

Holldack, Heinz, *Was wirklich geschah: Die diplomatische Hintergründe der deutschen Kriegspolitik* (Munich, 1949).

Langer, William L. and S. Everett Gleason, *The Challenge to Isolation, 1937–1940* (New York, 1952).

Lee, Dwight E., *Ten Years. The World on the Way to the War, 1930–1940* (Boston, 1942).

Magistrati, Massimo, *L'Italia a Berlino, 1937–1939* (Milan, 1956).

Namier, Lewis B., *Diplomatic Prelude 1938–1939* (New York, 1948).

Namier, Lewis B., *Europe in Decay, A Study in Disintegration 1936–1940* (London, 1950).

Neumann, Franz, *Behemoth: The Structure and Practice of National Socialism* (New York, 1942).

Nevins, Allan, *The New Deal and World Affairs. A Chronicle of International Affairs, 1933–1945* (New Haven, 1950).

Padelford, Norman J., *International Law and Diplomacy in the Spanish Civil War Strife* (New York, 1939).

Rauch, Basil, *Roosevelt: From Munich to Pearl Harbor* (New York, 1950).

Ripka, Hubert, *Munich, Before and After* (London, 1939).

Schuman, Frederick L., *Europe on the Eve: The Crises of Diplomacy, 1933–1939* (New York, 1939).

Schuman, Frederick L., *Night Over Europe* (New York, 1941).

Seton-Watson, Robert W., *Britain and the Dictators* (Cambridge, 1939).

Seton-Watson, Robert W., *From Munich to Danzig* (London, 1939).

Toscano, Mario, *Le origini del patto di acciaio* (Florence, 1956).

Toynbee, Arnold T., *The Eve of War* (London, 1958).

van der Easch, P., *Prelude to War. The International Repercussions of the Spanish Civil War, 1936–1939* (The Hague, 1951).

Wheeler-Bennett, John W., *Munich, Prologue to Tragedy* (New York, 1948).

Wiskemann, Elizabeth, *The Rome-Berlin Axis. A History of the Relations Between Hitler and Mussolini* (London, 1949).

The Second World War and its aftermath have had the effect of bringing out in unmistakable fashion the result of the process that

was initiated in 1914, the decline of the European Powers to positions
of at best second rank. The correspondingly clear emergence of American power and the acceptance by America of the world-strewn responsibilities that go with the American position make it difficult to
separate European diplomacy from that of America. The books listed
below therefore refer to American no less than to European affairs;
some of them have lasting value, but a good many will inevitably be
superseded with the passage of time; no more than a useful selection
from a vast number of possible titles is attempted in the following list.

Abetz, Otto, *Das offene Problem, ein Rückblick auf zwei Jahrzehnte deutscher Frankreichpolitik* (Cologne, 1951).

Assman, Kurt, *Deutsche Schicksaljahre: Historische Bilder aus dem
zweiten Weltkrieg und seiner Vorgeschichte* (Wiesbaden, 1950).

Betts, Reginald., ed., *Central and South East Europe, 1945–1948*
New York, 1950).

Bourbon-Parma, Xavier Prince de, *Les accords secrets franco-
anglais de décembre 1940* (Paris, 1949).

Bouthilier, Yves, *Le drame de Vichy*, 2 vols. (Paris, 1950–1951).

Browder, Paul, *The Origins of Soviet-American Diplomacy*
(Princeton, 1953).

Camps, Miriam, *European Unification in the Sixties: From the Veto
to the Crisis* (New York, 1966).

Carmoy, Guy de, *The Foreign Policies of France, 1944–1968*
(Chicago, 1970).

Churchill, Winston S., *The Second World War*, 6 vols. (Boston,
1948–1963).

Clark, W. Hartley, *The Politics of the Common Market* (Engle-
wood Cliffs, 1967).

Clay, Lucius D., *Decision in Germany* (Garden City, 1950).

Devillers, Philippe, *Histoire du Viet-Nam de 1940 à 1952* (Paris,
1952).

Diebold, William, Jr., *The Schuman Plan; a Study in Economic
Cooperation* (New York, 1959).

Doussinague, José Maria, *España tenia razón (1939–1945)* (Madrid,
1950).

Eden, Anthony, *The Memoirs of Anthony Eden*, 3 vols. (Boston,
1960, 1962, 1965).

Erfurth, Waldemar, *Der finnische Krieg, 1941–1944* (Wiesbaden,
1944).

Feis, Herbert, *The Spanish Story: Franco and the Nations at War*
(New York, 1948).

Feis, Herbert, *Churchill, Roosevelt, Stalin. The War They Waged
and the Peace They Sought* (New York, 1966).

Fontaine, André, *History of the Cold War*, 2 vols. (New York,
1968–1969).

Fotitch, Constantin, *The War We Lost* (New York, 1948).

Gardner, Richard N., *In Pursuit of World Order: U. S. Foreign
Policy and International Organizations* (New York, 1946).

Gaulle, Charles de, *Mémoires de guerre*, 3 vols. (Paris, 1954–1959).

Gisevius, Hans B., *To the Bitter End* (Boston, 1947).

Goodrich, Leland M. and E. Hambro, *Charter of the United Nations: Commentary and Documents* (rev. ed., Boston, 1969).

Grosser, Alfred, *La Politique extérieure de la Ve. République* (Paris, 1965).

Grosser, Alfred, *La IVe. République et sa politique extérieure* (Paris, 1967).

Guariglia, Raffaele, *Ricordi, 1942–1946* (Naples, 1950).

Hassell, Ulrich von, *The von Hassell Diaries, 1938–1944* (Garden City, 1947).

Hytier, Adrienne, *Two Years of French Foreign Policy; Vichy, 1940–1942* (Geneva, 1958).

Khrushchev, Nikita S., *The Present International Situation and the Foreign Policy of the Soviet Union* (New York, 1962).

Kleist, Peter, *Zwischen Hitler und Stalin, 1939–1945* (Bonn, 1950).

Kogan, Norman, *Italy and the Allies* (Cambridge, Mass., 1956).

Kordt, Erich, *Wahn und Wirklichkeit. Die Aussenpolitik des dritten Reiches, Versuch einer Darstellung* (Stuttgart, 1948).

Langer, William L., *Our Vichy Gamble* (New York, 1947).

Langer, William L. and S. Everett Gleason, *The Undeclared War, 1940–1941* (New York, 1953).

Lenczowski, George, *Russia and the West in Iran, 1918–1948* (Ithaca, 1949).

Lenczowski, George, *The Middle East in World Affairs* (Ithaca, 1962).

Lukacs, John, *The Great Powers and Eastern Europe* (New York, 1953).

Lundin, C. Leonard, *Finland in the Second World War* (Bloomington, 1957).

Macmillan, Harold, *The Blast of War, 1939–1945* (New York, 1968).

Macmillan, Harold, *Tides of Fortune, 1945–1955* (New York, 1969).

Macmillan, Harold, *Riding the Storm, 1956–1959* (New York, 1971).

MacNeill, William H., *America, Britain and Russia. Their Cooperation and Conflict, 1941–1946* (London, 1953).

Mamatey, Victor S., *Soviet Russian Imperialism* (Princeton, 1964).

Mazour, Anatole C., *Finland Between East and West* (Princeton, 1956).

Meinecke, Friedrich, *The German Catastrophe* (Cambridge, Mass., 1950).

Mikolaiczyk, Nicholas, *The Rape of Poland* (New York, 1948).

Mills, Lennox A. *et al.*, *The New World of Southeast Asia* (Minneapolis, 1947).

Moret, Claude, *L'Allemagne et la réorganisation de l'Europe, 1940–1943* (Neuchâtel, 1944).

Mosely, Philip E., *The Kremlin and World Politics* (New York, 1960).

Neumann, William L., *Making the Peace, 1941–1945. The Diplomacy of Wartime Conferences* (Washington, 1950).

Northedge, Frederick S., *British Foreign Policy; The Process of Readjustment, 1945–1961* (London, 1962).

Rothfels, Hans, *The German Opposition to Hitler* (Chicago, 1948).

Rougier, Louis, *Mission secrète à Londres. Les accord Pétain-Churchill* (Paris, 1946).

Schlesinger, Arthur M., Jr., *A Thousand Days: John F. Kennedy in the White House* (Boston, 1965).

Schmidt, Paul, *Der Statist auf der Galerie, 1945–1950. Erlebnisse, Kommentare, Vergleiche* (Bonn, 1951).

Schramm von Thadden, Ehrengard, *Greichenland und die Grossmächte im zweiten Weltkrieg* (Wiesbaden, 1955).

Schumacher, Edgar, *Geschichte des zweiten Weltkrieges* (Zurich, 1946).

Seabury, Paul, *The Wilhelmstrasse: A Study of German Diplomats under the Nazi Regime* (Berkeley, 1954).

Seton-Watson, Hugh, *The East European Revolution* (New York 1951).

Sherwood, Robert E., *Roosevelt and Hopkins: An Intimate History* (rev. ed., New York, 1950).

Shulman, Marshall D., *Stalin's Foreign Policy Reappraised* (New York, 1965).

Snell, John L. *et al.*, *The Meaning of Yalta* (Baton Rouge, 1956).

Stettinius, Edward R., Jr., *Roosevelt and the Russians: The Yalta Conference* (Garden City, 1949).

Stimson, Henry L. and McGeorge Bundy, *On Active Service in Peace and War* (New York, 1948).

Stucki, Walter, *Von Pétain zur Vierten Republik: Vichy 1944* (Bern, 1947).

Taylor, Telford, *Sword and Swastika. Generals and Nazis in the Third Reich* (New York, 1952).

Ulam, Adam B., *Titoism and the Cominform* (Cambridge, Mass., 1952).

Umiatowski, Roman, *Poland, Russia and Great Britain, 1941–1945* (London, 1946).

Wiskemann, Elizabeth, *Germany's Eastern Neighbours: Problems Relating to the Oder-Neisse Line and the Czech Frontier Regions* (New York, 1956).

Woodhouse, Christopher M., *Apple of Discord* (London, 1948).

Woodward, Sir Ernest Llewellyn, *British Foreign Policy in the Second World War* (London, 1962).

Wuorinen, John H., ed., *Finland and World War II, 1939–1944* (New York, 1948).

Zinkin, Maurice, *Asia and the West* (New York, 1951).

Index of Names

Nahas Pasha, 585
Napoleon, 6, 9, 11, 12, 13 n., 14, 15, 17,
    41, 66, 690–691
Napoleon III, 84, 88 n., 92
    American Civil War and, 119
    armistice of Villafranca and, 101–104
    Austro-French Alliance and, 135–136
    Austro-Prussian War and, 129–130,
        131, 132–133
    Bismarck and, 129–130, 133, 134
    Cavour and, 99–107
    Francis Joseph and, 135
    Luxembourg and, 134
    Mexican intervention of, 120–121
    policy of, 82–83
    Polish insurrection of 1863 and, 113
    Rumania and, 108
    Spanish succession and, 137–138
    Suez Canal and, 111–112
Narvaez, General, 57
Nasser, Colonel, 654, 657
Nehru, Jawarharlal, 650
Nekludov, A., 282
Nemours, Duc de, 35
Nesselrode, Count, 77 n., 87
Neurath, Constantin, von, 492, 517
Nicholas I, Tsar, 31, 33, 34 n., 36–37, 45,
    73, 91–92
Nicholas II, Tsar, 221 n., 238, 249
Nicholson, Harold, 4 n., 7
Nixon, Richard M., 668, 671, 691
    reelection of, 694 n.
Nkrumah, Kwame, 667
Nomura, Ambassador, 567

Obrenovitch, Milosh, 43 n.
Obruchev, General, 211, 212
Orlando, Vittorio E., 363 n., 368–369
Orsini, Felice, 100 n.
Osman Pasha, 171
Otto of Bavaria, 48, 108, 109
Oudinot, General, 74 n.

Paléologue, Maurice, 327 n., 330
Palmerston, Henry J. T., 87 n.
    on Belgian independence, 35
    Congress of Paris and, 92 n.
    Denmark and, 128
    Don Pacifico affair and, 109
    Far East and, 61
    Frankfort Parliament and, 77
    on Italy, 70, 71, 105
    Near East and, 52, 53–55
    on Polish independence, 37
    Russia and, 88 n.
    Spain and, 57, 58
    Suez affair and, 111
    Switzerland and, 68
    Texas and, 60

Papen, Franz von, 464, 519 n.
Pascal, Blaise, 362
Pašić, Nicolas, 260, 433 n.
Paskievich, Ivan F., 73
Paul, prince of Yugoslavia, 558
Pedro, emperor of Brazil, 30–31, 56
Peel, Robert, 57 n.
Perry, Commodore, 114
Pétain, Marshal, 548, 554–555, 556,
    572 n., 578, 579
Peter, king of Serbia, 240
Peter the Great, 156
Peter II, king of Yugoslavia, 558
Pilsudski, Josef, 342, 344 n., 349, 371,
    470 n., 473
Pius IX, Pope, 97, 182–183
Poincaré, Raymond, on Balkans, 283 n.
    character of, 275
    defeat of, 398
    election of, 288
    fall of, 414
    foreign policy of, 284 n.–285 n., 442 n.
    on Germany, 389, 394–395, 418 n., 440
    Great Britain and, 278, 393, 402–403,
        421, 424
    on occupation, 442
    policy of, 161
    recall of, 421 n.
    on Ruhr, 397
    Russia and, 281, 282, 283, 325, 327,
        330
Polignac, Prince de, 30, 47
Politis, Nicolas, 414
Polk, James K., 60
Pompidou, Georges, 668
Primo de Rivera, General, 501
Princip, Gavrilo, 323
Prinetti, Giulio, 234
Pritchard, 63
Pu-yi, 458

Quisling, Vidkun A. L., 545

Radek, Karl, 428
Radetzky, Joseph W., 70, 71, 73
Radowitz, Joseph Maria von, 79, 166
Rashid Ali, 558 n.
Rathenau, Walter, 391 n.
Redcliffe, Lord Stratford Canning de,
    87, 88, 89
Reshid Pasha, 53
Reynaud, Paul, 525 n., 545, 546, 547, 548,
    563
Rhodes, Cecil, 215, 217, 227 n.
Ribbentrop, Joachim von, 517, 528,
    534–535, 537, 539 n., 542 n., 552, 557
Rich, Norman, 207
Richelieu, Duc de, 4, 24, 25, 28, 125
Riza Pahlevi, Shah, 586

Index of Subjects

748

INDEX OF SUBJECTS

Great Britain—(*Continued*)
pacifism in, 482
1936–1939
on *Anschluss*, 519
appeasement policies of, 514, 526–528, 531–532
Arab world and, 510
armaments of, 533
Baltic States and, 536
Czech problem and, 522–523, 524–528
Egypt and, 508–509
foreign policy of, 510–511, 512–513
France and, 535
Germany and, 499, 515, 538 n.
Greece and, 532
India and, 511 n.
Italy and, 515, 520–521, 529
Munich Agreement and, 525–528
on Nazi-Soviet Pact, 538 n.
Palestine and, 509–510
Poland and, 532, 536–540
Rumania and, 532, 535
Russia and, 511 n., 535–536, 538 n.
Spanish Civil War and, 503, 515, 520–521, 530
on Sudetenland, 538 n.
Turkey and, 532–553
1939–
Atlantic Pact and, 624–627
Baghdad Pact and, 654
Battle of Britain, 550–551
Burma and, 650
Casablanca Meeting and, 577, 580
Ceylon and, 650
China and, 581–582
in Cyprus, 653
decolonization by, 677–678, 681
at Dumbarton Oaks Meeting, 595 n.
Egypt and, 585, 607, 653, 655–657
empire of, 606, 650–651
Europe and, 685, 693–694
and European Economic Community, 694 n.
European Movement and, 620–622
France and, 547, 548, 549–550, 554–556, 578–580, 581, 591–592
Germany and, 616–619, 633–635
Greece and, 590, 596, 609–610
Iceland and, 545 n.
India and, 650–651
internal conditions of, 546, 597
Iran and, 586–587, 609 n.
Iraq and, 558 n., 608
on Japanese imperialism, 581, 587
Jordan and, 653
Lebanon and, 586
Middle East and, 607–609
Pakistan and, 650–651
Palestine and, 607–608

Great Britain—(*Continued*)
Paris Accords and, 642–643
policy of, 662
Portugal and, 581 n.
at Potsdam Conference, 596–597
power status after WW II, 574–577, 598
Russia and, 559, 576–577, 581, 594–596, 639, 644
Schuman Plan and, 623
on Second Front, 577, 580
Southeast Asia policy of, 642
at Summit Conference (1955), 644
Syria and, 586
Teheran Conference and, 584–585
Transjordan and, 608
Treaty of Brussels (1948) and, 620
United States and, 563–564, 566–567, 576
Vichy France and, 555, 578
WW II and, 304, 304 n.–305 n., 543, 568, 659
at Yalta Conference, 592–593
Great Leap Forward, 666 n.
Great Powers, empire and, 676
Greater East Asia Coprosperity Sphere, 566
Greece, Atlantic Pact and, 626
Balkan Wars and, 283, 284 n., 285, 289
Bulgaria and, 436
Congress of Berlin and, 175
Crimean War and, 109
Cyprus and, 653
Egypt and, 50–51
France and, 45–48, 55 n., 109, 532
Germany and, 558–559
Great Britain and, 55 n., 532, 590, 596, 609–610
independence of, 43–48
intervention in, 108–109
Italy and, 433, 436, 552–553, 558
Potsdam Conference and, 596
Russia and, 44–48, 109
in Smyrna, 377, 401
Treaty of Lausanne (1923) and, 403
Turkey and, 653
Turkish War of 1920, 401–404
United States and, 610
WW I and, 342, 375, 391 n.
WW II and, 559 n., 589
Greenland, 565 n.
Grosse Politik der Europäischen Kabinette 1871–1914, die, 159
Guadelupe Hidalgo, Treaty of (1848), 61 n.
Guam, 570
Guarantees, Law of (1871), 183

Hague Conference (1907), 254

Printer and Binder: The Murray Printing Company

85 86 87 88 89 90   20 19 18 17 16 15 14 13 12